ORGANIZATIONAL PSYCHOLOGY

ORGANIZATIONAL PSYCHOLOGY

A SCIENTIST-PRACTITIONER APPROACH

Steve M. Jex

JOHN WILEY & SONS, INC.

Library of Congress Cataloging-in-Publication Data:

Jex, Steve M.
    Organizational psychology : a scientist-practitioner approach / Steve M. Jex.
      p. cm.
    Includes bibliographical references (p.   ) and index.
    ISBN 0-471-37420-2 (cloth : alk. paper)
     1. Psychology, Industrial.   I. Title.

HF5548.8.J49 2002
158.7—dc21

                                        2001046962

Printed in the United States of America.

10 9 8 7 6 5 4 3 2 1

Contents

Preface

Organizations are complex social systems that sometimes perform remarkably well and sometimes fail miserably. Organizational psychology is a subfield within the larger domain of industrial/organizational psychology that seeks to facilitate a greater understanding of social processes in organizations. Organizational psychologists also seek to use these insights to enhance the effectiveness of organizations—a goal that is potentially beneficial to all.

This book is designed to provide students with a thorough overview of both the science and the practice of organizational psychology. It primarily serves as a text for a course in organizational psychology (graduate, or upper-level undergraduate), but could also meet the needs of an organizational behavior course. It will likely serve as a text for many graduate courses, so considerable effort has been invested to provide a solid research base. Equal effort was also made to write the book in a style that students will find enjoyable, accessible, and perhaps, at times, even entertaining.

The topical layout of the chapters is based on the various "levels" at which behavior occurs in organizations, and the processes that occur as people move through organizations. Chapters 1 through 4 provide an introduction to the field of organizational psychology, an examination of the most common research methods used to study behavior in organizations, and the processes by which employees are socialized into organizations and finally become productive members.

Chapters 5 through 8 offer an examination of the processes by which employees develop feelings of satisfaction and commitment toward the organization, an exploration of counterproductive behaviors that they may engage in, how they might come to view the workplace as stressful, and some theories of motivation.

Chapters 9 through 12 include an examination of the various methods that organizations use to influence the behavior of employees, leadership and influence processes, and group behavior. Readers will note that two chapters are devoted to groups. One is designed to provide an overview of basic social-psychological processes in groups, and the second is focused more specifically on the factors that impact group effectiveness.

Chapter 13 focuses on the processes governing interactions between groups. The final three chapters are focused on "macro" or organizational-level processes. These include the design of organizations, organizational culture, and organizational change and development.

UNIQUE FEATURES OF THE BOOK

One of my primary motivations for writing this book was to have a text that I could use in my own graduate organizational psychology course. Like many faculty who have taught such a course, I found that few textbooks were available, and those that were available did not seem to meet my course objectives. Therefore, in this book, I have tried to incorporate a number of features that I feel are important. Three of these features are briefly discussed below.

One feature that is different, compared to most books, is that there is a full chapter on research methodology and statistics (Chapter 2). I believe, as do many others, that research methodology is a viable field of study within organizational psychology. Many organizational psychologists are superb methodologists, and much of the research in organizational psychology makes methodological as well as substantive contributions. Another reason for including this chapter is that students must understand methodology if they are going to read the research literature in organizational psychology. This is important because most course instructors supplement text readings with empirical research articles.

A second unique feature of this book is that several topics are covered that are not traditionally part of organizational psychology. As examples, in Chapter 3, recruitment is discussed; in Chapter 4, a good deal of attention is given to research on the relationship between general mental ability and performance; and in Chapter 9, discussions of financial incentives and executive compensation are included. This was done largely because of my belief that there is considerable interrelationship between the "I" and the "O" sides of the broader field of industrial/organizational psychology. Separating them is useful for pedagogical purposes, but, in real organizations, there is considerable overlap.

A third feature of the book is my use of "Comments." Readers will note that the material is quite varied. Some Comments relate chapter material to current events, some

provide extended commentary on chapter material, some help the reader to get to know the author a little better, and some are even meant to lighten the mood. The underlying aim of all of these Comments is to *encourage students to think about and discuss the chapter material.* There is nothing more laborious than rote memorization of theories and research findings. However, when students begin to relate material from this book to their own experiences, or perhaps current events, learning ceases to be a chore and may even be quite exciting.

ACKNOWLEDGMENTS

Writing a textbook is a tremendous undertaking that obviously requires the help and support of many people. So many people contributed to this book, either directly or indirectly, that it would be impossible to properly acknowledge everyone. However, I will try my best to recognize those whose help was most instrumental in making this book a reality.

I would first like to express my sincere appreciation to the faculty of the industrial/organizational psychology program at the University of South Florida. Without the tremendous education provided by that program, I would never have had the knowledge to write this book in the first place. Of all the faculty there, I would especially like to thank Paul Spector for his help and continued support of my career over the years.

I have also been very fortunate, over the years, to have excellent colleagues and research collaborators who have enhanced my knowledge and shaped my thinking about many of the topics covered in this book. Two deserve special mention. Gary Adams has been a faculty colleague, research collaborator, and great friend who has contributed tremendously to this book. Gary has provided a number of excellent ideas that I have used in the book and, perhaps more importantly, provided me with a great deal of comic relief during the book-writing process.

Paul Bliese has been an active research collaborator and valued friend who has also contributed to this book in numerous ways. Paul's interest in multilevel issues in organizational research has had a tremendous impact on the way I think about organizations, and hopefully this will be reflected well in the book. Also, my decision to include a chapter on research methodology and statistics was largely due to Paul's convincing me that this was a vibrant area of inquiry that should not be left out.

I would also like to thank the people from John Wiley and Sons who facilitated the completion of this project. My editor, Jennifer Simon, provided very helpful guidance during all phases of the book, yet gave me a tremendous amount of freedom in deciding on its content. I am also very grateful for the work done by Isabel Pratt, who helped me take care of the many details that are necessary to bring a textbook into production.

The final acknowledgment, and in many ways the most important one, is to my family. My wife Robin carefully read drafts of all chapters and made a number of excellent suggestions that were incorporated into the final product. She has also been a tremendous source of love, encouragement, and inspiration during the writing process. Without Robin's help, this book would not have been completed. My two sons, Garrett and Travis, also provided a great deal of love and support during the writing process. They are also my two best friends, and serve as a constant reminder of what's really important in life.

Chapter One

Introduction to Organizational Psychology

The behavior of individuals in formal organizational settings has a tremendous impact on many aspects of our lives. Everything—the food we eat, the cars we drive, the houses we live in—depends on coordinated human effort. In fact, the impact is so great that we typically pay attention to behavior in formal organizations only when the results are either very good or very bad. For example, we take notice when a professional sports team is highly successful, or a business organization is extremely profitable, or corruption occurs in a government agency. Most of the time, however, the impact of behavior in formal organizations goes relatively unnoticed.

Organizational psychology is a field that utilizes scientific methodology to better understand the behavior of individuals in organizational settings. This knowledge is also applied, in a variety of ways, to help organizations function more effectively. This is important because effective organizations are typically more productive, often provide higher-quality services, and are usually more financially successful than less effective organizations. For private organizations, success often results in increased shareholder wealth and greater job security for employees. For public organizations such as police departments, municipal governments, and public universities, success means higher-quality services and cost savings to taxpayers.

More indirect benefits are also associated with enhanced organizational effectiveness and the success that often comes with it. Organizations' success provides employment opportunities, which facilitate the economic well-being of members of society. Also, in many instances, employees in successful organizations are more satisfied and fulfilled in their work than employees in less successful organizations. These positive attitudes may carry over to nonwork roles such as *parent* and *community member*. Consumers also benefit from enhanced organizational effectiveness because well-managed, efficient organizations often produce products and provide services at a much lower cost than their less successful competitors. Such cost savings are often passed on to consumers in the form of lower prices. In sum, everyone is a potential winner when organizations function effectively. Organizational psychology seeks to enhance the effectiveness of organizations through scientific research and the application of research findings.

WHAT IS ORGANIZATIONAL PSYCHOLOGY?

This book is designed to provide students with a comprehensive treatment of the science and practice of organizational psychology. In the most general sense, **organizational psychology** is *the scientific study of individual and group behavior in formal organizational settings*. Katz and Kahn, in their classic work, *The Social Psychology of Organizations* (1978), stated that the essence of an organization is "patterned" human behavior. When behavior is patterned, some structure is imposed on individuals. This structure typically comes in the form of roles (normative standards governing behavior) as well as a guiding set of values. An organization cannot exist when people just "do their own thing" without any awareness of the behavior of others.

Given Katz and Kahn's defining characteristic of organizations (e.g., patterned activity), it is easy to see that there are many organizations in this world. A group of five people who regularly play poker on Friday nights would fit this definition, as would a major multinational corporation. Therefore, to further define the field of organizational psychology, it is important to distinguish between *formal* and *informal* organizations. A formal organization is one that exists to fulfill some explicitly stated purpose, and that purpose is often stated in writing. Formal organizations also typically exhibit some degree of continuity over time; they often survive far longer than the founding members do. Business organizations obviously exhibit these defining characteristics of a formal organization, as do many other nonprofit organizations and government agencies.

In contrast, an informal organization is one in which the purpose is typically less explicit than for a formal organization. Going back to the previous example of five poker players, these individuals are obviously spending time together because they enjoy playing poker and, in all likelihood, each other's company. It is doubtful, though, that in this situation these goals are captured in writing, or even explicitly stated. It is also doubtful whether this small group would continue to exist if three of the five members moved to another city or simply lost interest in poker.

Organizational psychology is concerned with the study of *formal* organizations. That is not to say that the formal organizations of interest to organizational psychologists are always *business* organizations (a common misconception that I have noticed among many of my colleagues trained in other areas of psychology). Throughout the chapters in this book, many studies will be described that have been conducted in nonbusiness settings such as government agencies, universities, and nonprofit social service agencies.

Another point worth noting is that the focus on formal organizations does not preclude the study of *informal organizational*

COMMENT 1.1

ORGANIZATIONAL PSYCHOLOGY VERSUS ORGANIZATIONAL BEHAVIOR: WHAT'S THE DIFFERENCE?

MANY READERS, PARTICULARLY those who have received at least a portion of their training in a university business school, have heard of the field of *organizational behavior.* What is the difference between organizational psychology and organizational behavior? In all honesty, these two fields are much more similar than different—so much so, in fact, that many faculty who teach organizational behavior in business schools received their training in departments of psychology. Though less common, some faculty who teach organizational psychology received their training in business schools.

Despite the outward similarities, there are actually subtle differences between organizational psychology and organizational behavior. Moorhead and Griffin (1995) define organizational behavior as "the study of human behavior in organizational settings, the interface between human behavior and the organization, and the organization itself" (p. 4). If we focus only on the first part of this definition, it is impossible to distinguish organizational psychology from organizational behavior. However, we start to see a hint of where differences lie in the portion of the definition stating that organizational behavior is concerned with "the organization itself." Specifically, those schooled in organizational behavior are concerned not only with individual behavior in organizations, but also with macro-level processes and variables such as organizational structure and strategy. These are viewed as interesting and worthy of study in their own right.

Organizational psychology is also concerned with the impact of macro-level variables and processes, but only to the extent that such variables and processes have an impact on *individual behavior.* Thus, one subtle way in which organizational psychology and organizational behavior differ is that organizational behavior is a bit more "eclectic" in its focus than is organizational psychology. Much of the reason for this difference is that organizational behavior draws off a greater variety of disciplines than does organizational psychology. While organizational psychology draws largely from various subfields within psychology, organizational behavior draws not only on psychology but sociology, anthropology, economics, and labor relations, to name a few.

Thus, to answer the question of whether there is a difference between organizational psychology and organizational behavior, my answer would be: Yes, but it is a very subtle difference. Perhaps the best way to summarize the difference is to quote a comment from one of my professors when I began searching for faculty jobs after finishing my Ph.D. When I asked about the major difference between teaching in a business school and a psychology department, his only response was: "About $20,000 in salary."

Source: G. Moorhead and R. W. Griffin. (1995). *Organizational behavior: Managing people and organizations* (4th ed.). Boston: Houghton Mifflin Company.

processes, or even occasionally informal groups and organizations. We know, for example, that informal friendship ties exist in organizations, and they have important implications for the functioning of formal organizations

(Riordan & Griffith, 1995). In this same vein, processes that occur in informal groups and organizations may provide some insight into processes that occur in formal organizations. For example, the manner in which a status hierarchy develops in an informal group may help us to better understand the emergence of leadership in formal organizations.

Another point of clarification in the definition provided above has to do with the term *psychology* itself. Psychology is the scientific study of individual human behavior and mental processes. Two things are important to note about this definition. First, organizational psychologists use methods of scientific inquiry to both study and intervene in organizations. This simply means that organizational psychologists use a systematic data-based approach to both study organizational processes and solve organizational problems. The "data" used by organizational psychologists may come in a variety of forms, including survey responses, interviews, observations, and, in some cases, organizational records.

Second, organizational psychology is intellectually rooted in the larger field of psychology. The most important implication of this connection to the broader field of psychology is that *organizational psychology focuses on individual behavior*. This statement may seem odd, given that a substantial portion of this text is devoted to both group and organizational-level processes. What it means is that regardless of the level at which some phenomenon occurs, *individual behavior is the most important mediating factor* (cf. Porras & Robertson, 1992). Thus, to understand the impact of group and organizational-level variables, we must focus on how they impact individual behavior. Groups and organizations don't behave; people do. This strong focus on individual behavior also serves to distinguish organizational psychology from other social science disciplines (e.g., sociology, economics, and political science) that attempt to explain organizational processes. It is also one way in which organizational psychology differs from the closely related field of organizational behavior (see Comment 1.1).

ORGANIZATIONAL PSYCHOLOGY IN CONTEXT

Although organizational psychology represents a legitimate field of study in its own right, it is part of the broader field of industrial/organizational (I/O) psychology. I/O psychology is defined as the application of the methods and principles of psychology to the workplace (Spector, 1999). Figure 1.1 provides a comparison of the topics that are typically of interest to those in the industrial and organizational portions of the field. Notice that the topics listed on the industrial side are those that are typically associated with the management of human resources in organizations. Contrast these with the topics on the organizational side, which are associated with the aim of understanding and predicting behavior within organizational settings.

Given this distinction between the industrial and organizational sides of the field, it is very tempting to polarize into different "camps" based on one's professional interests.

FIGURE 1.1

A Breakdown of Topics Associated with the Industrial and Organizational Sides of the Field of I/O Psychology

In fact, the author can distinctly remember fellow graduate-school students declaring that they were either an "I" or an "O." (Given the topic of this book, you can probably guess the author's choice!) Unfortunately, this "I" or "O" declaration is inconsistent with the reality that there is *considerable interdependence among the topics that constitute each of these subfields.*

To illustrate this point, let's say a life insurance company decides to develop a test to select people to sell insurance policies. To do so, this organization would likely conduct some form of job analysis to find out what exactly is involved in selling life insurance policies, develop performance criterion measures based on this job analysis, develop a selection test to measure things that are thought to be predictive of performance, and ultimately conduct a study to investigate whether performance on the selection test is correlated with the performance criterion measure (Cascio, 1998). Because all of these are "I" activities, what relevance does the "O" side of the field have for the life insurance company in this example? On first glance, it would appear to be very little. However, if you think about it, organizational topics are highly relevant. For example, after these life insurance agents are selected, they must be socialized into the culture of the specific agency in which they will be working, as well as the broader company culture (Bowen, Ledford, & Nathan, 1991; Kristof, 1996). Also, demands of life insurance sales may necessitate the hiring of individuals who will cope well with these demands (Jex, 1998). Thus, the organization needs to understand the unique stressors that are associated with this job, as well as the attributes that facilitate coping. As we will see, socialization and occupational stress are important topics within organizational psychology.

This point can also be illustrated by taking an "O" topic and describing the relevance of

the "I" side of the field. Let's say the U.S. Army is interested in improving decision-making and communication processes among the small groups that comprise special-forces units. Fortunately, in organizational psychology, there is considerable literature on group effectiveness and processes, and the Army could draw on these sources to help guide its efforts (e.g., Guzzo & Shea, 1992). Can issues that are relevant to the "I" side of the field be ignored? Absolutely not. To be effective, a group must have a certain mix of skills, abilities, and personality traits. Thus, regardless of the team processes that are taught to these units, care must be taken to select the right mix of individuals in the first place. It is also unlikely that decision-making processes would improve unless these teams receive accurate and timely performance feedback. Selection and performance appraisal, of course, are two of the major topics on the "I" side of the field.

THE SCIENTIST-PRACTITIONER APPROACH

Organizational psychology can and should be viewed as a science. In fact, much of the content of this book is based on scientific studies of behavior in both organizational and laboratory settings. Organizational psychology, however, is also concerned with the *application* of scientific knowledge to enhance the effectiveness of organizations. The **scientist-practitioner model** captures this interaction between generating scientific knowledge and the application of that knowledge for some practical purpose. At a very general level, the scientist-practitioner model states that science and practice are not independent and, in fact, often "feed off" each other (see Figure 1.2).

To illustrate how the scientist-practitioner model works, let's say the branch manager of

FIGURE 1.2
The Interactive Relationship between Science and Practice: The Essence of the Scientist-Practitioner Model

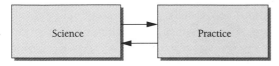

a bank is frustrated by high turnover among tellers. Fortunately, this individual may draw on the findings of many scientific investigations of turnover to guide his or her efforts to reduce it. It is also true that, in many cases, scientific investigations of organizational phenomena are motivated by the practical concerns of organizations. For example, the past decade has indicated a considerable rise in research on how organizations can assist employees in balancing the demands of both work and family domains (e.g., Adams, King, & King, 1996; Kossek & Ozeki, 1998). Although this research is certainly useful from a purely scientific standpoint, the primary factor motivating it is that organizations want to avoid losing valuable employees who have family responsibilities.

Within the general field of I/O psychology, the scientist-practitioner model has become so important that it serves as the underlying philosophy for most graduate training. Graduate training guided by the scientist-practitioner model suggests that, first and foremost, students need to learn the skills necessary to conduct scientific research. This explains why virtually all graduate programs in I/O psychology either require or strongly encourage training in statistics, research methodology, and psychological measurement. The other important implication of the scientist-practitioner model in graduate training is that students are typically provided with some opportunity,

through internships or other field experience, to apply what they have learned in "real world" settings (see Comment 1.2).

The scientist-practitioner model is also quite relevant to the field of organizational psychology, and thus was chosen as the guiding theme for this book. As will become evident as readers proceed through the chapters, research by organizational psychologists has greatly enhanced our understanding of behavior in organizations. For example, due largely to research by organizational psychologists and others, we now know much more about things such as group effectiveness, socialization of new employees, and goal-setting processes than we did even 10 years ago. At the same time, findings generated from scientific research in these areas have been used to guide interventions designed to help organizations become more effective.

The impact of the scientist-practitioner model can also be seen in the work settings and activities of those trained in organizational psychology. Many hold academic positions—typically, in departments of psychology or management. The primary job duties of most academicians are: teaching, scientific research, and service to one's academic department and university. However, many in academia also use their research skills to help organizations solve a variety of practical problems. My own academic career has certainly contained this blend of science and practice (see Comment 1.3).

The training of organizational psychologists who pursue academic careers is not drastically different from the training of those who pursue nonacademic careers. Consistent with the scientist-practitioner model, students in graduate programs in I/O psychology and related fields typically receive coursework in research methodology, statistics, and measurement, as well as in specific content areas

COMMENT 1.2

TRAINING SCIENTIST-PRACTITIONERS: THE ROLE OF PRACTICAL EXPERIENCE

MOST GRADUATE PROGRAMS in I/O psychology, as well as other related fields, incorporate some form of practical experience into their curriculum. This can be accomplished in a variety of ways. Many programs, for example, encourage students to participate in formal internship programs in corporations and consulting firms. Typically, internships span between six months and one year and essentially require that students work under the supervision of an experienced I/O psychologist. Other less formal ways of students' obtaining practical experience include class projects, working with faculty on research and consulting projects, and field-based practicum courses.

The major benefit of students' participating in field experiences is that they gain a chance to put what they've learned into practice in a real organization. Students also benefit in more subtle ways: they develop a greater understanding of how the "real world" actually works. Students with whom I have worked on field projects over the years are often surprised by things such as the speed at which organizations often want things done, as well as the importance of things such as building positive interpersonal relationships with "clients" in organizations. Many students have also commented that their methodological training often comes in quite handy as they work on these field projects.

Despite the many advantages of incorporating practical experience into graduate programs, there can be some disadvantages. The primary one experienced by doctoral programs is that, in some cases, students who take internships never finish their degree. Other problems that can occur are lack of competent supervision and, in some cases, the projects organizations give to students may not be meaningful. Despite these potential disadvantages, carefully monitored practical experience is usually a valuable component of graduate training. It is also an excellent way to promote the scientist-practitioner model to students.

(e.g., motivation, leadership, and so on). There are, however, some important components that future academicians need to incorporate into their graduate training. For example, it is important for those planning an academic career to become involved in research early in their graduate training. This increases the chances of gaining authorship of journal articles and conference presentations—something that definitely helps in a competitive job market. Research involvement also facilitates the development of close working relationships with faculty. These relationships are crucial in learning how to do research. Another essential component of the training of future academicians is teaching experience. Regardless of the type of institution in which one is employed, teaching is a major component of any academic position. Thus, graduate students who obtain significant teaching experience are much better prepared for academic positions than those with little or no experience.

Typical nonacademic employment settings for organizational psychologists include business organizations, consulting firms, non-profit research institutes, government agencies and research institutes, and even market

COMMENT 1.3

SCIENCE AND PRACTICE IN MY OWN CAREER

WHEN I REFLECT on my own career, the science-practice theme is very evident. Since receiving my Ph.D. in industrial/organizational psychology in 1988, I have carried on a very active program of research in the area of occupational stress. Thus, a good deal of what I do centers around the science. However, in addition to scientific activity, I have conducted a number of projects in organizations that have been designed to solve practical problems. For example, not long after starting my first job out of graduate school, I was the assistant investigator on a project conducted for the U.S. Army Research Institute. This project involved conducting an organizational assessment of the recruiting operations branch of the U.S Army. The Army was basically interested in ways that the recruiting branch could facilitate the training of field recruiters. Since that first project, I have worked with a number of organizations conducting applied research projects and developing training programs.

What have I learned from working with organizations? Probably most important, I have developed a great deal of respect for I/O psychologists who do applied work on a full-time basis. Applying research findings in organizational settings is tough work that requires considerable skill. Another thing I have learned is that, in most cases, *good science has practical value;* that is, when projects in organizations are conducted in a scientifically rigorous manner, organizations typically obtain much more useful information than when they are not. Finally, working in organizations has really convinced me of the viability of the scientist-practitioner model. The opportunity to do scientifically meaningful work that has practical value makes the field of I/O psychology very unique and exciting.

research firms. While actual job duties vary widely by setting, many organizational psychologists employed in nonacademic settings are involved in organizational change and development activities. This might involve assisting an organization in the development and implementation of an employee opinion survey program, designing and facilitating the implementation of team development activities, or perhaps assisting top management with the strategic planning process. The other major activity of those employed in nonacademic settings is research. This is particularly true of those employed in nonprofit research institutes, government research institutes, and market research firms. Given the diversity of these settings, it is difficult to pin down the exact nature of the research that is conducted.

However, in the most general sense, these individuals conduct scientific research that is designed to have some practical benefit to the organization or even to society in general.

To prepare for a nonacademic career, graduate students need training in many of the same areas as those pursuing academic careers. These include courses in research methodology, statistics, measurement, and several substantive topical areas. There is one important difference, however: It is essential for students planning nonacademic careers to obtain practical experience during their graduate training. This experience can often be gained by assisting faculty with consulting projects, or, in some cases, through formal internship programs (see Comment 1.4). Obtaining practical experience is crucial not only because it

COMMENT 1.4

PRACTICUM EXPERIENCE AT THE UNIVERSITY OF WISCONSIN OSHKOSH

ONE OF THE most important features of the graduate program in I/O psychology at the University of Wisconsin Oshkosh is the practicum course that is required of all second-year students. The purpose of this course is to provide students an opportunity to apply, in actual organizational settings and under the supervision of faculty, what they learned during the first year.

Typically, local organizations approach the I/O program faculty with some proposed organizational need that might be met by a student project. Examples of some of the projects that have been done in practicum include: employee opinion surveys, training needs assessment, customer service satisfaction surveys, and performance appraisal system development. After an organization has expressed a need, students typically meet with a representative from that organization to obtain more concrete information about the projects. This is typically followed by the submission, to that organization, of a formal proposal that includes the nature of the work to be done, the time frame under which the work will be done, and all of the "deliverables" that the organization will receive at the conclusion of the project.

The vast majority of students who graduate from the I/O program at the University of Wisconsin Oshkosh feel that the practicum experience was the most valuable component of their education. Furthermore, for some students, practicum experiences have led directly to permanent employment. By having the experience of applying what they have learned in classes, students are well prepared to meet the challenges of being a Master's-level I/O practitioner.

enhances a student's credentials, but because it provides valuable opportunities to apply what has been learned in graduate courses.

HISTORICAL INFLUENCES IN ORGANIZATIONAL PSYCHOLOGY

The year 1992 marked the hundredth anniversary of the field of psychology. To mark this centennial, much was written about the history of industrial/organizational psychology. This section, therefore, will not provide a detailed, comprehensive history of the field of organizational psychology. Rather, the intent is to provide a relatively concise summary of some of the people and historical events that have shaped the field.

Historical Beginnings

As Katzell and Austin (1992) point out, interest in the behavior of individuals in organizational settings undoubtedly dates back to ancient times: "In the organizational field, perhaps the earliest recorded consultant was the Midianite priest, Jethro, who advised his son-in-law, Moses, on how to staff and organize the ancient Israelites (Exod. 18)" (p. 803). *Formalized* attempts to study and influence such behavior, however, have a much more recent history.

To understand the more recent historical roots of organizational psychology, we must first examine the beginnings of the broader field of industrial/organizational psychology. Based on most historical accounts of the development of the field of I/O psychology, the industrial side of the field was much quicker to develop than the organizational side. Chronologically, the beginnings of the field of I/O psychology can be traced to work, during the early part of the twentieth century, by pioneers such as Hugo Munsterberg, Walter Dill Scott, and Walter Bingham. Most of the work at that time dealt with topics such as skill acquisition and personnel selection. Very little work dealing with the organizational side of the field was conducted. Table 1.1 provides a chronological summary of some of the major events that shaped the development of the field of organizational psychology in the twentieth century.

Ironically, the beginnings of the organizational side of the field can largely be traced to the work of several nonpsychologists. Perhaps the best known of these was Frederick Winslow Taylor, who developed the principles of **scientific management** (Taylor, 1911). Although the term *scientific management* typically conjures up images of time-and-motion study, as well as piece-rate compensation, it was actually much more than that. Scientific management was, to a large extent, a *philosophy* of management, and efficiency and piece-rate compensation were the most visible manifestations of that philosophy. When one looks past these more visible aspects of scientific management, three underlying principles emerge: (1) those who *perform* work tasks should be separate from those who *design* work tasks; (2) workers are rational beings, and they will work harder if provided with favorable economic incentives; and (3) problems in the workplace can and should be subjected to empirical study.

In considering the underlying principles of scientific management described above, the first principle is certainly contrary to much of the thinking in the field of organizational psychology today. The second principle, namely that employees will respond to financial incentives, has actually received considerable support over the years (Locke, 1982). The third principle, empirical study, is clearly the one that establishes the link between scientific management and what eventually became organizational psychology. In this respect, Taylor was a pioneer by employing scientific methodology to study production-related processes. (Most of his studies dealt with cutting sheet metal.) It should be noted, however, that

TABLE 1.1
A Chronological Summary of the Major Historical Influences on the Field of Organizational Psychology during the Twentieth Century

Early 1900s	Development and growth of Scientific Management (Taylor); beginning of the scientific study of organizational structure (Weber)
1920s–1930s	Hawthorne Studies; growth of unionization; immigration of Kurt Lewin to the United States
1940s–1950s	WWII; publication of Vitele's book *Motivation and Morale in Industry*; development of the "Human Relations" perspective; Lewin conducts "action research" projects for the Comission on Community Relations and establishes the Research Center for Group Dynamics at M.I.T.
1960s–1970s	U.S. involvement in Vietnam; Division 14 of the APA is changed to "Industrial/Organizational Psychology"; "multi-level" perspective in organizational psychology; increasing attention to nontraditional topics such as stress, work-family conflict, and retirement.
1980s—1990s	Increasing globalization of the economy; changing workforce demographics; increasing reliance on temporary or contingent employees; redefining the concept of a "job."

despite the impact of scientific management, many of Taylor's ideas met with a great deal of controversy (see Comment 1.5).

Another early nonpsychologist who contributed greatly to the development of organizational psychology was Max Weber. Weber's academic training was in law and history, but his legacy is largely in the field of organizational design. Weber is best known for his development of the notion of "bureaucracy" as an organizing principle. The basic idea of bureaucracy is that organizations should be designed so that employees know exactly what they are supposed to be doing, and the lines of authority are clearly stated. Another major principle of bureaucracy was that advancement and rewards should be based on merit and not on things such as nepotism or

---

COMMENT 1.5

FREDERICK WINSLOW TAYLOR: FATHER OF SCIENTIFIC MANAGEMENT

FREDERICK WINSLOW TAYLOR was born in 1856 in Germantown, Pennsylvania, a suburb of Philadelphia. Taylor was the son of affluent parents and spent a great deal of his childhood traveling in Europe. Perhaps the biggest turning point in Taylor's life came when, at the age of 18, he turned down the opportunity to study at Harvard, and instead accepted a position as an apprentice at the Enterprise Hydraulic Works in Philadelphia. Taylor worked there for two years before moving to Midvale Steel. He prospered at Midvale, working his way up to the supervisory ranks by the age of 24. It was during his time at Midvale that Taylor developed an interest in work methods and procedures—an interest that would lead to the famous pig iron experiments and ultimately to the development of Scientific Management.

The impact of Scientific Management during the early part of the twentieth century cannot be overstated. Most manufacturing was designed according to Scientific Management principles; in some cases, even white-collar jobs had elements of this approach. For Taylor, the emergence of Scientific Management meant a great deal of professional success and notoriety. Taylor eventually left Midvale, worked for several other organizations, and ultimately went out on his own and became one of the first management consultants. Many organizations contracted with Taylor to help them implement Scientific Management principles.

Despite these successes, Taylor's later years were not happy. Taylor's wife, Louise, suffered from chronic ill health, and Taylor himself was ill a great deal. In addition, Scientific Management came under fire, primarily due to the charge that it was inhumane to workers. In fact, this controversy became so great that, in 1912, Taylor was forced to testify before a congressional committee investigating the human implications of Scientific Management. This controversy took a toll on Taylor, both mentally and physically. He died in 1915 at the age of 59.

Regardless of the controversy that surrounded Taylor's Scientific Management, there is no denying its impact. For organizational psychology, the impact of Taylor was not so much in the principles he espoused, but in the methods that he used to develop those principles. By using data to solve work-related problems, Taylor pioneered an approach that has become a major part of modern organizational psychology and many other related fields.

Source: R. Kanigel. (1997). *The one best way: Frederick Winslow Taylor and the enigma of efficiency.* New York: Viking.

social class. Many principles of bureaucracy are taken for granted today and are even looked at with a bit of disdain, but these ideas were quite innovative at the time they were proposed by Weber.

Like Taylor, Weber was a pioneer because he went beyond merely giving advice about organization and management issues, and he subjected many of his ideas to empirical investigation. In addition to studying organizational design, Weber wrote extensively on organizational topics such as leadership, power, and norms at a time when these topics were largely ignored by psychologists. Willingness to study organizational issues empirically is one of the major defining characteristics of the field of organizational psychology and thus represents an important aspect of Weber's legacy (see Comment 1.6).

COMMENT 1.6

MAX WEBER: A PIONEER IN THE STUDY OF ORGANIZATIONS

MAX WEBER WAS born in 1864 in the Hanseatic town of Erfurt (which is now part of Germany) but spent the majority of his childhood in Berlin. Although Weber's parents were not wealthy, their social circles included many academicians, businessmen, artists, and politicians. Thus, Weber spent his early years in a richly intellectual environment. As a young man, Weber entered Heidelberg University to study law, although he never became a practicing lawyer. Instead, he completed his doctoral dissertation on medieval trading companies in 1889, and eventually secured a university appointment in Berlin. He moved back to Heidelberg in 1896, and, shortly after, suffered a nervous breakdown that plagued Weber's academic career for several years. During this period, Weber traveled extensively and ultimately resumed his scholarly work.

Following his travels, Weber completed influential essays on methods and procedures for studying social behavior, as well as the Protestant ethic. These essays were followed by a series of studies on legal institutions, religious systems, political economy, and authority relations. For organizational psychology, the studies of authority relations were especially significant because out of these came the well-known "principles of bureaucracy."

Weber's academic career was temporarily put on hold when World War I began in 1914. Although too old to fight, Weber contributed to the war effort by serving as a hospital administrator and as a member of a government commission examining tariff problems. During the latter part of the war, he resumed the scholarly work that eventually led to the book *Economy and Society*. Following the war, Weber tried unsuccessfully to establish a career in politics, something that evidently disappointed him greatly. He died in 1920, at the age of 56.

As a scholar, Weber was unique in two respects. First, his work represented the blending of the fields of law, history, and the social sciences. Thus, his work was clearly interdisciplinary in nature. Second, Weber was an excellent methodologist. Unlike many scholars of his era, Weber provided extensive documentation of his research findings, and he recommended that researchers attempt to unravel the causal factors underlying events. His methodological influence has perhaps been most evident in sociology and history, but has undoubtedly impacted psychology as well.

Source: F. Parkin. (1982). *Max Weber.* London: Routledge.

The Field Takes Shape

Despite the early work of Taylor and Weber, and others, the vast majority of effort in "Industrial" psychology in the early twentieth century was focused on what were described earlier as industrial topics. The event that changed that—an event many see as the beginning of organizational psychology—was the Hawthorne studies. The Hawthorne studies, a collaborative effort between the Western Electric Company and a group of researchers from Harvard University, took place between 1927 and 1932 (Mayo, 1933; Whitehead, 1935, 1938). The original purpose of the Hawthorne studies was to investigate the impact of environmental factors—such as illumination, wage incentives, and rest pauses—on employee productivity. Given the time period in which the Hawthorne studies were initiated (early 1920s), these topics were central to the dominant mode of managerial thought at the time: scientific management.

What made the Hawthorne studies so important to the field of organizational psychology were the unexpected, serendipitous findings that came out of the series of investigations. Perhaps the best known were the findings that came from the illumination experiments. Specifically, the Hawthorne researchers found that productivity increased regardless of the changes in level of illumination. This became the basis for what is termed the **Hawthorne effect,** or the idea that people will respond positively to any novel change in the work environment. In modern organizations, a Hawthorne effect might occur when a relatively trivial change is made in a person's job, and that person initially responds to this change very positively but the effect does not last long.

The significance of the Hawthorne studies, however, goes well beyond simply demonstrating a methodological artifact. For example, in subsequent studies, Hawthorne researchers discovered that work groups established and enforced production norms. In fact, it was found that those who did not adhere to production norms often met with very negative consequences from the other members of the work group, and that employees responded very differently to various methods of supervision. The overall implication of the Hawthorne studies, which later formed the impetus for organizational psychology, was that *social factors impact behavior in organizational settings.* This may seem a rather obvious conclusion today, but when considered in the historical context, it was a major finding. Those who focus only on the specific conclusions published by the Hawthorne researchers, as well as the methodological shortcomings of this research (e.g., Bramel & Friend, 1981; Carey, 1967), miss the much larger implications of this research effort.

During roughly the same time period in which the Hawthorne studies took place, another important historical influence on organizational psychology occurred: unionization. This is somewhat ironic, considering that I/O psychology, in general, is often viewed warily by unions (Zickar, 2001). However, the union movement in the United States during the 1930s was important because it forced organizations to consider, for the first time, many issues that are largely taken for granted today. For example, organizational topics such as participative decision making, workplace democracy, quality of worklife, and the psychological contract between employees and organizations are rooted, at least to some degree, in the union movement. Many of these issues were addressed in collective bargaining agreements in unionized organizations. Many nonunionized organizations were forced to address these issues due to the *threat* of unionization.

During the period of union growth in the 1930s, another event occurred that would prove to be very significant for the development of the field of organizational psychology: Kurt Lewin fled Nazi Germany and ultimately took a post at the University of Iowa Child Welfare Research Station. By the time he immigrated to the United States, Lewin was already a prominent social psychologist who had a variety of research interests, many of which were relevant to the emerging field of organizational psychology. Lewin's ideas, for example, have had a major impact in the areas of group dynamics, motivation, and leadership. Perhaps Lewin's greatest contribution was his willingness to use research to solve practical problems in both organizational and community settings. The term **action research,** which is typically associated with Lewin, refers to the idea that researchers and organizations can collaborate on research and use those findings to solve problems. The scientist-practitioner model can be traced to the action research model and thus stands as one of Lewin's most important contributions to the field (see Comment 1.7).

A Period of Growth

World War II had a tremendous impact on the growth of organizational psychology. For example, one of the results of World War II was that women were needed to fill many of the positions in factories that were vacated by the men called into military service. Also, shortly after World War II in 1948, President Harry S. Truman made the decision to pursue racial integration of the military. Both events were extremely important because they represented initial attempts to understand the impact of diversity on the workplace, a topic that has become quite pertinent in recent years.

World War II also served as the impetus for major studies of morale and leadership styles. Although Hollywood has managed to portray a somewhat idealized version of WWII, the U.S. military experienced problems with low morale and even desertion. Thus, troop morale and the influence of leadership were issues of great practical importance during this time.

Another very important event in the development of organizational psychology was the publication of Morris Viteles' book *Motivation and Morale in Industry* (1953). This was significant because Viteles' 1932 book, *Industrial Psychology,* had contained very little on the organizational side of the field, largely because there simply wasn't much subject matter at that time. Thus, the 1953 book signified that the organizational side of the field had finally "arrived" and had a significant role to play in the broader field of industrial psychology. It was also during the post-WWII period that the **human relations perspective** emerged within the field. Those who advocated this perspective (e.g., McGregor, 1960) argued that the way organizations had traditionally been managed kept employees from being creative and fulfilled on the job. During this time, for example, Herzberg conducted his studies of job design and job enrichment, and major research programs investigating both leadership and job satisfaction were conducted. By the early 1960s, organizational psychology was clearly an *equal partner* with the industrial side of the field in terms of the research topics studied and the activities of those in nonacademic settings (Jeanneret, 1991).

Another broader social factor impacted the development of organizational psychology during the 1960s and early 1970s: the U.S. involvement in the Vietnam War, which led to many cultural changes in America and in other countries. During this period, for example, many young people began to question the wisdom of societal institutions such as education, government, and the legal system.

COMMENT 1.7

KURT LEWIN: THE PRACTICAL THEORIST

KURT LEWIN WAS born in 1890 in the village of Mogilno, which was then part of the Prussian province of Posen (now part of Poland). Lewin's father owned a general store, as well as a small farm, so the family was prosperous although not wealthy. In 1905, Lewin's family moved to Berlin, largely to gain better educational opportunities than were available in Mogilno. Lewin entered the University of Frieberg in 1909, initially with the goal of studying medicine. His distaste for anatomy courses contributed to Lewin's abandoning the goal of becoming a physician. He switched his interest to biology. This led to a transfer first to the University of Munich and ultimately to the University of Berlin, where he eventually earned his doctorate in 1916. After returning from military service during World War I, he began his academic career.

The years at Berlin were very productive, and Lewin's work became quite influential. At this time, Lewin began to develop an interest in the application of psychology to applied problems such as agricultural labor, production efficiency, and the design of jobs. Lewin became quite interested in scientific management, particularly the impact of this system on workers. Lewin and his family left Germany in 1933 due to the rise of the Nazi party. He initially received a temporary appointment at Cornell University, and ultimately moved to the University of Iowa Child Welfare Research Station. While at Iowa, Lewin conducted influential studies on a variety of topics, including child development, the impact of social climates, and leadership. Following his years at Iowa, Lewin became deeply involved in the Commission on Community Relations, which was established by the American Jewish Congress. During his involvement, Lewin initiated a number of "action research" projects aimed at enhancing understanding of community problems such as racial prejudice, gang violence, and integrated housing. Remarkably, during this same time, Lewin also founded the Research Center for Group Dynamics at MIT. Lewin's work at the Center continued until his death in 1947, at the age of 56.

In retrospect, it is hard to imagine anyone having a greater impact on the field of organizational psychology than Kurt Lewin. His ideas continue to influence the study of a number of areas such as employee motivation, leadership, group dynamics, and organizational development. However, perhaps Lewin's most enduring legacy was his innovative blending of science and practice.

Source: A. J. Marrow. (1969). *The practical theorist: The life and work of Kurt Lewin.* New York: Basic Books.

Many, in fact, suspected that the federal government was not truthful about many important details of the war. Furthermore, subsequent accounts of the war by historians have proven that many of these suspicions were justified (e.g., Small, 1999). People at that time also began to feel as though they should have much more freedom to express themselves in a variety of ways (e.g., hairstyles, dress, speech).

For organizations, the cultural changes that arose out of the 1960s had major implications. In essence, it was becoming less and less common for people to blindly follow authority. Therefore, organizations had to find methods of motivating employees, other than simply offering financial incentives or threatening punishment. It was also becoming more and more common for employees to seek fulfillment in areas of their life other than work. Thus, it was becoming increasingly difficult to find employees who were willing to focus exclusively on work.

Maturity and Expansion

From the early 1970s into the 1980s, organizational psychology began to mature as a field of study. For example, during the early 1970s, the name of Division 14 of the American Psychological Association (APA) was formally changed from "Industrial Psychology" to "Industrial/Organizational Psychology." Also during this period, organizational psychologists began to break significant new ground in both theory and research. As just a few examples, Salancik and Pfeffer (1978) proposed Social Information Processing Theory (SIP) as an alternative to more traditional need-based theories of job satisfaction and job design. Also, roughly during this period, organizational psychology began to "rediscover" the impact of personality and dispositions on things such as job attitudes (Staw & Ross, 1985) and perceptions of job-related stress (Watson & Clark, 1984).

Another noteworthy development that took hold during this period, and continues today, was the recognition that behavior in organizations is impacted by forces at the group and organizational levels (e.g., James & Jones, 1974; Rousseau, 1985). This "multilevel" perspective has had major implications for the field in guiding theory development as well as statistical methodology (e.g., Dansereau, Alutto, & Yammarino, 1984; James, Demaree, & Wolf, 1984). During this same period, organizational psychologists began to devote increasing attention to what could be called "nontraditional" topics. For example, more

literature began to appear on work/family issues (e.g., Greenhaus & Buetell, 1985), job-related stress and health (Beehr & Newman, 1978), and retirement (Beehr, 1986). This willingness to explore nontraditional topics was significant because it served as evidence that the interests of organizational psychologists had broadened beyond purely management concerns.

RECENT PAST AND BEYOND

From the late 1980s to the present, a number of trends have impacted and will continue to impact the field of organizational psychology. If one takes a global perspective, perhaps the most significant event of this period was the breakup of the Soviet Union and the eventual fall of many Communist regimes. These extraordinary events have implications for organizational psychology because a number of the nations that embraced democracy during this period have also attempted to establish free market economies. As many of these new democracies have found, managing and motivating employees in state-owned businesses is quite different from doing so in a free market economy (Frese, Kring, Soose, & Zempel, 1996; Puffer, 1999; Stroh & Dennis, 1994). The science and the practice of organizational psychology have the potential to help these nations make this difficult economic transition.

Another important trend, both in the United States and worldwide, is the change in the demographic composition of the workforce. The world population is aging rapidly and becoming more ethnically diverse. One of the implications of these demographic shifts is that organizational psychologists will likely devote much more time and attention to understanding the process of retirement (e.g., Adams & Beehr, 1998). Organizational psychologists will likely help organizations as they assist employees in making the retirement transition. The increasing level of cultural diversity will also have wide-ranging implications. Organizational psychologists will increasingly be called upon to investigate the impact of cultural differences on organizational processes such as socialization, communication, and motivation.

A third trend that has become widely evident in recent years is the move away from highly specific jobs, and toward more temporary, project-based work. Some have labeled this "dejobbing" (Bridges, 1994). This trend has a number of implications for organizational psychology. At the most fundamental level, this trend has impacted and will continue to impact the "psychological contract" between organizations and employees. What does an organization owe its employees? What do employees owe the organization they work for? In the past, the answers to these questions were rather straightforward; now, they have become increasingly complex.

Another implication of this trend is that many individuals in the future will not be "employees" in the way we typically use that word today. Rather, in the future, it will become increasingly common for individuals to hire themselves out on a project or "per diem" basis. This trend suggests a number of interesting and challenging issues for organizational psychologists. How does an organization maintain a consistent culture and philosophy with a relatively transient workforce? Is it possible to motivate temporary employees to perform beyond an average level of performance? At the present time, we simply do not know the answers to these and many other questions.

The trends discussed above represent only a subset of those that will impact organizational psychology in the twenty-first century. Other current issues that will continue to impact the field include technological change, increasing use of telecommuting and other

flexible work arrangements, and increased globalization, to name a few. Considering all of these trends, it is clear that the work world of the future will be highly complex and fast-paced. This may seem rather intimidating, but it is also a very exciting prospect for the field of organizational psychology because it will allow for truly groundbreaking research and practical applications. In fact, this is one of the most exciting times in history to be involved in the science and practice of organizational psychology.

THE CHAPTER SEQUENCE

A textbook should function as a tour guide for the student. In my experience, both as a student and course instructor, the best way to guide is in a logical sequential fashion. The sequence of chapters in this book was developed with this consideration in mind. The chapters in Part I provide introductory material on the field of organizational psychology as well as its methodological foundations. Some students (and maybe even some instructors) may find it unusual to have a chapter on research methodology. I've included it for three primary reasons. First, understanding research methodology is fundamental to understanding many of the concepts and research findings discussed throughout the text. Second, research methodology is a legitimate area of inquiry within organizational psychology. In fact, some of the most important research within organizational psychology in recent years has been methodologically oriented. Finally, as a course instructor and supervisor of student research, I have found that students can never have too much methodological training.

The first seven chapters focus on the behavior of individuals in organizational settings. A close examination of these chapters reveals a sequential ordering. It is assumed that individuals are initially socialized into an organization (Chapter 3), become productive members of that organization (Chapter 4), and derive some level of satisfaction and commitment (Chapter 5). It is also recognized that individuals may engage in behaviors that are counterproductive to their employer (Chapter 6), and that work may have a negative effect on the health and well-being of employees (Chapter 7).

The next three chapters focus on the mechanisms that organizations use to influence employees' behavior. To this end, Chapter 8 covers the major motivation theories in organizational psychology. In Chapter 9, we examine the various ways in which organizations utilize theories of motivation to actually influence employees' behavior. Chapter 10 examines the other primary mechanism that organizations use to influence behavior, namely leadership. This chapter also examines the power and influence processes that are at the core of leadership.

In the next three chapters, the focus of the book shifts from the individual to the group level. This is very important, given the increased reliance on teams in many organizations. Chapter 11 introduces the basic concepts underlying group behavior. Chapter 12 describes the factors that have the greatest impact on group effectiveness. In Chapter 13, the dynamics underlying intergroup behavior are examined.

In the final three chapters, the focus shifts from the group to the organization—the "macro" level. Chapter 14 reviews several theoretical approaches used to define an organization and examines approaches to organizational design. Chapter 15 probes the concepts of organizational culture and climate. Chapter 16 describes the variety of ways in which organizations engage in planned change with the assistance of behavioral science knowledge.

One topic that readers will notice is *not* the focus of any one chapter is international or cross-cultural issues. This book examines cross-cultural issues in the context of the various topics covered in the chapters. This was done intentionally because I believe cross-cultural findings are best understood and assimilated in the context of specific topics.

CHAPTER SUMMARY

Organizational psychology is the scientific study of individual and group behavior informal organizational settings. While it is a legitimate field of study in its own right, organizational psychology is actually part of the broader field of Industrial/Organizational (I/O) psychology. Organizational psychologists use scientific methods to study behavior in organizations. They also use this knowledge to solve practical problems in organizations; this is the essence of the scientist–practitioner model, the model on which most graduate training in I/O psychology is based. Thus, those with training in organizational psychology are employed in both academic and nonacademic settings. Historically, organizational psychology was slower to develop than the industrial side of the field. The event that is usually considered the historical beginning of organizational psychology was the Hawthorne studies, although many other events and individuals have helped to shape the field over the years. A constant thread through the history of the field is the dynamic interaction between science and practice; in most cases for the betterment of organizations and their employees.

SUGGESTED ADDITIONAL READINGS

Dunnette, M. D. (1990). Blending the science and practice of industrial and organizational psychology: Where are we and where are we going? In M. D. Dunnette & L. M. Hough

(Eds.), *Handbook of industrial and organizational psychology* (2nd ed., Vol. 1, pp. 1–38). Palo Alto, CA: Consulting Psychologists Press.

Hyatt, D., Cropanzano, R., Finfer, L. A., Levy, P., Ruddy, T. M., Vandaveer, V., & Walker, S. (1997). Bridging the gap between academics and practice: Suggestions from the field. *Industrial-Organizational Psychologist, 35,* 29–32.

Kanigel, R. (1997). *The one best way: Frederick Winslow Taylor and the enigma of efficiency.* New York: Viking.

Chapter Two

Research Methods and Statistics

Because organizational psychology is a science, research methodology and statistical analysis are extremely important. Organizational psychologists routinely design scientific investigations to answer theoretically based research questions about behavior in organizational settings. As will be shown, these methods may range from simple observation of behavior to elaborate field-based quasi-experimentation. The data from such studies are then analyzed using a variety of statistical methods to test the validity of predictions.

Research methodology and statistical analysis are also crucial to the practice of organizational psychology. For example, organizational psychologists often use systematic research methods to provide organizational decision makers with information regarding employees' attitudes. In other cases, research methodology and statistical analysis are used to evaluate some intervention designed to enhance organizational effectiveness. An organization may want to know, for example, whether a team development intervention will enhance the functioning of work groups. This question, and others like it, can be answered with the aid of typical research methods and statistical analyses used in organizational psychology.

In addition to facilitating the science and practice of organizational psychology, research methodology and statistical analysis have both emerged as legitimate fields of study in their own right. Some organizational psychologists study topics such as job satisfaction, motivation, and organizational change; others have devoted their attention to methodological and statistical issues. For example, there are organizational psychologists who investigate the validity of self-report measures as well as the statistical methods used to detect moderator variables. Both topics will be discussed later in the chapter.

The purpose of this chapter is to provide a basic introduction to the methods organizational psychologists use to collect data, as well as the statistical techniques used to analyze it. From the student's perspective, research methodology and statistics are often viewed with some degree of apprehension. Even at the graduate level, methodology and statistics courses are often the most feared. Despite these negative perceptions, research methodology and statistics courses are probably the most valuable part of graduate training. Students who are well grounded in research methodology and statistics are in the best position to read and critically evaluate the research literature. They also possess a set of skills that are quite valuable, regardless of the setting in which they choose to work.

METHODS OF DATA COLLECTION

There are literally thousands of research questions that have been, and continue to be, explored by organizational psychologists. Are employees who perceive a high level of autonomy in their work likely to be highly satisfied with their jobs? Does a high level of conflict between work and family responsibilities lead to poor health? Does job performance remain consistent over time? Regardless of the research question being asked, there is a need for relevant data to be collected if the question is ever to be answered. In this section, four data collection methods will be discussed. These include observational meth-

ods, survey research, experimentation, and quasi-experimentation.

Observational Methods

Observational methods actually encompass a variety of strategies that may be used to study behavior in organizations (Bouchard, 1976). **Simple observation,** the most basic of these strategies, involves observing and recording behavior. If one wishes, for example, to investigate decision-making processes used by corporate boards of directors, one might observe these individuals during quarterly meetings and record relevant observations. These observations may reveal that the chairperson has more input into decisions than other board members, or that younger board members have less input into decisions than their more experienced counterparts.

Simple observation is useful as a data collection method because it allows behavior to be captured in its natural context. This allows the researcher to avoid the problem of **reactivity** (changing the phenomenon of interest in the process of measuring it). This is only a *potential* advantage, however, because the presence of an observer could cause research participants to act differently than they normally would. One way to address this issue is to establish rapport with research participants to the point where they are comfortable enough with the researcher to act naturally. Another option would be to observe behavior *unobtrusively.* Many retail stores use this method; they send "mystery shoppers" to stores in order to measure the quality of customer service. The use of unobtrusive observations raises ethical concerns, however, because when it is used, research participants typically are not able to make an informed choice as to whether they wish to participate in the research.

The primary disadvantage of simple observation is that it is a very labor-intensive activity. Observing and making sense of behavior takes a great deal of time and effort. It is also true that observations are often subjective and may be impacted by the observer's biases. Nevertheless, simple observation can often be quite useful, particularly in the very preliminary stages of a research program. Also, from a practical perspective, managers may find the information generated from observational studies easier to understand, and therefore more useful, than numerical data.

A variant of simple observation that may be useful in some cases is **participant observation.** Participant observation is essentially the same as simple observation except that the observer is also a participant in the event he or she is studying. If, in the previous example of studying corporate boards of directors, the researcher were also a *member* of the board being studied, this would be participant observation. Participant observation can be highly useful, particularly when being a participant in an event provides the researcher with information that may not be obtained otherwise. A good example of the use of participant observation is Van Maanen's (1975) investigation of police recruits as they made the transition from the training academy to regular police work. In conducting this study, Van Maanen participated in the police academy training as a recruit, and thus became a participant in the event being studied. By doing this, he undoubtedly was able to gather information that would have been unavailable through the use of other methods (see Comment 2.1).

Despite the potential advantages of participant observation, this method also carries some risks. The biggest risk is that the researcher, by taking on the role of participant, may change the phenomenon under investigation. This is somewhat ironic, considering

that the general *advantage* of observational methods is that they reduce the risk of reactivity. Being a participant may also lead the researcher to lose his or her objectivity. As previously stated, all observations are subject to distortion, but assuming the role of a participant may compound the problem. In Van Maanen's (1975) study, this problem was dealt with by supplementing his observations with survey data.

A third observational method for studying behavior in organizations is the use of **archival data** sources. Archival data represent any form of data or records that are compiled for purposes that are independent of the research being conducted (Webb, Campbell, Schwartz, Sechrest, & Grove, 1981). The use of archival data is more prevalent in organizational psychology, at least compared to simple or participant observation, because of the sheer abundance of archival data sources. Within organizations, records are typically kept on many employee behaviors such as job performance, absenteeism, turnover, and safety, to name a few. In addition, the governments of many countries maintain databases that may be relevant to the study of behavior in organizations. In the United States, for example, the Department of Labor produces the *Dictionary of Occupational Titles (DOT),* which contains information on the working conditions of a vast number of occupations. This database has been used in several investigations of behavior in organizations (e.g., Schaubroeck, Ganster, & Kemmerer, 1994; Spector & Jex, 1991). Recently, the *DOT* has been supplemented by a more extensive database in the form of the Occupational Information Network (O*NET). This represents an improvement over the *DOT* because the occupations that comprise the O*NET are more up-to-date, and the dimensions on which these occupations are described are more extensive. To date, only a few studies have used O*NET

THE PROS AND CONS OF QUALITATIVE RESEARCH METHODS

WITHIN THE GENERAL field of psychology, and organizational psychology in particular, qualitative data collection methods such as observation are not widely used. In other fields such as sociology and anthropology, qualitative methods are used quite frequently. In psychology, we make much greater use of surveys and, to a lesser extent, experimentation and quasi-experimentation (Sackett & Larsen, 1990). In talks with colleagues over the years, the typical disadvantages associated with qualitative methods have been: they are too labor-intensive and too many biases are associated with the observational process.

Unfortunately, because of these disadvantages, many in psychology fail to see many of the positive features of qualitative data collection methods. Chief among these is that observation typically provides a much richer description of whatever one is trying to study than questionnaire data do. For example, observing a group working together for a week is probably more meaningful than knowing group members rate the group's cohesiveness as 4.3 on a 1–6 scale. Another advantage of most qualitative data collection methods is that they do not require research participants to provide assessments of either themselves or

the work environment. For example, we may be able to determine, through observations, that an employee has a great deal of autonomy built into his or her job. If we were to *ask* the employee several questions about job autonomy via a questionnaire, the employee's responses might be biased because of a temporary mood state or overall job satisfaction.

In reality, researchers do not have to make "either/or" decisions in choosing between qualitative and quantitative research methods. For example, in conducting employee opinion surveys, I typically use closed-ended questionnaire items, but I also include space at the end of the survey for employees to write comments that are then analyzed for content. This allows for quantitative analysis of the closed-ended survey items, but employees can express their opinions in their own words. Written comments may also reveal very useful suggestions to organizational decision makers.

Source: P. R. Sackett and J. R. Larsen, Jr. (1990). Research strategies and tactics in industrial and organizational psychology. In M. D. Dunnette & L. M. Hough (Eds.), *Handbook of industrial and organizational psychology* (2nd ed., Vol. 1, pp. 419–490). Palo Alto, CA: Consulting Psychologists Press.

as an archival data source in the same manner as the *DOT* (e.g., Primeau, 2000), but it is likely that more will follow.

The use of archival data offers several advantages to researchers. First, many archival databases are readily available to the public and can be accessed quite easily—in many cases, via the Internet. Second, archival data are nonreactive. Archival data typically are not collected for the researcher's purpose, so there is no chance that participants will dis-

tort responses in a way that would impact the validity of the research. Finally, when archival data are used to measure employee behaviors, such records are usually less subject to distortion than self-reports of the same behavior.

Despite these advantages, the use of archival data may present several problems. One is that archival data are often only *indirect* measures of the phenomenon that is of interest to the researcher. Using databases such as the *DOT* or O*NET to measure characteristics of employees' jobs illustrates this problem quite well. Information contained in both of these databases is collected at the *occupation* level, so using it may mask important differences between individuals who may have the *same* occupation but perform substantially *different* work, or perform under very different conditions. For example, the job experiences of a nurse employed in a rural health clinic may be substantially different from those of a nurse employed in a large urban hospital.

Another potential problem is that the accuracy of archival data is often questionable. Organizations differ widely in the precision of their record-keeping practices. Furthermore, there may be instances where it is actually in an organization's interest to distort records. For example, organizations may underreport accidents or other negative incidents in order to avoid negative publicity or increases in insurance costs. The best course of action when using any form of archival data is to insist on some form of evidence supporting the accuracy of the information.

Survey Research

By far, the most widely used form of data collection in organizational psychology is survey research (Scandura & Williams, 2000). Survey research simply involves asking research participants to report about their attitudes and/or behaviors, either in writing or verbally. This form of research is extremely common in our society and is used to gather information for a wide variety of purposes. Most readers have probably participated in some form of survey research.

Before describing the general steps involved in conducting a survey research project, it is useful to consider the purposes of survey research. In many cases, survey research is conducted to provide purely descriptive information. For example, the top management team in an organization may wish to know the current level of employee job satisfaction, or a government agency may want to assess the income level of working adults. Survey research is also conducted to test hypotheses regarding the relationships between variables. For example, a researcher may want to assess whether employees who perceive a great deal of autonomy in their jobs also report a high level of job satisfaction. In this case, the researcher is less concerned with the *level* of autonomy or job satisfaction than with the relationship between these two variables.

As shown in Figure 2.1, the first step in conducting a survey research project is to identify the variables that one will be measuring. For many research projects, the variables

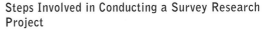

FIGURE 2.1

Steps Involved in Conducting a Survey Research Project

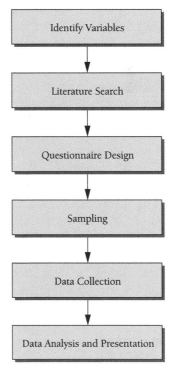

will be directly linked to the research question one is examining. If a researcher were interested in the relationship between interpersonal conflict on the job and employees' satisfaction with their jobs, these would obviously be the variables measured. In many applied projects in organizations, the choice of variables to be measured is based on the concerns of upper management personnel or, in some cases, a cross-section of employees from all levels. This is often achieved through the use of **focus groups** consisting of either top managers or groups of other employees. A focus group is a qualitative data-gathering technique that is often used to generate ideas during the preliminary stages of a research project. For example, to determine what to measure on a survey, a researcher might conduct a focus group with the top management of an organization. The researcher might begin the focus group session by posing a question—"What are the biggest concerns of employees in this organization?"—and noting the issues that come up during the ensuing discussion.

Once the researcher has decided on the variables that will be measured in a survey, the next step is to conduct an extensive search of the relevant literature. This is done to determine whether acceptable measures of the variables of interest exist. For many variables of interest to organizational psychologists, a variety of acceptable measures are available. Using previously developed measures saves a researcher considerable time; there is no need to "reinvent the wheel" each time a variable is measured. Using established measures in applied projects such as employee opinion surveys is often more difficult because many of the variables measured may be unique to a particular organization. In the author's experience, organizations often want survey items "customized," to enhance the relevance of the information.

Once a researcher has decided on the variables to be measured, the next step is to design the questionnaire or survey instrument. This step is extremely important because the quality of the questionnaire will strongly impact the integrity of the data generated. Designing a high-quality survey instrument is a time-consuming, painstaking process. Fortunately, there are excellent sources of information one can refer to for assistance in the questionnaire design process (e.g., Dillman, 2000). One general rule should guide the development of any questionnaire: It should be *easy for the respondent to complete.* Instructions should be easy to understand, response categories should be well defined, and the items should be clearly written. It is also important, in the questionnaire design process, to conduct some form of *pilot testing,* even if this involves simply asking a colleague to read through the questionnaire. Careful pilot testing may reveal unclear instructions, poorly worded items, or even misspellings.

After the questionnaire is designed and pilot tested, the next step is to determine specifically who the respondents will be. When research is conducted within organizations, this may involve simply including all employees. In other cases, it may be necessary to narrow the pool of responding employees. For example, if one were studying customer service behavior among employees, it would make sense to restrict the pool of respondents to those employees who have at least some contact with customers.

In cases where the number of potential respondents may be so large that it is impractical for the researcher to include everyone, some form of **probability sampling** may be utilized. The idea behind probability sampling is that the researcher selects a sample from a larger group (or population) in order to generalize the results to that larger group, with some margin of error (Fowler, 1984).

The most basic form of probability sampling is **simple random sampling.** This involves selecting members of a population such that everyone has an equal and nonzero probability of being included in the sample. An example of this would be if 200 employees from a large organization were randomly selected from a current employee directory to participate in an organizational survey.

Another form of probability sampling sometimes used is **stratified random sampling.** This essentially represents the application of simple random sampling within identifiable groups or "strata." The major reason for using stratified random sampling is to increase the precision of estimates (Fowler, 1984). The logic is that if estimates are made within strata and pooled, the result will be more precise than applying simple random sampling within an entire population. Stratified random sampling can also be used to increase the chances that the sample will closely mirror the population. If, for example, an organization consists of five different employee groups that are represented in equal proportions, *proportional* stratified random sampling can be used to increase the chances that the proportion of the job types in the sample will closely reflect the proportion in the organization.

A third form of probability sampling that may be useful in some cases is **cluster sampling.** What distinguishes this from the other two forms of sampling previously described is that the unit of sampling is no longer the individual but, instead, some larger unit or "cluster." An illustration of how cluster sampling can be used comes from a research project the author conducted several years ago for the U.S. Army Recruiting Command (US-AREC). This organization is very geographically dispersed and consists of multiple levels (brigades, battalions, companies, and stations). In the initial stages of the project, it

was decided that approximately 50 face-to-face interviews needed to be conducted with personnel at brigade, battalion, and company levels. Rather than randomly selecting individuals from these three levels, it was decided to first randomly select two battalions within each brigade. Two individuals were interviewed in each battalion, as well as in the company located closest to each battalion.

The primary advantage of cluster sampling is that it allows the researcher to cut down on travel time and expense. Imagine if simple random sampling had been used instead of cluster sampling in the previously described project. The 50 individuals selected to be interviewed may have been so geographically spread out that a separate trip would have been required to conduct each interview. The risk one runs in using cluster sampling is that the sample may not be as representative as would be the case if simple random sampling were used.

Once the researcher determines who the participants will be, the next step is to actually collect data. In collecting survey data, several options are available, and each option has advantages and disadvantages. With written organizational surveys, the *ideal* way to collect data is to have groups of employees complete the questionnaire in a centralized location and return the completed questionnaire to the researcher immediately after completion. This is ideal because it provides the best chance for a favorable response rate. A very low response rate is undesirable because it raises concerns about whether the survey results truly represent the target group. For example, in an organization where the author once worked, an employee opinion survey was conducted and the response rate was approximately 10%! This low response rate was revealing in and of itself, but it also raised questions about the validity of the information.

In some cases, centralized data collection is not possible because of employees' schedules or concerns about confidentiality. Other options that are used in some cases are: mailing questionnaires to employees' homes, or administering a questionnaire verbally by telephone, or via the Internet (see Comment 2.2). Although these methods are somewhat less desirable than centralized on-site data collection, there are actually many ways that researchers can use them and achieve very favorable response rates (e.g., Dillman, 2000).

The final step in conducting a survey research project is the analysis and presentation of the data. The analysis of survey data is dictated largely by the purpose of the survey. If the purpose is description (which is usually the case when organizations initiate survey research projects), analyses are relatively simple and straightforward. Descriptive indexes (e.g., means, ranges, percentages) will usually suffice in such situations. In cases where survey data are used for hypothesis testing, analyses are conducted to test hypothesized relations between variables. More detailed information on statistical analyses used in hypothesis testing will be discussed later in the chapter. However, it is worth noting here that survey data are typically best for assessing *covariation* among variables. Assessing causality

---

COMMENT 2.2

USE OF THE INTERNET FOR SURVEY DATA COLLECTION

As MOST READERS know, the Internet has had an enormous influence on many areas of our lives, including shopping, education, and even relationships. Given this influence, it is not surprising that many researchers have begun to make use of Internet-based surveys.

Dr. Gary Adams, one of my colleagues at the University of Wisconsin Oshkosh, recently used the Internet to conduct an employee opinion survey for a small software development company in southern Ohio. The employees from this company were able to access and complete the survey from a Web site. After employees completed the survey online, their responses were sent to a data file for processing. From a researcher's point of view, conducting survey research in this way is much more efficient than using paper-and-pencil survey forms because it eliminates the need to scan responses or, in some cases, to enter the responses by hand. From the respondent's point of view, the potential advantages of this form of data collection are that it is convenient, and it projects a higher level of privacy. Potential disadvantages of using the Internet to administer surveys (which were not true in this case) are the fact that all potential respondents may not have Internet access, and some of those who do may be lacking in computer literacy (Dillman, 2000).

Given the convenience of Internet-based surveys, this method of data collection is surely going to be used much more in the future. In fact, it's very possible that at some point, all surveys will be done in this manner. Hopefully, as this use picks up, researchers will investigate the limitations of this method and improvements will be made as needed. For instance, there is very little research on how the psychometric properties (e.g., reliability and validity) of Internet-based surveys compare to their paper-and-pencil counterparts.

Sources: Dr. Gary Adams, personal communication, May 26, 2000; and D. A. Dillman. (2000). *Mail and Internet surveys: The tailored design method* (2nd ed.). New York: Wiley.

from survey data is much more difficult because such data are usually collected at one point in time.

Experimentation

Another common form of data collection in organizational psychology is **experimentation.** An experiment is essentially a controlled situation that provides the researcher with the best opportunity, compared to other research methods, of assessing cause-and-effect relationships. This is important because the hallmark of any science is to detect and explain causal relationships.

Unfortunately, because "experiment" is a very common term, students are often confused about what constitutes a "true" experiment. According to Cook and Campbell (1979), there are essentially three characteristics that distinguish an experiment from other methods. These are: (1) manipulation of an independent variable and measurement of a dependent variable; (2) random assignment to experimental treatment conditions; and (3) maximum control by the experimenter. Let's examine each of these characteristics.

The term **independent variable** is used to designate the variable that is proposed to have some effect on other variables, and hence is typically of primary interest to the researcher. When the independent variable is "manipulated," this means that the research participants experience different *levels* of this variable. If a researcher were interested in the impact of feedback on performance, for example, the independent variable would be feedback. This variable could be *manipulated* by providing some research participants with feedback after performing a task, while providing no feedback to others.

The measurement of the **dependent variable** simply involves some record of the research participants' behavior or attitudes that may be impacted by the independent variable. Choice of dependent measures is often based on past research or convention. It is always important, however, to keep in mind that the dependent measure being used is really just an *operational definition* of a concept. For example, job satisfaction represents whether a person has a positive or negative feeling about his or her job or a job situation. If a five-item scale is used to assess job satisfaction, this measure is really being used to *represent* this conceptual definition.

The second defining characteristic of experimentation, **random assignment,** implies that research participants are assigned to *treatment conditions* (i.e., groups receiving different levels of the independent variable) in a random or nonsystematic fashion. Randomly assigning research participants can usually be accomplished quite easily—for example, by flipping a coin. The logic behind random assignment is that if research participants are assigned in a truly random fashion, it is *likely* that the different treatment groups will be similar in all ways except for the independent variable. This allows the researcher to isolate the independent variable as the cause of any differences between treatment groups on the dependent variable.

The third defining characteristic of an experiment, **maximum control,** simply implies that the manipulation of the independent variable and the measurement of the dependent variable are done under controlled conditions. The researcher tries to make sure that all variables other than the independent variable are held constant for the different treatment groups. Like random assignment, this is done to isolate the independent variable as the cause of any differences among the treatment groups. When experiments are conducted in laboratory settings, it is usually not too difficult for the researcher to achieve a desirable level of control. However, this is a much greater challenge when experiments are conducted in field settings.

Quasi-Experimentation

According to Cook, Campbell, and Perrachio (1990), a quasi-experiment is similar to a true experiment except that it lacks one or more of the essential features previously described. In organizational settings, the independent variable of interest often cannot be manipulated because it is under the control of the organization or may even be a naturally occurring event. Examples of independent variables that are usually under organizational control include training programs or the redesign of jobs. Naturally occurring events that may qualify as independent variables include computer shutdowns, changes in government regulations, or mergers. In all of these cases, the researcher has no control over which research participants receive which "treatments."

Quasi-experimental designs are also used in organizational settings because research participants often cannot be randomly assigned to treatment conditions. Assignment to training programs provides a good example of nonrandom assignment. Employees typically participate in training programs, either voluntarily or on the basis of an identified training need (Goldstein, 1993). Thus, in most cases, if a researcher were to compare training program participants to nonparticipants, it is quite possible that these two groups could differ in important ways.

Given the constraints that accompany quasi-experimentation, how do researchers set about proving that an independent variable has a causal impact on a dependent measure? One way is to measure and statistically control variables that may obscure the relationship between the independent and dependent variables. For example, if we know

that the average age of a group of employees receiving one level of the independent variable is higher than the age of groups receiving other levels, age can be measured and statistically controlled when comparing the groups. This would be using age as a **covariate.**

Other than statistical control, quasi-experimentation typically requires that researchers systematically identify and rule out alternatives to the independent variable when differences between treatment groups are found. According to Cook and Campbell (1979), there is a variety of explanations, other than the independent variable, that may lead to a difference between treatment groups in quasi-experimental designs. For example, treatment groups may be exposed to different historical events, they may change at different rates, or they may have differing views about participating in the research.

Regardless of the specific alternative explanation, a researcher conducting a quasi-experiment does not know for sure which of these are impacting his or her findings. However, it is often possible to assess the *plausibility* of different alternative explanations. For example, let's say a researcher conducted a quasi-experiment in which the job of bank teller was redesigned at one branch of a bank, but remained the same at another. Let's further assume that customer satisfaction is found to be higher at the branch where the job redesign took place. The job redesign may have caused the increase in customer satisfaction, but since this was not a true experiment, there may be alternative explanations. To rule out alternative explanations, the researcher could begin by comparing these two branches to see whether any preexisting differences between employees in the two branches could have caused the difference in customer satisfaction. If the employees at these two branches were similar in terms of tenure and overall job performance, these could be ruled out as alternative explanations for the findings. The researcher could also gather information on the nature of the customers who frequent each of the two branches. If customers at the two branches are demographically similar, for example, this could also be ruled out as an explanation of the difference in customer satisfaction. The researcher, in effect, plays detective in order to identify and rule out alternative explanations for his or her findings.

Choosing a Data Collection Method

Given the information presented about each method of data collection, the reader may wonder how to go about choosing which method to use. Unfortunately, there is no concrete formula for making this choice. Perhaps the best approach is to weigh the advantages and disadvantages of each method. As is illustrated in Figure 2.2, the primary advantage of observational methods is that they provide the researcher with an opportunity to study behavior in its natural context. Unfortunately, observational techniques tend to be highly labor-intensive.

Survey methodology allows the researcher to obtain data from a large number of participants at a relatively low cost. However, it is typically difficult to draw causal inferences from survey data, especially when the data are cross sectional. Experimentation provides the researcher the best way to assess causal relationships. In some cases, however, the generalizability of experimental findings may be questionable. Finally, quasi-experimentation, in many cases, offers the researcher a way to assess causal relationships in naturalistic settings. However, quasi-experiments may be difficult to conduct because researchers typically have little control in most field settings.

FIGURE 2.2

Summary of the Primary Advantages and Disadvantages Associated with Each of the Four Data Collection Methods

Observational Methods

Advantages	Disadvantages
• Behavior is captured in its natural context.	• May be highly labor intensive.
• Avoids the problem of "reactivity."	• Observations may be subject to bias.
• Some forms of observational data are readily available.	• Some forms of observational data only measure behavior indirectly.

Survey Research

Advantages	Disadvantages
• Allows the collection of data from large numbers of participants at low cost.	• Difficult to draw causal interferences from survey data.
• Survey data can typically be analyzed with very powerful statistical methods.	• Response rates for some forms of survey data are low.
	• Survey design is a difficult, time-consuming process.

Experimentation

Advantages	Disadvantages
• Best way to assess causal relationships.	• Generalizability of findings may be questionable.
• Best way to isolate the impact of a specific variable.	• Examining a variable in isolation may be unrealistic.
• Gaining compliance of participants is easier compared to survey research.	• Participants may not take the experimental situation serious.

Quasi-Experimentation

Advantages	Disadvantages
• Allows the researcher a way to access causality in naturalistic settings.	• Organizations may be reluctant to allow these to be conducted.
• An excellent way to evaluate the impact of organizational interventions.	• Researchers have very little control.

Given the advantages and disadvantages summarized in Figure 2.2, the choice of a data collection method depends largely on a researcher's objectives. If establishing causality is of primary importance, then experimentation is likely to be the method of choice. On the other hand, if capturing behavior in its natural context is the primary concern, then observation or quasi-experimentation may be

THE CASE FOR MULTIPLE DATA COLLECTION METHODS

UNFORTUNATELY, A SIGNIFICANT portion of research in organizational psychology suffers from what has been termed "mono-operation" bias. This means that, in many studies, all of the variables are measured using only *one* form of data collection. Often, this one form of data collection is a self-report questionnaire, although it does not have to be. For example, a study would suffer just as much from this form of bias if all variables were measured using simple observation.

Why is it a problem to measure all variables in a study with only one form of data collection? One obvious reason is that the relationships among variables may be inflated because they share a common method (e.g., common-method bias). Another way to view this issue is to think about the *positive* impact of using multiple forms of data collection in a single study. Let's say a researcher is interested in whether job autonomy is positively related to job satisfaction. Further assume that, in this

study, job autonomy is measured through a self-report measure completed by employees, and through archival information collected during a job analysis. Job satisfaction could be measured through a self-report measure and thorough observation of employees through their workday.

After these data are collected, we would likely find that the self-report autonomy measure would be positively related to the self-report job satisfaction measure. However, what if the archival measure of job autonomy is also related to the self-report job satisfaction measure? What if the self-report job autonomy is positively related to the observational measure of job satisfaction? If both of these results occur, this would most certainly strengthen the conclusion that job autonomy really does positively relate to job satisfaction. Thus, the real benefit of using multiple data collection methods is that it allows us to show relationships between variables in multiple ways.

preferred. Ideally, the best course of action is to use *multiple* methods of data collection (see Comment 2.3).

SPECIAL ISSUES IN DATA COLLECTION

Now that the most common methods of data collection have been described, we will explore, in this section, some important contemporary issues related to these methods. These issues include validity of self-report measures, generalizing laboratory findings to field settings, gaining access to organizations for data collection, and conducting research in different cultures.

Validity of Self-Reports

Self-report measures are so ubiquitous in organizational psychology that they are almost taken for granted. Employees are asked how much they like their jobs, how much variety they perceive in their work, how committed they are to their employing organization, and how anxious they feel about their jobs—just to cite a few questions. When any self-report measure is used, we are, in effect, taking it on faith that the information provided by the respondent is valid.

Self-report measurement is really based on two implicit assumptions. First, it is assumed that the respondents *know* the information we are asking for. Many of the questions asked in organizational surveys are subjective (i.e., there is no right or wrong answer), so it is reasonable to assume that respondents are aware of the information. Most people *know* whether they like their job, for example. In other cases, lack of knowledge may compromise the validity of self-report measures. For example, the author knows of a university that conducts an annual survey of the job-related activities of faculty. One of the items on this survey asks faculty to indicate the number of hours in a typical week they devote to course preparation, teaching, research, and university service. Most university faculty probably have only a very vague idea of the number of hours spent on each professional activity.

A second assumption underlying self-report measurement is that if respondents know the information asked by the researcher, they report it *truthfully*. Compared to researchers interested in some forms of behavior (e.g., drug use, criminal activity), organizational psychologists are relatively fortunate in this regard. Because most of the items on organizational surveys are not highly sensitive or invasive, employees probably respond truthfully to such items, provided they believe their responses will be held in confidence. In reality, however, employees' comfort level with surveys varies greatly. For example, when organizational researchers use self-reports to measure things such as absenteeism, turnover intentions, and other forms of counterproductive behavior, employees may be quite fearful of violations of confidentiality and therefore may not answer truthfully. In such cases, all a researcher can really do is take great care to reassure employees, and conduct the survey in a way that supports the promise of confidentiality. This might include having employees mail surveys to the researcher off-site, or perhaps not asking for any identifying information.

The situation that has generated the most controversy surrounding the use of self-report is when such measures are used to rate job and organizational conditions. According to Spector (1994), self-reports often do not correlate well with more "objective" measures of the work environment, such as ratings by job analysts or by others familiar with the same job (Spector, Dwyer, & Jex, 1988; Spector & Jex, 1991). Use of self-report measures is also controversial when such measures are correlated with other self-report variables. When this is the case, the correlations between such variables may possibly be inflated due to **common method variance**—a term that is used quite frequently but is rarely explicitly defined. Common method variance represents shared sources of measurement bias between two variables that can be directly tied to the method of measurement being used (Spector, 1987). As an example, let's say that a researcher is measuring two variables via self-report. Further assume that both of these measures, for some reason, are impacted by social desirability responding (Crowne & Marlowe, 1964)—that is, responses to items in both measures differ in their level of social desirability. This shared source of measurement bias may lead these two variables to be correlated, even if there is little or no underlying conceptual relationship between the two variables. In cases where these measures are conceptually related, the presence of common method variance will tend to *inflate* the magnitude of the relationship between the two variables.

Researchers should be concerned about common method variance, but empirical efforts to actually demonstrate its effects on relationships between variables have provided only mixed results. Spector (1987), for example, empirically investigated the prevalence of common method variance in the measurement of job characteristics and job satisfaction.

Based on an analysis of several data sets, Spector concluded that there was no strong evidence that correlations were inflated due to common method variance.

Spector's (1987) investigation prompted several attempts to replicate his findings; most of these attempts utilized more complex statistical techniques (e.g., Bagozzi & Yi, 1990; Williams & Anderson, 1994; Williams, Cote, & Buckley, 1989). A complete discussion of the findings of these studies is beyond the scope of this chapter, but the general conclusion of these studies was that the impact of common method variance is greater than Spector had estimated. However, as Brannick and Spector (1990) pointed out, there are problems in the use of complex statistical methodology to test for the effects of common method variance.

Another way to empirically assess the impact of common method variance is to compare correlations that contain a shared method to those without a shared method. Crampton and Wagner (1994) conducted a meta-analysis in which they summarized 42,934 correlations from studies using single and multiple methods. Overall, they found that correlations in which both variables were measured via self-report were not appreciably larger than other correlations. In the measurement of some variables, however, correlations based on a single source were larger than others. This suggests that the impact of common method variance is *real*; however, the magnitude of this effect varies widely, depending on the nature of the variables being measured.

Perhaps the best conclusion one can draw about the validity of self-report measures is that it depends primarily on the variable being measured and the research question being asked. For example, if one were interested in measuring employees' feelings about their jobs, then a self-report measure would be quite appropriate. On the other hand, if one

were interested in measuring employees' level of job autonomy, level of discretion in decision making, or (perhaps) workload, then relying exclusively on self-report measures is riskier. In all these cases, the researcher is really interested in characteristics of the *environment*, not those of the individual employee. When researchers wish to measure characteristics of the work environment, the best course of action is to use multiple measurement methods (e.g., Glick, Jenkins, & Gupta, 1986). Given the reliance of much organizational research on self-report measurement, it is likely that the pros and cons of self-report measurement are likely to be debated for quite some time (see Comment 2.4).

Generalizing Laboratory Findings

A common criticism of psychology is that it is a science based largely on laboratory studies that investigate the behavior of rodents and introductory psychology students. Organizational psychology tends to make less use of laboratory studies in comparison to other areas of psychology. Still, laboratory studies do account for a substantial portion of the research in both organizational psychology and I/O psychology in general (Locke, 1986; Sackett & Larsen, 1990; Scandura & Williams, 2000). The purpose of this section is to neither advocate nor discourage the use of laboratory investigations, but their use in organizational psychology raises some important issues. Perhaps the most important of these is the extent to which findings from laboratory investigations can be generalized to "real" organizational settings.

The strongest argument made against laboratory findings' generalizing to field settings is that laboratory situations lack realism. A university laboratory setting is not a real organization; thus, it lacks what is called **mundane realism.** Realism, however, must also be

COMMENT 2.4

THE SELF-REPORT CONTROVERSY

SELF-REPORT MEASUREMENT is undoubtedly the most common form of data collection in organizational psychology. It is also a form of data collection that has evoked a great deal of controversy, particularly when self-reports are used to measure *all* of the variables in a study. I have followed this issue for over a decade, primarily because it has a great deal of relevance to my own research program in occupational stress, since self-report measures tend to predominate.

On the positive side, self-reports allow us to measure something that is important in determining human behavior—namely, individuals' *perceptions* of their environment, their emotional states, and, in some cases, their views of other people. Self-report measurement is also very economical. In the time it might take to collect meaningful observations of 20 people, a self-report measure could be distributed to 100 times that many people.

The primary drawback to self-report measurement is that humans are not analytical instruments; thus, self-reports may not always produce accurate information. For example, when we ask employees to provide self-reports

of characteristics of their jobs, these ratings may be biased by internal mood states, social influences of coworkers, or stable internal dispositions (Spector, 1994). These same biases may also influence self-reports of emotional and affective states.

What is the most reasonable conclusion one can draw about self-report measures? In my opinion, it is that self-report measurement, like any other data collection method, has both advantages and disadvantages. Whether one uses self-report measurement should be dictated primarily by the variables one is trying to measure, which are ultimately dictated by the research question one is trying to answer. As a general rule, if one is primarily interested in *perceptions,* then self-report measurement is a logical choice. However, if one is interested in actual environmental conditions, then self-reports should be supplemented with other forms of data collection.

Source: P. E. Spector. (1994). Using self-report questionnaires in OB research: A comment on the use of a controversial method. *Journal of Organizational Behavior, 15,* 385–392.

considered from the perspective of the research participant. It is certainly possible to place a research participant in a situation that lacks mundane realism, yet create what is perceived as a very real situation. When this is the case, it can be said that there is a high degree of **experimental realism** for research participants. Many laboratory studies conducted over the years, particularly in social psychology (e.g., Milgram, 1974), have lacked mundane realism yet have retained a very high degree of experimental realism.

Another reason laboratory investigations may generalize has to do with the research participants. At the beginning of this section, it was remarked, somewhat facetiously, that laboratory investigations often utilize introductory psychology students. This often leads to criticism based on the fact that such individuals are different from the general population. For the study of many organizational issues, the use of college students as research participants actually may not compromise generalizability as much as one would assume.

College students, for the most part, represent the cadre of individuals who will hold many of the white-collar jobs in the future. Thus, they may be quite similar to such employees, both in terms of attitudes and abilities, even though they are obviously lacking in relevant organizational experience. By contrast, college students are probably a poor research sample if the aim is to generalize to employees holding blue-collar and manual labor jobs.

Despite these arguments for the generalizability of laboratory experiments, there are also important differences between laboratory and field settings. For example, the high level of experimental control in laboratory settings allows the researcher to isolate the impact of a variable in a way that is impossible in field settings because so many things are occurring that the impact of any single variable may be greatly diluted. Also, when variables are investigated in laboratory settings, they are taken out of their natural context. By taking a variable out of context, the researcher runs the risk of changing the nature of that variable. A good example of this is laboratory investigation of the effects of ambient temperature on aggression (e.g., Baron & Bell, 1976). In a laboratory setting, it is possible to completely isolate the impact of temperature. In natural settings, however, temperature increases often occur in conjunction with other variables such as loud noise and crowding.

Another important difference between laboratory and field investigations is that laboratory settings are typically short term (Runkel & McGrath, 1972). As a result, participants in laboratory investigations have very little time invested and have no reason to form any social ties with others. In contrast, employees in organizations have considerable time invested in their jobs, and often develop long-standing social ties with fellow employees. These differences may lead employees to react very differently to certain situations, as compared to participants in laboratory investigations.

A final important difference between laboratory and field settings is the nature of the tasks performed by research participants. Given the short-term nature of laboratory investigations, it is very difficult to match the complexity of the tasks performed by employees in real organizations. Thus, many laboratory studies ask participants to perform relatively simple tasks such as assembling tinker toys, solving anagrams, and putting together puzzles.

The pros and cons of laboratory investigations still leave us with the question of whether laboratory findings generalize to field settings such as organizations. Unfortunately, there is no definitive answer to this question, although it has been examined extensively (e.g., Berkowitz & Donnerstein, 1982; Dipboye & Flanagan, 1979). The most comprehensive analysis of this issue, relevant to organizational psychology, is contained in *Generalizing from Laboratory to Field Settings,* a book edited by Edwin Locke in 1986. The general conclusion one can draw from this book is that the results of *well-designed* laboratory investigations often do generalize to field settings. A well-designed laboratory investigation is one in which participants are highly engaged in the task being performed, and variable(s) of interest are well simulated. The reader should be cautioned, however, against concluding that *all* findings do or do not generalize. In the end, generalizability is an empirical question, and the best course of action is to replicate laboratory findings in field settings whenever possible.

Gaining Access to Organizations

One of the most challenging things about field research is simply gaining access to an organization for data collection. The author has known, over the years, many colleagues who have come up with interesting research questions, but could find no organization in which to collect data. Unfortunately, there is very little in the organizational literature to help guide researchers in their efforts to gain access to organizations. Thus, most of this section is based on both the author's experience as a researcher, and the experiences of fellow organizational researchers.

Before exploring ways to gain access to organizations, let us first consider reasons why organizations would *not* let a researcher gather data. Based on past experience, there are two primary reasons: (1) data collection usually requires employees' time, and (2) organizations are concerned that employees may divulge sensitive or proprietary information about the organization. This is particularly true of organizations that operate in very competitive industries (e.g., consumer products, high technology). In many organizations, the secrecy surrounding activities such as new product research diffuses to other activities, regardless of whether the concerns are valid.

Given these potential objections to the collection of research data, how can organizational researchers still gain access? Perhaps the most basic suggestion that can be made in this regard is: *Ask.* Many researchers who complain about lack of access have actually asked relatively few organizations for their cooperation. They simply *assume* that they will be unable to collect data. One way to enlist an organization is to contact several organizations by telephone and try to make contact with someone in the human resources department. Another approach is to "mass mail" to organizations, asking for cooperation. T. E. Becker (1992), for example, mailed letters to the presidents of 30 organizations asking for permission to collect data and eventually collected data in one of these.

General appeals or "cold calling" may result in a data collection opportunity, but it is often more advantageous to use established connections in organizations. Most people have family and/or friends who work in organizations, and such people may be in a position to either authorize the collection of data or put the researcher into contact with someone who has the authority to do so. This suggests that researchers should not be afraid to use established connections in organizations. Researchers should also invest time and energy to *develop* connections with people who can help with data collection in their organizations in the future. This often takes time and energy but, in the long run, the contact may result in excellent data collection opportunities (see Comment 2.5).

Let's now assume that a researcher has persuaded an organization to at least *consider* the possibility of data collection. How can a researcher convince an organization to actually go ahead with data collection? The most useful suggestion that can be made in this regard is: The researcher should offer the organization something in return for its cooperation. For example, researchers often provide a summary of the research findings to the organization, in return for its cooperation. Other researchers may offer to perform some consulting service at no cost to an organization. Organizations typically do not provide researchers access to their employees unless the access will provide some tangible benefit in return.

After an organization gives permission to collect data, there is often some negotiation between the researcher and the organization, regarding issues such as research design and measures. At this stage, researchers and organizations often clash, because of their differing goals and objectives. Researchers typically desire a high level of methodological rigor in their investigations because their ultimate goal is to

COMMENT 2.5

GAINING ACCESS TO ORGANIZATIONS: SOME EXAMPLES

As I wrote the section on gaining access to organizations, I thought of the various ways I have gained access to organizations in order to collect data. Like many researchers, I have used family connections. For example, I was able to gain access to an insurance company in Tampa, Florida, to conduct my Master's thesis research while in graduate school. My wife was employed there at the time. To this day, I can't figure out whether my wife was trying to advance science, or just wanted me to get out of graduate school! Another study I conducted, which was ultimately published in *Journal of Applied Psychology* (Jex, Beehr, & Roberts, 1992), was actually made possible through the efforts of my mother. This study was conducted at a hospital in Saginaw, Michigan (my hometown), where my mother was employed as a nurse. She introduced me to a person in the human resources department who was ultimately able to grant me access to all hospital employees. In this case, I think my mother's help was driven primarily by a desire to see her son get tenure. In addition to using family connections, I have gained access in many other ways. In some cases, current and former students have helped facilitate data collection efforts. I have also, on occasion, relied on former graduate school classmates, or other colleagues, to provide either data collection sites or useful contacts.

Is there any underlying theme when I think about the various ways in which I have gained access to organizations? The most obvious theme is that developing and maintaining relationships with people is important. This includes family, students, and professional colleagues. I'm not suggesting that relationships should be initiated only on the basis of what people can do for you. However, the fact is, it is much easier to ask someone for assistance if you've taken the time to maintain an ongoing relationship with him or her. The other important lesson I've learned over the years is simply to *ask*. We often assume incorrectly that family, friends, and colleagues do not want to be bothered helping with data collection. However, my experience has been that people often are very willing (and even flattered) to help if they're asked.

Source: S. M. Jex, T. A. Beehr, and C. K. Roberts. (1992). The meaning of occupational "stress" items to survey respondents. *Journal of Applied Psychology, 77,* 623–628.

publish their findings in peer-reviewed journals. Unfortunately, methodological rigor may be perceived by the organization as costly in a number of ways. For example, supplementing self-report measures with organizational records may be time consuming and pose ethical problems. It may also be impossible for an organization to allow a researcher the control needed for experimental or even quasi-experimental investigations. This is a tricky issue for researchers to navigate because just gaining access to organizations is such a challenge. The key is: The researcher must be willing to accommodate the organization, but not to such an extent that it compromises the scientific integrity of the investigation. Unfortunately, researchers often severely compromise the methodological rigor of studies without attempting to persuade organizations of its value. In most cases, a well-designed, methodological, rigorous study will not only help the researcher but will also be more informative to the organization (Campion, 1996).

Conducting Research in Different Cultures

Given increasing globalization, it is becoming more and more common for organizational psychologists to examine cross-cultural issues. Despite the value of cross-cultural research, data collection in this type of study may be challenged by a number of factors. For example, when self-report measures are used, these often must be translated from one language to another. This may seem rather simple; often, it is not. The typical procedure used to convert self-report measures into different languages is called **back translation.** This involves translating the items on a measure from one language to another (e.g., from English to Chinese), and then back to the original language. The researcher can then assess whether the items have retained their meaning to respondents after being translated from a different language.

Another issue that is often important in conducting cross-cultural research is sampling. Researchers conducting cross-cultural research often want to compare employees in one culture to employees in another, so it is important to have samples that are similar in all aspects except culture (Arvey, Bhagat, & Salas, 1991). For example, a researcher would typically want to select samples consisting of employees in the same industry who have approximately the same level of education.

Other than translation and sampling, researchers conducting cross-cultural research must be on the lookout for things that are specific to a given culture and may adversely affect data collection. For example, a researcher utilizing self-ratings of performance must be aware of the fact that, in oriental cultures, it is considered improper to rate oneself high in performance (Fahr, Dobbins, & Cheng, 1991). There may also be vast cultural differences in research participants' degree of comfort when they are asked to provide ratings of persons in positions of authority.

STATISTICAL METHODS IN ORGANIZATIONAL PSYCHOLOGY

Regardless of the method used, once data are collected, researchers are faced with the task of analyzing those data to assess whether their hypotheses are supported. Fortunately for organizational researchers, many statistical methods are available to help in making sense out of data. Because a comprehensive review of statistical methodology is beyond the scope of this chapter, we will review, in this section, the statistical methods that are used most frequently in analyzing research data.

Descriptive Statistics

The first thing a researcher needs to do after obtaining a set of data is to get a feel for general trends. For example, if we were to collect data on job satisfaction within an organization, two relevant questions might be: (1) What is the overall level of job satisfaction in the organization? (2) Are employees very similar in their levels of job satisfaction, or do they vary widely? To answer the first question, it is necessary to employ some descriptive measure of **central tendency.** The most commonly used measure of central tendency is the mean, which is calculated by simply adding up all of the scores on a variable and dividing by the total number of scores. Other common measures of central tendency include the *median* and *mode.* The median represents the score on a variable that splits the distribution into two equal halves. The median is useful as a supplement to the mean, in cases where a distribution contains extreme scores. Unlike the mean, the median is unaffected by the presence of extremely high or extremely low values. The mode is simply the most frequently occurring score and is typically not very informative unless there is a very dramatic preference for one response over others.

Measures of central tendency are useful because they provide information about the manner in which variables are distributed. This is important because most statistical tests are based on assumptions about the manner in which variables are distributed. Measures of central tendency are also valuable when organizational policy makers are assessing survey results. Figure 2.3, for example, contains a graphical representation of employee opinion survey data collected by the author and a colleague. Notice that this figure

is based on the mean values of four dimensions contained on the survey, but contains information that is potentially very useful to the organization. A quick perusal of this figure indicates relatively low satisfaction with the levels of communication and fairness in this organization. On the other hand, these employees appear to be committed to the organization and reasonably satisfied with their fringe benefits package. To the extent that this information can lead to interventions to enhance communication and fairness, it can provide organizations with some very tangible benefits.

In addition to measures of central tendency, researchers often want to know the level of uniformity in responses. Several measures of dispersion provide such information. The most basic measure of dispersion is the range, which is the difference between the highest and lowest value for a particular variable. It is often useful to compare the *observed* range for a given variable to the *possible* range. For example, if a variable is scaled such that it may range from 10 to 50 and the observed range is 30 to 50, this indicates potential problems with range restriction.

The range may be useful in identifying problems with range restriction, but it is still a very crude measure of dispersion. More precise and more commonly used measures of dispersion include the **variance** and **standard deviation**. The variance represents the degree to which scores vary about the mean. To calculate the variance, you simply subtract the mean from each score in a distribution, square each value, add up these squared values, and divide by the total number of scores. The standard deviation is simply the square root of the variance.

Given the way in which the variance and standard deviation are calculated, higher values indicate greater dispersion about the mean. The standard deviation is also useful

FIGURE 2.3

Graphical Representation of Mean Levels of Four Dimensions Measured in an Employee Opinion Survey.

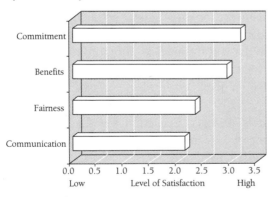

Notes: Communication = Satisfaction with amount of communication in the organization; Fairness = Satisfaction with level of fairness in the organization; Benefits = Satisfaction with current fringe benefit package; Commitment = Organizational commitment. Mean values may range from 1 to 4.

because it can be used in converting raw scores to **standard scores.** A standard score is simply the score on a given variable, expressed (in terms of its distance from the mean) in standard deviation units. The simplest form of standard score is a **z-score,** which is calculated by subtracting the mean from a raw score and dividing the result by the standard deviation. Standard scores can be useful in cases where the researcher wishes to compare a respondent's scores on different variables that may utilize different scales of measurement (see Comment 2.6).

A final type of descriptive measure that is typically used in any form of data analysis is **reliability.** In the most general sense, reliability represents the extent to which a variable is being measured without *error* (Nunnally & Bernstein, 1994). What is considered error, however, depends on the particular context in which a measure is being used. When multi-item measures are used, which is typically the case in organizational research, it is necessary to assess the **internal consistency reliability.** A measure of internal consistency reliability provides an estimation of the extent to which all items on a scale are measuring the same attribute. Suppose, for example, we constructed a five-item measure of job satisfaction. If internal consistency reliability were estimated to be very high, this would suggest that all five items were measuring the same thing.

In other cases, researchers must provide other reliability estimates. For example, if a variable is going to be assessed at multiple points in time, it is important for the researcher to show that the measure of the variable is not strongly impacted by random fluctuations over time. In this case, an appropriate form of reliability assessment would be **test-retest reliability,** which simply involves administering a measure at two different

<hr />

COMMENT 2.6

CONFESSIONS OF A STATISTICAL MINIMALIST

IN HIS INITIAL statement as editor of *Journal of Applied Psychology,* Philip Bobko referred to himself as a "statistical minimalist" (Bobko, 1995, p. 4) in describing his views on statistical analysis. What is a statistical minimalist? Perhaps the best way to understand this is to consider more of Bobko's editorial statement. Specifically, he advised potential authors: "Please look at 'simple' statistics, such as means, standard deviations, correlations, effect sizes, and so forth. And do not just look at them; consider them when attempting to understand and explain what's going on. I believe that one can often (usually?) learn more by looking at these simple statistics with a critical and understanding eye than one can learn by computing the newest fashion in statistics with an amazed eye" (p. 4).

The important point that Bobko was trying to make in this editorial is that even relatively simple descriptive statistics are important if one's goal is to understand their data. I think a more subtle message here is that the choice of statistical methods to use should be driven by the question being asked, not by the latest fad. Although not always the case, it is often possible to answer important research questions without resorting to overly complex statistical analyses.

Source: P. Bobko. (1995). Editorial. *Journal of Applied Psychology, 80,* 3–5.

points in time and calculating the correlation between these scores. If this correlation is high, it suggests that the measure is not strongly impacted by random temporal fluctuations.

Another form of reliability assessment, **interrater reliability,** may be necessary in cases where multiple raters are utilized to assess some attribute of a person (e.g., performance) or the environment (e.g., job characteristics). There are many ways to assess interrater reliability, but they all basically allow the researcher to assess whether the ratings provided by different raters are *similarly ordered*. The researcher can also assess whether raters agree on the absolute value of the ratings. This issue will be discussed in greater detail in the final section of the chapter, which deals with aggregation and levels of analysis issues.

Tests of Mean Differences

After assessing descriptive measures, the researcher should hopefully be able to conclude that there are no major distributional problems, and that all variables are measured with a minimal amount of error. If this is indeed the case, the next step is to perform some analysis to test whatever hypotheses are being proposed. There are many different types of hypotheses; a common type of hypothesis involves testing differences in the mean level of a given variable. For example, a researcher may hypothesize that employees in white-collar jobs have higher organizational commitment than blue-collar employees, or that the performance of groups that participate in team-building activities is higher than that of groups that do not participate. In this section, we cover the two most common statistical tests of mean differences.

Before describing these statistical tests, it is useful to provide a brief overview of the logic behind tests of statistical significance.

Regardless of the statistical test being used, a test of statistical significance essentially involves establishing a rule for distinguishing chance from nonchance outcomes. All statistical significance tests begin with the assumption of what is termed the *null hypothesis,* which is another way of saying there is no effect. Assuming that the null hypothesis is true, it is possible for a variety of research outcomes to occur simply on the basis of chance. Thus, the researcher needs some decision rule for determining whether a given result represents a chance occurrence or a legitimate scientific finding. The standard used most often for distinguishing chance from nonchance— the one that has come to be adopted in the behavioral sciences over the years—is 5%. Assuming that the null hypothesis is true, if the probability of a research outcome occurring by chance is 5% or less, scientists typically conclude that it is a legitimate scientific finding (e.g., they reject the null hypothesis). Thus, when the statement is made that a finding is "significant at the 5% level," the researcher is saying that it is very unlikely that the finding observed is a chance occurrence.

When testing mean differences, the simplest scenario is testing the difference between two groups. For example, a researcher may wish to test whether the average age of those who participate in training and development activities differs from those who choose not to participate. The statistic most commonly used in this situation would be a **t-test.** The magnitude of the t statistic depends on the absolute difference between means relative to the level of variation within the groups being compared. Thus, even if the absolute difference between the means is substantial, a high degree of variation *within* the different groups will keep the t value at a relatively low level, and will lead to the conclusion that there is no meaningful difference between the groups.

There are other instances in organizational research where the means of more than two groups must be compared. For example, a researcher might want to compare the mean level of job satisfaction in several different work groups that have and have not participated in team development activities. In this case, the statistical procedure used would be **analysis of variance.** The general purpose of analysis of variance is to assess the ratio of the variation between different groups, relative to the variation within groups. To perform an analysis of variance, it is necessary to calculate several different variance estimates or **mean-squares.** These are used to estimate the variance *between* groups and the variance *within* groups. The actual test of statistical significance employed in analysis of variance is the **F-test,** which is simply a *ratio* of the variance between groups to the variance within groups. When an F is statistically significant, this indicates that the ratio of variance between groups to the variation within groups is very unlikely to have occurred by chance, given the null hypothesis. Recall that the same basic logic is employed with the t-test. If a statistically significant F is found in analysis of variance, this indicates that there is *some* difference among the means in the groups of interest, although it does not tell the researcher *which* means are different. To figure this out, it is necessary to employ follow-up tests to assess the difference within each possible pair of means.

Given the basic logic behind the analysis of variance, this statistical procedure can be used a variety of ways. For example, different forms of analysis of variance can be used to assess: (1) the impact of multiple independent variables, (2) repeated measures of dependent variables, and (3) the impact of multiple dependent variables. Readers interested in more detailed information on analysis of variance procedures should consult Keppel (1982).

Correlation and Regression Analysis

Given the prevalence of cross-sectional field surveys in organizational research, hypotheses must often be tested by assessing the covariation among the variables of interest. The most commonly used statistical index of covariation is the **Pearson product-moment correlation coefficient.** The correlation coefficient can range from +1.00 to −1.00, but typically falls in between these values. The larger the absolute value of a correlation coefficient, the greater the degree of covariation. This degree is often expressed by squaring the correlation coefficient to obtain the amount of shared variation between two variables. For example, if the correlation between two variables is .30, they share 9% of their variance in common [e.g., $(.30)^2$]. When the sign of a correlation is positive, this simply means that two variables covary in the same direction. A negative sign, by contrast, indicates that two variables covary in opposite directions.

The correlation coefficient is useful in testing many hypotheses in organizational research, but it provides very limited information about *causal* relationships. For example, if job satisfaction were correlated with job autonomy, this could be due to the fact that high job autonomy causes one to be more satisfied. It could also be that a high level of job satisfaction causes one to see greater levels of autonomy in his or her job. It is also possible that two variables may be correlated primarily because of the influence of a third variable. If this is the case, it is said that the relationship is *spurious.* In the job satisfaction–job autonomy example, these variables could be spuriously related because both are influenced by the relationship one has with one's supervisor.

Correlational analysis is also limited by the fact that only two variables may be examined at a time. In many instances, a researcher may be interested in the extent to which *several* variables are related to some other variable of interest. For example, a researcher may be interested in the degree to which pay, length of service, level of performance, age, and job type all contribute to employees' overall satisfaction with their employing organization. One way to address this question would be to examine the correlation between job satisfaction and each of these variables individually. Unfortunately, such an analysis does not provide the researcher with information about the extent to which this entire *set* of variables is related.

The statistical procedure that is used to assess the relation of a set of variables (called *predictors*) to another variable (called the *criterion*) is **multiple linear regression** or, simply, multiple regression. Multiple regression is useful because it provides a quantitative estimate of the amount of covariation between a set of predictors and a criterion variable. This is assessed by the multiple R statistic, which is analogous to the correlation coefficient. In most instances, however, researchers report the *squared* value of multiple R, which serves as a measure of the amount of variance in the criterion variable that is explained by a set of predictors.

Multiple regression is also useful because it allows the researcher to assess the relative impact of each predictor in explaining the criterion variable. When a set of predictors is used to estimate a criterion variable, the criterion is estimated to be a linear function of the predictor set. The general form of this equation is:

$$Y = A + B_1 X_1 + B_2 X_2 + \ldots + B_k X_k$$

where Y is the criterion variable that is being predicted, the Xs represent the predictor variables, A is a constant, and each B-value represents the weighting of a given predictor or the extent to which it contributes to the prediction of the criterion. The advantage of using these statistical weights, as opposed to correlations, is that they are calculated in a way that takes into account the intercorrelations among the other predictor variables in the set. Thus, one way to interpret the B-values in multiple regression is that they represent the *unique* contribution of a given variable to the prediction of some criterion measure.

Beyond correlation and regression analysis, many other related methods can be employed for data analysis. Most of these fall under the general category of **multivariate methods** (e.g., Tabachnick & Fidell, 1983) and, due to their complexity, are not covered in this chapter. These methods are quite useful to the researcher, particularly in field investigations. However, like all statistical methods, they should be used only if necessary to test a given hypothesis.

Meta-Analysis

A final form of statistical analysis that is being used increasingly in organizational research is **meta-analysis.** Meta-analysis essentially involves the quantitative summary of research findings and is typically used in research domains where a considerable number of studies have been conducted (Rosenthal, 1991). For example, meta-analyses have been conducted on the relation between job satisfaction and job performance (Podsakoff & Williams, 1986), the effects of role stressors (Jackson & Schuler, 1985), and the impact of job characteristics (Fried & Ferris, 1987). In all three cases, so many studies have been conducted over the years that it would be difficult to provide an accurate qualitative summary of the findings.

Statistically, meta-analysis essentially involves averaging correlation coefficients. Before these correlations are averaged, however, researchers typically control for a number of **statistical artifacts**—factors that may lead to differences in the findings between studies. Probably the most basic statistical artifact is sample size. Studies with larger sample sizes need to be weighted more heavily when averaging correlations compared to those with smaller sample sizes. Another common statistical artifact controlled in meta-analyses is measurement unreliability. Earlier in the chapter, reliability was defined as the degree to which a variable is measured without error. When measurement procedures are *unreliable,* this means that they contain considerable error. This is important because it sets a lower boundary on the degree to which a variable can be correlated with other variables. Controlling for unreliability puts all variables on a "level playing field" in terms of measurement error.

The other common statistical artifact controlled in meta-analyses is **range restriction.** In some studies, correlations between variables may be reduced because the values do not cover the entire possible range. This may occur because of a variety of factors (e.g., Johns, 1991), but it always serves to limit the magnitude of correlations. When researchers control for range restriction, they are essentially estimating what the correlations would be if the variables of interest were measured without any range restriction problems.

Once all relevant statistical artifacts are controlled, two important statistics are typically calculated in meta-analysis. Most researchers calculate some overall estimate of the correlations between variables. This estimate represents the mean correlation after controlling for the impact of important statistical artifacts, and it provides a good estimate of the "true" correlation between variables. The other statistic typically calculated in meta-analysis is the amount of variation in correlations that remains after important statistical

artifacts are controlled. Usually, after important statistical artifacts are controlled, there is a relatively small amount of variation between studies' findings. However, if there is still a substantial amount of variation, factors other than statistical artifacts may be contributing to the differences in findings between the studies. Such factors are called **moderator variables.** Some of the more typical moderator variables examined in meta-analyses include aspects of the study design, characteristics of the research samples, and specific measures used to assess key variables.

SPECIAL ISSUES IN STATISTICAL ANALYSIS

At this point, readers should have a basic understanding of some of the more typical statistical methods used in organizational psychology. The purpose of statistical methodology is to help researchers answer questions (e.g., it is a means to an end), but statistics and quantitative methodology is a vibrant field of inquiry in and of itself. In fact, within organizational psychology, many researchers focus on statistical and methodological issues. Because of this focus, several issues in statistical methodology have surfaced over the years and have been the subject of inquiry and debate. In this section, we briefly review four important contemporary issues in the use of statistical methodology in organizational research.

Statistical Power in Organizational Research

Statistical power refers to the sensitivity of statistical tests to detect meaningful treatment effects. To use an analogy, one might think of the statistical power of different tests in the same way as differences between types of microscopes. An inexpensive microscope purchased from a toy store provides some magnification, but many objects cannot be detected (e.g., viruses). In contrast, an expensive electron microscope provides a very high level of magnification and allows the detection of even extremely small particles.

Several factors contribute to statistical power (Cohen, 1992). One is sample size. All things being equal, larger sample sizes provide higher levels of statistical power. A second factor impacting power is **effect size,** or the relative strength of the effect a researcher is trying to detect. There are actually several ways to express effect size, but probably the easiest way to explain it is based on the size of correlations. Generally speaking, if the true correlation between two variables is small, it is harder to detect than when the true correlation is large. Smaller-effect sizes require a more powerful "microscope" for detection.

A third factor that impacts statistical power is the **alpha level** chosen in statistical significance testing. The alpha level represents the cutoff for distinguishing chance from non-chance findings. Recall, from the previous discussion of statistical significance testing, that 5% has become the conventional rule in the behavioral sciences. The reason that the alpha level is set so low is to reduce the probability of committing a **Type I Error,** or falsely concluding that one has uncovered a legitimate scientific finding. In an organizational setting, an example of committing a Type I Error would be falsely concluding that a training program had a positive effect on employee performance. In contrast, a **Type II Error** is committed when a researcher fails to detect a legitimate effect when it is present. In the previous example, this would involve conducting a statistical test and falsely concluding that a useful training program had no impact on employee performance (see Comment 2.7).

As the alpha level becomes more stringent (e.g., 1%), this reduces the chance of committing a Type I Error, but also tends to reduce

power and hence increases the chances of committing a Type II Error. In contrast, a more liberal alpha level (e.g., 10%) tends to increase power, although this comes at the cost of an increase in the probability of committing a Type I Error.

A final factor impacting power is measurement error. Specifically, higher levels of measurement error are associated with low levels of power. This is simply due to the unsystematic nature of measurement error.

Given the previously described determinants of statistical power, let us now consider the level of statistical power in organizational research. Mone, Mueller, and Mauland (1996) examined this issue in a meta-analysis of the level of power in 26,471 statistical tests from 210 research studies conducted between 1992 and 1994. These authors also explored common practices with respect to the assessment of power prior to conducting research.

The results of the meta-analysis were revealing—and, in fact, somewhat troubling. Given that an acceptable level of statistical power is considered to be 80% (e.g., there is an 80% chance of detecting a true effect; Cohen, 1992), the authors found that across all effect sizes, an acceptable level of power was achieved only 50% of the time. What this means is that across all studies in this meta-analysis, researchers assume a 50% chance of failing to detect a true effect when it is present. This suggests that many studies conducted in organizational research are *underpowered.*

Low statistical power is extremely problematic when researchers are attempting to detect small effect sizes. When Mone et al. (1996) calculated the level of statistical power for small effect sizes, it was found that the percentage of studies achieving an acceptable level of power was only 10%! That is, the vast majority of studies attempting to detect small effects are grossly underpowered. What makes

COMMENT 2.7

TYPE I VS. TYPE II ERROR: WHICH IS THE GREATEST SIN?

GIVEN THE FACT that the alpha level is typically set at .05 or, in some cases, even .01, one would assume that committing a Type I error is a bad thing. Recall that when a Type I error is made, a researcher concludes that finding a scientifically meaningful when it really is not. Why is this bad? From a scientific point of view, Type I errors are bad because they lead us down "blind alleys," and ultimately may lead to faulty theories. From a practical point of view, a Type I error may lead an organization to spend a considerable amount of money on a training program that ultimately is not effective. Given these negative effects of a Type I error, we want to minimize the chance that one will occur, so we set alpha at a very low level.

Unfortunately, in minimizing the chances of Type I error, we increase the chances of Type II error. As you recall, Type II error is committed when a researcher *fails* to uncover a legiti-

mate scientific effect. Is it better to make a Type II than a Type I error? It really depends on the situation. Let's say, for example, that a researcher is testing a drug that could potentially neutralize the HIV virus. It would obviously be bad if this researcher were to falsely conclude that this drug was effective (e.g., commit a Type I error). However, consider the implications of committing a Type II error in this case. If this drug is effective, and research does not show it, a great chance to reduce human suffering has been missed.

Ultimately, research should be designed to *balance* the risks of both Type I and Type II errors. To minimize the risk of Type I error, alpha levels should be set sufficiently low, and proper statistical procedures should be used. On the other hand, Type II error can be minimized primarily by employing adequate sample sizes and reliable measures.

this finding disturbing is that small effects are very common in organizational research, due to the vast number of variables impacting employees in organizations.

The results of the survey of authors were also revealing. Perhaps the most important finding was that 64% of the authors surveyed reported that they do not perform any type of power analysis prior to conducting a study. One reason frequently cited for this was that, in many cases, researchers have little or no control over sample sizes in field research. Thus, even if a power analysis indicated that a larger sample size would be desirable, it would not be possible to increase. Many authors in this survey also noted that scholarly journals do not insist on power analysis during the review process, although there are

some exceptions (e.g., Campion, 1993). This is unfortunate because scholarly journals serve an important "gate keeping" function, and insistence on power analysis would serve to heighten awareness of this issue. As it stands right now, there are probably many meaningful effects in organizational psychology that go undetected due to low statistical power.

Detection of Moderator Variables

Recall from the section on meta-analysis that a moderator variable is any variable that changes the relationship between two other variables (James & Brett, 1984). More specifically, the relationship between two variables differs at different levels of the moderator variable. In organizational psychology, many theories contain provisions for moderator variables; thus, it is important to understand the statistical procedures used for assessing whether moderated relationships exist.

There are actually several ways to test moderator effects (e.g., see James & Brett, 1984), but the most commonly used procedure is through the use of multiple regression analysis (J. Cohen & Cohen, 1983). In this procedure, which is known as **cross-product regression,** the researcher first enters the *independent* variable into the regression equation. In the next step, the *moderator* variable is entered. In the final step, the cross-product of the independent variable and moderator is entered. The cross-product term is created by multiplying the independent variable by the moderator for each respondent. If the variation explained by the cross-product term is statistically significant, a moderated relationship is present. This means that the relationship between the independent variable and the dependent variable differs as a function of the moderator. This is usually shown visually by plotting the relationship at high (one standard deviation above the mean) and low (one standard deviation below the mean) levels of the moderator. Figure 2.4 illustrates how this is done. In this case, self-efficacy moderates the relationship between work hours and psychological strain. Notice that, when self-efficacy is low, there is a positive relationship between work hours and psychological strain. In contrast, when self-efficacy is high, there is essentially no relationship between these two variables.

The procedure for detecting moderator variables is rather straightforward, but, in practice, the actual detection of moderators is difficult, primarily because the detection of moderator effects is a notoriously low-power statistical test. The major reason is that moderator effects are typically small, since the

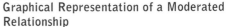

FIGURE 2.4
Graphical Representation of a Moderated Relationship

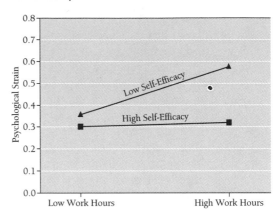

Source: S. M. Jex and P. D. Bliese. (1999). Efficacy beliefs as a moderator of the impact of work-related stressors: A multilevel study. *Journal of Applied Psychology, 84,* 349–361. Copyright © 1999 by the American Psychological Association. Reprinted with permission.

variance explained by a moderator effect is that which is left over after taking into account both the independent variable and the moderator. Often, little variance is left over for the moderator to explain. Power is also reduced when the independent variable and the moderator are strongly correlated and, in the case of dichotomous variables (e.g., race, gender), when the proportion differs greatly from 50/50 (Aguinis & Stone-Romero, 1997).

What can be done to increase the power of moderator tests? Given the previous general discussion of statistical power, researchers testing moderator effects should try to employ large samples and reliable measures. A somewhat more controversial way to increase power is to increase the alpha level beyond the conventional .05. Recall that the alpha level represents the researcher's decision rule for distinguishing chance from nonchance findings. If a less stringent alpha level of .10 is adopted, for example, this means that results with a 10% or lower probability of occurring by chance are considered legitimate treatment effects.

Given the low power associated with moderator tests, the decision to adopt a less stringent alpha level would appear to be logical. It is not extremely unusual to find researchers using alpha levels of .10 in moderator tests (e.g., Jex & Elacqua, 1999), but the practice is not widespread. Why is this the case? It is likely due to the fact that the .05 level is so ingrained in our thinking. Most students are taught that an alpha level beyond .05 is "cheating," and they are extremely reluctant to raise it.

Beyond statistical considerations in the detection of moderator effects, it is always good practice to have a solid *theoretical* rationale before searching for moderators. Often, moderator variables that are very intuitively appealing may not be theoretically justified.

Statistical methodology will never compensate for poor theory development (see Comment 2.8).

Use of Causal Modeling

Over the past 20 years, a statistical technique that has become increasingly popular in organizational psychology—and many other fields—is **causal modeling** (James, Mulaik, & Brett, 1982). The basic logic behind causal modeling is that the researcher derives a set of predictions about how a set of variables relate to one another, and tests all of these relations simultaneously. In practice, this is typically done through the use of either **path analysis** or **structural equation modeling.** With path analysis, the variables that constitute a causal model are the actual variables that are measured. This is illustrated in the path model depicted in Figure 2.5. Variables A and B lead

---

COMMENT 2.8

THE ELUSIVE MODERATOR EFFECT

As will become evident as readers make their way through this book, many theories in organizational psychology propose moderator hypotheses; that is, certain relationships between variables may hold under some conditions, but not under others. Moderator variables are important in theory development because they allow us to specify the precise conditions under which some phenomenon may occur. They also may have a great deal of practical value by providing an organization with guidance about whether there are certain conditions under which interventions such as job redesign may work.

Despite the theoretical and practical value of moderator variables, they are very difficult to demonstrate empirically. This is primarily due to the fact that moderator variables typically explain a small portion of the variance in dependent measures and, as a result, the statistical power to detect these effects is very often inadequate. Thus, in many cases, researchers propose theoretically sound moderator hypotheses yet "come up empty" when they test for these effects. What can researchers do to avoid this fate? The most logical steps one can take to increase the statistical power of moderator tests are: employ large sample sizes, utilize reliable measures, adopt a reasonable alpha level, and try to cut down on extraneous sources of variation.

FIGURE 2.5
Simple Path Model

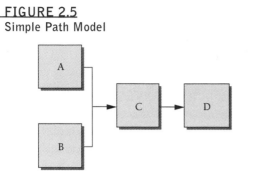

to variable C, which in turn leads to variable D. Structural equation modeling is similar to path analysis except that the variables comprising the causal model are *latent* rather than *measured* variables. A latent variable is a hypothetical variable that is purported to cause the interrelationships among measured variables. As an example, verbal ability is a latent variable that typically leads to high intercorrelations among tests such as word analogies, reading comprehension, and verbal expression. An example of a structural equation model is contained in Figure 2.6. The circles are meant to denote latent variables, and the boxes represent measured variables. For

example, the measured variables A₁ and A₂ are indicators of the latent variable A, and so on. Notice that this is essentially the same model depicted in Figure 2.5. The only difference is that the proposed relationships are among latent rather than measured variables.

Once a model is proposed, the researcher seeks to assess whether the model "fits" the actual data. There are actually several indexes of model fit, but the logic behind most of these is very similar. When a model is proposed, the researcher is placing certain restrictions on the covariation among the variables of interest. Based on these restrictions, an expected covariance matrix of relations among variables in the causal model can be calculated. This expected covariance matrix is then compared to the actual covariation among the variables in the proposed model. When a model is said to "fit the data well," this means that the actual covariation among the variables closely matches that which would be expected, based on the proposed relations among the variables.

Causal modeling is a powerful technique because it allows the researcher to simultaneously test all the relations comprising an entire

FIGURE 2.6
Simple Structural Equation Model

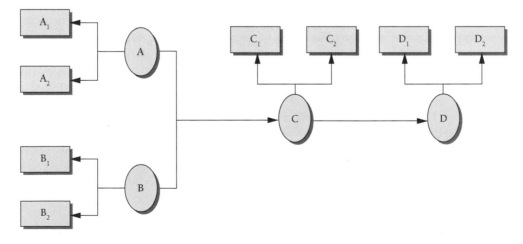

theoretical model. With correlation and regression analysis, it is only possible to test "parts" or individual segments of a theoretical model. The use of causal modeling, however, has been somewhat controversial. Many such controversies are technically beyond the scope of this chapter and are related to parameter estimation methods and the assessing model fit. Some, however, have questioned whether this technique has been overused, and whether model tests have been too data driven and not grounded enough in theory.

Like any statistical technique, causal modeling is neither *good* nor *bad*. If applied properly, it can be a very useful part of an organizational psychologist's statistical tool kit. Generally speaking, causal modeling is most powerful when the model being tested has a strong theoretical base. It is only at this point that a researcher has enough insight to propose the complex set of interrelations among variables that comprises most causal models. Thus, it is usually not appropriate to use causal modeling early in a theoretically based research program.

Aggregation and Levels of Analysis

A recent trend in organizational psychology is the exploration of variables at multiple levels of analysis; that is, researchers have increasingly become interested in the impact of variables that are conceptualized not only at the individual level but also at group and even organizational levels. Researchers have also become interested in how variables at different levels of analysis impact each other. This latter type of investigation is known as **cross-level analysis.**

Exploring multiple levels of analysis obviously presents researchers with some important theoretical issues (e.g., Chan, 1998; K. J. Klein, Dansereau, & Hall, 1994). However, with these theoretical considerations come statistical considerations. Let us first consider the issue of **aggregation.** When data are aggregated, this simply means that one value is used to represent the unit of aggregation. An example of this would be: using the mean level of job satisfaction within a work group to represent "group-level satisfaction." Note that when we aggregate, all individual differences within the unit of aggregation are suppressed.

When is it appropriate to aggregate individual responses? Generally speaking, researchers must be prepared to justify aggregation on three different levels. First, there must be *theoretical* justification. The issue here is whether the variable created through aggregation is theoretically meaningful. In the example provided in the previous paragraph, the researcher would need to make the case that the average level of job satisfaction within a work group is a theoretically meaningful variable.

If aggregation is theoretically justified, the researcher must provide some *methodological* justification for the decision to aggregate. This has to do with the measurement of variables. In many cases, individual responses are aggregated because items make reference to respondent perceptions of the unit of aggregation. For instance, if a researcher were to measure organizational climate (James & Jones, 1974), the items should make reference to the *organization* and not the individuals responding. This suggests that researchers should make the decision to aggregate before data are collected.

The third way that researchers must be prepared to justify aggregation is *statistically.* In most instances where individual responses are aggregated, the researcher is doing so in order to measure some attribute of the unit of aggregation. For example, a researcher may want to measure the level of cohesiveness in a group, or the level of trust within an organization. In such cases, it is incumbent upon the researcher to justify aggregation by showing some statistical evidence of agreement in responses within the unit of aggregation. If respondents within a group do not agree on the level of cohesiveness within the group, it usually makes little sense to average their responses. There are several ways to measure interrater agreement, but the most frequently used method has become the r_{wg} statistic (James et al., 1984).

Besides aggregation, the other major issue confronting researchers exploring multiple-level issues is statistical analysis. In any research investigation, the choice of statistical analysis is driven by the research question being asked. Thus, in some cases, the analysis of multilevel data is relatively straightforward. For example, if a researcher were interested in the relation between group cohesiveness and group performance, it would make sense to examine the correlation between aggregate-level measures of both of these variables. The only drawback to this approach, of course, is that it greatly reduces sample size, and, hence, statistical power.

In other instances, the analysis of multilevel data is more complex because researchers wish to retain the effects of multiple levels within the same analysis. For example, a researcher may be interested in estimating the relative contribution of individual-level versus group-level effects. In some cases, researchers may be interested in exploring the impact of group or organizational-level variables on the relation between individual-level variables. Fortunately, statistical procedures are available to researchers, to allow the analysis of data at multiple levels.

To explore the relative contribution of group and individual effects, a statistical technique that has been used frequently is **within and between analysis (WABA)** (Dansereau, Alutto, & Yammarino, 1984). WABA is useful because it allows the researcher to *simultaneously* examine relationships between variables

at the individual and group levels. To examine cross-level relations, a statistical technique that is becoming increasingly popular is **random coefficient modeling** (Byrk & Raudenbush, 1992). Random coefficient modeling can be used, for example, to test whether the magnitude of relations between individual-level variables (represented by regression coefficients) differs as a function of some aggregate level variable. While both of these techniques are very useful, they are also very complex, and they require the use of special computer software. However, if used appropriately, both can help researchers untangle the complexity of multilevel data.

CHAPTER SUMMARY

This chapter explored the methodological and statistical foundations of organizational psychology. As was shown, organizational psychologists have several options when collecting data about behavior in organizations. These range from simple observation methods to highly complex quasi-experimental investigations. The most frequently used technique, however, is survey research.

In the collection of data in organizations, several important issues must be considered. For instance, researchers need to be cognizant of the limitations of self-report measures, and aware of limits on the generalizability of research findings across research settings. When cross-cultural research is attempted, researchers must be attuned to issues of language and sampling. A more practical issue is simply gaining access to organizations to collect research data.

A variety of statistical methods were discussed that can be used to analyze data once they are collected. These range from simple descriptive statistics to more complex correlation and regression analysis. The choice of any statistical technique is dictated by the nature of the question the researcher is attempting to answer.

In the statistical analysis of data, a number of important issues must be considered. Researchers should be aware of the importance of statistical power and attempt to maximize it whenever possible. This is particularly true when researchers are interested in demonstrating the effect of moderator variables. Complex statistical techniques, such as causal modeling, can be useful tools to organizational researchers, provided they are used judiciously and are based on sound theory. The exploration of multilevel data has become increasingly popular in organizational psychology in recent years. Researchers conducting multilevel analysis must be prepared to justify aggregation, and must choose the analytical technique that best represents the substantive issue of interest.

SUGGESTED ADDITIONAL READINGS

Dane, F. C. (1990). *Research methods.* Pacific Grove, CA: Brooks-Cole.

Hays, W. L. (1988). *Statistics* (4th ed.). Fort Worth, TX: Harcourt Brace Jovanovich.

Kirk, R. C. (1982). *Experimental design: Procedures for the behavioral sciences* (2nd ed.). Pacific Grove, CA: Brooks-Cole.

McCall, M. W., Jr., & Bobko, P. (1990). Research methods in the service of discovery. In M. D. Dunnette & L. M. Hough (Eds.), *Handbook of industrial and organizational psychology* (2nd ed., Vol. 1, pp. 381–418). Palo Alto, CA: Consulting Psychologists Press.

Ostroff, C. (1993). Comparing correlations based on individual-level and aggregated data. *Journal of Applied Psychology, 78,* 569–582.

Schaubroeck, J., & Kuehn, K. (1992). Research design in industrial and organizational psychology. In C. L. Cooper & I. T. Robertson (Eds.), *International review of industrial and organizational psychology 1992* (pp. 99–121). Chichester, England: Wiley.

Stone, E. F., Stone, D. L., & Gueutal, H. G. (1990). Influence of cognitive ability on responses to questionnaire measures: Measurement precision and missing response problems. *Journal of Applied Psychology, 75,* 418–427.

Tabachnick, B. G., & Fidell, L. S. (1996). *Using multivariate statistics* (3rd ed.). New York: HarperCollins.

Chapter Three

Attraction and Socialization

The lifeblood of any social organization is people. For example, a university must have faculty, an auto manufacturer must have design engineers, and a professional football team must have players. Thus, to remain viable, organizations must periodically bring in new employees and train them to become full-fledged organizational members. To begin this process, organizations must first attract potential employees and determine whether their qualifications match organizational needs. Once employees enter an organization, they must be trained not only to perform job-specific tasks, but also to learn the culture of the organization. Taken together, this entire process can be viewed collectively as attraction and socialization.

This chapter begins with an examination of the recruiting process from the perspective of both the organization and the applicant. Organizations use a variety of methods to recruit potential employees, and a number of factors can impact the success of recruiting

efforts. Regardless of the methods used, organizations must be careful not to turn off potentially valuable employees during this process. Applicants, or potential employees, also evaluate potential employers. In general, potential employees attempt to make some determination of the extent to which they "fit" with an organization.

The focus of the chapter then shifts to employee socialization. Once a recruit accepts employment and becomes an "official" organizational member, a process begins in which the new employee is transformed from an "outsider" to a full-fledged organizational member. Organizational psychologists have examined the socialization process in an effort to understand the various tactics organizations use to socialize new employees, determine what employees learn as they are socialized, and describe the tactics new employees use to obtain information during the socialization process.

The chapter concludes with a discussion of the impact of diversity on employee socialization. In contemporary organizations, it is quite common for new employees to enter organizations with demographic characteristics, experiences, and values that are far different from those of the majority of employees. Because of this, it may be especially difficult for such individuals to be fully socialized into an organization. Fortunately, there are steps an organization can take to deal with the impact of diversity on the socialization process.

THE RECRUITMENT PROCESS: AN ORGANIZATIONAL PERSPECTIVE

The aim of recruiting is to generate a large pool of *highly qualified* applicants so that the organization can select those who stand a good chance of becoming productive and successful employees. In college athletics, for example, coaches typically spend most of the off-season recruiting highly prized high school athletes. Although recruiting is usually not considered an "organizational" topic, it is covered briefly in this chapter because it is strongly related to socialization. Successful recruiting increases the chances that the new employees an organization selects will fit well into the culture of the organization and will be socialized more successfully.

Recruitment Planning

Organizations typically do not recruit new employees in a random fashion. Rather, an organization's recruiting efforts are typically based on careful planning as to: (1) the number of employees that will be needed in various jobs, (2) when these new employees will be needed, and (3) the present and future supply of potential employees in the labor market. An organization that understands these three elements of planning will be able to focus its recruiting efforts much more effectively. According to Cascio (1998), this crucial first step in the recruitment process is known as **recruitment planning**.

What type of information does an organization need to develop a sound recruitment plan? First and foremost, recruitment planning should coincide with an organization's **strategic planning**. A strategic plan can be thought of as an organization's plan for "where we're going" and "how we're going to get there." Strategic planning must be linked to recruitment planning because strategic plans often have clear implications for staffing needs. As an example, let's say the coach of a professional football team decides to replace an offensive system that relies heavily on running plays with one that relies primarily on passing. This change in strategy will require players with different skills and thus will have implications for recruiting. The coach would want to focus on obtaining a highly talented quarterback and corps of receivers, either through the college draft or by other means (e.g., trades or free-agent signings).

Another factor that should be considered in developing a recruitment plan is **succession planning**. Succession planning involves making some projections as to the likelihood of turnover within various job categories. This is often done on the basis of projected retirements, but may be based on other factors as well (i.e., employees in limited-term jobs, employees returning to school). Based on these projections, an organization can often gear its recruiting efforts toward attracting individuals who have the skills necessary to perform the work of those who may be leaving the organization. As with any prediction, there is some degree of uncertainty in succession planning. For example, since there is no mandatory retirement age for most occupations, organizations are often uncertain as to the retirement plans of senior employees.

A third consideration in recruitment planning is the skills and abilities of current employees. Many organizations ask current employees to periodically complete what is known as a **skills inventory.** A skills inventory may ask employees to document their job experiences, continuing education (if any), and special skills and competencies. If current employees possess the skills and abilities needed by an organization, there is obviously less need to recruit from outside sources. This is important because filling positions internally has certain advantages (i.e., less adjustment for the employee and less cost for the organization) and may create positive incentives for employees.

A final piece of information that is useful for developing a recruitment plan is some assessment of the supply of labor for various job categories. This type of information can often be obtained relatively easily from government agencies, trade associations, and, in some cases, professional organizations. In the field of I/O psychology, for example, the Society for Industrial and Organizational Psychology (SIOP) collects information about the supply of labor in the profession. The basic question an organization is seeking to answer is whether the supply of employees in different job categories is very plentiful or very scarce. For example, the supply of attorneys in the United States has grown to the point where they are quite plentiful in the labor market. In contrast, software developers and computer programmers are in relatively short supply.

Labor market information is useful because it will influence the approach an organization will take in its recruiting efforts, as well as the choice of specific recruiting sources. To fill jobs for which labor is in short supply, organizations may need to be highly aggressive in their recruiting efforts and perhaps offer other incentives (e.g., sign-on bonuses) to attract new employees. Such recruiting efforts may require the assistance of executive search firms and may be international in scope. In contrast, when the supply of labor is plentiful, organizations may be able to devote fewer resources to recruiting efforts, and may adopt a much less aggressive approach. For example, if many unskilled manual labor positions are open, organizations may rely on referrals from current employees or simply invite walk-in applicants.

Recruiting Methods

Assuming that an organization has developed a sound recruitment plan, the next step is to choose some methods of recruiting. A key decision for any organization that plans to recruit new employees is whether to invite applications from *internal* and *external* sources. The primary form of internal recruiting is advertising to current employees (i.e., through job postings). As stated earlier, recruiting internally has many advantages. Internal transfers and promotions are less expensive than bringing in new employees, may provide positive incentives for current employees, and may require less training for those employees who apply and are accepted.

On the other hand, new employees from the outside may bring a fresh perspective to the organization. Also, some organizations may be forced to hire outsiders because their current employees have not acquired the skills necessary to perform a given job.

Compared to a current workforce, external recruiting sources are much more plentiful, as indicated in Table 3.1. Although a specific recruiting source may be required because of the nature of the job, some general comments can be made about recruiting sources. For example, the most frequently used recruiting source is some form of advertising—typically, in print or electronic media.

The recruiting sources listed in Table 3.1 indicate considerable variation in cost. The least costly recruiting sources are typically walk-ins and employee referrals. In addition to their low cost, employee referrals may be attractive because these applicants typically possess greater knowledge of the organization than other applicants do. This may explain why employees who are referred by organizational members tend to have lower levels of turnover, compared to others (Gannon, 1971; Reid, 1972). An obvious danger in reliance on employee referrals is that it may perpetuate nepotism, and the result may be an overly homogeneous workforce.

The most costly recruiting methods are: the use of employment agencies and, to a lesser extent, on-campus recruiting. It should be emphasized, however, that the cost of a recruiting source must be weighed against other factors. For example, most organizations are willing to incur the cost of employment agencies or executive search firms when they must select high-level senior executives. Poor hiring decisions at this level may cost an organization millions of dollars. For lower-level positions, though, it would be difficult for an organization to justify that level of expenditure.

Other than cost, how else can organizations evaluate the potential usefulness of different recruiting sources? Two commonly used indexes are **yield ratios** and **time lapse data**. A yield ratio is simply the *total number* of candidates generated by a given recruiting source (newspaper ads, for example), relative to the

---

TABLE 3.1
Typical External Recruiting Sources Used by Organizations

1. *Advertising:* newspapers (classified and display), technical and professional journals, direct mail, television, the Internet, and (in some cases) outdoor advertising.
2. *Employment agencies:* federal and state agencies, private agencies, executive search firms, management consulting firms, and agencies specializing in temporary help.
3. *Educational institutions:* technical and trade schools, colleges and universities, co-op work/study programs, and alumni placement offices.
4. *Professional organizations:* technical societies' meetings, conventions (regional and national), and placement services.
5. *Military:* out-processing centers and placement services administered by regional and national retired officers' associations.
6. *Labor unions.*
7. *Career fairs.*
8. *Outplacement firms.*
9. *Walk-ins.*
10. *Write-ins.*
11. *Company retirees.*
12. *Employee referrals.*

Source: W. F. Cascio. (1998). *Applied psychology in personnel management* (5th ed.). Upper Saddle River, NJ: Prentice Hall. Reprinted by permission of Pearson Education, Inc., Upper Saddle River, NJ.

number of *qualified* candidates. From an organization's perspective, an ideal recruiting source is one that delivers a large number of candidates who are well qualified for the position the company is attempting to fill. This allows the organization to be highly selective in making its hiring decisions.

Time lapse data represent estimates of the time it takes to go from one step to the next in the recruiting and hiring process. For example, organizations may estimate the time needed for each step that takes place between the initial contact with an applicant and the time when he or she is employed by the organization. Time lapse data help an organization identify "bottlenecks" in the recruitment process that may cause applicants to lose interest (see Comment 3.1). When those bottlenecks are identified, an organization can sometimes take steps to speed up the process; however, this is not always possible. For example, recruitment for government jobs that require security clearance has to be quite lengthy, to allow for background investigations.

COMMENT 3.1

RESEARCH ON RECRUITING

BECAUSE OF THE importance of recruiting, there has been considerable research on it over the years (see Rynes, 1991). One theme is very evident in recruiting research: the *recruiter* is not a key factor in whether an applicant decides to accept employment with an organization. Rather, the nature of the job and other conditions of employment (e.g., salary, benefits, and promotion potential) appear to be much more important. The one thing about recruiters that does appear to be important, however, is their knowledge of the job that an applicant is seeking. This may be the reason that organizations often select technical specialists to recruit in their technical specialty.

Another very clear theme in the recruiting literature—the way organizations treat applicants during the recruiting process—is important. For example, if an organization treats applicants rudely, or is very lax about keeping them informed, this approach will turn off applicants and make them less likely to accept an offer of employment. Why is this the case? Most recruiting researchers contend that, during the recruiting process, applicants form an impression of a potential employer. Thus, when an applicant is not treated well during the recruiting process, negative "signals" tell the applicant what the organization would be like as an employer.

In summary, research has shown that, in comparison to many other factors, recruiting does not have a large impact on applicants' decision making. Nevertheless, the recruiting process is important, largely because, if not done well, it has the potential to turn off applicants. Organizations should strive to employ knowledgeable recruiters who treat applicants with respect. It is also imperative that organizations attempt to avoid lengthy time delays, and to maintain contact with applicants during the recruitment process.

Sources: S. L. Rynes. (1991). Recruitment, job choice, and post-hire consequences: A call for new research directions. In M. D. Dunnette and L. M. Hough (Eds.), *Handbook of industrial and organizational psychology* (2nd ed., Vol. 2, pp. 399–444). Palo Alto, CA: Consulting Psychologists' Press; and S. L. Rynes, R. D. Bretz, Jr., and B. Gerhart. (1991). The importance of recruitment in job choice: A different way of looking. *Personnel Psychology, 44,* 487–522.

THE RECRUITMENT PROCESS: THE APPLICANT'S PERSPECTIVE

From the organization's perspective, the recruitment process involves trying to "put our best foot forward" in order to favorably impress potential employees. Applicants are also trying to make a favorable impression on the organizations they contact. At the same time, we know that applicants are trying to determine which organizations are most attractive to them. In this section, we examine how, and on what basis, applicants make such judgments about organizations.

In a very general sense, when applicants evaluate potential employers, they are typically making some judgment as to whether they "fit" with these organizations. An applicant is really asking himself or herself: "Can I see myself doing this job in this organization?" This question can obviously be answered on many levels; thus, some explanation is needed as to the bases on which applicants' assessments of fit are made. On one dimension, the applicant's skills and abilities must match the skills and abilities required to perform a given job (Kristof, 1996). To perform the job of auto mechanic, for example, a person needs mechanical aptitude, the skills necessary to perform automotive repairs, and, in many cases, formal training.

Assuming that an applicant does possess the necessary job-relevant skills and abilities, what other bases does that applicant use to assess his or her fit with a particular organization? Research on applicants' decision making reveals that several factors are used by applicants to judge whether they would fit in a particular organization. According to Schneider's (1987) **Attraction–Selection–Attrition** framework, applicants are attracted to and stay in organizations with cultures that are compatible with their personalities. This explains why members of organizations, and even work groups, tend to be rather homogeneous in terms of personality (George, 1990; Jordan, Herriot, & Chalmers, 1991; Schaubroeck, Ganster, & Jones, 1998; Schneider, Smith, Taylor, & Fleenor, 1998).

To simply say that applicants are attracted to organizations with cultures that are compatible with their personalities is a rather imprecise statement. Such a statement begs the question: What aspects of personality, and what aspects of organizational culture? To address this question, Judge and Cable (1997) investigated the relationship between the Big Five personality traits (neuroticism, extraversion, openness to experience, agreeableness, and conscientiousness) and job applicants' attraction to organizations with different cultural profiles. Organizational culture can be thought of as the underlying values and basic assumptions that guide much of the behavior of organizational members. (See Chapter 15 for a more extensive examination of organizational culture.)

The results of this study showed that applicants were attracted to organizations with cultural profiles that were congruent with their personalities. As an example of how this works, consider the personality trait of "conscientiousness." A person who is highly conscientious is dependable and achievement-oriented, and plans well. Judge and Cable's (1997) study showed that those who are highly conscientious prefer organizations with cultures that can be described as highly detail-oriented, and that place an emphasis on tangible outcomes. This may very well be due to the fact that highly conscientious individuals are meticulous about their work and are likely to produce tangible outcomes.

Applicants may also judge their fit to a particular organization on the basis of commonality in perceived *values*. Values simply represent things that are important to people and organizations. Suppose that a person places a strong emphasis on the value of individual achievement. It is unlikely that this person would be attracted to an organization that places a strong emphasis on the value of teamwork and collective achievement. Several studies have in fact demonstrated that applicants are attracted to organizations that they perceive to have values similar to their own (Chatman, 1991; Dawis, 1990). The major implication is that an organization must be careful to convey accurate information to applicants regarding its values. Obviously, though, applicants base their judgments of an organization's values on more than just recruiting materials. For example, applicants may base such judgments on information from others, encounters with the organization (e.g., as a customer), and the way the organization is portrayed in the media. A broader implication is that organizations must clarify their values and attempt to operate in a way that is consistent with those values. These findings suggest that value clarification is also a useful exercise for applicants (see Comment 3.2).

COMMENT 3.2

VALUE CLARIFICATION: WHAT WOULD YOU WALK THE I-BEAM FOR?

VALUES REPRESENT THINGS or ideas that are important to people. For one person, acquiring material wealth may be extremely important; for another, the most important thing might be to help other people. There is evidence that when people search for jobs, careers, and organizations, values play a very important role. That is, people want their work lives to be compatible with their values.

Despite the importance of values, many people never take the time to seriously clarify what their values are. However, value clarification occurs very quickly when people have to make choices. A humorous beer commercial on television illustrated this principle very well. In the commercial, two college-age men, at a grocery-store checkout, discover they do not have enough money to pay for all of their groceries. They start putting back the groceries, and are eventually left with two items— beer and toilet paper. They still do not have enough money, so they are forced to purchase *either* the beer or the toilet paper. As some readers will remember, they decide to buy the beer but of course request *paper* rather than plastic bags. (I'll leave it to the reader's imagination to figure out why!)

I encountered an interesting value clarification exercise while participating in a training seminar about two years ago. The person leading the seminar described a situation in which an I-beam approximately six inches wide was placed between the roofs of two skyscrapers that were about 50 feet apart. Needless to say, walking across this I-beam would be extremely dangerous. She then asked one of the seminar participants whether he would walk across this I-beam if $100,000 were waiting at the other end. When he quickly responded "No," she then asked whether he had any children. When he replied that he had two sons, ages 5 and 3, she asked whether he would walk this I-beam if his five-year-old son were stranded on it. As you might guess, his response was now an unequivocal "Yes." Few situations in life require such dramatic value clarification. However, it is a good way to begin thinking about what one really values in life. So the next time you're unsure about your values, asking yourself "What would I walk the I-beam for?" might provide some useful answers.

In addition to personality and values, applicants may make other assessments of fit, based on a variety of other factors. For example, an applicant may have strong feelings about work-family issues, and thus actively seek membership in an organization that is very progressive regarding work-family initiatives. Some people seek membership in organizations for more ideological reasons. As an example, in the 1990 book *By Way of Deception: The Making and Unmaking of a Mossad Officer,* Victor Ostrovksy describes how becoming an agent in the Mossad, Israel's secretive intelligence organization, appealed to his Zionism and his strong belief that Israel must constantly be on guard against its enemies (Ostrovsky & Hoy, 1990).

ORGANIZATIONAL SOCIALIZATION

Assuming that an organization is able to attract a pool of highly qualified applicants, it will obviously utilize some selection procedures, make offers to applicants, and ultimately end up with new employees. When someone is hired, a process of socialization is required to transform the new "outsider" employee into a full-fledged organizational member. In this section, organizational socialization is defined, models of the organizational socialization process are reviewed, and tactics used by both organizations and newcomers during the socialization process are described. The concluding section examines the impact of diversity on organizational socialization efforts.

Defining Organizational Socialization

Organizational socialization represents the process by which an individual makes the transition from "outsider" to "organizational member." What does a person have to learn in order to make this transition successfully?

According to Van Maanen and Schein (1979), in the broadest sense, socialization represents the process by which new members can *learn the culture of an organization*. Thus, socialization is synonymous with the process of **acculturation** of new organizational members. Socialization has also been defined (a bit more narrowly) as the process by which new members learn the task-related and social knowledge necessary to be successful members of an organization (Louis, 1990). In this case, socialization is very much concerned with new employees' learning job-related tasks and getting along with members of their immediate work group.

One of the most comprehensive definitions of organizational socialization was provided by Chao, O'Leary-Kelly, Wolf, Klein, and Gardner (1994). Their definition, which contains six dimensions, encompasses elements of task-related learning, knowledge of the social climate, and culture transmission. These six dimensions are presented in Table 3.2.

The first dimension proposed is *history.* As a person becomes socialized into an organization, he or she gradually becomes familiar with an organization's long-held customs and traditions. Many organizations provide newcomers with this information during their initial orientation. New employees at Walt Disney World, for example, learn about the legacy of Walt Disney himself and the traditions of the organization in their initial

---

TABLE 3.2

Six Dimensions of Organizational Socialization (Chao et al., 1994)

---

1. History.
2. Language.
3. Politics.
4. People.
5. Organizational goals and values.
6. Performance proficiency.

---

training, which is called "Traditions 101" (Peters & Waterman, 1982).

The second dimension of socialization is *language*. All organizations utilize some terminology and jargon that are familiar only to organizational members. Some of this language may be required by the dominant profession within an organization (e.g., a law firm), but some is organization-specific. Newcomers to military organizations quickly learn about the reliance on military-specific terminology and acronyms. For example, "presentations" are referred to as "briefings," and "assignments" are referred to as "missions." With respect to acronyms, some readers may recall a hilarious scene in the movie *Good Morning, Vietnam* where the actor Robin Williams manages to squeeze every possible military acronym into one sentence. Having worked as a contractor for the U.S. Army in the past, the author can personally attest to the reliance on acronyms in the military (see Comment 3.3).

A third aspect of socialization is *politics*. As newcomers become socialized into an organization, they gradually begin to understand the politics or "unwritten rules" that govern behavior within the organization. For example, this may involve learning how to get things done, how to obtain desirable work assignments, and who the most influential people in the organization are. Such things may appear to be obvious at first, but they may actually be more complex. In many organizations, newcomers often find that power and influence are only moderately related to hierarchical level. For example, it is not unusual for clerical employees to be very influential because they can control the flow of information and access to those at higher levels of the organizations.

COMMENT 3.3

ACRONYMS AND MILITARY CULTURE

ONE OF THE biggest shocks for civilians who work for or with the military is the heavy reliance on acronyms in the military. For example, the person you are working most closely with is your POC (Point of Contact), and when someone goes to another location temporarily, he or she is TDY (Temporary Duty). I first encountered military acronyms during work on a year-long project for the United States Recruiting Command (USAREC, of course). Evidently, the people we were working with on this project were concerned about our lack of understanding of military acronyms; they provided us with a booklet explaining the meaning of all military acronyms. I knew we were in trouble because the booklet was about an inch thick! However, once we learned some of the more important acronyms, we actually became quite comfortable with this form of communication.

After several years of not working for the military, I began an association with Walter Reed Army Institute of Research (WRAIR) in 1996 that eventually led to an appointment as a Guest Scientist, which I still hold. Although the work I have done with WRAIR is quite different than with USAREC, the use of acronyms still predominates. I have actually asked some Army personnel why the military uses so many acronyms. Although most of those I have talked to don't know for sure, the consensus is that acronyms were adopted because they facilitate speed of communication, something that might be critical during an actual military operation.

The fourth dimension of socialization is *people.* Most organizational newcomers typically belong to some group or unit, so they must establish and maintain good working relationships with others. This may involve establishing friendships both within the work group and in the organization as a whole. Although such contacts may be important in and of themselves, they also may help a newcomer to understand the history and politics of the organization. In many universities, for example, this process is facilitated by pairing new faculty with senior faculty mentors. These mentoring relationships are important in helping newcomers to adjust to their new surroundings, make contacts within the university, and understand the history of the institution.

The fifth dimension is *organizational goals and values.* Although members of organizations do not become robots who blindly follow orders, they must learn the goals and values of the organization and, to some extent, assimilate them as their own. An employee working for McDonald's, for example, must learn to get at least somewhat "fired up" about the prospect of satisfying customers. As stated earlier, some of this learning is accomplished in the attraction stage because employees tend to be attracted to organizations that they identify with ideologically. However, applicants typically do not have a *complete* grasp of the goals and values of an organization until they become regular employees.

The final dimension of socialization, according to Chao et al. (1994), is *performance proficiency.* All organizational newcomers must learn to perform their jobs proficiently or they will not be able to maintain their membership for long. Building performance proficiency is a complex process that involves developing an understanding of one's job duties, as well as acquiring the specific skills necessary to perform them. As will be shown later in this chapter, a consistent theme in the organizational socialization literature is that this dimension is the top priority of new employees when they initially enter an organization. This is understandable; rewards and other future opportunities within the organization are often contingent on performance.

The Socialization Process: An Organizational Perspective

The process of organizational socialization can be viewed from two distinct perspectives: (1) the organization and (2) the newcomer. When viewed from an organizational perspective, the focus is on the stages newcomers pass through during the socialization process, and the tactics used by organizations to get them through these stages. When viewed from the perspective of the newcomer, the focus is on the ways in which newcomers learn about and make sense of their new organizational environment. In this section, we examine socialization from an organizational perspective.

Organizational psychologists have tended to view socialization largely in terms of stages that new employees pass through during the socialization process. Feldman (1976, 1981) proposed what has become the most influential stage model of organizational socialization. This model is presented in Figure 3.1.

The first stage in this model is **anticipatory socialization,** which refers to processes that occur before an individual joins an organization. This form of socialization typically occurs during the recruitment phase, when applicants gather information about the organization and make some assessment of whether they would "fit" within it. In some cases, however, anticipatory socialization may occur much earlier than the recruitment phase. For example, people often have an opportunity to "try out" certain occupations

FIGURE 3.1
Feldman's (1981) Model of the Stages of
Organizational Socialization

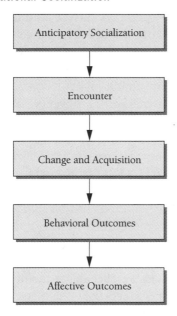

Source: D. C. Feldman. (1981). The multiple socialization of organization members. *Academy of Management Review, 6,* 309–318. Reprinted by permission of the Copyright Clearance Center.

through internships, summer jobs, or other related experiences. According to Feldman (1981), anticipatory socialization is most valuable when an applicant has a realistic picture of the organization and the job he or she will be performing. In fact, much research has been done on the value of realistic job previews (RJPs), which prepare new employees for the realities of the jobs they will be performing (e.g., Wanous, 1989). Related to this, it is also desirable if the applicant actually has the skills and abilities that are congruent with the job being sought, and has needs and values that are congruent with the organization.

As the newcomer moves into the organization and becomes an official member, the **encounter** stage begins. According to Feldman (1981), the encounter stage represents

the point at which the newcomer begins to see the job and organization as they really are. For a number of reasons, this period may require considerable adjustment. The newcomer may have to balance the demands placed on him or her by the organization with family demands. A new attorney in a large law firm, for example, may find that new associates are expected to work in excess of 80 hours per week if they want to eventually become partners. This is also the time when the new employee is learning the demands of his or her role within the organization. Often, this simply requires clarification of role responsibilities with one's supervisor, but it may also involve mediating conflicting role demands.

After new employees become acclimated to their new roles, they eventually reach the stage labeled by Feldman as **change and acquisition.** At this point, the employee has become fairly comfortable with his or her new role both in terms of performing required job tasks and, perhaps more importantly, adjusting to the culture of the organization. At this point, an employee is "firing on all cylinders," so to speak. For an attorney, this would be the point at which he or she is handling a number of cases and is comfortable doing so. During the change and acquisition phase, the new employee has also come to some resolution regarding role demands; that is, the employee has gained, from his or her supervisor and coworkers, a good understanding of what is and is not expected. At this point employees are also able to achieve some reasonable balance between their work and their personal lives.

To a large extent, when the change and acquisition stage is reached, the new employee has become "socialized," at least according to the model. To assess the *extent* of socialization, Feldman included behavioral and affective outcomes within the model. At a behavioral level, the extent of socialization can be assessed by whether an employee is capable of carrying out his or her role-related assignments. For example, we would hardly consider the socialization process successful if an employee were unable to perform his or her job.

A second behavioral index of socialization is the extent to which an employee is spontaneously innovative in carrying out role responsibilities, and is cooperative with other employees. According to Van Maanen and Schein (1979), when an employee is socialized into a new role, this may take the form of **custodianship, content innovation,** or **role innovation.** A custodial approach requires simply performing a role exactly "as written," with little or no deviation. Most readers have undoubtedly heard the phrase "It's not in my job description." Content innovation and role innovation, on the other hand, imply that the new role occupant may introduce changes into the content or even into the nature of the role. An example of content innovation might be a physician's informing patients directly about the results of lab tests rather than having nurses do this. An example of role innovation might be: expanding the role of production workers to include not only product assembly, but also quality control and perhaps even communication with product end users. Feldman's model proposes that putting one's stamp on the new role being occupied is an aspect of socialization.

A third behavioral index of the extent of socialization is turnover. If an employee leaves an organization, one could certainly make the case that this represents a breakdown in the socialization process (Feldman, 1981). This is only partially true, however; turnover may occur because of plentiful job opportunities (Carsten & Spector, 1987), or because an employee has exceptional skills and thus may have opportunities in other organizations (Schwab, 1991). It is also possible for an

employee to remain in an organization but resist being fully socialized (see Comment 3.4).

Affective outcomes associated with socialization refer to things such as attitudes toward work, level of motivation, and involvement in one's job. According to Feldman's model, when employees are successfully socialized, they tend to exhibit higher levels of job satisfaction, internal work motivation, and job involvement. As with turnover, these outcomes may also be impacted by many factors and are thus imperfect indicators of socialization.

Feldman's (1981) model, which describes the stages employees go through during the socialization process, has received empirical support (e.g., Feldman, 1976), but it does not explicitly describe the tactics organizations use to socialize newcomers. For example, how does a police department "break in" new recruits after they graduate from the training academy? How does a major league baseball team help a talented minor league player make the transition to playing at the major league level? How does a university help a new professor make the transition from graduate school to faculty status?

The most comprehensive description of socialization *tactics* was provided by Van Maanen and Schein (1979) in their review of the organizational socialization literature. According to these authors, socialization tactics can be described according to the six dimensions that are presented in Table 3.3. Note that these are not specific tactics, per se, but they form a very useful *framework* for understanding specific tactics. As can be seen, organizations may opt to socialize new organizational members *collectively* or *individually.* As an example of collective socialization, an organization might bring in a group of new recruits and put them through an extensive training course together. In state police departments, for example, large groups of individuals are typically hired at the same time, and these

COMMENT 3.4

ORGANIZATIONAL SOCIALIZATION AND CONFORMITY

As NEWCOMERS BECOME socialized into an organization, they begin to understand the organization's culture. Furthermore, once they understand an organization's culture, they begin to assimilate that culture. Thus, it is assumed that one of the signs that an organization is not successful in socializing new employees is turnover. Those who do not conform to an organization's culture end up leaving that organization. This may be true in some cases but, in others, nonconformists end up staying in an organization.

Based on what we know about turnover, there may be situations in which an individual does not embrace the culture of an organization, yet has few other employment options. The nonconforming employee may simply learn ways to cope with working in such an organization. There may also be individuals who do not embrace the culture of an organization, yet may work there for a variety of reasons— compensation, geographical preferences, or

simply because it's easier than looking for another job. Such employees may also find ways to cope with working for an organization that they do not fit into.

There may be cases, however, where an employee does not conform and the organization must adapt. If an employee is unusually talented, or possesses a very rare skill, an organization may be forced to put up with a certain degree of nonconformity. For example, several professional basketball teams have put up with the unconventional behavior and appearance of Dennis Rodman because of his rebounding skill. In addition, for several years, the Dallas Cowboys allowed Deion Sanders to pursue a professional baseball career even though he was regarded as one of the best cornerbacks in the National Football League. It is important to note, though, that these examples are exceptions. Employees in *most* organizations can rarely get away with similar levels of nonconformity.

individuals subsequently attend a training academy as a group or cohort. Among the clear advantages of collective socialization are: It is more economical from the organization's perspective, and it provides opportunities for

newcomers to develop a sense of cohesion and camaraderie among themselves. A potential danger of collective socialization is that it is most likely to produce only a custodial orientation among newcomers; that is, newcomers socialized in this manner may not be particularly innovative in performing their roles.

Examples of individual socialization would include skilled apprenticeship programs and, in a more general sense, mentoring. This form of socialization is typically used when the information a newcomer must learn is very complex, and when socialization takes place over a long period of time. Compared to group socialization, individual socialization allows an organization somewhat more control over the

TABLE 3.3

Van Maanen and Schein's (1979) Six Dimensions of Organizational Socialization Tactics

Collective	Individual
Formal	Informal
Sequential	Random
Fixed	Variable
Serial	Disjunctive
Investiture	Divestiture

information passed on to the newcomer, and this is more likely to produce outcomes that are desired by the organization. For example, Van Maanen and Schein (1979) point out that those socialized individually will be more likely to be innovative in the way they carry out their roles, as compared to those socialized collectively.

Despite the apparent value of individual socialization, there are some drawbacks. One obvious drawback is that individual socialization is expensive. For a senior manager to give one-on-one mentoring to a management trainee, or for a master plumber to work with a journeyman is time-consuming and expensive. Also, in some cases, a custodial role orientation encouraged by collective socialization is more desirable than innovation. For example, if a police officer does not follow proper procedures when making an arrest, the chances of obtaining a conviction may be very slim. Also, if soldiers do not adhere strictly to agreed-on rules of engagement during peacekeeping missions, their actions may result in violations of international law.

The second dimension depicted in Table 3.3 is *formal* versus *informal*. Police recruits' attendance at a residential training academy is an example of formal organizational socialization (e.g., Van Maanen, 1975). Note from the previous discussion that this is also collective socialization, although all forms of formal socialization need not be collective. For example, doctoral students are being socialized into their chosen professions in the context of a formal program of study. Within doctoral programs, however, much of the socialization takes place during informal interactions between students and their faculty mentors. The most common form of informal socialization is the very familiar "on-the-job" training. The new employee is not distinguished from more experienced colleagues, but his or her initial performance expectations are obviously lower.

According to Van Maanen and Schein (1979), formal socialization tends to be used in situations where newcomers are expected to assume new ranks or achieve a certain status in an organization, where there is a large body of knowledge for newcomers to learn, or when errors on the part of a new employee may put others (including the newcomers themselves) at risk. This would certainly apply to many law enforcement jobs, as well as many forms of professional training (e.g., law, medicine, dentistry). Informal socialization, on the other hand, is most typical when it is necessary for a newcomer to quickly learn new skills and work methods, or to develop highly specific practical skills. This would apply to a wide variety of workers, such as convenience store clerks, restaurant employees, and production employees in manufacturing.

Formal socialization assures the organization that all newcomers have a reasonably comparable set of experiences. In professions such as law, medicine, and dentistry, the commonality in educational programs ensures that those entering these professions have a common base of knowledge. A potential drawback of formal socialization is that it is associated with a custodial approach to one's role. In many cases, some innovation is desirable even if the role occupant has to acquire a fairly standard set of facts and knowledge. Physicians may, at times, need to deviate from doing things "by the book" in order to provide high-quality care for their patients. Informal socialization, in contrast, often allows them to develop their own unique perspective on their role, and to introduce changes when they are able to perform independently. As a graduate student, the author was assigned to teach courses, but was provided with very little instruction on how to teach. Although this "sink or swim" approach was somewhat difficult at the time, it also provided the opportunity to develop a unique teaching style and a perspective on the teaching role (see Comment 3.5).

Socialization tactics can also be viewed in terms of whether they are *sequential* versus *random*. For example, to become a physician, one is required to complete a clearly defined sequence of steps: undergraduate training, medical school, internship, and residency. In contrast, for many management positions in organizations, socialization is more random because there is no clear sequence of steps that one must follow. Rather, over time, one gradually acquires the skills and experiences necessary to assume progressively higher levels of managerial responsibility.

According to Van Maanen and Schein (1979), a sequential approach to socialization is typically used when employees are being socialized to move up through a clearly defined organizational hierarchy. In the Army, for example, an officer cannot assume the rank of Colonel before passing through lower-level ranks such as Captain, Major, and Lieutenant Colonel. Because of these clearly

---

COMMENT 3.5

SOCIALIZATION INTO ACADEMIA

FOR MOST PROFESSORS, socialization begins during graduate training and continues into the first job out of graduate school. Traditionally, socialization into academia has been a rather informal process; newcomers essentially navigate their own way through. That was certainly the case for me, when I was first asked to teach an introductory course in I/O psychology as a graduate student. Aside from receiving a textbook and some sample syllabi, I was pretty much left to my own devices to run my course as I saw fit. Although I have no doubt that help would have been available had I asked for it, I don't recall ever seeking it out. This same basic approach was used when I began my first academic position out of graduate school. Other than some very general guidelines and occasional advice from a kind senior colleague, I was pretty much left alone to navigate my way through the first years of academia.

In recent years, there has been a trend in many universities to institute formal mentoring programs for new faculty and for graduate students seeking academic careers (Perlman, McCann, & McFadden, 1999). In the case of graduate students, formal instruction is provided in teaching and in working with students. New faculty mentoring programs typically involve assigning new faculty to a more senior faculty mentor. A mentor may provide advice on things such as teaching, beginning a research program, the tenure process, and even navigating university politics. Do formal mentoring programs produce better quality faculty? This is a difficult question to answer because few, if any, programs have been systematically evaluated. However, one would assume that most new faculty probably find such programs helpful. The only potential downside to formal mentoring is that if it is *too* formal, it may decrease the creativity and individuality of new faculty. Although there is a certain amount of comfort in having a senior colleague there to provide advice in difficult situations, navigating those difficult situations alone can result in a great deal of growth and development for new faculty.

Source: B. Perlman, L. I. McCann, and S. H. McFadden. (1999). How to land that first teaching job. In B. Perlman, L. I. McCann, and S. H. McFadden (Eds.), *Lessons learned: Practical advice for the teaching of psychology.* Washington, DC: The American Psychological Society.

defined steps, sequential socialization tends to produce more of a custodial than an innovative role orientation. In many organizations, for example, employees must "put in their time" at headquarters if they hope to obtain promotions in the future. When socialization is more random, however, new employees may be exposed to a greater variety of views and opinions regarding their role. As a result, such individuals may be more innovative regarding their specific role responsibilities or perhaps even the way their role fits into the organization.

Socialization efforts may also be distinguished in terms of being *fixed* versus *variable*. When socialization is fixed, a newcomer knows in advance when certain transition points will occur. In many entry-level management training programs, for example, new employees know in advance that they will be rotated through the organization for a specific period of time before being granted a permanent assignment. When socialization is variable, the organization does not tell the new employee when transitions will occur. Instead, the message often given is that a new assignment will be forthcoming "when we feel you're ready to handle it," and no specifics are given as to how and when readiness will be determined.

Fixed socialization patterns are most typically associated with changes in an employee's hierarchical status. In academic institutions, for example, faculty rank is determined in this fashion. Typically, a fixed number of years must be invested before a faculty member can move from assistant to associate, and, finally, to full professor. In contrast, it is unlikely that a fixed period of time can be specified before a newcomer in an industry is fully accepted and trusted by his or her coworkers. Another difference is that, unlike variable socialization, fixed socialization is more likely to facilitate innovative role

responses. Variable socialization tends to create anxiety among new employees, and such anxiety acts as a strong motivator toward conformity. Variable socialization also keeps new employees "off balance" and at the mercy of socializing agents within the organization. At first glance, this may appear ideal from the organization's perspective, but it can backfire. If an organization is very arbitrary or vague about the speed of a new employee's career progression, highly talented employees may simply leave for better jobs.

Socialization efforts may also be distinguished as being *serial* or *disjunctive*. When socialization occurs in a serial fashion, experienced members groom newcomers to assume similar types of positions in the organization. In most police departments, for example, recruits fresh from academy training are paired with veteran police officers who help them to "learn the ropes." In addition to fulfilling a training function, serial socialization serves to pass on the culture of the organization from one generation to the next. For example, during the socialization process, experienced employees often pass on the history and folklore of the organization to newcomers. Disjunctive socialization, in contrast, occurs when new recruits do not follow in the footsteps of their predecessors, or where no role models are available. This would occur when a new employee occupies a newly created position, or one that has been vacant for some time.

According to Van Maanen and Schein (1979), serial socialization is more likely than disjunctive socialization to facilitate social acceptance into an organization. In many organizations, it is often necessary to "come up through the ranks" in order to be truly accepted by others. Serial socialization is also useful in situations where moving up in the organizational hierarchy requires some continuity in skills, values, and attitudes. In the military, for example, a person coming from the civilian world might have the necessary managerial and technical skills to assume a high-level rank. However, such a person would likely have difficulty due to a lack of the understanding of military culture and traditions that is needed for such a position.

Serial and disjunctive socialization also differ in that serial socialization is more likely than disjunctive socialization to be associated with a custodial role orientation. Disjunctive socialization, on the other hand, is more likely to facilitate innovation. Both approaches to socialization, however, carry certain inherent risks. The custodial role orientation facilitated by serial socialization is desirable if the experienced member of the organization—the person doing the socializing—does his or her job well. If this is not the case, a serial approach to socialization may perpetuate a "culture of mediocrity" within the organization. This can be seen when professional sports teams are consistently unsuccessful and veteran players who are used to losing pass this expectation to newcomers.

An advantage of disjunctive socialization is that it may allow a newcomer to define his or her role in a very innovative and original manner. This, however, requires considerable personal initiative on the part of the employee. An employee who is not highly motivated, or who perhaps lacks confidence, may flounder if socialized in this manner. Newcomers socialized in this manner may also become influenced by persons in the organization who do not have particularly desirable work habits. If disjunctive socialization is used, organizations may have to do considerable screening during the hiring process, and carefully monitor those who participate in the socialization process.

The final dimension of organizational socialization tactics depicted in Figure 3.3 is the distinction between an *investiture* approach versus a *divestiture* approach. When investi-

ture socialization is used, the organization capitalizes on the unique skills, values, and attitudes the newcomer brings to the organization. The organization is telling the newcomer: "Be yourself" because becoming a member of the organization does not require one to change substantially. Many organizations attempt to communicate this message during orientation programs and in a variety of other ways (e.g., giving employees discretion over how they do their jobs). Perhaps the most powerful way to communicate this message is simply via the way the newcomer is treated in day-to-day interactions. If a newcomer is punished for any display of individuality, this suggests that the organization does not want to capitalize on that employee's unique characteristics.

When divestiture socialization is used, an organization seeks to fundamentally change the new employee. An organization may wish to make the new employee forget old ways of doing things, and perhaps even old attitudes or values. Put differently, the organization is not building on what the new employee brings to the job; instead, it seeks a more global transformation. The first year of many forms of professional training involves a good deal of divestiture socialization. During the first year of doctoral training in many fields (including psychology), for example, students are taught to view problems from a scientific perspective and to base their judgments on empirical data. For many students, this is a form of divestiture socialization because they typically have not thought this way prior to entering graduate training. More dramatic examples of divestiture socialization are used in organizations such as religious cults, radical political groups, and organized crime families. In these cases, new members may be required to abandon *all* forms of personal identity and give their complete loyalty to the organization (see Comment 3.6).

COMMENT 3.6

THE ULTIMATE IN DIVESTITURE SOCIALIZATION

SAMMY ("THE BULL") Gravano became famous (or infamous) when his testimony eventually led to a long prison term for well-known New York Mafia boss John Gotti. In Peter Maas's 1997 book *Underboss: Sammy the Bull Gravano's Story of Life in the Mafia,* Gravano describes how he rose through the ranks of the Mafia and eventually became a "made guy," or official member of the criminal organization. Perhaps the most interesting part of his story, at least with regard to organizational socialization, was the ceremony that marked Gravano's official involvement. According to Gravano, during this ceremony, he pledged his unquestioning loyalty to the Mafia, and was made to understand that he was always to be ready to respond to the needs of the organization.

For those who, like Gravano, take this oath, the criminal organization essentially becomes their whole life—even more important than their family. Obviously, most legitimate organizations do not require this level of commitment and loyalty from their members. Nevertheless, organizations do vary quite widely in the degree to which new members must conform to new attitudes or ways of thinking.

Source: P. Maas. (1997). *Underboss: Sammy the Bull Gravano's story of life in the Mafia.* New York: HarperCollins.

According to Van Maanen and Schein (1979), divestiture socialization is most prevalent when recruits first enter an organization, or when they are striving to gain social acceptance. For example, a new law-school graduate may dramatically change many of his or her attitudes and assumptions during the first transition to practicing law. Changes in lifestyle and spending habits may also be necessary in order to gain social acceptance among other attorneys in a law firm. Failure to make such changes may lead to social isolation and perhaps to disillusionment with one's chosen profession.

Van Maanen and Schein's (1979) model has proven to be quite useful in facilitating an understanding of the organizational socialization process. Furthermore, Van Maanen and Schein cite considerable empirical support for many of the propositions in the model. However, a number of things about this model must be kept in mind. First, although the

tactics represented by each of the models are described as though they are discreet forms of socialization, in reality they represent opposite ends of a continuum. As an example, most socialization efforts are neither completely formal nor informal; they fall somewhere in between. A related point is that the socialization tactics described in this section occur in combination. An organization may socialize new recruits individually, using an informal, serial approach. This highlights the complexity of the organizational socialization process and suggests a possible reason why it is difficult to predict the outcomes of socialization.

Finally, despite the complexity of organizational socialization tactics, making them explicit is quite useful for organizations. If managers are aware of the tactics that are available for socializing new recruits, the socialization process can be managed more effectively. Organizations can choose those methods of socialization that are likely to provide the most desirable outcomes to both the organization and the new recruit.

The Socialization Process: A Newcomer Perspective

Despite the value of early work on organizational socialization (Feldman, 1976, 1981; Van Maanen, 1975; Van Maanen & Schein, 1979), this literature had a major gap. Socialization was viewed almost exclusively from an organizational point of view, or as something the organization "does to" the newcomer. Thus, very little work focused on how newcomers make sense of the complex maze of technical and interpersonal information they confront during the socialization process. There was also very little work suggesting that newcomers *proactively* seek information during this process.

In more recent work on organizational socialization, the focus has shifted quite dramatically to the organizational newcomer. More specifically, organizational psychologists have become quite interested in how newcomers gather information about their new organizations. According to Miller and Jablin (1991), newcomers actively seek information during organizational socialization, and they do so in a number of ways. Figure 3.2 presents a model developed by Miller and Jablin to describe the complex process of newcomers' information-seeking process. As can be seen in the first step in this model, one factor that initially determines information seeking is the newcomer's perceptions of uncertainty. Generally speaking, newcomers put more effort into information seeking when they perceive a great deal of uncertainty in the environment. Newcomers' perceptions of uncertainty depend on a multitude of factors such as the nature of the information one is seeking, individual differences and contextual factors, availability of information sources, and, ultimately, the level of role conflict and ambiguity one experiences. In actual organizations, the degree of uncertainty varies considerably.

A second factor that may influence the choice of newcomers' information-seeking tactics is the *social costs* associated with these tactics. Social costs really center on the image newcomers want to project to others in the organization, such as supervisors and coworkers. Most readers have probably had the experience of beginning a new job and having coworkers say, "If you have any questions, just ask," or "There's no such thing as a stupid question." Although experienced employees may be completely sincere in making these statements, newcomers may still feel uncomfortable when they must repeatedly ask questions of supervisors or coworkers. In doing so, one incurs an obvious social cost: appearing incompetent in the eyes of one's supervisor and/or coworkers. When the social costs of information seeking are high, newcomers tend to use less overt information-seeking tactics and are more likely to seek out nonthreatening information sources.

Based on perceptions of uncertainty and of the social costs of information seeking, newcomers choose from a variety of information-seeking tactics. The most straightforward tactic newcomers use to obtain information is **overt questioning.** If a new employee does not know how to use a copy machine, he or she can simply ask someone how to use it. Of all the possible information-seeking tactics, overt questioning is clearly the most efficient. It is also the most likely to yield useful information, and may even help the newcomer to develop rapport with others. Despite these advantages, newcomers may incur considerable social costs by using overt questioning because they run the risk of appearing incompetent

FIGURE 3.2
Miller and Jablin's (1991) Model of Newcomer Information Seeking Behavior

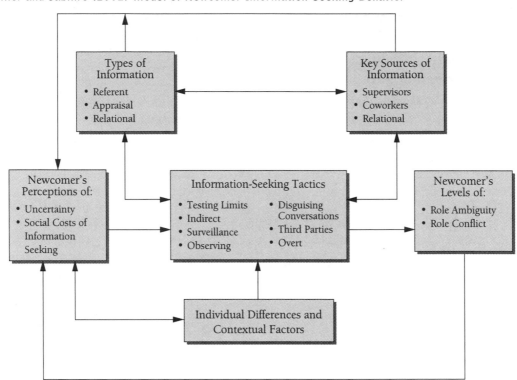

Source: V. D. Miller and F. M. Jablin. (1991). Information seeking during organizational entry: Influences, tactics, and a model of the process. *Academy of Management Review, 16,* 92–120. Reprinted by permission of the Copyright Clearance Center.

and may be viewed as an annoyance by some coworkers. Such costs obviously depend on the number of times the same question is repeated and, to some extent, the manner in which the questions are asked. If an employee continues to ask coworkers how to use a copy machine after six months on the job, or rudely demands such assistance, this would likely be seen as an annoyance.

Another information-seeking tactic newcomers may use is **indirect questioning:** not asking someone to provide the *exact* information that is needed, but asking a question that gets at it indirectly instead. For example, a new employee hired for a sales position may eventually want to move into a position in the

organization's human resources department. As a new employee, this person may feel uncomfortable directly asking his or her supervisor about the possibility of obtaining a transfer. As an alternative, the new employee may casually ask a question this way: "I have a friend who works for XYZ Corporation and he was initially hired as a purchasing agent but eventually transferred into market research. Does that type of thing happen much here?" By using this approach, the employee reduces the risk of offending his or her supervisor by asking what could be perceived as an inappropriate question. Unfortunately, this type of question may not generate the most accurate information. In the newcomer's organization, transfers from purchasing to market research may be common, but going from sales to human resources is very rare.

A somewhat riskier information-seeking tactic, **testing limits,** is used by newcomers. This involves creating situations in which information targets must respond. For example, if a new employee is uncertain about whether attendance at staff meetings is mandatory, he or she may deliberately not attend one week and await the supervisor's reaction. If there is no negative reaction, the employee may presume that attendance is not mandatory. On the other hand, if his or her supervisor reprimands the employee, this signals that attendance is important and should be viewed as mandatory. Assuming that the employee attends subsequent meetings, this one infraction is unlikely to have a negative impact.

Newcomers may also seek information through **disguised conversations.** This involves initiating a conversation with someone for a hidden purpose. A new employee may be uncertain about whether employees in the organization are expected to bring work home on the weekends, but is uncomfortable asking about this directly. To obtain the information, the newcomer may strike up a conversation with a fellow employee about what he or she did during the weekend. If the fellow employee states that he or she spent time on a work-related project, this suggests to the newcomer that the organization expects employees to bring work home.

Disguised conversations can be useful because they save the newcomer from having to ask potentially embarrassing questions of others. In the previous example, the newcomer may worry that he or she will be seen as a "slacker" by fellow employees if bringing work home on the weekend is the norm. On the other hand, if this is *not* the norm, the newcomer may worry that he or she will be perceived as trying to make others look bad

(i.e., a "rate buster") if this question is asked directly. The major disadvantage of disguised conversations is that the newcomer has little control over the response of the information source. That is, the fellow employee in the previous example may be very vague and not divulge whether he or she spent any time working.

One of the major nonverbal information-seeking tactics used by newcomers is **observation.** For example, organizational newcomers typically become keenly aware of the behaviors that are rewarded and punished in the organization. Although newcomers will typically utilize observation to obtain many types of information, they will rely most heavily on this tactic when the social costs of asking the information source directly are high. A new employee may be uncomfortable directly asking his or her supervisor what is considered to be outstanding performance. Observing others may be the safest route to acquiring this information.

Closely related to observation is the use of **surveillance** to gather information. The primary distinction between surveillance and observation is that surveillance is more dependent on retrospective sense making, and is more unobtrusive than observation. A newcomer may use surveillance to try to understand organizational norms with regard to the length of the workday. To do this, he or she may pay close attention to the behavior of fellow employees near the end of the day. The use of surveillance allows the newcomer to obtain important information while avoiding the social costs of asking potentially embarrassing questions (e.g., "What hours do we work?"). Unfortunately, this is somewhat risky because the newcomer has no control over the target under surveillance. Thus, newcomers tend to use surveillance in situations of extremely high uncertainty. Newcomers will also tend to use surveillance to a greater degree to obtain information from coworkers rather than supervisors. Newcomers typically have less opportunity to obtain information from supervisors in this manner, and the behavior of coworkers has more information value than supervisory behavior.

A final information-seeking tactic contained in Miller and Jablin's (1991) model is the use of **third parties,** or seeking information from those other than the primary source of information. The use of third parties actually encompasses several of the information-seeking tactics described above. For example, an employee who is unsure whether a supervisor is pleased with his or her performance may directly or indirectly ask coworkers for their opinions. Like other indirect tactics, acquiring information in this way spares an employee potential embarrassment. In the previous example, if the employee's supervisor has *not* been pleased with his or her performance, asking the supervisor about this directly would obviously be uncomfortable. As with all indirect information-seeking tactics, however, new employees run the risk of receiving inaccurate information by not going directly to the most relevant information source. In the author's experience, bitter conflicts in organizations are often started because people do not go to each other directly to obtain information. As anyone who has played the game "Telephone" knows, second-hand information may be highly distorted.

Having described the major information-seeking tactics used by newcomers, the next issue addressed in Miller and Jablin's (1991) model is the various outcomes associated with information-seeking tactics. At a general level, different information-seeking tactics provide newcomers with information that varies in both quantity and quality. According to Miller and Jablin, this is manifested primarily in newcomers' levels of *role ambiguity* and *role conflict*. Role ambiguity simply means that an employee is uncertain about his or her role responsibilities. For example, role ambiguity may result if a supervisor is very unclear about performance standards.

Role conflict, on the other hand, occurs when information obtained from different sources is inconsistent. This might occur, for example, if a newcomer receives mixed messages from a supervisor and coworkers, regarding performance standards. Levels of role ambiguity and conflict are typically highest when newcomers rely on indirect or covert tactics to acquire information. Because these tactics are far removed from the most relevant information source, they provide newcomers with the least opportunity to verify the accuracy of the information they obtain. Given that both role ambiguity and role conflict are associated with negative outcomes (e.g., Jackson & Schuler, 1985), organizations need to create an environment in which newcomers feel comfortable using direct information-seeking tactics, such as overt questioning.

Since Miller and Jablin's (1991) review, there has been considerable research on the many aspects of newcomers' information seeking. Ostroff and Kozlowski (1992), for example, examined the relationship between the types of information acquired during socialization, and the use of different information sources. These authors proposed that newcomers use different information sources to acquire different types of information. To acquire task-related information, it was expected that testing (e.g., proposing different approaches to one's supervisor) or experimentation (e.g., performing one's job tasks in different ways and evaluating the effects) would be relied on most heavily. To obtain information about group processes, however, it was expected that coworkers would be the most useful information source. The most important source of information about roles was expected to be observation of the behavior of others.

This study also examined a number of outcomes of the socialization process, as well as changes in the socialization process over time. New employees who considered themselves more knowledgeable about their job-related tasks, role demands, group-level dynamics, and the organization as a whole were expected to: be more satisfied with their jobs; be committed to and feel more adjusted to their organization; experience fewer stress-related symptoms; and report lower levels of turnover intent. Over time, knowledge in all areas was expected to increase. The authors proposed that knowledge of the group would initially be greatest but knowledge of the task would equal it over time. Knowledge of the organization as a whole was expected to be the slowest to develop.

Based on data collected at two points in time from 219 individuals who had been business and engineering majors in college, most predictions in this study were supported. For example, observing the behavior of others, which was used most for acquiring knowledge, was followed by interpersonal sources (coworkers and supervisors), experimentation, and objective referents (e.g., consulting written manuals). Also, as predicted, different information sources were used, depending on the type of information respondents were trying to acquire. For information about the role being performed, respondents relied more heavily on supervisors than on coworkers, but tended to rely more on coworkers for information about the internal dynamics of their work group. To obtain information about the task, experimentation was used to a greater extent than interpersonal sources such as supervisors or coworkers.

In terms of knowledge of different domains, at Time 1 respondents reported that knowledge about the group was greater than knowledge of the task, role, and organization. This pattern had changed somewhat at Time 2. At this point, knowledge of the task had surpassed knowledge of the role and group, and knowledge of the organization remained the lowest. There was only one area in which knowledge changed from Time 1 to Time 2; respondents reported becoming more knowledgeable about the task.

When relationships among information acquisition, knowledge, and outcomes were examined, a number of trends emerged. At both points in time, acquiring knowledge from one's supervisor was associated with higher levels of job satisfaction and commitment, and lower levels of turnover intent. Interestingly, acquiring knowledge from coworkers was associated with high levels of satisfaction and commitment, and low levels of stress and turnover at Time 1, but these relations are not supported at Time 2. This finding suggests that supervisors are a constant source of information, whereas coworkers may initially be very influential but their influence wanes over time. Acquiring information from observing others and through experimentation was positively related to stress-related symptoms. This may be due to the fact that observing others may provide unclear information and thus may result in role ambiguity. Acquiring information through experimentation may be stressful because it may often result in failure, at least when job tasks are first being learned.

Respondents who believed they possessed more knowledge about all of the domains reported higher levels of satisfaction, commitment, and adjustment. However, the two that stood out as most strongly related to these outcomes were *knowledge of task* and *role domains*. It was also found that correlations were stronger between level of knowledge and outcomes than they were between sources of information and outcomes. The implication is that, for newcomers to feel adjusted, it is important that they feel knowledgeable about both their job-related tasks and their work group role. *Where* this information is acquired is less important than the fact that it *is* acquired.

When changes in the relationship among information sources, knowledge, and outcomes were examined, it was found that newcomers who increased the information obtained from supervisors over time also experienced positive changes in satisfaction, commitment, and adjustment. This further reinforces the importance of the supervisor as an information source during the socialization process. It was also found that positive changes in task knowledge were associated with positive changes in both commitment and adjustment and effected a reduction in stress. This finding reinforces the importance of task proficiency to the adjustment of the newcomer.

Ostroff and Kozlowski's (1992) study has a number of important implications. Consistent with Miller and Jablin's (1991) model, the results suggest that newcomers use different methods to acquire different types of information. The results also clearly show that supervisors are important information sources for employees, although newcomers may initially rely just as much on coworkers. Perhaps the most important lesson from this study is: Acquiring task knowledge is of paramount importance to the adjustment of new employees. Thus, organizations need to make sure that new employees receive proper training and, in some cases, on-the-job coaching in order to increase their task knowledge over time. A related implication is that organizations should not overload new employees with ancillary duties.

In another longitudinal study of the socialization process, Morrison (1993) collected data, at three points in time, from 135 new staff accountants. In this study, it was proposed that newcomers acquire a number of types of information, most of which were comparable to those in Ostroff and Kozlowski's (1992) study. For example, Morrison (1993) proposed that newcomers acquire information on how to perform their job-related tasks. Newcomers also acquire what Morrison described as referent information, or information about one's role. Newcomers also must acquire information about how they are performing their jobs (labeled Performance Feedback). In many cases, newcomers need to acquire what may be described as normative information, or information about the norms within the organization. Finally, newcomers need to acquire social information, or information about their level of social integration into their primary work group.

In addition to describing the types of information acquired, this study proposed that there are multiple ways of acquiring each type of information. Consistent with past socialization research, it was proposed that information could be acquired from one's supervisor or from an experienced peer; through monitoring others' behavior; by responses to direct inquiries; or from available written sources. Consistent with Ostroff and Kozlowski (1992), the dimensions of socialization examined were task mastery, role clarification, acculturation, and social integration.

Newcomers seeking greater amounts of technical information and performance feedback were expected to exhibit higher levels of task mastery than newcomers seeking lesser amounts of this information. It was also expected that newcomers seeking greater referent information and performance feedback would report experiencing higher levels of role clarity. With respect to acculturation, it was expected that this would be associated with seeking greater amounts of normative information, and social feedback from others. Finally, social integration was also expected to be highest among those seeking greater amounts of normative information and social feedback.

The results of this study partially supported the hypotheses. For example, it was found that technical information (from both supervisors and peers) and written feedback were statistically significant predictors of task mastery. Interestingly, though, the direction of the relation between technical information from peers and task mastery was *negative*. This may be due to the fact that peers may not always have an adequate mastery of the technical information that is sought by newcomers.

It was also found that to facilitate role clarification, newcomers tended to make use of referent information, performance feedback (through inquiries), and consultants' written feedback. For example, a person new to a work group may pay attention to cues from group members as to whether his or her role performance is satisfactory; informally solicit feedback from the supervisor; and take advantage of written feedback from the initial performance review. Using these information sources makes sense because they are most likely to be relevant to employees' role-related activities.

Social integration was related primarily to the use of normative inquiries and monitoring activities. This finding suggests that new employees may feel uncomfortable when they must ask for direct feedback from either peers or supervisors, in their efforts to determine their level of social integration. Indeed, it is unlikely that most people would feel comfortable asking fellow employees directly about the degree to which they are liked and whether they "fit in" with the work groups. Written sources of feedback would not provide this type of information either.

Finally, for the acculturation dimension, the only significant predictor was monitoring. To some extent, this finding mirrors the findings with regard to social integration. To learn about the culture of the organization, a new employee must primarily observe others in the organization and how things are done. This is likely due to the complexity of culture, but may also be due to the potential social costs associated with more direct forms of information seeking. Because culture is generally taken for granted or internalized (e.g., Schein, 1990), newcomers may run the risk of embarrassment by asking directly about things many experienced organizational members consider to be obvious or mundane. Overall, Morrison's (1993) study, like that of Ostroff and Kozlowski (1992), suggests that newcomers use a variety of information-seeking tactics, and they use different tactics for acquiring different types of information.

Unfortunately, neither of the studies just described examined whether information seeking during the socialization process has an impact on the *success* of newcomers. It is clear, for example, that newcomers seek and acquire information, and that they use different information sources to acquire different types of information. What is less clear, however, is whether employees who increase their knowledge over time are ultimately more successful than employees who acquire less information.

Chao et al. (1994) addressed these issues in a longitudinal study of 182 engineers, managers, and professionals, conducted over a three-year period. Career success in this study was measured by respondents' levels of personal income and career involvement. With respect to personal income, the only socialization dimension that was predictive was knowledge about the politics of the organization. Employees who developed the greatest knowledge of organizational politics tended to have the highest incomes. This may be due to the fact that those who become very knowledgeable about the politics of the organization may be most likely to make the contacts and form the alliances needed to reach levels in the organizational hierarchy that are associated with high levels of income.

In terms of career involvement, the only socialization dimension that was predictive was knowledge of the goals and values of the organization. Specifically, those who indicated having a great deal of knowledge of the goals and values of the organization reported higher levels of career involvement than those with less knowledge. Looking at this another way, it is difficult for new employees to become highly involved in their careers if they are unsure of what their employers are trying to accomplish. Taken together, these findings suggest that certain aspects of socialization may contribute to affective outcomes (Ostroff & Kozlowski, 1992), and other aspects may be more important in determining success.

Another interesting finding from this study was that *changes* in the socialization dimensions were related to *changes* in both measures of career success. Thus, for employees to sustain a high level of success over time, they must continually increase their knowledge in crucial areas of socialization. This finding suggests that, to sustain a high level of success over time, one must never stop learning. Thus, organizations should provide learning opportunities for employees and, when possible, design work in a way that allows employees to learn (Parker & Wall, 1998).

Given the shift in focus of recent socialization research to newcomer information-seeking strategies (e.g., Miller & Jablin, 1991), the influence of other socializing agents and methods has been de-emphasized (e.g., Van Maanen & Schein, 1979). As a result, much less is known about the *combined* effect of newcomers' information-seeking strategies and the behavior of others (e.g., peers and supervisors), in explaining the socialization of organizational newcomers. Bauer and Green (1998) examined this

issue in a very ambitious longitudinal study of 205 newcomers, 364 of their coworkers, and 112 of their managers. Like past socialization research, this study examined newcomer information seeking, several dimensions of socialization (feelings of task proficiency, role clarity, and feelings of being accepted by one's manager), and socialization outcomes such as performance, job satisfaction, and organizational commitment. What makes the study unique, however, is that the behaviors of managers which are designed to facilitate socialization were also examined. Thus, this study addresses the need for a dual perspective.

As with the research previously discussed, it was expected that the type of information sought by newcomers and provided by managers would match socialization outcomes. For example, it was predicted that task-oriented information seeking and managers' clarifying behavior would be related to feelings of task proficiency and role clarity. For feelings of acceptance by one's manager, it was expected that the best predicators would be social information sought by the newcomer, as well as managers' supporting behaviors. For outcomes, it was expected that feelings of task proficiency would predict performance, and feelings of acceptance by one's manager would be predictive of both job satisfaction and organizational commitment. A final prediction examined in this study was that the effects of both information-seeking tactics and managerial behavior on socialization outcomes would be mediated by newcomers' perceived level of socialization.

The results of this study showed that only managerial clarifying behavior at Time 2 predicted role clarity at Time 3. This same result occurred for predicting performance efficacy at Time 3. These findings are interesting because they seem to contradict recent socialization research that has placed such a strong emphasis on the information-seeking tactics of newcomers. Rather, these findings suggest that the behavior of managers is the most important factor, at least for these outcomes. With respect to feelings of acceptance by one's manager at Time 3, the only variable that was predictive was managers' supportive behavior at Time 2. Again, employees' information seeking had no impact on this measure. With respect to the mediational hypotheses, no support was found for the mediating role of socialization on the relation between newcomers' information seeking and outcomes. There was, however, evidence that feelings of task proficiency and role clarity fully mediated the relationship between managerial behavior and performance. Role clarity and feelings of acceptance partially mediated the relation between managerial behaviors and organizational commitment. These findings suggest that behaviors of managers, such as providing clarification and support, have a positive impact on things such as newcomers' performance and affective outcomes, but only to the extent that they facilitate the socialization process.

The broader implication of Bauer and Green's (1998) study is that the behavior of individual managers toward new employees is a critical factor in employee socialization. As stated earlier, this study is also noteworthy because the recent organizational socialization literature has focused so heavily on information-seeking tactics and knowledge acquisition of newcomers. Earlier work on organizational socialization focused heavily on the *organizational* attempts to socialize newcomers. This suggests that a more balanced view of organizational socialization is needed—that is, socialization is the result of a complex *interaction* between socializati-on tactics used by organizations, and the information-seeking and sense-making processes of newcomers. Ignoring either the organizational or the newcomer perspective provides a limited picture of the organizational socialization process.

A final issue regarding the newcomer perspective is the expectations that newcomers bring to the socialization process. As Feldman's (1981) model showed, there is a period of *anticipatory socialization* prior to newcomers' formal entry into the organization. One way that prior expectations have been examined is through the study of **realistic job previews (RJPs)** (Wanous, 1989; Wanous, Poland, Premack, & Davis, 1992). As was stated in the earlier section on recruiting, the basic idea behind realistic job previews is that, prior to organizational entry, the newcomer is given a realistic preview of what the job will entail, even if some of this information is negative. Despite the intuitive appeal of RJPs, meta-analyses have shown that they have a very small impact on turnover (McEvoy & Cascio, 1985; Reilly, Brown, Blood, & Malatesta, 1981).

Another approach to dealing with newcomers' expectations is to focus information at a more general level. For example, Buckley, Fedor, Veres, Weise, and Carraher (1998) conducted a field experiment that evaluated the effect of what they described as an **expectation lowering procedure (ELP)** among a sample of 140 employees recently hired by a manufacturing plant. The ELP consisted of lecturing the new employees on the importance of realistic expectations, and how inflated expectations can lead to a number of negative outcomes. This study also included one condition in which employees were provided with an RJP. This allowed the researchers to test the impact of an RJP against the more general ELP.

The results of this study indicated that both the RJP and ELP had positive effects. For

COMMENT 3.7

HOW TO DEVELOP REALISTIC EXPECTATIONS

THERE IS CONSIDERABLE research evidence to support the value of having a realistic picture of the job one will be performing, as well as life in the organization in which one will be working. Despite the value of realistic expectations, many readers might be wondering how to gain this type of information while still in college. Many students do so through internships, participation in cooperative education programs, and summer employment. Many university placement offices post (and keep records of) these types of jobs at local, national, and international levels.

A somewhat less conventional way to obtain information is to set up an *informational interview* with a member of the profession you wish to pursue, or an employee of the organization you would like to work for. This involves simply contacting such an individual and asking for about 30 minutes of his or her time. Before the meeting, it's a good idea to prepare a list of questions about the profession or the organization. Although time may not always permit an informational interview, professional people are often very willing to talk about their profession to an eager college student.

example, employees in those two conditions initially had lower expectations than those who received neither intervention, although there was no difference after six months. Most importantly, lower levels of turnover and higher levels of job satisfaction were found in the RJP and ELP conditions, compared to those receiving neither intervention. It was also found that expectations mediated this effect; that is, both RJP and ELP interventions lowered turnover because they first lowered employees' expectations.

An important implication of this study is that organizations may not have to develop job-specific realistic previews for newcomers in order to facilitate realistic expectations. Rather, the expectations of newcomers can be changed to be more realistic by more general interventions of the type conducted by Buckley et al. (1998). From a practical point of view, this is encouraging because developing RJPs is more time-consuming than more general interventions such as ELP. RJPs must be job-specific; thus, many RJPs must be

developed, depending on the number of jobs in an organization. The more general point to be gleaned from this study is that newcomers do much better when they come into a new organization with realistic expectations of both their jobs and their future life within the organization. Thus, it's always a good idea to have as much information as possible before choosing a job or career (see Comment 3.7).

THE IMPACT OF DIVERSITY ON ORGANIZATIONAL SOCIALIZATION

Jackson, Stone, and Alvarez (1992) reviewed the literature on the impact of diversity on socialization into groups and came up with a number of propositions, many of which are relevant to the broader issue of organizational socialization. According to these authors, the primary dilemma posed by diversity is that many individuals who are perceived as "different" must still be socialized and assimilated into organizations. This would be the case, for example, if a female executive were to be promoted to an all-male top management group. Not only does such an individual tend to stand out, but it may also be difficult for such individuals to become accepted and seen as "part of the team." According to Jackson et al., this occurs simply because people tend to like, and feel more comfortable around, persons perceived to be similar to themselves (e.g., Byrne, 1971).

Because people are attracted to, and feel more comfortable with, those who are similar to themselves, those perceived as different are often put at a disadvantage during the socialization process. According to Jackson et al. (1992), newcomers who are dissimilar are often less likely to form the social ties and receive, from experienced organizational members, the feedback necessary to assimilate well into organizations. Experienced organizational members may not deliberately exclude those who are demographically different, but there is a subtle tendency to shy away from such individuals. This often puts women and racial minorities at a disadvantage because, in many organizations, the most influential members are white males.

How can organizations facilitate the socialization of a demographically diverse workforce? Jackson et al. (1992) suggested a number of strategies that might help to facilitate the socialization process. For example, they recommended that when several minority employees enter an organization at the same time, collective socialization processes should be used, if possible. Recall from Van Maanen and Schein's (1979) description of organizational socialization tactics, collective socialization has the benefit of generating a high level of communication and support among those socialized in the same cohort. This type of socialization may help women, racial minorities, and perhaps older employees feel less isolated,

and may facilitate the development of social support networks within the organization.

Another recommendation of Jackson et al. (1992) is for organizations to develop training programs aimed at newcomers *and* established organizational members. For newcomers, such training programs might be aimed at increasing awareness of some of the problems they may face in the socialization process, and helping them to develop coping strategies. For established organizational members, such training may help to increase awareness of some of the challenges women and racial minorities face when they are being assimilated into the organization. As Jackson et al. point out, however, such "diversity training" programs may have the unintended consequence of highlighting the *differences* rather than the *similarities* between people. It is also possible that if such programs are forced on employees, they may create *less* favorable attitudes toward diversity.

A third recommended strategy is the use of valid procedures in the selection of female and minority employees. Assimilating any newcomer into an organization will be much easier if the individual has the skills and abilities needed to do the job (Ostroff & Kozlowski, 1992). Although socialization of female and minority employees may initially be difficult, organizations are usually pragmatic enough to eventually accept those who are capable of performing their jobs well and making a positive contribution. This also suggests that no one benefits when organizations hire and promote unqualified individuals on the basis of gender or racial preferences. This became very obvious to the author several years ago when teaching a course composed primarily of African Americans, many of whom worked in professional positions in the auto industry. When the issue of racial quotas was discussed during class, the vast majority of these African American students were strongly opposed to this method of addressing past racial discrimination. Most expressed a strong desire to be seen as having "made it" on the basis of their own talents, and not because of a government-mandated program.

Finally, performance appraisal and reward systems can go a long way toward assimilating female and racial minority employees into organizations. For example, managers in organizations should be evaluated, at least to some degree, on the extent to which they develop *all* of their subordinates. If female and minority employee subordinates continually have a difficult time adjusting, this should reflect poorly on the evaluation of a manager. If an organization rewards on the basis of the performance of work groups, it is in a group's best interest to maximize the talents of *all* group members, regardless of gender, race, or age. This may explain the relative success of the military, at least in comparison to civilian organizations, in providing opportunities for racial minorities (Powell, 1995). "Mission accomplishment" is the highest priority in military organizations, and those who contribute positively to the mission are likely to be rewarded and accepted, regardless of race.

CHAPTER SUMMARY

In this chapter, we examined the ways that organizations attract new organizational members, and the process by which they are socialized. Organizations utilize a variety of methods to recruit potential newcomers; the choice of method is dependent on a number of factors such as the nature of the job, cost, relative quality of candidates generated, and time considerations. Regardless of the method chosen, recruiting research suggests that organizations are best served by providing recruits with accurate information and treating them with respect and courtesy.

Recruiting obviously is not a one-sided process. Job seekers, who are the targets of organizational recruiting efforts, evaluate the messages put out by organizations and make some judgment as to the attractiveness of the organization. Research suggests that judgments of organizational attractiveness are made primarily on the basis of job seekers' judgments of "fit" with the organization. That is, job seekers make some judgment as to whether several aspects of the organization fit with their abilities, values, and personality. The major implication for organizations is that it is in their best interest to provide an accurate portrayal of their culture to potential employees.

Once an individual is hired, the process of organizational socialization begins. Although many definitions of socialization have been provided, most see it as the extent to which a new employee is able to do his or her job, get along with members of the work group, and develop some understanding of the culture of the organization. Organizations may use a variety of tactics to socialize organizational newcomers. The choice of tactics depends, to a large extent, on the nature of the job a newcomer will assume in the organization and the ultimate goals of the socialization process.

Like recruiting, socialization is a two-way process. Organizational newcomers actively seek information about the organization and may use a variety of tactics in order to obtain information. The choice of tactics depends largely on the level of uncertainty, the nature of the information being sought, and the perceived social costs of obtaining it. A consistent finding in recent socialization research is that newcomers initially put their efforts into obtaining information that will help them to perform their job tasks competently, and will enable them to get along with members of their immediate work group. Once they are able to perform their job tasks competently, the focus of information seeking shifts to broader issues such as the culture of the organization.

A final issue examined was the impact of diversity on the socialization of organizational newcomers. Those perceived as "different" by established organizational members may face a number of unique challenges in the socialization process. In the extreme, such individuals run the risk of being marginalized and never really fitting in. Organizations can, however, take steps to facilitate the socialization of older employees, females, and racial minorities. Through facilitating the development of support networks, providing training programs, using valid selection procedures, and placing an emphasis on performance and employee development, organizations can make sure that these individuals are accepted and their talents are fully utilized.

SUGGESTED ADDITIONAL READINGS

Barber, A. E. (1998). *Recruiting employees: Individual and organizational perspectives.* Thousand Oaks, CA: Sage.

Major, D. A., Kozlowski, S. W. J., Chao, G. T., & Gardner, P. D. (1995). A longitudinal investigation of newcomer expectations, early socialization outcomes, and the moderating effects of role development factors. *Journal of Applied Psychology, 80,* 418–431.

Schein, E. H. (1964). How to break in the college graduate. *Harvard Business Review, 42,* 68–76.

Schneider, B., Kristof, A. L., Goldstein, H. W., & Smith, D. B. (1997). What is this thing called fit? In N. Anderson & P. Herriot (Eds.), *Handbook of selection and appraisal* (2nd ed., pp. 393–412). London: Wiley.

Chapter Four

Productive Behavior in Organizations

As new employees gradually become acclimated, they eventually reach a point where they are capable of engaging in behavior that contributes positively to organizational goals and objectives. As examples, an accountant becomes capable of handling the tax returns of several clients of an accounting firm, a retail store employee becomes capable of operating a cash register with minimal supervision, and a scientist becomes capable of independently carrying out his or her own original research investigations. The behaviors described in the examples may be thought of collectively as *productive behavior,* which is the focus of this chapter.

After thoroughly defining productive behavior, the chapter shifts to a discussion of job performance. This is, by far, the most common form of productive behavior in organizations, and organizational psychologists have devoted considerable attention to its study. Much work, for example, has been enlisted in simply understanding what is meant by job performance,

and in determining performance dimensions that are common across jobs.

We then discuss the causes of job performance. For example, considerable work has been devoted to determining the relative contribution of abilities, skills, motivation, and situational factors in explaining performance differences. As researchers have found, the interaction among all of these predictors is complex. Fortunately, the amount of research done allows us to draw some fairly definitive conclusions—at least about individual differences that determine performance.

We will focus on a number of issues that organizational psychologists have grappled with as they studied job performance in organizations. These will include measuring job performance, understanding organizational factors that restrict performance variability, and understanding variability in performance over time. These issues are vital because they impact our ability to predict and influence employee job performance in organizations.

A second form of productive behavior occurs when employees do things that are not required in their formal job descriptions. For example, organizations may at times need employees to provide assistance to each other, even though this activity is not part of their formal job descriptions. These types of behaviors have been defined as organizational citizenship behaviors (OCBs). Research into OCB has focused primarily on understanding the factors that lead employees to perform OCBs.

The third form of productive behavior is innovative. For example, to remain competitive, a computer manufacturer may need employees to consistently design new computer models that have innovative designs and features. There is considerable research on creativity in the general psychological literature, but organizational psychologists have also examined organization-specific innovation and creativity. Like other forms of productive behavior, innovation and creativity result from a complex interaction between characteristics of individual employees and the organizational environments in which they work.

DEFINING PRODUCTIVE BEHAVIOR

For the purposes of this chapter, productive behavior is defined as *employee behavior that contributes positively to the goals and objectives of the organization.* When an employee first enters an organization, there is a transition period in which he or she is not contributing positively to the organization. For example, a newly hired management consultant may not be generating any billable hours for his or her consulting firm. From an organizational perspective, a new employee is actually a liability because he or she is typically being compensated during this unproductive period. The organization is betting, however, that, over time, the new employee will reach a point where his or her behavior contributes positively to the organization. When productive behavior is viewed in financial terms, it represents the point at which the organization begins to achieve some return on the investment it has made in the new employee. In the sections that follow, we take an in-depth look at three of the most common forms of productive behavior in organizations: job performance, organizational citizenship behavior (OCB), and innovation.

Job Performance

Job performance is a deceptively simple term. At the most general level, it can be defined simply as "all of the behaviors employees engage in while at work." Unfortunately, this is a rather imprecise definition because employees often engage in behaviors at work that have little or nothing to do with job-specific tasks. For example, in a study of enlisted military personnel, Bialek, Zapf, and McGuire (1977) found that less than half of the work time of these individuals was spent performing tasks that were part of their job descriptions. Thus, if performance were defined simply in terms of employee behaviors performed while at work, many behaviors that have no relation to organizational goals would be included (see Comment 4.1). On the other hand, if job performance were confined *only* to behaviors associated with task performance, much

COMMENT 4.1

WHAT DO PEOPLE ACTUALLY DO AT "WORK"?

BASED ON SOME estimates, it appears that, during a typical workday, people may spend as much as half of their time doing things that are not directly related to their actual job tasks. I find this quite intriguing. In particular, I wonder what people *do* during the other half of their day, when they're not working on job-related tasks. Being a good scientist, I wanted to collect some data to examine this question so I kept track of the things that I do, during a typical day at work, that are not directly related to my primary duties of teaching, research, and service. Although this list is not meant to be generalizable to other occupations, it might provide some insight into how academicians spend their time. Here goes:

1. Walking to the university center coffee shop to purchase a *grande cappuccino*.
2. Walking to the vending machine to purchase a can of soda.
3. Walking to the main psychology department office to check my mail.
4. Standing in the hall outside my office and discussing a recent NBA playoff game.
5. Calling a heating company to check on the status of a claim filed due to damage to (our air conditioner was damaged during a hailstorm).
6. Standing in the hall outside the psychology department office, talking with colleagues about tenure and promotion standards.

I could add to it, but this list probably provides a representative sample of the things that I do at "work" when I'm not working. Given the size of the list, did I accomplish nothing on that particular day? Not necessarily. For me, and for many other people, when the decision is made to channel effort into job-related tasks, a great deal can be accomplished in a relatively short period of time. Furthermore, if *all* we did was spend time on work-related tasks, the work environment would probably be much less enjoyable, and ultimately, people might not be as productive.

Source: H. Bialek, D. Zapf, and W. McGuire. (1977, July). *Personnel turbulence and time utilization in an infantry division* (Hum RRO FR-WD-CA 77-11). Alexandria; VA: Human Resources Research Organization.

---

productive behavior in the workplace would be excluded.

According to J. Campbell (1990), job performance represents behaviors employees engage in while at work. However, he goes a step further by stating that such behaviors *must contribute to organizational goals* in order to be considered in the domain of job performance. This definition is obviously more precise than simply defining performance as all behaviors

that employees perform at work. It is also not too restrictive; job performance is confined only to behaviors directly associated with task performance.

In defining job performance, it is important that we distinguish it from several related terms. According to J. Campbell (1990), job performance should be distinguished from *effectiveness, productivity,* and *utility.* Effectiveness is defined as the evaluation of the *results* of an employee's job performance. This is an important distinction because employee effectiveness is determined by more than just job performance. For example, an employee who is engaging in many forms of productive behavior may still receive a poor performance rating (a measure of effectiveness) because of performance rating errors, or simply because he or she is not well liked by the person assigned to do the rating.

Productivity is closely related to both performance and effectiveness, but it is different because productivity takes into account the cost of achieving a given level of performance or effectiveness. For example, two salespeople may perform equally well and ultimately generate the same level of commissions in a given year. However, if one of these individuals is able to achieve this level of sales at a lower cost than the other, he or she would be considered the more productive of the two. A term that is closely related to productivity, and is often used interchangeably, is *efficiency*. This refers to the level of performance that can be achieved in a given period of time. If a person is highly efficient, he or she is achieving a lot in a relatively short period of time. Given that "time is money," one can consider efficiency a form of productivity. Some organizations, in fact, are highly concerned with efficiency. United Parcel Service (UPS), for example, places a strong emphasis on the efficiency of the truck drivers who deliver packages to customers.

Finally, utility represents the *value* of a given level of performance, effectiveness, or productivity. This definition may seem redundant alongside the description of effectiveness. Utility is somewhat different, though; an employee may achieve a high level of effectiveness (i.e., the results of his or her performance are judged to be positive), but utility still could be low. An organization simply may not place a high value on the level of effectiveness

achieved by the employee. In large research universities, for example, faculty research productivity and grant writing are typically given higher priority than teaching performance. Consequently, it is possible to be denied tenure at such universities even though one is a superb teacher.

At first glance, distinguishing among performance, effectiveness, productivity, efficiency, and utility may appear to be a rather trivial exercise. On the contrary, these distinctions are extremely important if one is interested in understanding and ultimately predicting performance. Many studies in organizational psychology purport to predict "performance" when they are actually predicting "effectiveness" or "productivity" (Jex, 1998). Employees typically have more control over performance than they do over effectiveness or productivity, so studies often fail to adequately explain performance differences among employees. This gap may ultimately lead to erroneous conclusions about the determinants of performance differences.

Models of Job Performance

Efforts to model job performance are aimed at identifying a set of performance dimensions that are common to *all jobs*. Given the vast number of jobs that exist in the world of work, it is hard to imagine why anyone would undertake an attempt to model job performance. However, modeling job performance is vitally important because so much research and practice in organizational psychology centers around performance prediction. A major reason for studying many of the variables that we do (e.g., motivation, leadership, stress) is their potential impact on performance. Two models of job performance are described here.

J. Campbell (1990, 1994) proposed a model that allows performance on all jobs to be broken down into the eight dimensions listed in Table 4.1. The first dimension in this model, **job-specific task proficiency**, represents behaviors associated with the core tasks that are unique to a particular job. For example, behaviors such as counting money, recording deposits, and cashing checks would represent some of the job-specific tasks of a bank teller. On the other hand, examples of the core job tasks of a teacher at a day-care center may include scheduling activities, maintaining discipline, and communicating with parents.

The second dimension in this model is labeled **non-job-specific task proficiency.** This dimension is represented by behaviors that must be performed by some or all members of an organization, but are not specific to a particular job. For example, the primary job-related activities of a college professor are teaching and research in a given substantive area (e.g., physics). However, regardless of one's specialty, most professors are required to perform common tasks such as advising students, serving on university committees, writing grants, and occasionally representing the university at ceremonial events such as commencement.

The third dimension is labeled **written and oral communication task proficiency.** Inclusion of this dimension acknowledges that incumbents in most jobs must communicate either in writing or verbally. For example,

a high school teacher and an attorney obviously perform very different job-specific tasks. Both, however, must periodically communicate, both orally and in writing, in order to do their jobs effectively. A high school teacher may need to communicate with parents regarding students' progress, and an attorney may need to communicate with a client in order to verify the accuracy of information to be contained in a legal document such as a trust or divorce agreement.

The fourth and fifth dimensions are labeled **demonstrating effort** and **maintaining personal discipline,** respectively. Demonstrating effort represents an employee's level of motivation and commitment to his or her job tasks. Regardless of whether one performs the job of dentist, firefighter, or professional athlete, it is necessary to exhibit some level of commitment to one's job tasks. It may also be necessary at times to demonstrate a willingness to persist in order to accomplish difficult or unpleasant tasks. Professional athletes, at times, may have to "play through" nagging injuries in order to help their teams. Maintaining personal discipline is simply the degree to which employees refrain from negative behaviors such as chronic rule infractions, substance abuse, or other forms of unproductive behavior. Taken together, these two dimensions essentially represent the degree to which an employee is a "good citizen" in the workplace.

The sixth dimension is labeled **facilitating peer and team performance.** One aspect of this dimension is the degree to which an employee is helpful to his or her coworkers when they need assistance. This could involve assisting a coworker who is having trouble meeting an impending deadline, or perhaps just providing encouragement or boosting the spirits of others. This dimension also represents the degree to which an employee is a "team player," or is working to further the goals of his or her work group. As J. Campbell

TABLE 4.1
J. Campbell's (1990, 1994) Taxonomy of Higher-Order Performance Dimensions

1. Job-specific task proficiency
2. Non-job-specific task proficiency
3. Written and oral communication task proficiency
4. Demonstrating effort
5. Maintaining personal discipline
6. Facilitating peer and team performance
7. Supervision/Leadership
8. Management/Administration

(1990) points out, this dimension would obviously have little relevance if one worked in complete isolation. Today, when so many companies place strong emphasis on teamwork, this is more the exception than the rule (see Comment 4.2).

The seventh and eighth dimensions are labeled **supervision/leadership** and **management/administration,** respectively. Both of these dimensions represent aspects of job performance that obviously apply only to jobs that carry some supervisory responsibilities. Whether one is a supervisor in a retail outlet, a hospital, or a factory, certain common behaviors are required. For example, supervisors in most settings help employees set goals,

---

COMMENT 4.2

BEING A GOOD TEAM MEMBER

OF THE EIGHT dimensions of job performance described in Campbell's (1990) model, one of the most interesting, and potentially most important, is "Facilitating peer and team performance." One obvious reason is that more and more organizations are making use of **teams** for both projects, and even as a basis for organizational structure. Given this greater use of teams, it is not surprising that much recent organizational research has focused on team effectiveness. However, one aspect of team effectiveness that has not been given great attention is identifying the characteristics of a good team member. According to Susan Wheelan, in her book *Creating Effective Teams: A Guide for Members and Leaders,* there are a number of behavioral characteristics of effective team members. These include:

Not blaming others for group problems

Encouraging the process of goal, role, and task clarification

Encouraging the adoption of an open communication structure

Promoting an appropriate ratio of task and supportive communications

Promoting the use of effective problem-solving and decision-making procedures

Encouraging the establishment of norms that support productivity, innovation, and freedom of expression

Going along with norms that promote group effectiveness and productivity

Promoting group cohesion and cooperation

Encouraging the use of effective conflict management strategies

Interacting with others outside of the group, in ways that promote group integration and cooperation within the larger organizational context

Supporting the leader's efforts to facilitate group goal achievement

This list is obviously not meant to be exhaustive, but it provides a clue as to the specific behaviors that constitute team-related performance. As is evident from the list, most of these behaviors transcend technical specialties and even organization types. This is consistent with Campbell's notion that there is a general set of performance dimensions.

Source: J. P. Campbell. (1990). Modeling the performance prediction problem in industrial and organizational psychology. In M. D. Dunnette and L. M. Hough (Eds.), *Handbook of industrial and organizational psychology* (2nd ed., Vol. 1, pp. 687–732). Palo Alto, CA: Consulting Psychologists Press; and S. A. Wheelan. (1999). *Creating effective teams: A guide for members and leaders.* Thousand Oaks, CA: Sage.

teach employees effective work methods, and more generally attempt to model good work habits. Many supervisory positions also require a multitude of administrative tasks such as monitoring and controlling expenditures, obtaining additional resources, and representing one's unit within an organization.

When we consider each of these dimensions of job performance, it becomes clear that all eight dimensions would not be relevant for all jobs. In fact, J. Campbell (1990) argued that only three (core task proficiency, demonstrating effort, and maintenance of personal discipline) are major performance components for *all* jobs. This model is still quite useful because it provides a common metric for examining performance across jobs. For example, using this model, we could compare employees from two completely different jobs on the dimension of *demonstrating effort.* Having such a common metric is tremendously helpful in trying to understand the general determinants of job performance.

A second model of job performance was proposed by Murphy (1994). The model was specifically developed to facilitate an understanding of job performance in the U.S. Navy, but the performance dimensions are also relevant to many civilian jobs. As can be seen in Table 4.2, this model breaks performance down into four dimensions instead of eight. The first of these is labeled **task-oriented behaviors,** which closely mirrors the job-specific task proficiency dimension in

J. Campbell's (1990, 1994) model. It is also reasonable to assume that, for supervisory jobs, this label would include the dimensions related to supervision and management/administration. In essence, this represents performing the major tasks associated with one's job. The second dimension, labeled **interpersonally oriented behaviors,** represents all of the interpersonal transactions that occur on the job. For example, they might include a retail store clerk answering a customer's question, a nurse consulting a doctor about a patient's medication, or an auto mechanic talking to a service manager about a repair that must be done on a car. Because many interpersonal transactions in the workplace are task-related, this dimension mirrors *facilitating peer and team performance,* in J. Campbell's (1990, 1994) model. Not all interpersonal transactions in the workplace are task-related. For example, employees may start off Monday mornings with "small talk" about what they did over the weekend. This dimension therefore also represents the extent to which employees generally maintain positive interpersonal relations with coworkers. This aspect of job behavior is not explicitly part of J. Campbell's (1990, 1994) model, although it is clearly an important aspect of performance (see Comment 4.3).

The third dimension, **down-time behaviors,** represents behaviors that may lead the job incumbent to be absent from the worksite. These include counterproductive behaviors such as drug and alcohol abuse, and other violations of the law. They are considered aspects of performance because an employee with a substance abuse problem, for example, may be frequently absent from work and is therefore not performing well. A closely related set of behaviors is included in the fourth category, **destructive/hazardous behaviors.** These would include such things as safety violations, accidents, and sabotage. The down-

TABLE 4.2

Murphy's (1994) Dimensions of the Performance Domain

1. Task-oriented behaviors
2. Interpersonally oriented behaviors
3. Down-time behaviors
4. Destructive/Hazardous behaviors

COMMENT 4.3

MAINTAINING POSITIVE INTERPERSONAL RELATIONS AT WORK

MAINTAINING POSITIVE INTERPERSONAL relationships with others is a performance dimension that is rarely noticed unless someone is unable to do it. Research over the years has shown, relatively consistently, that interpersonal conflict is perceived negatively by employees and leads to a number of negative outcomes (e.g., Spector & Jex, 1998). Specifically, when there are frequent interpersonal conflicts in the work environment, employees tend to dislike their jobs and feel anxious and tense about coming to work.

Another aspect of interpersonal relations that has been explored less frequently, but may be just as important, is the impact of interpersonal relations on promotions in organizations. Having worked in two corporations and taught many courses over the years, a frequent theme I have heard is that relatively few individuals fail to get promoted due to lack of technical skills. More often than not, a lack of mobility in organizations is due to an inability to get along

with others. In fact, many organizations invest considerable amounts of money in individual coaching programs that are often aimed at individuals who have a great deal of technical prowess but are lacking in interpersonal skills. Why is it so important to get along with others in organizations? The likely reason is that much of what gets done in any organization gets done through *people*. If someone has a hard time getting along with others, it is quite possible that he or she will have a hard time gaining others' cooperation and assistance—factors that are often necessary to get things done in organizations.

Source: P. E. Spector and S. M. Jex. (1998). Development of four self-report measures of job stressors and strain: Interpersonal Conflict at Work Scale, Organizational Constraints Scale, Quantitative Workload Inventory, and Physical Symptoms Inventory. *Journal of Occupational Health Psychology, 3,* 356–367.

time behaviors and destructive/hazardous behaviors dimensions are most closely related to the dimension of maintaining personal discipline, in J. Campbell's (1990, 1994) model. In some cases, though, destructive/hazardous behaviors may result from a lack of effort (e.g., not taking the time to put on safety equipment), so this dimension may overlap with the demonstrating effort dimension in Campbell's model.

Compared to J. Campbell's (1990, 1994) eight-dimension model, Murphy's (1994) four-dimension model is somewhat less useful, for two reasons. First, this model was developed to explain job performance—specifically, among U.S. Navy personnel. Campbell's objective was to describe performance in a broader spectrum of jobs, although his model could certainly be used to

describe job performance among military personnel. Second, the performance dimensions described by Murphy are considerably broader than those described by Campbell. Because they are so broad, it is more difficult to determine the factors that led to differences among employees on these performance dimensions. Despite these disadvantages, this model again provides us with a set of dimensions for comparing performance across jobs.

Determinants of Job Performance

In trying to explain behavior such as job performance, organizational psychologists have at times engaged in heated debates over the relative impact of the person versus the environment (e.g., nature versus nurture). In such cases, these debates are resolved by the rather commonsense notion that most behaviors are the result of a complex interaction between characteristics of people and characteristics of the environment.

Generally speaking, differences in job performance are caused by the interaction among ability, motivation, and situational factors that may facilitate or inhibit performance. Thus, for an employee to perform well, he or she must possess job-relevant abilities. Ability alone will not lead to high levels of performance, though, unless the employee is motivated to do so, and does not experience severe situational constraints. Of course, in some cases, a high level of one of these three factors will compensate for low levels of the others (e.g., a highly motivated employee will overcome situational constraints), but usually all three conditions are necessary.

This section begins with an examination of a well-known theoretical model of the determinants of job performance, followed by an exploration of empirical evidence on determinants of job performance. Given the vast number of factors that impact job performance, the exploration of the empirical literature will be limited to *individual differences* or characteristics of persons that explain performance differences. Environmental factors that impact job performance (e.g., leadership, motivation, and situational constraints) will be covered in more detail in subsequent chapters.

J. Campbell (1990, 1994) proposed that job performance is determined by the interaction among **declarative knowledge, procedural knowledge/skill,** and **motivation** (see Figure 4.1). Declarative knowledge is simply knowledge about facts and things. An employee with a high level of declarative knowledge has a good understanding of the tasks that are required by his or her job. As an example, a medical technician with a high level of declarative knowledge *knows* the steps necessary to draw blood from a patient. According to Campbell, differences in declarative

FIGURE 4.1
Campbell's (1990, 1994) Model of the Determinants of Job Performance

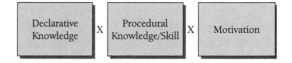

Adapted from J. P. Campbell. (1990). Modeling the performance prediction problem in industrial and organizational psychology. In M. D. Dunnette and L. M. Hough (Eds.), *Handbook of industrial and organizational psychology* (2nd ed., Vol. 1, pp. 687–732). Palo Alto, CA: Consulting Psychologists Press. Modified and reproduced by permission of the publisher.

knowledge may be due to a number of factors, such as ability, personality, interests, education, training, experience, and the interaction between employee aptitudes and training. Many forms of professional and academic training, at least in the early stages, stress the acquisition of declarative knowledge. The first year of medical school, for example, requires considerable memorization of information about human anatomy and physiology.

Once an employee has achieved a high degree of declarative knowledge, he or she is in a position to acquire a high level of procedural knowledge/skill. When this is achieved, the employee understands not only what needs to be done but also how to do it, and is able to carry out these behaviors. A medical technician who has achieved a high level of procedural skill or knowledge not only knows the steps involved in drawing blood, but is also able to *perform* this task. According to Campbell, differences in the acquisition of procedure knowledge/skill are determined by the same factors that lead to differences in declarative knowledge. In academic and professional training, the acquisition of procedural knowledge/skill tends to be emphasized at later stages or, typically, after a sufficient degree of declarative knowledge has been acquired. Medical training, for example, becomes more "hands on" during the third and fourth years.

When an employee has reached a high level of procedure knowledge/skill, he or she is *capable* of high levels of job performance. Stated differently, at this point, an employee has *performance potential*. Whether this potential actually leads to high levels of job performance depends on motivation. This, according to J. Campbell (1990, 1994), reflects an employee's choices regarding (1) whether to expend effort directed at job performance, (2) the level of effort to expend, and (3) whether to persist with the level of effort that is chosen. Thus, even if an employee has achieved a very high level of procedural knowledge/skill, low motivation may prevent it from being translated into a high level of performance. For example, a highly capable employee may simply decide not to put forth any effort, may not put in *enough* effort, or may put forth the effort but lack the willingness to sustain it over time.

The primary value of J. Campbell's (1990, 1994) model is that it states, in precise terms, the factors within the person that determine performance, and the interplay among those factors. Furthermore, it has received empirical support (e.g., McCloy, Campbell, & Cudeck, 1994). The model also reminds us that the interaction among the factors that determine performance is complex. For example, a high level of motivation may compensate for a moderate level of procedural knowledge/skill. On the other hand, a low level of motivation may negate the potential benefits of a high level of procedural knowledge/skill. This model can also be used to generate ideas and hypotheses about performance and its determinants (see Comment 4.4).

Given all the factors that have been proposed to explain differences in job performance, a logical question may be: What is the relative contribution of all of these factors to

COMMENT 4.4

THE INTERACTION BETWEEN DECLARATIVE AND PROCEDURAL KNOWLEDGE

Is DECLARATIVE KNOWLEDGE a necessary precondition to obtaining procedural knowledge? That is, do you have to know *about* something in order to know how to *do* something? For some tasks, it is fairly obvious that declarative knowledge is a precursor to procedural knowledge. For example, it would be very difficult to fly a jet airplane if one had absolutely no knowledge of jet propulsion.

For some types of human performance, however, it is unclear whether declarative knowledge must precede procedural knowledge. For example, it is not unusual for athletes to understand how to do things but not necessarily know the principles behind what they are doing (perhaps that's where Nike came

up with the slogan "Just Do It"). There are also instances of great musicians who are unable to read music but are able to play musical compositions based on their auditory memory.

Perhaps those instances when one can achieve procedural knowledge without first obtaining declarative knowledge are relatively rare. However, it would be useful to develop a greater understanding of the interaction between these two forms of knowledge. Because many training and educational programs are based on the premise that declarative knowledge must come first, a greater understanding of this interaction may pave the way for interesting new training and educational methods.

performance? Indeed, so much research has examined this question over the years that a comprehensive review of this literature is clearly beyond the scope of the chapter. It is possible, however, to draw some conclusions, at least with respect to individual difference predictors of performance. As stated earlier, situational factors that impact performance will be covered in other chapters.

By far the one individual difference variable that has received the most attention as a determinant of job performance is **general cognitive ability.** Numerous definitions have been offered, but the common element in most definitions of general cognitive ability is that it reflects an individual's capacity to process and comprehend information (Murphy, 1989b; Waldman & Spangler, 1989). As a determinant of job performance, research has consistently shown, over many years, that general cognitive ability predicts performance over a wide range of jobs and occupations. The most comprehensive demonstration of this was a recent meta-analysis conducted by Schmidt and Hunter (1998), in which nearly 85 years of research findings on various predictors of job performance are summarized. Their analysis indicated that the corrected correlation between general cognitive ability and performance across jobs was .51—that is, over 25% of the variance in performance across jobs is due to differences in general cognitive ability. This does not take into account other factors that may impact job performance (e.g., motivation, leadership, and situational constraints), so this finding is truly impressive.

Why is general cognitive ability such a key to explaining differences in job performance? According to Schmidt, Hunter, and Outerbridge (1986), the intermediate link between general cognitive ability and job performance is **job knowledge**; that is, employees who possess higher levels of general cognitive ability

tend to develop a greater understanding of their job duties than individuals with lower levels. For example, a very intelligent airplane pilot would likely possess greater knowledge of all that goes into flying a plane than a pilot who was less intelligent. In essence, those with high levels of cognitive ability are able to extract more relevant information from the job environment than those with lower levels of general cognitive ability.

Another consistent finding in this literature is that general cognitive ability is a better predictor of performance in jobs that have a high level of complexity compared to jobs lower in complexity (e.g., Hunter, Schmidt, & Judiesch, 1990). Although there is no standard definition, most researchers agree that job complexity is strongly influenced by the mental demands and information-processing requirements placed on job incumbents (Wood, 1986). For example, the job of a corporate executive requires the use of "higher-order" cognitive skills such as planning and synthesizing large amounts of information. On the other hand, the job of a convenience store clerk typically requires what might be considered "lower level" cognitive skills such as following established guidelines and procedures. General cognitive ability predicts good performance in complex jobs, primarily because such jobs place higher-level information-processing demands on incumbents. Thus, compared to those with lower levels, incumbents who possess high levels of general cognitive ability are better able to meet those demands.

Another individual difference variable has been examined frequently as a general predictor of job performance: job experience. It would seem logical that a person with a higher level of relevant job experience would perform better than others who possess little or no job experience. Empirical evidence has, in fact, shown that experience, like general cognitive ability, is positively related to job performance over a wide range of job types (McDaniel, Schmidt, & Hunter, 1988; Schmidt & Hunter, 1998). Like general cognitive ability, the relation between experience and job performance appears to be mediated by job knowledge (Schmidt et al., 1986). This relation is also moderated by job complexity. For example, McDaniel et al. (1988) found that experience was a better predictor of performance in *low* rather than *high* complexity jobs. They attributed this difference to the fact that *experience* is really the only preparation for low-complexity jobs. For example, there is no way to learn how to perform the job of convenience store clerk other than by actually working at it. With high-complexity jobs, however, education may compensate for a lack of experience. Note that the form of this interaction effect is exactly the opposite of that found for general cognitive ability.

There is also evidence that the importance of job experience in explaining performance differences tends to diminish over time. For example, McDaniel et al. (1988) found that the correlation between experience and performance was strongest in samples where the average level of job experience was less than three years, but the correlation was considerably less for samples where the average level of experience was higher. This suggests that there is a "law of diminishing returns" with respect to the impact of job experience on job performance.

Research on the impact of job experience on job performance should be viewed cautiously, however, because most studies have measured job experience as the number of years in an organization or job. Quinones, Ford, and Teachout (1995) pointed out that job experience can be viewed not only in terms of *quantity* but also in terms of *quality*. Years of experience is a quantitative measure of experience. If job experience is viewed

qualitatively, this has to do with the job tasks performed and the relevance of situations one has been exposed to on the job. For example, if an individual has several years of experience as an accountant, but has conducted few field audits, that person will not necessarily perform better in an auditing position than an individual who has less general accounting experience.

Building on the work of Quinones et al. (1995), Tesluk and Jacobs (1998) proposed that job experience can also be viewed in terms of both the *density* and *timing* of job-related experiences. When experience has high density, the employee is exposed to many "developmental experiences" in a relative short period of time. These may include increased responsibilities, and perhaps even being required to perform under very difficult conditions. The timing dimension has to do with the fact that certain experiences might have more, or less, developmental value, depending on whether they occur at the beginning, middle, or latter stage of one's career. For most employees, mistakes have a greater developmental impact when they occur at the early (as opposed to later) stages of one's career. The more important point from the work of Quinones et al. (1995) and Tesluk and Jacobs (1998) is that job experience is a complex variable, and much theoretical and empirical work needs to be done before we fully understand and appreciate it (see Comment 4.5).

Along with general cognitive ability and job experience, the other individual difference variable that stands out as a predictor of performance over a wide range of jobs is the personality trait of **conscientiousness** (Barrick & Mount, 1991; Ones, Viswesvaran, & Schmidt, 1993). A person who is conscientious can be described as dependable, goal-oriented, planful, and achievement-oriented. Barrick and Mount (1991) found that the corrected correlation between conscientiousness

COMMENT 4.5

WHAT IS JOB EXPERIENCE?

JOB EXPERIENCE IS a variable that is used so frequently in organizational psychology that it is easy to forget about it. Typically, most researchers don't pay too much attention to it because they are measuring it either for descriptive purposes, or to use as a control variable in statistical analyses. In the vast majority of studies, experience is measured simply as the number of months or years that a person has been employed in a particular job or in a particular organization.

In a recent review, Tesluk and Jacobs (1998) pointed out that organizational or job tenure is not likely to capture the complexity of job experience. They point out, for example, that the same length of tenure may be very different in terms of both the density and the timing of job-related experiences. A good example of the density dimension would be a surgeon performing in a war zone. This individual would typically be doing surgeries around the clock, and would thus acquire more surgical experience in three months than a surgeon at a regular civilian hospital would acquire in twice the time. A good example of timing would be a manager's having to take over a poorly performing department immediately after completing his or her training. Such an experience would undoubtedly have a greater impact on this individual now than it would later in his or her career.

Many organizations recognize complexity of experience and attempt to structure the assignments of high-potential managers in a way that maximizes their developmental value. For the most part, however, researchers have treated experience in a very simplistic fashion. In the future, this is likely to be a very fruitful area of research in organizational psychology.

Source: P. E. Tesluk and R. R. Jacobs. (1998). Toward an integrated model of work experience. *Personnel Psychology, 51,* 321–355.

and performance, across a wide variety of jobs, was .22. Ones et al. (1993) found that the mean corrected correlation between integrity tests (which many presume are measures of conscientiousness) and job performance, across jobs, was .34.

There are two explanations as to why conscientiousness is a robust predictor of performance. According to Schmidt and Hunter (1998), the variable that links conscientiousness and job performance is job knowledge. Recall that this was the same variable proposed to mediate the relation between both general cognitive ability and experience and performance. In this case, however, the process has to do primarily with motivation rather than with ability. Individuals who are highly conscientious presumably put time and effort into acquiring high levels of job knowledge, and hence will perform better than those who are less conscientious.

Another explanation for the relation between conscientiousness and performance is goal setting. Barrick, Mount, and Strauss (1993) found, in a study of sales personnel, that goal setting mediated the relation between conscientiousness and job performance. Specifically, those who were highly conscientious exhibited a greater proclivity for setting performance-related goals than those who were less conscientious. This proclivity for setting goals facilitated, in turn, higher levels of job performance. This adds to the findings of Schmidt and Hunter (1998) regarding why highly conscientious people tend to perform well, regardless of the job.

At this point, the major conclusion to be drawn is that the most important individual difference variables impacting job performance are general cognitive ability, job experience, and conscientiousness. Furthermore, the primary mechanisms linking these variables to job performance are job knowledge and, to a lesser extent, goal setting. Finally, many of these relations appear to be impacted by job complexity. Figure 4.2 summarizes these propositions.

Readers will undoubtedly note that Figure 4.2 does *not* contain a number of situational factors such as motivation, leadership, and organizational climate. This was done largely for pedagogical reasons because the link between these situational factors and performance will be covered in later chapters. It is important to note, however, that although few studies have examined the *joint* effect of individual

FIGURE 4.2
Summary of the Most Important Individual Difference Predicators of Job Performance

differences and situational factors, it has been demonstrated empirically that both do contribute to job performance (e.g, Colarelli, Dean, & Konstans, 1987; Day & Bedeian, 1991). Thus, organizations must do more than simply hire smart, experienced, conscientious people in order to facilitate high levels of employee performance.

SPECIAL ISSUES IN THE STUDY OF JOB PERFORMANCE

By this point, readers have (I hope) developed an understanding of the complexity of job performance and its determinants. Because of this complexity, a number of factors come into play when organizational psychologists attempt to document the relationship between job performance and other variables. In this section, three of the most important complicating factors are discussed: (1) the measurement of job performance, (2) restriction in the variability of job performance, and (3) instability in job performance over time.

Measurement of Job Performance

By definition, job performance is *behavior,* so job performance is rarely measured directly. More typically, what is measured is some *external assessment* of job performance. According to Murphy (1989a), performance can be assessed in eight different ways: (1) paper/pencil tests, (2) job skills tests, (3) on-site hands-on testing, (4) off-site hands-on testing, (5) high-fidelity simulations, (6) symbolic simulations, (7) task ratings, and (8) global ratings. By far, the two most common methods of performance assessment in organizations are ratings of employees' performance on specific tasks, and ratings of overall performance on the job.

The literature on performance rating is vast (e.g., Landy & Farr, 1980; Murphy &

Cleveland, 1990), and will not be reviewed in detail here. Two general points, however, can be made. First, there are many potential sources of error in performance ratings. For example, a rater may not have an adequate opportunity to observe performance; ratings may be biased by the degree to which the rater likes or dislikes the ratee; or different raters may employ different internal performance standards. These are just three of many potential sources of error. Rating errors are problematic because they ultimately mask meaningful differences in actual job performance, and thus may weaken the relationship between job performance and other variables.

A second point is that steps *can* be taken to reduce error in performance ratings. For example, rater training has been shown to increase accuracy in performance ratings (Pulakos, 1984). Another way to circumvent the problems with performance ratings is to seek more "objective" performance measures, such as output produced or sales commissions. Unfortunately, these more objective performance measures may have serious flaws of their own. The most obvious flaw is that most are really measures of *effectiveness* or *productivity* and not actual job performance (J. Campbell, 1990). Another disadvantage is that employees may lack control over objective performance indicators. For example, even a very skilled real estate salesperson would probably not sell many houses if the mortgage interest rates rose to 20%.

The major point of considering performance measurement is simply that we must always keep in mind that *performance* is not the same thing as the *measurement of* performance. Furthermore, because measuring anything will inevitably involve some degree of error, our understanding of performance and our ability to predict it will always remain imperfect.

Restriction in the Variability of Job Performance

For a variety of reasons, the variability in performance levels within organizations is often restricted. To better understand restriction in performance variability, it is useful to distinguish between **artifactual restriction** in performance variability and **true restriction.** Artifactual restriction in performance variability results from things such as errors in performance ratings, or the performance measurement system. Even though there may be real differences among employees' levels of job performance, these may be masked because of an error in the performance rating process. True restriction in performance variability, on the other hand, occurs when measures of performance are relatively accurate but there is a true lack of meaningful variation in actual job performance. In this section, reasons for true restriction in performance variability are discussed.

According to Peters and O'Connor (1988), there are four reasons why variation in individual performance may be restricted. First, organizations simply may have very low performance standards. If organizations do not expect much, this standard will tend to discourage high levels of performance, and employees will gravitate toward "minimally acceptable" levels of performance. The end result of this process is often a great reduction in the variability of performance. A good example is the commonly held stereotype that performance standards for government employees are low. Many readers have probably heard the expression "Good enough for government work," which implies that work must only be done at a minimally acceptable level.

A second factor, which is related to low performance standards, is that organizations vary in the degree to which they value high levels of individual job performance. Organizations either may fail to recognize the contributions of those who perform well, or tolerate individuals who consistently perform poorly. Some organizations may even inadvertently create situations in which low levels of performance are actually *rewarded,* and high levels of performance are *punished.* For example, in many organizations, employees who perform well are often "rewarded" with greater responsibility and heavier workloads, but receive no additional compensation or promotions. The author has also seen managers rid themselves of incompetent employees by recommending that they be promoted to positions in other departments.

A third factor restricting performance variability is the degree to which organizations excuse employees for low levels of performance. This factor is related to low performance standards but operates somewhat differently. According to Peters and O'Connor (1988), organizations may develop what they describe as a "culture of justification" (p. 117); that is, employees are routinely allowed to "explain away" instances of poor performance. A somewhat more irreverent way of describing this is the familiar acronym "CYA." Such a culture takes away the incentive to perform well and ultimately restricts performance to mediocre levels.

A final cause of restriction in performance variability, according to Peters and O'Connor (1988), is variation in organizational resources. Having limited resources often leads to situational constraints that ultimately reduce the variability in performance (Peters & O'Connor, 1980). For example, it is difficult for an auto mechanic to perform well if he or she has no tools. On the other hand, if organizational resources are extremely *plentiful,* this may also reduce the variability in performance. In this case, everyone in an organization may perform up to his or her full potential

and, as a result, the variability in performance will be restricted.

A somewhat different explanation as to why the variation in actual performance levels may be restricted is that selection and retention in organizations are not random processes. According to Johns (1991), most organizations require that employees pass through relatively rigorous screening processes before they are hired. For example, those who wish to become police officers typically must pass through a series of tests before even being selected for academy training. In many other occupations, such as law, medicine, and engineering, much of this screening is done by universities during professional training. As a result of these screening processes, the variation in skill and ability level among employees may be quite restricted, which may ultimately restrict the variability in job performance. Employees who perform poorly or simply do not fit well with an organization's culture often select themselves out and leave voluntarily (Schneider, 1987). Like formal socialization processes, this again tends to create uniformity in job performance.

Despite all of the factors that may restrict performance variability, empirical evidence suggests that performance variability in organizations is still meaningful. For example, Schmidt and Hunter (1998) point out that even though performance variability in organizations is somewhat restricted, a substantial portion still remains. If this were not the case, it is unlikely that selection tools such as cognitive ability tests, personality measures, and biodata instruments would be related to performance.

Instability in Job Performance over Time

There has been considerable debate, over the years, concerning the relative stability of performance criterion measures (e.g., Ackerman, 1989; Austin, Humphreys, & Hulin, 1989; Barrett, Caldwell, & Alexander, 1985; Henry & Hulin, 1987, 1989). Some contributors have claimed that performance is relatively stable over time; many others have argued (quite forcefully at times) that performance is more dynamic. The weight of the evidence seems to support the position that performance criteria are dynamic. For example, Deadrick and Madigan (1990) examined the stability in performance of sewing machine operators over time and found that the correlations between performance levels were quite strong when the time interval was very short. However, the correlation between performance at one point in time, and performance 23 weeks later, was considerably weaker. Thus, because of a variety of factors,

employee performance tends to fluctuate over time. In fact, this inconsistency may explain why people are so impressed when a high level of consistency is displayed. In sports, for example, great honors are bestowed on athletes for breaking records that indicate consistency and longevity (see Comment 4.6).

Ployhart and Hakel (1998) pointed out that although evidence supports the dynamic nature of performance, correlations between levels of performance at different points in time provide little insight into how the performance of individuals changes over time. Furthermore, we know very little about variables that predict distinct patterns of change in performance over time. To address this issue, these researchers examined eight years' worth of performance criterion data from a sample of 303 securities analysts.

COMMENT 4.6

CONSISTENCY OF PERFORMANCE IN BASEBALL

SOME OF THE most highly regarded records in the world of sports reflect consistency of performance. In baseball, for example, a record that has stood for over 50 years is New York Yankee Joe DiMaggio's 56-game hitting streak. More recently, Cal Ripken, Jr., of the Baltimore Orioles, made history by playing in 2,632 consecutive games. Why are these two records so highly regarded? DiMaggio's record is remarkable when one considers all of the factors that work against obtaining a base hit in that number of consecutive games. One would think that the skill of pitchers at the major league level, minor injuries, and general fatigue would make such a streak highly unlikely. Thus, this record is a reflection of DiMaggio's skill as a hitter, and his determination.

One reason Ripken's streak is so unusual is simply that few players last that long at the

major league level. It is also unusual for players to avoid serious injuries for that period of time. Furthermore, because of the number of games played in a major league season (162), and minor injuries, most players want an *occasional* day off. Thus, Ripken's streak is a reflection of a number of factors, including consistency in performance, rigorous off-season conditioning, and a high level of motivation.

What do these baseball records tell us about stability and consistency of performance? If anything, they highlight the fact that stability and consistency, over time, are more the exception than the rule. Because of external constraints, fluctuations in motivation, and just plain good/bad luck, performance in most domains is often quite variable. However, when it does remain consistent for a long period of time, it is often highly rewarded.

Using a statistical procedure known as **latent growth curve modeling,** which allows the modeling of patterns of change over time, they found that, on average, performance among these securities analysts approximated a basic learning curve. Initially, performance rose steadily; eventually, it reached a leveling-off point. They also found that, within the sample, not all curves were the same. For example, there were differences in how quickly performance initially accelerated. There were also differences in how quickly performance reached a leveling-off point. Most importantly, they found that patterns of change in performance over time were predictable; for example, those who described themselves as persuasive and empathetic exhibited the quickest initial rate of acceleration in sales. They also found that these two variables predicted whether there would be a drop in performance. Those who described themselves as persuasive were *more* likely to exhibit a drop in performance early in the second year of employment, and those describing themselves as empathetic were *less* likely to exhibit this drop. On a more substantive level, this finding suggests that exhibiting empathy toward clients may be a more effective sales technique than trying to persuade them.

Ployhart and Hakel's (1998) study provides important insight into the issue of performance stability. At least for the sample employed, it suggests that although performance is not stable over time, it does not fluctuate randomly. More importantly, this study suggests that it is possible to identify and statistically model patterns of change in performance over time. It also suggests that there may be individual differences that predict patterns of performance variability over time. An important practical implication of this possibility is that an organization may be able to identify a desired temporal pattern of performance and select individuals who are likely to exhibit

that pattern. For example, it may be possible to screen out individuals whose performance peaks very quickly and then declines.

Job performance variability over time can also be explained by characteristics of the job itself. Murphy (1989b) proposed that jobs are characterized by what he termed "maintenance" stages and "transition" stages. During maintenance stages, the tasks comprising the job become somewhat routine and automatic for the job incumbent. For example, once a person learns to drive an automobile, the steps necessary to perform this task become so routine that little conscious thought is required. When this level of proficiency is achieved, it is as if people are on "automatic pilot" when they are performing the task. This may explain why, during morning commutes over the years, the author has witnessed drivers applying makeup, eating breakfast, or reading newspapers!

When a job is in the transition stage, the tasks comprising the job become novel and the incumbent cannot rely on automatic routines while performing them. Transition periods in jobs may occur during the introduction of new technology or perhaps when a major change in laws impacts the job being performed. For example, due to new manufacturing technology, the jobs of many production employees have changed dramatically in the past 10 years (Parker & Wall, 1998). Also, many employees in nursing homes and other long-term healthcare facilities have recently experienced profound changes in their jobs because of changes in Medicare billing procedures (D. Campbell, 1999).

Murphy (1989b) notes that because transition periods require adjustments on the part of the employee, they lead to some level of disruption and instability in performance. Another consequence of transition points, according to Murphy, is that general cognitive ability is a more important determinant of performance during these periods (compared to performance during the maintenance period). This makes sense, given the well established finding that general cognitive ability is a stronger predictor of performance in complex jobs. If this is true, it follows that general cognitive ability should be more strongly related to performance during these periods. Unfortunately, this proposition has not as yet received empirical scrutiny.

ORGANIZATIONAL CITIZENSHIP BEHAVIOR

The second form of productive behavior to be discussed in this chapter is organizational citizenship behavior (OCB) (Organ, 1977, 1994). Generally speaking, OCB refers to behaviors that are not part of employees' formal job descriptions (e.g., helping a coworker who has been absent; being courteous to others), or behaviors for which employees are not formally rewarded. Even though such behaviors are not formally mandated by organizations, in the aggregate they are believed to enhance the effectiveness of groups and organizations (George & Bettenhausen, 1990; Katz & Kahn, 1978; Podsakoff, Ahearne, & MacKenzie, 1997). Recall from the previous models of job performance (J. Campbell, 1990, 1994; Murphy, 1994) that OCB is essentially a dimension of job performance, if we adopt a broad view of performance. It is covered as a separate form of productive behavior because it has been studied separately from "in-role" performance. Also, as will be shown, the antecedents of OCB are different from the antecedents of in-role performance.

According to Organ (1977, 1994), OCB in organizations can be categorized as five different types:

1. **Altruism** represents what we typically think of as "helping behaviors" in the workplace. This form of OCB is sometimes referred to as "prosocial behavior." An example of altruism would be an employee's voluntarily assisting a coworker who is having difficulty operating his or her computer.

2. **Courtesy.** This dimension of OCB represents behaviors that reflect basic consideration for others. An example of behavior within this category would be: periodically "touching base" with one's coworkers to find out how things are going, or letting others know where one can be reached.

3. **Sportsmanship** is different from other forms of OCB because it is typically exhibited by *not* engaging in certain forms of behaviors, such as complaining about problems or minor inconveniences.

4. **Conscientiousness** involves being a "good citizen" in the workplace and doing things such as arriving on time for meetings.

5. **Civic virtue** is somewhat different from the others because the target is the organization—or, in some cases, the work group—rather than another individual. An example of this form of OCB would be attending a charitable function sponsored by the organization.

Why do employees engage in OCB? There are actually three different explanations. According to the first, the primary determinant is positive affect, typically in the form of job satisfaction. Theoretically, this view comes from a fairly long history of social psychological research showing that a positive mood increases the frequency of helping and of other forms of spontaneous prosocial behavior (see George & Brief, 1992). Furthermore, positive mood and helping behavior are actually mutually reinforcing because helping others usually makes people feel good.

A second explanation for OCB has to do with cognitive evaluations of the fairness of employees' treatment by an organization.

This view is theoretically rooted in **Equity Theory** (Adams, 1965), which states that employees evaluate their work situations by cognitively comparing their inputs to the organization with the outcomes they receive in return. (Equity Theory will be covered in more detail in Chapter 8.) If employees perceive that the organization is treating them fairly or justly, then they are likely to reciprocate the organization by engaging in OCB. It seems, however, that certain forms of fairness or justice predict OCB better than others. For example, Moorman (1991) found that the best predictor of OCB was **interactional justice,** or the manner in which supervisors treat employees as they carry out organizational policies and procedures. In contrast, other studies have found that **procedural justice** is a better predictor of OCB than is **distributive justice** (e.g., Konovsky & Pugh, 1990). Procedural justice refers to employees' perceptions of the fairness of procedures used to make decisions such as pay raises; distributive justice refers to perceptions of fairness of the *outcomes* one receives as a result of those procedures.

A third explanation for OCB is that it is due to dispositions. According to this viewpoint, certain personality traits predispose individuals to engage in OCB. In other words, some people are naturally more helpful than others are. Compared to the first two explanations of OCB, the dispositional viewpoint has received much less attention in the OCB literature because proponents of this view have been vague as to the specific personality traits that should be related to OCB. This has been a criticism of dispositional explanations of other forms of employee attitudes and behavior (Davis-Blake & Pfeffer, 1989).

Other than affect, fairness, and dispositions, a handful of other factors have been proposed to impact the performance of OCB, although none of these has received extensive empirical scrutiny. For example, Chattopadhyay (1998) found evidence that OCB is impacted by the demographic composition of work groups. It has also been found that the performance of OCB may be impacted by other factors, such as job-related stressors (Jex, 1998; Jex, Adams, Bachrach, & Rosol, 2001) and employees' level of organizational commitment (Williams & Anderson, 1991).

To evaluate the relative impact of various antecedents of OCB, Organ and Ryan (1995) conducted a meta-analysis of 55 studies. Their results suggest that job satisfaction and perceived fairness were correlated with OCB at approximately the same magnitude. The results for dispositional predictors of OCB were rather disappointing, however. For example, personality traits such as conscientiousness, agreeableness, positive affectivity, and negative affectivity were all unrelated to OCB. As Figure 4.3 summarizes, the most logical conclusion to be drawn from Organ and Ryan's meta-analysis is that affective and cognitive influences combine in an additive fashion to determine OCB.

FIGURE 4.3
Summary of the Major Antecedents of Organizational Citizenship Behavior (OCB)

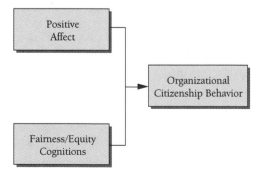

Special Issues in OCB Research

Since Organ (1977) first introduced the concept of OCB, there has been considerable research on the topic. As with most well-researched topics, many issues have generated controversy and debate among researchers in this area. In this section, four of these issues are discussed briefly.

The underlying premise behind OCB research is that this form of productive behavior is necessary in order for organizations to be effective (Katz & Kahn, 1978). What is typically argued is that if employees performed their jobs exactly as written, and did nothing beyond that, organizations would not be able to function effectively. Surprisingly, this claim had received virtually no empirical scrutiny until very recently. It has now been shown empirically, at least for groups, that OCB is positively related to effectiveness (Karambayya, 1989; Podsakoff at al., 1997). As would be expected, groups in which members engage in more OCBs tend to be more effective than groups in which members engage in fewer of these behaviors.

What is still not clear, from research on OCB and its effectiveness, is the direction of causality underlying this relationship. Researchers have largely operated under the assumption that OCB has a causal impact on group and organizational effectiveness. However, it is also possible that the direction of causality could be reversed. Members of effective groups may report high levels of OCB, regardless of whether they actually exist. When a group is successful, group members may perceive high levels of OCB as they bask in the glow of this success. In a related study, Staw (1975) found that group members' retrospective reports of group cohesiveness could be manipulated based on false feedback about group performance. In this study group,

members who were told that their group had been successful reported higher levels of cohesiveness than did group members who were told that their group had been unsuccessful. Using the same paradigm as Staw (1975), Bachrach, Bendoly, and Podsakoff (2001) recently found evidence that retrospective perceptions of OCB may be impacted by group performance. This issue will undoubtedly be addressed in future OCB research.

A second issue has become important in recent OCB research: the validity of the OCB concept itself. As originally defined by Organ (1977), OCB represents behavior that is above employees' formal job responsibilities, and for which there are no formal rewards. With regard to the first issue, it is becoming increasingly questionable that, in performing their day-to-day activities, employees make the "in-role" versus "extra-role" distinctions upon which OCB is based. This suggests that many employees view activities such as helping other employees, being courteous to others, and occasionally attending functions on behalf of their organization, as part of their formal role responsibilities. This is supported by Morrison (1994), who found, in a sample of clerical employees, that many behaviors that are considered OCB were classified by these employees as part of their normal in-role job responsibilities. She also found that there was very little correlation between employees' and supervisors' classifications of OCBs. Thus, many of the behaviors that *supervisors* consider OCB may simply represent employees' doing things that they consider to be part of their jobs.

Another interesting finding from Morrison's (1994) study was that employees were most likely to classify OCBs as in-role behaviors when they reported high levels of both job satisfaction and affective organizational commitment. Building on this finding, Bachrach and Jex (2000) conducted a laboratory study in which they used a mood induction procedure to investigate the impact of mood on the categorization of OCB for a simulated clerical position. In this study, it was found that inducing a positive mood state had no impact on classification of OCB. Interestingly, though, subjects who experienced a *negative* mood induction procedure classified *fewer* of the OCBs as being part of their regular role, compared to those in the positive or neutral mood conditions. These findings suggest that negative affect may result in a more narrow definition of one's role. Taken together with Morrison's (1994) study, these findings call into question the "in-role" versus "extra-role" distinction that has been implicit in OCB research.

A third issue in OCB research is whether employees really engage in OCB without the expectation that such behaviors will be rewarded. Despite Organ's (1977) initial claim, recent evidence suggests that this assumption may be rather questionable. For example, it has been shown empirically that performing OCB positively influences formal performance appraisals (Eastman, 1994), and it is doubtful that employees are unaware of this. According to Bolino (1999), when OCB is performed with the expectation of future rewards, it then becomes a form of **impression management** rather than truly altruistic behavior. Impression management behaviors are simply tactics people use to influence others' view of them. According to Bolino, OCB is most likely to be used as an impression management tool when it is highly visible to others, particularly those responsible for the dispensation of rewards. As an example, an employee may help other employees only when his or her supervisor is around to observe.

One could certainly argue that as long as OCB is performed, the motivation is irrelevant. However, the reasons behind such behavior are important if organizations want to

influence the performance of OCB. If employees perform OCB primarily because they are satisfied with their jobs, or feel that they have been treated fairly, organizations can influence the performance of OCB by treating employees fairly and taking steps to enhance satisfaction. On the other hand, if OCB is performed with the expectation of rewards, or for impression management purposes, organizations should directly or indirectly link rewards to the performance of OCB. In essence, this suggests that OCB should be explicitly recognized as another form of job performance.

The term **contextual performance** has been used to describe forms of job performance that are virtually identical to OCB (Borman & Motowidlo, 1993; Conway, 1999). The only difference is that proponents of the contextual performance concept argue that these behaviors should be used in formal performance evaluations, and as criteria in personnel selection. Many organizations do in fact recognize many forms of contextual performance. For example, evaluations of university faculty typically take into account not only teaching and research, but also more ancillary activities such as service to one's academic department and the university.

A final issue in OCB research is whether OCB will remain a viable concept in the workplace of the future. Bridges (1994), among others, has pointed out a clear trend in recent years: Organizations have been moving away from formal job descriptions. In fact, Bridges has predicted that the concept of a "job" will eventually cease to exist (see Comment 4.7). This has not occurred as yet, but it is true that the work of employees in many organizations has become increasingly project-driven, and their activities revolve more and more around project completion rather than fulfilling their job duties. Given this trend, one may ask whether the "in-role"/"extra-role" distinction upon which OCB rests will be relevant in the

COMMENT 4.7

A WORLD WITHOUT JOBS

WILLIAM BRIDGES, IN his 1994 book *JobShift: How to Prosper in a Workplace without Jobs,* argues that, in the near future, the concept of a "job" will cease to exist. That is, rather than having a formalized job description that lays out one's duties, each person in an organization will be given project-based objectives and expected to accomplish them. One of the implications of having no formalized jobs is that organizations will be able to make much greater use of temporary and contingent employees; that is, an organization will be able to bring in specialists on an "as needed" basis to complete specific projects. This will give organizations considerable flexibility and allow them to operate with much lower labor costs. Another implication of this trend is that more and more people will become "independent contractors" rather than permanent employees of a given organization.

According to Bridges, this trend toward doing away with jobs has thus far been most evident in organizations that operate in high-technology sectors. This is largely due to the speed at which things are done in these sectors, and the need for constant innovation. Will other types of organizations eventually do away with jobs? Although it's certainly possible, there are reasons to believe that many organizations will not do away with jobs. For example, defending the legal soundness of selection and promotion procedures depends, to large degree, on the *job*-relatedness of those procedures. Thus, an organization without job descriptions would be in a very difficult position if its selection and promotion procedures were challenged. One would also assume that unions would be very wary of doing away with job descriptions since they help in establishing wage rates and essentially serve as a "contract" as to the job duties employees are expected to perform.

Source: W. Bridges. (1994). *JobShift: How to Prosper in a workplace without Jobs.* Reading, MA: Addison-Wesley.

workplace of the future. Behaviors considered to be OCB will still be necessary in a "de-jobbed" environment, but employees in the future will tend to consider them "part of the job," at least to the extent that they facilitate project completion. As Morrison's (1994) study shows, this is already occurring but will probably become a more pronounced trend because many employees may not have formal job descriptions to guide their behavior.

INNOVATION IN ORGANIZATIONS

The third and final form of productive behavior to be examined in this chapter is innovation.

Like OCB, innovation is really an aspect of job performance, but it is unique enough that a distinct literature examining its antecedents has developed. Although no standard definition of innovations exists, this form of productive behavior may be thought of as instances in which employees come up with very novel ideas or concepts that further the goals of the organization. The most visible forms of employee innovation in organizations are new products and services, and there are many examples of these. The Dell Computer Company, for example, has been an innovator in the marketing and distribution of personal computers. Saturn has been an innovator in both the distribution and service of automobiles. Not all innovations, however, take the forms of products and services. For example, an employee or employees may come up with a unique organizational structure, a more efficient production method, or some other cost-saving administrative procedure.

In the organizational innovation literature, there are four distinct streams of research (Damanpour, 1991). Some researchers have examined the *process* by which employees come up with innovative ideas; others are more interested in determining the characteristics that distinguish highly innovative employees from others. Note that, in both cases, the focus is on the employee or employees responsible for the innovation. This view is also reasonably congruent with the definition of innovation proposed in this chapter. Innovation can also be viewed from a more macro perspective; that is, many innovation researchers focus on what is described as the "diffusion" of innovations throughout an organization. An example of this might be the manner in which computers come to be utilized company-wide. Other innovation researchers tend to focus on what can be described as the "adoption" of innovations. Viewed from this perspective, the focus is on an organization's initial decision on whether to adopt some innovation.

If innovation is viewed from the individual employees' perspective, a logical question is: Are there predictors of whether employees will be innovative? According to Amabile (1983), several variables are predictive of creative production in individuals. Because creativity and innovation are closely linked, these variables are also relevant for predicting innovation in organizational settings. According to Amabile, creativity is due to **task-relevant skills, creativity-relevant skills,** and **task motivation.**

The area of task-relevant skills is related to the previously discussed variable of general cognitive ability, but it is more than that. To be creative, an individual must have a high level of general cognitive ability, but must also have more specific abilities. For example, a scientist developing a new vaccine must not only be intelligent, but must also know specific information about the behavior of microorganisms and be able to apply this knowledge in his or her work. Specific knowledge and technical skills are dependent on a certain level of general cognitive ability. Often, however, individuals must acquire these through some type of formal education; for example, most successful scientists have completed graduate training in their respective fields. Creative talent may also be developed apart from formal education. In the creative arts, for example, many successful people learn through informal means such as one-on-one tutoring, or may even be self-taught.

Despite the importance of task-relevant skills, many people possess them but do not produce creative, innovative work. For example, despite the large number of individuals holding the PhD degree in industrial/organizational psychology and related fields (e.g., Organizational Behavior, Human Resource Management), a relatively small proportion become highly productive researchers (e.g., Long, Bowers, Barnett, & White, 1998; Ones & Viswesvaran, 2000). Keep in mind that individuals holding PhD degrees in these fields all have reasonably equivalent education and training, and have achieved a certain level of competence in their specialty. Why, then, are some highly productive while others are not? The answer to this question may lie in the area of creativity-relevant skills and task motivation.

Creativity-relevant skills are essentially "meta-skills" that individuals use in the creative process. One crucial skill in the creative process is a cognitive style that is conducive to creativity. According to Amabile (1983), creative people are able to understand the complexities in a problem and are able to "break set" during problem solving. Stated differently, being creative requires being able to see a problem from multiple perspectives and having the willingness needed to "break the mold" in order to solve a problem. A good historical example of this principle's *not* being applied can be seen in recent retrospective accounts of the Vietnam War (McNamara, Blight, Brigham, Biersteker, & Schandler, 1999). In hindsight, it is clear that American and North Vietnamese decision makers viewed the conflict from completely different perspectives and were unwilling to deviate from these perceptions. On the American side, Vietnam was viewed as the "First Domino" in a Communist plan to dominate Southeast Asia. The North Vietnamese, on the other hand, equated American intervention with the colonialism of the French. If either aide had been willing to deviate from these perspectives, it is possible that the conflict could have been settled before the war escalated to a level that was so destructive for both sides.

Another important creativity-relevant skill is a work style that is conducive to creativity. Creative people are able to concentrate their efforts on a given problem for long periods of time. Stated differently, *creativity requires hard work*. Creative people, for example, are often able to work long hours at a time without stopping. Another aspect of work style is that creative people are able to engage in what Amabile (1983) described as "productive forgetting"—the ability to abandon unproductive searches, and temporarily put aside stubborn problems. Clear examples of this can be found in the sciences, where "breakthroughs" are typically achieved only after many failures.

The creativity-relevant skills described up to this point may be acquired from training, but there are more dispositional factors that contribute to creativity. Although researchers have been unable to isolate a "creative personality," some personality traits do seem to be associated with creative activity. These include self-discipline, ability to delay gratification, perseverance in the face of frustration, independence, an absence of conformity in thinking, or lack of dependence on social approval.

The issue of task motivation has not been examined extensively in creativity research, largely because of the strong focus on intrinsic factors associated with creativity. It is likely, however, that at least some of the variation in creativity can be explained by the level and nature of the motivation one has toward the task being performed. According to Amabile (1983), creativity requires that individuals genuinely enjoy what they are doing, and perceive that they are performing the task because they want to, rather than because of external pressures. These perceptions of enjoyment and intrinsic motivation depend on one's initial level of intrinsic motivation toward the task being performed, the presence or absence of external constraints in the social environment, and the individual's ability to block out or minimize external constraints.

Given this discussion of the determinants of creativity in individuals, what can organizations do to foster creativity and innovation among employees? The short answer to this question is: Hire creative people. There certainly may be some merit to this suggestion, there are other things organizations can do. For example, to enhance creativity-relevant skills, organizations can provide training in the use of creative problem-solving methods such as brainstorming. A typical activity in such a training program might be for participants to come up with as many different uses for a paper clip as they can think of in five minutes (there are actually quite a few, if you think about it!). Such forms of training will obviously not completely compensate for a lack of innate ability; however, they may help talented employees realize their creative potential.

Another way that organizations can foster creativity and innovation is through influencing task motivation. A more comprehensive discussion of motivation is contained in Chapter 8, but, in the present context, there appear to be things organizations can do to enhance task enjoyment and intrinsic motivation. One way is to attempt to place employees into jobs that they genuinely enjoy. This is not always possible, but if it can be done, it can lead to higher levels of creativity. Another way organizations can enhance task motivation is through the identification and removal of external constraints (Peters & O'Connor, 1988). Even though some individuals may be able to temporarily circumvent external constraints, employees stand a greater chance of developing the intrinsic motivation necessary to be creative if they are not there in the first place.

As stated earlier, much of the innovation literature has adopted a macro focus; that is, researchers have focused on identifying characteristics of *organizations* that facilitate or impede the adoption or diffusion of innovation in those organizations. The most comprehensive examination of organizational-level predictors of the adoption of innovation was a meta-analysis by Damanpour (1991), in which he combined data from 23 studies. Before describing the findings from this meta-analysis, it is important to note that Damanpour distinguished between **technical innovations** and **administrative innovations.** Technical innovations pertain to innovations in products, services, and production process technology. An organization adopting a new production process would be adopting a technological innovation. Administrative innovations focus on organizational structure and administrative processes. An example of this would be an organization's decision to switch to a team-based organizational structure.

The results of this study suggest that there are several organizational-level predictors of innovation. The strongest predictor, not surprisingly, was technical knowledge resources. Organizations are more likely to adopt innovations when they have employees who possess the technical expertise to understand and facilitate the implementation process. A possible explanation for this finding is: Without technical expertise, there would be no innovations for organizations to adopt in the first place. Thus, an organization needs to hire individuals with high levels of technical knowledge.

The second most powerful predictor of innovation was the organization's level of specialization. An organization that is highly specialized, such as the manufacturer of a small number of products, likely has individuals with high levels of technical expertise. Having many technical specialists simply brings more talent to bear on important problems and may facilitate the cross-fertilization of ideas, both of which ultimately lead to innovation.

A third notable predictor of innovation identified in this meta-analysis was the level of external communication in an organization. Examples of this predictor would be technical experts' presenting their research findings at conferences and sharing their ideas with individuals in other organizations. Organizations that encourage frequent communication with the external environment are likely to increase the chances of bringing in innovative ideas from the outside. External communication also provides members of organizations with an opportunity to test the validity of their ideas on those outside of the organization. For those in many technical specialties, external communication may in fact be the *only* way to obtain unbiased feedback on their ideas.

A fourth predictor of innovation was identified as **functional differentiation.** A high level of functional differentiation simply means that distinct and identifiable functional specialties exist within an organization; that is, an organization with a high degree of functional differentiation may have a research and development division with a departmental structure based on technical specialties. A high level of functional differentiation leads to innovation because groups of employees who belong to the same functional specialty are better able to elaborate on ideas and hence to develop innovations. In many cases, this is helpful because specialty-based coalitions may help to facilitate administrative changes and innovations.

The four variables described above were the strongest predictors of innovation identified in this meta-analysis. Other less powerful, though statistically significant predictors of innovation were: professionalism (.17), centralization (−.16), managerial attitudes toward change (.27), administrative intensity (.22), slack resources (.14), and internal communication (.17). These results suggest that innovation is fostered by employees who have a strong identification with their profession, a low level of centralization, positive managerial attitudes toward change, a high concentration of administrative employees, available slack resources, and a high level of communication.

Given these findings, organizations wishing to encourage innovative behavior certainly need to recruit and hire the best technical talent possible. It is also important that organizations allow talented individuals to communicate with others outside of the organization, to develop and test ideas. This can be done through a variety of mechanisms: attending professional conferences, publishing in peer-reviewed journals, and, in some cases, bringing in experts from the outside. Ironically, some organizations are hesitant to do this, for fear that external communication will compromise proprietary information. This is particularly true for organizations operating in highly competitive industries (e.g., consumer products, food). This is a valid concern, but one could argue that the potential benefits of such forms of external communication far outweigh the risks.

Influencing managerial attitudes toward change is a complicated issue, but an organization can approach it in several ways. One way is to select management employees who have positive attitudes toward change. This may be difficult if the assessment must be done during the hiring process. Another approach may be to influence management attitudes through training and development activities. Ultimately, the most powerful influence on attitudes toward change is the way managers are treated. In many organizations, employees are punished for or discouraged from trying new things. Thus, the best way to improve attitudes toward change may be to encourage managers to try new things and to take risks. By doing this, organizations can take the threat out of change. Consequently, managers themselves may be more receptive to change and innovation.

CHAPTER SUMMARY

In this chapter, we examined productive behavior, or employee activities that contribute to the goals of the organization. The most common form of productive behavior in organizations is job performance, and this has been studied extensively for a number of years. There have even been attempts to describe dimensions of performance that are common to most jobs. Such efforts to model job performance continue to evolve, and they hold great promise in helping us to understand the substantive nature of job performance.

Far more research has been aimed at determining the causes of job performance. Research accumulated over the years has led to the conclusion that three variables stand out as predictors of performance, regardless of the job: (1) general cognitive ability, (2) level of job experience, and (3) the personality trait of conscientiousness. Furthermore, these variables appear to influence performance largely through the acquisition and utilization of job knowledge.

Because of its complexity, a number of factors complicate the attempts to predict job performance. These include the measurement of job performance, the amount of instability in job performance over time, and the fact that a number of forces tend to restrict the variability in job performance within organizations. Despite all of these complicating factors, organizational researchers have still learned much, over the years, about the determinants of job performance.

Organizational Citizenship Behavior (OCB) represents the second form of productive behavior examined in the chapter. Although it can take several forms, OCB is defined as behavior that is not part of employees' formal job responsibilities. Research has shown that employees engage in OCB primarily because of positive affect and perceptions of the level of fairness with which they are treated by the organization. Only recently have researchers begun to empirically examine the assumption that OCB enhances organizational performance, to question the "in-role/extra-role" distinction that lies at the heart of OCB, and to probe the underlying motivation for the performance of OCB.

The third form of productive behavior discussed was innovation. We examined the characteristics of individuals who are likely to engage in innovative or creative behavior, and we explored macro influences on the innovation process. Drawing on individual-level studies of creativity, it appears that creativity and innovation can be explained on the basis of domain-relevant skills, creativity-relevant skills, and task motivation. Macro-level studies suggest several influences on the innovation process in organizations. The most general predictors of innovation appear to be technical knowledge resources, external communication, and managerial attitudes toward change. As with individual-level attributes, organizations have several levels of influence at the macro level in order to encourage both the development and adoption of innovation.

SUGGESTED ADDITIONAL READINGS

Podsakoff, P. M., & MacKenzie, S. B. (1997). Impact of organizational citizenship behavior on organizational performance: A review and suggestions for future research. *Human Performance, 10,* 133–151.

Ree, M. J., Earles, J. A., & Teachout, M. S. (1994). Predicting job performance: Not much more than g. *Journal of Applied Psychology, 79,* 518–524.

Sackett, P. R., Gruys, M. L., & Ellingson, J. L. (1998). Ability-personality interactions when predicting job performance. *Journal of Applied Psychology, 83,* 545–556.

Wolfe, R. A. (1994). Organizational innovation: Review, critique, and suggested research directions. *Journal of Management Studies, 31,* 405–431.

Chapter Five

Job Satisfaction and Organizational Commitment

Everyday experience suggests that humans are *evaluative* creatures; they look at much of their experience in terms of liking and disliking. Most of us, for example, have developed very clear preferences regarding the people we socialize with, the activities we engage in, and even the foods we choose to eat. In the workplace, this propensity for evaluation leads employees to develop feelings of liking or disliking toward the jobs they are performing. Most people have *some* opinion, be it positive or negative, about their job and the organization in which they work.

One could argue that another human tendency is to develop feelings of attachment or commitment. Indeed, many of us develop feelings of commitment toward other people, ideas, and even institutions. In the workplace, this tendency is manifested as employees' level of commitment toward the employing organization. Employees may be committed to their employing organizations for varying reasons, but there is no doubt that such feelings of

commitment have important consequences for both the individual employee and the organization as a whole.

In this chapter, we cover two topics that many believe lie at the core of organizational psychology: (1) job satisfaction and (2) organizational commitment. Job satisfaction essentially represents employees' feelings of positive affect toward their job or job situation. Organizational commitment, which is closely related to job satisfaction, represents employees' feelings of attachment and loyalty toward an organization. Both of these variables have been studied extensively in organizational psychology, largely because they are related to a number of outcomes that are important for both theoretical and practical reasons.

JOB SATISFACTION

Job satisfaction is, without a doubt, one of the most heavily studied topics in organizational psychology, as well as in the broader field of industrial/organizational psychology. To emphasize this point, many authors, over the years, have referred to Locke's chapter in the *Handbook of Industrial and Organizational Psychology* (1976), where he reported that studies dealing with job satisfaction numbered in the thousands. That was approximately 25 years ago, so the figure cited by Locke has grown considerably by now. Incidentally, this high level of research attention has not escaped the notice of many inside and outside the field of I/O psychology. For example, the author, can remember a then graduate student, one of the non-I/O faculty stated that I/O psychology was defined as "One hundred and one ways to ask people how they like their jobs. . . . " Although this individual was being a bit facetious (he was actually being *very* facetious), there is certainly a grain of truth in his statement.

Defining Job Satisfaction

Job satisfaction is typically defined as an employee's level of **positive affect** toward his or her job or job situation (e.g., Locke, 1976; Spector, 1997). Along with positive affect, we can add both a *cognitive* and a *behavioral* component to this definition. The addition of these two components is consistent with the way social psychologists define attitudes (Zanna & Rempel, 1988). Job satisfaction,

after all, really is an employee's attitude toward his or her job.

The cognitive aspect of job satisfaction represents an employee's *beliefs* about his or her job or job situation; that is, an employee may believe that his or her job is interesting, stimulating, dull, or demanding—to name a few options. Note that although these represent cognitive beliefs, they are not completely independent of the previously described affective component. For example, a statement or belief that "My job is interesting" is likely to be strongly related to feelings of positive affect.

The behavioral component represents an employee's behaviors or, more often, **behavioral tendencies** toward his or her job. An employee's level of job satisfaction may be revealed by the fact that he or she tries to attend work regularly, works hard, and intends to remain a member of the organization for a long period of time. Compared to the affective and cognitive components of job satisfaction, the behavioral component is often less informative because one's attitudes are not always consistent with one's behavior (Fishbein, 1979). It is possible, for example, for an employee to dislike his or her job but still remain employed there because of financial considerations.

Theoretical Approaches to Job Satisfaction

A substantial portion of the research conducted on job satisfaction over the years has been devoted to explaining what exactly determines employees' levels of job satisfaction. Understanding the development of job satisfaction is certainly of theoretical importance to organizational psychologists. It is also of practical interest to organizations as they attempt to influence employees' level of job satisfaction and, ultimately, other important outcomes.

There are three general approaches to explaining the development of job satisfaction: (1) **job characteristics,** (2) **social information processing,** and (3) **dispositional** approaches. According to the job characteristics approach, job satisfaction is determined primarily by the nature of employees' jobs or by the characteristics of the organizations in which they work. According to this view, employees cognitively evaluate their job and organization and make some determination of their relative level of satisfaction.

Over the years, several models have been proposed to explain the precise manner in which job satisfaction develops in response to job conditions [see Hulin (1991) for a summary]. There are differences among these models, but the common theme running through most of them is that job satisfaction is largely determined by employees' comparison of what the job is currently providing them and what they would like it to provide. For each facet of a job—pay, working conditions, supervision—employees make some assessment of what they are *currently receiving.* These assessments are meaningful only when they are compared with what an employee feels he or she *should be receiving* from a particular facet. These perceptions are based on a number of factors: the employees' skills, the amount of time they have put into the job, and the availability of other employment opportunities.

If employees perceive what they are currently receiving to be at or above what they feel they should be receiving, then they are satisfied. If not, then feelings of dissatisfaction are evoked. As a relatively simple example of how this works, suppose an employee's current yearly salary is $42,000. If the employee believes that he or she should be receiving an annual salary of approximately $40,000, then the salary will evoke feelings of satisfaction. On the other hand, if the employee believes,

for some reason, that he or she deserves an annual salary of $100,000, then the current salary will evoke feelings of dissatisfaction.

The notion that job satisfaction depends on an employee's comparison of what he or she is currently receiving versus what is desired is reasonable. However, according to Locke (1976), this is an oversimplification because it does not account for the fact that employees differ in the importance they place on various facets of work. For one employee, it may be extremely important to have pay and fringe benefits that meet his or her expectations; for another, it may be essential to have a job that provides an opportunity for challenging assignments.

To explain how such differences impact the development of job satisfaction, Locke (1976) proposed what has become known as **range of affect theory.** The basic premise of range of affect theory is that facets of the work are differentially weighted when employees make their assessments of job satisfaction. For example, if pay is very important to an employee, the fact that his or her current pay is close to what was expected would have a large positive impact on his or her overall assessment of job satisfaction. In contrast, if pay is relatively unimportant, the fact that expectations were met or unmet would have a relatively small impact on employee job satisfaction.

The job-characteristics approach to job satisfaction is strongly ingrained in organizational psychology (e.g., Campion & Thayer, 1985; Griffin; 1991; Hackman & Oldham, 1980). Furthermore, the weight of empirical research from a variety of areas strongly supports the idea that characteristics of the job and the job situation are robust predictors of employees' level of job satisfaction (e.g., Fried & Ferris, 1987). Thus, by the mid-1970s, the job characteristics approach had clearly become entrenched as the dominant approach to job satisfaction within organizational psychology.

The first major challenge to the job characteristics approach came in the late 1970s in the form of Social Information Processing (SIP) theory (Salancik & Pfeffer, 1977, 1978). Salancik and Pfeffer criticized the job characteristics approach to job satisfaction on two counts. First, they proposed that the job characteristics approach was inherently flawed because it was based on the assumption that job characteristics were objective components of the work environment. According to these authors, jobs are "social constructions" that exist in the minds of employees and are not objective entities. Second, they pointed out that the job characteristics approach was based on the idea of need satisfaction. The problem with this, according to Salancik and Pfeffer, is that little evidence has supported the utility of needs in the prediction of employee outcomes.

Salancik and Pfeffer (1978) proposed two primary mechanisms by which employees develop a feeling of satisfaction or dissatisfaction. One of these mechanisms states that employees look at their behavior retrospectively and form attitudes such as job satisfaction in order to make sense of it. This view is based on Bem's (1972) **Self-Perception Theory,** which is a more general social-psychological theory of attitude formation. According to this view, for example, an employee who has been working in an organization for 30 years may say to himself or herself, "I've worked here for a long time, therefore I must really like my job . . . ."

The other explanation—the one most closely linked to social information processing theory—is that employees develop attitudes such as job satisfaction through processing information from the social environment. This view is based largely on Festinger's (1954) **Social Comparison Theory,** which states that people often look to others to in-

terpret and make sense of the environment. According to this view, for example, a new employee who happened to interact with other employees who were dissatisfied with their jobs would also likely become dissatisfied. The practical implication of this, of course, is that organizations must be careful not to allow new employees to be "tainted" by dissatisfied employees during the socialization process.

Within organizational psychology and other related fields, the initial development of Social Information Processing theory had a strong impact. This was undoubtedly due to the fact that the job characteristics approach had been dominant up to that point. As evidence of this impact, a flurry of research activity designed to test this theory was conducted in the late 1970s and throughout the 1980s, (e.g., Adler, Skov & Salvemini, 1985; O'Reilly & Caldwell, 1979; H. Weiss & Shaw, 1979; White & Mitchell, 1979). Most of these investigations found that social information, usually in the form of verbal comments about task characteristics, had at least as powerful an impact on job satisfaction and perceptions of task characteristics as the objective characteristics of the task. Field tests of Social Information Processing theory, however, have been much less supportive than laboratory investigations (e.g., Jex & Spector, 1989).

Given the inability to demonstrate Social Information Processing effects outside of laboratory settings, it is tempting to conclude that this is nothing more than an interesting laboratory phenomenon (e.g., Jex & Spector, 1988). However, common sense and everyday experience suggest that social information does play a role in the formation of our attitudes. If the impact of social influence is ubiquitous, why then is the influence of social information on job satisfaction so difficult to demonstrate outside of laboratory settings? According to Hulin (1991), laboratory investigations of social information processing effects are typically more successful than field studies because they grossly simplify the social influence process. For example, in most laboratory studies, subjects are given either "positive" or "negative" social information about the task they are being asked to perform. In organizational settings, employees rarely receive such discrete levels of social information about their jobs or organizations. For example, employees may receive social information covering a variety of levels of favorability, and may at times receive conflicting information from the same source. In the future, organizational psychologists must develop more creative ways of studying the impact of social information on job satisfaction (see Comment 5.1).

The most recent approach to explaining job satisfaction is based on **internal dispositions.**

The basic premise of the dispositional approach to job satisfaction is that some employees have a tendency to be satisfied (or dissatisfied) with their jobs, regardless of the nature of the job or organization in which they work. The use of dispositions to explain behavior and attitudes is often portrayed as a very recent phenomenon, but the dispositional approach to job satisfaction can actually be traced back to the work of Weitz (1952). Weitz was interested in whether an individual's general affective tendencies would interact with job satisfaction to impact turnover. Thus, Weitz was not interested in *explaining* job satisfaction by dispositions per se, but his work was clearly suggestive of that notion.

The study that brought about renewed interest in dispositions was Staw and Ross's (1985) investigation of the stability of job

COMMENT 5.1

SOCIAL INFORMATION PROCESSING RESEARCH

WHEN GERALD SALANCIK and Jeffrey Pfeffer introduced the Social Information Processing (SIP) approach to job satisfaction in the late 1970s, they caused a great deal of controversy among job satisfaction researchers. The reason for this controversy is that Salancik and Pfeffer challenged the widely held belief that job satisfaction was due primarily to characteristics of the jobs and organizations in which employees work. One of the results of this controversy was that different "camps" developed—those who favored the job characteristics approach, and those who favored the social information processing approach.

As so often happens when different "camps" develop, each tried to provide empirical evidence supporting its position. Thus, in the late 1970s and early 1980s, a number of the laboratory studies conducted essentially pitted the job characteristics and social information processing approaches against each other. More specifically, researchers manipulated characteristics of laboratory tasks and, at the same time, provided social cues (usually by using a confederate) about the desirability of the task. The objective was then to see which of these manipulations explained the most variance in task satisfaction.

What many of these so-called "race horse design" studies showed, not surprisingly, was that the task satisfaction of laboratory subjects was impacted by *both* task design and the social cues that were provided about the task. Since that time, researchers have generally accepted the fact that both job characteristics and social information have an impact on job satisfaction. In the future, the key is to determine the situations in which each of these (along with dispositions) may exert the greatest impact.

satisfaction among a national sample of working males. This study found that there was a statistically significant correlation between job satisfaction at one point in time, and job satisfaction seven years later. Because many of those in the sample had changed jobs—and, in some cases, careers—the authors argued that the level of stability that was found suggested that job satisfaction was at least partially determined by dispositions. Subsequent research by Staw, Bell, and Clausen (1986) provided even more impressive evidence of stability by showing that job satisfaction in adolescence was predictive of job satisfaction in adulthood.

Perhaps the most interesting evidence for the dispositional approach to job satisfaction was provided in a study conducted by Arvey, Bouchard, Segal, and Abraham (1989). In this study, the authors examined job satisfaction among pairs of monozygotic twins, and estimated the extent to which job satisfaction was similar within pairs. Using a statistic called the **intraclass correlation coefficient,** these authors found that approximately 30% of the variance could be attributed to genetic factors. Although this study was subsequently criticized on methodological grounds (e.g., Cropanzano & James, 1990), it is nevertheless consistent with a dispositional approach to job satisfaction.

A major limitation of early work on the dispositional approach to job satisfaction was that it was imprecise as to exactly which dispositions are related to job satisfaction (Davis-Blake & Pfeffer, 1989). Recall that Staw and Ross (1985) demonstrated that job satisfaction was stable over time, but they did not specify which dispositional traits accounted for this consistency. More recent dispositional research has focused on documenting relations between specific traits and job satisfaction. As an example, Levin and Stokes (1989) found that **negative affectivity** was negatively associated with job satisfaction, and explained variance that was independent of job characteristics. Negative affectivity is a dispositional trait having to do with the predisposition to experience negative emotionality and distress (Watson & Clark, 1984). It has also been found that positive analogues to negative affectivity, such as **dispositional optimism** and **positive affectivity,** are positively related to job satisfaction (e.g., Jex & Spector, 1996).

One issue that dispositional researchers as yet have failed to resolve is determining the practical implications of dispositional effects. At first glance, it might be assumed that if job satisfaction is linked to specific traits, organizations would be justified in using that information to select individuals who are likely to be satisfied. This recommendation, however, ignores the fact that situational effects still exert a stronger impact on job satisfaction than dispositions (e.g., Gerhart, 1987; Levin & Stokes, 1989). Also, given the fact that, in many instances, job satisfaction is not strongly related to performance (Podsakoff & Williams, 1986), selecting employees who are most likely to be satisfied may have adverse legal ramifications. More research is needed before dispositional findings are applied in organizational settings.

In this section, we have covered three general approaches to explaining employees' levels of job satisfaction in organizations: job characteristics, social information processing, and dispositions. After examining each of these approaches, it is tempting to ask: "Which of these approaches is correct?" The weight of empirical evidence favors the job characteristics approach, yet it would be premature to conclude that this approach is "right" and the other two approaches are "wrong." As was pointed out earlier, modeling social influence with a high degree of fidelity in laboratory settings is extremely difficult (Hulin, 1991). Furthermore, in the case of dispositions, research is still in its infancy, and much still needs to be learned. Thus, the most appropriate conclusion, which is summarized in Figure 5.1, is that job satisfaction is a joint function of job characteristics, social information processing, and dispositional effects.

Measurement of Job Satisfaction

Given the importance of job satisfaction to organizational psychologists, it is crucial to have viable measures available to measure this construct. It is impossible to study something if you can't measure it. Fortunately for organizational psychologists, several viable measures of job satisfaction are available for their use. In this section, four of the most widely used measures are described. However, before describing specific measures, we briefly review the process by which measures come to be seen as valid.

Although the measures that are described in this section are viewed as **construct valid** measures of job satisfaction, it is really incorrect to say that any measure *is* or *is not* construct valid. Construct validity is a matter of degree. The measures described in this section are associated with a high degree of construct validity evidence—in most cases,

accumulated over several decades. Because of this accumulated evidence, researchers can use these measures with a great deal of confidence that they are indeed measuring employees' levels of job satisfaction.

How do we provide evidence for the construct validity of a measure? In general, there are three tests of construct validity (D. Campbell & Fiske, 1959; Nunnally & Bernstein, 1994). First, for a measure to be construct valid, it must correlate highly with other measures of the same construct. Stated differently, a measure must exhibit **convergence** with other measures of the same construct. A second test of construct validity is that a measure must be distinct from measures of other variables. Another name for this is **discrimination.** A third way that researchers typically show evidence of construct validity is through theoretically grounded predictions; that is, researchers typically develop a theoretically based **nomological network** of proposed relationships between the measure being developed and other variables of interest. To the extent that these relations are support, the construct validity of the measure is supported.

Several measures are widely considered to be construct valid measures of job satisfaction. Again, they are not construct valid in an absolute sense. Rather, so much favorable evidence has accumulated over the years that they are widely accepted measures of the job satisfaction construct. Given the large number of construct valid job satisfaction measures currently in use, a comprehensive coverage would be beyond the scope of this chapter. However, a handful of job satisfaction measures have been used widely over the years. Four of these are described in this section.

One of the first measures of job satisfaction that enjoyed widespread use was the **Faces Scale** developed by Kunin in the mid 1950s (Kunin, 1955). As can be seen in

FIGURE 5.1

Summary of the Determinants of Job Satisfaction

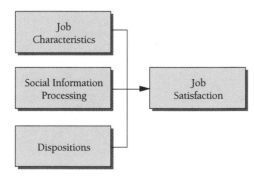

FIGURE 5.2
The Faces Scale of Job Satisfaction

Put a check under the face that expresses how you feel about your job in general, including the work, the pay, the supervision, the opportunities for promotion, and the people you work with.

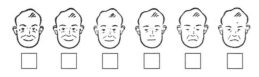

Source: T. Kunin. (1955). The construction of a new type of attitude measure. *Personnel Psychology, 8,* 65–67. Reprinted by permission.

Figure 5.2, this scale consists of a series of faces with differing emotional expressions. Respondents are asked simply to indicate which of the five faces best represents their feelings of *overall satisfaction* toward the job. The primary advantages of the Faces Scale are its simplicity and the fact that respondents need not possess a high reading level in order to complete it. This would be an excellent scale to use, for example, if a researcher were surveying a sample of employees who were known to have a very low level of education.

A potential disadvantage of the Faces Scale is that it does not provide the researcher with any information about an employee's satisfaction with different *facets* of the job. If an employee endorses one of the lower values on the Faces Scale (a "Frown"), this does not tell the researcher whether the source of this dissatisfaction is pay, supervision, or the content of the work itself. Thus, if a researcher is interested in pinpointing the source of satisfaction or dissatisfaction, the Faces Scale is of more limited value.

Another scale that has enjoyed extremely widespread use is the **Job Descriptive Index (JDI)** developed in the late 1960s by Patricia Cain Smith and her colleagues at Cornell University (P. C. Smith, Kendall, & Hulin, 1969). Sample items from the JDI are presented in Table 5.1. One thing to notice immediately is that the JDI is aptly named because the scale does require that respondents *describe* their jobs. Also, in contrast to the Faces Scale, users of the JDI obtain scores for various facets of the job and the work environment. The JDI provides scores for the individual facets of work, pay, promotion opportunities,

TABLE 5.1
Sample Items from the Job Descriptive Index (JDI)

Think of your present job. In the blank beside each word of phrase, write:

Y for "Yes" if it describes your job
N for "No" if it does not describe your job
? if you cannot decide

Work	*Pay*	*Promotions*
_____ Fascinating	_____ Barely live on income	_____ Opportunities somewhat limited
_____ Pleasant	_____ Bad	_____ Promotion on ability
_____ Can see results	_____ Well paid	_____ Regular promotions

Source: P. C. Smith, *The Job Descriptive Index, Revised.* Copyright, 1975, 1985, 1997, Bowling Green State University. Licensing for the JDI and related scales can be obtained from: Department of Psychology, Bowling Green State University, Bowling Green, Ohio 43403. Reprinted by permission.

supervision, and coworkers. Although some users of the JDI combine the facet scores to form an overall satisfaction index, this practice is not recommended by the developers of the JDI.

The primary advantage of the JDI is that a great deal of data supports its construct validity. Furthermore, research still continues in an effort to *improve* this scale (see Comment 5.2). Thus, the initial development and continued research on the JDI are exemplary. One consequence of this long-standing research effort is that considerable **normative data** on the JDI have been accumulated over the years. Thus, if a researcher or consultant were to use the JDI to measure job satisfaction among a sample of nurses, he or she would be able to compare their scores to a normative sample from the same occupation.

Norm group comparisons can often be extremely useful if top managers want to know how the satisfaction levels of their employees compare to those of employees in similar occupations or employees within the same industry.

Given the vast amount of research associated with the JDI, not many disadvantages are associated with this scale. One issue, however, has come up, over the years, in conjunction with the JDI: lack of an overall satisfaction scale. As stated earlier, in some cases, researchers merely wish to measure employees' levels of overall satisfaction, and the JDI does not allow for this. To address this issue, developers of the JDI created what is termed the **Job in General (JIG) Scale** (Ironson, Smith, Brannick, Gibson, & Paul, 1989). The JIG is modeled after the JDI except that it

COMMENT 5.2

THE LEGACY OF THE JDI

THE JOB DESCRIPTIVE Index (JDI) is undoubtedly one of the most popular and widely used measures of job satisfaction. One of the reasons for such wide use is the considerable research and development that has gone, and continues to go, into this instrument. The JDI was developed by Patricia Cain Smith and colleagues at Cornell University in the early 1960s. When Dr. Smith relocated from Cornell to Bowling Green State University in the mid-1960s, she founded the JDI research group, which consisted of both faculty and graduate students.

Over the years, the JDI research group has conducted research aimed at further refinement of the instrument, as well as development of national norms. This group continues such efforts to the present day, and has developed a number of other measures that are based on the JDI. The JDI research group at Bowling

Green has also served as a clearinghouse for research data using the JDI. As a result, the group has assembled an impressive data archive consisting of dozens of data sets, collected over a 25-year period, containing over 12,000 cases. Recently, the group has begun to make a portion of these data available, outside of Bowling Green, to researchers who are interested in job satisfaction and related areas such as occupational stress, retirement, and job design.

Overall, the JDI represents one of the most comprehensive and exemplary scale development efforts ever conducted in the field of industrial/organizational psychology. It also serves as a good example of how scale developers, and the entire field, can benefit by making data available to the research community.

Source: http://www.bgsu.edu/departments/psych/JDI.

consists of a number of adjectives and phrases about the *job in general* rather than about specific job facets. Because of its relatively recent development, considerably less is known about the psychometric properties of the JIG, as compared to the JDI. In the future, however, this is likely to be a widely used measure of overall job satisfaction within organizational psychology.

A third job satisfaction measure that has enjoyed widespread acceptance and use within organizational psychology is the **Minnesota Satisfaction Questionnaire (MSQ)**. The MSQ was developed by a team of researchers from the University of Minnesota at roughly the same time JDI was being developed (D. Weiss, Dawis, England, & Lofquist, 1967). The long form of the MSQ consists of 100 items that are designed to measure the 20 facets of work that are presented in Table 5.2. There is also a "short" form of the MSQ, consisting of 20 items. The short form, however, is not designed to provide facet satisfaction scores.

The items comprising the MSQ consist of statements about various facets of the job,

and the respondent is asked to indicate his or her level of satisfaction with each. For example, a respondent is presented with an item having to do with activity level, such as "Being able to keep busy all the time," and is asked to indicate his or her level of satisfaction with the statement. Compared to the JDI, the MSQ is more of an *affect-based* measure; that is, responses indicate liking or disliking rather than description.

Like the JDI, considerable research has gone into the development and construct validation of the MSQ. The MSQ also provides quite extensive information on employees' satisfaction with various facets of the job or work environment. As stated earlier, this type of information may be especially useful when organizations are conducting internal employee opinion surveys. For example, if it is found that satisfaction with a certain facet is much lower compared to the others, this suggests that an organization may need to makes changes in this area. The only major disadvantage of the MSQ is its length. At 100 items, the full version of the MSQ is very difficult to

TABLE 5.2
A Listing of the Facets Measured by the Minnesota Satisfaction Questionnaire (MSQ)

Activity	Ability utilization
Independence	Company policies and practices
Variety	Compensation
Social status	Advancement
Supervision (human relations)	Responsibility
Supervision (technical)	Creativity
Moral values	Working conditions
Security	Coworkers
Social service	Recognition
Authority	Achievement
Supervision (human relations)	Company policies and practices

Source: D. J. Weiss, R. V. Dawis, G. W. England, and L. H. Lofquist. (1967). *Manual for the Minnesota Satisfaction Questionnaire* (Minnesota Studies in Vocational Rehabilitation, No. 22). University of Minnesota, Minneapolis.

administer, especially if a researcher wishes to measure other variables. Even the shortened version (20 items) is still considerably longer than many other measures of satisfaction available.

A final job satisfaction measure that has not been used as extensively as the others described, but has considerable evidence supporting its psychometric properties, is the **Job Satisfaction Survey (JSS).** This scale was originally developed by Spector (1985) as an instrument to measure job satisfaction levels of Human Service employees. The JSS consists of 36 items designed to measure nine facets of the job and work environment. The facets measured by the JSS are listed in Table 5.3.

Compared to the other measures described in this section, the JSS is fairly typical; that is, the items represent statements about a person's job or job situation. Respondents are then asked to indicate the extent to which they agree with each item. Given this type of scaling, the JSS is more similar to the JDI because it is more descriptive in nature than the MSQ. Unlike the JDI, however, an overall satisfaction score can be computed for the JSS by summing the facet scores.

Compared to the JDI and MSQ, not as much supporting data are available for the JSS, but the evidence supporting the psychometric properties of this scale is still impressive

(Spector, 1997). Furthermore, Spector has assembled a fairly comprehensive normative database for the JSS; it includes a variety of job types, many different organizations, and even different countries.

Correlates of Job Satisfaction

Although job satisfaction is interesting for its own sake, researchers and managers are interested in job satisfaction primarily because of its possible relationship to other variables of interest. Given the sheer volume of research on job satisfaction that has been conducted over the years, it would be nearly impossible to discuss all of the correlates of job satisfaction. Thus, this section describes relations between job satisfaction and four types of variables that have both theoretical and practical importance: attitudinal variables, absenteeism, employee turnover, and job performance.

Attitudinal Variables. By far, job satisfaction has been found to correlate most strongly with other attitudinal variables. These variables reflect some degree of liking or disliking; that is, they are affective in nature. Examples of common attitudinal variables used in organizational research include job involvement, organizational commitment (described later in the chapter), frustration, job tension, and

<u>TABLE 5.3</u>
A Listing of the Facets Measured by the Job Satisfaction Survey (JSS)

Pay	Promotion
Supervision	Benefits
Contingent rewards	Operating procedures
Coworkers	Nature of work
Communication	

Source: P. E. Spector. (1997). *Job satisfaction: Application, assessment, causes, and consequences.* Thousand Oaks, CA: Sage. Reprinted by permission of Sage Publications, Inc.

feelings of anxiety. Notice that all of these variables, to a large degree, reflect levels of affect. For job involvement and organizational commitment, this affect is positive. The other variables reflect feelings of negative affect.

Considerable empirical research has supported the relationship between job satisfaction and attitudinal variables. For example, in a comprehensive meta-analysis of 124 published studies, Mathieu and Zajac (1990) found that the corrected correlation between organizational commitment and job satisfaction was .53. It has also been found that job satisfaction is positively related to a multitude of other measures that reflect positive affect, such as job involvement, positive mood, and organization-based self-esteem, to name a few (e.g., Spector, 1997). With respect to negative attitudes, numerous occupational stress studies have shown that job satisfaction is strongly and negatively related to variables such as frustration, anxiety, and tension (Jackson & Schuler, 1985; Jex & Spector, 1996; Spector & Jex, 1998).

While there is little debate that job satisfaction is related to other attitudinal variables, the precise mechanisms underlying many of these relations remain unclear because much of the research on job satisfaction has relied on self-report measures and cross-sectional designs. For example, a high level of job satisfaction may *cause* employees to have other positive feelings toward their jobs, and may lead to lower levels of negative feelings. Conversely, it is also possible that other positive and negative attitudes *cause* high or low levels of job satisfaction. For example, a high level of job involvement, coupled with a low level of frustration, may lead employees to feel satisfied toward their jobs. It is also possible that such relations are the result of shared common causes such as job conditions (Fried & Ferris, 1987; Jackson & Schuler, 1985; Mathieu & Zajac, 1990).

Absenteeism.   The study of absenteeism is important for both theoretical and practical reasons. From a theoretical perspective, absenteeism represents a common way in which employees may withdraw from their jobs (Hulin, 1991). From a practical perspective, absenteeism is a very costly problem to many organizations. When employees are absent, work may not get done or may be performed by less experienced employees.

It is certainly intuitively plausible that an employee's absence from work would be one reaction to a high level of job dissatisfaction. Despite its intuitive plausibility, empirical research has provided only weak support for the relation between job satisfaction and absenteeism. For example, Hackett and Guion (1985) conducted a meta-analysis of 31 studies and found the corrected correlation between job satisfaction and absenteeism to be only −.09. This suggests that job satisfaction may play some role in employee absences, but that role is marginal.

Hackett and Guion (1985) offer a number of explanations for the weak relation between job satisfaction and absenteeism. One reason is the measurement of absenteeism itself. Although at first glance absenteeism would appear to be a rather simple variable, it is actually quite complex. For example, when measuring absences, one can distinguish between *excused* and *unexcused* absences. Excused absences would be allowed for events such as illnesses and funerals. In unexcused absences, the employee simply does not show up at work. One could argue that job satisfaction would be more likely to play a role in unexcused than in excused absences.

Another reason for the weak relation between satisfaction and absenteeism is that job satisfaction represents a *general* attitude, while absenteeism is a specific form of behavior. For example, a person's attitude toward organized religion (a general attitude) would probably not be a good predictor of attendance at a worship service on one particular day. According to the **Theory of Reasoned Action** (Ajzen & Fishbein, 1977; Fishbein, 1979), a complex pathway links general attitudes (such as job satisfaction) to actual behavior. For example, variables such as subjective norms and attitudes toward the behavior in question also come into play when linking attitudes and behavior. Thus, job satisfaction may be weakly related to absenteeism because of a failure to account for unmeasured variables such as normative standards surrounding attendance, as well as attitudes toward being absent from work.

Finally, an issue that absenteeism researchers typically confront is that absenteeism is a behavior that has a low **base rate** (i.e., it doesn't occur frequently). Predicting a variable with a low base rate is problematic because most of the statistical procedures used by organizational psychologists, particularly correlation and regression analysis, are based on the assumption that variables are normally distributed. In most instances in organizational research, the variables examined are not *exactly* normally distributed, but they do not deviate so far that conventional statistical procedures are seriously biased. However, in the case of absenteeism, distributions may be so skewed that the true relationship between job satisfaction and absenteeism is seriously underestimated when commonly used statistical procedures are used.

Employee Turnover. Another correlate of job satisfaction that is of considerable interest to both researchers and managers is employee turnover. Some turnover in organizations is inevitable and, in some cases, may even be desirable. However, very high levels of turnover can be costly to organizations since they must begin the process of recruiting, selecting, and socializing a new employee. High levels of turnover may also have an adverse impact on the public image of an organization, and hence increase the difficulty of recruiting.

Give the importance of turnover, organizational psychologists have devoted considerable attention to understanding its antecedents. Although some of the work on turnover has been aimed at simply documenting its relation with job satisfaction, much more has been aimed at modeling the role job satisfaction plays in employees' turnover decisions. One of the earliest, and ultimately most influential, models of the turnover process was developed by Mobley (1977). As can be seen in Figure 5.3, this model proposes that employees' decisions to leave a job are complex and consist of multiple stages. In the first stage, an employee evaluates his or her existing job and, depending on this evaluation, experiences either satisfaction or dissatisfaction. After this evaluation, if the employee is satisfied, the process is unlikely to go further. If the employee is dissatisfied, however, this may lead to thoughts of quitting his or her job. Notice, however, that the model allows for the possibility that employees may express job dissatisfaction through other forms of withdrawal, or by simply putting forth less effort.

Once a dissatisfied employee begins to think about quitting his or her job, the next step in the model is some cognitive evaluation of whether a search will be successful, and the various costs associated with quitting the present job. Even if a person is extremely dissatisfied with a job, leaving entails certain costs—moving to a new location and perhaps giving up benefits accrued in the present job. If an employee decides either that a search would be unsuccessful, or that the cost of leaving the job is too high, the process will end and the employee may simply find ways to adapt to the present situation.

On the other hand, if the employee believes that a search will be successful, and the

FIGURE 5.3
Mobley's Model of the Turnover Process

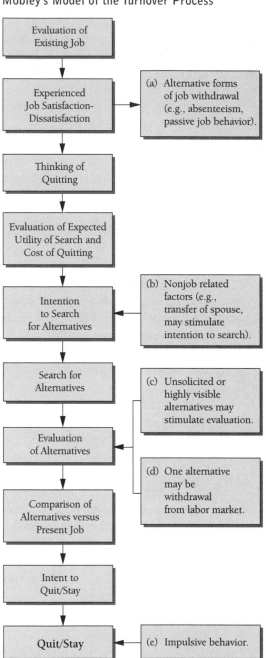

Source: W. H. Mobley. (1977). Intermediate linkages in the relationship between job satisfaction and employee turnover. *Journal of Applied Psychology, 62,* 237–240. Copyright © 1977 by the American Psychological Association. Reprinted with permission.

costs associated with leaving are not prohibitive, he or she will then progress to the next stage in the model: an intention to search for alternatives. This is the point at which a person begins planning the job search, and, in all likelihood, an intention to search will translate into actual search behavior. The employee may scan newspaper ads, seek the services of an employment agency, or attend job fairs, hoping to find alternative employment opportunities. The model allows for the possibility that the intention to search will be motivated by factors other than job dissatisfaction (e.g., desire to live in another location).

After searching for alternatives, a person may find that none is available. This outcome obviously depends on a person's level of qualifications and the availability of jobs in his or her profession. If a person finds no alternatives, he or she may have no choice but to adapt to the present job. If alternatives are available, the next step is to evaluate them. It is also possible that an individual may be presented with employment alternatives suggested in unsolicited offers.

In evaluating different employment alternatives, the model proposes two standards of evaluation. Alternatives are evaluated against the employee's internal standards for judging the acceptability of jobs, as well as his or her present job. Given these two evaluative standards, it is possible that alternatives may exceed a person's internal standards, yet still not measure up to his or her present job. If this is the case, the job search may remind the employee that the "Grass is not necessarily greener on the other side," and the present job may be viewed in a more favorable light. Another possibility, which is acknowledged in the model, is that the individual may withdraw from the labor market completely. For example, a dissatisfied employee may decide to become a stay-at-home parent.

The job search may also result in one or more alternative employment offers that are perceived to be more attractive than the present job. According to the model, if this is the case, the person forms *intentions* regarding whether to quit the present job. Why don't people automatically quit their present job if a better alternative is found? Based on the previously discussed Theory of Reasoned Action, a person may decline a more attractive job offer simply because he or she does not have a positive attitude toward the act of changing jobs. Normative influences may come into play as well. For example, a person may come from a family in which both parents worked for the same organization during their entire careers, and thus may experience subtle (or not so subtle) normative pressure to remain employed with the same organization and not be a "job hopper."

Another reason that intentions may not translate into actual behavior is that the *act* of quitting one's job is much different from the *idea* of quitting. In Figure 5.3, Mobley's (1977) model proposes that, relatively early in the process, an employee should evaluate the costs associated with quitting. It is important to note, however, that early in the process, "quitting" is an abstract concept and not a concrete choice that a person is faced with. Thus, although the model is not very explicit, some reevaluation of the costs of quitting one's job is likely to take place between the intention to quit and the actual quitting. A person may get "cold feet" when faced with a concrete job offer, and may decide that the costs associated with leaving the present job for a better one are not worth it after all. As a final note, the model allows for the possibility that the decision to quit may be made impulsively. Perhaps some readers have had the experience of making an "on-the-spot" decision to quit a job.

Empirical research over the years has supported Mobley's model in two ways. First, studies that have tested the original model, or variants of it, have generally provided support (e.g., Hom, Caranikas-Walker, Prussia, & Griffeth, 1992; Michaels & Spector, 1982; Mobley, Griffeth, Hand, & Meglino, 1979). The model has been supported more indirectly through studies examining the correlation between job satisfaction and turnover. Carsten and Spector (1987) conducted a meta-analysis of 42 studies and found that the corrected correlation between job satisfaction and turnover was −.24. The corrected correlation between behavioral intentions and actual turnover was .32. One would expect intentions to be more strongly correlated with turnover than with job satisfaction because intent is a more proximal cause of job satisfaction (see Figure 5.3).

These authors also examined, albeit indirectly, whether the availability of employment alternatives would impact the relationship between job satisfaction and turnover. Specifically, the authors obtained data on the levels of unemployment that existed in the localities at the time when data for each of the studies were collected. As expected, the corrected satisfaction–turnover andintentions–turnover correlations were both stronger during periods of low (as opposed to high) unemployment. This is presumably due to the fact that alternative employment opportunities are much more plentiful when unemployment is low.

These findings are consistent with the role that job satisfaction is proposed to play in the turnover process. In fact, when one considers that job satisfaction is actually a very distal cause of turnover, and turnover is a low base rate event, an overall corrected correlation of −.24 between these two variables is actually quite remarkable. At a more conceptual level, these findings suggest that the desire to find more satisfying work is often a driving force behind job changes. Therefore, organizations wishing to keep turnover to manageable levels cannot ignore job and organizational conditions that impact job satisfaction.

Job Performance. The third correlate of job satisfaction is job performance. Of the numerous variables that researchers have correlated with job satisfaction over the years, job performance has perhaps the longest history. In fact, the attempt to link job satisfaction with job performance can actually be traced back as far as the Hawthorne Studies. Based on their findings, the Hawthorne researchers came to the relatively naïve conclusion that one way to make employees more productive was to make them more satisfied. Stated differently, "A happy worker is a productive worker." This notion that job satisfaction impacted job performance became widely accepted and helped to usher in what was described in Chapter 1 as the "Human Relations" movement within organizational psychology.

Toward the end of the 1950s and in the early 1960s, another trend in organizational psychology—reliance on cognitive processing models—would eventually change the prevailing views on the relationship between job satisfaction and job performance. Vroom's (1964) Expectancy Theory, for example, proposed that employees would put forth more effort if they believed that effort would translate into high levels of performance, and higher performance would lead to valued outcomes. If performance is viewed from this perspective, there is no reason to assume that job satisfaction should play a causal role in determining job performance. On the other hand, if high levels of job performance ultimately lead to desirable outcomes, employees should be most satisfied with their jobs when they perform well and are rewarded for it. If viewed from this perspective, one would conclude that job performance *causes* job satisfaction. Thus, rather than trying to make employees happy, organizations would be

much better off helping employees develop the skills they need to perform well, and linking rewards to performance.

Unfortunately, much of the early debate surrounding the relation between job satisfaction and job performance was based on opinion instead of empirical data. That basis began to change in the 1970s and 1980s, when there were more empirical investigations of the relation between job satisfaction and job performance. In the mid-1980s, many of these empirical studies were summarized in comprehensive meta-analyses by Iaffaldano and Muchinsky (1985) and, later, by Podsakoff and Williams (1986). In the Iaffaldano and Muchinsky investigation, the corrected correlation between job satisfaction and job performance was found to be .17. Podsakoff and Williams (1986) obtained very similar results.

Podsakoff and Williams (1986) also found that the satisfaction–performance relation was moderated by the degree to which rewards were linked to performance. In studies where rewards were closely tied to performance, the corrected correlation between job satisfaction and performance was .27. In contrast, in studies where rewards were not closely tied to performance, the corrected correlation was weaker ($r = .17$). This moderator effect is important because it suggests that when job satisfaction and performance are related, the most plausible causal sequence is from *performance to job satisfaction,* rather than the reverse. More specifically, if rewards are tied closely to performance, job satisfaction may be a natural byproduct of receiving rewards.

Based on the accumulated empirical research, it is tempting to conclude that the job satisfaction–job performance relationship is relatively trivial. However, according to Ostroff (1992), this conclusion may be erroneous because the vast majority of studies examining the relationship between job satisfaction and job performance have been conducted at the *individual* level of analysis. Ostroff points out that although employees who are highly satisfied with their jobs may not necessarily perform better than employees who are more dissatisfied, this relation may be stronger at the organizational level of analysis; that is, *organizations* in which employees are highly satisfied will tend to perform better than *organizations* in which employees are highly dissatisfied. When employees are highly satisfied, they may not be more productive as individuals, but may nevertheless engage in behaviors that facilitate the effectiveness of the organization as a whole.

Ostroff (1992) tested this hypothesis by examining relations between job satisfaction and several performance indexes in a national sample of 298 junior and senior high schools. As can be seen in Table 5.4, aggregate-level job satisfaction was significantly related to every performance indicator, and the magnitude ranged from −.11 to .44. Many of these correlations are considerably higher than those found in individual-level studies (Iaffaldano & Muchinsky, 1985; Podsakoff & Williams, 1986). Interestingly, Ostroff argued that, at the organizational level, satisfaction likely *causes* higher levels of performance, which is counter to individual-level studies (Podsakoff & Williams, 1986). Unfortunately, since this study was cross-sectional, the issue could not be addressed.

Job Satisfaction: A Cross-Cultural Perspective

Like many issues in organizational psychology, the study of job satisfaction has taken place primarily in the United States and Western European countries. This is obviously a "blind spot" in our knowledge because work is a universal activity, and, presumably, so is the development of positive or negative feelings toward work. In this section, we briefly examine recent evidence on the possibility of cross-cultural differences in levels of job

TABLE 5.4
Correlations between Organization-Level Job Satisfaction and Organization-Level Performance Measures

Performance Measure	Correlation
Reading achievement	.30
Math achievement	.31
Social science achievement	.24
Percentage of students passing courses	.20
Administrative performance	.24
Percentage of students dropping out	−.28
Percentage of students attending	.24
Percentage of students with discipline problems	−.27
Vandalism costs (in dollars)	−.11
Student satisfaction with teachers	.24
Overall student satisfaction	.44

Note: All correlations are statistically significant beyond the .05 level.
Source: C. Ostroff. (1992). The relationship between satisfaction, attitudes, and performance: An organization-level analysis. *Journal of Applied Psychology, 77,* 963–974. Copyright © 1992 by the American Psychological Association. Adapted with permission.

satisfaction, and potential reasons for these differences.

Given the dearth of cross-cultural research in general, relatively few studies have examined cross-cultural differences in job satisfaction. For example, Griffeth and Hom (1987) found that Latin American managers were more satisfied than European managers. In a comparison of Dominican and American employees working for the same company, Marion-Landis (1993) found that the Dominicans were more satisfied than their American counterparts. Several studies have also shown that Japanese employees tend to be less satisfied than American employees (e.g., P. B. Smith & Misumi, 1989).

Direct cross-national comparisons in job satisfaction are interesting, but they provide very little insight into why those differences exist. To understand the basis of such differences, it is useful to frame the issue in terms of the three approaches to job satisfaction discussed at the beginning of this chapter. When viewed from the job characteristics perspective, there are several plausible explanations for cross-cultural differences in job satisfaction. For example, there is considerable evidence of cross-cultural differences in **values.** Hofstede (1984) investigated differences in values—including **individualism/collective, masculinity, power distance,** and **uncertainty avoidance**—in 40 different countries. The individualism/collectivism dimension reflects the extent to which people are concerned with their own interests and needs, rather than those of other people or of members of important collective units (e.g., family, work group, and so on). Masculinity reflects the degree to which there is a focus on achievement and performance as opposed to the well being and satisfaction of others. Power distance reflects the degree to which those with high levels of authority and status are distinct from those with lower levels.

Finally, uncertainty avoidance reflects the extent to which people are comfortable working in uncertain environments.

Hofstede's (1984) findings have shown rather clearly the existence of cross-national differences on each of these four values. For example, the United States and countries in Western Europe tend to place a very high value on individualism, while Hispanic and Oriental countries tend to place a relatively high value on collectivism. With respect to masculinity, it has been found that Scandinavian countries tend to place a relatively high value on this dimension, compared to other countries. Power distance tends to have very high value in Hispanic countries, but the opposite is true in countries such as Australia and Israel. Uncertainty avoidance was found to be highest in countries such as Greece and Portugal, and lowest in Singapore and Denmark.

The primary implication of these cross-national differences in value preferences is that cross-cultural differences in job satisfaction may be due to differences in what employees *desire* from their jobs. Recall from the beginning of this chapter that job satisfaction has been purported to result from a comparison between what people perceive their jobs provide and what they desire. Thus, when viewed from this perspective, cultural differences can be at least partially attributed to the fact that employees in different cultures seek different things from their jobs, and may place different levels of importance on different job facets.

While there is undoubtedly some merit to this argument, cross-cultural differences in job satisfaction may also be impacted by cross-national differences in actual job conditions. Because of economic and political differences, employees in different countries may differ greatly in the quality of their on-the-job experiences. In the former Soviet Union, for example, it is unlikely that employees in state-run organizations had much decision-making authority over many aspects of their jobs. In contrast, employees in countries that embrace free-market economics typically have greater participation in decision making and are more strongly encouraged to engage in proactive behaviors.

Cross-cultural differences can also be viewed through the lens of the social information-processing approach to job satisfaction. For example, it is possible that in addition to value differences, cross-cultural differences may exist in the degree to which social influence processes are salient to employees. One might speculate that in an individualistic society such as the United States, social information may have a relatively minimal impact, and job satisfaction may be only weakly related to prevailing cultural values. In contrast, in a more collectivist society such as Japan, social influence processes may be much more important.

Compared to the job characteristics and social information processing approaches, the dispositional approach to job satisfaction would appear to be less helpful in explaining cross-cultural differences in job satisfaction. However, it is possible that the prevalence of certain dispositional traits that impact job satisfaction may differ across cultures. As yet, little empirical work in cross-cultural psychology has addressed this issue.

ORGANIZATIONAL COMMITMENT

In addition to feelings of satisfaction or dissatisfaction, employees may develop feelings of *attachment* or *commitment* toward the organization in which they are employed. As with satisfaction or dissatisfaction, a strong case can be made that the tendency to develop attachment or commitment ties extends far beyond the workplace. For example, people

commit to each other through marriage and other forms of kinship. Many people also faithfully commit themselves to activities such as exercising, institutions such as churches, and political ideologies such as democracy. Given these vast numbers of commitments, it is not surprising that employees also develop feelings of commitment and attachment toward the organizations in which they work.

Defining Organizational Commitment

At a very general level, **organizational commitment** can be thought of as the extent to which employees are dedicated to their employing organization and are willing to work on its behalf, and the likelihood that they will maintain membership. Note that, in this general definition, one can distinguish between what has been termed *affective* commitment and what has been described as *behavioral* commitment (Mowday, Porter, & Steers, 1982). Commitment represents both the feelings and the behavioral tendencies that employees have toward the organization.

Meyer and Allen (1991) further refined the definition of organizational commitment by pointing out that there can be multiple *bases* of commitment—that is, employees may be committed for different reasons, and these reasons constitute unique forms of commitment. They proposed a three-component model of commitment consisting of **affective, continuance,** and **normative** commitment. Affective commitment reflects the extent to which employees identify with the organization and feel a genuine sense of loyalty toward it. In contrast, continuance commitment is based on employees' perceptions of the relative investments they have made in the organization, and the relative costs associated with seeking membership in another organization. Normative commitment is based on an employee's feeling of obligation to the organization, wherein remaining a member is the morally right thing to do.

In addition to having multiple bases, employee commitment may be focused at different levels within the organization and may even be directed to outside groups. For example, an employee may feel a sense of commitment toward his or her organization as a whole, the primary work group to which he or she belongs, and perhaps the leader of this group. Many employees in organizations also feel a sense of commitment toward the profession to which they belong. For example, physicians who work for Health Maintenance Organizations (HMOs) are likely to have some level of commitment to their employing organization, but are committed to the medical profession as well.

Given that commitment has multiple bases and foci, this suggests that there are a number of distinct forms of commitment. Meyer and Allen (1997) illustrate this in a matrix in which the three bases of commitment (affective, continuance, and normative) are crossed with six distinct foci. As can be seen in Figure 5.4, an employee may have feelings of affective, continuance, or normative commitment toward any number of foci within the organizational

environment. This reflects the fact that, for employees in most organizations, commitment is a multidimensional, complex construct. Thus, if one were to come up to an employee and ask, "How committed are you?" the employee would most likely have a multipart answer.

Development of Organizational Commitment

What determines employees' level of commitment toward their organization? Given the complexity of the organizational commitment construct, this is not an easy question to answer. Most researchers have approached this issue by examining the development of each of the three bases of commitment proposed by Meyer and Allen (1991). If one considers affective commitment, a logical supposition might be that employees will tend to develop this type of commitment if they perceive that the organization is being supportive and/or treating them in a fair manner (Meyer & Allen, 1991). In fact, research has shown that affective commitment is positively related to variables such as perceived organizational support (POS) and procedural justice. POS simply represents the extent to which the

FIGURE 5.4
The Relationship between Bases and Foci of Commitment

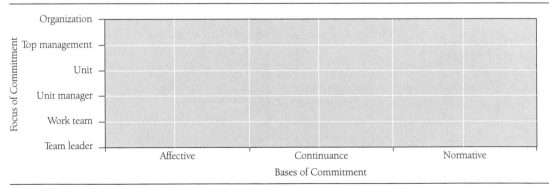

Source: J. P. Meyer and N. J. Allen. (1997). *Commitment in the workplace: Theory, research, and application.* Thousand Oaks, CA: Sage. Reprinted by permission of Sage Publications, Inc.

organization is seen as helpful to the employee; in effect, it is "on the employee's side." Recall from the previous chapter that procedural justice reflects the fairness of the procedures organizations use in dealing with employees.

Another factor that may impact the development of affective commitment is whether the organization is seen as a source of rewarding outcomes. Research has shown, for example, that a positive relationship exists between affective commitment and variables such as job scope, participative decision making, job autonomy, and perceived competence (Meyer & Allen, 1997). One way to interpret such findings is based on a belief that employees develop feelings of affective commitment if they see the organization as a place where they feel they are important and competent.

Another way some researchers have sought to explain affective commitment is through behavioral commitment and retrospective sense making. Put differently, one might say that employees develop feelings of affective commitment as a retrospective mechanism to justify their tenure in the organization and the level of effort they have expended on its behalf. This explanation of commitment is consistent with Salancik and Pfeffer's (1978) Social Information Processing theory, described earlier in the chapter. In general, retrospective explanations of affective commitment have met with very limited support. However, as Meyer and Allen (1997) point out, this mechanism is quite subtle and thus may be very difficult to test empirically.

Compared to affective commitment, explaining the development of continuance commitment is much more straightforward. Most explanations of continuance commitment rely on H. Becker's (1960) notion of "side bets" as a mechanism committing one to a course of action. If, for example, a person has wagered a bet that he or she would lose 20 pounds over the next six months, this would commit the person to that course of action. When this concept is applied to the workplace, we can see very clearly that, over time, employees accumulate a number of "side bets" that commit them to their current employer. For example, the accrual of seniority means that employees may be entitled to special benefits or privileges. If the employee were to leave and work for another employer, such benefits would be forfeited. Also, many employees develop numerous social relationships with their coworkers, and these bonds help to facilitate feelings of belonging and comfort. These feelings would be forfeited in a switch to another employer.

Another proposed determinant of continuance commitment is the extent to which employees *perceive* other viable alternatives to the present employer. The word *perceive* is italicized because it really doesn't matter whether *actual* alternatives exist; the important thing is an employee's perceptions. Perceptions of alternatives may be impacted by things in the environment, such as the unemployment rate, but may also be affected by other, more subjective factors. For example, an employee's perception of his or her overall competence, level of training, and mobility will all enter into the perception of alternatives. As one might guess, continuance commitment will tend to be higher among employees who perceive few alternatives to the present employer.

Compared to affective and continuance forms of commitment, much less is known about the development of normative commitment. According to Meyer and Allen (1997), personal characteristics and the nature of an employee's transactions with the organization may impact the development of normative commitment. At a personal level, individuals may differ in terms of whether their early socialization emphasized the development of strong loyalty and a sense of moral obligation to their employer. They also point out that the organization may attempt to instill in employees, during the initial socialization process, a strong sense of moral obligation to the organization.

Perhaps the most powerful determinant of normative commitment is ultimately the manner in which an organization treats its employees. When employees enter an organization, an implicit agreement, or a **psychological contract,** exists between them and the organization (e.g., Schein, 1980). A psychological contract essentially represents an employee's perceptions of what he or she feels is reasonable treatment as a member of the organization. One would assume that normative commitment is highest when an employee perceives the organization as honoring its end of the psychological contract. More research, however, is needed before more conclusions can be drawn about the development of this form of commitment.

Measurement of Organizational Commitment

As with most subjective attitudinal variables, organizational commitment is measured with self-report scales. Historically, the first organizational commitment scale to gain widespread use was the Organizational Commitment Questionnaire (OCQ; Mowday, Steers, & Porter, 1979). The original OCQ primarily reflected what Meyer and Allen (1991) described as affective commitment and, to a lesser extent, normative commitment. The original OCQ also contained one item measuring an employee's turnover intentions. The inclusion of this item prompted criticism, particularly when the OCQ was used to predict turnover. Most researchers who have used the OCQ in recent years have eliminated the turnover intent item. In many cases,

researchers have also used shorter versions of the original measure.

In general, there is evidence that the OCQ has desirable psychometric properties. Mathieu and Zajac (1990), in their meta-analysis of 124 organizational commitment studies, reported that the mean internal consistency reliabilities for various forms of the OCQ were all over .80. In this same study, the OCQ was found to correlate appropriately with conceptually related variables, thus providing some support for its construct validity. The major limitation of the OCQ is that it measures primarily the affective component of organizational commitment, and thus provides very little information on the continuance and normative components. This is an important limitation because these different forms of commitment are associated with different outcomes.

More recently, Allen and Meyer (1990) developed an organizational commitment measure that contains three subscales that correspond to the affective, continuance, and normative components of commitment. An example of an affective commitment is: "This organization has a great deal of personal meaning to me." An example of a continuance commitment item is: "It would be too costly for me to leave my organization in the near future." Finally, an example of a normative commitment item is: "I would feel guilty if I left my organization now."

Because the Allen and Meyer (1990) scale has been developed more recently than the OCQ, comparatively less evidence has accumulated to support both its reliability and validity. However, the evidence accumulated to date has been very encouraging. For example, Meyer and Allen (1997) reported that the median internal consistency reliabilities for the affective, continuance, and normative commitment scales are .85, .79, and .73, respectively. They also report that all three scales have exhibited reasonably high levels of temporal stability.

In terms of construct validity, there is also impressive supporting evidence. For example, several studies have supported the three-factor structure of the scale (summarized in Meyer & Allen, 1997). There is also evidence that these forms of commitment are empirically distinguishable from related constructs such as job satisfaction, values, and occupational commitment. The construct validity of Meyer and Allen's measure has also been supported by the pattern of its relationships with other variables. (These will be described in more detail in the next section.) The important point is that the three subscales corresponding to the three different forms of commitment appear to correlate with other variables in an expected manner.

Other than the OCQ and the Allen and Meyer (1990) scales, a handful of other measures of organizational commitment have surfaced, but none has been used extensively. One recent measure worth noting was developed by T. Becker (1992). In this study, organizational commitment was measured in terms of multiple bases (as per Meyer and Allen) *and* multiple foci. Few other studies have done this, so there is little empirical evidence on the viability of this approach to measuring commitment. However, in the future, it may be useful to measure commitment in this fashion if, indeed, different outcomes are associated with different combinations of bases and foci of commitment.

Correlates of Organizational Commitment

As with job satisfaction, researchers and managers are interested in organizational commitment largely because of its relationship with other variables. In this section, we briefly review evidence on the relationship between organizational commitment and attitudinal variables, absenteeism, turnover, and performance.

Attitudinal Variables. Given Meyer and Allen's (1991) distinction among affective, continuance, and normative commitment, the correlates of each of these forms of commitment are examined separately. Affective commitment has been shown to be strongly related to other work-related attitudes. As mentioned earlier in the chapter, Mathieu and Zajac (1990) found that the mean corrected correlation between affective organizational commitment and job satisfaction was .53. Other consistent attitudinal correlates of affective commitment found in this meta-analysis included job involvement (.36), occupational commitment (.27), union commitment (.24), and stress (−.29).

Compared to affective commitment, less empirical work has examined the relation between attitudinal correlates of either continuance or normative commitment (Meyer & Allen, 1997). Based on the little evidence that is available, however, it appears that continuance commitment is correlated with many of the same variables as affective commitment, yet there are some important differences. Mathieu and Zajac (1990), for example, found that affective commitment was more strongly related to job satisfaction and job involvement than was continuance commitment. Given the dearth of research on normative commitment, very little can be concluded about its relation with other attitudinal variables.

Absenteeism. Compared to attitudinal correlates, much less evidence exists on the relation between each form of organization commitment and absenteeism. Mathieu and Zajac (1990) found that the corrected correlation between affective commitment and attendance was .12 and the correlation with lateness was −.11. These findings suggest that those with high levels of affective commitment tend to exhibit lower levels of absenteeism, but this trend is quite weak. Recall from the previous section that the correlation between absenteeism and job satisfaction is of a similar magnitude (e.g., Hackett & Guion, 1985). As with job satisfaction, this weak relationship may be due to variation in the measurement of absenteeism, as well as more general issues in attitude–behavior consistency. Also, from a conceptual point of view, a high level of affective commitment indicates a *desire* to contribute to an organization—a desire that may at times be negated by situational contingencies.

Again, compared to affective commitment, little evidence exists on the relations between either continuance or normative commitment and absenteeism. Studies that have been done, however, have shown neither of these forms of commitment to be related to absenteeism (Meyer & Allen, 1997). From a conceptual point of view, these findings are somewhat surprising. For example, if an employee's commitment is of the continuance variety, it in his or her best interest to attend work on a regular basis; failure to do so could jeopardize his or her membership in the organization. This argument of course is based on the assumption that organizational policy is such that frequent absenteeism would be met with negative consequences. With respect to normative commitment, frequent absenteeism would seem to be inconsistent with commitment based on a strong moral obligation toward one's employing organization. Given the little research that is available, both of these possibilities await examination in future research.

Employee Turnover. With the nature of organizational commitment, considerably more evidence exists on the relation among all three forms of commitment and turnover, compared to other outcomes. As might be expected, research has generally shown a negative relation among all three forms of commitment and turnover (Allen & Meyer, 1996; Mathieu & Zajac, 1990). The fact that all forms of commitment are negatively associated with turnover would appear to be a positive thing for organizations. However, this may not be true in some cases. For example, consider an employee who remains in an organization primarily because he or she has a high level of continuance commitment. Is this necessarily good for the organization, or even for the employee? Such an individual may adopt an attitude of doing the bare minimum and may be very unhappy in his or her job. The same may be true for an employee who remains in an organization primarily out of a sense of moral obligation (e.g., normative commitment).

Job Performance. Much research over the years has investigated the relation between organizational commitment and job performance. In general, affective commitment has been shown to be positively related to job performance, although the magnitude of this relation is not strong (Mathieu & Zajac, 1990; Meyer & Allen, 1997). Determining the mechanism(s) behind these relations is difficult, however, because these studies have used a wide variety of performance criterion measures. For example, some have used supervisors' ratings of overall performance (e.g., Konovsky & Cropanzano, 1991), others have used objective indexes such as cost control (e.g., Shim & Steers, 1994), and others have utilized self-ratings of performance (e.g., Baugh & Roberts, 1994). One commonality among these studies, however, is that the relation between affective commitment and performance is mediated by employees' effort. Employees who possess high levels of affective commitment *tend to work harder and exert more effort than employees who possess lower levels of affective commitment.* In some cases, this higher level of effort will translate into higher levels of performance, although this is not always the case (J. Campbell, 1990, 1994).

This link between affective commitment and effort suggests that commitment is positively related to performance when employees possess adequate ability, when performance is primarily determined by motivation, and when employees have some level of control over performance. This explains why researchers have generally found that affective commitment predicts organizational citizenship behavior (OCB) better than in-role performance (Meyer & Allen, 1997; Organ & Ryan, 1995). Recall from the previous chapter that because OCB is largely motivationally based, employees have greater control over it than they do over in-role performance.

Compared to affective organizational commitment, considerably less research has examined the performance-related implications of either continuance or normative commitment. Meyer and Allen (1997) point out, however, that most of the available empirical research has shown that neither of these forms of commitment is strongly related to either in-role performance or OCB. Furthermore, it is difficult to come up with a conceptual justification for why they would be related to performance. For example, there is no reason why continuance commitment would prompt an employee to exert high levels of effort or go appreciably beyond his or her required job duties.

It is somewhat more plausible that high levels of normative commitment would engender high levels of effort toward organizational goals. One can also make an equally plausible counter argument that commitment based on employees' feelings of obligation will not necessarily lead to greater levels of

effort on behalf of the organization. To the contrary, one can even imagine that an employee who feels compelled to remain in an organization out of a sense of obligation may even grow to resent that organization and perhaps be compelled to engage in counterproductive behaviors (see Chapter 6).

Practical Applications of Commitment Research

One way to view the applications of organizational commitment research is to examine various ways in which organizations may engender high levels of commitment among their employees. Meyer and Allen (1997) describe several different human resources policies that may impact employee commitment. For example, it has long been recommended that during the selection and recruitment processes, organizations provide realistic information to potential employees (Wanous, 1973). Retention has typically been cited as the rationale for using realistic job previews, but Meyer and Allen point out that realistic job previews may also engender employee commitment. Employees who are provided with candid information will presumably feel that the organization has "laid its cards on the table," and the employees are able to make informed choices about whether to join the organization. Such feelings of free choice may enhance employees' feelings of commitment to the organization.

Providing realistic job previews may also facilitate commitment for more symbolic reasons. If an organization is honest, even about the undesirable aspects of a job, recruits have a signal that the organization is going to treat them in a fair and honest manner in the future. When these recruits become employees, they will likely "reciprocate" such honesty and fairness with high levels of commitment. Conversely, if an employee feels that he or she was provided with an overly positive picture of the job prior to being hired, this signals a lack of fairness and honesty in the organization.

After employees enter an organization, their initial socialization and training experiences may have a strong impact on their ultimate level of commitment. Recall from Chapter 3 that organizations use a multitude of strategies to socialize new employees (Van Maanen & Schein, 1979), and that new employees may use a variety of strategies to obtain information (Miller & Jablin, 1991). Meyer and Allen (1997) point out that an *investiture* approach to socialization is likely to lead to greater feelings of organizational commitment than a *divestiture* approach. Recall that when an investiture approach is used, the organization does not require the newcomer to completely give up his or her old self. Rather, the organization allows the newcomer to be a full-fledged member while still maintaining some individuality. What message does this convey? The newcomer receives a message of affirmation and a willingness, on the part of the organization, to respect the rights of employees. Employees will often respond to this message with greater feelings of commitment toward the organization.

A divestiture approach to socialization, in contrast, requires the newcomer to essentially give up many aspects of his or her prior identity and "fall in line" in order to assume full membership in the organization. This form of socialization may suggest to the newcomer that the organization is "elite," and that achieving membership should be viewed as a great privilege. On the other hand, it may also convey an unhealthy mistrust of outsiders and a condescending view of newcomers. Given these mixed messages, it would seem possible that divestiture socialization could lead to either very high or very low levels of commitment.

In most recent empirical research on the socialization process (e.g., Chao, O'Leary-Kelly, Wolf, Klein, & Gardner, 1994; Ostroff & Kozlowski, 1992), a consistent finding is that the greatest initial concern of newcomers is to acquire task-related information. Before newcomers learn about things such as the political climate of the organization, they want to be able to carry out their job-related tasks in a competent manner. Given these initial concerns, organizations must make sure that new employees receive the training they need in order to do their jobs. Such training may require a formal training program or more informal on-the-job coaching activities.

Training may enhance organizational commitment because it conveys to newcomers that the organization is supportive and has a vested interest in their success. Another reason is: If training ultimately facilitates an employee's success, this will likely result in positive outcomes for the employee (e.g., pay increases, promotions). If employees recognize that the training they have received has contributed to their success, they are likely to be grateful to the organization. Such feelings of gratitude may very well enhance the employee's affective or normative commitment.

Training may also contribute to enhanced feelings of continuance commitment. If an employee received training that was highly specific to a particular organization, this would greatly enhance the cost associated with leaving the organization. As an example, much of the training that military personnel receive is so highly specialized that it does not transfer well to civilian jobs. For some individuals, this may enhance feelings of continuance commitment and ultimately contribute to a decision to pursue a long-term military career.

Given this apparent tradeoff between providing general versus highly specific training, which course of action should an organization choose? Training that is highly transferable will likely engender feelings of affective commitment toward the organization. A potential drawback, however, is that such training often *does* enhance employees' marketability. Highly specific training will enhance employees' job performance, and thus may have the potential to enhance feelings of affective or normative commitment. This form of training may also heighten feelings of continuance commitment, and thus enhance employee retention. However, organizations probably do not want employees to remain in the organization primarily because of feelings of continuance commitment. Ultimately, it is probably best for organizations to have some balance between general and organization-specific training programs.

The development of internal promotion policies is another area in which organizations can make tangible use of organizational commitment research. As Meyer and Allen (1997) point out, promoting from within an organization facilitates higher levels of commitment among employees. If an organization does pursue an internal promotion policy, some important issues must be addressed. Perhaps most important, any internal promotion initiatives should be publicly made available to all employees. If employees see internal promotion practices as being unfair and secretive, the unintended effect may be a reduction of employees' commitment. It also makes little sense to make promotional opportunities available to employees if the organization fails to help them acquire the skills necessary to be competitors for such opportunities. As was discussed above, skill acquisition can certainly be facilitated by formal training programs. However, to provide employees with meaningful developmental experiences, organizations may utilize other methods, such as lateral transfers or job rotation.

Organizations often utilize organizational commitment research in the area of compensation and benefits. Although there is some degree of variation, most organizations tie their forms of compensation to employee tenure. It is quite common, for example, for organizations to require that employees accrue some minimum years of service before they can be vested in pension programs and receive matching contributions in 401(k) savings plans. Such requirements may enhance commitment, but it is primarily of the continuance variety. Thus, having such requirements may induce employees to remain in the organization but will not necessarily motivate them to work harder on its behalf.

A more creative way that organizations may use compensation to enhance employees' commitment is through the use of profit sharing or employee stock ownership plans (ESOPS; Lawler & Jenkins, 1992). The idea behind such plans is that employees benefit from the increased profitability of the organization as a whole. This presumably helps employees to see "the big picture" and work for the good of the entire organization. It is also possible that such compensation programs may enhance all three forms of organizational commitment. Having "ownership" in the organization may evoke feelings of pride and identification that may ultimately facilitate the employee's affective commitment. Feelings of ownership may also evoke a strong sense of responsibility and moral obligation toward the organization; hence, normative commitment may be heightened. Because employees in such compensation systems stand to lose financially if they leave the organization, continuance commitment may also be enhanced.

Another method of compensation that may impact organizational commitment is **skill-based pay**. In skill-based pay systems, employees' compensation is determined, at least to a degree, by the number of skills they possess (Murray & Gerhart, 1998). The reasoning behind skill-based pay is that having employees with multiple skills will allow greater staffing flexibility within an organization. Presumably, it also gives employees a sense of accomplishment as they acquire new skills and competencies. Like profit sharing and ESOPs, skill-based pay programs may enhance employees' feelings of all three forms of organizational commitment. To the extent that organizations help employees acquire skills, employees may feel that the organization is being supportive and may then develop feelings of affective commitment. This may also evoke feelings of obligation toward the employer, and thus enhance feelings of normative commitment. Finally, if an employee in a skill-based pay program considers leaving the organization, it is possible that he or she would not receive the same "credit" for these skills in another organization. Thus, continuance commitment may be heightened.

CHAPTER SUMMARY

In this chapter, we examined employee job satisfaction and the related topic of organizational commitment. Both topics are important, for theoretical and practical reasons. Job satisfaction is generally defined as employees' feelings of affect toward their job or job situation, but may also contain cognitive and behavioral components. Traditionally, the characteristics of jobs, and other aspects of the work environment, have explained differences in job satisfaction. In general, job satisfaction tends to be highest when the characteristics of a job match the employees' expectations in areas that are deemed important. In recent years, it has been proposed that job satisfaction is due to cues from the social environment, as well as stable dispositions. In reality, job satisfaction is likely the result of a complex

interaction among job characteristics, social cues, and dispositions.

Given the way job satisfaction is defined, the vast majority of measures of job satisfaction have come in the form of self-reports. Measures range from the very general Faces scale to other measures that allow researchers to assess employees' satisfaction with various facets of the work environment. As with any scales, measures of job satisfaction must be evaluated on the basis of *construct validity*. Two scales for which considerable evidence of construct validity has accumulated are: the Job Descriptive Index (JDI) and the Minnesota Satisfaction Questionnaire (MSQ). More recently, the Job Satisfaction Survey (JSS) has shown considerable potential as a valid measure of job satisfaction.

Research has shown that job satisfaction is consistently related to other measures of positive and negative affect. Evidence suggests, however, that job satisfaction is only a very weak predictor of absenteeism. Job satisfaction has been found to be related to turnover, albeit indirectly and only when employees perceive the existence of alternative employment opportunities. In general, research suggests that the relationship between job satisfaction and job performance is not strong. Under certain conditions, such as when rewards are directly tied to performance, there is evidence that the two may be more strongly related. Evidence also suggests that job satisfaction is a much better predictor of organizational citizenship behavior than it is of in-role performance. It has also been shown that the satisfaction–performance relationship may be more tenable at the aggregate rather than the individual level.

Organizational commitment reflects employees' feelings of loyalty toward the organization and their willingness to maintain membership. Employees may be committed because they have positive feelings toward the organization (affective), because they realize that the costs of leaving outweigh the benefits (continuance), or because they feel morally obligated to stay (normative). Affective and normative commitment can be explained largely on the basis of equity theory. Feelings of commitment represent employees' desire to reciprocate what they consider fair and equitable treatment at the hands of the organization. Continuance commitment, on the other hand, is due largely to employees' perceptions of "sunk costs" and the extent of alternatives.

Historically, the most popular measure of organizational commitment has been the Organizational Commitment Questionnaire (OCQ). A major limitation of the OCQ, however, is that it measures only affective commitment. More recently, Allen and Meyer (1990) have developed a scale that measures all three forms of commitment. Although this scale is relatively new, evidence to date has shown that it has excellent psychometric properties. This scale will likely be the most widely used measure in future organizational commitment research.

Commitment has also been studied in order to predict other variables. Affective commitment has been found to be consistently related to other attitudinal variables. Research, however, has not supported a strong link with absenteeism. This form of commitment has been found most strongly related to turnover—a finding that is not surprising, given the nature of this construct. Affective commitment appears to be related to performance only to the extent to which it increases employee effort. Although considerably less research has been conducted on continuance and normative commitment, most studies have shown that these are primarily related to turnover.

Commitment research also has a number of practical applications. Organizations may impact employees' feelings of commitment during the socialization process, as well as through other human resources management policies. In general, human resources management practices that convey a high level of organizational support tend to be associated with high levels of affective and normative commitment. Practices that increase employees' "sunk costs" tend to engender feelings of continuance commitment. Organizations are typically best served by achieving some balance among affective, continuance, and normative commitment among their employees.

SUGGESTED ADDITIONAL READINGS

Judge, T. A. (1992). The dispositional perspective in human resources research. *Research in Human Resources Management, 10,* 31–72.

Judge, T. A., Locke, E. A., Durham, C. C., & Kluger, A. N. (1998). Dispositional effects on job and life satisfaction: The role of core evaluations. *Journal of Applied Psychology, 83,* 17–34.

Meyer, J. P., Allen, N. J., & Smith, C. A. (1993). Commitment to organizations and occupations: Extension and test of a three-component conceptualization. *Journal of Applied Psychology, 78,* 538–551.

Sanchez, J. I., Korbin, W. P., & Viscarra, D. M. (1995). Corporate support in the aftermath of a natural disaster: Effects on employee strains. *Academy of Management Journal, 38,* 504–521.

Chapter Six

Counterproductive Behavior in Organizations

Employees typically behave in ways that contribute positively to the goals of their employing organizations. That is, employees perform their jobs very well, occasionally go above and beyond the call of duty, and may even come up with highly innovative and creative ideas. Employees tend to engage in such productive behaviors because organizations are selective in their hiring and, as we will see in subsequent chapters, often set up motivational and leadership systems that encourage such forms of behavior.

Employees may also, at times, engage in behaviors that run counter to organizational goals. Common forms of counterproductive behavior in organizations include ineffective job performance, absenteeism, turnover, and unsafe behavior. Less common forms of counterproductive behavior include antisocial behaviors such as theft, violence, substance use, and sexual harassment. Although less common, these forms of behavior may be quite destructive and ultimately costly to organizations.

This chapter examines counterproductive behavior in organizations. In covering these forms of behavior, the emphasis will be on understanding both the causes and the consequences of such behaviors. A related objective is to explore ways in which an organization can eliminate these behaviors or at least keep them at a level that is not too destructive to the goals of the organization.

DEFINING COUNTERPRODUCTIVE BEHAVIOR

Most readers have probably received poor service at a restaurant, or experienced the inconvenience of a long wait, brought about by poor scheduling or staffing shortages, at a doctor's office. While obviously annoying, these experiences represent relatively mild forms of counterproductive behavior in organizations. More dramatic forms of counterproductive behavior, such as criminal activity or violence, may have very negative consequences and become very newsworthy events. For example, when a government employee commits espionage, national security may be compromised, and media attention surrounding such a crime is typically intense. Likewise, when a disgruntled employee enters an organization and randomly guns down several coworkers, lives are permanently altered, and the event receives considerable media attention.

The specific examples in the preceding paragraph are all different, but each represents a form of **counterproductive behavior** in organizations. For the purposes of this chapter, counterproductive behavior will be defined as *behavior that explicitly runs counter to the goals of an organization*. This definition is intentionally quite general and is based on a number of underlying assumptions. For example, it is assumed that organizations have multiple goals and objectives. A major goal of private organizations is profitability, but such organizations may have many others as well. These may include a high level of customer service, a harmonious work environment, and the reputation of being socially responsible. According to the above definition, any employee behavior that makes it more difficult for an organization to achieve any of its goals is counterproductive.

The above definition also makes no assumption regarding the *motives* underlying counterproductive behavior. A retail employee who steals merchandise from his or her employer is obviously doing it intentionally and, most likely, for personal gain. On the other hand, it is entirely possible for an employee to engage in counterproductive behavior without intending to. For example, an employee who is poorly trained or lacking in ability may *want* very badly to perform well, but may not accomplish that goal.

Finally, the above definition makes no assumption as to the *causes* underlying counterproductive behavior. Recall from Chapter 4 that productive behaviors likely result from a complex interaction between characteristics of individuals and characteristics of the environment. This same perspective is adopted in the examination of counterproductive behavior. In fact, one can make a strong argument for a person-by-environment interaction for literally all forms of counterproductive behavior. When an employee performs his or her job poorly, this may be due to limited ability, but may also be partially caused by poor task design. Likewise, when an employee engages in a violent act at work, this may be due to deep-seated psychiatric problems, but may also be exacerbated by an authoritarian organizational climate.

Based on the definition provided above, there are undoubtedly many forms of counterproductive behaviors in organizations. In organizational psychology, however, only a handful of these behaviors have received empirical scrutiny. The most commonly studied counterproductive behaviors have been: ineffective job performance, absenteeism, turnover, and accidents. These will be covered in some depth in the present chapter. More recently, organizational researchers have begun to examine several other forms of counterproductive behavior that are less common but are potentially more devastating to organizations. These include actions such as theft, violence, substance use, and sexual harassment. They are discussed in somewhat less detail at the end of the chapter.

INEFFECTIVE JOB PERFORMANCE

Most people who go to work each day *want* to do their jobs well. This desire is linked to a variety of reasons. High levels of performance are often associated with positive tangible outcomes such as merit increases, cash bonuses, promotional opportunities, and the like. Performing well may also lead to more intangible rewards such as praise and admiration from others, and a heightened sense of personal accomplishment. Despite all the logical reasons for performing well, some employees do not perform up to par. Ineffective job performance is often a difficult issue for organizations, for a number of reasons. For example, in many cases, it may be difficult for an organization to detect ineffective performance in the first place. Once detected, it is often challenging to diagnose the cause of the performance problem. Finally, organizations often struggle with the issue of how to respond to, and prevent, instances of ineffective performance. Each of these issues is discussed below.

Detection of Ineffective Performance

Recall from Chapter 4 that models of job performance propose that behaviors constituting job performance may be categorized into a number of different types, such as core tasks that are specific to the job, and more general or peripheral tasks. Ideally, all organizations would have in place performance measurement systems that would allow assessment of the many behaviors that constitute the performance domain. If this were the case, a routine performance appraisal would be quite useful in the detection of ineffective performance. Unfortunately, performance measurement systems typically provide information about the *impact* of employee behavior.

Performance-related data that organizations typically collect may be classified into three different types: **personnel data, production data,** and **subjective evaluations.** Personnel data include items such as absences, sick days, tardiness, disciplinary actions, and safety violations. Some of these, as will be shown later in the chapter, are counterproductive behaviors for which personnel data provide a direct measure. Personnel data may also, at times, provide useful information in the diagnosis of performance problems. For example, an employee who is absent or late frequently may be having trouble meeting deadlines.

Production data provide an organization with useful information about tangible outcomes associated with job performance. The most commonly used form of production data is probably sales commission, although production indexes may be used in many other settings. As a means of detecting ineffective job performance, there are clearly advantages using production data. Such data provide organizations with an objective performance metric that an employee cannot dispute (i.e., numbers don't lie). Such data are also typically not costly to obtain because they are often collected for multiple purposes.

A potential drawback with production data is that they often provide an overly simplistic view of employee performance. A salesperson may exhibit reduced sales commissions in a particular year, yet these numerical data provide an organization with little information about the source of the performance problem. Also, in the author's experience, reliance on production data may lead supervisors to adopt a somewhat callous attitude toward subordinates who are experiencing a performance problem. The response to reduced sales commissions may be: "Increase your sales, or else!"

By far the most common form of employee performance data comes in the form of subjective appraisals. Most typically, an employee's immediate supervisor(s) completes some performance appraisal instrument on an annual or semiannual basis. In considering subjective appraisals, it is important to keep in mind that what is actually being measured in most cases is the *result* of employees' behavior, or, more specifically, employee **effectiveness** (Pritchard, 1992). To be sure, some organizations may invest the time and effort required to develop and implement elegant behaviorally based performance appraisal systems. Most organizations, however, still tend to rely on performance appraisal instruments that utilize rather general dimensions of employee performance and engage in rather minimal efforts to train raters (Cascio, 1998).

As a method of detecting ineffective performance, subjective appraisals have certain advantages when compared to either personnel data or production indexes. A supervisor's thoughtful consideration of an employee's performance may provide considerable insight into ineffective employee performance compared to more quantitative indexes. Also, if appraisals are performed well and the information is regularly transmitted to employees (e.g., Meyer, Kay, & French, 1965), they may *prevent* ineffective performance before it occurs (see Comment 6.1).

Despite these potential advantages, subjective appraisals are often of marginal value in the detection of ineffective performance. Because many organizations still utilize performance appraisal instruments that assess very global performance dimensions, such ratings may often fail to reveal performance problems. Also, despite the considerable technical advances in performance appraisal methodology over the past 25 years (e.g., Borman, 1991; Murphy & Cleveland, 1990), many organizations still administer performance appraisals very poorly or simply ignore them.

Causes of Ineffective Performance

Let's assume for the moment that an instance of ineffective performance has been detected. A salesperson has failed to meet his or her quota for three consecutive months; a clerical employee repeatedly makes mistakes on his or her word-processing assignments; a university professor repeatedly receives negative assessments of his or her teaching performance. In each of these cases, we know that the employee is not performing up to par. What is often not known is *why* the employee is performing poorly.

In most organizational settings, the underlying causes of ineffective performance are often unclear. As a result, the cause(s) of ineffective performance must be determined by attributional processes; that is, after observing some instance of ineffective performance, a supervisor must determine the cause(s) of this behavior. **Attribution theory** suggests that people make use of several pieces of information when determining the causes of another person's behavior (Kelley, 1973). For instance, people examine the consistency of behavior over time, between different settings or contexts, and in comparison to others. Thus, if an instance of poor performance were encountered, a supervisor would ask questions such as: What has this employee's performance been like in the past? Does he/she perform poorly on all aspects of the job or just certain ones? Is the level of performance poor in relation to others' performance?

COMMENT 6.1

THE IMPORTANCE OF PERFORMANCE FEEDBACK

WITHOUT A DOUBT, one of the *least* favorite tasks of managers and supervisors is conducting annual or semiannual performance reviews. This is particularly true when an employee is performing poorly. Ironically, though, performance reviews have the potential to provide the greatest benefit to those employees who are not performing well—provided they are done well.

Research on conducting performance reviews has shown that there are several attributes of an effective performance review. One of the most important of these, particularly for a poorly performing employee, is that the tone of the review should be constructive rather than punitive. An employee who is performing poorly is likely to respond much more favorably to a supervisor who says, "What can I do to help you improve?" than to a supervisor who lists all of the things that the employee is doing poorly.

It is also very important that the feedback provided to an employee is specific and is focused on behavior. Telling a poorly performing employee that he or she has a "bad attitude" doesn't provide that employee with much diagnostic information. On the other hand, telling the same individual that he or she often does not thank customers after completing a transaction is much more specific and, more importantly, is something the individual can change.

Finally, research has also shown that *performance* reviews should be conducted separately from *salary* reviews. When the performance and salary reviews are conducted together (which is common), most people tend to focus disproportionately on the size of their salary increase. Unfortunately, what ends up receiving much less attention in comparison is performance feedback and, if necessary, suggestions for improvement. This is particularly unfortunate for employees performing poorly; these individuals stand to benefit the most from focusing on performance.

Source: H. H. Meyer, E. Kay, and J. R. P. French, Jr. (1965). Split roles in performance appraisal. *Harvard Business Review, 43,* 123–129.

Based on the processing of all this information, a supervisor is likely to make some determination as to the cause of the ineffective performance. Generally speaking, if the ineffective performance is consistent over time and settings, and is seen as poor in relation to others, a supervisor would likely conclude that the ineffective performance was due to a lack of ability or motivation, both of which are *internal* to the employee. In contrast, if the ineffective performance is not a consistent pattern over time and settings, and is not seen as being poor in relations to others, a supervisor would likely conclude that the ineffective performance was due to factors *external* to the individual (e.g., poor task design, interruptions).

One of the problems with the attribution process is that people are not always accurate and may, in fact, hold certain biases in assessing the causes of others' behavior. The best known of these is termed the **fundamental attribution error** (Ross, 1977) and refers to the bias toward attributing the causes of others' behavior to internal, as opposed to external, causes. Although the reasons for this bias are complex, the basic issue is that, in most situations, *people are more distinctive than the situations they are in.* Thus, when any behavior occurs, there is a tendency to focus on personal (as opposed to situational) factors being the cause.

There is evidence that managers and supervisors may bring such attributional biases to a diagnosis of ineffective performance, although several factors may influence it. For example, in a laboratory study, Mitchell and Kalb (1982) found that supervisors who lacked experience in the tasks their subordinates performed tended to attribute poor performance to internal causes. In contrast, those with more task experience tended to make more external attributions. In another laboratory study, Ilgen, Mitchell, and Frederickson (1981) found that supervisors who were highly interdependent with subordinates tended to make more external attributions for ineffective performance; supervisors who saw little interdependence tended to make more internal attributions.

Understanding the attributional processes involved in determining the causes of ineffective performance is important because such attributions may have a strong impact on supervisory *responses* to ineffective performance. For example, if a supervisor sees the cause of the ineffective performance as being poor task design, his or her response may be completely different than if it is seen as due to a lack of effort. Ilgen et al. (1981) found that supervisors responded to ineffective performance more favorably when they attributed it to external (versus internal) causes. It has also been shown clearly that supervisors react much less favorably to ineffective performance when they perceive it as being caused by a lack of motivation, as opposed to a lack of ability (Podsakoff, 1982).

For the moment, we'll take as a given that determining the cause(s) in effective performance often requires the use of imperfect attributional processes. What then are the most common causes of ineffective performance? To answer this question, it is useful again to think back to Chapter 4 and the discussion of the causes of productive behaviors, such as job performance. Based on this vast literature, it can be concluded that ineffective performance may be due to employees' inability to perform their job effectively (e.g., lack of ability, lack of skills, or poor training), lack of willingness to perform effectively (e.g., unwilling to put forth or sustain effort, or putting efforts in the wrong direction), or aspects of the environment that prevent the employee from performing well (e.g., poor task design, ineffective coworkers).

In examining each of these causes of ineffective performance, it is possible to pinpoint tangible organizational activities that may contribute to them. For example, **selection errors** may result in organizations' hiring individuals who lack either the skills or the abilities necessary to perform their jobs. Selection errors may also be evidenced when employees possess the requisite skills and abilities necessary to perform their jobs, but simply do not fit well into the culture of the organization (Kristof, 1996).

How can organizations avoid selection errors? At the risk of sounding overly simplistic, organizations simply need to put a systematic effort into employee hiring. While many organizations clearly do this, many others do not. More to the point, many organizations simply fail to gather and utilize data that would help them make more informed hiring decisions. Although a complete exploration of the employee selection is clearly beyond the scope of this chapter (see Cascio, 1998, for complete coverage), selection errors may often be avoided by the systematic use of tests, personal history information, and background/reference checks.

Another way in which organizations may contribute to ineffective performance is through **inadequate socialization and training.** As was pointed out in Chapter 3, when employees first enter an organization, they typically need to be taught specific job-related skills, as well as more general information about the culture of the organization. Employees who receive either inadequate training or no training at all may be set up for failure when they enter an organization. In such an environment, only those who have very high levels of ability and self-confidence may survive.

With respect to socialization, organizations may make a number of errors that could lead to poor performance among employees. Specifically, failing to provide new employees with information about important aspects of the culture of the organization may lead to failure. For example, if the culture of an organization is such that timely completion of work is highly valued, a new employee may inadvertently perform poorly by not completing work on time. Typically, this type of situation is resolved when the new employee realizes the value of timeliness.

A more problematic situation occurs when new employees receive "mixed signals" about the culture of the organization. In the author's experience, this is a typical problem for faculty at medium-size regional universities. Because such institutions offer some graduate programs (typically at the Master's degree level), some faculty and administrators feel that an organizational culture that places a strong emphasis on research is appropriate. On the other hand, many of these institutions have historically placed a strong emphasis on undergraduate teaching, so many others feel that the culture should primarily emphasize teaching excellence. Although such differences in philosophy may sometimes lead to insightful dialogue, they may also prove to be very confusing to new faculty members who must decide where to focus their efforts.

Another potential cause of ineffective performance is rooted in organizational reward systems. More specifically, organizational reward systems may inadvertently discourage employees from performing well, and may actually perpetuate poor performance. Although it is difficult to estimate it precisely, there is probably considerable variation in the extent to which organizations reward employees on the basis of performance (Lawler & Jenkins, 1992). For example, monetary raises may be "across the board," and employees may be rewarded primarily for length of tenure. In other cases, merit pay systems may exist, but are administered in such a way that employees are unable to see any connection between rewards and performance. Is it impossible for employees to perform well under these conditions? Not necessarily. If rewards are not based on performance, an employee may perform well out of personal pride, or perhaps because he or she wishes to remain a member of the organization. Over time, however, employees working under such systems may question the value of performing well, and, in some cases, those who perform well may receive more attractive offers from other organizations (Schwab, 1991).

In some cases, employees may want to perform well but are prevented from doing so because of constraints in the environment. For example, an employee's job tasks may be designed in a way that makes it difficult to perform well, or in a way that is incompatible with the organization's reward systems (Campion & Berger, 1990; Campion & Thayer, 1985). For example, if it is crucial for an employee to make independent judgments in order to perform effectively, it would not make sense to design the job in a way that denies this employee decision-making authority. Even if tasks are designed properly, other constraining forces in the work environment may hinder performance (Peters & O'Connor, 1980; Spector & Jex, 1998). For example, employees may be unable to perform well because of interruptions from others, poor tools or equipment, and perhaps poor information from others.

Management of Ineffective Performance

Given the multitude of factors that may contribute to ineffective performance, managers need to investigate the causes of ineffective performance when it occurs. As was pointed out earlier (e.g., Ilgen et al., 1981; Mitchell & Kalb, 1982), managers often assume that the cause of ineffective performance lies with the individual employee, particularly when managers lack task experience. To the extent that such attributions are incorrect, they may lead to misguided efforts to correct such behavior. Thus, as a first step toward investigating ineffective performance, managers should *talk to the employee*. Perhaps more importantly, such discussions should involve considerable *listening* on the part of the manager (Meyer et al., 1965).

Depending on the outcome of the conversation with the poorly performing employee, a number of corrective actions may be utilized by the manager to improve performance. In some cases, it may be possible to improve an employee's performance through relatively straightforward **training interventions.** For example, if an employee is consistently producing poor-quality written reports, a logical way to improve performance might involve some form of training aimed at improving his or her written communication skills. In other cases, the underlying cause(s) of ineffective performance may not be as obvious. Let's say, for example, that a real estate salesperson is failing to produce acceptable commissions. For a sales manager to accurately diagnose the cause of this particular performance problem (assuming, of course, that interest rates are not 20%!), he or she may need to actually observe the employee trying to close a sale.

This type of activity may be thought of as **on-the-job coaching** of the employee. Coaching is a form of training, but it is much more extensive and time-consuming. The manager who provides coaching to employees is engaged in a form of active learning that may involve examining all aspects of the employee's performance-related behavior. In the example above, coaching activities may consist of observing the employee during sales presentations, determining how the employee organizes his or her time, passing on suggestions or "tricks of the trade" that may help the employee perform well, and ultimately following up to see whether performance improves.

Another option in dealing with ineffective performance is the use of **counseling** and **employee assistance programs (EAPs)** (Cartwright & Cooper, 1997; Swanson & Murphy, 1991). Employees do not "compartmentalize" their lives; thus, problems outside of work may manifest themselves in the workplace. Marital or financial problems may have a negative impact on the performance of even highly competent employees. If this option is considered, however, managers must be very careful how they approach the employee. Even if such efforts are well-intentioned, the suggestion that employees need to seek such services may be met with considerable resistance on the part of an employee. Despite these potential caveats, providing counseling or EAPs may be very useful ways of dealing with some instances of ineffective performance.

Up to this point, the methods of addressing ineffective performance have focused primarily on *changing the behavior of the employee*. However, ineffective performance may also be due to environmental factors such as environmental constraints or poor task design. In fact, some management experts, most notably W. Edwards Deming, have argued that the *primary* cause of ineffective performance lies in the environment and not with individual employees. What, then, can be done if the cause of poor performance lies in the work environment?

As a first step, managers can attempt to identify factors in the work environment that are obviously constraining employee performance. This identification may include relatively simple steps, such as asking employees to report things that consistently make it difficult for them to do their jobs. More systematic ways of identifying environmental constraints may include **reengineering** and **task analysis.** Reengineering is a comprehensive organizational change intervention that involves, among other things, systematically tracking the steps involved in completing administrative actions or procedures (Hammer & Champy, 1993). For example, an insurance company could track all of the steps a claims adjuster must follow after customers with homeowners' insurance policies report damage to their homes. The information gleaned from this type of analysis may reveal, in these administrative procedures, "bottlenecks" that may be partially responsible for ineffective performance. In the example above, a claims adjuster who is unable to settle claims in a timely manner may be having difficulty receiving the initial report of the claim.

Task analysis is aimed at examining the content of the job-specific tasks of employees (Levine, 1983). Task analysis information can be collected in a variety of ways: interviews with job incumbents; observing job incumbents, and even managers, performing the job; and so on. The information generated by a systematic task analysis can be quite useful in the management of ineffective performance. With a better understanding of the job tasks, it may become apparent that something in the environment is constraining performance. For example, a task analysis for the job of auto mechanic may reveal that some of the tools needed to perform some required tasks are either in poor condition or are often unavailable to the employee. Task analysis may also reveal poor job design. For example, a task analysis might reveal that a manager is performing many tasks that could be delegated, which would then free up his or her time for more crucial activities.

Preventing Ineffective Performance

As is evident by now, organizations have a variety of ways of dealing with ineffective performance when it occurs. Ideally, though, organizations prefer to prevent ineffective performance before it occurs. A first step toward preventing ineffective performance is the utilization of scientifically based selection programs. There is considerable evidence that some variables—most notably, general cognitive ability, conscientiousness, and prior experience—predict performance across a variety of job types (Barrick & Mount, 1991; Schmidt & Hunter, 1998). Thus, it would seem to be in an organization's best interest to employ rigorous selection programs to ensure that employees enter with the skills, abilities, and personality traits necessary to perform their jobs.

Although rigorous selection may go a long way toward the prevention of performance problems, it is certainly not a panacea. Thus, once employees enter an organization, steps must be taken to nurture employees' skills and abilities so they are translated into performance (Colarelli et al., 1987). As stated earlier, one way of addressing this issue is through proper training and socialization. The manner in which organizations conduct initial training and socialization varies widely. Organizations that take the time to properly socialize and train new employees clearly stand a good chance of avoiding performance problems in the future.

Another important step toward the prevention of performance problems is having a systematic performance measurement and feedback system. That is, organizations should regularly measure performance and share this information with employees. This helps to keep employees on track with respect to performance, and serves to communicate performance expectations. In many cases, ineffective performance may simply be due to the fact that employees do not know what the organization (or their immediate supervisor) expects. Regular performance evaluations also signal to employees that *performance matters.*

A final step organizations can take to prevent performance problems is by responding appropriately to performance differences. When employees perform well, they should be rewarded for it. Granted, employees will not necessarily perform *poorly* if they believe a high level of performance is not appreciated. However, if rewards are unrelated to performance, many employees will perform their jobs in a minimally acceptable manner, and will be unlikely to engage in extra role behaviors. These responses, in the long run, may be even more destructive than ineffective performance.

Perhaps of equal importance is an organization's response to consistent patterns of ineffective employee performance. This may occur in cases where the organization has repeatedly tried to help a poorly performing employee, but performance does not improve. Perhaps an employee simply lacks the ability to perform the job, or is not motivated to improve. In the former case, a possible option would be to transfer the employee to a less demanding job. In doing this, however, organizations must be careful not to give the appearance that the poorly performing employee is being rewarded. More to the point, such transfers should not be promotions.

How should organizations respond when poor performance is primarily due to a lack of motivation? In such cases, organizations often use what has been termed **progressive discipline** (Mitchell & O'Reilly, 1983); that is, an employee is initially given a verbal warning when performance is not up to par. If the poor performance continues, this step is usually followed by progressively more serious consequences such as written reprimands, unpaid suspensions, and, ultimately, termination. The decision to terminate an employee is obviously difficult for organizations and deserves special mention here. Like any disciplinary measure, consideration must be given to the reasons behind the poor performance, as well as the seriousness of the consequences (Klaas & Wheeler, 1990; Liden et al., 1999). Terminating an employee should be done only in situations where reasonable efforts to help an employee improve have failed, or where poor performance has very negative consequences.

EMPLOYEE ABSENTEEISM

The second form of counterproductive behavior examined in this chapter is employee absenteeism. Recall from the previous chapter that absenteeism was discussed, but only as a potential consequence of job dissatisfaction and low organizational commitment. In this section, we approach absenteeism from a somewhat broader perspective and examine other predictors, as well as various ways in which organizations can reduce the incidence of employee absenteeism.

Defining and Measuring Absenteeism

Absenteeism appears to be a relatively simple variable to define and measure; that is, absenteeism can be defined simply as *not attending work.* However, defining absenteeism in such a general way is problematic when the goal is to predict and control absenteeism. In the absenteeism literature, researchers typically make some distinctions with respect to the *types* of absences. For example, a distinction is often made between excused and unexcused absences. Excused absences would be those due to reasons that the organization deems as acceptable (e.g., illness). In contrast, unexcused absences would be those that are either due to unacceptable reasons or cases where employees have not followed proper procedures (e.g., calling in to one's supervisor). What is considered an unacceptable absence obviously varies from organization to organization. However, most organizations would probably not look favorably on an employee who simply does not show up for work and has no acceptable reason for an absence.

Making distinctions regarding the reasons for absenteeism is important because different types of absences may be caused by different variables. To underscore this point, Kohler and Mathieu (1993) examined a number of predictors of seven different absence criterion measures among a sample of urban bus drivers and found different predictors for different criteria. For example, they found that absences due to nonwork obligations (e.g., caring for children, transportation problems) were most strongly related to variables such as dissatisfaction with extrinsic features of the job, role conflict, role ambiguity, and feelings of somatic tension. On the other hand, absences due to stress reactions (e.g., illnesses) were most strongly related to dissatisfaction with both internal and external features of the job, feelings of fatigue, and gender (women were absent more frequently).

Kohler and Mathieu's study shows that absenteeism is a multidimensional construct. This suggests that efforts to develop theoretical models of absenteeism must take this into account; thus, different types of absenteeism may have quite different antecedents. From a practical point of view, these findings provide

some helpful guidance to organizations interested in reducing employee absenteeism. For example, if an employee is frequently absent due to childcare problems or unreliable transportation, it may be possible for an organization to provide tangible assistance in these areas. On the other hand, reducing absences due to illness may be possible through interventions such as stress management and health promotion.

To measure absenteeism, the most common indexes are **time lost measures** and **frequency measures** (Hammer & Landau, 1981). When a time lost measure is used, absenteeism is represented by the number of days or hours that an employee is absent for a given period of time. As an example, if an employee is absent from work three days over a three-month period, that employee's level of absenteeism would be three days or 24 hours (assuming that each workday is eight hours).

If a frequency metric is used, absenteeism represents the number of absence *occurrences* for a given period of time. An occurrence can range from one day to several weeks. In the previous example, if each of the three days that the employee is absent occurs in a different month, the time lost and the frequency metrics would be identical. However, if the employee was absent for three *consecutive* days, the absence would be recorded as only *one occurrence* if a frequency metric is used.

Although both time lost and frequency measures of absenteeism have been used in studies of absenteeism (e.g., Hackett & Guion, 1985; Steel & Rentsch, 1995), time lost measures are generally more desirable because they exhibit greater variability than frequency measures (Hammer & Landau, 1981). Thus, it is generally more difficult to predict absenteeism when using frequency-based absenteeism measures.

Another important issue in the measurement of absenteeism is the time frame used to aggregate absences. In terms of aggregation periods, studies can be found in which absenteeism data are aggregated over periods ranging from as short as one month to as long as four years (Hammer & Landau, 1981; Steel & Rentsch, 1995). The primary advantage to using longer aggregation periods is that the distributions of such measures are not as likely to be skewed as those from shorter periods. Given that absenteeism is a low base-rate event even for relatively long periods of time, aggregating absenteeism data over a very short period of time may pose researchers with some vexing statistical problems.

Predictors of Absenteeism

To a large extent, organizational psychologists have focused on *affective* predictors of absenteeism, such as job satisfaction and organizational commitment. As was shown in Chapter 5, however, the predictive power of affective variables is somewhat inconsistent. Furthermore, meta-analytic reviews have generally found the relationship between affect and absenteeism to be rather weak (e.g., Hackett, 1989; Hackett & Guion, 1985; Mathieu & Zajac, 1990). These findings are undoubtedly due to a number of factors, such as the multidimensional nature of absenteeism, choice of measurement indexes, choice of aggregation periods, and so on. In this section, we go beyond affective variables and review other predictors that have been explored in the absenteeism literature.

As a first step toward understanding absenteeism, it is useful to consider employee attendance decisions in a general sense. According to Steers and Rhodes (1978), two general factors—the ability to attend and the desire to attend—determine employees' attendance. *Ability to attend* is obviously

determined by an employee's health but may also be due to factors such as nonwork responsibilities, reliability of transportation, and weather. The *desire to attend* work is determined to a large extent by employees' feelings about the organization or job, but may also be due to other factors. For example, an employee may like his or her job but choose not to attend because of some more attractive nonwork alternative. For example, an employee may choose to be absent on a particular day in order to go Christmas shopping.

Based on this view of absenteeism, three nonaffective variables seem to stand out as consistent predictors of absenteeism. For example, it has been rather consistently found that women are absent more frequently from work than are men (Farrell & Stamm, 1988; Steel & Rentsch, 1995; VandenHeuvel & Wooden, 1995). Based on Steers and Rhodes (1978), this is probably because women are more likely than men to be in situations that constrain their *ability* to attend work. For example, it has been shown that, even in dual-career situations, women tend to assume primary responsibility for childcare and household chores (Hochschild, 1989).

Another important nonaffective predictor of absenteeism is the nature of an organization's **absence control policies**. Some organizations are quite lenient; they choose not to even record employees' absences. At the other extreme, some organizations require extensive documentation for the reason for absences, and they respond with strict disciplinary actions when employees are absent frequently. As one might expect, the frequency of absenteeism tends to be lower in organizations that have more strict absence control policies (Farrell & Stamm, 1988; Kohler & Mathieu, 1993; Majchrzak, 1987). It is important to note, however, that simply having a strict absence control policy in place may not always reduce absenteeism. For example, Majchrzak (1987) found that in Marine Corps units where the absence control policy had been communicated clearly and applied consistently, unauthorized absences were reduced significantly over a six-month period. In contrast, absences remained constant in units where no policy existed, or where the policy was not communicated clearly.

Another nonaffective predictor of absenteeism that has begun to receive attention only recently is **absence culture.** The term has been defined by Chadwick-Jones, Nicholson, and Brown (1982) as "the beliefs and practices influencing the totality of absence frequency and duration—as they currently occur within an employee group or organization" (p. 7). There are two things to note about this definition. First, absence culture is clearly a group or organization-level construct, and thus must be measured at the appropriate level (e.g., group or organization). Second, because organizations typically consists of multiple groups, several absence cultures may in fact be operating simultaneously in the same organization.

Given that normative standards serve as an important guide for the members of any social unit (Hackman, 1992), one would expect that group members' absenteeism would tend to be consistent with the prevailing absence culture. That is, one would expect absenteeism to be more prevalent in groups where the prevailing culture is very tolerant of absences. In contrast, when the culture is very intolerant, one would expect absences to be less frequent. If absence behavior runs counter to the prevailing absence culture, a group member runs the risk of informal sanctions or, possibly, ostracism by other group members.

The concept of absence culture (and its proposed impact on absenteeism) is quite consistent with what is known about the impact of norms in groups. Unfortunately, to date, there has been relatively little empirical investigation of the absence culture construct or of its effects on absenteeism. One exception is a study in which Mathieu and Kohler (1990) examined the impact of group-level absence rates on individual absences. Using a sample of transit operators employed by a large public transit authority, they found that the level of absences in the various *garages* in which these employees worked predicted absenteeism using a time-lost measure.

A more direct test of the effect of absence culture comes from a study conducted by Martocchio (1994). Unlike the method in the Mathieu and Kohler (1990) study, Martocchio actually assessed absence culture within groups and investigated the impact of this variable on absenteeism. Based on a sample of clerical employees at a Fortune 500 company, Martocchio found that group-level beliefs regarding absenteeism (e.g., absence culture) were predictive of individual employees' absenteeism, measured in terms of the frequency of paid absences. Only individuals' beliefs regarding absenteeism predicted the frequency of unpaid absences.

Based on the limited research to date, it appears that absence culture holds considerable promise as a cause of absenteeism (see Comment 6.2). When combined with previous research on affective predictors and absence control policies, a reasonably clear picture of employee absenteeism begins to emerge. Employees who are dissatisfied and who lack commitment have a tendency to be absent from work. Whether these feelings of negative affect actually lead to absences may depend on other factors, such as organizational absence policies and the prevailing norms (regarding absenteeism) in the work group. Figure 6.1 summarizes the factors that have been shown to influence employee absenteeism.

COMMENT 6.2

ABSENCE CULTURE: A NEW FOCUS IN ABSENTEEISM RESEARCH

FOR MANY YEARS, absenteeism research has focused on affect (most typically, in the form of job satisfaction) as the primary driving force behind absenteeism. Recently, however, absenteeism researchers have begun to shift their focus to organizational and group-level norms surrounding absenteeism. *Absence culture* is the term used to refer to such norms, and there is some evidence that it is a predictor of individuals' absenteeism.

Research on absence culture is relatively new, however, and many unanswered questions still surround this construct. For example, what determines absence culture in the first place? Is it shaped by characteristics of individual group members, or is it a byproduct of the actual level of absenteeism within a group? Another issue that has not been ex-

plored is whether absence culture has a greater impact on some individuals than on others. It is possible, for example, that individuals who have a strong need for approval from their fellow group members would adhere more strictly to group absence norms than individuals who do not.

Perhaps the most important issue yet to be explored is whether organizations can *change* the absence culture of a group. Although only speculative, possible ways to do this might be: changing the composition of a group, redesigning the group's work to make it more interesting, or altering absence control policies.

Given all these unanswered questions, there is likely to be a great deal of interesting research on absence culture. Who knows, maybe *you* will end up conducting some of it!

FIGURE 6.1
Summary of the Major Determinants of Employee Absenteeism

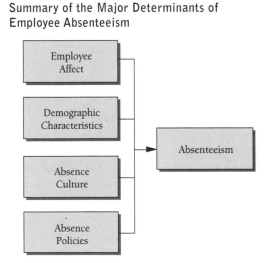

Cross-Cultural Differences in Absenteeism

Like most phenomena studied by organizational psychologists, absenteeism has been studied largely in samples of either American or Western European employees. Despite calls for cross-cultural absenteeism research (e.g., Martocchio & Harrison, 1993), few studies have examined cross-cultural differences in absenteeism. One notable exception is a recent study by Johns and Xie (1998). Employees from the People's Republic of China and from Canada were compared on a number of aspects of absenteeism, such as perceptions of their own absence levels in comparison to those in their work groups; manager–subordinate agreement on absence norms; and legitimacy of reasons for absenteeism.

The most notable cross-cultural difference found in this study was that Chinese employees were more likely than Canadians to generate estimates of their own absenteeism that favored their work group. This suggests that absence norms may be a more powerful predictor of absenteeism among the Chinese. Along these same lines, it was found that Chinese managers were in greater agreement with their work groups on absence norms than were Canadian managers. Finally, with respect to reasons for absence, the Canadians were less likely than the Chinese to see domestic reasons as a legitimate excuse for absences. In contrast, the Chinese were less likely than the Canadians to see illness, stress, and depression as legitimate excuses.

Johns and Xie (1998) attributed their findings to well-documented differences in values between Western and Eastern societies. Most notably, in Eastern societies, the strong collectivist orientation suggests that social norms regarding such behavior may have a more powerful effect than they do in Western societies. This may also explain why those in collectivist societies may see absences due to family reasons as more legitimate than do those in more individualistic societies. In contrast, in Eastern societies, norms surrounding the expression of feelings may prohibit absenteeism based on poor mental or physical health. The results of this study are provocative; they suggest that cross-cultural absenteeism research may be a fruitful area of research in the future.

Preventing Absenteeism

Based on the empirical absenteeism literature, organizations may choose to prevent employee absenteeism in a number of ways. Generally, prevention of absenteeism can focus on (1) making attendance more rewarding to the employee; (2) making absenteeism less attractive to the employee; and (3) helping to reduce constraints on employee attendance. Each of these approaches is discussed below. If organizations seek to reduce absenteeism by making attendance more rewarding, this may be accomplished through several interventions. For example, organizations may choose to redesign employees' jobs (Griffin, 1991), provide greater opportunities for participation in decision making (Spector, 1986), or perhaps provide employees with higher levels of support (Eisenberger, Huntington, Hutchison, & Sowa, 1986). Organizations that use this approach will essentially be trying to reduce absenteeism by making the work environment more appealing to employees.

Organizations can also make attendance more attractive through absence control policies. For example, some organizations compensate employees for some percentage of their unused sick days. In other companies, sick days may be "banked" and used for other purposes. As an example, the author's present employer allows employees to use accumulated unused sick time to pay for health care coverage during retirement. One of the more creative ways to make attendance more attractive to employees is illustrated in a study by Pedalino and Gamboa (1974). Employees were issued a poker card every day they attended work and, at the end of the month, the person with the best hand won a pool of money. Notice that, in all of these examples, employees are not *punished* for being absent from work. Rather, the policies operate such that employees are *rewarded* for consistently attending work.

The second approach to reducing absenteeism is to make absenteeism unattractive to employees. If absence control policies contain no disincentives for frequent unauthorized absences, it is possible that employees will take advantage of this. Thus, organizations should have in place absence control policies that have negative consequences for frequent unauthorized absenteeism. These may include loss of pay, written reprimands, and, in extreme cases, termination.

Another potential way to make absenteeism unattractive is through the various absence cultures that develop within organizations. As has been shown, the prevailing norms and beliefs regarding absenteeism may have an impact on the absence behavior of individuals (e.g., Martocchio, 1994). Unfortunately, very little evidence reveals the manner in which absence cultures develop; thus, organizations have little guidance on how to influence them. Potential ways to impact absence cultures, based on the group dynamics literature (e.g., Forsyth, 1999; Hackman, 1992), may include fostering high levels of within-group cohesion and supporting high-level performance norms.

A final way in which organizations may reduce absenteeism is to help remove barriers to attendance. As shown by Kohler and Mathieu (1993), some absences may be due to nonwork factors such as unreliable transportation and child-care issues. Organizations may be able to assist employees by providing benefits such as day care, "sick child" services, and eldercare referrals. Assistance can also be provided at the community level by making affordable public transportation available. In Washington, DC, for example, many people rely on the Metro transit system for transportation to and from work. Without this system, people in the metropolitan Washington, DC, area who lack the financial means to afford personal transportation would have much greater difficulty attending work.

EMPLOYEE TURNOVER

Like absenteeism, employee turnover was discussed in the previous chapter as a correlate of job satisfaction and organizational commitment. Furthermore, compared to absenteeism, empirical evidence has shown that employee affect is a stronger predictor of turnover decisions. Therefore, the focus in this section will be to examine employee turnover from a more macro perspective (e.g., the impact of turnover on organizations), explore nonaffective predictors of turnover, and, finally, explore a recent model that has applied behavioral decision theory to the study of turnover.

The Impact of Turnover on Organizations

Like many variables explored in this book, employee turnover has been studied from a very *micro* perspective; that is, researchers have sought to enhance the understanding of individual-level decision-making processes that characterize turnover decisions. Organizational researchers have generally paid much less attention to examining the impact of employee turnover on organizational effectiveness. Abelson and Baysinger (1984), employing this macro perspective, distinguished between what they term **optimal** and **dysfunctional turnover.** Optimal turnover occurs when poorly performing employees decide to leave an organization. These authors also suggest that, in some cases, turnover may be optimal even if high-performing employees leave. Their logic is rooted in cost–benefit analysis. Sometimes it is *not* in an organization's best interest to retain a high-performing employee, because of the costs of retaining that individual. At other times, it may be possible to match a competing salary offer, but such an increase may have such a negative impact on the morale of other employees that retaining the employee is not justified.

Like optimal turnover, dysfunctional turnover can be viewed in multiple ways. If the *rate* of turnover is extremely high, this can be very dysfunctional for organizations. Those with high rates of turnover must incur costs associated with constantly having to recruit and train new employees. A consistently high rate of turnover may also serve to tarnish the image of the organization and thus make it even harder to attract new employees. In most industries, there are organizations that have a reputation of "chewing up and spitting out" employees.

Turnover may also be dysfunctional if a high percentage of those who leave are good employees. As stated above, the cost of retaining high-performing employees may be prohibitive; thus, keeping such employees is more costly than releasing them. However, some organizations may have an opportunity to retain a valuable employee but take no steps to do so. Another mistake, sometimes made by organizations, is assuming that salary is the only reason an employee is considering leaving. This may be true in some cases, but there are often other reasons why an employee may consider seeking employment elsewhere. An employee may be seeking other professional challenges, wish to have greater autonomy over his or her work, or perhaps desire to work for an organization that is more supportive of its employees. Organizations often are able to address these non-salary issues and thus prevent turnover.

Another way to view the impact of turnover on organizations is to distinguish between what might be termed **avoidable turnover** and **unavoidable turnover.** Turnover is avoidable when there are steps that an organization could have taken to prevent it. As argued above, this is somewhat subjective and involves weighing the costs of losing employees versus the benefits of retention. Unavoidable turnover, on the other hand, is illustrated by situations in which an organization clearly cannot prevent an employee from leaving. This may occur when an employee's spouse is transferred to another location, or when there

is simply no need for the employee's services. In other cases, turnover may be unavoidable simply because an employee decides to withdraw from the labor force.

Nonaffective Predictors of Turnover

One nonaffective predictor that has actually received a fair amount of attention in the turnover literature is performance. Based on the discussion above, it is in an organization's best interest if turnover is highest among lower-performing employees. Furthermore, empirical evidence has supported such a negative relation between performance and turnover (e.g., McEvoy & Cascio, 1987; Williams & Livingstone, 1994), although this relation is not strong. The relative weakness of the performance-turnover relation may be due to a number of factors. As Hulin (1991) has argued quite forcefully, turnover is a low-base-rate event, and studies employing typical parametric statistical procedures may underestimate the true relation between turnover and other variables. This becomes even more problematic when performance is examined as a predictor of turnover because, due to a variety of factors, the variability in job performance measures may be severely restricted (e.g., Jex, 1998; Johns, 1991).

A more substantive variable that may impact the performance-turnover relation is organizational reward contingencies. One of the assumptions underlying the prediction that performance is negatively related to performance is that low performers will receive fewer organizational rewards than high performers. Because of this, low-performing employees are more likely to become dissatisfied and seek employment elsewhere. Given that organizations vary widely in the extent to which they reward on the basis of performance, this would certainly account for the weak performance-turnover relation. Furthermore, in one recent meta-analysis of the performance-turnover relation (Williams & Livingstone, 1994), the average correlation between performance and turnover was strongest in studies conducted in organizations where rewards were tied to performance.

A third factor that may impact the performance-turnover relation is the *form* of this relationship. As in most studies in organizational psychology, it has been assumed that the performance-turnover relation is *linear.* Jackofsky (1984), however, has argued that the performance-turnover relation may in fact be **curvilinear** and best described by a U-shaped function. This means that turnover should be highest among employees performing at very low and very high levels. Jackofsky (1984) argued that, in most cases, very low performers are not going to be rewarded very well and thus may become dissatisfied. As performance moves toward medium levels, employees are probably being rewarded at a level that keeps them from becoming extremely dissatisfied, and thus seeking alternative employment. As performance increases, however, there is a greater likelihood that employees will have attractive alternative employment opportunities and thus may be more likely to leave an organization. This may even be true in organizations that reward on the basis of performance. Employees who are extremely talented may be receiving top salaries in a particular organization, but organizations simply may not be able to match what another organization is willing to pay in order to lure the employee away.

To date, Jackofsky's (1984) curvilinear hypothesis has not received a great deal of empirical investigation, although it has received some support. Schwab (1991) investigated the relation between performance and turnover among faculty at a large university, and obtained findings that indirectly support a nonlinear relation between performance and

turnover. Specifically, among nontenured faculty, there was a negative relation between performance (measured by number of publications) and turnover. In contrast, among tenured faculty, there was a positive relation between performance and turnover.

The negative relation between performance and turnover among nontenured faculty is most likely due to the fact that low-performing individuals, knowing they probably will not receive tenure, leave before this decision is made. Among tenured faculty, those performing at low levels are more likely to remain with the organization because their jobs are secure, and they are likely to have relatively few alternatives. High-performing tenured faculty, in contrast, may have very attractive employment alternatives, including salaries that their current employer simply cannot match. Because universities are often limited in the extent to which they can counter outside employment offers, highly talented tenured faculty may often be lured away (see Comment 6.3).

In addition to Schwab's (1991) study, more direct tests of the curvilinear hypothesis have supported this relationship (e.g., Trevor, Gerhart, & Boudreau, 1997), as did the previously mentioned meta-analysis conducted by Williams and Livingstone (1994). Trevor et al. (1997) also found that this curvilinear relation is more pronounced if salary growth is low and rates of promotion are high. When salary growth is low, both low and high performers have the most to gain by seeking other employment. When rates of promotion are high, low performers are likely to be dissatisfied and look elsewhere. High performers who are promoted rapidly are going to be more marketable in the external labor market than high performers who are promoted more slowly.

A second nonaffective variable that may impact turnover is the external labor market. Most people do not leave their present job

COMMENT 6.3

COUNTERING SALARY OFFERS

LET'S SAY THAT you're unhappy with your present salary and want a large pay raise. One strategy for getting this pay raise is to look for another job in the hopes that you will receive a more attractive offer, which your present employer will then match. Will this strategy work? Although it certainly is possible that your present employer will match the competing offer, there are actually many reasons *not* to match it. One reason may simply be that your employer can't afford to pay the salary that you are being offered by the competing organization. In professional sports, this occurs frequently when small-market teams have to part with players who become free agents. Another reason may be that, although they have the financial resources to match the offer, doing so would completely disrupt the internal equity of the salary structure. For example, if matching the competing offer means that you will be paid higher than your boss, then you probably won't get it. Finally, some organizations simply have a standing policy that they do not match competing job offers. Although such a policy may cause an organization to lose valuable employees, one could also argue that it protects the organization from being "blackmailed" into paying people more than they are worth.

until they have secured other employment, so turnover should be highest when job opportunities are plentiful. Empirical research that examined the direct relation between labor-market variables and turnover has produced mixed results. For example, Steel and Griffeth (1989) performed a meta-analysis and found the corrected correlation between perceived employment opportunities and turnover to be relatively modest ($r = .13$). Gerhart (1990), however, found that a more objective index of employment opportunities (regional unemployment rates) predicted turnover better than perceptions of employment opportunities. The fact that these findings are at odds suggests that the objective state of the external labor market, and individuals' perceptions of opportunities, may operate independently to influence turnover decisions.

Steel (1996), in a sample of U.S. Air Force personnel, examined the impact of objective labor market indexes and perceptions of employment opportunities on reenlistment decisions. The results of this study showed that reenlistment decisions could be predicted with a *combination* of perceptual and objective labor market variables. Turnover was highest among individuals who reported that they had strong regional living preferences and believed there were a large number of employment alternatives. The one objective labor market measure that predicted reenlistment was the historical retention rate for each Air Force occupational specialty in the study. Those in occupational specialties with high retention rates were more likely to reenlist.

Although Steel's study is quite useful in combining perceptual and objective data, its generalizability may be limited by its use of a military sample. In civilian organizations, employees are not bound to a certain number of years of service; thus, they may leave the organization at any time. One might surmise that labor market conditions (both objective and perceptive) might be more salient for military personnel because they have a window of opportunity; they can choose between staying or leaving the organization. As with any finding, generalizability is ultimately an empirical issue. Thus, these findings must be replicated in a nonmilitary setting.

A final variable—job tenure—may directly and indirectly impact turnover. As discussed in the previous chapter, longer job tenure is associated with higher levels of continuance commitment and, hence, lower levels of turnover (Meyer & Allen, 1997). Job tenure may also have an indirect effect because turnover may be impacted by different variables at different points in an employee's job tenure. Dickter, Roznowski, and Harrison (1996) examined both job satisfaction and cognitive ability as predictors of quit rates, in a longitudinal study conducted over a period of approximately four years. Their findings indicated that the impact of job satisfaction on turnover is strongest when employees have been on the job about one year, and this effect gradually decreases over time. It was also found that a high level of cognitive ability was associated with decreased risk of turnover. However, as with job satisfaction, this relationship diminished over time.

The results of Dickter et al. (1996) suggest that job satisfaction may drive turnover decisions early in an employee's job tenure. However, as an employee builds up job tenure, the costs associated with leaving one's employer become greater. Also, as job tenure increases, it is likely that a greater number of nonwork factors will come into play when one is deciding whether to leave one's present employer. For example, employees with children in school may not wish to change jobs if doing so involves a geographical move.

The fact that cognitive ability has less impact on turnover over time is also significant. Given that cognitive ability is associated with job performance (e.g., Schmidt & Hunter, 1998), this supports the notion that the relation between performance and turnover is nonlinear only among those who have been

employed a relatively short period of time. Performance may not be related to turnover among longer-tenured employees for a number of reasons. For example, the level of performance among those who stay in an organization may be restricted, and this may prevent performance from being related to turnover among this group. This essentially represents a **self-selection effect.**

It is also possible that true performance differences exist among longer-tenured employees, but other factors are at work. For example, when employees have been employed in an organization for several years, managers may be reluctant to highlight their performance differences. It is also possible that, over time, the experience employees gain may compensate for what they may be lacking in cognitive ability.

An Alternative Turnover Model of the Turnover Process

As discussed in the previous chapter, Mobley's (1977) model of the turnover process, and variants of it, have dominated the turnover literature for the past 25 years. Although there are some differences among these models, they all basically have two things in common. First, all propose that *employee affect plays a key role in the turnover process.* That is, a lack of satisfaction or feelings of low commitment set in motion the cognitive processes that may eventually lead an employee to quit his or her job. Second, because of the emphasis on employee affect, an implicit assumption in most turnover models is that *employee turnover is usually due to willingness to get away from the present job rather than attraction to other alternatives.*

According to Lee and Mitchell (1994), the dominant process models in the turnover literature have been useful, but they have also ignored some basic properties of human decision-making processes. Based largely on behavioral decision theory (Beach, 1993), they developed the **Unfolding Model** of the turnover process. A basic assumption of the Unfolding Model is that people generally do not evaluate their job or job situation unless forced to do so. Lee and Mitchell refer to events that force people to evaluate their jobs as "shocks to the system." Shocks may be, but are not necessarily negative events (e.g., a major layoff). A shock is simply any event that forces an employee to take stock and review his or her job situation. For example, a promotion may also be a shock to the system, according to Lee and Mitchell's definition.

Once an employee experiences a shock to the system, a number of outcomes are possible. One possibility is that the employee may have a preprogrammed response to the shock, based on previous experience. For example, an employee may have previously worked in a company that was acquired by a competitor, and decided it was best to leave the company. If this same event happens in later years, the employee may not even have to think about what to do; he or she may simply implement a preprogrammed response.

Where a preprogrammed response does not exist, an employee would engage in **controlled cognitive processing** and consciously evaluate whether the shock that has occurred can be resolved by staying employed in the current organization. To illustrate this point, Lee and Mitchell (1994) provide the example of a woman who becomes pregnant unexpectedly (a shock to the system). Assuming that this has not happened before, this woman would probably not have a preprogrammed response (quit or stay), and most likely would not have a specific job alternative. Rather, she would be forced to evaluate her attachments to both the organization and her career. Such an evaluation may also involve deciding whether continuing to work in the organization is

consistent with her image of being a competent mother.

A third type of situation involves a shock to the system without a preprogrammed response, but with the presence of specific job alternatives. An example of this situation would be where an employee receives an unsolicited job offer from another organization. This job offer may be considered a shock to the system because it forces the employee to think consciously about his or her job situation and to compare it to the outside job offer. Note that, in this type of situation, the employee may be reasonably happy in his or her job but may ultimately leave because another job is simply *better*.

A final alternative is where there is no shock to the system but turnover is "affect initiated"—that is, over time, an employee may simply become dissatisfied with his or her job for a variety of reasons. For example, the job may change in ways that are no longer appealing to the employee. Alternatively, the employee may undergo a change in his or her values or preferences, and may no longer see the job as satisfying. According to Lee and Mitchell (1994), once a person is dissatisfied, this may lead to a sequence of events, including reduced organizational commitment, more job search activities, greater ease of movement, stronger intentions to quit, and a higher probability of employee turnover. This proposed sequence of events is very consistent with dominant affect-based models of the turnover process (e.g., Mobley, 1977).

Lee and Mitchell's (1994) Unfolding Model is relatively new, so it has not received nearly the empirical scrutiny of more traditional affect-based process models. However, recent empirical tests of this model have met with some success (Lee, Mitchell, Holtom, McDaniel, & Hill, 1999; Lee, Mitchell, Wise, & Fireman, 1996). As with any model, it is likely that further refinements will be made as more empirical tests are conducted. Nevertheless, the Unfolding Model does represent an important development in turnover research.

Accidents

Accidents represent a very serious and costly form of counterproductive behavior in organizations. For example, in the United States alone, the most recent estimate is that accidents cost organizations $145 billion per year (U.S. Department of Health and Human Services, 2001). Another indication of the importance of safety in the workplace is that many nations have enacted legislation dealing with safety standards, and many have also created government agencies to oversee it. In the United States, for example, the Occupational Safety and Health Act provides employers with a set of legal standards regarding safety in the workplace. This legislation also led to the creation of the Occupational Safety and Health Administration (OSHA) to enforce employment safety and health standards.

Determinants of Accidents

Research on accidents has a long history, although organizational psychologists have not conducted much of it. For example, industrial engineers have focused on the design of machinery and the physical layout of the workplace as possible causes of workplace accidents (Wickens & Hollands, 2000). Within psychology, early accident research focused largely on developing a profile of "the accident-prone employee." This research identified a number of characteristics that were correlated with accidents, but researchers were never able to consistently document a cluster of characteristics that were consistently associated with accident prevalence (see Hansen, 1988). A major problem with

much of this research was that it was largely devoid of any theoretical underpinnings.

Research examining personal characteristics associated with accidents has become more theoretically grounded over the years, and, in fact, has yielded some useful results. For example, Hansen (1989) examined a combination of demographics, personality traits, and ability as predictors of accident frequency among employees of a large petrochemical processing company. The results of this study provide some interesting insight into personal characteristics associated with accidents. For example, tenure was *negatively* related to accident frequency. This may be due to a number of factors such as general inexperience, lack of training, and, possibly, emotional maturity levels.

Two personality traits stood out as predictors of accident involvement. The first was an index labeled *General Social Maladjustment*. This measure includes a variety of negative characteristics such as law breaking, immaturity, substance abuse problems, and disregard for other people—to name a few. As might be expected, those scoring high on this index were more likely to be involved in accidents than those scoring lower. The other trait that was found to be correlated with accidents was an index labeled *Distractibility*. As the label suggests, this measure captures the extent to which people have trouble concentrating, and whether their attention can be easily diverted. Those scoring higher on this index were more likely to be involved in accidents, compared to those scoring lower.

Inexperience can be remedied with the passage of time, but the other predictors of accidents identified by Hansen pose a greater problem to organizations. Employees who are maladjusted and highly distractible may be difficult to "turn around" with respect to safety behavior. Such individuals may be very unwilling to comply with safety-related rules (e.g., wearing safety equipment), and may simply lack the concentration needed to follow procedures. It is important to note that such employees, at least with regard to maladjustment, may also be prone to other forms of deviant behavior (Ones et al., 1993). Thus, the best way to address these characteristics may be at the stage of employee screening and selection.

In recent years, there has been a noticeable shift in accident research, from investigating characteristics of individual employees, to characteristics of group and organizational climates. **Safety climate** has been defined as the prevailing norms and values surrounding safety issues in an organization. Essentially, two questions can be answered if the safety climate of an organization is known: Is employee safety considered a high-level organizational priority? and Does this get communicated to employees through formal organizational policies and managerial actions?

Because safety climate is a relatively new concept, relatively little empirical research has been aimed at measuring it or documenting its impact on accident frequency. The research conducted to date, however, has yielded promising results. Hofmann and Stetzer (1998) found that a positive safety climate may lead employees to take more personal responsibility for safety. Hofmann and Morgeson (1999) also found that high commitment to safety and greater safety communication (two important aspects of safety climate) were associated with lower accident rates.

This recent shift in emphasis toward safety climate is important for a number of reasons. At a general level, it offers a potentially productive departure from a long history of accident research that has clung rather dogmatically to individual characteristics as predictors. This is not to say that individual characteristics have no bearing on accidents; for example, the results of Hansen's (1989)

study would suggest otherwise. However, given the considerable effort that has gone into the investigation of individual predictors, the actual insight gained about accidents and accident prevention has been rather disappointing.

Safety climate research also represents a recognition that employees work in a social context. Thus, information communicated via the social environment may have a powerful impact on employees' behavior. Granted, research on safety climate is still in its infancy and a number of issues are still to be resolved (e.g., Does safety climate operate equally at the group and organizational levels? How does safety climate develop in the first place? Do personal characteristics of employees interact with safety climate to impact actual safety behavior?). Despite these unresolved issues, this represents a fruitful new approach that may yield considerable insight into safety and ultimately provide organizations with concrete guidance on reducing the incidence of workplace accidents.

Accident Prevention

Given the research reviewed, an organization can take one of four different approaches to the prevention of accidents. First, based on human factors and industrial engineering research, an organization may choose to focus on physical factors. For example, an effort might be made to make equipment and other features of the physical environment safer for employees. This approach can be quite useful, given that some accidents can be prevented by better equipment design. It may also be quite costly; depending on the modifications that may be needed within the physical environment.

A second approach, and one that is used frequently, is **behavior modification** that encourages employees to use safe work practices and discourages employees from being unsafe. This involves the use of reinforcements for safe behaviors and the use of sanctions or punishment for unsafe behaviors. An organization, for example, might offer cash bonuses to employees who have the best safety records in a particular year. On the negative side, organizations may take disciplinary actions (e.g., written reprimands, suspensions) against employees who engage in unsafe work practices or who consistently have poor safety records.

There is actually a fair amount of empirical evidence supporting the effectiveness of behavior modification as a means of promoting safety in organizations. Komaki and colleagues, for example, have conducted a number of studies demonstrating the effective use of behavior modification in several organizations (e.g., Komaki, Barwick, & Scott, 1978; Komaki, Heinzmann, & Lawson, 1980). Overall, these studies have shown that the use of positive reinforcement or incentives can have a powerful effect on safety in organizations.

A third approach is to use selection as a means of screening out employees who are likely to be unsafe. If unsafe behavior is viewed as part of a general pattern of deviant antisocial behavior, then organizations may have a number of useful predictors at their disposal. For example, based on Hansen's (1989) study, described earlier, general social maladjustment and distractibility would appear to be two predictors that organizations could use to screen out employees who may have poor safety records. On the positive side, organizations may consider the use of personality traits such as conscientiousness in selection (Barrick & Mount, 1991; Tett, Jackson, Rothstein, 1991) as a positive step toward improving safety.

A final method of preventing accidents is by changing or improving the safety climate of the organization. Unfortunately, because research on safety climate is still in its infancy,

organizations have relatively little guidance as to how to change the safety climate. Some possible ways of doing this might be: publicizing the importance of safety within the organization, and making supervisors and managers accountable for the safety records within their units (Hofmann & Morgeson, 1999). Over time, as more research on the safety climate construct is conducted, organizations will likely be provided more guidance in their efforts to improve safety climate.

LESS COMMON FORMS OF COUNTERPRODUCTIVE BEHAVIOR

Up to this point in the chapter, we have covered what might be described as most *common* forms of counterproductive behavior in organizations. Most organizations must deal with ineffective employee performance, absenteeism, turnover, and employee safety issues. These, however, are clearly not the only forms of counterproductive behavior in organizations. In this concluding section, we explore less common but no less important forms of counterproductive behavior in organizations. They are: employee theft, workplace violence, substance use, and sexual harassment.

Employee Theft

Most employees do not steal from their employers. In fact, the vast majority of employees approach their work with a great deal of honesty and integrity. Nevertheless, employee theft does occur with enough frequency to be problematic for many organizations. For example, it has been estimated that approximately 35% of employees steal from their employers, and the financial losses from theft are in the billions (Kuhn, 1988). Furthermore, because the costs of employee theft are typically passed on to consumers, the impact of employee theft reaches far beyond the organizations in which it occurs.

Employee theft may be defined simply as "employees taking from the organization things that don't belong to them." Based on this definition, theft could range from relatively minor acts, such as employees taking inexpensive office supplies, to more serious forms such as a government employee's theft of classified documents. Most of the literature on employee theft has focused on what could be described as "moderate" forms of employee theft: retail store employees stealing merchandise, or convenience store employees skimming money from the cash register.

A review of the literature on the causes of employee theft reveals essentially two themes. The first, and by far the strongest, is that theft is due largely to characteristics of the individual (e.g., Jones & Boye, 1992; Ones et al., 1993). Furthermore, publishers of integrity tests have conducted much of this research. This is potentially problematic because such organizations may lack the motivation to rigorously evaluate the predictive capabilities of their products. Despite these concerns, Ones et al.'s (1993) meta-analysis showed fairly clearly that integrity tests do in fact predict employees' theft. Because integrity tests most likely measure the personality trait of "conscientiousness," this suggests that the employees most likely to steal are those who are unreliable and generally lack self-discipline. Jones and Boye (1992), however, point out that low employee conscientiousness may be only partially responsible for employee theft. They contend that low conscientiousness will lead to theft only among employees who have very tolerant attitudes toward theft and other forms of dishonesty.

A second theme in the literature suggests that employee theft may be a form of *retaliation* against unfair or frustrating organizational conditions. Greenberg (1990), for example,

conducted a study in which a pay-reduction policy was implemented in two separate locations of a large manufacturing organization. In one of these locations, little explanation was provided as to why the policy was being implemented, and this explanation was given with little remorse or sensitivity. In the other location, however, management provided employees with a more extensive explanation as to why the policy had to be adopted, and did so with much greater sensitivity. As predicted, the rate of theft in the plant where the inadequate explanation was provided was significantly higher compared to the plant given the adequate explanation and a third plant where no pay reduction had been implemented.

According to Spector (1997b), employee theft may also be caused by organizational conditions that induce frustration among employees. Frustration is essentially the emotion evoked in people when things in the environment are blocking their goals. In organizations, these barriers may include environmental constraints such as poor equipment, unnecessary rules and regulations, and other policies that end up wasting employees' time. Thus, Spector has proposed that employees may vent their frustrations toward the organization through acts of theft and sabotage. As with many relations, the link between frustration and theft may be impacted by other factors. For example, employees who are frustrated may feel like stealing but do not act on such impulses either because they have no opportunity or they are afraid of the consequences of such behavior. According to Spector (1997b), one variable that may moderate the relation between frustration and theft is employees' **locus of control**. Locus of control represents beliefs regarding the control people have over reinforcements in their lives (Rotter, 1966). A person described as having an *internal* locus of control generally believes that he or she has control over reinforcements. In contrast, an *external* locus of control is associated with the belief that one has little control over reinforcements.

The potential moderating effect of locus of control on the relation between frustration and theft is depicted in Figure 6.2. As can be seen, this model proposes that frustration is most likely to lead to destructive behaviors such as theft among employees who have an *external* locus of control. Those with an external locus of control tend to respond to frustration through theft and other forms of destructive behavior because they do not believe that frustrating organizational conditions can be changed through more constructive means. In contrast, those with an internal locus of control are more likely to believe that they are able to change frustrating organizational conditions constructively. These individuals, for example, may choose to exert their influence through participative management practices or labor–management committees. Spector's (1997b) hypothesis has received some empirical scrutiny and in

general has been supported (Chen & Spector, 1992; Spector & O'Connell, 1994; Storms & Spector, 1987).

Organizations wishing to reduce employee theft should certainly consider carefully screening applicants for characteristics such as low levels of conscientiousness, unreliability, or highly tolerant attitudes toward theft and forms of deviance. These characteristics may also be discerned indirectly though careful consideration of applicants' employment histories, and through reference checking. Organizations should also take a hard look at the internal organizational environment. If employees are often treated unfairly, or in a very arbitrary manner, this may signal that an organization is at risk for theft and other forms of antisocial behavior. Also, if employees are often thwarted in their efforts to perform their jobs, and thus frustration is high, organizations should explore ways to reduce organizational constraints.

Workplace Violence

Like employee theft, workplace violence is a relatively infrequent event. However, in recent years, there has been an alarming increase in the number of violent incidents in the workplace. For example, it has recently been estimated that, in the United States, nearly two million people, each year, may experience physical attacks in the workplace (Barling, 1996). Even more alarming is the fact that homicides are the second leading cause of job-related deaths (U.S. Bureau of Labor Statistics, 1999).

Like other phenomena that either have been or will be covered in this book, what is considered workplace violence is quite broad. For the purposes of this chapter, workplace violence is defined as *physical acts of aggression by members of an organization, carried out in organizational settings*. Notice that no attempt is

FIGURE 6.2
Spector's Model of the Impact of Locus of Control on the Relationship between Frustration and Counterproductive Behavior

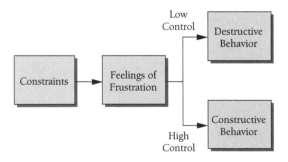

Source: P. E. Spector. (2000). *Industrial and organizational psychology: Research and practice* (2nd ed.). New York: John Wiley & Sons, Inc. Reprinted by permission.

made to specify or restrict the *target* of the aggression. For example, a violent act could be directed at a fellow employee, one's supervisor, or even a customer. However, our focus here is on the behavior of *employees in organizations* who commit acts of violence. Restricting the focus in this way obviously rules out attacks by customers, or by acquaintances, that take place in the workplace. These incidents, while obviously counterproductive, do not constitute counterproductive behavior of employees in organizations.

To explain violent acts on the part of employees, there have generally been three foci: (1) the physical environment; (2) characteristics of the individual; and (3) the organizational environment. If the focus is on the physical environment, we are able to draw on the social psychological literature that has linked aggression to violent cues in the environment as well as things that induce frustration (Worchel, Cooper, Goethals, & Olson, 2000). Considerable research has also linked stress-related symptoms to monotonous machine-paced work (e.g., Broadbent, 1985), although this work has not focused on aggression or violence as an outcome.

Given that little empirical research has examined the link between the physical environment and workplace violence, we can only speculate that environment may play a role. However, it is interesting to note that some of the most highly publicized acts of violence on the part of employees have taken place in work environments that many would consider somewhat noxious. In the U.S. Postal Service, for example, much of the work is highly monotonous and paced by the speed of machines. Factories and other manufacturing facilities are often noisy and hot. This link is obviously pure speculation, but over time, as more data are collected about violent incidents, it may be possible to assess more clearly the contribution of the physical environment.

A second focus in the workplace violence literature is identification of the characteristics of those who may be predisposed to violent acts. It has been suggested that persons who are loners, are paranoid, have a fascination with weaponry, and have few friends may be at risk for violent acts in the workplace (Johnson & Indvik, 1994). Unfortunately, little empirical data can be offered to support this claim. A somewhat more fruitful way to approach this issue is to examine personality characteristics that may identify the potential for violence. For example, many publishers of integrity tests have claimed that "unreliability" or "organizational deviance" scales are associated with a variety of counterproductive workplace behaviors, violence being among them (Hogan & Hogan, 1989).

A more indirect way to investigate the role of personality characteristics is through biographical or personal history information. The most obvious cue related to violence potential would be a past history of workplace violence or violations of the law. In some jurisdictions, organizations may be prohibited from obtaining such information prior to hiring a new employee. However, a routine background check may reveal prior acts of violence. Organizations should obviously consult an employment expert in order to make sure that preemployment background checks are within the law.

A third focus of workplace violence research has viewed the organizational environment as a possible factor precipitating violent acts. Much of what can be said here mirrors the previous section on theft. Organizations that treat employees unfairly and ignore their frustrations may be at greater risk for violence than organizations that emphasize fairness and support (Greenberg, 1990; Spector, 1997b). There may be some merit to this argument, but it must be remembered that, even in the most punitive organizations, very *few* employees engage in acts of violence. Thus, a negative organizational environment will probably not have a strong main effect on the incidence of workplace violence. Rather, the best way to think of the contribution of the organizational environment is in combination with personal factors. For example, a person who is prone to aggression and violence may take out his or her frustrations through violent acts if treated in an unfair or arbitrary manner by the organization.

Substance Use

The use of alcohol and illicit drugs is clearly a serious social problem. Substance use is related, either directly or indirectly, to negative outcomes such as traffic fatalities, domestic abuse, and violent crime. Because the workplace is reflective of general societal trends, one should not be surprised that substance use is considered a serious form of counterproductive organizational behavior. In examining substance use in organizations, it is important to be clear that the vast majority of research has not investigated *on-the-job* substance use. Rather, most research has examined either the job-related causes or the consequences of substance use that occurs off the job.

Research examining the *impact* of substance use in organizations has produced some fairly consistent findings. For example, it has been shown that employees who are problem drinkers and users of illicit drugs may exhibit a number of negative outcomes such as performance decrements, increased absenteeism, greater frequency of accidents, greater job withdrawal, and more antagonistic behavior toward others (Ames, Grube, & Moore, 1997; Blum, Roman, & Martin, 1993; Lehman & Simpson, 1992; Normand, Lempert, & O'Brien, 1994). Given these findings, the more pressing issues appear to be:

(1) identifying those who may have substance use problems, and (2) deciding what to do when employees show signs of substance use problems.

With respect to prediction of substance use, basically this issue has been approached in two ways. As with theft and violence, substance use is seen by many as part of a more general pattern of antisocial behavior (e.g., Hogan & Hogan, 1989). Given this conceptualization, efforts have been made to predict substance use based on personality traits more generally associated with antisocial behavior. McMullen (1991), for example, found that the Reliability scale from the Hogan Personality Inventory (HPI; Hogan & Hogan, 1989) was negatively related to self-reports of both off- and on-the-job substance use among college students. Interestingly, in this same study, in an applicant sample, this scale distinguished those who passed and those who failed a urinalysis drug screening.

Other than personality, research has also investigated personal characteristic predictors in the form of personal history. Lehman, Farabee, Holcom, and Simpson (1995) investigated a number of personal background characteristics as predictors of substance use among a sample of municipal workers, and produced a number of meaningful findings. Those at the greatest risk for problem substance use were young males who reported low self-esteem, had a previous arrest history, came from a family with substance use problems, and tended to associate with substance-using peers.

Another line of inquiry has examined environmental predictors of substance use. In this line of research, the variable that has been examined most is stressful job conditions. For the most part, this research has shown that although holding a stressful job may increase one's risk of substance use, this effect does not appear to be large (e.g., Cooper, Russell,

& Frone, 1990). A more recent line of inquiry has examined the social norms surrounding substance use in organizations. Recall that this idea has also been explored, with some success, in the study of both absenteeism and accidents. An example of this type of research can be seen in a study by Bennett and Lehman (1998), in which the impact of a workplace drinking climate was measured. It was found that in groups where a drinking climate was positive, individuals reported higher levels of both their own and coworkers' drinking activity. These findings suggest that social factors within work groups, and perhaps even within professions, may contribute to problem drinking.

Based on the empirical research, what can organizations do to prevent substance use among employees? As with prevention of theft and violence, one measure that appears to have some merit is the use of preemployment screening. Given the multitude of counterproductive behaviors that are associated with low conscientiousness (e.g., Hogan & Hogan, 1989; Ones et al., 1993), assessing this trait would appear to have some merit. In addition to personality testing, a thorough preemployment background check would also be a logical step toward preventing substance use problems (Lehman et al., 1995). As stated earlier, organizations obviously must make sure that such checks do not violate the rights of applicants.

Another method of preventing substance use has become increasingly popular: requiring applicants, and even current employees, to submit to drug screening, most typically through urinalysis. Drug screening is both expensive and controversial (Rosen, 1987), so organizations must think very carefully about its use. On the positive side, urinalysis may allow organizations to identify applicants or employees who have substance use problems. Furthermore, the mere presence

of a drug-screening program may serve as a powerful deterrent to those considering substance use.

Drug screening, however, carries with it a number of disadvantages as well. According to Rawlinson (1989), screening tests can cost up to $90 per subject, a figure that has undoubtedly increased considerably since 1989. Other than cost, another potential problem with drug screening is that organizations may turn off potentially valuable employees. There is evidence that attitudes toward drug testing are quite variable and may be impacted by various features of the specific program. For example, research has shown that people are not strongly opposed to the use of preemployment drug testing for jobs in which the safety of others could be put at risk by a drug-using employee (Murphy, Thornton, & Reynolds, 1990), but have less favorable attitudes toward jobs without these characteristics. Research has also shown that attitudes toward drug screening programs are more positive when such programs are seen as procedurally fair (Konovsky & Cropanzano, 1991). Important procedural issues in drug testing include the basis on which employees or applicants are required to submit to such tests, as well as whether retesting is allowed.

A final issue with drug testing—and perhaps the most critical issue—is an organization's response to confirmed employee substance use. An organization essentially has two choices in deciding how to respond to such employees: *punishment* or *treatment*. Some organizations have what could be described as "zero tolerance" policies with respect to drug use. In the military, for example, evidence of illicit drug use will automatically disqualify a recruit and will result in immediate disciplinary action against active duty personnel. In other cases, when substance use problems among employees are discovered, organizations seek to provide these individuals with treatment—typically, through Employee Assistance Programs (EAPs) and referrals. Note that these two responses, punishment and treatment, need not be mutually exclusive. An organization may suspend an employee as punishment, yet allow reinstatement after the completion of treatment.

Although cogent arguments can be made for either approach, research suggests that drug testing is viewed more favorably if those identified as having substance use problems are provided with at least some form of treatment (Stone & Kotch, 1989). The provision of treatment makes a drug-testing program appear to have a greater level of fairness compared to those that have only punitive outcomes. A possible downside to treatment is that an organization may run the risk of conveying an overly tolerant attitude toward substance use. In dealing with substance use, an organization is best served by pursuing a policy that combines clearly stated consequences with compassionate options that assist with treatment and recovery.

Sexual Harassment

During the past decade, sexual harassment has become a highly visible issue in organizations ranging from corporations to universities. Although it had been an issue for some time, the event that did much to heighten public awareness of sexual harassment was the U.S. Senate's confirmation hearing of Supreme Court Justice nominee Clarence Thomas, in October 1991. At the start of these televised hearings, the focus was on Thomas's judicial philosophy as reflected in past writing and decisions. The hearings took an unexpected turn when Anita Hill, a relatively unknown law professor, came forward with allegations of sexual harassment against Thomas. As Hill testified about the sordid details of Thomas's behavior, and Thomas subsequently denied them, a very intense public dialogue regarding sexual harassment in the workplace was sparked.

Sexual harassment, a form of illegal sexual discrimination, is prohibited by Title VII of the 1964 Civil Rights Act. Sexual harassment may come in many forms but is defined as: "unwelcome sexual advances, requests for sexual favors, and other verbal or physical contact when (a) submission to the conduct is either explicitly or implicitly a term or condition of an individual's employment, (b) submission to or rejection of such conduct by an individual is used as a basis for employment decisions affecting that individual, and/or (c) such conduct has the purpose or effect of unreasonably interfering with work performance, or creating an intimidating, hostile, or offensive working environment" (Equal Employment Opportunity Commission, 1980). The term **quid pro quo sexual harassment** is often used to denote situations where an employee's advancement or performance is adversely impacted by refusing the sexual advances of a supervisor or other employee who exerts power over the employee. This form would apply primarily to the first two parts of the definition provided above.

The second form of sexual harassment, often referred to simply as **hostile work environment,** refers primarily to the third part of the definition. In this form, there is no overt attempt to manipulate or threaten. Rather, the existence of sexual harassment is based on the general behavior of others in the workplace. Vulgar comments, telling "off-color" jokes, the display of pornographic images, and even nonverbal gestures that elicit discomfort may provide the basis for sexual harassment based on the hostile work environment argument. This category is important because it highlights the fact that even behavior intended to be for fun can be perceived as offensive to others. Destructive intent is not a prerequisite for sexual harassment.

Organizational research on sexual harassment has examined a number of issues, including prevalence (Fitzgerald, Drasgow, Hulin, Gelfand, & Magley, 1997), causes (Gruber, 1998; Gutek, Cohen, & Konrad, 1990), ways to respond to sexual harassment allegations, and methods of prevention (Fitzgerald, 1993). This research suggests that sexual harassment is prevalent, and that it is most likely to be experienced by women who are in positions of unequal power and heightened visibility in relation to men. Women in such situations are typically required to interact frequently with men, and therefore are at greater risk for harassment.

With respect to organizational responses, the literature is clear that organizations are much better off when they investigate such incidents objectively (as opposed to denying them). When an allegation of sexual harassment is brought forward, organizations have a responsibility to take such allegations seriously. At the same time, individuals accused of sexual harassment have the right to an objective, unbiased inquiry into the matter. In some cases, organizations may err by categorically dismissing all sexual harassment charges. At the other extreme, in the effort to eradicate sexual harassment, organizations may unfairly treat those accused as "guilty until proven innocent" and deny them due process. Given the serious consequences associated with such charges, the best course of action is a careful assessment of the facts.

One way that organizations can prevent sexual harassment is to have in place a clearly articulated sexual harassment policy. Such a policy serves the dual purposes of letting employees know what is considered sexual harassment and the steps an organization will take if harassment occurs. Letting employees know what is considered sexual harassment is often easier said than done. Given the wording of sexual harassment statutes, employees may often be confused as to what is considered sexual harassment. However, based on the author's experience, getting people to agree on what is appropriate and inappropriate behavior in mixed-gender company may not be nearly as difficult as it may seem. Given common sense and knowledge of the prevailing societal codes of morality, the vast majority of adults know what is and what is not proper behavior in mixed-gender company. Ignorance is not a viable defense against charges of sexual harassment.

Sexual harassment policies also need to communicate to employees that sexual harassment is a serious matter and that those who engage in such behavior will encounter severe consequences. Ultimately, however, the most powerful way to communicate organizational sexual harassment policy is through an organization's response to such behavior. If organizations respond to such behavior in a manner that is consistent with their policy, and do so regardless of the parties involved, this sends the powerful message that the organization will not tolerate such behavior. On the other hand, organizations that choose to ignore this issue run the risk of sending employees a very confusing message about sexual harassment. At best, this communicates ignorance and indifference. At worst, this may convey a message that the organization approves of such behavior and is willing to "look the other way" when it occurs.

CHAPTER SUMMARY

This chapter examined counterproductive behaviors, or those actions on the part of employees that explicitly run counter to the goals of an organization. The most common form of counterproductive behavior is ineffective job performance. Nevertheless, ineffective performance is often difficult to detect due to external constraints on performance and deficiencies in organizational performance measurement systems. Based on models of job performance, ineffective performance may be due to characteristics of the employee as well as environmental factors. Organizations may respond to poor performance in a number of ways, including training, coaching, and, if all else fails, punishment. A key issue in deciding the response to poor performance is the underlying causes of performance difficulties.

Absenteeism and turnover are the other two most common forms of counterproductive behavior in organizations. Absenteeism has long been viewed by organizational psychologists as a behavioral response to negative feelings about one's job or job situation. Over time, however, this somewhat narrow view has given way to a broader view of the causes of absenteeism. The most promising of these appears to be group norms regarding absenteeism. This is due largely to the recognition that absenteeism is a complex phenomenon and thus may be impacted by a variety of factors.

Like absenteeism, turnover has been viewed largely as a response to negative affect. Here too, more contemporary turnover research has expanded and investigated other nonaffective predictors of turnover. The external labor market, as well as employees' job performance, are two nonaffective variables that have been shown to have an important impact on employee turnover. Another important advance in this area is the use of findings from behavioral decision theory to model the turnover process.

Less common forms of counterproductive behavior examined in the chapter included accidents, theft, violence, substance use, and sexual harassment. Many years of research have failed to uncover a clear profile of the "accident-prone" employee, but more recent research in this area has provided some important insights. The "safety climate"

within an organization, in particular, appears to be an important key to accident frequency. Attention to this climate, coupled with a focus on the physical environment and characteristics of employees, is likely to be the best strategy for preventing accidents in organizations.

Theft and violence, when considered together, can be considered "antisocial" behaviors in organizations. Although both are relatively low-frequency events, they can nevertheless be quite damaging to organizations. Like most forms of behavior, these can be explained by characteristics of both the employee and the environment. With respect to theft, considerable evidence has accumulated suggesting that employees with a combination of a low level of conscientiousness and tolerant attitudes toward theft are most likely to steal. Research has been much less conclusive about personal characteristics indicative of violence, although it is likely that violence is often indicative of underlying psychopathology.

With respect to environmental characteristics, there is some evidence that treating employees unfairly, and failing to address frustrations, may heighten the risk of antisocial behavior. This is particularly the case when employees believe they have no control over events that impact them. Thus, organizations wishing to prevent antisocial behavior should combine thorough preemployment screening with efforts to treat employees fairly and remove barriers to performance.

Substance use is a form of counterproductive behavior that may be quite damaging, particularly when employees perform dangerous work or are entrusted with the safety of others. The causes of substance use are complex; however, it is interesting to note that personality traits predictive of other forms of antisocial behavior are also predictive of substance use. Prediction and prevention of substance use often pose a dilemma for organizations because issues of employee privacy and public relations are involved.

The final form of counterproductive behavior examined in this chapter was sexual harassment. Sexual harassment may occur in the form of direct acts, or more indirectly through behaviors that, in the aggregate, create a "hostile work environment." Research has shown that women are typically the victims of sexual harassment, and it is most likely to occur in work situations in which women are in the minority and fill positions of lower power than men. The best way to prevent this form of counterproductive behavior is to have in place a clearly articulated sexual harassment policy, and to heighten employees' awareness of the issue. When accusations of sexual harassment do occur, organizations should have in place fair and unbiased methods of investigation and be willing to take punitive action if necessary.

SUGGESTED ADDITIONAL READINGS

Braverman, M. (1999). *Preventing workplace violence.* Thousand Oaks, CA: Sage.

Gavin, M. B., Green, S. G., & Fairhurst, G. T. (1995). Managerial control strategies for poor performance over time and the impact on subordinate reactions. *Organizational Behavior and Human Decision Processes, 63,* 207–221.

Hom, P. W., & Griffeth, R. W. (1995). *Employee turnover.* Cincinnati, OH: Southwestern.

Martocchio, J., & Judge, T. A. (1994). A policy capturing approach to individuals' decisions to be absent. *Organizational Behavior and Human Decision Processes, 57,* 358–386.

Piotrkowski, C. (1998). Gender harassment, job satisfaction, and distress among employed white and minority women. *Journal of Occupational Health Psychology, 3,* 33–43.

Chapter Seven

Occupational Stress

Occupational stress is a topic that has generated a tremendous volume of research in a surprisingly short period of time (Beehr, 1995; Jex, 1998). It is also a topic that has been the focus of a great deal of popular media attention, and it comes up frequently in everyday conversation. (Who *doesn't* have a stressful job!) Despite all this attention, the scientific study of occupational stress does not have a long history. Furthermore, despite the considerable progress that has been made over the years, we still have much to learn about the dynamics of stress in organizations.

A question that is frequently asked about occupational stress is: Does it really have an aversive effect on individuals and organizations, or are those who study occupational stress "making mountains out of molehills"? There is evidence that being consistently exposed to stressful work conditions is harmful to employees and may have a negative impact on organizational effectiveness. Consider, for example, that the amount of money extracted from the U.S. economy due to occupational

stress has been estimated in the billions of dollars (e.g., Aldred, 1994; Ivancevich & Matteson, 1980; Matteson & Ivancevich, 1987; Mulcahy, 1991). Such estimates are based on the assumption that stress plays a role in negative outcomes such as increased healthcare costs, higher rates of absenteeism and turnover, more on-the-job accidents, and reduced productivity.

Another indication of the harmful effects of occupational stress is the increasing trend toward stress-related workers' compensation claims (National Council on Compensation Insurance, 1988, 1991). In the past, compensation for work-related injuries was limited to *physical* injuries caused by some *physical* event or stimulus. Increasingly, however, more and more states are recognizing the legitimacy of physical and even psychological injuries that may be caused by some stressful aspect of the work environment that is not physical in nature (e.g., an overly demanding supervisor).

Occupational stress is also important because of its impact on society as a whole. It is unlikely that a person experiencing constant stress on the job will function effectively in his or her other roles, such as husband/wife, parent, neighbor, and community member. Failure to perform these roles effectively may not have direct economic costs but may, in the long run, have a tremendously negative impact on society. Thus, occupational stress is clearly not the "cause of all societal ills," but it does have an important and real impact on individuals, organizations, and society.

A BRIEF HISTORY

The earliest scientific investigations related to the field of occupational stress were conducted by the well-known physiologist Walter Cannon in the early part of the twentieth century (e.g., Cannon, 1914). Cannon was a pioneer in the investigation of the relationship between emotions and physiological responses, and is perhaps best known for having coined the term **homeostasis.** Homeostasis represents the body's effort to restore normal physiological functioning when some deviation is required. When the body is exposed to extreme cold, for example, the physiological changes that are evoked are designed to maintain a constant internal body temperature. Stressful conditions on the job are typically perceived as aversive events that require some adaptive response designed to return the employee to normal functioning.

The first actual scientific investigations of stress are attributed to Hans Selye (1956), who is considered by many to be the "Father of Stress." Selye, an endocrinologist, was conducting research on reproductive hormones in animals. During the course of this research, he was required to expose these animals to a number of aversive stimuli, such as temperature extremes and radiation. While doing this, Selye observed a great deal of predictability in these animals' efforts to adapt to the aversive stimuli. From this, Selye reasoned that humans do much the same in their efforts to cope with the challenges of everyday life, and he developed the **general adaptation syndrome** to describe this process.

The general adaptation syndrome consists of three distinct stages: alarm, resistance, and exhaustion. In the alarm stage, the physiological resources of the body are mobilized, in wholesale fashion, to deal with an impending threat. In the resistance stage, the body recognizes that not all of its resources may be needed, and thus continues to mobilize only those that are necessary. Finally, in the exhaustion stage, the body realizes that its physiological resources are depleted and, as a result, makes another attempt to mobilize. If this second attempt at mobilizing physiological resources does not neutralize the threat, this may lead to permanent damage to the organism, or what Selye termed "diseases of adaptation."

Selye's work was undoubtedly pioneering, but it must be remembered that he focused primarily on *physiological* reactions to aversive *physical* stimuli. He was not focusing on stress in the *workplace*. The first large-scale program of research focusing exclusively on stress in the workplace was undertaken at the University of Michigan's Institute for Social Research in the early 1960s. What is particularly noteworthy about this research effort is that the focus was on **psychosocial factors** in the workplace that may be stressful to employees. Psychosocial factors represent aspects of the work environment having to do with interactions with other people. In particular, the Michigan researchers focused much of their attention on what they termed **role stressors** (to be discussed in more detail later in the chapter), which are aversive working conditions associated with behaviors expected of each employee in an organization (e.g., Caplan, Cobb, French, Harrison, & Pinneau, 1975; Kahn, Wolfe, Quinn, Snoek, & Rosenthal, 1964).

Despite the contributions of the University of Michigan research program, occupational stress did not attract a lot of interest among organizational psychologists in the late 1960s and early 1970s. This changed in 1978, due in large part to a comprehensive review and analysis of the occupational stress literature. The authors of the review, which appeared in the journal *Personnel Psychology,* were Terry Beehr and John Newman. The Beehr and Newman (1978) compilation is generally regarded as an important scholarly work and has been cited frequently, but its greatest contribution may have been to alert those in the field of organizational psychology that occupational stress was an issue worthy of attention.

Evidence of the impact of Beehr and Newman's review can be seen in the steep increase in the volume of occupational stress research after its publication (Beehr, 1995, 1998). Since then, several books, chapters, and comprehensive reviews have continued to summarize this vast literature (e.g., Beehr & Bhagat, 1985; Cartwright & Cooper, 1997; Ivancevich & Matteson, 1980; Jex, 1998; Jex & Beehr, 1991; Kahn & Byosiere, 1992; Sullivan & Bhagat, 1992).

APPROACHES AND TERMINOLOGY

Organizational psychologists have certainly contributed much to the study of occupational stress, but a perusal of the occupational stress literature will show that important contributions have also been made by physicians, clinical psychologists, engineering psychologists, labor economists, epidemiologists, and nurses, to name a few. To capture the interdisciplinary nature of occupational stress, Beehr and Franz (1987) proposed that occupational stress can be approached from four different perspectives: (1) medical, (2) clinical/counseling, (3) engineering psychology, and (4) organizational psychology. The distinguishing feature of the **medical approach** to occupational stress is a focus on the contribution of stress in the workplace to employee health and illness. When viewed from this perspective, stressful aspects of the work environment may be considered pathogenic agents that contribute to disease conditions. Not surprisingly, many researchers who approach occupational stress from this perspective are physicians or have received their academic training in some other health-related field (e.g., health education, nursing, or public health).

The **clinical/counseling approach** to occupational stress emphasizes the impact of stressful working conditions on mental health outcomes (e.g., depression, anxiety). Beehr and Franz (1987) also point out that, compared to the others, this approach tends to focus more on *treatment* than on *research.* That is, rather than focusing on *why* stressful work conditions lead to problems, adherents of this approach tend to focus on developing methods to relieve stress-related symptomatology (e.g., Beehr, Jex, & Ghosh, 2001). As one would expect, the clinical/counseling approach is dominated by those trained in clinical or counseling psychology.

The **engineering psychology approach** to occupational stress focuses on sources of stress that originate from the physical work environment. Examples of these might include work schedules, pace of work, or perhaps the design of employees' workstations. This emphasis on the physical environment as a source of stress is not surprising, given that the discipline of engineering psychology (also termed *human factors*) focuses on the interface between employees and the physical environment. Another distinctive feature of this approach, according to Beehr and Franz (1987), is that it emphasizes the performance-related implications of stress in the workplace. It is also true, though not pointed out by Beehr and Franz, that much of the occupational stress research guided by this approach has examined health-related outcomes such as physiological changes (Frankenhaeuser, 1979) or fatigue (Sparks, Cooper, Fried, & Shirom, 1997).

The **organizational psychology approach** to occupational stress is characterized by a number of distinctive features. For one thing, this approach tends to focus on what were previously defined as *psychosocial* sources of stress in the workplace. This implies two things. First, this approach tends to focus heavily on **cognitive appraisal**, or the process by which employees perceive the work environment and decide whether it is stressful. Second, as was pointed out earlier, this approach tends to focus on sources of stress that emanate from interactions with others (e.g., they are social in nature). Another distinguishing feature of this approach, as compared to the others, is that researchers tend to be interested in the impact of occupational stress on employee outcomes that directly impact organizational effectiveness.

OCCUPATIONAL STRESS TERMINOLOGY

Like any field of study or discipline, occupational stress has adopted (and, at times, struggled with) unique terminology. In this section, the terminology used in occupational stress research is briefly reviewed. No term has evoked more controversy and discussion than the term "stress" itself (see Comment 7.1). It can be defined in a number of ways, but researchers have tended to adopt a *stimulus, response,* or *stimulus–response* definition. A stimulus definition implies that stress is some type of force acting upon the individual. In everyday conversation, this definition might be reflected in the following sentence: "Bob has had his share of stress at work during the past year." Notice that, in this statement, the term *stress* is used to refer to negative aspects of the work environment that may be troublesome to the individual.

A response definition implies that stress is synonymous with the way in which employees *react* to stressful job conditions. Consider the following statement: "Barbara is feeling a lot of stress because of her upcoming performance review." *Stress* is used here to represent the *feelings* that are evoked by something in the work environment that the employee obviously considers aversive.

When a stimulus–response definition is used, the term *stress* is used merely to refer to the overall process by which the work environment may negatively impact employees. Rather than using the term stress to mean anything, the term **stressor** is used to represent aspects of the work environment that may require some adaptive response on the part of employees. For example, one might note that a person appears to be experiencing many stressors on his or her job. (Later in the chapter, a number of common organizational stressors will be described.)

The other term associated with the stimulus–response definition, **strain**, refers to a multitude of maladaptive ways employees may react to stressors. For example, one

COMMENT 7.1

THE MEANING OF THE WORD "STRESS"

LIKE MANY OTHER researchers in various fields of study, occupational stress researchers have struggled considerably with terminology over the years. Variance in terminology makes it more difficult for researchers to communicate and more generally decreases the rate of progress within any scientific endeavor. This can also be a big problem if those who participate in occupational stress studies have their own definitions of important terms and concepts.

Several years ago, I conducted a study, in collaboration with Terry Beehr and Cathy Roberts, in which we were interested in a simple question: "How do survey respondents tend to interpret the word 'stress' when it is used on self-report questionnaires?" Our data seemed to indicate that respondents had a ten-dency to use what is termed a "response" definition. In other words, if you ask people about their current "stress level," chances are they will answer in terms of the *reactions* they are having to the stressful conditions they are experiencing in their job.

The practical implication of this study is actually quite simple: Unless there is a compelling reason to do so, it is probably not a good idea to use the word "stress" in questionnaire items. If it is used, researchers should be very clear as to how they are defining it.

Source: S. M. Jex, T. A. Beehr, and C. K. Roberts. (1992). The meaning of occupational "stress" items to survey respondents. *Journal of Applied Psychology, 77,* 623–628.

might observe that because of working long hours (a stressor), an employee appears to be showing a great deal of strain. Occupational stress researchers typically classify strains in three categories: psychological, physical, and behavioral. Psychological strains include affective or emotional responses to stressors. Common examples of these from the occupational stress literature include anxiety and frustration (Spector, Dwyer, & Jex, 1988), hostility (Motowidlo, Packard, & Manning, 1986), and depression (Heinisch & Jex, 1997).

Physical strains include responses that are related to employees' physical health and well-being. These have received considerable attention in recent years (e.g., Ganster & Schaubroeck, 1991) because of the escalating costs associated with healthcare. The most common method of measuring physical strain has been self-reported physical symptoms (e.g., Frese, 1985; Spector & Jex, 1998). Other methods that can be found in the occupational stress literature include the assessment of physiological indexes (Fried, Rowland, & Ferris, 1984; Schaubroeck & Merritt, 1997), and diagnosed disease conditions (Sales & House, 1971).

Behavioral strains have been explored the least in occupational stress research. This is likely due to the difficulties associated with obtaining behavioral indexes, as well as a lack of understanding the many forms of behavior in organizations (e.g., Campbell, 1990). Perhaps the most relevant form of behavioral strain in organizations is impaired job performance. The majority of occupational stress studies that have examined the impact of stressors on job performance have measured it through the use of supervisory ratings (Jex, 1998). Other behavioral strains that have been examined, with varying degrees of success, include absenteeism, turnover, and substance abuse.

OCCUPATIONAL STRESS MODELS

As was pointed out in Chapter 2, a theoretical model is simply an attempt to describe the relevant variables impacting some phenomenon and the relations among these variables. Theoretical models are often quite useful in guiding behavioral science research and its applications. Over the years, a number of theoretical models of occupational stress have been developed to help guide both research and organizational efforts to reduce stress. Those that have had the greatest impact are described below.

Institute for Social Research (ISR) Model

One of the earliest occupational stress models came out of the previously mentioned program of research at the University of Michigan's Institute for Social Research (French & Kahn, 1962; Katz & Kahn, 1978). For this reason, it has come to be known as the ISR model of occupational stress. As can be seen in Figure 7.1, this model begins with the *objective environment*. This essentially includes anything in an employee's work environment: the number of hours worked, the amount of responsibility, the extent to which interaction with others is required, and so on.

The next step in this model is labeled the *psychological environment*. At this step, according to the model, the employee perceives the objective environment. The employee at this

FIGURE 7.1
The ISR Model of Occupational Stress

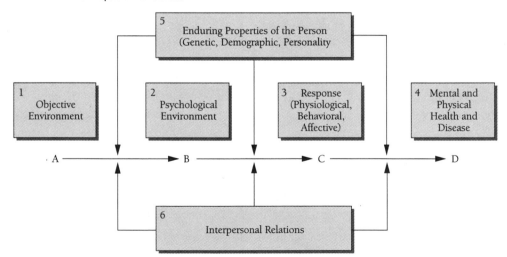

Adapted from: D. Katz and R. L. Kahn. (1978). *The social psychology of organizations* (2nd ed.). New York: Wiley. Reprinted by permission.

point is appraising aspects of the work environment and making some judgment as to whether it is threatening (Lazarus, 1966). As was stated in the previous discussion of approaches to occupational stress, the appraisal process is a key component of the organizational psychology approach.

Once the environment is appraised, the model proposes that the result may be *immediate physiological, behavioral, and emotional responses* on the part of the employee. Physiological changes that are commonly evoked by stressful stimuli include increases in heart rate, blood pressure, and respiration (Fried et al., 1984). Immediate behavioral responses may include decreased effort, or perhaps an inability to concentrate (Jex, 1998). Emotional responses may include increases in both anxiety and depressive symptoms, and a decrease in job satisfaction (Heinisch & Jex, 1997; Spector et al., 1988).

Depending on the severity and duration of the immediate responses, the result may be *adverse changes in mental and physical health*. For example, an employee whose initial response to a stressor (such as an impending deadline) is increased anxiety may end up feeling anxious all the time. On the physical side, an employee who experiences a short-term elevation in blood pressure in response to this same stressor may eventually develop chronic hypertension or coronary heart disease.

The next two components in the ISR model (5 and 6) are meant to illustrate the impact of individual differences on all of the processes depicted in the model. For example, people obviously differ considerably in terms of genetic makeup, demographic characteristics, personality traits, and the quality of their interpersonal relations with others. Furthermore, any or all of these may impact the manner in which people perceive the

objective environment, their immediate responses to perceived stressors, and, ultimately, whether stressors lead to adverse mental and physical health.

The ISR model has served as a conceptual guide for a substantial portion of the occupational stress research conducted over the years, and therefore it has been quite influential. Perhaps the greatest weaknesses of this model are its generality and simplicity. The model does not provide *specifics* about each of the steps in the process. One could also argue that important variables and processes have been left out of the model. For example, the model does not explicitly account for employees' efforts to cope with stressors, or acknowledge that stressors may impinge on the employee from outside of the organization.

McGrath's Process Model

After the ISR model was proposed, several others were put forth and emphasized different aspects of the occupational stress process. McGrath, for example, in his *Handbook of Industrial and Organizational Psychology* (1976), proposed a theoretical model that focused heavily on the performance-related implications of occupational stress. As shown in Figure 7.2, McGrath's model conceptualizes the stress process as a four-stage, closed-loop process.

The first stage, as in the ISR model, represents situations that employees encounter in organizations. These situations are then perceived via cognitive appraisal processes. As in the ISR model, when these perceptions are negative, this signals the presence of stressors.

At the next stage, McGrath's model diverges somewhat from the ISR model. Notice that after a situation is appraised, the model proposes that individuals make *decisions* about how they will respond to the stressor. Once a

FIGURE 7.2
McGrath's Process Model of Occupational Stress

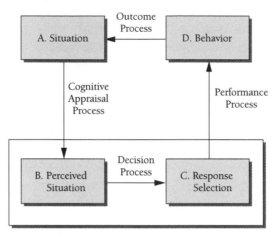

Adapted from: J. B. McGrath. (1976). Stress and behavior in organizations. In M. D. Dunnette (Ed.), *Handbook of industrial and organizational psychology* (pp. 1351–1396). Chicago: Rand McNally. Reprinted by permission.

decision is made, the individual then engages in some form of overt behavior. Such behavior may have negative implications for performance (e.g., reducing effort), although this may not always be the case. For example, an employee confronted with a stressor (e.g., conflict with a coworker) may choose a more adaptive response (e.g., talking rationally to the person) and alter the situation in a favorable manner.

Though not as influential as the ISR model, McGrath's model does have some very positive features. Chief among these is the recognition that responses to stressors involve *conscious choices* on the part of employees. By explicitly incorporating decision making in the model, McGrath was somewhat ahead of his time. As will be shown in Chapter 8, recent theories of motivation have clearly embraced the idea that choice and decision making are important determinants of motivation and, ultimately, of performance (see also Kanfer, 1992).

Beehr and Newman's Facet Model

In addition to providing a comprehensive review of the occupational stress literature, Beehr and Newman (1978) proposed a model of the occupational stress process. The primary reason for proposing this model, according to these authors, was to serve as a guide to categorizing the occupational stress literature. As can be seen in Figure 7.3, this model proposes that the occupational stress process can be broken down into a number of "facets" that represent categories of variables to be studied. Going from left to right in the model, the *Personal* facet represents the stable characteristics that employees bring with them to the workplace. Examples of variables included here would be demographic characteristics (e.g., age, gender, race) and personality.

The *Environmental* facet, in contrast, represents those stimuli in the work environment that individual employees must confront. Variables comprising this facet would include

FIGURE 7.3
Beehr and Newman's Facet Model of Occupational Stress

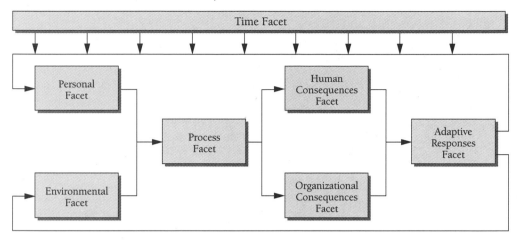

Adapted from: T. A. Beehr and J. E. Newman. (1978). Job stress, employee health, and organizational effectiveness: A facet analysis, model, and literature review. *Personnel Psychology, 31,* 665–699. Reprinted by permission.

characteristics of the work performed (e.g., level of complexity) as well as the nature of job-related interpersonal relations. It is in the *Process* facet that characteristics of the person and the situation interact. This is the point at which employees appraise the work environment and ultimately decide whether it is harmful.

After the environment is appraised, if the employee perceives stressors to be present, there may be a variety of consequences for both the individual employee and the organization as a whole. The *Human Consequences* facet represents the multitude of ways in which employees may respond to stressors that primarily have implications for each individual employee (e.g., health problems, substance abuse). In contrast, the *Organizational Consequences* facet represents employee responses that primarily have implications for organizational functioning (e.g., higher rates of absenteeism and turnover, impaired employee job performance).

Depending on the consequences for the individual and the organization, some re-

sponse may be required. The *Adaptive Response* represents efforts on the part of individuals and organizations to respond adaptively to stressors. An adaptive response for an individual may be to exercise when he or she feels tense or anxious. An organization may respond to increased absenteeism by instituting flexible work hours.

The final facet in this model is *Time*. As is evident from Figure 7.3, this facet has an impact on all other facets in the model. It exhibits recognition of the fact that the process of employees' appraising the environment, determining what aspect(s) are stressful, and ultimately responding to those perceived stressors, is embedded in a temporal context. In some cases, this process may be very short; at other times, it may occur over a period of several years. As Beehr and Newman (1978) aptly pointed out, this is probably the least understood of all the facets because of the reliance on cross-sectional research designs. (See McGrath and Beehr, 1990, for a more extensive discussion of the role of time in occupational stress research.)

Demands–Control Model

A model of occupational stress that is much more limited in scope than the others presented to this point is known simply as the Demands–Control model. This model, which was proposed by Robert Karasek in the late 1970s, posits that the most stressful situations in the workplace are those in which employees face heavy job demands but, at the same time, are given little control over their work. [Karasek (1979) used the term "Job Decision Latitude" to denote control.] A good example would be the situation of a typical factory worker in the Scientific Management era. Recall from Chapter 1 that one of the major principles of Scientific Management was to provide production employees with challenging goals, usually in the form of production standards. At the same time, proponents of Scientific Management argued that these same employees should have little control over things such as the design of work methods and the scheduling of rest breaks. Factory employees during this period also had little control over the reliability of machinery or the motivation levels of their fellow employees.

Most research using the Demands–Control model as a theoretical framework has examined health and physiological outcomes (e.g., Fox, Dwyer, & Ganster, 1993; Karasek, Baker, Marxer, Ahlbom, & Theorell, 1981; Perrewe & Ganster, 1989). This limits the scope of the model somewhat, although it is certainly possible that the scope of the Demands–Control model could be broadened. In fact, some research that tested the Demands–Control model has investigated psychological outcomes (e.g., Spector, 1987a).

It is also worth mentioning that recent tests of the Demands–Control model have shown that the interaction between job demands and control may be more complex than Karasek originally proposed. Most notably, Schaubroeck and Merritt (1997) found, in predicting blood pressure, that the interaction between demands and control that is predicted by Demands–Control theory was observed only for employees who reported high self-efficacy. This suggests that having control over one's work tasks is helpful to an employee only if he or she feels able to perform those tasks (i.e., has high self-efficacy).

Person–Environment Fit Model

This model of occupational stress actually has implications for many organizational phenomena (e.g., selection, socialization). The historical roots of the Person–Environment (P–E) Fit approach can be traced back to Kurt Lewin and his notion of *interactional psychology*. Lewin believed that human behavior is a function of the interaction between characteristics of the person and characteristics of the situation. One aspect of this interaction that is relevant to occupational stress is the degree to which there is a *fit* between the person and the situation. According to this approach, an employee perceives the work environment as stressful when there is a lack of fit (Caplan, 1987; French, Caplan, & Harrison, 1982).

The general notion of P–E Fit is rather simple but there are many ways in which fit (and misfit) between an employee and the work environment can occur. According to Kristof (1996), fit (and misfit) may indicate the degree to which an employee's skills and abilities match the requirements of the job he or she is performing. An employee who lacks the skills and abilities necessary to perform a job may feel overwhelmed and inadequate. Conversely, when job requirements are well below an employee's capabilities, the results may be boredom, frustration, and dissatisfaction. In either case, it is very likely that such an employee will perceive the job as stressful.

The concept of P–E Fit (and misfit) may also occur at a more "macro" level of analysis. More specifically, one can speak of the degree of fit between characteristics of the employee and characteristics of the organization. For example, suppose an employee who places a very high value on individual accomplishment goes to work for an organization that places a very high value on teamwork. This would obviously be a poor fit and it is likely that such an individual would ultimately find working in such an environment stressful.

The P–E Fit approach has proven to be quite useful to occupational stress researchers. Over the years, considerable refinements have been made both in conceptualizing fit (e.g., Edwards, 1994; Kristof, 1996) and in the statistical analysis of P–E fit data (Edwards & Parry, 1993). Perhaps the major limitation of the P–E fit approach is that, compared to the *Environment* component, we seem to be much further ahead in the measurement of the *Person* component of the model. That is, psychologists have devoted considerable time and energy to conceptualizing and measuring individual characteristics such as abilities, skills, and personality. Far less attention has been given to conceptualizing and measuring unique characteristics of organizations.

Comparison of Occupational Stress Models

Now that four of the most widely used occupational stress models have been described, some comparison of the relative merits of each is in order. In terms of usefulness, all of the models presented have some merit. However, over the years, the ISR model and the model proposed by Beehr and Newman (1978) have guided the bulk of occupational stress research. This suggests that both models have served as "road maps" to guide oc-

cupational stress researchers' efforts. It is relatively easy to use each of these models to guide a specific research investigation or to clarify the focus of a stress-related organizational intervention.

Of all the occupational stress models, the Demands-Control model (Karasek, 1979) has clearly received the most empirical scrutiny, and the results have been mixed (e.g., Fox et al., 1993; Perrewe & Ganster, 1989; Spector, 1987). As was stated earlier, this may be due to the fact that the conditions under which demands and control interact are more complex than those Karasek originally proposed (e.g., Schaubroeck & Merritt, 1997). The P–E Fit approach has also received a fair amount of empirical testing, though not all of this testing has been in the context of occupational stress research. In this case, the results have generally been favorable (e.g., Kristof, 1996).

WORKPLACE STRESSORS

A stressor represents anything in the job or organizational environment that requires some type of adaptive response on the part of the employee. One of the difficulties in covering stressors is simply deciding which ones to describe when there are so many in the workplace. The stressors covered in this section represent two general types: (1) those that have been commonly studied or have received considerable attention in the occupational stress literature, and (2) those that have received less attention but have more recently become the focus of attention.

Commonly Studied Stressors

Role Stressors. In the history of occupational stress research, role stressors have been given more attention, by far, than any other type. A "role" is essentially a set of the behaviors that are expected of an individual. Most people have multiple roles (e.g., parent, employee, student, spouse), so it stands to reason that people also have multiple sets of role demands. In complex social systems such as organizations, roles serve the important function of bringing order and predictability to the behavior of individuals (Katz & Kahn, 1978). At a more micro level, roles help individual employees to gauge whether they are doing what they are supposed to be doing.

Employees in organizations receive role-related information through both *formal* and *informal* sources. In many organizations, the most common formal source of role-related information is a written job description. Other common sources are verbal and written communications with one's immediate supervisor. All of these formal sources may provide important information, but they may also be limited in defining an employee's role. For example, written job descriptions are often very general and become outdated quickly. In addition, supervisors' job knowledge may be lacking, and communication is often imprecise.

To compensate for limitations in formal sources of information, employees may look to *informal* sources as they define their organizational roles. These may include informal interactions with coworkers at the same level, as well as encounters with subordinates and with persons outside the boundaries of the organization (e.g., customers, suppliers, regulatory agencies). The term **role set** encompasses the various sources of information, formal and informal, that employees utilize in defining their roles in organizations.

The communication of role-related information should be a smooth process in which the various members of a role set provide clear and consistent information to employees. However, we know that this does not always happen. When role-related information is unclear, this may lead to a stressor known as **role ambiguity** (Kahn et al., 1964; King & King, 1990). In the most general sense, role ambiguity exists when an employee is unsure of what he or she is supposed to do. This uncertainty can be manifested in a variety of ways: unclear performance standards (Beehr, Walsh, & Taber, 1980), uncertainty regarding scheduling and work methods (Breaugh & Colihan, 1994), and so on. A common example of role ambiguity experienced by students is professors' lack of clarity regarding grading standards.

Another common problem that may occur is a lack of consistency in the role-related information provided by members of an employee's role set. When this occurs, the stressor that often results is known as **role conflict** (Kahn et al., 1964; King & King, 1990). Role conflict usually results from inconsistent information or conflicting demands provided by different members of an employee's role set. It is also possible that the *same* individual within an employee's role set may communicate inconsistent information or requests over time. For many college professors, their teaching responsibilities and research activities form a common source of role conflict. The more time they spend on teaching, the less time they have available for research, and vice versa.

A third role stressor that has been examined, though not nearly as much as role ambiguity and conflict, is **role overload.** This stressor is defined by Jones, Flynn, and Kelloway (1995) as occurring when "an employer may demand more of an employee than he or she can accomplish in a given time, or simply, the employee may perceive the demands of work as excessive" (p. 42). Given the generality of this definition, it is possible that an employee may feel overloaded for two reasons. First, feelings of role overload may be due to the sheer volume of the demands emanating from an employee's role set (this is referred to as *quantitative* role overload). During tax season, for example, many accountants experience this type of role overload. Second, role overload may be due to the difficulty of the demands, relative to the skills and abilities of the employee (this is referred to as *qualitative* role overload). This form of role overload is becoming very common in all of the armed services because the skill requirements of new technology often exceed those of enlisted personnel.

A great deal of occupational stress research has been grounded in role theory, so it is not surprising that more empirical research has been done on role stressors than on any of the other stressors covered in this chapter. Several meta-analyses have been conducted to summarize this vast literature (Abramis, 1994; Fisher & Gitelson, 1983; Jackson & Schuler, 1985; Tubre, Sifferman, & Collins, 1996). Overall, the results from these meta-analyses have been quite consistent in showing that role ambiguity and role conflict are correlated with a variety of strains. Table 7.1, for example, shows corrected correlations from Jackson and Schuler's study. As can be seen, high levels of role ambiguity and role conflict are associated with low job satisfaction, high anxiety

and tension, and a higher probability of turnover. Correlations with behavioral outcomes such as absenteeism and job performance, however, are very small.

Compared to role ambiguity and role conflict, much less research has examined the effects of role overload. The few studies that have been done, however, have shown this stressor to be related to higher levels of both psychological and physical strain (e.g., Caplan et al., 1975; Caplan & Jones, 1975; Jex, Adams, Elacqua, & Bachrach, 1998). Interestingly, some evidence suggests that quantitative role overload may actually be positively associated with job performance (Beehr, Jex, Stacy, & Murray, 2000). Employees who perform their jobs well may receive a disproportionate share of work assignments. Also, in some jobs (e.g., sales), the volume of work one has to contend with is directly proportional to one's success.

Workload. Workload can be defined as the amount of work an employee has to do in a given period of time. This definition, however, is deceptively simple. For example, it is necessary to distinguish between *perceptions* of workload and *objective* workload. In a purely objective sense, two employees may have

TABLE 7.1

Corrected Correlations between Role Stressors and Both Affective and Behavioral Outcomes

Outcome	Role Ambiguity	Role Conflict
Job satisfaction	-.46	-.48
Tension/Anxiety	.47	.43
Turnover intent	.29	.34
Absences	.13	-.02
Performance ratings	-.12	-.11

Source: S. E. Jackson and R. S. Schuler. (1985). A meta-analysis and conceptual critique of research on role ambiguity and role conflict in work settings. *Organizational Behavior and Human Decision Processes, 36,* 16–78. Adapted by permission of Academic Press.

exactly the same volume of work but perceive their respective workloads quite differently. Another complicating factor in attempting to understand the impact of workload is that it is cyclical. Employees in retail stores, for example, experience a sharp increase in workload as the end-of-year holiday season approaches, but this peak is followed by a decline in January. Finally, as with role overload, it is necessary to distinguish between the sheer volume of work one is required to perform (quantitative workload) and the difficulty of that work (qualitative workload).

In general, studies of the impact of workload have focused heavily on physical outcomes. In one of the earliest studies of workload, Buell and Breslow (1960) found that working more than the typical 40 hours per week doubled the chances of mortality from coronary heart disease in men. Subsequent research, over several years, has shown that working long hours is associated with a variety of indicators of ill health, although the effects appear to be rather modest (Sparks et al., 1997). The negative physical effects associated with long hours are most likely due to physiological changes that occur during periods of overwork. According to research conducted in Sweden by Frankenhaeuser (1979), the level of adrenaline and other catecholamines increases predictably during periods of long work hours. If these adrenal hormones remain consistently elevated over an extended period of time, the risk of a number of illnesses may increase. To date, however, longitudinal research linking cyclical elevations in adrenal hormone levels to illness is lacking (Jex & Beehr, 1991).

In addition to physical strains, studies have examined both the psychological and the behavioral effects using a variety of workload indexes. Spector and Jex (1998) recently summarized the results of several studies that examined perceived workload, and found it to be related to high anxiety and frustration, reduced job satisfaction, and increased turnover intentions. These authors also found that perceived workload was *positively* related to job performance ratings. Recall that this was also true for quantitative role overload (Beehr et al., 2000), suggesting that not all stressors lead to negative outcomes. In the long run, however, this relationship might be detrimental. Employees who perform well and thus have to shoulder a disproportionate share of the workload may eventually tire of such conditions and leave the organization.

Interpersonal Conflict. Most jobs require at least a minimal amount of interaction with other people (e.g., coworkers, customers, and contractors). Such social interactions are often a source of satisfaction and personal fulfillment (Nielsen, Jex, & Adams, 2000; Riordan & Griffeth, 1995). Interactions with others can also make work more stressful if **interpersonal conflict** (Keenan & Newton, 1985; Spector, 1987), defined as negatively charged interactions with others in the workplace, develops. Negative interactions can range from something as minor as a momentary dispute over a parking space to heated arguments (see Comment 7.2). At extreme levels, interpersonal conflicts may even escalate to physical violence (O'Leary-Kelly, Griffin, & Glew, 1996).

Research suggests that there may be several potential causes of interpersonal conflict. Perhaps the most widely cited precursor to conflict is competition (Forsyth, 1999). In many organizations, employees must compete for rewards such as pay raises, promotions, and competitive budget allocation processes (e.g., the more Department A receives, the less Department B receives). This policy of one person's (or department's) gain is another's loss often fosters a high level of competition.

COMMENT 7.2

THE COMPLEXITY OF INTERPERSONAL CONFLICT

INTERPERSONAL CONFLICT IS a stressor that has not been studied for a long period of time but has been shown to negatively impact employees (e.g., Spector & Jex, 1998). In fact, in conversations with people working in organizations, I have found that this represents a *very* important stressor. People strongly dislike coming to work when they don't get along with others, or when fellow employees are embroiled in conflicts.

Given the effects of interpersonal conflict, it is important that occupational stress researchers get a better handle on all of the forms in which interpersonal conflict can manifest itself in organizations. Most studies, to date, have assessed relatively mild forms of interpersonal conflict. However, we know that what constitutes interpersonal conflict ranges widely from minor arguments to physical violence.

Another aspect of interpersonal conflict that has yet to be explored is its active versus passive forms. Active conflict, which has been the focus of most of the research, includes arguments and saying rude things to others. More passive forms of conflict might include not returning a fellow employee's phone calls, or perhaps "forgetting" to invite a coworker to a meeting.

In summary, interpersonal conflict is an important variable that is much more complex than current research would seem to indicate. A great deal more conceptual work needs to be done before we are able to get a clear picture of the impact of interpersonal conflict in organizations.

Source: P. E. Spector and S. M. Jex. (1998). Development of four self-report measures of job stressors and strain: Interpersonal Conflict at Work Scale, Organizational Constraints Scale, Quantitative Workload Inventory, and Physical Symptoms Inventory. *Journal of Occupational Health Psychology, 3,* 356–367.

Another factor that may lead to interpersonal conflict is rude or contentious behavior on the part of employees. This may occur, for example, when one person tries to influence another through threats or coercion (Falbe & Yukl, 1992). As Falbe and Yukl point out, employees who are the target of contentious influence tactics typically do not respond favorably; in fact, they may retaliate. In either case, the odds that interpersonal conflict will occur are heightened.

Interpersonal conflict may also occur in response to behavior that is not intentionally directed at another individual but ultimately has a negative effect. An example of this type of behavior is "free riding" in-groups (Albanese & Van Fleet, 1985; Roberts, 1995). Free riding occurs when one or more members of a work group do not "pull their weight" and, as a result, other group members must pick up the slack. Those who must pick up the slack may resent the free rider, and this resentment may ultimately come out in the form of strained interpersonal relations. What's important to note about this example is that the person who is *perceived* to be a free rider may have had no intention of angering his or her fellow group members. This person, in fact, may not even realize that he or she is free riding.

Compared to role stressors, considerably less research has been conducted on the effects of interpersonal conflict in organizations. Probably the most comprehensive summary of the impact of interpersonal conflict was provided by the previously described meta-analysis by Spector and Jex (1998). This meta-analysis showed that interpersonal conflict is correlated with a number of psychological, physical, and behavioral strains. The most notable finding from the meta-analysis was that interpersonal conflict was most strongly related to feelings of anxiety at work. This would appear to be a logical finding, given that anxiety is an emotion felt in anticipation of future problems and challenges (Spielberger, 1979). Those who experience high levels of interpersonal conflict at work may spend time ruminating over the possible effects of past conflicts, and may worry over future conflicts before they even occur.

Organizational Constraints. Organizations have a vested interest in facilitating the job performance of their employees. The more effective individual employees are, the more effective the organization will ultimately become. However, anyone who has worked in any organization knows that organizational conditions do not always facilitate performance. In fact, organizational conditions may even detract from or constrain employee performance. For example, it is not unusual for employees to have difficulty doing their jobs because of unnecessary rules and procedures, a lack of resources, or interruptions from fellow employees.

Peters and O'Connor (1980) used the term "situational constraints" to describe a variety of organizational conditions that may prohibit employees from performing up to their capabilities. (In this section, the term **organizational constraints** is used in recognition of the fact that constraints are not always tied to specific situations.) To more fully define organizational constraints, Peters and O'Connor (1988) proposed a classification system consisting of 11 different categories of organizational constraints. These include: (1) job-related information, (2) budgetary support, (3) required support, (4) time and materials, (5) required services and help from others, (6) task preparation, (7) time availability, (8) the work environment, (9) scheduling of activities, (10) transportation, and (11) job-related authority.

For any of these categories of constraints, the inhibiting effect on performance may be due to *unavailability, inadequacy,* or *poor quality* (or some combination of these). Consider the category of "job-related information." Employees, in some cases, may lack the information needed to accomplish job-related tasks. In other cases, there may be information available, but not enough to accomplish required tasks. In still other cases, there may be plenty of information available, but the information is of such poor quality that it is of limited value; hence, employee performance is constrained.

Since Peters and O'Connor (1980) first introduced the concept, many studies have examined relations between organizational constraints and a variety of stress-related outcomes. In fact, so many studies have been conducted that two recent meta-analyses have summarized their findings (Spector & Jex, 1998; Villanova & Roman, 1993). The specific outcomes examined in these meta-analyses differ somewhat, but the major conclusion from both is that organizational constraints are most strongly related to negative emotional reactions on the part of employees. These include things such as job dissatisfaction, frustration, and anxiety.

One finding is common to both meta-analyses (which is somewhat puzzling): the *lack* of a relation between organizational constraints and job performance. Organizational constraints are things in the environment that inhibit performance, so one would expect a much stronger relation. Peters and O'Connor (1988), however, point out that, in most organizations, several factors work against such a relation. For instance, performance appraisals are often conducted poorly and may ultimately restrict the variability in such measures (Cascio, 1998). Also, in many organizations, performance standards are very low, and employees are offered little incentive to perform above these standards.

Perceived Control. The idea that humans desire control over their environment, and will go to great lengths to maintain even the illusion of control, has been well documented in the behavioral sciences literature (e.g., Averill, 1973; Friedland, Keinan, & Regev, 1992). Compared to the other stressors covered in this chapter, perceived control is much more general and thus can be manifested in a variety of ways. According to Spector (1986), the two most common ways that perceived control is manifested in organizations are through **job autonomy** and **participative decision making.** A high level of job autonomy indicates that an employee has discretion over how his or her job tasks are to be performed, and perhaps over things such as starting and ending times (Hackman & Oldham, 1980). As an example, university professors have considerable autonomy (some would say, too much!) over many aspects of their jobs, while manual laborers and convenience store clerks typically have little autonomy.

Participative decision making is defined by Lowin (1968) as an organizational form of decision making in which those responsible for implementing decisions have some input in their formulation. This participation could take a variety of forms but is most typically identified with labor–management committees, quality circles, job enrichment, and other shared governance policies (Cotton, 1995). As an illustration of how participative decision making might be carried out, the author and a colleague recently assisted a medium-size producer of dairy products in conducting a company-wide employee opinion survey. All phases of this project were conducted in collaboration with an "Employee Committee," which consisted of approximately 12 individuals, from several divisions of the company, who were responsible for representing the interests and views of their fellow employees.

Like other stressors covered in this section, meta-analyses have summarized the effects of both job autonomy and participative decision making. For example, Spector (1986) summarized the findings of 88 studies conducted between 1980 and 1985. A summary of the results of this meta-analysis is provided in Table 7.2. As can be seen, both manifestations of perceived control are positively correlated with job satisfaction and negatively related to a number of strains. For example, employees who perceive a lack of control also tend to report being emotionally distressed and experiencing physical symptoms; exhibit lower levels of performance; and are more likely to quit their jobs.

Since Spector's (1986) investigation, other meta-analyses have focused more specifically on participative decision making (e.g., Wagner, 1994; Wagner & Gooding, 1987). Most of the outcomes examined in these meta-analyses, with the exception of job satisfaction and job performance, are not relevant to occupational stress. However, in both studies, participative decision making was strongly and positively related to job satisfaction, suggesting that a *lack* of participation may lead to negative attitudinal reactions.

TABLE 7.2
Corrected Correlations between Two Measures of Perceived Control and Affective, Health, and Behavioral Outcomes

Outcome	Job Autonomy	Participation
Job satisfaction	.37	.44
Emotional distress	−.37	−.18
Physical symptoms	−.33	−.34
Turnover intent	−.26	−.20
Turnover	−.25	−.38
Performance	.26	.23

Source: P. E. Spector. (1986). Perceived control by employees: A meta-analysis of studies concerning autonomy and participation at work. *Human Relations, 39,* 1005–1016. Copyright © The Tavistock Institute, 1986. Reprinted by permission of Sage, Ltd.

Contemporary Organizational Stressors

The stressors discussed in the previous section are those that have received the greatest attention in the occupational stress literature. These stressors are also somewhat "timeless" in that they have been present in the workplace for many years and will likely be there for quite some time into the future. The stressors covered in this section, in contrast, have received comparatively less attention because their increased importance is related to more recent trends. These contemporary stressors include work–family conflict, mergers and acquisitions, layoffs and job insecurity, and emotional labor.

Work–Family Conflict. Conflict between work and family is certainly not a new stressor. In recent years, however, several trends have indicated that work–family conflict has indeed increased in importance as a stressor. For example, in the United States, more than 60% of families need day care because of parental work demands (Covey, 1997). Fifty years ago, that figure was less than 20%. Also, extended families are becoming more

geographically dispersed and generally are having less contact with each other, compared to previous generations. Thus, it appears that, for employees today, the demands from work and family domains are competing more than ever. At the same time, sources of support that have traditionally been available to help balance those demands (i.e., extended family) are increasingly unavailable.

In describing work–family conflict, most researchers make the distinction between what is termed **work–family conflict,** and what is termed **family–work conflict.** Work–family conflict occurs when the demands of *work* interfere with one's *family* responsibilities. For example, an unexpected meeting late in the day may prevent a parent from picking up his or her child from school. In contrast, family–work conflict occurs when the demands of *family* interfere with one's *work* responsibilities. A very common example would be a parent's need to leave his or her work in order to take care of a sick child.

Another distinction often made in the work–family conflict literature is between **time-based conflict** and **strain-based conflict.** With time-based conflict, the time demands in one domain make it more difficult to attend to one's responsibilities in the other. Since the typical workweek is now well over 40 hours per week (Sparks et al., 1997), this is often the reason why work interferes with family. This would be "time-based, work–family conflict." On the other hand, family demands can be very time-consuming and may interfere with work. Any parent of infant or preschool children would certainly attest to the time demands associated with this role. This would be "time-based, family–work conflict."

Strain-based conflict occurs when the "strain" due to stressors in one domain impairs a person's functioning in the other. Like time-based conflict, this can occur in two directions. For example, if a person is anxious and tense because of an increase in his or her workload, this response may have a negative impact on the quality of interactions with family members. In contrast, an employee who is emotionally distraught over having to care for an elderly parent may have difficulty concentrating on work, and his or her performance may suffer. A summary of the various forms of work–family conflict is presented in Table 7.3.

Work–family conflict is a relatively new research domain, so there has not been a tremendous volume of empirical research. However, the volume of work–family conflict research has increased so rapidly, in recent years, that a recent meta-analysis was performed on the impact of work–family conflict (Kossek & Ozeki, 1998.). The major finding from this meta-analysis was that work–family and family–work conflict were both negatively associated with job and life satisfaction. Interestingly, though, work–family conflict was more strongly correlated with both job and life satisfaction than was family–work conflict. The major implication of this finding is that employees may find it more stressful to have their work interfere with their family life than the reverse. Another interesting finding from this study was that work–family conflict was more strongly related to job and life satisfaction among women than it was among men. Thus, when the demands of work interfere with family responsibilities, women evidently find it more stressful than do men. This may reflect the fact that despite recent societal changes, women still take on a greater share of family responsibilities than men do (Hochschild, 1989).

Mergers and Acquisitions. The trend for organizations to engage in mergers and acquisitions started in the mid-1980s and has continued since. Mergers occur when two separate organizations combine to form one. An acquisition, on the other hand, occurs when one company (which is typically larger)

TABLE 7.3
A Taxonomy of Different Forms of Work-Family Conflict

		Direction of Conflict	
Basis of Conflict	*Time*	Time-Based, Work-Family Conflict	Time-Based, Family-Work Conflict
	Strain	Strain-Based, Work-Family Conflict	Strain-Based, Family-Work Conflict

obtains a controlling financial interest in another company (which is typically smaller). The acquirer then assumes a dominant role over the acquired. Hogan and Overmeyer-Day (1994) point out that, in practice, it is often difficult to clearly distinguish between mergers and acquisitions. Acquiring organizations often want to convey the impression that the two organizations are equal partners. Given this fuzzy boundary, mergers and acquisitions are discussed here as one stressor.

According to Hogan and Overmeyer-Day (1994), much of the research on mergers and acquisitions has focused on the financial and strategic implications of these transactions. A somewhat smaller body of literature has examined the stress-related implications (e.g., Buono & Bowditch, 1989; Rentsch & Schneider, 1991; Schweiger & DeNisi, 1991). Related research efforts have also been aimed at recommending strategies to help employees cope with mergers and acquisitions (e.g., Ivancevich, Schweiger, & Power, 1987).

From the limited empirical literature, the most reliable stress-related correlates of mergers and acquisitions are employees' feelings of anxiety, uncertainty, and job insecurity. Considering that even rumors of mergers and acquisitions evoke considerable speculation among employees as to how the merger or acquisition will be handled, this finding is not surprising. Ivancevich et al. (1987) recommended that organizations engaging in mergers and acquisitions should make an effort to communicate to employees as much information as possible. Given that mergers and acquisitions will continue in the future, more research is needed on the stress-related implications of this important organizational activity.

Layoffs and Job Insecurity. Like mergers and acquisitions, layoffs became a fact of life in the 1980s. A survey by the American Management Association indicated that 66% of U.S. firms with more than 5,000 employees reported reducing their workforce through layoffs in the late 1980s (Henkoff, 1990). This trend continued into the 1990s and is likely to continue for years to come (Kozlowski, Chao, Smith, & Hedlund, 1993).

Layoffs are somewhat different from the other stressors discussed in this chapter. Like the other stressors, layoffs occur in an organizational context, but their most direct impact is felt outside of the organizational context (Leana & Feldman, 1992). It is important to note, though, that layoffs often impact those who do *not* lose their jobs. Employees who survive layoffs may have feelings of vulnerability, and even guilt (Brockner, Grover, Reed, & DeWitt, 1992; Brockner, Grover, Reed, DeWitt, & O'Malley, 1987), and may experience an increase in workload because the amount of work typically stays the same.

How do layoffs impact those who lose their jobs? The evidence is rather unequivocal: Job loss is bad for one's mental and physical health. For example, research over the years has shown that job loss is strongly related to psychological strains such as depression and loss of self-esteem (Cvetanovski & Jex, 1994; Jex, Cvetanovski, & Allen, 1994; Leana & Feldman, 1992). Job loss has also been shown to have a negative impact on physical health (Kasl & Cobb, 1970, 1980).

Research has shown rather clearly that the negative impact of job loss is mitigated by reemployment (Eden & Aviram, 1993; Vinokur, van Ryn, Gramlich, & Price, 1991). Also, the manner in which individuals cope with job loss may have an important effect on whether the effect is negative. For example, Wanberg (1997) found that unemployed individuals who employed **active coping** techniques (e.g., they actively searched for employment) fared better than those who avoided looking for work. An obvious reason is: Active coping is likely to speed reemployment.

Compared to the direct impact of job loss, less is known about the impact of job insecurity. With respect to emotional reactions, those who survive a layoff may respond with reduced trust and commitment toward their employing organization (Buch & Aldrich, 1991). Seeing fellow employees laid off may signify a potential breach of the implicit "psychological contract" between employees and the organization (Morrison & Robinson, 1997). Layoff survivors may also find that their job duties have been expanded, leading to feelings of being overworked (Byrne, 1988; Tombaugh & White, 1990).

Another issue may confront layoff survivors: To remain employed, they may be forced to accept job transfers that require relocation. This may be very difficult, particularly for dual-career families (Gupta & Jenkins, 1985). Children may also perceive job insecurity in parents, and such perceptions may have a negative impact. For example, Barling, Dupre, and Hepburn (1998) found that college students perceived their parents' job insecurity, and these perceptions were associated with attitudes about the world of work. Students who perceived high levels of job insecurity among their fathers reported lower levels of both the Protestant work ethic (i.e., hard work pleases God) and humanistic work beliefs. Given the prevalence of layoffs in recent years, the long-term implications of these findings are troubling (see Comment 7.3) and suggest that more research on job insecurity is needed.

Emotional Labor.   During the past 50 years, the structures of the U.S. economy and the economies of other countries have changed dramatically. Once dependent on heavy manufacturing, the service sector now dominates the economies of the United States and many other nations. This shift undoubtedly has enormous implications for many organizational phenomena, but it has clearly changed the content of people's jobs. As a result, many employees are faced with a very different set of stressors than were their forefathers who worked in factories a half-century ago.

The term **emotional labor,** initially coined by Hochschild (1979, 1983), refers to the emotional demands that employees face on the job. Emotional labor can take many forms, but two stand out as being particularly relevant to the study of occupational stress. In the first form, employees are forced to confront negative emotions. Examples of this would occur when a grocery store clerk must interact with a dissatisfied customer or when a physician must interact with a grieving family. In another relevant form of emotional labor, an employee may be forced to suppress his or her true emotional state in order to further the goals of the organization. Many occupations have "display rules" that tell the employee the appropriate emotion to display to customers or clients (Ekman, 1973). Employees who work directly with the public encounter this type of situation every day. A waiter at a restaurant may be having a bad day but must be pleasant to customers because his job demands it.

Research on emotional labor is still relatively new, but there is evidence linking it to stress-related outcomes. The most common stress-related outcome associated with emotional labor has been emotional exhaustion (Ashforth & Humphrey, 1993; Jackson, Schwab, & Schuler, 1986). Higher emotional labor requirements are associated with heightened feelings of emotional exhaustion. Ashforth and Humphrey, however, point out that the relation between emotional labor and emotional exhaustion (and possibly other

COMMENT 7.3

THE IMPACT OF OCCUPATIONAL STRESS ON CHILDREN

IN A RECENT study, Barling, Dupre, and Hepburn (1998) found that parental job insecurity had a negative impact on children's beliefs about the value of hard work as well as beliefs about humanistic values in the workplace. Stated differently, parents' job insecurity led their children to question the value of hard work and to believe that the workplace was rather cold and unforgiving.

This study is interesting for two reasons. First, the occupational stress literature offers very little data on the impact of stressors beyond the person experiencing them. It seems logical, though, that if an employee is experiencing stressors at work, the effects of these stressors will be felt by his or her spouse and children. People cannot simply block out work when they leave. Second, this study suggests that children whose parents worry about job security may develop a rather cynical attitude toward the workplace and may question whether there is any value in hard work. This finding is troubling, because hard work and commitment *are* needed for societies to be productive.

Perhaps, as time goes by and people do not expect to be with one employer for a long period of time, job insecurity will become less of an issue, and children may be less impacted by it. However, in the meantime, the study by Barling et al. (1998) reminds us that children are keen observers of their parents' work lives, and they form many long-lasting attitudes based on these observations.

Source: J. Barling, K. E. Dupre, and C. G. Hepburn. (1998). Effects of parents' job insecurity on children's work beliefs and attitudes. *Journal of Applied Psychology, 83,* 112–118.

strains) may be quite complex. For example, if the emotional display rules of a job are congruent with how an employee is *actually* feeling, this may not be harmful. Being cordial to a customer will not be difficult for a salesperson who is in a good mood. Morris and Feldman (1996) also point out that the stress-related impact of emotional labor may differ depending on (1) the frequency of emotional displays required, (2) the extent to which an employee is required to strictly adhere to display rules, and (3) the variety of emotional expressions required.

Emotional labor appears to be a very fruitful area for further occupational stress research, considering the large number of service sector employees. It also may be useful to broaden the scope of emotional labor research to include jobs outside of the service sector, because even these jobs may have differing emotional display rules that impact employees.

REDUCING THE IMPACT OF WORKPLACE STRESSORS

To this point, the focus of the chapter has been on understanding the relationship between specific stressors and strains (i.e., understanding what is stressful on the job). At this point, we shift the focus to examining ways to use that knowledge to improve the quality of life of employees in the workplace. Organizational efforts to reduce the impact of job-related stressors generally take one of five forms: (1) stress management training,

(2) reduction of stressors, (3) alternative work schedules, (4) family-friendly benefits, and (5) health and fitness programs. Each of these approaches is discussed below.

Stress Management Training

Perhaps the most common method of combating the effects of workplace stressors is referred to as **stress management training** or, more commonly, stress management (Murphy, 1984). Stress management training is designed to help provide employees with the resources necessary to cope more effectively when they are faced with stressors. Note that the purpose of stress management training is *not* to eliminate or even minimize the stressors themselves; their existence is basically taken for granted.

The content of stress management training programs varies widely from organization to organization (Beehr et al., 2001; Bellarosa & Chen, 1997), but there are some common program components. For example, most programs have some educational component; that is, employees are provided with information regarding the nature of stress and its effects. It is also very common for such programs to include some form of training that is designed to help employees reduce the physical effects of stressors. In many cases, this involves some form of **relaxation training,** in which employees learn to release the muscular tension that often accompanies stressful encounters at work. Among other interventions, in **biofeedback training,** employees learn to control physiological responses to stressors such as heart rate and respiration, with the aid of physiological monitoring equipment (Smith, 1993).

Another common component of stress management training programs involves teaching techniques that are designed to help employees alter their appraisal of the work environment. As noted at the beginning of this chapter, the manner in which the work environment is cognitively appraised is a key factor in determining whether it is considered a stressor. One commonly used method of accomplishing this is Meichenbaum's (1977) **Stress-Inoculation Training,** which consists of three distinct phases.

In the first phase, participants are provided with information about stress, as well as a conceptual framework for understanding the phases of the treatment that will follow. In the second phase, participants learn and rehearse various coping strategies, which are typically taught in the form of "self-statements." The idea underlying this phase is that people often engage in dysfunctional self-statements when they encounter stressors, and these may ultimately exacerbate the effect of the stressor. As an example, before making an important sales presentation, a person may say to himself or herself: "I'm no good at speaking in front of other people . . . ." Needless to say, negative self-statements make the situation more uncomfortable. According to Meichenbaum (1977), it is possible to replace such negative self-talk with more functional statements. For example, when making a sales presentation, the person could instead learn to say: "One step at a time; you can handle the situation" (p. 155). This type of self-statement is likely to be more functional and can have a calming effect on the individual.

The final phase of Stress Inoculation is referred to as "Application Training." In this phase, participants learn to apply and use positive self-statements in everyday situations. This involves developing an awareness of situations that are perceived as stressful and of the negative self-statements that accompany such situations. Once this is done, participants learn to substitute self-statements that facilitate coping. One thing to note about this process: consistent use of these positive

self-statements may require considerable practice and rehearsal.

Reduction of Stressors

Another approach to reducing the effects of stressors is to attempt to reduce the levels of the stressors themselves. This approach is much less popular than stress management training. However, if an organization is truly interested in reducing the effects of stressors, this approach has greater potential for improving employees' well-being and quality of life, rather than simply treating the *effects* of stressors (Hurrell, 1995).

There may be many interventions that would reduce stressors; some may even have a preventative effect. Examples might include (but are not limited to) redesigning a job to increase autonomy (Griffin, 1991; Hackman & Oldham, 1980), providing employees with opportunities for greater participation in organizational decision making (Lowin, 1968; Wagner, 1994), training managers to communicate more effectively with subordinates, and training employees to use more effective conflict resolution techniques.

The interventions mentioned above, when implemented in organizations, are typically not labeled as "stress reduction" efforts. In many cases, these interventions are offered as training programs, or as part of a comprehensive organizational development strategy (see Chapter 16). The result of many organizational development interventions, however, is a decrease in stressors and, consequently, an increase in employees' well-being. This point is illustrated very clearly in a study conducted by Schaubroeck, Ganster, Sime, and Ditman (1993) in which a Responsibility Charting intervention in a university was evaluated. Responsibility Charting is an activity that is typically conducted during team-building interventions. It helps a work group clarify who is responsible for what, within the group (French & Bell, 1995). One of the effects of Responsibility Charting, found in this study, was a reduction in role ambiguity.

Alternative Work Schedules

In many cases, stressors are the result of time-based conflicts. For example, an employee may be required to be at home when his or her child arrives home from school in the afternoon. Unfortunately, this may conflict with regular work hours. To help employees cope with this form of conflict, an increasing number of organizations are implementing policies allowing **alternative work schedules.** An alternative work schedule is defined as any deviation from the typical five-day, 8:00–5:00 or 9:00–5:00 work schedule. Given this rather broad definition, there are numerous forms alternative work schedules can take. The two most typical forms are **flextime** and the **compressed workweek.**

In a typical flextime arrangement, all employees are required to be present during some portion of the day. This time period is referred to as the "core hours." Beyond the core hours, employees are allowed to choose their own hours, as long as they work an eight-hour day and their choice of hours is relatively consistent. To illustrate, an organization could mandate that all employees must be present between 10:00 A.M. and 3:00 P.M. Beyond these core hours, an employee may choose to start work at 7:00 A.M. and leave work at 3:00 P.M. An employee also has the option of starting his or her workday at 10:00 A.M. and leaving work at 6:00 P.M.

Because many organizations have adopted flextime arrangements (Johnson & Packer, 1987), a number of empirical studies have evaluated the impact of this form of alternative scheduling (e.g., Pierce & Newstrom, 1982; Pierce, Newstrom, Dunham, & Barber,

1989). Most of these empirical studies have found that employees respond positively to flextime arrangements in terms of job satisfaction, performance, and absenteeism. Pierce and Dunham (1992), however, suggested that flextime arrangements that have a small number of core hours and allow for changes in the pattern of hours are likely to be most appealing to employees.

In a typical compressed workweek arrangement, employees work four 10-hour days instead of five eight-hour days. In such an arrangement, an employee could work four consecutive days (e.g., Monday through Thursday) or arrange to have a day off in the middle of the week. Evidence on the effects of compressed scheduling suggests that, like flextime, such arrangements have a positive effect because they allow employees greater scheduling flexibility (Latack & Foster, 1985; Pierce & Dunham, 1992). One potential problem with compressed scheduling, however, is that the fatigue associated with working longer days may offset the increased flexibility (Goodale & Aagaard, 1975). According to Pierce and Newstrom (1992), the best way to avoid this problem is to implement the compressed schedule so that employees work four days and then have four days off. The key to making compressed scheduling work is to allow employees enough time to recover from the longer days.

Family-Friendly Benefits

To help employees cope with the often conflicting demands of work and family, many organizations offer what have been termed "family-friendly" benefits. There is no standard definition of what constitutes a family-friendly benefit. Generally, these benefits are specifically designed to help employees balance the demands of work and family. Typical family-friendly benefits include flexible spending accounts, child care and elder care referrals, part-time work options, and on-site day care facilities.

Unfortunately, a widely held misconception about family-friendly benefits is that they are exclusively for women. Such benefits may be more salient to women (Kossek & Ozeki, 1998), but they are designed to benefit both men and women. In fact, in a recent survey of human resources executives, Milliken, Martins, and Morgan (1998) found that the percentage of females in an organization was not indicative of whether an organization offered family-friendly benefits. This study found that the best predictor was whether the executives felt that work–family issues would impact organizational effectiveness.

There is considerable testimonial evidence on the value of family-friendly benefits, but methodologically rigorous evaluations have been rare. Thomas and Ganster (1995), for example, conducted a study of the stress-related impact of family-friendly benefits among hospital employees. They found that those who worked in organizations offering family-friendly benefits reported higher levels of job satisfaction and lower levels of depression and somatic complaints. They were also found to have lower cholesterol than employees working in organizations that did not offer such benefits. This study also showed that family-friendly benefits, particularly flexible schedules, have a positive impact because they enhance employees' perceptions of control and reduce feelings of work–family conflict.

One final point—one that complicates evaluation of the impact of family-friendly benefits—must be considered: the implementation of such benefits is often at the discretion of individual managers. As a result, the mere *existence* of a family-friendly benefit does not guarantee that all employees will have equal access. For example, an organization may institute a policy that makes it possible for employees to switch from full-time to part-time status. If this policy is at the discretion of individual managers, all employees may not have the opportunity to benefit. This raises the general point that perhaps the key to helping employees balance the demands of work and family does not lie in "official" solutions such as family-friendly benefits (Goff, Mount, & Jamison, 1990). Rather, the most important factor may be the flexibility, understanding, and compassion of individual managers.

Health and Fitness Programs

An increasing number of organizations are offering a variety of programs designed to improve employees' health and fitness. Such programs can range from something as simple as providing information about health-related topics, to extensive on-site fitness facilities (O'Donnell, 1986). For most organizations, the primary motivation for offering health and fitness programs is to reduce employees' healthcare costs (Falkenberg, 1987; Jex, 1991). Indeed, several studies conducted over the years have shown that health and fitness programs do reduce healthcare costs (see Pelletier, 1991 for a summary). Another common reason is that employees who are healthy and physically fit are less likely to be absent due to illness. As with healthcare costs, there is empirical evidence showing that health and fitness programs do indeed lead to reductions in employee absenteeism (Cox, Shephard, & Corey, 1981; Kerr & Vos, 1993; Tucker, Aldana, & Friedman, 1990).

Some studies have also attempted to link participation in health and fitness programs to outcomes such as psychological strain (e.g., anxiety, depression, and job satisfaction). Compared to the studies examining healthcare costs and absenteeism, evidence linking fitness programs to psychological strain is much more equivocal. According to Jex and Heinisch (1996), this is largely due to methodological

flaws in the design of many studies examining the impact of health and fitness programs. For example, many such studies do not employ control groups. Even in studies that do employ control groups, fitness program participants often drop out prior to program completion, or participate at a very minimal level.

Perhaps the most accurate conclusion to be drawn about health and fitness programs is that they are useful for improving the physical health of employees and, as a result, may lead to decreased absenteeism. Based on the available empirical evidence, however, it is unclear whether participation in health and fitness programs has a great deal of impact on other stress-related outcomes. In the future, methodologically sound evaluations of health and fitness programs will be needed to provide more definitive evidence on this issue.

CROSS-CULTURAL OCCUPATIONAL STRESS RESEARCH

The majority of what we know about occupational stress comes from studies of employees in the United States and, to a lesser extent, Great Britain, Germany, and Scandinavia. As a result, very little evidence exists regarding basic issues such as whether occupational stress models generalize across cultures, whether cultural factors impact on reactions to stressors, and whether there are cultural differences in coping strategies. In this final section of the chapter, three studies that have attempted to explore such cross-cultural issues are described. These studies were chosen because they represent examples of issues in occupational stress that readily lend themselves to cross-cultural research.

Very little evidence exists regarding the generalizability of occupational stress theories. This is not a trivial issue, given that most occupational stress theories have been developed in the United States or other Western countries. Xie (1996) examined this issue by testing Karasek's (1979) Demands–Control model in the People's Republic of China (PRC). According to Xie, it would be tempting to predict that Karasek's model would not apply in a collectivist nation like the PRC, since this model focuses on personal control. However, as Xie points out, there are clear differences between blue- and white-collar workers within the PRC. Blue-collar workers ". . . are generally less educated and less exposed to Western influences. Therefore, they are more likely to maintain the traditional values which impede the desire of individuals for personal control" (p. 1600). White-collar workers, on the other hand, have had greater exposure to Western values, one of which is valuing personal control. These individuals, compared to blue-collar workers, have also benefited much more from recent economic changes in the PRC.

Based on a sample of 1,200 respondents, the interaction between demands and control that would be predicted by Karasek's model was found only for white-collar employees for most of the outcomes in the study. This supports Xie's hypothesis and suggests, more importantly, a potential limitation on this very popular occupational stress model. Schaubroeck and Merritt (1997) also found that this model was supported only for those with high self-efficacy.

Another important issue that lends itself to cross-cultural research is whether there are cultural differences in the perceptions of stressors. This issue was addressed in a cross-cultural study of role stressors among managers from 21 nations, conducted by Peterson et al. (1995). These authors found that perceptions of role stressors (ambiguity, conflict, and overload) varied considerably across nations. They also found that levels of role

stressors could be predicted from characteristics of different national cultures. Perceptions of role stressors differed with respect to power distance (degree of segregation by levels of power), level of masculinity, degree of individuality, and degree to which individuals try to decrease uncertainty.

For example, managers from nations low in power distance (e.g., industrialized, Western countries) reported high levels of role ambiguity and low levels of role overload. The pattern of results was exactly the opposite in nations characterized as high on power distance (e.g., Latin American and Far Eastern countries). This finding suggests that Western managers may not have problems with the sheer volume of work but may be uncertain about their responsibilities. Non-Western managers, in contrast, may be clear about their responsibilities but see the sheer volume of work as a stressor.

These findings, according to Peterson et al. (1995) suggest that "Role conflict, ambiguity, and overload contain a core of meaning wrapped up in the nature of formal relationships within formal organizations." (p. 447). The mistake often made in occupational stress research is to assume that the *meaning* of organizational events is consistent across cultures. In the future, more of this type of cross-cultural comparative research may reveal other important differences in stressors across cultures.

A final example of recent cross-cultural occupational stress research was provided in a study by Van De Vliert and Van Yperen (1996) in which cross-national comparisons in role overload were examined. These authors contended that the cross-national differences in role overload reported by Peterson et al. (1995) could be explained, at least in part, by cross-national differences in ambient temperature. That is, nations characterized as low in power distance by Peterson et al. were located in geographical areas in which the ambient temperature tended to be comparatively higher. They proposed that differences in ambient temperature, rather than in power distance, could have led to differences in reports of role overload.

These authors reanalyzed the data from Peterson et al. (1995), along with two other cross-cultural data sets. It was found, as predicted, that controlling for ambient temperature eliminated the relationship between power distance and role overload. Thus, these authors concluded that the relationship between power distance and role overload might be due entirely to cross-national differences in ambient temperature. These findings suggest that certain cultural characteristics may be determined, to a certain degree, by climate, and that such characteristics may then impact organizations.

In summary, this section has provided a brief sampling of recent cross-cultural occupational stress research. The three studies are different, but the clear message from all three is that cultural factors may play an important role in the stress process. Many of the theories and models that were once thought to be universal may not be. As organizations continue to expand globally, the importance of further cross-cultural occupational stress research cannot be overstated.

CHAPTER SUMMARY

This chapter examined occupational stress, a topic that is becoming increasingly important both to organizations and to society as a whole. The roots of occupational stress research can be traced to the early twentieth century, although the first large-scale research program did not begin until the 1960s. Furthermore, a great deal of occupational stress research has been conducted only within the past 25 years.

Occupational stress researchers have, at times, struggled with terminology. This is largely due to the fact that the study of occupational stress has always been interdisciplinary in nature. Organizational psychology has certainly contributed, but important contributions have also been made by those in medicine, clinical psychology, and engineering psychology.

Several models of the occupational stress process have been proposed over the years, and four of these were discussed. The ISR model is probably the most influential because it has guided a great deal of occupational stress over the years. Other models discussed included McGrath's Process Model, Karasek's Demands–Control Model, Beehr and Newman's Facet Model, and, finally, the P-E Fit Model.

Stressors represent things in the job or organization that require some type of adaptive response on the part of employees. The most commonly studied stressors are those associated with employee roles, although researchers have also examined workload, interpersonal conflict, organizational constraints, and perceived control. Stressors that have increased in importance in recent years include work–family conflict, mergers and acquisitions, job insecurity, and emotional labor.

Organizations wishing to reduce the impact of stressors have generally tried to do so in five different ways. The most common method is the development of stress management training programs that teach employees how to cope more effectively with stressors. Other less common methods include reducing stressors, offering alternative work schedules, making family-friendly benefits available, and offering employees health and fitness programs.

Occupational stress has clearly lagged behind in cross-cultural research. Recently, however, there appears to be some progress in this area. For example, research conducted in the People's Republic of China has shown that the Demands–Control Model may not apply to all cultures. It has also been shown that culture may have an impact on the types of stressors that are perceived. A great deal more cross-cultural research is needed, however.

SUGGESTED ADDITIONAL READINGS

Bliese, P. D., & Halverson, R. R. (1996). Individual and nomothetic models of job stress: An examination of work hours, cohesion, and well-being. *Journal of Applied Social Psychology, 26,* 1171–1189.

Fried, Y., & Tiegs, R. B. (1995). Supervisors' role conflict and role ambiguity differential relations with performance ratings of subordinates and the moderating effect of screening ability. *Journal of Applied Psychology, 80,* 282–291.

Spector, P. E., & O'Connell, B. J. (1994). The contribution of individual dispositions to the subsequent perceptions of job stressors and job strains. *Journal of Occupational and Organizational Psychology, 67,* 1–11.

Xie, J. L., & Johns, G. (1995). Job scope and stress: Can it be too high? *Academy of Management Journal, 38,* 1288–1309.

Chapter Eight

Theories of Motivation

Motivation is concerned with a question: Why do people "do what they do?" Whether we realize it or not, all of us are "naïve scientists" who often attempt to figure out the motives behind the behavior of others. We may read a newspaper and wonder why a person committed a violent crime, or perhaps why an athlete maintained a consistently high level of performance during his or her career. Within organizational psychology, the study of employee motivation represents one of the most important topics in the discipline, and there are several reasons for this. First, motivation is a key to understanding many forms of behavior in organizations. Understanding what motivates employees helps us to understand the dynamics underlying such important behaviors as job performance, absenteeism, turnover, and even counterproductive behaviors.

Second, an understanding of the dynamics underlying various forms of behavior enhances our ability to *predict* these same behaviors. For example, if an organization's leaders understand the motivation underlying performance, they can predict their employees' future performance. This is important when organizations are initially selecting new employees, but it may also be helpful when current employees are being considered for promotional opportunities. Some organizations may also want to predict whether employees will engage in counterproductive behaviors.

A final reason to study employee motivation is that understanding the motives behind behavior is an important first step toward influencing it. For example, if an organization knows that employees are highly motivated by financial incentives, this knowledge can be

209

used to influence performance. All organizations, in one way or another, attempt to influence employees' behavior. Organizations that are armed with a clear understanding of motivation are in a better position to influence employee behavior than are organizations that lack this knowledge.

This chapter provides an overview of the theories of motivation that have been most influential in organizational psychology. In Chapter 9, we will examine how motivation theories are applied within organizations to influence employee behavior. Before examining specific motivation theories, however, we will briefly review the important issue of *what* motivation actually is and how it is defined. As will become evident, this is important because different theories conceptualize motivation in somewhat different ways.

DEFINING MOTIVATION

According to Kanfer (1990), motivation is a **hypothetical construct**; we cannot see it or feel it. We *can* observe the effects or byproducts that are indicative of differing levels of motivation. To use an analogy, motivation is a bit like gravity. We cannot see or feel gravity, but its effects would become very clear if one were to jump out a window of a five-story building.

According to Pinder (1998), motivation determines the *form, direction, intensity,* and *duration* of work-related behavior. Thus, by observing these dimensions of behavior, we can draw some conclusions about the impact of motivation on employees' behavior. Based on Pinder's proposition, a major question for organizational psychologists studying employee motivation is: What *dependent variable* should be studied in empirical research? As readers will see, common dependent measures for theories of motivation include employees' *effort, choice,* or, in some cases, *persistence.* Some

researchers have chosen to use *performance* as the dependent measure. Strictly speaking, this is incorrect because motivation represents only one of many determinants of performance. For example, an employee may be highly motivated but perform poorly because of a lack of ability, or because of certain constraints in the environment.

A final issue to consider in defining and understanding employee motivation is determining what forms of behavior organizations wish to influence. This will become particularly important when applications of motivation theories are described in Chapter 9, but it is also important in understanding different motivation theories. As will be shown, motivation theories can be distinguished in terms of whether they ultimately predict outcomes most relevant to performance, employee citizenship, or simply the propensity to maintain organizational membership.

THEORIES OF MOTIVATION

Given the importance of motivation in psychology, numerous theories of human motivation have been developed over the years. Many of these, however, either were not developed to explain behavior in the workplace, or are simply difficult to apply in the work domain. The theories that are covered in this chapter have been developed *specifically* to explain employee motivation or have been applied successfully to the study of work behavior.

It is possible to place motivation theories into four general categories:

1. Need-based theories explain work motivation in terms of the extent to which employees satisfy important needs in the workplace.
2. Job-based theories place the source of motivation primarily in the content of jobs that employees perform.

3. Cognitive process theories emphasize the decisions and choices that employees make when they allocate their efforts.
4. The behavioral approach emphasizes principles of learning.

Need-Based Theories

By definition, a "need" indicates some deficient state within an individual. We know, for example, that humans *need* things such as oxygen and water in order to survive. Psychologists have also proposed that humans have psychological needs that serve to drive much of human behavior. Murray (1938), for example, was one of the first psychologists to propose a systematic taxonomy of human needs. He proposed that these needs are evoked by different stimuli in the environment, and subsequently drive behavior.

Maslow's Need Hierarchy. Building on the work of Murray (1938), Maslow (1943) proposed his well-known **Need Hierarchy** as an explanation of the forces driving human behavior. It is important to note that Maslow's theory was *not* designed specifically to explain behavior in the workplace. Rather, Maslow attempted to create a "universal" theory that would explain the driving forces behind all purposeful behaviors. It is also important to consider that Maslow developed his Need Hierarchy based largely on clinical observations rather than systematic empirical research. Despite these caveats, Maslow's theory has become quite influential in a variety of areas of psychology, including organizational psychology.

Figure 8.1 presents the five need levels that comprise Maslow's Need Hierarchy. At the bottom of the hierarchy are **physiological needs.** This level represents the need for food, oxygen, and water—things that are physiologically necessary to sustain life. These needs are at the lowest level because they will motivate behav-

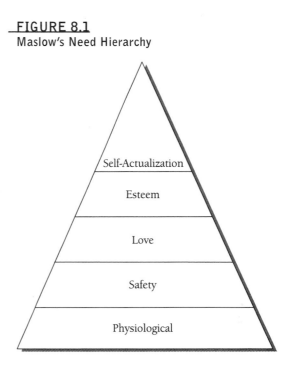

FIGURE 8.1
Maslow's Need Hierarchy

Self-Actualization

Esteem

Love

Safety

Physiological

ior only if they are *unsatisfied.* Thus, a person who lacks such basic necessities will be motivated primarily to obtain them. The closest most of us have come to being motivated by physiological needs is a late-night excursion to a fast-food restaurant. In some parts of the world, however, basic physiological sustenance is one of the major forces driving not only work behavior, but many other behaviors as well.

When physiological needs are satisfied, a person then "moves on" to the next level in the hierarchy: **safety needs,** which include things such as shelter from the elements and protection from predators. As with all needs, Maslow proposed that safety needs would motivate behavior only to the extent that they are unmet. Compared to physiological needs, it is a bit easier to illustrate how safety needs may motivate work behavior. For example, work may allow a person to provide his or her family with adequate housing in a safe neighborhood, as well as the security of having a guaranteed retirement income.

If safety needs are satisfied, the next level that becomes salient is **love needs.** This level represents the need to form meaningful social relationships with others and the desire to feel a sense of belonging. Although love needs may be satisfied in a variety of ways, for most people work represents an important context for satisfying this type of need. People often develop close social ties with coworkers, and derive considerable satisfaction from this affiliation. These social ties may also help employees to cope with many of the negative aspects of the work environment (Cohen & Wills, 1985).

After love needs are met, the next level that becomes important in motivating behavior is **esteem needs.** Esteem needs are linked to a desire to feel a sense of competence and mastery. As with social/belongingness needs, esteem needs may potentially be satisfied in a variety of ways. For example, one may feel a sense of esteem or competence by being a good parent, cultivating a productive garden, or having a neat and clean house. For many people, the workplace represents a primary setting in which esteem and competence needs are satisfied. For example, an accountant may feel a sense of pride and accomplishment when he or she completes a client's tax return quickly and accurately.

The highest need level that can be reached, in Maslow's hierarchy, is **self-actualization.** According to Maslow (1943), to self-actualize is to realize one's potential and "become what one is capable of becoming." Maslow pointed out that few people ever completely "satisfy" the need for self-actualization. Compared to the other levels of needs, self-actualization is a bit more difficult to describe because people differ considerably in how they define self-actualization. Nevertheless, it is certainly possible that work could provide the opportunity for self-actualization. A teacher, for example, may feel actualized by educating future generations.

When viewed as a complete theory, Maslow's Need Hierarchy is certainly intuitively appealing and represents an insightful statement about human nature. The theory, however, has fared very poorly as a predictor of work behavior (Locke & Henne, 1986). Empirical research has not supported the number of levels in the theory or the notion that lower levels in the hierarchy must be satisfied before higher-level needs will motivate behavior (e.g., Hall & Nougaim, 1968). Thus, in recent reviews of motivation theory (e.g., Ambrose & Kulik, 1999; Austin & Vancouver, 1996; Kanfer, 1990), Maslow's theory is covered primarily for historical value and because it has served as the basis for more elaborate theories of work motivation.

ERG Theory. The most direct descendant of Maslow's Need Hierarchy was Alderfer's (1969) ERG Theory of motivation. The acronym ERG stands for "existence," "relatedness," and "growth." Essentially, Alderfer collapsed Maslow's five need levels into three. Existence encompasses both the physiological and the safety/security needs from Maslow's theory. Relatedness corresponds to the social/belongingness level in Maslow's theory. Growth represents the esteem and self-actualization levels from Maslow's theory.

ERG theory also deviates from the Need Hierarchy in other important ways. Unlike Maslow's theory, ERG Theory allows for the possibility that needs do not have to operate in a strict hierarchical fashion (Alderfer, 1969). For example, an artist may be trying to scratch out a living and, at the same time, to achieve his or her artistic potential. ERG also allows for the possibility that people may *regress* if their needs at one level are not satisfied. Suppose an artist fails to achieve his or her potential.

According to Alderfer, such a person may become more focused on satisfying "lower level" needs. The artist may become focused on making friends and connecting with people socially. Recall that Maslow's theory is focused only on moving up through the hierarchy of needs. It says little about situations in which needs are thwarted.

When it was first proposed, ERG Theory was seen as an improvement to Maslow's theory, but it has fared only a little bit better in terms of empirical support. Alderfer's (1969) original work supported the theory, but subsequent tests have offered only mixed support (e.g., Wanous & Zwany, 1977). However, like Maslow's theory, ERG Theory has served as a foundation for future theories in which need satisfaction is proposed to be a central component.

Need for Achievement Theory. A third need-based theory of motivation, Need for Achievement Theory (Atkinson, 1964; McClelland, 1965), has proven to be somewhat more useful than the two previously discussed. Need for Achievement draws its historical roots from the early work of Murray (1938). However, rather than focusing on multiple needs, the emphasis has been primarily on the Need for Achievement in explaining differences between people in goal-directed behavior.

The work of McClelland and others has identified some consistent distinguishing characteristics of those who have a high need for achievement. For example, they tend to choose moderate levels of risk, have a strong desire for knowledge of results or feedback, and have a tendency to become very absorbed in their work. In the work environment, this may be reflected in the tendency of such individuals to set moderately difficult performance goals, seek jobs that readily provide performance feedback, and perhaps work long hours.

McClelland also proposed that Need for Achievement has consequences for entire societies as well as for individuals. For example, in his book *The Achieving Society,* McClelland (1961) proposed that societies differed in terms of their absolute level of Need for Achievement, and that such differences may explain differences in economic growth. Thus, one way to promote economic development in poor countries, according to McClelland, is to promote higher levels of Need for Achievement among native or indigenous populations.

Compared to the other two need-based theories, Need for Achievement Theory is clearly narrower in focus. Rather than try to account for all needs and all forms of behavior, this theory focuses on only one need and a very specific form of behavior (e.g., achievement). This tighter focus makes Need for Achievement Theory somewhat more useful in organizations. For example, if a manager knows that one of his or her subordinates has a high need for achievement, this knowledge may be useful in determining job assignments and the frequency with which performance-related information should be communicated.

The narrow focus of Need for Achievement Theory is also problematic in some respects. McClelland acknowledged that factors other than Need for Achievement impact behavior, but these factors are not explicitly part of the "nomological net" surrounding the Need for Achievement construct. It is important to keep in mind, however, that in explicating the Need for Achievement construct, McClelland was not attempting to develop a full-blown theory of human motivation.

Summary of Need-Based Theories. Perhaps the most accurate conclusion to be drawn about need-based theories is that they have not succeeded well in predicting purposeful behavior in organizations. As a result, they have generally fallen out of favor within organizational psychology. Does this mean that we can summarily dismiss need-based theories? Probably not. History tells us that the field of psychology is a bit like the world of fashion. What's out of favor today may resurface tomorrow, albeit in a different form. Perhaps one or more of the need-based theories discussed in this section will be refined in the future, and need-based theories will then return to prominence (see Comment 8.1).

Job-Based Theories of Motivation

Need-based theories of motivation are based on the premise that human behavior is directed largely by a desire to satisfy needs. Job-based theories take this one step further; they propose that the key to understanding motivation lies in the *content of employees' jobs*. Job-based theories are closely related to need-based theories, due to the fact that need

satisfaction is often offered as an explanatory mechanism linking job content and motivation. Job-based theories, however, are more likely than need-based theories to have been developed specifically for the workplace. Also, focusing on job content as the lever for influencing behavior is inherently more practical than focusing on need satisfaction.

Motivation-Hygiene Theory. From a historical perspective, the first job-based theory to appear on the scene was Herzberg's **Motivation-Hygiene Theory** (Herzberg, 1968). The basic premise behind Herzberg's theory, as with all job-based theories, was that the primary source of motivation in the workplace was the content of people's jobs. At the time that Motivation-Hygiene Theory was developed, most organizations were highly influenced by Scientific Management. Recall that the primary method of motivation in Scientific Management was through compensation

---

COMMENT 8.1

DO HUMANS REALLY HAVE PSYCHOLOGICAL "NEEDS"?

THEORIES OF MOTIVATION that emphasized need satisfaction once strongly dominated the field of organizational psychology. Over time, however, need theories have generally fallen out of favor. At the present time, they are considered more for their historical value than anything else. One obvious reason for this demise is that need theories have not stood up well under empirical scrutiny. Another reason is that the concept of psychological "needs" is rather controversial.

Although it is rather easy to make a case that humans have physiological needs, the idea that psychological needs exist is more debatable. For example, it could be argued that although things such as social belonging are

"valued," people typically do not suffer dire consequences if they have less social contact than they desire. On the other hand, it has been shown that social isolation may lead to certain forms of psychopathology and contribute to developmental disabilities (e.g., Bowlby, 1973). From this point of view, one could mount a rather convincing argument that psychological needs do exist. Ultimately, need theories may have been unsuccessful at explaining work behavior simply because a workplace represents one of many settings in which a person could satisfy his or her needs.

Source: J. Bowlby. (1973). *Separation: Anxiety and anger.* New York: Basic Books.

and financial incentives. Herzberg, and others, were of the opinion that financial incentives had the power to "motivate" people in the sense that they kept them on the job and perhaps prevented them from complaining. To truly motivate people, according to Herzberg, the content of the jobs that people perform was the key.

Herzberg proposed that the work environment could be divided into two general categories. The first of these, he labeled **hygiene factors.** Included were aspects of the work environment, such as pay, fringe benefits, relations with coworkers, and essentially everything else that is distinct from the content of an employee's work. Herzberg used the term "hygiene factors" because these factors are necessary to keep employees from being dissatisfied but do not have the power to truly motivate them. To use a health-related analogy, maintaining proper dental hygiene does not make a person's teeth any *better,* but it *prevents* problems such as tooth decay and gum disease.

Herzberg labeled the second category of the work environment **motivators.** In contrast to hygiene factors, motivators reside primarily in the *content* of a person's job. Motivators include things such as the amount of challenge inherent in one's work, the amount of discretion one has in carrying out one's job tasks, and perhaps how intrinsically interesting the work is. According to Herzberg, in order to motivate an employee, an organization must design work in a way that builds in motivators and thus makes work content intrinsically rewarding to employees. A summary of hygiene factors and motivators is contained in Figure 8.2.

In terms of empirical support, Motivation-Hygiene Theory has not fared particularly well. Herzberg, Mausner, and Snyderman (1959) provided what has probably been the strongest support for Motivation-Hygiene Theory. In

FIGURE 8.2
Summary of Hygiene Factors and Motivators

Hygiene Factors	Motivators
Pay	Level of Challenge
Fringe Benefits	Level of Autonomy or Discretion
Relations with Coworkers	Intrinsic Interest
Physical Working Conditions	Opportunities for Creativity

their study, engineers and accountants employed by the City of Pittsburgh were asked to describe critical incidents that were illustrative of being "very satisfied" or "very dissatisfied." Consistent with Motivation-Hygiene Theory, hygiene factors were mentioned more often than motivators when describing dissatisfaction. The reverse was true when describing satisfaction.

After the Herzberg et al. (1959) study, other attempts were made to test the theory (summarized by Locke, 1976), but most were unsuccessful. Since the mid-1970s, very little research has used Motivation-Hygiene Theory as a framework. (For an exception, see Maidani, 1991.) The reason most analysts have given for the inability to replicate the theory is the critical incident method used in Herzberg's original study. Specifically, in describing critical incidents, respondents tended to attribute highly satisfying incidents to aspects of the job that were most closely associated with themselves (e.g., the degree of challenge in the job) and to attribute dissatisfying incidents to aspects of the work environment that were most closely associated with others (e.g., social relations with coworkers). Thus, many have argued that Herzberg's findings represented a methodological artifact rather than support for Motivation-Hygiene

Theory. [See Locke (1976) for an example of one of the most vigorous criticisms of the theory.]

Despite the lack of empirical support for his theory, one can certainly argue that Herzberg was a pioneer because he was one of the first organizational psychologists to focus on job content as a source of employee motivation. This point has often been lost over the years. In focusing on the methodological shortcomings of Motivation-Hygiene Theory, many in the field have failed to give Herzberg credit for being ahead of his time and providing the foundation for many practices that are commonplace in organizations today.

Job Characteristics Theory. Although Herzberg was one of the first to emphasize the importance of job content in motivating employees, his theory had some important limitations. For example, Motivation-Hygiene Theory was rather imprecise as to *how* to build "motivators" into employees' jobs. Herzberg also provided no tangible measures of these job dimensions. Another problem with Motivation-Hygiene Theory is that it was based, at least implicitly, on the assumption that all employees want the same things from their work.

Job Characteristics Theory (Hackman & Oldham, 1976, 1980), to a large extent, addressed the deficiencies in Motivation-Hygiene Theory and has become the most influential job-based theory of motivation in organizational psychology. Before describing its major components, we should note that Job Characteristics Theory has evolved over several years. For example, Turner and Lawrence (1965) proposed the concept of **Requisite Task Attributes**—essentially, a set of job dimensions that they believed to be motivating to employees. Building on this work, Hackman and Lawler (1971) proposed what is generally considered the most immediate precursor to what

eventually became Job Characteristics Theory. Job Characteristics Theory extended this earlier work by proposing the mediating linkages between job characteristics and outcomes, and by specifying moderators of individual differences.

As can be seen in Figure 8.3, the starting point in the theory is labeled **core job dimensions.** These represent characteristics of a person's job and include the following dimensions: **skill variety, task identity, task significance, autonomy,** and **feedback.** Skill variety represents the extent to which a job requires that a person must use many different skills. A good example of a job with high skill variety would be that of a corporate executive. A person performing this job may have to utilize quantitative skills to prepare a budget, interpersonal skills to manage conflicts among others, and high-level analytical skills to develop a long-term strategic plan. On the other end of the spectrum, a manual labor job may require primarily heavy lifting, and a very minimal amount of independent judgment.

Task identity represents the extent to which a job requires that a person must complete a whole identifiable piece of work, as opposed to a small fragment of it. Conducting research is an example of a job with high task identity because it requires a person to be involved in all steps in the process: reviewing the literature, developing measures, collecting and analyzing data, and writing a report. Low task identity might be found in a traditional assembly-line job. An employee may be responsible for adding one part to a product, and thus will have only a vague idea of how he or she contributes to the finished product.

Task significance represents the degree to which performing the job is important or "counts for something." In a sense, all jobs in the workforce are important, but it is possible to argue that some are more significant than others. For example, most readers would

FIGURE 8.3
Job Characteristics Theory of Motivation

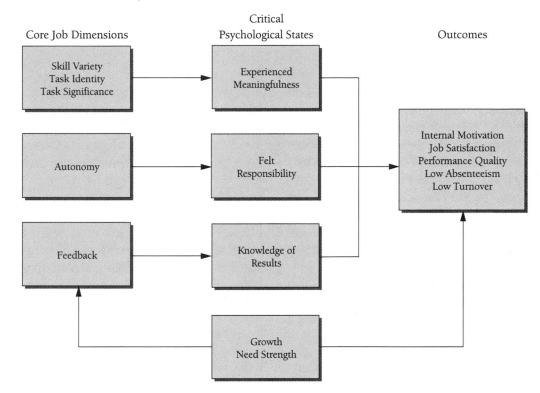

Source: J. R. Hackman and G. R. Oldham. (1980). *Work redesign.* Reading, MA: Addison-Wesley. Reprinted by permission of Pearson Education, Inc. Upper Saddle River, NJ.

probably agree that the task significance for a research scientist studying the molecular structure of the HIV virus is higher than that of a clerk in a retail store. Nevertheless, this core job dimension is still a bit more subjective than the other two.

Autonomy represents the degree to which employees have control and discretion over things such as how they perform their job tasks and schedule their work. Comparatively speaking, college professors represent a professional group with an extremely high level of autonomy. As most readers know, professors have considerable control over their hours of work, choice of work activities, and method of approaching their work activities.

At the other extreme might be a person performing telemarketing. Most telemarketing companies provide very explicit instructions (e.g., scripts) to telemarketing representatives, and instruct them not to deviate from these instructions.

The final core job dimension, feedback, represents the extent to which performing a job provides information about the performance of the job incumbent. As a rule, comedians know very quickly whether their audience considered a particular joke funny. Dead silence and a sea of blank stares are pretty good indicators that a joke has "bombed." At the other extreme, years may pass before a corporate executive receives feedback about certain aspects of his or her performance. For example, the "correctness" of a decision to enter a new market may not be known until the company has been in that market for several years.

Notice in Figure 8.3 that the core job dimensions are immediately linked to the next step, which is labeled **critical psychological states.** These states represent what employees experience, on a psychological level, by performing a job with a given set of core job dimensions. According to the model, when jobs have high levels of skill variety, task identity, and task significance, the corresponding psychological state is **experienced meaningfulness.** Having these three dimensions present leads employees to psychologically experience their jobs as meaningful.

The critical psychological state associated with autonomy is labeled **felt responsibility.** If an employee has autonomy over how he or she performs a job, this will evoke feelings of responsibility for the outcomes that result from that work. An executive who has complete autonomy to determine the strategic direction of an organization will also likely feel a strong sense of responsibility for the success or failure of that organization. Conversely, an employee who simply "follows orders" is unlikely to feel a great deal of responsibility for the outcomes of his or her work.

The core job dimension of feedback is linked to the critical psychological state of **knowledge of results.** Thus, an employee whose job provided considerable feedback will psychologically possess knowledge of the results of his or her performance. Conversely, employees who receive little feedback have a correspondingly vague knowledge of the results of their performance.

According to the next step in the model, critical psychological states are linked to **personal and work outcomes.** This means that experiencing the three previously described

critical psychological states will lead to a number of outcomes, one of which is high internal work motivation. Note also, in Figure 8.3, that the critical psychological states are also associated with high levels of job satisfaction and performance quality, and low levels of absenteeism and turnover.

The final aspect of Job Characteristics Theory is the role of **growth-need strength.** Growth-need strength represents the extent to which employees see their job as a mechanism for satisfying "growth" needs such as personal achievement and self-actualization (Alderfer, 1969; Maslow, 1943). The specific role played by growth-need strength is that of moderating the relations between the core job dimensions and the critical psychological states, and between the critical psychological states and the personal and work outcomes. More specifically, Hackman and Oldham proposed that the core job dimensions will evoke the critical psychological states *only* for those with a high level of growth-need strength. Similarly, the theory proposed that the critical psychological states will lead to the proposed personal and work outcomes *only* among those who have a high level of growth-need strength. For those with a low level of growth-need strength, core job dimensions will have little impact on critical psychological states, and these states will have little impact on outcomes.

Over the years, Job Characteristics Theory has been subjected to considerable empirical testing. Fried and Ferris (1987) conducted a comprehensive meta-analysis of job characteristics studies and reported a number of findings that were supportive of Job Characteristics Theory. For example, all of the core job dimensions were found to be related to outcomes such as job satisfaction, motivation, absenteeism, and turnover. Fried and Ferris's data, however, are a bit more equivocal with respect to the role of the critical psychological states proposed by Hackman and Oldham. Specifically, the core job dimensions do not correlate predictably with their proposed critical psychological states. In addition, the magnitude of the correlations between the core job dimensions and the critical psychological states is not stronger than with outcomes. This is important because if the critical psychological states are key mediators, as proposed by Hackman and Oldham, the core job dimensions should be more strongly correlated with them than with more distal outcomes (Baron & Kenny, 1986).

Although the Fried and Ferris (1987) meta-analysis is informative, very few studies have tested the Job Characteristics Model as a whole. This was done in Hackman and Oldham's (1975, 1976) early work, but most researchers after that have tested only parts of the theory. One exception is a study in which Champoux (1991) tested the entire theoretical model utilizing canonical correlation analysis. The results of this study supported both the causal flow of the model and the proposed moderating effects of growth-need strength. Subsequent studies, however, have been less supportive of the moderating effects of growth-need strength (Evans & Ondrack, 1991; Johns, Xie, & Fang, 1992; Tiegs, Tetrick, & Fried, 1992), as well as the mediating impact of the critical psychological states (e.g., Renn & Vandenberg, 1995).

Campion's Multidisciplinary Approach. One of the assumptions underlying the two previously described job-based theories was that job content appeals to employees at a psychological level, and this, in turn, results in positive employee outcomes. This would appear to be a valid assumption, but it is also true that employees view their jobs from more than just a psychological/motivational perspective. Consistent with this point, the design of jobs is an issue that is of interest to other disciplines such as industrial engineering, human factors/ergonomics, and biomechanics.

Based on this notion, Campion developed the **Multidisciplinary Approach to Job Design** (Campion & McClelland, 1991; Campion & Thayer, 1985). Strictly speaking, this is not a *theory* of motivation; rather, it is an approach to guide the design and redesign of jobs. It is covered as a theory here because the different approaches that are described by Campion ultimately represent a *desire for different end states*. Thus, even though this is typically presented only as a method of job design, at its core it is really a theory of motivation.

According to Campion, organizations can use four different approaches to design jobs, and each approach is associated with certain outcomes for both individual employees and the organization as a whole. As can be seen in Table 8.1, the **motivational** approach has

TABLE 8.1
A Summary of the Four Approaches to Job Design, from Campion's Model

Job Design Approach	Associated Disciplines
Motivational	Organizational psychology; human resources management
Mechanistic	Industrial engineering
Biological	Ergonomics: biomechanics
Perceptual motor	Human factors engineering

been emphasized by those in psychology and closely related fields (e.g., human resources, organizational behavior). Recall from the previously described job-based theories, the emphasis is on making job content intrinsically interesting and meaningful to employees. Positive outcomes associated with approach include increased job satisfaction, internal motivation, higher-quality performance, and fewer withdrawal behaviors. Designing jobs in this fashion also comes at a cost. For example, these types of jobs are more complex and thus may require higher skill levels, longer training periods, and higher levels of compensation. Such jobs may also be stressful because of the high levels of responsibility and the complexity of the interpersonal interactions that are required.

The next job design approach presented in Table 8.1 is **mechanistic.** This approach derives its roots from scientific management and, in more modern times, has been the province of industrial engineering. Consistent with scientific management, the emphasis in the mechanistic approach is to design jobs with maximum efficiency in mind. Job tasks are simplified and work cycles are generally made to be short. The primary benefit of the mechanistic approach is that employees performing jobs designed in this way will be efficient, particularly if one defines efficiency in terms of speed of production. Jobs designed in this fashion will also, generally, be easier to staff, and training time will be short due to low-level skill requirements. The primary disadvantage of the mechanistic approach is that jobs designed in this way may foster boredom and alienation among employees, which ultimately could lead to a number of counterproductive behaviors such as absenteeism, lack of effort, and even sabotage.

The third approach to job design presented in Table 8.1 is **biological.** This approach is focused on designing jobs to maximize the physical comfort of employees. Those training in ergonomics and biomechanics tend to emphasize this form of job design. By emphasizing employees' physical comfort in the design of jobs, organizations may reap important benefits such as reduced health care costs and lower numbers of workers' compensation claims. These outcomes may ultimately translate into higher levels of job satisfaction, but designing jobs in this fashion may require a considerable investment on the part of the organization. There may also be instances where employees' physical comfort detracts from their performance, particularly in tasks that require sustained attention to detail and vigilance.

The fourth and final approach to job design in Table 8.1 is **perceptual motor.** In this case, jobs are designed primarily with task-related information-processing demands in mind. As such, this approach tends to be emphasized primarily by those trained in human factors engineering. The primary advantage of this approach is that it may cut down on errors and fatigue, particularly for jobs that have heavy information-processing requirements. Airline pilots, air traffic controllers, and anesthesiologists are three groups whose jobs would be relevant. Despite these advantages, a potential drawback to this approach might be high levels of boredom, if information is highly simplified. Also, like the biological approach, this approach to job design may require considerable research and development costs.

Beyond specifying the four different approaches to job design, the underlying message in Campion's model is that decisions regarding job design require that organizations weigh certain costs and benefits, and ultimately make some trade-offs. For example, if efficiency is a very high priority within an organization, the mechanistic approach would probably be preferred, despite its inherent

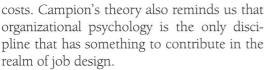

costs. Campion's theory also reminds us that organizational psychology is the only discipline that has something to contribute in the realm of job design.

Since it has been developed more recently, much less empirical work has been done on the Multidisciplinary Approach than on Job Characteristics Theory. It appears, however, that many of the premises of this theory have been supported. For example, Campion and McClelland (1991) found that job changes according to the different disciplinary orientations led to many of the predicted outcomes. Also, Campion and Berger (1990) demonstrated that redesigning jobs according to different approaches had a number of predicted implications for compensation. Over time, it is likely that more research will examine many of the propositions in this useful approach to job design.

Summary of Job-Based Theories. When viewed in a historical context, job-based theories represent a major theoretical breakthrough in organizational psychology. Prior to Herzberg, much of motivational theory within organizational psychology was focused on need satisfaction. Furthermore, outside of the field, because of the influence of Scientific Management, much of the theory and practice in motivation was focused only on the use of financial incentives. This is not to say that financial incentives are irrelevant. Rather, the advent of job-based theories led to the realization that job content can have a potent impact (positive or negative) on people.

A problem that is common to all three job-based theories is that all assume, to a large extent, that job content is an objective attribute (Salancik & Pfeffer, 1977). It has been shown, however, that "objective" indexes of the work environment often do not correlate well with self-report measures of the same attributes (e.g., Spector & Jex, 1991). Another

weakness in the job-based theories described in this section is that they are somewhat deficient with regard to *process* issues. For example, in Job Characteristics Theory, the core job dimensions lead employees to experience critical psychological states, and these states lead to a number of outcomes. The theory is not very explicit, however, as to the reasons underlying these propositions. Given the time period in which Job Characteristics Theory was developed (mid-1970s), and the proposed moderating role of growth-need strength, one might deduce that the mechanism is need satisfaction (Hackman & Oldham, 1976). However, it is also possible that jobs high on the core job dimensions also have higher levels of compensation and prestige. Both of these factors, rather than need satisfaction, may be necessary for the steps in the model. The more general point is that by focusing so heavily on job content, these theories have come up a bit short on the processes by which job content is translated into outcomes.

Cognitive Process Theories of Motivation

Another way that we can view employee motivation is in terms of the **cognitive processes** underlying motivation. Cognition, of course, means *thought*. What are some of the thought processes that go along with employee motivation? As readers will see in the theories described in this section, employees *make judgments* about how fairly they are being treated, *choose* where they will direct their efforts, and are able to *anticipate* future rewards associated with different levels of goal accomplishment. An understanding of these cognitive processes provides a great deal of insight into employee motivation.

When one looks at the history of psychology, the closest the field has ever come to having what might be described as a "dominant paradigm" was during the 1960s and 1970s, when behaviorism was at the height of its popularity. The author can remember, for example, taking Introductory Psychology in the mid-1970s and being told that psychology is the study of *observable behavior only*. Thought processes such as decision making and choice were not considered under the realm of psychology, because these could not be directly observed.

This view began to change in the late 1970s, and the changes ushered in what many have referred to as the "Cognitive Revolution" in psychology. During this period, psychologists began to focus on the thought processes underlying phenomena such as problem solving, choice, and even psychopathology. Another factor that facilitated the development of cognitive process theories was the growth in computer use. This is important because with this revolution came an increasing trend, particularly in memory research, to equate human information processing with computer information processing. As readers will notice, the "mind as computer" metaphor is evident, particularly in the more recent cognitive process theories of motivation.

Equity Theory. According to Homans (1958), humans tend to view social interactions as being much like economic transactions. That is, we tend to view relationships with others, as well as transactions with institutions (e.g., work, government), in terms of what we give and what we receive. Based on this notion, **social exchange theory** was developed to explain how we weigh and balance what we give and receive from social exchanges (Kelley & Thibaut, 1978).

Equity Theory is a type of social exchange theory that focuses on how people determine the fairness of social exchanges (Adams, 1965). Although Equity Theory can really be applied to any form of social exchange, in describing this theory we focus on the work context. A basic assumption of Equity Theory is that employees bring to the workplace what they perceive to be a number of *inputs*. Given that Equity Theory focuses on cognition, an input is essentially anything an employee decides it is. Job-relevant inputs would include things such as a person's academic credentials, years of prior experience, and job-related skills, as well as the level of effort given to his or her employer.

The other important component of Equity Theory is *outcomes*. Outcomes represent those things that an employee feels he or she is receiving from the employment relationship. The most tangible of these is monetary compensation, but outcomes may also include intangibles such as praise from one's supervisor, feelings of accomplishment, or even feelings of camaraderie among one's coworkers. Like inputs, outcomes are cognitive representations, and thus may differ from employee to employee.

According to Adams (1965), employees cognitively compare their *ratio* of inputs-to-outcomes to the perceived *ratio* of some comparative standard. A comparative standard could be another employee employed in the same job in the same organization, someone performing a similar job in a different organization, or perhaps even the focal employee at a different point in time. If an employee perceives that the ratio of his or her inputs to outcomes is *equal* to the ratio of the comparative other, a **state of equity** is said to exist. This means that the employee is reasonably satisfied with the current exchange relationship with his or her employer. When these ratios are different, however, a **state of inequity** is said to exist. In this case, the employee is not satisfied with the current state of the exchange relationship, and therefore is motivated to bring it back into balance.

According to Equity Theory, the most common form of inequity is referred to as **underpayment**. This occurs when the ratio of inputs to outcomes is perceived as less favorable than the comparative standard. For example, if an employee perceives that he or she is working much harder than a fellow employee who is paid the same salary, this may engender feelings of underpayment. According to Adams (1965), an employee can use a number of strategies in an attempt to restore equity when feelings of underpayment exist. These strategies are summarized in Table 8.2.

One way for an employee to restore equity would be to attempt to increase his or her outcomes. In the example given above, the employee could go to his or her supervisor and ask for a raise in order to compensate for his or her higher level of work effort. This may have the effect of restoring equity if the employee is successful, but it may also be risky. If the employee's request for a raise is denied, he or she may feel worse than before. This is especially true if the employee regards the effort required to request the raise as an additional input.

In a second strategy to restore equity, the employee may reduce his or her inputs so that the ratio becomes equal to that of other workers, and the underpayment is rectified. For example, an employee may reduce his or her effort to a level that is perceived as commensurate with outcomes. This strategy also carries some degree of risk. Reduced effort on the part of an employee may be perceived negatively by a supervisor or by his or her coworkers. This may, in turn, result in even fewer outcomes for the employee.

A third strategy is to cognitively adjust one's perceptions of inputs and outcomes in a way that restores equity. For example, an employee may cognitively reevaluate his or her outcomes and decide that they are more favorable than was first thought. The employee could also reevaluate his or her inputs and decide that they do not have as much value as first thought, or perhaps decide that there are additional outcomes that were not considered initially. The inputs and outcomes

TABLE 8.2
A Summary of the Mechanisms That Can Be Used to Restore Equity

Mechanism	Example
Increasing outcomes	Asking one's supervisor for an increase in salary
Reducing inputs	Decreasing the level of effort devoted to work tasks
Cognitive adjustments	Changing the perception of the value of one's inputs or outcomes, to restore equity
Changing the "comparative standard"	Choosing a different person to compare the ratio of inputs to outcomes
Leaving the field	Obtaining a job that provides a more favorable ratio of inputs to outcomes

of the comparison standard may also be cognitively adjusted in order to bring the two ratios into balance.

Of all the strategies listed in Table 8.2, cognitive adjustment of the perceptions of inputs and outcomes clearly requires the least amount of effort on the part of an employee, and is the least risky. For example, the employee does not have to make an effort to increase his or her outcomes, and does not incur the risk that goes along with reducing his or her inputs. A potential drawback with this strategy is that it may result in an employee's being taken advantage of. There *are* situations in organizations where people are treated unfairly, and cognitively adjusting one's perceptions does not change unfair treatment.

The fourth possibility listed in Table 8.2 is that an employee who perceives underpayment may change his or her "comparative standard" so that the ratio is perceived more favorably. For example, if the author were to use a professional baseball player as a comparative standard in making equity judgments, this would undoubtedly lead to strong feelings of inequity, at least with regard to salary. On the other hand, changing the comparative standard to "associate professors in psychology departments" would provide a greater chance of restoring equity. Keep in mind, though, that even within the same occupation or profession, multiple comparisons may be possible. For example, among academic I/O psychologists, distinctions can be made between those in psychology departments and those in business schools. Even within psychology departments, a distinction can be made between those teaching is doctoral programs and those employed at the master's level (see Comment 8.2).

A final way that an employee may respond to underpayment inequity was described by Adams (1965) as "leaving the field," or withdrawing from the inequitable exchange. In an employment setting, this would typically take the form of employee turnover, although it could take more subtle forms. For example, an employee who is feeling inequitably treated may psychologically withdraw from the organization. This may simply involve very minimal participation or reduced feelings of organizational commitment. As Adams pointed out, leaving the field is a step that is typically taken after other methods of resolving inequity are exhausted. In certain cases, however, this may be an employee's best option. For example, if there is little chance that equity can be restored, it may be best for an employee to seek other employment.

Recall that Equity Theory also proposes that feelings of inequity will arise when the ratio of a person's inputs to outcomes is more favorable to the comparative standard. This is referred to as *overpayment*. Given that feelings of underpayment largely represent feelings of unfairness or injustice, how then can we describe the quality of feelings of overpayment? According to Adams (1965), feelings of overpayment are uncomfortable, as are feelings of underpayment. Qualitatively, feelings of overpayment are probably best described as *guilt* rather than unfairness.

According to Adams (1965), an employee experiencing overpayment may use the same basic strategies that can be used to restore equity when feelings of underpayment exist. For example, one could *increase* one's inputs to make them proportional to one's outcomes, attempt in some way to *decrease* one's outcomes, cognitively adjust one's inputs or outputs, change the comparative standard, or even leave the exchange. Of all these strategies, the most common is cognitive adjustment, most likely because it is easier and more feasible than most of the others.

In general, research has supported Equity Theory very well, particularly with respect to

COMMENT 8.2

SALARY EQUITY IN PROFESSIONAL SPORTS

ONE AREA IN which the effects of Equity Theory can be observed quite readily is professional sports. It's almost comical, for example, to see a professional athlete who is being paid $5 million per year complain bitterly that he is being treated unfairly because he is not being paid $10 million. Most of us would be ecstatic to be paid even a fraction of either of those amounts. However, if one keeps in mind the "comparative standard" used by a professional athlete, such feelings of inequity become much easier to understand. More specifically, highly paid professional athletes compare their earnings to *other highly paid professional athletes of the same stature*. When these types of comparisons are made, the fact that one is a multimillionaire is really irrelevant. What's important is how one's salary compares to these other players.

A related issue that Equity Theory can help to explain is how highly paid professional athletes reconcile the fact that they are paid a great deal more than physicians, teachers, scientists, and others who perform work that is extremely important to society. Here's one somewhat speculative answer. A major league baseball player making $10 million may reason that he is deserving of this because of all the years he spent developing his skills, the years he spent playing in the minor leagues, and the fact that his career could be ended at any time by an injury. In Equity Theory terms, what this player is doing is cognitively adjusting his inputs relative to his outcomes.

the *underpayment* condition. It has been shown, for example, that perceptions of underpayment inequity are unpleasant and will motivate employees to do something about the inequity (e.g., Greenberg, 1990; Lord & Hohenfeld, 1979). In recent years, equity theorists have distinguished between equity with respect to the *outcomes* employees receive, and the *procedures* used to determine those outcomes. Perception of the equity of one's outcomes is referred to as **distributive justice**. The term **procedural justice** is used to denote perceptions of equity with respect to the procedures used to determine outcomes (Folger & Cropanzano, 1998). This distinction has proven to be quite useful because these two forms of justice have been shown to be associated with somewhat different outcomes (e.g., Sweeney & McFarlin, 1997).

The weakest support for Equity Theory has typically come from studies that have examined the overpayment condition (Pritchard, 1969). While it has been shown in a laboratory setting that feelings of overpayment can be induced (e.g., Lawler, Koplin, Young, & Fadem, 1968), there is very little evidence of this effect in organizational settings. This may be due to the fact that the whole notion of overpayment is rather questionable. At least with respect to salary, it simply may be unlikely that many people see themselves as *overpaid*. It is also possible that people may be able to cognitively adjust their perceptions very quickly to alleviate feelings of overpayment. For example, a person who is being paid what he or she considers too much may rationalize this by adjusting his or her perceptions of inputs (e.g., "My experience is a little better than I thought") or outputs ("With today's prices, that salary is not as great as it seems").

Expectancy Theory. One of the things that is unique about humans, at least with respect to cognition, is their ability to anticipate the future and adjust their behavior accordingly. Expectancy Theory is based on this uniquely human characteristic, and is focused on the cognitive processes that drive employees' decisions regarding where they will direct their efforts (Vroom, 1964, 1995). The basic premise of Expectancy Theory is that employees will generally direct their efforts toward behaviors or courses of action when:

1. There is a high probability that they will be able to perform the behavior if they try.
2. There is a high probability that the behavior or course of action will lead to some outcome.
3. The outcome that will result from the behavior or course of action has value to the person.

If any of these three conditions is lacking, a person is unlikely to direct his or her efforts toward that particular course of action.

According to Vroom (1964, 1995), the belief that one's efforts will allow one to perform a given behavior is referred to as **expectancy** and is typically denoted as effort-to-performance ($E \rightarrow P$). Because expectancy is a belief about the future, Vroom proposed that this is a probability function and, as such, may range from 0 to 1. An expectancy of zero essentially means there is no way that a person's efforts will result in a given level of performance. In contrast, an expectancy of close to 1 indicates that an employee has considerable confidence that if he or she puts forth effort, a given level of performance can be achieved. Expectancy beliefs may be based

on a number of factors: a person's innate ability, his or her level of training, or the existence or lack of significant performance constraints.

The belief that a given behavior or level of performance will be associated with a given outcome is referred to as **instrumentality** and is typically denoted as performance-to-outcome ($P \rightarrow O$). Like expectancy, instrumentality is a probability function. For example, an employee may perceive the instrumentality for the relationship between a given level of performance and a pay increase to be zero if salary raises are across the board or are determined by collective bargaining. On the other hand, a high instrumentality would indicate a strong possibility that a given level of performance would be rewarded with a given pay increase. Instrumentality beliefs are based, to a large extent, on stated organizational reward policies (i.e., the existence of merit pay), but are also based on the manner in which such policies are carried out.

The value of the outcomes that an employee may obtain is referred to as **valence**. According to Vroom, because of a number of factors, people differ on the value they attach to outcomes that can be obtained for different levels of performance. One person, for example, may place a high value on monetary compensation; thus, a high raise may have considerable valence. Another person, in contrast, may place greater value on feelings of mastery and praise from others. One interesting thing about valence is that it can take on *negative* values, and this has implications for predicting the direction of effort. Consider, for example, all of the things that may occur if an employee performs his or her job very well. Pay raises, praise from one's supervisor, recognition from others, and feelings of accomplishment are outcomes that most people would find at least moderately desirable. In contrast, those who perform their jobs well often end up having to perform a greater proportion of the work, and their higher salaries may encounter resentment from fellow employees. These outcomes would be considered by most people to be at least moderately *undesirable*.

Vroom proposed that Expectancy, Instrumentality, and Valence can be combined, in equation form, to explain employee motivation. This equation is presented in Table 8.3. The variable that this equation predicts is labeled **force.** This simply represents the level of effort that an employee will direct toward a given level of performance. Readers should be clear that force is *not* the same as performance. A person may direct his or her efforts in a way that is consistent with Expectancy Theory, yet not perform well because of a lack of innate ability or perhaps performance-related constraints.

As is shown in Table 8.3, for each possible outcome that can result from a given level of performance, instrumentality is multiplied by the valence. These values are then summed, and this sum is then multiplied by expectancy. Given this equation, force will be highest when employees believe that effort will lead to a given level of performance, and that the level of performance will lead to valued outcomes. Conversely, if any of these values are near zero, the motivational force will be considerably lower. For example, let's say an employee believes there is a high probability that effort will

TABLE 8.3
The Equation Representing How the Components of Expectancy Theory Interact to Determine Motivational Force

$$F = E \,(\Sigma \, I \times V)$$

F = Motivational force
E = Expectancy (E→P)
Σ = Summing over all possible outcomes
I = Instrumentality (P→O)
V = Valence

lead to a given level of performance, and that the outcomes that are possible are highly valued. If this employee does not believe that these outcomes are contingent on performance (e.g., instrumentality is low), then force will be low.

As another example, consider an employee who believes that effort will lead to a given level of performance, and that performance will lead to a number of outcomes. In this case, force may still be low if the outcomes have little value to the employee. The possibility of a promotion, or perhaps of praise, does not mean much to the employee.

Finally, an employee could believe that performance leads to highly valued outcomes, but he or she does not believe that the effort will lead to performance (e.g., expectancy is low). For example, many marathon runners believe that setting a world record would lead to a number of highly valued outcomes (e.g., money, fame, feelings of accomplishment), yet do not believe they can achieve this level of performance, even with considerable effort.

Since the development of Expectancy Theory by Vroom in 1964, it has become one of the dominant motivational theories in organizational psychology. As a result, considerable research has examined expectancy theory predictions. Van Eerde and Thierry (1996) performed a meta-analysis of 77 studies that have tested Expectancy Theory predictions, and examined the correlations between expectancy theory components and outcomes such as performance, effort, intention, preference, and choice.

The results of this study showed mixed support for Expectancy Theory. For example, although individual components such as expectancy and instrumentality were correlated with a number of outcomes, multiplying terms together, as suggested by Expectancy Theory, did not result in greater prediction. Another important finding from this meta-analysis was that correlations based on studies employing **within-subjects designs** were stronger than correlations from studies employing **between-subjects designs.** In a within-subjects design, Expectancy Theory would be used to predict a *particular individual's* choice among different levels of performance or different courses of action. In a between-subjects design, Expectancy Theory would be used to predict performance or effort from a large number of individuals. This finding supports the contention that the theory is useful in predicting how people will direct their efforts when faced with a number of different choices (e.g., Mitchell, 1974; Muchinsky, 1977).

In addition to direct empirical tests, Expectancy Theory has received indirect support from studies that have examined the impact of financial incentives (Jenkins, Mitra, Gupta, & Shaw, 1998; Lawler, 1990; Lawler & Jenkins, 1992). Although financial compensation will be discussed in greater depth in Chapter 9, suffice it to say that considerable evidence has shown that financial incentives can be a powerful motivator. Although this in itself does not constitute direct support for Expectancy Theory, it is certainly consistent with many of its propositions.

Goal-Setting Theory. The idea that human behavior is motivated and regulated by goals and aspirations has long been recognized by psychologists (Austin & Vancouver, 1996). Thus, like Expectancy Theory, the conceptual underpinnings of Goal-Setting Theory can be traced back many years. Organizational psychologists, most notably Edwin Locke, have elaborated on the basic notion of goal setting and have described how this drives behavior in organizations.

Before describing the specifics of Goal-Setting Theory, it is important to consider *why* goals motivate employees' behavior. According to Locke (1968), goals have motivational value for three reasons:

1. Goals serve to direct our attention and focus our efforts in a particular direction. A student who has a goal of obtaining an "A" grade in a course is likely to direct much of his or her attention toward that course.
2. Goals help us to maintain task persistence. This is important because, in many cases, people will fail or get sidetracked when they are trying to accomplish something.
3. The existence of goals tends to facilitate the development of task strategies. For example, the student in item 1 above may devise very innovative methods of studying his or her course material, in order to enhance retention.

Having described the functions served by goals, we now examine the attributes of goals that make them motivating. One attribute that has been supported very strongly over the years (e.g., Locke & Latham, 1990a) is **goal difficulty.** Generally speaking, goals that are difficult are more motivating than easier goals. For example, a salesperson is going to be more motivated if he or she has a goal of making $100,000 in commission, rather than a goal of $50,000.

The second attribute that must be present for a goal to have motivational value is **goal acceptance.** To a large extent, goal acceptance hinges on a person's belief that a goal is *attainable.* If a person does not believe he or she can attain a particular goal, this goal will probably not be accepted. Over the years, it has been suggested that employee participation in goal setting is a necessary condition for goal acceptance. Latham and Locke (1991), however, point out that evidence has shown that assigned goals can be just as motivating as jointly set goals, as long as they are accepted.

The third condition necessary for goals to be motivating is **goal specificity.** Goals are much more motivating when they specify a particular level of performance (e.g., "Sell 20 cars in the next month"), as opposed to being vague (e.g., "Be a good salesperson"). Because of the importance of goal specificity, many goal setting studies have what is referred to as a "do your best" condition in which participants are given no concrete performance goals.

Fourth, it has generally been recognized that employees must receive feedback in order for goals to motivate performance. Attaining a goal is often an incremental process; thus, it is important that employees receive feedback regarding their progress. Furthermore, according to Latham and Locke (1991), the relation between goals and feedback is actually reciprocal; that is, feedback helps employees to keep on track with respect to goal attainment. Conversely, the existence of goals helps to put feedback into a meaningful context.

In terms of research support, goal setting is one of the most well-supported theories in all of organizational psychology. Over 30 years, research has supported the motivational value of goals in both laboratory and field settings (e.g., Locke & Latham, 1990a, 1990b). Because of this wide support, the focus in the past 10 years has largely been on explaining the mechanisms underlying goal setting, as well as identifying boundary conditions of the theory.

With respect to mechanisms underlying goal setting, considerable research has been conducted on the goal commitment, goal acceptance, feedback, and self-efficacy (Ambrose & Kulik, 1999). It has been found, for example, that monetary incentives can be used to enhance goal commitment and

acceptance (Wright, 1992), and that both feedback and self-efficacy are necessary conditions for goal setting to be effective (Latham & Locke, 1991).

In terms of boundary conditions, several studies have indicated that goal setting may not work in all situations. Because goals tend to narrow one's focus, they may actually be counterproductive in situations where an employee may need to alter a poorly designed task (Staw & Boettger, 1990). Also, those who are assigned specific goals may be less likely to spontaneously help coworkers (Wright, George, Farnsworth, & McMahan, 1993). This tendency for goals to lead to "tunnel vision" may be counterproductive in organizations of the future, since it has been predicted that role boundaries will be much less well defined (Bridges, 1994).

Another boundary condition of goal setting is that there may be a "law of diminishing returns" with respect to the number of goals that an employee can use to guide his or her behavior. As the number of goals begins to increase, the probability of conflict between goals increases (Gilliland & Landis, 1992). Furthermore, when an employee has a large number of goals, the probability increases that he or she will not even be able to keep track of them all. Given that goal specificity is a key element of the theory, it is unlikely that an employee will be able to retain the specifics of an excessive number of performance-related goals.

A final boundary condition that has been examined in recent years is task complexity. Research has shown that goal setting may be more effective for simple (as opposed to complex) tasks (Mone & Shalley, 1995). The most frequently cited reason for this is that, if they are going to motivate performance, goals require a portion of a person's cognitive resources (e.g., Kanfer, Ackerman, Murtha,

Dugdale, & Nelson, 1994). Devoting cognitive resources to goals will have a detrimental effect when one is performing a complex task (i.e., preparing an annual budget). Also, when goal setting is used for complex tasks, goals are often set at inappropriate levels. Setting very *distal* goals will probably not be very helpful when one is performing a complex task. For example, if a research scientist were to set a very distal goal (e.g., "I want to obtain three scientific breakthroughs in the next 10 years"), this may have very little impact on performance. On the other hand, if a person performing this job were to set more *proximal* goals (e.g., "Read three important research articles this week"), this could potentially facilitate task performance. Given the increasing complexity of future jobs, this is an issue that clearly warrants more attention in goal-setting research.

Control Theory. In many areas of psychology, a trend in recent years has been to explain behavior in terms of *self-regulation* mechanisms. **Control theory** represents a very general theory that attempts to explain self-regulation processes underlying motivation (Carver & Scheier, 1981; Powers, 1973a, 1973b, 1978). Most treatments of control theory in the organizational literature cover it primarily in the context of goal setting, because it has been used rather extensively to explain the mechanisms underlying goal setting (e.g., Klein, 1989). Given this fact, control theory is not covered extensively in this section.

According to Powers (1973a), any control system consists of four distinct parts:

1. A *sensor* is a component that gathers important information about the control system. For humans, the sensor represents one's observations and perceptions.
2. A *standard* represents some state that a system attempts to maintain or achieve. In

terms of motivation, this would most likely be some type of goal, such as a level of performance or perhaps a more general aspiration (e.g., wanting to become a doctor).
3. A *comparator* or discriminator represents the mechanism by which information that is obtained by the sensor is compared to the standard. For example, a person may cognitively compare his or her rate of progression toward a desired goal.
4. An *effector* represents the mechanism by which the system can interact with its environment. With humans, the effector mechanism makes it possible; for example, to adjust one's effort if it is determined that progression toward a given goal is too slow.

Control theory conceptualizes motivation as an ongoing process by which people cognitively monitor their progress toward some goal or standard, and may make adjustments based on whether they are making progress toward that goal or standard. Given its generality, control theory could be used to explain essentially any form of purposeful behavior (e.g., weight loss, progress in psychotherapy, accumulation of wealth). As stated earlier, organizational psychologists have used control theory primarily as a means of explaining the mechanisms underlying goal setting (e.g., Klein, 1989; Lord & Hanges, 1987), although it has also been used in other areas such as occupational stress (e.g., Edwards, 1992).

According to Klein (1989), control theory augments goal setting in many ways. For example, control theory provides a more elegant description of the process by which feedback impacts goal-setting processes. In control theory terms, feedback represents a *sensor* that facilitates the process by which an individual compares his or her performance to the goal, and makes adjustments as necessary. Control theory also provides a plausible explanation of why a person may revise his or her goals in the face of repeated failure.

Beyond the implications for goal setting, control theory also serves as a useful framework for examining many other types of behavior in organizations. For example, an employee who suddenly begins to put forth more effort may be doing so because he or she feels that the current level of effort matches what is considered to be the effort of a "good employee." An employee who decides to change jobs may feel that the current job does not match his or her perception of what a job should be providing. Finally, an employee may decide to decrease his or her hours at work and spend more time at home because this is more congruent with his or her perception of being a "good parent."

Given the generality of control theory, little research has been aimed at testing it specifically. However, the overwhelming support for goal-setting theory over the years certainly bodes well for the viability of control theory. In the future, there is likely to be more research on goal setting performed from a control theory perspective. It is also quite possible that organizational researchers will examine other employee behaviors from a control theory perspective.

Summary of Cognitive Process Theories. Compared to other theories of motivation, the primary advantage of cognitive process theories is that they provide a more detailed view of the mechanisms underlying motivation. To use an analogy, cognitive process theories have allowed us to put work motivation under a microscope. Rather than simply knowing that an employee will work hard to fulfill esteem needs, cognitive process theories help us to understand the choices and decisions that employees make during this

process. Thus, cognitive process theories have most definitely enhanced our understanding of work motivation.

Despite the value of understanding the processes underlying work motivation, one might ask whether some cognitive process theories have reduced motivation to such a "micro" level that it is counterproductive. Such fine-grained analyses have the feel of being scientifically rigorous and objective, but it may be unrealistic to think that we can understand something as complex as human motivation in such detail. This also increases the danger that such theories will be perceived as inaccessible to the very group they are supposed to help: managers in organizations. In the future, greater effort needs to be put into delineating the practical implications of cognitive process theories.

THE BEHAVIORAL APPROACH TO MOTIVATION

The underlying assumption of the behavioral approach to motivation is that *behavior is largely a function of its consequences.* For example, when working with laboratory animals, the frequency with which a rat presses a bar is largely a function of the consequences of performing that behavior. If the consequence is positive for the rat (e.g., a food pellet), this will *increase* the probability of the behavior's occurring in the future. On the other hand, if the consequence is either negative (e.g., an electric shock) or neutral (e.g., nothing happens), this will *decrease* the probability of the behavior's occurring in the future.

The behavior of people in work settings is much more complicated than the behavior of laboratory rats. However, at a very basic level, the general principle described above also governs behavior in organizations; that is, people in organizations generally try to behave in ways that result in positive outcomes, and avoid behaving in ways that produce negative or neutral outcomes. In the remainder of this section, we will examine some of the mechanisms underlying behavioral explanations of motivation in organizations.

One of the major principles that can be used to influence behavior in organizations is **reinforcement.** Reinforcement can be defined as any stimulus that increases the probability of a given behavior. If an employee writes a good report and receives verbal praise from his or her supervisor, the verbal praise could be considered reinforcement. Readers will notice that this definition is not conceptual; rather, we define reinforcement primarily in terms of its *function*.

One of the key issues in the use of reinforcement to influence behavior is how it is administered. According to Luthans and Kreitner (1985), **schedules of reinforcement** describe various strategies that can be used to administer reinforcement. A general distinction that can be made about reinforcements is between those that are *continuous* and those that are *intermittent*. If reinforcement is provided continuously, this simply means that a person is constantly receiving reinforcement for his or her actions. This type of reinforcement schedule is rarely used in organization, but may have some use when new employees are initially learning their jobs. For example, a supervisor may initially reinforce a new employee every time he or she successfully completes a work assignment.

An obvious problem with continuous reinforcement is that it is inefficient for the organization. Also, if reinforcement is provided continuously, it may eventually lose value to the employee. Thus, in most cases, reinforcement in organizations is provided according to intermittent schedules. One common form of intermittent reinforcement is a *fixed-interval* schedule—the administration of reinforcement according to predictable time periods. Paying employees once a month is an example of such a schedule in an organization. A key decision to be made when using a fixed-interval schedule is the length of time between administrations of reinforcement. For example, when employees are first learning a task, it is common for intervals between reinforcement to be very small. Gradually, however, the intervals between administrations of reinforcement become larger. That is, an employee may receive a compliment or other reward perhaps once every few days.

A *variable-interval* reinforcement schedule is also the administration of reinforcement over time. However, unlike the fixed-interval schedule, when a variable interval schedule is used, the time interval between administrations of reinforcement varies. For example, an employee may receive compliments from his or her supervisor twice in the same week, but may not receive another compliment during the next three weeks. The power of variable reinforcement lies in the fact that the employee does not know exactly when it is coming. Some rewards cannot be administered this way (e.g., salary), but variable schedules can be a powerful way to motivate behavior using other, more intangible reinforcers.

Intermittent reinforcement can also be administered based on the behavior that is desired; such schedules are referred to as **ratio schedules.** For example, in a laboratory setting, a rat may receive a food pellet for pressing a bar a certain number of times. In an organizational setting, an employee may receive a reward based on the performance of a given behavior (e.g., selling a car). If a *fixed ratio* schedule is used, reinforcement is administered after a behavior has been performed a given number of times. For example, at the university where the author is currently employed, faculty are granted a release from teaching one course (a highly valued reward) for every six thesis committees they chair.

As with the fixed-interval schedule, a key decision is the number of behaviors that must be performed before the employee may receive the reward. For chairing thesis committees, the decision was based primarily on equating the time involved in this activity with the time involved in teaching a semester-long course. In many cases, however, the number of behaviors required to obtain reinforcement has to do with the skill level of employees. For example, when employees are first learning a task, the number of behaviors required to obtain reinforcement will generally not be very high. Over time, as the employee becomes more skilled, more behaviors are typically required in order to obtain reinforcement.

When a *variable ratio* reinforcement schedule is used, reinforcement is also administered based on the behavior performed. However, unlike the fixed-ratio schedule described above, the number of behaviors required to obtain reinforcement varies. An employee may be reinforced after performing a given behavior twice, and then not reinforced again until the behavior is performed five more times. Some readers will recognize this as the reinforcement schedule on which gambling is based. Given the number of people who become addicted to gambling, it is fair to say that this is a very powerful schedule of reinforcement. Like the variable interval schedule described above, some rewards cannot be administered according to this schedule for ethical reasons. However, rewards such as praise and recognition certainly can be, and often are, administered in this manner.

A second major principle of the behavioral approach to motivation is that of **punishment** or any consequence that has the effect of reducing the probability of a behavior. In organizational settings, punishment may be used to influence behavior, but typically is used much less often than reinforcement. The most common use of punishment in organizations is to *decrease the frequency of counterproductive behaviors.* Thus, it is probably most accurate to say that the way punishment motivates behavior is by discouraging the performance of negative behavior. The most common forms of punishment in organizations are: docking employees' pay, suspension, demotion, being given undesirable work assignments, and, in extreme cases, termination.

Although punishment may have a powerful effect, there are things to consider before organizations use it to influence employee behavior. For example, although punishment may produce the desired outcome in the short run, it may also produce considerable resentment and distrust among employees. In addition, it is well known that punishment tends to *suppress* undesirable behavior rather than eliminate it completely. Another danger in using punishment to influence behavior is that an organization may adopt it as the primary mode of influence. Typically, in this mode, employees are not praised when they do something well but are punished when they do something wrong.

In many cases, the behavior of employees in organizations may meet with neither positive nor negative consequences—that is, nothing happens. This phenomenon is known as **extinction.** The impact of extinction on organizational behavior may be positive or negative, depending on the nature of the behavior under consideration. For example, if an employee is rude and obnoxious during meetings, extinguishing such behavior is positive. On the other hand, if an employee is very helpful to others and never receives any acknowledgment, there is a chance that the positive behavior will be extinguished. Of course, in such cases, some employees may feel a sense of internal satisfaction and thus may keep performing helpful behaviors for that reason. However, when such behavior is no longer internally rewarding, it may cease.

Probably the most important implication of extinction is that organizations must think about the behaviors they want to encourage, and the behaviors they want to see minimized. Too often, rewards in organizations are administered in a way that encourages behaviors that are only minimally important, and extinguishes those that are the most crucial to organizational success. Consider, for example, an organization that administers rewards primarily on the basis of seniority. In behavioral terms, such an organization is saying that the most valuable commodity is the length of service of employees. Under this type of system, an employee who performs very well but has not been employed a long period of time has little incentive to maintain a high level of performance.

In many companies, behavioral principles are used in training employees to learn new skills and to adopt new behaviors. Particularly when an employee is learning a novel behavior, the behavioral principle of **shaping** comes into play. Essentially, shaping has to do with the reinforcement of successive approximations of a particular behavior, rather than the entire behavioral sequence. Probably the best example of the use of shaping is in the training of animals. Readers who have been to Sea World have undoubtedly enjoyed the tricks performed by sea lions and killer whales. To teach those tricks, trainers must work many hours and reinforce the slightest movements that are seen as leading to the ultimate behavior.

In organizational settings, shaping may be used in ways that have implications for employee motivation. For example, when employees are first learning job tasks, reinforcing "successive approximations" of ultimate task

performance will keep an employee from getting discouraged. In many academic departments, faculty are often reinforced for taking *preliminary steps* that may lead to desired outcomes, such as publication and external grants. By reinforcing behaviors such as building relationships with those at funding agencies, and establishing collaborative relationships with other researchers, it is hoped that such activities will ultimately lead to grants and publications.

A final behavioral principle that has important implications for motivation is **feedback.** When employees engage in any form of behavior (or in performance-related behavior in particular), it is helpful to have some feedback about that behavior. Feedback has motivational value, particularly when it is positive. Most employees enjoy hearing positive feedback when they perform well, and such feedback often serves as an incentive to maintain a high level of performance. Feedback can also have considerable diagnostic value when employee performance is lacking. When an employee is performing poorly, feedback serves the important function of letting the person *know* that he or she is seen as not performing well. Sometimes, it is quite obvious when performance is lacking (e.g., a comedian tells a bad joke), but in many cases, it is not (e.g., a manager who is making poor strategic decisions). Thus, in many instances, feedback about performance must be given by some external agent or the employee simply will not know that he or she is performing poorly.

Perhaps the most important diagnostic function of feedback is that it communicates to employees where specific performance deficiencies exist. Simply having the knowledge that one is not performing well is certainly useful. However, it is more useful to receive feedback on what *specific aspects* of performance are lacking. Once these aspects are established, it is possible to go even further and diagnose the root cause of the performance problem.

In organizations, the *application* of behaviorism is known as **Organizational Behavior Modification (OBM),** and this approach has been used to influence a number of behaviors, such as safety, suggestive selling, and production efficiency. In general, evidence supporting the effectiveness of OBM is impressive (Weiss, 1990). That is, using behavioral principles has been shown to impact the behaviors listed above in ways that are favorable for organizations. One limitation of OBM, and thus of the behavioral approach, is that it appears to work best when it is applied to relatively simple forms of behavior. That is, when jobs are relatively simple, it is much easier to keep track of desirable and undesirable behaviors, and apply reinforcement accordingly. With more complex tasks, however, this becomes much more difficult to do.

As an example, suppose we tried to use reinforcement principles to motivate a scientist who is working on mapping the entire human genetic structure. Because of the complexity of this type of scientific activity, it would likely be quite difficult to get a good handle on all of the steps necessary to ultimately accomplish this goal. Also, because progress in this type of scientific activity is very slow and incremental, reinforcement may be so infrequent that it would have little impact on motivation.

Another issue has been raised about behaviorism: the ethics underlying this approach. Some critics, for example, have charged that by systematically analyzing the contingencies underlying behavior and manipulating the environment to impact behavior, people are robbed of their choice and free will. B. F. Skinner, in his 1971 book, *Beyond Freedom and Dignity,* countered such charges by stating that environmental contingencies will govern behavior whether or not we choose to intervene. Behaviorism, in his view, represented nothing more than a systematic attempt to use those environmental contingencies in a way that was beneficial to society.

THE PRACTICAL VALUE OF MOTIVATION THEORIES

Having reviewed what are generally considered to be the major theories of employee motivation, we now ask: How valuable are these theories to managers in organizations? There is no way, for example, to rank-order the theories in this chapter in terms of practical value. However, it is possible to draw some general conclusions about the four general types of theories described. Generally, Need Theories probably fare the worst, among the four different general approaches to motivation. Needs may be highly specific to individual employees, so it may be extremely difficult for a manager to either figure out a given employee's level of need satisfaction or take steps to respond to it. Also, because a given need may be satisfied in multiple ways, motivating on this basis would be quite time-consuming and cumbersome for managers.

Job-based theories, in contrast, fare considerably better in terms of practical value. Job content is something that most managers can relate to, and in fact have some control over. Thus, if a manager sees that an employee lacks autonomy in his or her job, steps may be taken to increase autonomy. On the other hand, in some cases, changing a person's job is simply not practical. For example, job content may be governed by a union contract, or perhaps changing one employee's job would have such wide-ranging effects throughout an organization that the cost would be prohibitive.

Cognitive process theories may also have considerable practical value, although the exact value varies considerably for each theory. Expectancy Theory, for example, has much to offer managers in designing reward systems and in the diagnosis of performance problems; that is, performance-based rewards will be effective only if employees are able to see a connection between their performance and the level of rewards they attain (e.g., Instrumentality). Similarly, a performance problem may be linked to a belief that effort will make no difference (e.g., low expectancy), a belief that performance will make no difference (e.g., low instrumentality), or the fact that an employee simply does not value the rewards that an organization is providing. Goal-setting theory has also proven to be very useful and, in fact, is employed extensively in organizations.

Equity Theory, at least in its original form, probably has less practical value than Expectancy Theory and Goal Setting. Because perceptions of inputs and outcomes represent cognitions, they may be highly individualized and thus may be of little help to managers in motivating people. Also, readers will recall that many Equity Theory predictions are negative; that is, Equity Theory predicts that in some situations employees will reduce effort, or perhaps even leave a situation, in order to resolve feelings of underreward. However, for most managers, motivation is a *positive* enterprise and trying to prevent negative behaviors is not nearly as useful.

The behavioral approach to employee motivation may also be very useful to managers. Principles of behaviorism are relatively easy for most managers to grasp, even if they do not have behavioral science training. Particularly when jobs are not highly complex, it is not difficult to determine the contingencies governing different behaviors. Finally, from a practical point of view, the best thing about the application of behavioral principles is that *it works.*

Well-articulated and well-supported theories provide managers with considerable informed guidance as they attempt to motivate employees. If no theories of motivation were available, managers' attempts to motivate people would essentially be random, or perhaps would be based on each manager's idiosyncratic view of the world. In the next chapter, we examine how these motivation theories are applied in organizations in order to influence a multitude of employee behaviors.

CHAPTER SUMMARY

In this chapter, we reviewed what are considered the major theories of motivation in organizational psychology. These theories were organized into four general categories: Need-Based Theories, Job-Based Theories, Cognitive Process Theories, and The Behavioral Approach. According to Need-Based Theories, motivation is largely rooted in the human desire to satisfy needs. Theories falling under this category included Maslow's Need Hierachy, Alderfer's ERG Theory, and Achievement Motivation Theory. In general, support for Need-Based Theories has been rather weak, due largely to the difficulty of conceptualizing and measuring needs.

According to Job-Based Theories, the content of employees' jobs is the key factor impacting motivation. Theories covered under this category included Herzberg's Motivation-Hygiene Theory, Job Characteristics Theory, and Campion's Interdisciplinary Approach to Job Design. Job-Based Theories have proven quite useful and have generally been supported much better than Need-Based Theories. One problem that plagues Job-Based Theories is the distinction between objective and subjective attributes of jobs.

Cognitive Process Theories are aimed at describing the cognitive processes involved in employee motivation. These theories, for example, focus on things such as decision making, levels of aspiration, and self-regulation. Theories discussed under this category included Equity Theory, Expectancy Theory, Goal Setting, and Control Theory. Although all of these theories have been supported, Goal Setting has clearly received the greatest support and has had the most impact within organizations. In the future, as Cognitive Process Theories become more complex, a challenge will be to translate these into a form that can be readily used by managers.

The Behavioral Approach to employee motivation involves using principles adapted from behaviorism in order to influence behavior in organizations. The principle used most frequently is reinforcement, although others, such as punishment, shaping, and extinction, may be used in certain situations. Applications of the behavioral approach in organizations, in the form of Organizational Behavior Modification (OBM), have produced impressive results. This approach, however, appears to work best in situations where the jobs being performed are not highly complex.

In the concluding portion of the chapter, we examined the value of motivation theories to managers in organizations. This may vary from theory to theory, but it was concluded that in general, motivation theories can be quite useful to managers. Specifically, theories provide managers with a "road map" for motivating employees. Without motivation theories, managers would be forced to rely entirely on intuition and their own implicit theories of human behavior.

SUGGESTED ADDITIONAL READINGS

George, J. M. (1995). Asymmetrical effects of rewards and punishments: The case of social loafing. *Journal of Occupational and Organizational Psychology, 68,* 327–338.

Griffin, R. W., & McMahan, G. C. (1994). Motivation through work design. In J. Greenberg (Ed.), *Organizational behavior: The state of the science* (pp. 23–43). Hillsdale, NJ: Erlbaum.

Kanfer, R., & Heggestad, E. D. (1997). Motivational traits and skills: A person-centered approach to work motivation. In L. L. Cummings & B. M. Staw (Eds.), *Research in organizational behavior* (Vol. 19, pp. 1–56). Greenwich, CT: JAI Press.

Wright, P. M., O'Leary-Kelly, A., Cortina, A., Klein, H., & Hollenbeck, J. (1994). On the meaning and measurement of goal commitment. *Journal of Applied Psychology, 79,* 795–803.

Chapter Nine

Organizational Applications of Motivation Theory

For any organization to be successful, employee behavior must be channeled in directions that contribute positively to that success. For example, a car dealership wants its salespeople to work hard to sell cars; an elementary school wants its teachers to strive to educate students. Organizations also want to *prevent* employees from engaging in behaviors that stand in the way of organizational success. For example, a construction company wants to discourage its employees from being late to work, and an auto manufacturer wants employees to refrain from drug use on the job.

The purpose of this chapter is to build on Chapter 8 by describing the various ways in which organizations apply motivation theories in order to influence employee behavior. It should be noted at the outset that the methods described in this chapter are not the *only* ways that organizations can influence behavior. Indeed, an organization could manipulate, coerce, and even physically threaten its employees in order to influence their behavior.

However, in the long run, these methods tend to have undesirable effects. Thus, organizations typically use more positive methods.

This chapter describes methods that are either directly or indirectly based on the theories of motivation described in Chapter 8. An obvious advantage of doing this is that it serves to maintain continuity from chapter to chapter. A more important reason, which will hopefully be brought out in this chapter, is that methods of influence that are firmly grounded in well-supported motivation theories are generally more effective than those based purely on intuition or speculation.

SOME BASIC ASSUMPTIONS

Before getting into specific methods that organizations use to influence employees' behavior, it is useful to examine some basic assumptions surrounding this process. One underlying assumption, which is so basic that we rarely question it, is that an organization has the *right* to influence the behavior of its employees. In essence, the relationship between organization and employee is viewed as a "psychological contract" whereby each is entitled to certain things (e.g., Morrison & Robinson, 1997). From an employee's perspective, the employment relationship typically carries with it certain entitlements such as pay, fringe benefits, and, possibly, other perquisites. In return, an organization expects employees to behave in ways that benefit the organization. When their behavior is not benefiting the organization, employees are expected to modify their behavior.

Another assumption is that employees have at least some freedom of choice as to whether they will engage in behaviors that positively or negatively impact the organization. If employees had no freedom of choice, organizations would have very little to do in the way of "motivating" their employees. In fact, if employees had no freedom of choice, all an organization would have to do is order employees to behave in ways that supported organizational goals. This would obviously make life much simpler in organizations. (It would also make for a very short Chapter 9.) In reality, though, employees in most organizations do have some level of control. Certain forms of behavior (i.e., attending work) may be required to maintain organizational membership. The choice to go beyond them typically rests with the employee.

A third assumption underlying applications of motivation theory is that there are no major internal or external constraints on employees' behavior. Internal constraints would be things such as a lack of job-relevant skills or abilities among employees. As was shown in Chapter 4, motivation is only *one* determinant of productive behavior in organizations. When an organization attempts to influence employees' behavior through compensation, for example, it is assumed (not always correctly) that employees have the skills and abilities necessary to perform their jobs well.

External constraints, on the other hand, represent things in the external organizational environment that make it difficult for employees to translate their skills and abilities into performance (Peters & O'Connor, 1988). Although situational constraints is a topic that has typically been explored in the occupational stress literature (see Chapter 7), it is relevant here as well. When organizations attempt to motivate employees by providing higher levels of job autonomy, for example, an implicit assumption is that there are no organizational conditions blocking the increase in autonomy.

A final underlying assumption of organizational attempts to motivate employees is that behavior is at least somewhat malleable. Put differently, it is assumed that *people are capable of changing their behavior.* This seems like a fairly common sense notion, but the evidence in the psychological literature regarding behavior change is not clear-cut. For example, Hellervik, Hazucha, and Schneider (1992) conducted an extensive review of the behavior change literature and concluded that, in general, empirical evidence supports the notion that behavior is amenable to change. They were quick to point out, however, that behavior

---

COMMENT 9.1

CAN PEOPLE CHANGE?

BEHAVIOR CHANGE IS an important issue that has been studied and debated by psychologists for many years. The importance of behavior change, however, goes far beyond psychology and other behavior sciences. For example, people's views about behavior change have implications for the relationships that we develop with others and, in many cases, public policy decisions. Many people also spend a considerable amount of money in order to change what they consider to be undesirable behaviors (e.g., smoking, overeating, and being sedentary).

What does psychological research have to say about behavior change? Hellervik, Hazucha, and Schneider (1992) conducted a comprehensive review of the behavior change literature and came up with a number of interesting conclusions. The good news is that research evidence generally supports the notion that it is possible for people to change behavior. Their review contained studies showing evidence that people are able to change behaviors such as level of knowledge, job performance, safety behavior, and mental health. However, their review also showed that behavior change is complex and depends on a number of factors—perhaps most

importantly, the behavior one is trying to change. For example, it is unlikely that underlying traits such as cognitive ability and personality traits can be changed. On the other hand, much simpler things, such as interpersonal skills, probably can be modified.

Another important conclusion from this review is that behavior change is not easy. People have to be motivated to change, and interventions designed to change behavior need to be well designed and, in many cases, need to take place over a fairly long period of time. So, yes, it is possible for people to change some forms of behavior, but such change does not occur overnight. Failing to recognize this could lead to problems if organizations either attempt to change behaviors that cannot be modified, or fail to use proper interventions to change other behaviors that must be modified.

Source: L. W. Hellervik, J. F. Hazucha, and R. J. Schneider. (1992). Behavior change: Models, methods, and a review of the evidence. In M. D. Dunnette and L. M. Hough (Eds.), *Handbook of industrial and organizational psychology* (2nd ed., Vol. 3, pp. 823–895). Palo Alto, CA: Consulting Psychologists Press.

---

cannot be changed *quickly* or *easily* (see Comment 9.1).

BEHAVIORS ORGANIZATIONS ATTEMPT TO INFLUENCE

Figure 9.1 contains four forms of behavior that are most typically targeted by organizational influence attempts. If we take a sequential view of motivation, organizational attempts to influence behavior begin before employees actually become organizational

members. Specifically, organizations first try to influence behavior during the *attraction* stage. Through tangible means such as salary and benefits, and more intangible things such as promotion potential and organizational image, organizations seek to influence skilled individuals to seek membership in the organization, and ultimately to become members of the organization.

Once an individual becomes an employee, there are a number of behaviors that organizations attempt to influence. The most

FIGURE 9.1
Types of Behaviors That Are Typically the Focus of Applications of Motivation Theories in Organizations

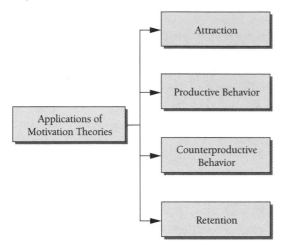

visible of these, and the one that has been explored the most in the motivation literature, is *productive behavior.* Organizations want employees to perform their in-role tasks well and, in some cases, go beyond and perform extra-role behaviors. They would also like employees to come up with innovative and creative ideas for the organization's benefit, and, given the increasing competition and rates of change, organizations often want employees to learn new things and periodically update their skills.

This strong focus on performance in the motivation literature has unfortunately shifted the focus away from other behaviors the organizations wish to influence. For example, organizations obviously want to discourage employees from being absent frequently, and from engaging in a multitude of *counterproductive behaviors* such as theft, substance use, and sabotage—to name a few. Although we typically don't think of these behaviors as the focus of organizational motivation programs, they really are in the sense that

organizations are trying to persuade employees *not* to engage in them.

Another behavior that is frequently the focus of organizational applications of motivation theory is *retention.* In comparison to other behaviors, motivating employees to retain their membership in an organization is a bit different because it requires that the organization must balance a number of factors. As is often the case with compensation, an organization may be in the position of having to make difficult choices when deciding which employees are worth retaining, and how much the organization is willing to pay to keep them. If an organization retains one employee by providing a large pay increase, this may very well prompt other employees to look elsewhere. Thus, an organization is often in the unenviable position of having to weigh the cost of internal harmony against the cost of a skilled employee's leaving.

Regardless of the behavior organizations wish to influence, applying motivation theories involves some *choice* on the part of an organization, and such choices are often value driven. For example, the founder of an organization may make a very conscious choice to reward his or her employees on the basis of performance. In other cases, the values communicated by motivational practices are far more *implicit* and, in some cases, are in conflict with the espoused values of the organization (Kerr, 1975; Lawler, 1990). Many organizations *say* they value performance and even institute reward systems that are meant to reflect this philosophy. However, despite the espoused value of performance, rewards in many organizations are only very weakly related to performance. Thus, in exploring the application of motivation theories, we must keep in mind that such applications always involve important value-ladened choices on the part of organizations.

ORGANIZATIONAL REWARD SYSTEMS

By far, the most common method of motivating and influencing employee behavior is through **organizational reward systems.** There could potentially be an infinite number of ways an organization could reward its employees, so it is useful to distinguish between two types of rewards: tangible and intangible. Tangible rewards are those that are most familiar to readers: salary, fringe benefits, and bonuses. Intangible rewards include things such as recognition, praise, and increased freedom for employees. Tangible rewards will be discussed first.

Tangible Rewards

One misconception within organizational psychology, perhaps due to the rise of job-based theories over the years, is that money does not motivate people in the workplace (Flannery, Hofrichter, & Platten, 1996; Lawler, 1990). Quite to the contrary, few people would work for an organization for no salary. Furthermore, people engage in a variety of illegal behaviors, ranging from selling illegal drugs to selling government secrets, primarily to make money. Why is money important? In a general sense, money is obviously important because it provides the means for people to purchase life's necessities and luxuries. In the workplace, employees' salaries are important because they communicate something about the employees' value to the organization. Within a given organization, if one employee has an annual base salary of $20,000 and another employee is paid $100,000, it is fairly evident that the second employee is more highly valued than the first. Salary is also important because many people use it as at least an indirect barometer of their career success. For example, a person may define "success" as having a six-figure salary before the age of 40.

Despite the importance of pay, it is also true that pay is one of many motivating factors in the workplace. In fact, when people are asked about the most important things they are looking for in a job, pay tends to be ranked lower than things such as a chance to do interesting work, and an opportunity to use their skills (Hugick & Leonard, 1991).

As an attraction mechanism, pay can be highly effective. According to Gerhart and Milkovich (1992), research evidence shows that organizations that adopt a strategy of paying top dollar for talent have greater success in attracting skilled employees than organizations choosing not to do so. The reasons for this would appear to be rather obvious. When all other things are equal, many applicants will choose to work for an organization that pays them well. In addition, organizations that pay premium salaries tend to develop a positive reputation; thus, more applicants will be attracted to them (see Comment 9.2).

Despite the apparent utility of paying top salaries to attract top talent, this strategy can be quite risky for organizations. Given the high payroll costs involved, those hired must perform extremely well in order to justify this cost (Lawler, 1990). In addition, if several organizations within the same industry adopt this strategy, salaries may be driven to a much higher level than would be warranted by normal market forces (e.g., scarcity of labor). This has clearly been the case in professional sports, where salaries have reached astronomical levels. It has become increasingly difficult for "small market" teams to compete for talent and ultimately to be successful. It should be noted, also, that many teams with huge payrolls have been unsuccessful (see Comment 9.3).

COMMENT 9.2

BEING KNOWN AS A HIGH-PAYING COMPANY

It's clear from the compensation literature that organizations known to pay very high wages tend to be more successful in recruiting employees, compared to organizations that are less generous. On the surface, the reason for this seems rather obvious: Who doesn't want a high salary? Paying high wages also helps with recruiting, for other reasons. For example, the fact that an organization pays well may be seen by potential employees as a sign that the organization "takes care of its employees," and may even give the organization a somewhat elite image among potential applicants. Attracting a great number of applicants may allow an organization to be highly selective, and, ultimately, to hire the best talent available.

So why don't all organizations attempt to be known as high-paying companies? One reason is that many organizations simply can't afford the expense. Paying premium wages is costly, and that cost tends to compound over

time. Typically, only large organizations and those that have been extremely successful can afford to have such high payroll costs. Another reason some organizations do not choose this strategy is that wages can get out of control if many organizations in the same industry choose to adopt this strategy. In fact, this strategy may drive wages to a level that is out of line with the skills and talents of those who are being hired. (See the section on executive compensation.) Furthermore, when organizations are paying everyone well, employees must be able to contribute almost immediately, and there may be little time for newcomers to ease into their roles.

Source: B. Gerhart and G. T. Milkovich. (1992). Employee compensation: Research and practice. In M. D. Dunnette and L. M. Hough (Eds.), *Handbook of industrial and organizational psychology* (2nd ed., Vol. 3, pp. 481–569). Palo Alto, CA: Consulting Psychologists Press.

Pay is also frequently used as a mechanism for motivating behaviors such as performance and retention in organizations. The most common way of doing this is through **merit pay**; that is, employees receive an annual percentage increase in their pay, based on the outcome of a formal performance review (Lawler & Jenkins, 1992). Ideally, in a merit pay system, employees who receive the most favorable performance reviews receive the greatest percentage increases. From an organizational viewpoint, the hope is that employees will see the connection between performance and the size of their annual increase.

According to Lawler and Jenkins (1992), there is ample evidence that a *well-designed* and *properly administered* merit pay program

can be highly effective in motivating employees. Merit pay systems, however, are often not effective because they are either poorly designed or administered improperly. A clear theme in the compensation literature is that pay systems should be designed to support the strategic objectives of an organization (Flannery et al., 1996; Lawler, 1990; Wilson, 1995). Thus, if an organization's strategy is focused on customer service, the merit pay system should encourage positive customer service behavior. A common mistake in many organizations is that very little thought is put into exactly what behaviors are being encouraged by the merit pay system.

For the proper administration of a performance-based merit pay system, three factors

COMMENT 9.3

CAN MONEY BUY ORGANIZATIONAL SUCCESS?

BESIDES THE HIGH costs that go along with paying high wages, this strategy is risky for another reason: An organization paying high wages must be very successful in order to justify those costs.

In professional sports, this is a particularly relevant issue, given the fact that salaries have become so high and success is so cut and dried. Do teams that pay enormous salaries to players tend to be more successful than teams paying lower salaries, due either to a lack of resources or simply a refusal to pay high salaries? There are certainly a number of examples to support this hypothesis. In major league baseball, the New York Yankees have traditionally had one of the higher payrolls, and have been quite successful of late. In professional basketball, the Chicago Bulls were quite successful during the period when they had one of the highest paid players (Michael Jordan) on their team.

There are, however, notable examples of professional sports teams that have been unsuccessful in trying to spend their way to success. In professional football, for example, the San Francisco 49ers in 1999 had the distinction of having one of the highest payrolls and one of the worst records in the conference. In their case, injuries, combined with age-related declines, contributed to this dubious distinction. In professional baseball, the Baltimore Orioles spent a considerable amount of money on free-agent players in 1999, and ended up losing nearly as many games as they won.

In professional sports, as with any other type of organization, buying a deep supply of talent is necessary but not always sufficient for success. Thus, organizations need to be concerned not only with acquiring talent, but with things such as how that talent will mesh together, and how to design a system in which that talent will be best used.

are particularly crucial. First, for such a system to work, an organization *must be able to accurately measure and document performance differences among employees.* This can be done in some companies, but, more often, it is nearly impossible to do with any level of accuracy, particularly when jobs require a great deal of collaboration or interdependence. If performance cannot be accurately measured and documented, a performance-based merit pay system will be doomed to failure. In fact, where performance cannot be measured well, a performance-based merit system may do more harm than good because employees may see merit-pay decisions as being very arbitrary.

Second, the system must be administered fairly; that is, employees must believe there is

some validity to the performance-based pay decisions that result from the system (Eskew & Hennenman, 1996; Scarpello & Jones, 1996). This is obviously related to, but goes beyond, the first point. Fairness involves not only the accuracy of performance measurement, but also whether employees perceive that merit increases reflect actual performance differences. This obviously mirrors the actual administration of the merit pay system, but it also depends heavily on communication. In many cases, merit pay procedures are ineffective simply because organizations fail to adequately explain the basis for merit increases.

Third, for a merit pay system to motivate performance, the amount of money available to fund merit increases has to be enough to allow the amount of the increases to be perceived as meaningful. According to Lawler (1990), a percentage increase needs to be large enough to be meaningful to employees. What is seen as a meaningful pay increase is somewhat subjective; it depends on many factors, such as the current rate of inflation and what other comparable organizations are paying. However, a clear trend, during the past 20 years, has been for organizations to reduce the size of merit pay increases (Lawler & Jenkins, 1992). Thus, many merit pay systems that are well designed in some respects have only a negligible impact on employee performance simply because the amount of the merit increases is not meaningful to employees.

As an alternative or supplement to merit pay, some organizations have shifted toward pay for performance, through the use of **incentive pay.** In a typical incentive pay system, an employee's pay is directly linked to a quantifiable level of performance. The most common form of incentive pay, which dates back to Scientific Management, is piece-rate compensation. Under a typical piece-rate system, employees are paid a certain amount based on the number of products or parts produced. It is also common, in piece-rate systems, for employees to have a chance to earn "bonuses" by producing at a very high level. For sales jobs, a familiar form of incentive pay is described as sales commissions.

Bonuses are another way that organizations often attempt to tie pay to performance. In principle, bonuses are very similar to incentive pay; however, bonuses are often given out based on different criteria. For example, a manager may receive an annual bonus that is contingent on his or her department's meeting a given performance goal. Another difference is that bonuses are often distributed as lump-sum payments,

whereas incentive pay is typically distributed from paycheck to paycheck.

Compared to merit pay, an advantage of incentive pay and bonus compensation is that both are more concretely tied to performance. For example, a real estate agent knows that variations in his or her paycheck are linked to the number of homes sold. A manager who receives an annual bonus typically knows *why* it is being paid. Because of the timing of merit pay, it is often difficult for employees to draw any connections between their increase and their performance. Another advantage, at least with lump-sum bonuses, is that they are more psychologically meaningful to employees. When an employee receives a 5% merit increase (which is fairly typical), this makes only a negligible difference in take-home pay and is often taken for granted. In contrast, a lump-sum payment of 5% of one's annual salary is more likely to attract the attention of the employee.

Incentive pay and bonuses are also advantageous to organizations for financial reasons because these systems make it much easier for the organizations to link their labor costs with their ability to pay (Lawler, 1990). For example, under incentive and bonus systems, employees are paid well when the organization is financially successful. During lean years, however, incentive and bonus payments are much lower.

At least in the case of incentive pay, research clearly supports a positive impact on performance. Jenkins, Mitra, Gupta, and Shaw (1998) found, in a meta-analysis of 39 studies conducted in both laboratory and field settings, that the corrected correlation between financial incentives and performance *quantity,* over all studies, was .34. Financial incentives had no impact on performance quality. This meta-analysis also revealed that the impact of financial incentives was greatest in experimental simulations and when studies were conceptually grounded in either expectancy or reinforcement theory. It has also been shown that financial incentives work well in comparison to other methods of increasing employee productivity (Guzzo, Jette, & Katzell, 1985).

Despite the positive aspects of incentives and bonuses, some clear negatives are associated with these methods of motivating employees' performance. Though not a problem in all incentive and bonus systems, some of these systems can lead to very adversarial relations between employees and management. Historically, this has been most typical in the implementation of piece-rate compensation systems. In a typical piece-rate system, employees are expected to produce a certain amount, considered the "standard," and are paid more if they produce more than the standard. In many companies, there is considerable disagreement over what is an appropriate standard, and employees may intentionally slow down production while the standard is being determined. Management sometimes exacerbates this problem by arbitrarily raising the standard if they feel that the employees are making too much money. Ultimately, the focus can be more on "beating the system" than on increasing productivity.

Problems may also occur when some jobs in an organization are covered by incentive and bonus systems and others are not. The employees who do not work under such plans may resent the employees who do. Employees who work under such a system may be reluctant to accept a transfer to other job responsibilities for which they may be better suited, because they would have to take a pay cut to do so.

One thing that merit pay, incentives, and bonuses all have in common is that most are typically based on *individual employees'* performance. Many of today's organizations, however, want employees to take a broader perspective and focus their efforts on enhancing the success of the work group or organization. One of the most common ways that organizations tie rewards to organizational performance is through **employee stock ownership plans,** commonly referred to as ESOPs (Rosen, Klein, & Young, 1986). Although the ownership of stock is often associated only with executive compensation, many organizations make wider use of this form of compensation. Perhaps the most notable example of this policy is Wal-Mart discount stores, where hourly employees have always been allowed to purchase stock in the company.

From an organization's point of view, there are many advantages to having employees share an ownership stake though stock purchases. For example, if an organization is performing well financially, this can be an excellent way to attract talented employees. Also, because the value of stock often appreciates in value over time, employees may lose out financially if they leave the organization after a short period of time. Therefore, stock ownership can also be a way of enhancing retention. It is also possible that stock ownership will encourage positive attitudes and a sense of responsibility among employees (Klein, 1987)—things that many organizations try to promote by designating employees as "owner-representatives." Finally, from a purely financial point of view, having employees own stock is beneficial because it is a good way for an organization to raise capital and thus avoid hostile takeovers from larger organizations or investors (Lawler & Jenkins, 1992).

One thing that ESOPs probably do *not* do well, however, is motivate employees' performance. With the exception of high-level executives, most employees are unable to see a strong connection between their own performance and the organization's stock price. This has been particularly true in recent years' increased volatility in financial markets. Furthermore, in most ESOP plans, participation is not based on performance. The only criterion employees must meet before they are able to purchase shares of company stock is that they must be employed for a certain period of time (six months, for example).

Organizations also attempt to motivate employees' organizational performance through **profit-sharing** and **gain-sharing** programs. According to Florkowski (1987), in a typical profit-sharing program, an organization designates a target profit margin that it wishes to achieve. When profits exceed this target margin, a percentage of these "excess" profits is shared with employees. For example, if an organization decides that a 5% profit margin is acceptable and the actual profit margin is 7%, a portion of the additional 2% is shared with employees. Profit sharing has the potential to decrease competition and enhance cooperation among employees. Employees under such a system stand to gain much more by working together for the good of the organization as a whole, rather than trying to outdo each other. Also, like ESOPs, profit sharing may help in attracting and retaining high-quality employees. Although there has not been a great deal of research evaluating profit sharing, there is some evidence that it is associated with such positive effects as enhanced organizational productivity and positive employee attitudes (Florkowski, 1987; Florkowski & Schuster, 1992).

Profit sharing, however, is also unlikely to be a powerful motivator of individuals' performance. As with ESOPs, most employees fail to see a strong connection between their own behavior and the profitability of their organization. Some organizations can address this issue by basing profit-sharing payments on divisional or even unit profitability, although this can't always be done. The other problem with profit sharing as a motivational tool is that profit-sharing programs often pay out only once or twice a year. Thus, even if an employee is able to see the connection between his or her performance and profits, the temporal lag between performance and the profit-sharing payment makes it very difficult for such payments to have much motivational impact.

Gain sharing is similar to profit sharing in that some portion of pay is based on the performance of the organization as a whole. According to Lawler (1990), however, it is different in two respects. First, the payments made to employees from gain-sharing programs are based on *cost savings* rather than on profits. For example, an organization might determine, based on past data, that losing 10% of cost, due to production defects, is acceptable. Given this 10% target, if a lower percentage can be achieved, some portion of the additional savings will go to employees.

Second, gain sharing is a comprehensive organizational change intervention; profit sharing is strictly a compensation program. Given the objectives of gain sharing, this makes sense. Cost reduction typically requires the efforts of individuals at many levels of an organization's hierarchy; thus, input from all employees is vital.

Evidence on the effects of gain-sharing programs has been positive (e.g., Hatcher & Ross, 1991; Petty, Singleton, & Connell, 1992). Specifically, such programs have been shown to result in significant cost reductions, and may in fact have positive effects on employees' attitudes. It is much easier for employees to see the connection between their behavior and cost reduction, as opposed to their impact on stock prices or profit margins. Also, compared to profit sharing, gain sharing represents a more fundamental change in management values, so employees working under gain-sharing programs may find that many other aspects of their work situation improve.

One potential drawback to gain sharing is that, in some cases, it is difficult for an organization to establish cost-reduction benchmarks. If an organization is relatively new, for example, or has not collected a great deal of historical data, the cost reduction benchmarks that are set may be regarded by employees as being arbitrary. If this is the case, such a plan may do a great deal more harm than good. Gain sharing can only work if the cost-reduction benchmarks are seen as being objective. If they are seen as being arbitrary, employees may feel a great deal of resentment.

Up to this point, all the forms of tangible compensation that have been described involve either direct cash payments to employees or the prospect of some future payment. However, not all forms of tangible compensation involve direct cash payments to employees. **Fringe benefits** represent a significant portion of most employers' total compensation costs—most typically, they are around 30% (U.S. Chamber of Commerce, 1991). The most typical fringe benefits offered by employers include health and dental insurance, some form of life insurance coverage, and pension benefits. Some organizations also offer their employees benefits such as 401(k) plans, vision coverage, and tuition reimbursement.

Unfortunately, very little research has examined the motivational impact of fringe benefits. However, the research that has been done suggests that their impact may be fairly minimal. Often, employees simply lack knowledge about their organization's fringe benefits program (Milkovich & Newman, 1990), and they typically underestimate its financial value

(Wilson, Northcraft, & Neale, 1985). Given that barrier, it is hard to imagine that fringe benefits would have much motivational value.

Fringe benefits, however, can have a positive impact on the attraction and retention of employees (Gerhart & Milkovich, 1992). For example, given the high cost of health care, even small differences in health coverage plans can have significant financial implications for employees. Thus, a very good health coverage plan may potentially provide an organization with a competitive advantage when it tries to attract employees and is reasonably competitive with respect to salary. The same can also be said for retirement and pension plans.

With regard to retention, pension plans probably have the greatest impact because the value and portability of one's benefits often depend on organizational tenure. Organizations must deal with one question, however: Is it desirable to attempt to retain employees primarily on the basis of their "sunk costs" in a pension program? Such plans may help to retain employees, but employees who remain in an organization primarily for that reason may not be highly productive or particularly motivated (Meyer & Allen, 1997).

Another common form of noncash compensation comes in the form of **perquisites**, more commonly know as "perks." The specific perks offered by organizations vary widely and depend, to a large extent, on the level of each employee. For example, for servers in fast-food restaurants, typical perks include meal discounts and free uniforms. Most retail stores offer employees discounts on merchandise. At the other end of the spectrum, perks for high-level executives can reach almost outrageous proportions. For example, it is not unusual for executives to receive perks such as country club memberships, free use of a company-owned resort, transportation to and from work, and travel via a corporate aircraft. Organizations have cut back on executive perks in recent years, due to changes in tax laws, but most executives are still treated very well by their organizations (see Comment 9.4).

As with fringe benefits, very little research has examined the impact of perks in organizations. It is doubtful, however, that perks have a great impact on employees' day-to-day behavior because, for most people, perks represent a relatively small portion of their compensation. In addition, within most industries, the nature of the perks provided to employees is fairly standard. For high-level employees, however, perks may make a difference, particularly when a company needs their skills. For example, to lure away an executive from a competing firm, an organization may attempt to "sweeten the deal" with perquisites. This is also a very common practice in professional sports. For example, when the Los Angeles Dodgers signed free-agent pitcher Kevin Brown in 1998, a clause in his contract called for unlimited use of a corporate jet to fly to his home in Georgia.

Intangible Rewards

Although organizations often reward employees with tangible things such as money and fringe benefits, these represent only a subset of the rewards organizations may use to influence employees' behavior. Many organizations recognize employees' performance with what can be described as *intangible rewards*. An intangible reward is defined as one from which the employee does not realize financial or material gain. Although clearly not as powerful as financial rewards, intangible rewards are used frequently and, in many cases, are highly valued by employees.

One of the most common intangible rewards in organizations is a combination of

---

COMMENT 9.4

EXECUTIVE PERKS: LIFE IS GOOD AT THE TOP

PERQUISITES ("PERKS" FOR short) are special privileges that employees receive over and above their salary and fringe benefits. For most employees, perks represent a relatively small and insignificant portion of the their total compensation. For high-level executives, however, perks can represent a significant portion of total compensation and may be quite lavish. Common perks for executives include a car and driver, country club membership, use of company-owned vacation properties, first-class travel privileges, and separate dining facilities, to name a few. In many organizations, top executives are almost treated like royalty.

In recent years, however, organizations in the United States have become somewhat less extravagant in granting perks to executives. One of the reasons for this is that, in the mid-1990s, the Internal Revenue Service ruled that some perks represented a form of income to executives and thus were subject to income tax. Another reason is that more and more organizations are trying to create an egalitarian atmosphere in which all employees are treated equally. Granting lavish perks only to executives serves to highlight status differences within organizations, and thus runs counter to an egalitarian philosophy. Finally, public outrage over executive compensation in general has probably led organizations to be a bit more judicious about the perks they grant to executives.

Despite these cutbacks, perks still offer a very comfortable existence to executives in most organizations.

recognition and awards. In some companies, recognition and citations come with tangible rewards attached, but the tangible reward is often less meaningful to the employees than the recognition and appreciation that are conveyed. For example, many organizations formally recognize employees after a certain number of years of service, or when they have achieved some change in status, such as a promotion. Awards may also be given out for specific work-related accomplishments such as coming up with a novel work process or a cost-saving measure.

Another frequently used intangible reward is **praise.** For example, a supervisor may verbally praise a subordinate when a work assignment is well done. The use of praise should have some impact on an employee's behavior because it is likely that praise from one's immediate supervisor has some reinforcement value (Latham & Huber, 1992) and may enhance employees' feelings of competence (Bandura, 1986). Key issues, however, are the timing and sincerity of supervisory praise. Praise is likely to have the greatest impact when it follows closely after the desired behavior. If a supervisor praises a subordinate for a report that was written six months earlier, this is likely to have little effect on the employee. The effect will undoubtedly be much greater if the praise is delivered on the day after the report is completed.

Praise from a supervisor is also much more effective if employees believe that it is sincere. Undoubtedly, a number of factors can determine sincerity, but two are particularly important. The first has to do with the frequency with which praise is given out. If a supervisor is constantly praising his or her subordinates, the motivational value of this praise will likely diminish over time. On the other hand, if praise is very rarely given out, subordinates may become highly suspicious on those few occasions when they do receive

it. Thus, for praise to be effective, supervisors must strike a balance between giving too much or too little praise.

A related issue, though no less important, is the level of performance that must be achieved in order to receive praise. If supervisors heap lavish amounts of praise on subordinates for mediocre performance, this will decrease the value of praise when high levels of performance are actually achieved. Praise is also typically more effective if employees feel that they have some control over the behavior for which they are being praised (Koestner, Zuckerman, & Olsson, 1990). It is unlikely, for example, that an employee would be impacted if praise were given for something he or she had little control over.

Another intangible reward that organizations sometimes use to motivate employees is **status symbols.** Status symbols are simply ways that organizations communicate an employee's worth or value to the organization. Typical status symbols include the size and location of one's office, an impressive-sounding title, and, in some areas, the location of one's parking space. Unfortunately, there is very little research on the impact of status symbols on employees' behavior. One would assume, however, that these probably do not have a great deal of impact on employees. Most people tend to take status symbols for granted, although they may be happy with them initially. Also, status symbols often go hand in hand with other more tangible forms of compensation.

A final intangible reward that organizations sometimes use to influence employees' behavior is **increased autonomy and freedom.** Over time, as employees become more proficient and demonstrate that they can be trusted, supervisors may grant them increased autonomy and freedom (Spector, Dwyer, & Jex, 1988). This may be done in a number of ways. For example, supervisors may give employees broad latitude on how they perform their work, and perhaps allow employees the freedom to choose their own hours or even to work at home on occasion. Although supervisors granting this type of autonomy and freedom do not see it as being a reward, it is quite possible that subordinates do see it that way.

One of the clear benefits of granting increased autonomy and freedom is that it will likely enhance job satisfaction and perhaps decrease employees' stress (e.g., Fried & Ferris, 1987; Spector, 1986). It is also possible that this will enhance performance and retention, although little empirical evidence exists to support either outcome. Granting increased autonomy and freedom may have a positive effect on performance, especially when employees are highly talented and motivated. Increased autonomy and freedom may help these employees to reach their full potential.

Autonomy and freedom may contribute to retention as well. Often, autonomy and freedom are perks that employees have acquired over time by demonstrating their talent and loyalty within an organization. Thus, if an employee were to leave his or her present organization, it is unlikely that the same degree of autonomy and freedom would be present at the new company, at least initially. The autonomy and freedom that employees have in a given career keep them from taking other career paths. This is undoubtedly one of the reasons why many university professors choose to stay in academia rather than pursue more lucrative careers in business or government. When people have experienced a great deal of freedom in their jobs, it is very difficult to give it up, even if they will be paid significantly more.

Executive Compensation

Up to this point, we have covered the major types of rewards that organizations use to influence employees' behavior. These same rewards are typically used to influence the behavior of executives, but the compensation of executives is quite unique, for a number of reasons. One reason is the *amount* of compensation of executives, compared to other employees. Although executive salaries vary by type of organization, it is not at all unusual for the total compensation of executives in private organizations to exceed several million dollars per year (Crystal, 1995).

Other than the sheer amount of compensation, another difference is that executives' compensation is typically based more on the performance of the organization than is the compensation of other employees. In fact, executives may receive 50% or more of their total compensation in the form of bonuses, or through stock options. Bonuses are often determined by the profitability of the company; typically, the company must perform well for an executive to benefit handsomely from exercising his or her stock option. Thus, compared to other organizational employees, a greater portion of executives' compensation is at risk if the organization does not perform well (Gomez-Mejia, 1994).

Given the high level of compensation that is received by executives, many have raised the issue of whether this reward is deserved (e.g., Crystal, 1991). Arguments in favor of high executive salaries typically center around two facts: (1) high-level executive skills are in relatively short supply, and (2) decisions made by these individuals can have a tremendous financial impact on an organization and its shareholders.

On the other hand, it has also been argued that executive compensation packages have become excessive and are out of line with the actual impact that executives have on organizational effectiveness (Barkema & Gomez-Mejia, 1998; Crystal, 1991). According to this argument, executive skills are scarce but not scarce enough to warrant the levels of compensation currently given to executives. For example, even though the salaries of professional athletes are often viewed as excessive, it could be argued that the skills possessed by these individuals are much rarer than the skills possessed by executives. For example, it is likely that far fewer people possess the basketball skills of Michael Jordan or the baseball skills of Alex Rodriguez, in comparison to the administrative skills of Michael Eisner.

Another reason for treating executive compensation separately is that, even within the same organization, the processes typically used to set executive compensation levels are often quite different from those used to determine compensation for other employees. According to Crystal (1991), high-level executive compensation packages typically result from negotiations between the executive and the compensation subcommittee of the organization's board of directors. This negotiation process is often aided by an outside compensation consultant who determines whether the board is compensating the executive at a level that is commensurate with executives employed at comparable organizations.

Given these procedures for determining executive compensation levels, there may be reasons why executives are at a distinct advantage in this process. Members of corporate boards of directors are often executives who inhabit the same social circles as the organization's executives. Such similarity may positively bias board members in favor of the executives. Also, many board members have their compensation determined in the same fashion, so it is certainly in their interest to have members of their peer group well compensated. Thus, members of corporate boards may not be the most objective judges of what is a fair level of compensation. Interestingly, recent research has not shown a relationship between the composition of compensation

committees and executive compensation (Daily, Johnson, Ellstrand, & Dalton, 1998), a finding these authors attribute to recent pressure from shareholders to curb executives' salaries.

Another aspect of this process that often favors executives is the use of external compensation consultants. As stated earlier, the role of a compensation consultant is typically to assess an executive's compensation in relation to the compensation of executives in comparable organizations. On the surface, then, it would appear that compensation consultants would be the most objective players in the whole process. Keep in mind, however, that compensation consultants must give their recommendations to executives and board members who typically want to see the level of executives' compensation rise. If a compensation consultant does not recommend a highly lucrative compensation package, he or she may not be hired the next time compensation is determined (Crystal, 1991).

Within organizational psychology, research on executive compensation is relatively new, although some consistent findings have begun to emerge. For example, it has been found, relatively consistently, that the amount of executives' compensation is only weakly related to the performance of organizations (Finkelstein & Hambrick, 1988; Gerhart & Milkovich, 1990). This finding would appear to be a bit disconcerting, given the vast amounts of money paid to executives. However, it could simply be a statistical artifact, due to the restriction of range in executive salaries. It may also be due to the fact that even though executives are important, their actions represent one of a multitude of factors that contribute to organizational success. For example, even if top executives make sound strategic decisions, these will not lead to success if an organization lacks the necessary talent, at lower levels, to translate these decisions into higher levels of profitability. Organizations are also impacted by a number of external forces that are outside of executives' control: economic cycles, changes in government regulations, shifts in consumer preferences, and so on.

Another stream of research has begun to examine the various determinants of executive compensation. One fairly consistent finding is that executive compensation is positively related to organizational size (Finkelstein & Hambrick, 1988; Gomez-Mejia, 1994; Gomez-Mejia & Welbourne, 1989). Larger organizations have greater financial resources, and thus are simply able to pay higher salaries than small organizations. It has also been found that executives appear to be paid, to a large extent, based on the amount of discretion they have over decision making in their organization (Finkelstein & Boyd, 1998). This makes a good deal of sense, considering that when executives have a great deal of discretion in decision making, they have a much greater chance of impacting (positively or negatively) organizational performance

We return now to a question that was asked about other types of compensation: What impact does it have on employees' behavior? It appears fairly obvious that executive compensation has a great deal of impact on attraction. In fact, without such compensation packages, most organizations would find it difficult to attract high-level executive talent. The impact of executive compensation on attraction is closely tied to its impact on retention; that is, organizations must compensate executives very well in order to retain their services. There are, however, certain ways that executive compensation packages can be structured to have a greater impact on retention. For example, when granting an executive stock options, a board of directors has some discretion over the length of time the stock shares must be held before the executive may sell them (Crystal, 1991). Thus, to retain an executive, a board may specify a relatively long period of time before the stock options may be exercised.

Another common way for corporate boards to enhance executive retention is by granting executives so-called "golden parachutes"—lucrative pension benefits that are contingent on remaining with the organization for a given period of time. Although job tenure is a feature built into most pension programs, with executives the stakes are so high that remaining with an organization may make a difference of millions of dollars in pension benefits. However, some executives may be so wealthy that the loss of pension benefits may mean very little if another organization is more competitive with its offer of compensation.

Finally, does executive compensation have any impact on performance? As stated earlier, there is a very weak connection between the amount of an executive's compensation and organizational performance. However, because so many factors contribute to organizational performance, it is still possible that compensation *does* motivate executives. Executive compensation packages are typically heavily loaded with stock options, and such packages are likely to motivate executives to make decisions that will increase stock prices. This can obviously be done through increasing profits, but may also be done by more negative means such as layoffs or ill-advised acquisitions.

MOTIVATION THROUGH THE DESIGN OF WORK

Although reward systems represent the major mechanism for influencing employees' behavior, organizations also attempt to motivate employees through the design of work; that is, they try to design employees' jobs, departmental structures, and even whole organizations in ways that engender high employee involvement and motivation. In this section, we focus primarily on the design of employees' jobs as a motivational tool used in organizations. More macro-level approaches to the design of work will be covered in Chapter 14.

Job Design: A Brief History

According to Moorhead and Griffin (1998), prior to the nineteenth century, most nations were agrarian societies. Families farmed and were largely self-sufficient. Gradually, this model of self-sufficiency gave way to what might be described as "general craft" work. Specifically, people gradually reduced their production of food and instead concentrated their efforts on the production of goods (e.g., clothing, furniture) that were then traded for food. Over time, this "general craft" model gave way to greater specialization. For example, in the production of clothing, people began specializing in weaving, sewing, and tailoring.

The single event that had the greatest impact on the design of work was the Industrial Revolution, which occurred in the United States in the late 1800s, and had spread throughout Europe in the late 1700s and early 1800s. With the Industrial Revolution came systematic study of job specialization by men such as Adam Smith and Charles Babbage. Their work ultimately led to the development of the assembly line and, eventually, to the introduction of Taylor's Scientific Management system. As readers may recall, the primary motivational mechanism used in Scientific Management was compensation; employees were paid on the basis of the amount they produced. Job design was also a key part of motivating employees under the Scientific Management system. To the extent that jobs were designed so employees could maximize their efficiency, this would lead t o higher wages because employees were

being paid on the basis of how much they produced.

Due largely to worker dissatisfaction over Scientific Management, there eventually emerged an approach to work design that is typically identified with the Human Relations school of thought. According to advocates of this approach, work should be designed in ways that provide employees with an opportunity to have input and to fully maximize their skills and abilities. A major assumption behind this approach was that people work not only to make money but also for more intrinsic reasons such as intellectual stimulation and creative expression. Although a number of work design interventions came out of the Human Relations movement, a common thread running through most was that jobs were designed to be more interesting and to give employees greater discretion over work-related decisions.

Since the Human Relations era, the focus has been on refining this basic approach. For example, Hackman and Oldham's (1980) Job Characteristics Model brought greater specificity to the design of jobs and produced a tool for the diagnosis of the motivational properties of jobs (the Job Diagnostic Survey). More recently, Campion's interdisciplinary approach to job design has represented the melding of approaches to job design that come from disciplines other than organizational psychology. We now consider specific approaches to the design of work.

Humanistic Job Design

One of the simplest forms of humanistic job design is **job rotation.** With job rotation, the actual content of jobs is not changed; however, employees are allowed to periodically rotate among different jobs. The reasoning behind job rotation is that performing different jobs will provide an employee with greater variety and, perhaps, an opportunity to learn new skills. Although job rotation has been shown to produce some positive outcomes and is still used (Campion, Cheraskin, & Stevens, 1994), the content of employees jobs does not actually change.

A second approach to job design, stemming directly from humanistic principles, is **job enrichment**. The term *job enrichment* was first coined by Frederick Herzberg and was used to describe those aspects of people's jobs that were labeled as "motivators." (Recall the description of Motivation-Hygiene Theory in the previous chapter.) Motivators were linked to the content of people's work, such as the amount of control workers had over decisions, the level of intellectual challenge in the work, and the level of creativity workers were able to use in performing the work. Job enrichment represented an attempt to build greater levels of "motivators" into jobs and, hence, to make them more motivating.

The primary mechanism used for the enrichment of jobs was termed **vertical loading**, which simply means providing employees with more tasks to perform, as well as greater freedom and discretion as to how they perform those tasks. As an example of how vertical loading might work, the job of a janitor might be vertically loaded by allowing this individual to schedule his or her cleaning tasks and to assume responsibility for ordering new cleaning supplies. In this way, the job has been changed by adding tasks and allowing the employee to assume the responsibility for tasks that may have been previously performed by a supervisor.

Although few empirical studies have evaluated the design of jobs according to Herzberg's principles of job enrichment, there is some indication that this approach was successfully implemented in some organizations. For example, Ford (1973) reported positive outcomes, such as increased productivity and reduced

turnover, resulting from the enrichment of clerical jobs at AT&T. Texas Instruments also had a great deal of success with the enrichment of janitorial jobs (Weed, 1971).

Not all of the early job enrichment programs were successful, however (Griffin & McMahan, 1994). One of the reasons is that early job enrichment programs were conducted under the assumption that everyone would be motivated by having their jobs enriched. Given the vast number of ways in which humans differ, this would appear to be a rather naïve assumption at best. Early job enrichment represented a rather narrow and imprecise way of designing jobs to enhance motivation. Although vertical loading may make sense in some cases, there may also be other ways that jobs could be changed in order to enhance motivation. It is largely in response to these two criticisms of job enrichment that the next approach to job design evolved.

The Job Characteristics Approach to Job Design

As you'll recall from Chapter 8, Hackman and Oldham's (1980) Job Characteristics Theory posits that most jobs can be described according to these "core" dimensions: autonomy, variety, significance, feedback, and identity. Furthermore, to the extent that these core dimensions are present, people will tend to experience their jobs as psychologically meaningful, feel a sense of responsibility about their work, and have an understanding of how they are performing their jobs. If people experience these positive psychological states, a number of positive outcomes will occur, one of which is high internal motivation. Hackman and Oldham proposed that this model would only be applicable for those with high growth-need strength and, more recently, it has been proposed that satisfaction with the work context (e.g., pay, working conditions) is also a key moderator. For over the past 25 years, Job Characteristics Theory has served as the theoretical foundation for a great deal of applied work on job design in organizations. It is to that aspect of Job Characteristics Theory that we now direct our focus.

According to Hackman and Oldham (1980), an important first step in any potential job redesign effort is some form of *diagnosis* of the job (or jobs) within an organization that might be the target of such an effort. Fortunately, in the course of developing Job Characteristics Theory, Hackman and Oldham also developed the **Job Diagnostic Survey (JDS),** which can be used to measure each of the components in the theory. Fortunately, the JDS has undergone a number of refinements over the years and, at present, is a reasonably good psychometric instrument (see Comment 9.5).

COMMENT 9.5

THE JOB DIAGNOSTIC SURVEY

IN THE COURSE of developing Job Characteristics Theory, Hackman and Oldham also developed the Job Diagnostic Survey (JDS) to measure the major components of the theory (Hackman & Oldham, 1975). The development of the JDS was important for job redesign because it provided a means of measuring the attributes of jobs that might need to be changed.

Over the years, a great deal of research has been conducted on the psychometric properties of the JDS, and, in general, the results have been favorable. That is, the scales measuring core job dimensions and other variables in the theory have been shown to be reliable (Fried & Ferris, 1987). Evidence on the validity of the JDS has been somewhat more mixed (e.g., Fried, 1991; Rentsch & Steel, 1998; Spector & Jex, 1991), although in general the JDS appears to be a construct valid measure of the attributes of jobs.

The only substantive modification in the JDS over the years was made in one of the items in the autonomy subscale. Idaszak and Drasgow (1987) identified a problem in the autonomy measure that was due to a negatively worded item. Subsequently, most users of the JDS have eliminated this problem by wording all three items in a positive direction.

Even though the JDS is certainly not perfect, it has served organizational psychologists well as the primary method of measuring the components of Job Characteristics Theory. This has facilitated research on the theory and helped greatly with the diagnosis and redesign of many jobs over the years.

Sources: J. R. Hackman and G. R. Oldham. (1975). Development of the Job Diagnostic Survey. *Journal of Applied Psychology, 60,* 159–170.

Y. Fried and G. R. Ferris. (1987). The validity of the job characteristics model: A review and meta-analysis. *Personnel Psychology, 40,* 287–322.

Y. Fried. (1991). Meta-analytic comparison of the Job Diagnostic Survey and the Job Characteristics Inventory as correlates of work satisfaction and performance. *Journal of Applied Psychology, 76,* 690–697.

J. R. Rentsch and R. P. Steel. (1998). Testing the durability of job characteristics as predictors of absenteeism over a six-year period. *Personnel Psychology, 51,* 165–190.

P. E. Spector and S. M. Jex. (1991). Relations of job characteristics from multiple data sources with employee affect, absence, turnover intentions, and health. *Journal of Applied Psychology, 76,* 46–53.

J. R. Idaszak and F. Drasgow. (1987). A revision of the Job Diagnostic Survey: Elimination of a measurement artifact. *Journal of Applied Psychology, 72,* 69–74.

When used for a preliminary diagnosis, the most important thing to look for is the pattern in the measures of the five core job dimensions. Let's say, for example, that a group of employees holding similar clerical positions completed the JDS, and the pattern of results resembled those in Figure 9.2. In this case, the scores that we see reflect a reasonably high level of significance, variety, and feedback. However, it is rather clear that the employees performing this job feel that they lack both autonomy and identity. In clerical jobs, it is not unusual for incumbents to have little autonomy over how their work is done, and the low identity may reflect a feeling that they are only contributing to the goals of the organization in a very narrow way.

Now that a diagnosis has been done and we have some indication of how a job might be changed, Hackman and Oldham (1980) recommend that the next step is to assess the feasibility of job redesign. Although a number of factors impact feasibility, the general categories to look at are the *employees* and the *organizational system*. With respect to employees, a major issue is whether employees want their jobs redesigned. Also, because job redesign often increases the skill requirements of jobs, the skill levels of employees must be taken into account. If employees either do not want job redesign, or possess very limited skills, job redesign is unlikely to be successful.

Some of the organizational factors that would likely weigh in the decision of whether to pursue job redesign would be: the presence of union representation of employees, the prevailing management philosophy of the organization, and the likely cost of redesigning jobs. Although the presence of a union does not automatically mean that jobs cannot be redesigned, it does make it much more difficult because collective bargaining agreements often cover the content of jobs that employees perform. Thus, if an organization decides to redesign jobs, a union may see this as the organization's attempt to get more work out of its members without raising their pay.

The prevailing management and control mechanisms in an organization are important because job redesign interventions often involve granting employees greater discretion over how they perform their jobs. Thus, at some level, job redesign often requires that managers and supervisors delegate some of their authority to subordinates. If the prevailing management philosophy in an organization is very authoritarian, there is a good chance that most forms of job redesign will not work; they simply will not fit the organization. Thus, the prevailing management culture within an organization must not view delegation of authority as a negative thing if job redesign is to work.

Redesigning jobs in an organization can be a costly undertaking. Job redesign often necessitates the use of outside consultants, requires training employees in new skills and work methods, and may introduce changes in jobs that interface with those being redesigned. Generally speaking, if an organization must completely redesign its production

FIGURE 9.2
Sample Profile of Core Job Dimension Scores from the Job Diagnostic Survey (JDS)

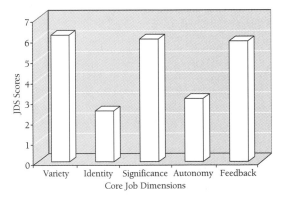

processes or technology in order to redesign a job or set of jobs, this may make the cost of job redesign prohibitive.

When the conditions in an organization appear to favor job redesign, a major choice organizations face is how to implement this change. Although it is possible to simply mandate the redesign of jobs, it is generally advisable to involve those organizational members who are major **stakeholders** in the job redesign process. A stakeholder is anyone who may be impacted by the redesign of a job. The obvious set of stakeholders in any job design effort are job incumbents—workers whose lives will be changed by the redesign of the job. Other common stakeholders are supervisors, union representatives, and anyone else in the organization who must regularly interact with job incumbents. There is no standard way to involve stakeholders, but a common mechanism is to create a temporary committee or task force composed of major stakeholders to provide oversight of the job redesign process.

Assuming that there is cooperation from major stakeholders, the next step in this process is to decide on specific changes to be made in jobs. These changes should obviously be driven by the initial diagnosis. It is also useful to have additional information about the job (from a job analysis, if available). According to Hackman and Oldham (1980), jobs can be redesigned in a number of different ways, depending on the core job dimension that one is trying to enhance. A common method of changing jobs, and one that is really based on the principle of job enrichment, is **vertical loading**. In the Job Characteristics Theory approach to job redesign, vertical loading is essentially the same as it was in Herzberg's approach; that is, employees are given more tasks and greater levels of control and discretion over how they perform their job duties.

If one thinks back to Job Characteristics Theory, vertically loading a job could impact nearly all of the core job dimensions, although the greatest impact is typically increased autonomy, because employees are provided with higher levels of discretion. However, this intervention may potentially have a positive impact on the other core dimensions of skill variety, task identity, and task significance. Skill variety is often enhanced because when one has greater control, this often necessitates the use of skills that were previously not used. Task identity may be enhanced because vertical loading often makes it possible for employees to complete a whole cycle of work rather than a small fragment. Task significance is enhanced because when a job is vertically loaded, it is often easier for an employee to see the importance of the work he or she is performing.

Another common job design intervention based on Job Characteristics Theory is **combining tasks**. This simply involves combining small, specialized tasks into larger units of work. For example, a clerical employee whose job has involved primarily word processing may have filing and phone coverage added to his or her job duties. Combining tasks undoubtedly has the greatest impact on the core job dimension of skill variety because the employee is doing different things that may require different skills. It is possible, however, that combining tasks may also impact task identity if the combination of tasks represents a more integrated experience for the employee.

A third intervention based on Job Characteristics Theory is that of **forming natural work units**. This is similar to combining tasks, but, in practice, operates quite differently. Forming natural work units involves giving an employee responsibility for a logical, identifiable body of work. For example, an insurance company could redesign the jobs of claims adjusters so that instead of handling claims on an ad hoc basis, each adjuster could have primary responsibility for the claims of a certain group of clients. This type of job change often allows higher levels of task identity to be built into jobs because when natural work units are formed, employees are more likely to complete a job from "start to finish" and to see the job as an integrated whole. This intervention also has the potential to increase task significance because doing an integrated piece of work helps employees to see the "big picture"—that is, to understand how their work contributes to the more general mission of the organization.

A fourth job redesign intervention is **establishing client relationships.** This simply involves making it possible for an individual who is performing a job to interface directly with internal or external customers. A manufacturer may use this type of intervention by providing a phone number on a finished product so that, if there is a problem, the customer can contact the individual or team that produced the product. From the employees' perspective, this may enhance autonomy by giving the job somewhat of an entrepreneurial feel. It also has the potential to enhance skill variety, since the skills necessary to interface with customers may be quite different from those required for other aspects of the job. Establishing client relationships is also an excellent way to build greater levels of feedback to any job.

A final intervention based on Job Characteristics Theory is **opening feedback channels.** This simply involves redesigning a job in a way that provides employees with an opportunity to receive feedback on their performance. In manufacturing, this may simply involve providing employees with access to quality control data on a regular basis. It may also involve the elimination of feedback from supervisors, in favor of direct feedback to employees. This intervention is targeted specifically at the core job dimension of feedback.

Hackman and Oldham (1980) reported the results of several studies that showed the successful implementation of job redesign based on Job Characteristics Theory, and others were published over the years (e.g., Griffin, 1991; Griffin & McMahan, 1994; Parker & Wall, 1998). Generally speaking, redesigning a job based on Job Characteristics Theory has been shown to have a fairly robust effect on job satisfaction (i.e., satisfaction tends to increase when jobs are redesigned), although the impact on actual job performance is somewhat mixed. Griffin, for example, found, in a redesign of the jobs of bank employees, that immediately after the job redesign, performance actually went *down*. Over time, however, performance ultimately exceeded initial levels. This suggests that it may take time for employees to learn redesigned jobs, but ultimately redesigning jobs may enhance performance.

Despite the successes, Hackman and Oldham (1980) also note instances where the redesign of jobs based on Job Characteristics Theory has been unsuccessful (e.g., Frank & Hackman, 1975). Although there may be numerous reasons for job redesign failures, there are likely to be some common themes. For example, organizations often do not anticipate the complexities of job redesign. A common mistake in this regard is failing to anticipate "ripple effects," or the wider impact when a job is redesigned. For example, when a job is vertically loaded, many of the decisions that were previously in the hands of the supervisor are "passed down" to the employee. If supervisors are not informed of this at the beginning of a job redesign project, they may ultimately not be cooperative.

A second common reason for difficulties in job redesign is failure of the organization to do the necessary preliminary work. For example, if a proper diagnosis is not conducted, a job may be redesigned when it does not need to be or when employees do not want it. An organization may also make the mistake of failing to involve key stakeholders in the job redesign process. If, for example, an organization were to attempt to redesign a job without consulting a union, it is very likely that the redesign would not be successful.

The Interdisciplinary Approach to Job Redesign

Given its relatively recent development, far less has been written about the *application* of the interdisciplinary approach, at least in comparison to Hackman and Oldham's (1980) Job Characteristics Theory. Nevertheless, this approach could be and has been used successfully in organizations. When job design is guided by the interdisciplinary approach, the first step in the process is a thorough diagnosis of the job(s) that are being considered for redesign. In the process of developing the interdisciplinary approach, Campion and colleagues developed the **Multimethod Job Design Questionnaire** to assess jobs on each of the four disciplinary approaches (e.g., Campion & Thayer, 1985), although recent research suggests that it measures more than four dimensions (Edwards, Skully, & Brtek, 1999). This instrument can be used, for example, to highlight whether a job may be lacking on the motivational, mechanistic, biological, or perceptual motor approaches to job design. A diagnosis may indicate, for example, that a job is well designed for efficiency and speed of information processing, but lacks characteristics that will facilitate internal motivation and physical comfort.

If a job is lacking in one or more of the four approaches to job design, an organization must decide whether the costs of enhancing the job on that approach would be offset by the benefits of improvement. In some cases, the choice is relatively obvious.

For example, if a job is lacking on the biological approach, and several workers' compensation claims have been filed as a result, an organization may have little choice but to improve the physical comfort level of those performing this job.

In other cases, however, the choices are not as clear-cut. For example, if a job is lacking on the motivational approach, enhancing it may lead to desirable outcomes such as high job satisfaction and internal motivation, and decreased absenteeism and turnover. Changing a job in this manner, however, also may increase the skill requirements, which may force the organization to pay higher wages (Campion & Berger, 1990). In some cases, this is a trade-off that is favorable for an organization; in other cases, it is not.

Assuming that a diagnosis was performed and an organization decided to enhance a job on any of the four approaches to job design, how would the organization do it? In the motivational approach, the previous section on the Job Characteristics Theory approach to job design answers the question. Making changes—such as vertical loading, combining tasks, forming natural work units, establishing client contact, and opening feedback channels—will likely maximize outcomes associated with this approach. However, these changes may result in a number of costs to the organization, such as increased skill requirements, longer training times, and, possibly, higher wages.

Changing jobs to enhance the mechanistic job design dimension is rather unfamiliar to organizational psychologists, but is still done frequently by industrial engineers. In many cases, this involves **time and motion study** to assess whether the job in question has been designed efficiently (e.g., Salvendy, 1978). Such a study may reveal, for example, that the way the job is currently designed allows for a number of unnecessary motions, and efficiency is being compromised. Elimination of these wasted motions may result in much greater efficiency; hence, productivity may be enhanced. Often, mechanistic redesign also involves redesigning incentive systems so that employees are motivated to use these more efficient work methods and procedures.

Redesign of a job to enhance the biological approach may be initiated by the organization or, in some cases, by an individual employee who is having physical difficulties such as back problems or repetitive motion injuries (Hollenbeck, Ilgen, & Crampton, 1992; May & Schwoerer, 1994). This type of redesign typically begins with some form of ergonomic assessment of the job(s) in question. This involves an analysis of the job by an individual trained in ergonomics or, in some cases, in occupational health. What such a person would be looking for obviously depends on the particular job being analyzed. However, common problems in ergonomic job design often include the existence of repetitive motions or the design of the work station. For many clerical jobs, the height of the desk and the positioning of a worker's computer are key variables that one would assess for possible improvement. Depending on the problem that is identified, there may be a number of ways to enhance ergonomic job design. For example, some jobs can be changed by eliminating some repetitive motions. For other problems, the solution may lie in the redesign or replacement of equipment or work stations. Frequently, the solution to an ergonomic problem may be quite expensive.

If an organization were to enhance a job on the perceptual motor component, this would typically involve some analysis of the job by an expert trained in Human Factors or Engineering Psychology (Wickens & Hollands, 2000). In analyzing the job, such a professional would be largely focusing on the nature of the information the incumbent must work with, and how this information is presented. This type of analysis sometimes indicates that the incumbent is simply being required to process too much information; thus, changes may be recommended to reduce information load. Such an analysis may reveal rather straightforward changes that can be made in a job or in the work aids (e.g., computers) associated with the job. However, changes in information presentation may be quite involved and expensive. The problem may not be the *amount* of information being processed, but the way it is being presented to the incumbent. For example, in the design of automobile instrument panels and computer software, it has been found that information is easier to process when it is presented as icons or symbols, as opposed to text.

ORGANIZATIONAL DISCIPLINARY PROCEDURES

To this point, we have covered methods by which organizations attempt to motivate employees to engage in productive behaviors. Another use of motivation theory is to discourage employees from engaging in counterproductive behavior. In Chapter 5, on counterproductive behavior, interventions aimed at curbing specific behaviors such as absenteeism, accidents, drug use, and workplace violence were briefly discussed. Therefore, the focus of this section will be on more general organizational disciplinary procedures.

Progressive Discipline

Although specific disciplinary procedures vary widely across organizations, it is quite common for organizations to have what have been described as **progressive disciplinary procedures.** A progressive disciplinary procedure indicates a progression in the severity of the consequences when a work site has continuing or escalating infractions (Arvey & Jones, 1985). For example, such a progressive approach may be applied to safety violations in a manufacturing plant. The first safety-related violation may result in a verbal warning to the offending employee. If more safety-related violations occur, the consequence may increase in severity; a written warning may be followed by a formal written reprimand, a suspension, and eventually, if enough violations occur, dismissal.

What determines the specifics of a progressive disciplinary policy? One obvious factor is the nature of the behavior an organization is attempting to discourage. When counterproductive behaviors are relatively mild, an organization can tolerate a number of infractions before severe consequences are handed out. However, for some behaviors, even one instance cannot be tolerated. For example, most reasonable people would probably agree that an organization cannot tolerate an employee's assaulting a coworker, or blatant forms of sexual harassment. For such behaviors, an organization may opt for a "zero tolerance" policy and terminate an employee at the first infraction.

Another important factor that must be considered when determining a disciplinary policy is the legal environment. Many union contracts contain clauses dealing with employee discipline (Bemmels & Foley, 1996). Some organizations may want to be tough on certain forms of counterproductive behavior, but may be constrained by either the terms of a collective bargaining agreement or a threat of litigation brought by a union. Organizational disciplinary procedures must also be consistent with state and federal laws governing employment. Legislation in some states may constrain an organization from disciplining specific forms of counterproductive behavior. As an example, alcohol and drug abuse meet the criteria for being disabilities under the terms of the Americans with Disabilities Act of 1990. Organizations are probably much more likely to exhibit tolerance by providing employees with treatment for alcohol and drug abuse problems, even if they would like to adopt more punitive measures.

Unfortunately, relatively little is known about the impact of progressive disciplinary procedures. Despite this lack of empirical evidence, it is likely that the effectiveness of progressive disciplinary procedures depends on a number of factors. One important factor is whether employees are aware of these disciplinary procedures. This may seem like a rather obvious point, but organizations vary widely on their effectiveness in communicating policies to employees. It is possible that an organization could have a progressive disciplinary procedure and its employees are simply unaware of it. If employees don't know about a policy, there is little chance that it will impact their day-to-day behavior.

When disciplinary policies are applied, those procedures must be fulfilled in a fair manner (Trevino, 1992). Put differently, it is important to have policies applied with a degree of **procedural justice.** It is also important, in the implementation of disciplinary procedures, that employees are treated with respect and dignity. This often involves providing an employee with an opportunity to "tell his or her side of the story" and rebut any accusations. The term used to describe this form of fairness is **interactional justice.**

In an effort to be fair, some organizations have developed formalized grievance procedures to redress employees' complaints regarding disciplinary procedures. In many cases, grievance procedures are mandated by collective bargaining agreements, although that is not always the case (McCabe, 1988). Some organizations voluntarily create grievance procedures that closely resemble those contained in collective bargaining agreements. Although grievance procedures vary by organization, most typically allow employees to file formal grievances if they feel they have been unfairly disciplined. After such a filing, grievance procedures normally allow for disputes to be settled informally. If this is not possible, more formal procedures are used.

As with disciplinary policies, grievance procedures work best when employees perceive them to be fair, and when employees who utilize the grievance procedures are treated with respect (Bemmels & Foley, 1996). Grievance procedures regarding disciplinary actions can often be avoided if an employee and his or her immediate supervisor can resolve the dispute informally (Cleyman, Jex, & Love, 1993; Klaas, 1989).

CHAPTER SUMMARY

This chapter covered the most common applications of motivation theory in organizations. Without a doubt, the most widely used mechanism that organizations use for motivating behavior is reward systems. Tangible rewards include merit pay, incentive pay, bonuses, fringe benefits, perquisites, and status symbols. Research, over the years, has shown that tangible rewards such as pay *can* be very powerful motivators of employee behavior. In many organizations, however, the way in which these reward systems are administered makes it very difficult for employees to make the connection between rewards and performance.

Organizations also motivate employees through the use of a number of intangible rewards such as recognition, praise, and high levels of job autonomy. Compared to the impact of tangible rewards, much less is known about the impact of intangible rewards. Some research and considerable anecdotal evidence, however, suggest that these may often be powerful motivators. It is doubtful that intangible rewards can substitute for low levels of tangible rewards, however.

Compensation of executives was treated as a separate topic, primarily because the manner in which executives are compensated differs greatly from that of rank-and-file employees. Executives' compensation is typically much more dependent on organizational performance than is the compensation of other employees. Research has shown that the size of executive compensation packages is positively related to organizational size and to the amount of discretion executives have in decision making. Thus, it appears that, to a large degree, executives are paid based on the potential impact of their decisions on organizational performance.

The most troubling finding in the executive compensation literature is that executive compensation is largely unrelated to organizational performance. This has led to very heated public criticism of what are seen as excess levels of compensation among executives. Despite such criticisms, it is very unlikely that the level of executive compensation will go down appreciably. The procedures that are used to determine these compensation practices appear to be firmly entrenched. Also, to compete for executive talent, organizations often have little choice but to pay these high levels of compensation.

Other than reward systems, the other major method of motivating employees is through the design of work. The basic idea is that the content of people's jobs may have a profound impact on whether they are motivated. Approaches to motivation through the design of work have evolved considerably. The oldest was described as the humanistic approach, which was typified by Herzberg's job enrichment. This approach involved primarily building high levels of control and discretion into jobs. Job enrichment was applied successfully, but it eventually gave way to the job characteristics approach. This approach involves changing jobs in order to build in greater levels of the core job dimensions from Job Characteristics Theory. Most recently, Campion's interdisciplinary approach to job design has suggested a number of ways that jobs can be changed to enhance a variety of outcomes, some of which are relatively unfamiliar to organizational psychology. Regardless of the approach taken, it should always be remembered that job redesign is a complex undertaking that requires careful advance planning and, often, considerable financial resources.

Organizations also use motivation theory to discourage other forms of behavior. The most typical way of doing this is through the use of progressive disciplinary policies. Such policies differ by organization. Their actual content depends on factors such as the behavior being discouraged, collective bargaining agreements, and other legal constraints. Ultimately, the success of a progressive disciplinary policy depends on how well it is communicated and whether it is applied consistently and in a fair manner.

Many organizations often develop grievance procedures to accompany progressive disciplinary measures. These allow for employees to dispute disciplinary actions if they are not considered fair. As with progressive disciplinary procedures, the effectiveness of grievance procedures depends on whether they are seen as fair by employees. In many cases, formal grievance procedures can be avoided if supervisors and subordinates are open to informal problem solving.

SUGGESTED ADDITIONAL READINGS

Dunford, B. B., & Devine, D. J. (1998). Employment at-will and employee discharge: A justice perspective on legal action following termination. *Personnel Psychology, 51,* 903–934.

Kelly, J. (1992). Does job re-design theory explain job re-design outcomes? *Human Relations, 45,* 753–774.

Mitchell, T. R., & Mickel, A. E. (1999). The meaning of money: An individual difference perspective. *Academy of Management Review, 24,* 568–578.

Mitra, A., Gupta, N., & Jenkins, G. D., Jr. (1997). A drop in the bucket: When is a pay raise a pay raise? *Journal of Organizational Behavior, 18,* 117–137.

Westphal, J. D. (1999). Collaboration in the boardroom: Behavioral and performance consequences of CEO-board social ties. *Academy of Management Journal, 42,* 100–110.

Chapter Ten

Leadership and Influence Processes

Leadership is a topic that has been of interest to organizational psychologists for several decades. Indeed, volumes have been written about leadership, though not all have been products of organizational psychologists. Authors ranging from business executives to collegiate athletic coaches have written books about what it takes to succeed as a leader. Because much of leadership involves getting things done through other people, power and influence represent core activities of leaders. In fact, power and influence are deemed so vital to leaders that some authors have defined leadership largely as a form of influence (Yukl, 1989).

In this chapter, we examine leadership, as well as power and influence processes. Coverage of the general approaches to leadership is followed by descriptions of well-known leadership theories. Consistent with recent advances in the study of leadership, the chapter devotes much more attention to "contingency" approaches to leadership, in comparison to those

that focus exclusively on the traits and behaviors of leaders.

Compared to other treatments of leadership, this chapter is somewhat unique in that power and influence are covered in the same chapter as leadership theories. This was done intentionally to acknowledge that *the essence of leadership is influencing other people's behavior.* Whether one is leading a church congregation, a Fortune 500 corporation, or a major league baseball team, much of what one does involves influencing others' behavior. Furthermore, a leader's success in influencing others, as well as the means by which he or she chooses to do so, will depend heavily on the amount and nature of power held. Power and influence are clearly the "nuts and bolts" of leadership.

DEFINING LEADERSHIP

If you were to pick 10 people at random and ask them to define *leadership,* there is a good chance that you would get a variety of definitions. According to Yukl and Van Fleet (1992), leadership is difficult to define because of the complexity of the leadership process. Because leadership involves interactions between leaders and subordinates (typically, the members of a work group), leadership can be viewed in many ways. For example, we can view leadership as consisting of the *behaviors* that are enacted by the group leader. These may include organizing the work, obtaining resources for the group, providing encouragement to group members, and ultimately evaluating the group's output (Guzzo & Shea, 1992).

On the other hand, one could just as easily view leadership as a series of *functions* that need to be carried out in order for a group to be effective. The nature of a group's task may need to be clarified, resources may need to be obtained, the spirits of group members occasionally may need lifting, and the group's output must eventually be evaluated. These functions can be but don't necessarily have to be performed by a leader. Any group member with relevant expertise may help to provide task clarification, or someone with an outgoing personality may motivate others. By viewing leadership in this way, we are saying that it resides within groups, and not with one specific individual.

Definitions of leadership often differ in whether they emphasize leadership behaviors or the *results* of those behaviors. Ideally, when a leader attempts to influence his or her

subordinates, these individuals do what the leader wants, and do it willingly. Sometimes, however, an influence attempt by a leader will result only in grudging compliance or may even be actively resisted by subordinates. According to some definitions of leadership, compliance or resistance does not represent "true" leadership. On the other hand, according to other definitions of leadership, influence attempts that lead only to compliance or resistance still represent leadership, albeit unsuccessful leadership.

Another issue that complicates the task of defining leadership is the frequent distinction between "leadership" and "management." A leader, some have argued, is a person who obtains commitment from his or her subordinates and, in some cases, may even inspire them. A manager, on the other hand, is someone who makes sure the "trains run on time," and primarily obtains compliance from his or her subordinates. A manager is someone who doesn't make things worse for his or her work group, but doesn't get them too excited either. Interestingly, the leadership–management distinction is much more of an issue in the popular leadership literature than it is among leadership scholars. This may explain the fact that the author has observed groups of managers express very strong feelings about the issue (see Comment 10.1).

Despite all the factors that complicate the meaning of leadership, it is possible to identify some common ground among the numerous definitions. Yukl and Van Fleet (1992) define leadership as "a process that includes influencing the task objectives and strategies of an organization, influencing people in the organization to implement the strategies and achieve the objectives, influencing the group maintenance and identification, and influencing the culture of the organization." (p. 149). This definition is summarized in Figure 10.1.

COMMENT 10.1

MANAGEMENT VERSUS LEADERSHIP

LIKE MANY AREAS in organizational psychology, leadership has had its fair share of problems with definition of important terms and constructs. One issue that often comes up, particularly among those who work in organizations, is the distinction between "management" and "leadership." A manager is typically defined as an individual who engages in traditional administrative behaviors such as planning, helping to organize the work of subordinates, and exerting control over their behavior. A leader, on the other hand, is a person who not only fulfills required administrative functions, but also is able to inspire and motivate employees to strive for excellence, and, at times, facilitates meaningful change in organizations.

One of the reasons that I find this "management vs. leadership" distinction interesting is that it seems to be more of an issue for employees, and less of an issue for leadership researchers. Although recent theories, such as charismatic and transformational leadership,

address this issue to some degree, leadership researchers have not focused a great deal of effort on it. In contrast, I have found that, in courses I have taught during the past 10 years, the issue is always raised and discussed with a great deal of enthusiasm. To most people, at least in my experience, managers and leaders are distinct groups.

If people do indeed distinguish between management and leadership, and have strong feelings about it, this suggests two things to me. First, employees in organizations want to work for people who are true leaders and are not there just to perform administrative duties. Second, there is a shortage of real leaders in organizations. There may be many reasons for this; it may be due to the fact that real leaders are often agents of change. If those in positions of authority simply carry out administrative duties, this allows an organization to maintain the status quo, and no pressure for change is created.

There are several things to note about this definition. First, obviously, is the fact that leadership involves the influencing of others' behavior. Second, leadership is viewed as a *process* and not as an *outcome*. It is possible, based on this definition, for a leader to engage in unsuccessful influence attempts. Third, this definition implies that leadership requires a variety of skills. Influencing task objectives and strategy may require strong analytical and conceptual skills; influencing people to *implement* those strategies and objectives requires interpersonal and persuasive skills. Finally, leaders are frequently important agents of change in organizations. Changing the culture of an organization is a tall order, although it may be necessary at times, if an organization

is to survive. Because of the influence they have, leaders are often in the best position to facilitate cultural change.

The Importance of Leadership

What exactly do leaders do that is so important? Leaders are often needed to provide **strategic direction and vision** to groups and, in many cases, to entire organizations. Work group members are often too busy with routine task completion, and with meeting deadlines, to think about where the group is headed in the future. In many groups, strategic planning and visioning activities are shared among group members, but the leader is typically the focal point of such efforts. In a

FIGURE 10.1
Summary of Yukl and Van Fleet's (1992) Definition of Leadership

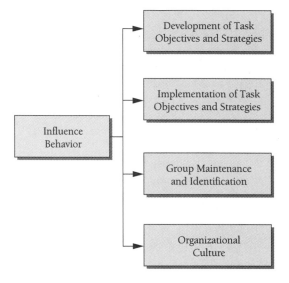

sense, then, leaders help organizations to channel productive behavior in directions that are beneficial and that meet relevant strategic objectives.

Another important function of leaders, particularly those in small groups, is to engage in **motivation and coaching** behaviors. Even highly experienced employees occasionally need encouragement and, in some cases, help in solving difficult work-related problems. As with strategic planning and visioning, motivation and coaching activities could potentially be shared among the members of a group. However, it is often more efficient, as well as less confusing for group members, to have one individual who is primarily responsible for fulfilling these functions. In most cases, that person is the leader.

A third important function of leaders in organizations is **enforcement and interpretation of organizational policies.** For most employees, leaders serve as "linking pins" to people in higher levels of the organization (Likert, 1967). Because of this concept,

leaders often are required to interpret and enforce organizational policies. Again, it is certainly possible that a group could informally "police itself," but having a formally designated leader makes it much more likely that organizationally mandated rules and procedures will be followed.

Finally, leaders are important because they are typically responsible for **obtaining resources for groups.** Leaders essentially represent the interests of their work group within the broader organizational environment. Because of this, groups often rely heavily on the persuasive skills of leaders to obtain resources for task completion. Without a leader, the members of a group may all be trying to obtain resources and, at times, may get in each other's way.

The four leadership functions just mentioned are not meant to be exhaustive, but they make a fairly compelling case for the importance of leadership. Furthermore, with organizations becoming flatter, skilled leadership is even more crucial to the success of organizations. In flatter organizational structures, leaders have a much wider span of control (e.g., they supervise a larger number of employees), and the impact of each leader's behavior is much greater than in organizations with a great many levels. Thus, *leadership is very important, if not vital, to the success of an organization.*

GENERAL APPROACHES TO LEADERSHIP

Like many of the topics covered in this book, leadership has been of interest for centuries, although much of the early writing on leadership came from philosophers, historians, and political scientists. Only within the past half-century have organizational psychologists become heavily involved in the study of leadership. During this time, distinct approaches to the study of leadership have evolved. In this section, we review three of these approaches: the trait approach, the behavioral approach, and the contingency approach.

The Trait Approach

The basic premise behind the trait approach to leadership is actually quite simple: Those who are effective leaders possess traits that are different from those who are less effective leaders. Leadership research guided by the trait approach is aimed primarily at identifying traits that discriminate between effective and ineffective leaders. Indeed, a good deal of early leadership research was based on the trait approach. [For summaries, see Mann (1959) and Stogdill (1948).]

Unfortunately, early trait-based leadership research failed to generate a definitive profile of the traits that characterized "the effective leader," partly because some of the "traits" explored by these early leadership researchers (e.g., physical characteristics and gender) were not based on sound theoretical reasoning. In addition, the aim of most of these early leadership researchers was to use traits to distinguish *effective* from *ineffective* leaders. Given that numerous variables influence leaders' effectiveness, it is understandable that using traits alone to predict effectiveness met with only limited success.

Because traits did not predict leader effectiveness well, and because, within psychology, emphasis shifted to environmental influences on behavior, the trait approach to leadership generally fell out of favor in the 1940s and 1950s. Trait-based leadership research was still conducted but was clearly a much less dominant approach to leadership than it previously had been. Over time, however, the trait approach to leadership resurfaced and made important contributions to the study of leadership, primarily due to two factors. First,

researchers eventually decreased the emphasis on the prediction of leader effectiveness, in favor of predicting **leader emergence.** In group situations where there is not a formally designated leader, someone within the group eventually assumes the leadership role. Leadership emergence is simply the process by which this occurs.

The trait approach has also made great strides in identifying traits that predict leader emergence (Foti & Rueb, 1990; Zaccaro, Foti, & Kenney, 1991). Those who are more intelligent, have higher needs for dominance, are high self-monitors, and are socially perceptive tend to emerge as leaders when no leader has been formally designated. This profile suggests that emergent leaders are able to: (1) accurately "read" the social dynamics of a situation, and (2) adapt their behavior to meet those social demands. Although not yet researched in the trait literature, it is plausible that such individuals are also more likely to end up in leadership positions when formal selection procedures are used. Longitudinal studies of managerial effectiveness would certainly suggest that this is the case.

Second, trait-based leadership research has made a comeback because the traits investigated in more recent research have been more theoretically plausible. According to Yukl and Van Fleet (1992), several traits have been identified that predict managerial effectiveness and advancement within organizations. These include a high energy level, stress tolerance, integrity, emotional maturity, and self-confidence. Given the nature of managerial work, it is easy to see how these traits would be related to success, especially when they are compared to things such as physical characteristics or gender.

Although much has been done to revive the trait approach to leadership, there are still many questions that trait researchers have yet to answer. For example, what are the practical implications of trait leadership theory? One would assume that the practical value of this approach lies mainly in the area of selection for leadership positions, but that has not been fully articulated by trait researchers. Another issue that has not been fully addressed by trait researchers is the impact of various *combinations* of traits within work groups. What happens, for example, if a group consists of *several* individuals who possess traits indicative of leadership emergence? Do these individuals share leadership functions, or do they compete for this role? Despite these potential shortcomings, the trait approach, particularly in recent years, has advanced our understanding of leadership processes considerably.

The Behavioral Approach

Due largely to shortcomings of early trait research, the focus of leadership research shifted to the behaviors that seem to distinguish effective from ineffective leaders. The best known taxonomy of leader behavior was developed by Ralph Stogdill and Edwin Fleishman and their colleagues at Ohio State University (e.g., Fleishman, Harris, & Burtt, 1955). According to these researchers, leadership behavior could be broken down into two basic categories: (1) **initiating structure** and (2) **consideration.** Leader behaviors that comprise the initiating structure dimension are aimed at facilitating the task performance of groups. Examples might include organizing work for subordinates, communicating performance expectations, and making sure that subordinates' behavior stays focused on the tasks that they are performing.

Consideration is represented by behaviors that are designed to show subordinates that they are valued and that the leader cares about them as people. Examples of this dimension include showing an interest in subordinates'

families, "touching base" with subordinates periodically to see how things are going, and being understanding when problems occur.

During roughly the same time period when the Ohio State leadership studies were conducted, other researchers were involved in efforts to provide meaningful classifications of leader behavior. For instance, Rensis Likert and his colleagues at the University of Michigan made the distinction between **job-centered leadership behavior** and **employee-centered leadership behavior** (Likert, 1961). Blake and Mouton (1964) made a similar distinction between **concern for production** and **concern for people** in the development of their managerial grid. Note that all of these reflect a basic distinction between leader behaviors designed to facilitate task completion, and leader behaviors designed to enhance interpersonal harmony in a group.

Despite the apparent parsimony of classifying leader behaviors into two broad categories, a number of issues were still unresolved. For instance, some argued that these two dimensions were largely independent (e.g., Blake & Mouton, 1964). In other words, a leader could simultaneously exhibit behaviors indicative of initiating structure and consideration. Others argued that these two forms of leader behavior are negatively related (e.g., Likert, 1961). For example, initiating structure behaviors were performed at the expense of consideration, and vice versa.

Another issue was that some leader behaviors were difficult to classify as strictly initiating structure or strictly consideration. For instance, a leader may make a point of talking to each subordinate each day, to see how things are going. This could certainly be viewed as consideration because it provides the leader with an opportunity to express concern for these subordinates. These informal chats may also help to keep subordinates focused on their work-related tasks, and may provide an opportunity to exchange important task-related information with the leader. Thus, the behaviors leaders engage in may be more complex than this two-dimensional classification would suggest.

Finally, an issue that has plagued the behavioral approach from the beginning is that researchers were never able to identify a set of leader behaviors that were consistently associated with effectiveness. This suggests that there is no "universal" set of leader behaviors that will facilitate leader effectiveness in all situations. Rather, the behaviors that are needed from a leader will vary from situation to situation. This realization led to the contingency approach to leadership, which will be described next.

The Contingency Approach

The contingency approach is based on the assumption that the relationship between leader behaviors and traits and effectiveness depends on characteristics of the particular situation the leader is in. The task of a leader, according to the contingency approach, is to first "read" the situation to determine what behaviors would be most appropriate. Once this is determined, the leader has to adjust his or her behavior to meet the demands of the situation.

To illustrate how the contingency approach works in practice, let's say that a leader has been asked to take charge of a group consisting of five highly skilled and experienced design engineers. In this type of situation, the leader would probably *not* have to do a great deal of teaching and performance-related coaching. In fact, if the leader tried to do this, the group members might consider him or her an annoyance. Instead, the leader in this situation would be more effective if he or she concentrates on obtaining resources for the group, facilitates professional development

activities for group members, and periodically makes an effort to boost the morale of the group.

Now consider a different leader who is in charge of a group of five design engineers who are all recent college graduates. A good deal of this leader's behavior will be focused on task clarification, teaching, and performance-related coaching. In a group like this, these activities would not be considered an annoyance at all; in fact, they would probably be welcomed. To be effective in this situation, a leader would have to be very "hands on" with his or her subordinates. If a leader in this situation spent the bulk of his or her time negotiating for resources within the organization, or remained very distant from the group members, he or she would probably not be successful.

Most leadership theories developed during the past 30 years are contingency theories. Thus, it is accurate to say that the field of leadership has accepted the general premise behind contingency theories. Less consensus, however, has been given to many of the specifics of the contingency approach. For example, there is not a great deal of consensus regarding the specific aspects of the situation that leaders must "read" in order to adjust their behavior. For example, several contingency theories propose that "subordinates" are one such factor, but there is not a great deal of agreement on *what specific aspects of subordinates* are the most important.

Another area of disagreement surrounding contingency theories has to do with the behaviors that leaders must exhibit in order to be successful. As readers will see, contingency theories differ in the level of adaptability they ascribe to the leader. In some theories (e.g., Fiedler, 1967), it is proposed that leaders have a predetermined leadership style that is not subject to a great deal of modification. Other contingency theories (e.g., House,

1971), however, propose that leaders are fully capable of adapting their behavior to different situations. This really speaks to the more basic issue of the malleability of behavior, which was discussed in the previous chapter (e.g., Hellervik, Hazucha, & Schneider, 1992). Based on that literature, the weight of the evidence suggests that leaders are capable of modifying their behavior to meet situational demands. What is not nearly as clear is what, specifically, leaders are supposed to do in response to the situations they face.

MODERN THEORIES OF LEADERSHIP

Most leadership theories developed within the past 30 years can be classified as contingency theories. In this section, we examine the contingency leadership theories that have been most influential in the leadership literature. Influence is defined in terms of the research generated by the theories, as well as the impact that the theory has had on the practice of leadership within organizations.

Fiedler's Contingency Theory

The basic premise behind Fiedler's contingency theory is actually quite simple. Like all contingency theories, it proposes that the success of a leader depends on the interaction between characteristics of the situation and characteristics of the leader. According to Fiedler, **situation favorability** depends on the three factors illustrated in Figure 10.2. The first of these, *leader–member relations,* reflects the extent to which a leader gets along well with his or her subordinates. Generally speaking, situations are more favorable for leaders when they get along well with subordinates, and, conversely, less favorable if leader–member relations are poor.

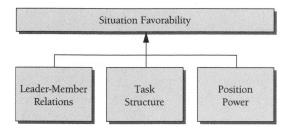

FIGURE 10.2
Determinants of Situation Favorability in Fiedler's Contingency Theory

The next situational attribute, *task structure,* reflects whether the subordinates working under a leader are working on a task that is very straightforward and structured (e.g., it produces 50 widgets per day), or whether the task is vague and unstructured (i.e., "Develop innovative products"). Subordinates may find a lack of structure challenging but, from a *leader's* perspective, having a high degree of structure is more favorable than having a low degree. When task structure is high, the leader is required to spend less time clarifying the task for subordinates, and decisions are typically much easier to make.

The third determinant of situation favorability is the *position power* of the leader—the amount of formal authority that a leader has over his or her subordinates. Some degree of authority is inherent in all leadership positions, but the *amount* of authority actually varies considerably. Some leaders are granted the authority to assign subordinates to different jobs, to evaluate their work, and to dismiss those who are not performing well. However, leadership positions do not always carry a great deal of authority. A good example is the chairperson of an academic department. A chairperson is technically "in charge" of an academic department, but this person has very little formal authority beyond that of supervisors in many other types of organization.

From a leader's perspective, a high rather than a low position is desirable. When position power is high, subordinates will typically do what the leader wants, and the leader does not have to exert a great deal of influence. Subordinates could just be doing this out of fear; still, things are less complicated for the leader. When a leader's position power is *low,* subordinates may still do what they want, but the leader may have to expend a great deal of effort to make that happen. Consider, for example, the chairperson of an academic department, who is trying to persuade a tenured faculty member to teach a class that this individual does not want to teach. The chairperson must spend time and effort to persuade this individual to teach the course, and perhaps may have to offer something in return (a course release in the future).

Given these three situational attributes, and the fact that each has two levels, it is possible to come up with eight unique situations (called "octants") in terms of favorability. These are illustrated in Figure 10.3. The most *favorable* situations for leaders are those in which leader-member relations are good, task structure is high, and position power is high. In this type of situation, a leader gets along well with his or her subordinates, is directing a group of employees working on a well-defined task, and has a great deal of formal authority. From a leader's perspective, what could be better? A leader can then spend his or her time on activities such as strategic planning, acquiring resources for the group, and perhaps helping subordinates to develop their skills.

At the other end of the spectrum, the least favorable situations for leaders are those in which leader-member relations are poor, task structure is low, and the leader has very low position power. From a leader's perspective, what could be worse? The fact that the leader does not get along well with his or her

FIGURE 10.3

Summary of the Eight Octants Which Represent Differing Degrees of Situation Favorability

L-M Relations	(P)
Task Structure	(L)
Position Power	(L)

Low Situation Favorability

L-M Relations	(G)
Task Structure	(L)
Position Power	(L)

L-M Relations	(P)
Task Structure	(H)
Position Power	(L)

L-M Relations	(P)
Task Structure	(L)
Position Power	(H)

Moderate Situation Favorability

L-M Relations	(G)
Task Structure	(H)
Position Power	(L)

L-M Relations	(G)
Task Structure	(L)
Position Power	(H)

L-M Relations	(P)
Task Structure	(H)
Position Power	(H)

L-M Relations	(G)
Task Structure	(H)
Position Power	(H)

High Situation Favorability

| P | = Poor | H | = High |
| G | = Good | L | = Low |

subordinates is likely to be unpleasant. However, when combined with a very vague and unstructured task and a very low level of authority, this is even worse. A leader in this situation may have to spend the bulk of his or her time trying to influence or negotiate with subordinates in order to get anything accomplished. Furthermore, there is no guarantee that such influence attempts will be successful. The leader will have considerably less time available for things such as strategic planning, resource acquisition, or employee development.

In between these extremes are six other situations that Fiedler referred to as having "moderate" favorability for the leader. In the interest of brevity, all of these moderately favorable situations will not be described. However, as an example of a moderately favorable situation, a leader may have good leader–member relations, high task structure, and *low* position power vis-à-vis his or her subordinates. From the leader's point of view, these situations are inherently more complex than situations of either very high or very low favorability.

The second portion of Fiedler's theory has to do with the characteristics of the leader. According to Fiedler, leaders can be reliably distinguished in terms of whether they are "task-oriented" versus "relationship-oriented." To measure this task versus relationship orientation in leaders, Fiedler and his colleagues developed the **Least Preferred Coworker (LPC) Scale** (Fiedler, 1967). As can be seen in Table 10.1, the LPC Scale consists of 18 pairs of adjectives. Respondents completing this scale are asked to think of a person with whom they currently work or have worked in the past, and with whom they have had the most difficulty in getting work done. A high LPC score indicates that a leader has described his or her least preferred coworker in relatively favorable terms. This in-

dicates that the leader is relationship-oriented because he or she is able to rate this coworker favorably, even though the individual is not seen as someone who would facilitate task accomplishment. In contrast, a low LPC score indicates that the least preferred coworker is described in relatively unfavorable terms. This indicates that the leader is task-oriented, according to Fiedler, because this coworker's negative impact on task accomplishment overrides any positive qualities this person may possess.

Fiedler proposed that leaders who are task-oriented (herein referred to as Low LPC leaders) are most successful in either highly favorable or highly unfavorable situations. In highly favorable situations, a Low LPC leader will basically leave things alone and not try to introduce major changes. He or she will also not try to "get into people's heads" and become very close to them interpersonally. This type of leader behavior simply is not needed. In contrast, when situations are highly unfavorable, a Low LPC leader is probably the only type that will get anything done. In these situations, leaders' attempts to develop strong interpersonal ties will likely fall flat and will ultimately reduce the chances of any form of task accomplishment.

When situations are moderately favorable, Fiedler proposed that leaders who are relationship-oriented (herein referred to as High LPC leaders) are most effective. The logic here is that moderately favorable situations are not "black and white." Such situations often require some interpersonal finesse, and a High LPC leader has this trait. Let's say, for example, that a leader is in a moderately favorable situation: Leader–Member relations are good, but Task Structure and Position Power are low. A High LPC leader is needed because the leader may have to rely heavily on his or her relationships with subordinates in order to clarify the task and ultimately get things done.

TABLE 10.1
Least Preferred Coworker (LPC) Scale (Fiedler, 1967)

Over the course of your life you have probably worked in many groups with other people on your job, in community groups, church groups, athletic teams, etc. Some of your coworkers may have been very easy to work with in attaining the group's goal, while others were less easy to work with.

Think of the person in your life with whom you worked least well. He or she may have been someone you knew in the past or someone you work with now. The person does not have to be the person you like least well, but should be the person with whom you have the most difficulty getting the job done. In this scale you will be describing this person. You do not need to give the person's name.

Following are pairs of words which are opposite in meaning, such as "Very Neat" and "Not Neat." Between each pair of words are eight blanks to form a scale.

__EXAMPLE__: In describing the person with whom you least like to work, if you ordinarily think of him or her as being "Quite Neat," you would put an "X" in the space marked 7.

If you ordinarily think of this person as being only "Somewhat Neat," you would put your "X" in the space above the 6.

If you think of this person as being "Slightly Untidy," you would mark the space above the 4.

If you would think of this person as being "Very Untidy" (or not neat), you would put your "X" in space 1.

Look at the words at both ends of the line before you mark your "X." Work rapidly, your first answer is likely to be your best one (there are no right or wrong answers, though).
Please do not omit any items, and mark each item only once.

Now use the scale to describe the person with whom you find it hardest to get the job done.

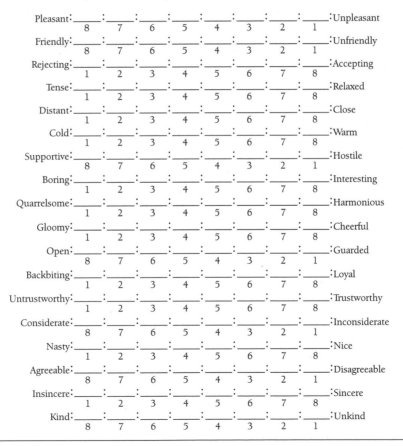

Note: 1 = least descriptive of the Least Preferred Coworker; 8 = most descriptive of the Least Preferred Coworker.
Source: F. E. Fiedler. (1967). *A theory of leadership effectiveness*. New York: McGraw-Hill. Used with permission of the author.
Scores on the LPC Scale can range from 18 to 144. A score of 56 or less indicates that a person is a task-oriented leader; a score of 63 or above indicates that a person is relationship-oriented. Scores between 56 and 63 indicate that a person's leadership style cannot be determined.

A Low LPC leader would be unsuccessful in this situation, primarily because he or she may not see the complexities in the situation and may simply demand performance. The relationship between LPC and situational favorability is summarized in Figure 10.4.

Considerable research has been done on Fiedler's contingency theory over the years, and the evidence is mixed. For example, it has been found that leader LPC scores predict performance in situations of differing favorability in a way that is consistent with the theory (Chemers, 1983; Chemers, Hays, Rhodewalt, & Wysocki, 1985), but other tests have not been supportive (e.g, Schriesheim & Kerr, 1977; Vecchio, 1977). The most comprehensive test of contingency theory to date was a meta-analysis conducted by Schriesheim, Tepper, and Tetrault (1994). This study found that the differences in mean performance levels of High versus Low LPC leaders in different octants generally supported Fiedler's theory. However, in terms of absolute levels of performance, the results were less supportive. For example, in highly favorable situations, it was found, as predicted by Fiedler's theory, that Low LPC leaders outperformed High LPC

leaders. However, the performance of High LPC leaders was still above the mean, which is consistent with the idea of "mismatch" proposed by Fiedler. Schriesheim et al. (1994) recommended that "organizations without the ability or interest in situational engineering might consider just trying to make all leadership situations highly favorable (Octant 1)" (p. 571).

Other than the equivocal support, the portion of Fiedler's theory that has been the source of greatest criticism is the LPC Scale. Many, for example, have questioned the logic behind the measurement strategy (e.g., McMahon, 1972; Theodory, 1982). In fact, having given the LPC Scale to students for several years, the author has found that they are often confused by the instructions. A more serious problem is the lack of support for the construct validity of this scale. Recall from Chapter 2 that construct validity reflects whether a measure is measuring the intended construct or attribute. Strong support for the construct validity of the LPC Scale simply does not exist.

At this point in time, Fiedler's theory no longer represents one of the major theoretical approaches used by leadership researchers. Even so, it is a valuable theory because it has generated a great deal of research on leadership. It has also served as the basis for **Cognitive Resource Theory** (Fiedler & Garcia, 1987), which states that groups draw on the different cognitive resources from the leader, depending on the situation. This is a relatively new approach, and not a great deal of work has been done on it as yet. It does seem to be a promising approach, though, and ultimately may be more useful than Fiedler's original theory.

Path–Goal Theory

Path–Goal Theory represents a very ambitious attempt to blend leadership and employee

FIGURE 10.4

Effectiveness of High versus Low LPC Leaders at Different Levels of Situation Favorability

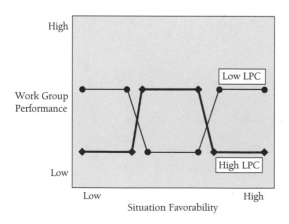

motivation into one theory (House, 1971; House & Mitchell, 1974). The basic idea behind Path–Goal Theory is that the role of a leader is really to help his or her subordinates become successful. House actually stated this in Expectancy Theory terms (Vroom, 1964); specifically, if a leader is successful, subordinates' level of expectancy (the perception that effort will lead to performance) is raised. Stated differently, the function of leaders is to show subordinates the "path to the goal."

Path–Goal Theory states that a leader must be able to adapt his or her leadership style to the subordinates being supervised and the situation. House proposed that, to be successful, a leader must be capable of utilizing the four different leadership styles: directive leadership, supportive leadership, achievement-oriented leadership, and participative leadership

Directive leadership focuses on making sure that subordinates know what they are supposed to be doing, and perhaps clarifying task responsibilities. A leader who meets with subordinates once a week to give out work assignments is exhibiting directive leadership. **Supportive leadership** represents behaviors that are aimed at showing concern and caring for subordinates. A leader who makes it a point to ask about a subordinate's sick child is exhibiting supportive leadership.

Achievement-oriented leadership represents behaviors that are aimed at helping employees to improve their performance and ultimately perform better. A leader may exhibit this leadership style in a number of ways, such as providing on-the-job coaching, setting challenging goals, making sure training and development opportunities are available, and seeing to it that subordinates have the resources they need in order to be successful. Finally, **participative leadership** represents behaviors that are aimed at getting the input of subordinates on work-related matters. A

leader who regularly seeks the input of subordinates before making important decisions is exhibiting this form of leadership.

Having described the four leadership styles, the next issue is to determine when each of these leadership styles should be used. Path–Goal Theory proposes that leaders should consider two situational factors when they are deciding on the appropriate leadership style: (1) characteristics of one's subordinates, and (2) characteristics of the work environment. With respect to subordinates, the two key factors that a leader must consider are perceived ability and personality. In considering perceived ability, what would be the most appropriate leadership style for subordinates who perceive themselves as having limited job-related abilities? For these subordinates, a leader would probably need to be quite directive, because these individuals likely would want to know exactly what to do. Participative leadership may not be emphasized because individuals who perceive their abilities to be limited may not have a great deal to contribute. Achievement-oriented and supportive leadership would probably be used to varying degrees, depending on other characteristics of the subordinates.

When subordinates perceive themselves as having a great deal of task-related ability, a leader would probably need to put relatively little emphasis on directing. Instead, the leader may need to strongly emphasize achievement-oriented and participative leadership. Those who perceive their ability to be high may have a strong desire to further develop that ability; thus, achievement-oriented behaviors would be called for. These subordinates may also have a great deal to contribute, so it would be in the leader's best interests to solicit input and ideas from these individuals. Supportive leadership would likely be used in varying degrees, depending on other characteristics of subordinates.

The second subordinate characteristic that leaders need to consider when deciding on a leadership style is personality. This is obviously a broad category, but one personality trait that Path–Goal Theory deems important is subordinates' **locus of control.** According to Rotter (1966), locus of control reflects relatively stable individual differences in beliefs regarding control of external reinforcements. A person with an *internal* locus of control believes that he or she has a great deal of control over reinforcements. Such a person, for example, would believe that working hard would be a good thing to do because it would lead to positive outcomes. Persons with an *external* locus of control believe that reinforcements in their life are due to external forces such as luck, fate, or, perhaps, powerful people.

As a leader, managing an individual with an internal locus of control would probably require an emphasis on achievement-oriented and participative leadership, and comparatively less on directive and supportive leadership. An employee with an internal locus of control believes that he or she has control over reinforcements, and hence is also likely to believe that if performance is increased, then positive rewards will result. Facilitating this process requires the use of achievement-oriented leadership. Also, because those with an internal locus of control ("internals") may also perform well (Spector, 1982), it is often in the best interest of the leader to seek input from such individuals through participative leadership.

Those with an external locus of control will likely need greater direction from the leader; thus, directive leadership behaviors will be needed. Also, it is very likely that those with an external locus of control ("externals") will need more support from the leader, compared to internals. Having an external locus of control has been shown to be associated with negative mental health outcomes (e.g., Spector, 1982; Storms & Spector, 1987); thus, externals may often be more anxious, frustrated, and dissatisfied than internals.

In addition to the characteristics of subordinates, Path–Goal Theory proposes that leaders must focus on characteristics of the work environment when they are determining the most appropriate leadership style. One aspect of the situation that is important, according to Path–Goal Theory, is the prevailing norms regarding authority and leadership within an organization. This is really an aspect of an organization's culture and reflects, for example, prevailing views on issues such as employee involvement and participation, the extent to which employees should take the initiative to solve work-related problems, and whether managers should get involved in subordinates' personal lives. In an organization that strongly values employee involvement and participation, a participative leadership style would fit much better than in a very autocratic organization. Similarly, in an organization that places a great deal of emphasis on employee self-reliance, a very directive style of leadership would probably not fit very well. On the other hand, achievement-oriented and participative styles would be very compatible.

Task structure, a second characteristic of the work environment, is important in determining the most appropriate leadership style. If a leader is directing a group that is working on a highly structured task (i.e., producing a very simply product), there would probably be little need for the leader to adopt a directive or a participative leadership style because members of the group know exactly what they're supposed to do. In contrast, when a task is highly unstructured (i.e., developing a new product), a leader may at times have to be directive, but may also need to be participative in order to help the group figure out how best to approach the task.

The final environmental characteristic proposed by Path–Goal Theory is the nature of the work group one is leading. For example, in some groups, the task of providing direction is done by experienced members of the group rather than the leader. If this is the case, the leader does not need to be directive but could emphasize other leadership styles. Essentially, this means that the leader's behavior needs to "add value" to the behaviors being performed by members of the group.

Given the nature of Path–Goal Theory, it is difficult to test in its entirety. However, tests of various parts of the theory have been relatively successful (e.g., Wofford & Liska, 1993). More research on this theory is needed before more definitive statements can be made about its validity. The practical implications of Path–Goal Theory come primarily in the area of management training and development. Specifically, managers need to be trained to recognize meaningful differences among their subordinates, as well as important aspects of the work environment, and have to learn to use the different leadership styles proposed by Path–Goal Theory. It also may have implications for selection and placement. For example, if a leader is very good at developing subordinates (i.e., providing achievement-oriented leadership), an organization may wish to place this person in charge of a group consisting of a number of young, high-potential employees. Conversely, if a leader is very adept at participative leadership, an organization may want to place this person in charge of a group that must make many consensus decisions.

Vroom–Yetton–Jago Model

The Vroom–Yetton–Jago model (Vroom & Jago, 1988; Vroom & Yetton, 1973) is a contingency theory of leadership that focuses on one aspect of leadership: decision making. This model is also more *prescriptive* than the other theories discussed; that is, this theory is focused on providing leaders with a set of guidelines for which decision-making style to adopt. According to this model, leaders will be more effective to the extent that their decision-making style is compatible with the situations they are in.

The first component of the Vroom–Yetton–Jago model to consider is the various styles that a leader could use in making a decision. As can be seen in Table 10.2, in the first decision-making style (AI), the leader makes a decision alone after considering relevant information. The next decision-making style (AII) also involves the leader's making the decision alone, but, in this case, information is obtained from subordinates before making the decision. Decision-making style CI involves sharing the problem with each subordinate individually, and then making the decision alone. Decision-making style CII involves sharing the problem with subordinates as a group and then making the decision alone. The final decision-making style (GII) involves making the decision by group consensus.

According to the model, leaders must analyze a situation for the presence or absence of the following attributes, in order to determine which decision-making style is most appropriate: (1) the need for a quality decision; (2)

TABLE 10.2
Decision-Making Styles Proposed by the Vroom-Yetton-Jago Model of Leadership

AI—Leader makes the decision alone after considering the relevant information.

AII—Leader makes the decision alone after obtaining relevant information directly from subordinates.

CI—Leader shares the problem with each subordinate individually and then makes the decision alone.

CII—Leader shares the problem with subordinates as a group and then makes the decision alone.

GII—The decision is made by group consensus.

whether the leader has sufficient information to make the decision alone; (3) the degree to which the problem is structured; (4) whether subordinates' acceptance is needed for implementation; (5) whether subordinates will accept the leader's decision; (6) the degree to which subordinates share the organization's goals; (7) whether there will likely be conflict among subordinates as to the most preferred decision; and (8) whether subordinates have enough relevant information to make a decision on their own.

According to the model, these eight situational attributes will determine a "feasibility set" of decision-making types. The feasibility set simply represents those decision-making types that may be appropriate for a given situation. Figure 10.5 shows how this process works. Notice that these situational questions are asked in a sequential fashion that resembles a flowchart. Specifically, the leader's response to each question narrows the feasibility set until eventually one decision-making style is recommended. For a leader to use this theory, he or she would simply answer each of the questions about the decision to be made, and, ultimately, a preferred method of decision making would emerge.

Research on the Vroom–Yetton–Jago model has shown that managers are more effective when they adopt decision-making styles that are consistent with the model's prescriptions (Margerison & Glube, 1979; Paul & Ebadi, 1989; Vroom & Jago, 1988). However, a major methodological limitation of most tests of the model is that they have relied primarily on retrospective descriptions of decisions made by managers. This raises the question of whether managers revise their recollections of decisions in a way that is consistent with the model. More recent research that has not relied on retrospective reports (Field & House, 1990; Parker, 1999) has provided more limited support for the theory.

From a practical point of view, the Vroom–Yetton–Jago model is one of the more useful leadership theories that has been developed. Compared to other theories, this model provides leaders with some specific guidelines for making decisions, rather than merely describing leadership processes. The biggest problem with the Vroom–Yetton–Jago model is that it tends to oversimplify the conditions under which leaders make decisions. For example, in many cases, it is difficult for a leader to provide "Yes–No" answers to the questions posed earlier. Further revisions of this model will be needed to overcome these weaknesses.

Leader–Member Exchange (LMX) Model

Anyone who has been part of a work group, or has been a leader of one, knows that everyone is not always treated the same. To the contrary, leaders typically develop a unique relationship with each subordinate, and some of these relationships are more positive than others. Based on this idea, Dansereau, Graen, and Haga (1975) developed the **Vertical Dyad Linkage Model** of leadership. The term "Vertical Dyad" was originally used to describe this theory because of its emphasis on the unique relationship between leaders and subordinates. Over time, however, the name of the theory eventually became "Leader–Member Exchange" because this relationship is really one that reflects social exchange between the leader and the subordinate.

According to Dansereau et al. (1975), within work groups there are typically two sets of employees: the "in-group" and the "out-group." The in-group consists of employees who are trusted confidants of the leader. These are typically individuals who perform well, have a desire to assume greater levels of responsibility, and simply get along well with the leader. Members of the out-group consist

FIGURE 10.5
The Recommended Decision-Making Sequence Proposed by the Vroom-Yetton-Jago Model

A. Does the problem possess a quality requirement?
B. Do you have sufficient information to make a high-quality decision?
C. Is the problem structured?
D. Is acceptance of decision by subordinates important for effective implementation?
E. If you were to make the decision by yourself, is it reasonably certain that it would be accepted by your subordinates?
F. Do subordinates share the organizational goals to be attained in solving this problem?
G. Is conflict among subordinates over preferred solutions likely?

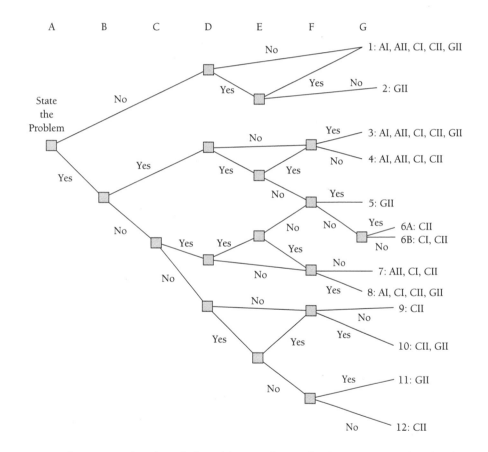

Source: V. H. Vroom and P. W. Yetton. (1973). *Leadership and decision-making* Pittsburgh, PA: University of Pittsburgh Press. Copyright © 1973 by University of Pittsburgh Press. Reprinted with permission.

of the group of subordinates who have more formal relationships with the leader. Members of the in-group are typically privy to more information from the leader than are members of the out-group, and are also given more discretion over how to do their jobs. Members of the out-group typically are individuals who may not perform as well, may not desire a great deal of responsibility, or simply may not get along as well with the leader as do members of the in-group.

Gradually, less emphasis has been placed on the "in-group"/"out-group" distinction, and more emphasis is on how leader–subordinate relationships develop over time (Graen, 1976). According to Graen (1976), when a subordinate is first assigned to a leader, the leader has relatively limited information as to this person's capabilities. Thus, over time, the leader tests the subordinate by giving him or her assignments of increasing responsibility. To the extent that the subordinate is successful, a positive exchange relationship develops. From the subordinate's point of view, there may be some degree of negotiation as to specific role responsibilities. Other factors that influence the development of this exchange relationship are: perceived similarity between subordinates and leaders, as well as the level of interpersonal attraction (Liden, Wayne, & Stilwell, 1993). Exchange relationships are likely to be most positive when subordinates are competent, when they and the leader perceive some degree of mutual similarity, and when subordinates and leaders like each other.

What are the consequences of the exchange relationship that develops between a subordinate and a leader? Gerstner and Day (1997) conducted a meta-analysis of 79 studies that examined correlates of Leader–Member Exchange. They found that LMX was positively related to job performance, job satisfaction, and organizational commitment,

and negatively related to outcomes such as turnover and role stressors. One of the most perplexing findings in their meta-analysis was the relatively small correlation between leaders' and subordinates' reports on the quality of the exchange relationship (corrected $r = .37$). Thus, although leaders and subordinates tend to agree on the quality of the relationship that exists between them, this level of agreement is not great. At present, it is unclear why agreement on the quality of the exchange relationship is not higher, what factors influence agreement, or the impact of disagreements over the quality of the exchange relationship.

LMX Theory is useful for both theoretical and practical reasons. In terms of theory, it presents leadership in a more realistic light, compared to many previous theories. Subordinates are not simply passive recipients of leaders' influence. In terms of practical implications, LMX Theory suggests that it is desirable for leaders to develop positive exchange relationships with their subordinates. This may not be possible 100% of the time, but organizations may be able to facilitate the development of high-quality exchange relationships by training managers in such skills as communicating with subordinates, providing feedback, and engaging in coaching activities.

In the future, LMX Theory faces a number of challenges. One of the most important of these is continued refinement of what actually constitutes the "exchange relationship" itself. To measure the exchange relationship, Liden and Maslyn (1998) recently developed a scale that consisted of four distinct dimensions: (1) Affect, which represents the levels of mutual interpersonal attraction between a leader and subordinate; (2) Loyalty, which represents the amount of public support provided by each member of the leader–subordinate dyad; (3) Contribution, which represents what each member of the leader–subordinate dyad contributes positively to the goals of the organization; and (4) Professional respect, which represents the degree to which each member of the leader–subordinate dyad has built a reputation, within and/or outside of work, because he or she excels in his or her line of work. Previous LMX scales have treated it as a one-dimensional construct.

Another challenge for LMX Theory is expansion of its scope. For most people, the unique relationship they develop with their immediate supervisor is one of the most important dimensions of their work experience. As such, it may impact many aspects of that experience. For example, Kokotovich, Jex, and Adams (2000) found that a high-quality LMX buffered the relationship between role ambiguity and job satisfaction. Employees reporting a high-quality LMX actually reacted positively to role ambiguity. Recent studies have suggested that the LMX may interact with the cognitive ability of employees to impact creativity (Tierney, Farmer, & Graen, 1999).

Charismatic and Transformational Leadership

These last two leadership theories are the newest to be developed, and those for which the least amount of research is available. Nevertheless, they represent interesting and promising approaches to leadership that may eventually become quite influential. Because these two approaches to leadership are highly similar, they will be discussed together.

The idea of Charismatic and Transformational leadership is that there are certain leader behaviors and traits that not only influence subordinates but may also inspire them to perform well beyond their capabilities. Another defining characteristic of Charismatic and Transformational leadership is that both have the potential to induce meaningful change in

organizations. The term that is typically used to describe the *opposite* of Charismatic and Transformational leadership is **Transactional leadership.** A transactional leader is one who makes sure that subordinates get the job done and follows the rules of the organization. Transactional leaders, however, do not inspire subordinates or facilitate meaningful change in organizations.

The general idea of Charismatic and Transformational leadership is certainly interesting, but what exactly does a Charismatic or Transformational leader do? One task that is often cited in this regard is **providing a vision.** According to House (1977), a vision is a very generalized ideal state that typically represents shared values and often has moral overtones. An example of a vision for a university might be *to enlighten the students;* a vision for a military organization might be *to uphold freedom around the world;* a vision for an auto manufacturer might be *to enhance the mobility of society.* A vision applies to all members of the organization and can thus serve as a general "rallying point" for everyone. Many examples of leaders, particularly in t he political arena, can be distinguished on the presence or absence of vision (see Comment 10.2)

A second attribute of Charismatic and Transformational leadership is **vision implementation.** Having a vision is not very meaningful if a leader is not able to persuade others to implement that vision. Vision implementation is aided by the leader's being able to clearly articulate his or her vision (e.g., a vision cannot be implemented if subordinates do not know what it is), and being able to get others excited about it. When one thinks of great leaders in many fields of endeavor, a common characteristic is that they are excellent communicators who are able to engender an almost fanatical devotion among their followers.

COMMENT 10.2

THE "VISION THING"

ONE OF THE key components of Charismatic and Transformational leadership is *vision*. A vision is essentially an ideal or desirable end state that often has moral overtones. A leader with vision "stands for something" and has a sense of purpose that is communicated to his or her followers.

Vision has become particularly important in the political arena. When candidates run for national office, the vision that they are able to communicate to voters can literally make or break their chances of being elected. In 1980, Ronald Reagan defeated Jimmy Carter for the U.S. Presidency largely based on the vision that he communicated to the American public. Reagan's vision, based heavily on conservative principles, struck a chord with voters who wanted lower taxes and a stronger national defense. Whether or not one agreed with Reagan's "vision," there is no denying that he communicated it well and was quite successful at convincing the public to embrace it.

Just as having a vision propelled Ronald Reagan to victory, a *lack* of vision may have been one of the major reasons George H. Bush lost the presidency to Bill Clinton in 1992. Although Bush showed excellent crisis management skills during the Gulf War, he was unable to articulate a coherent vision in the way Reagan did many years earlier. For many voters, it was difficult to tell exactly what Bush stood for. Clinton, in contrast, was very successful at communicating a vision based on economic opportunity, and in many instances seemed to connect with voters much better on a personal level. The end result was that Clinton won a convincing victory over Bush and third-party candidate Ross Perot.

The third attribute of Charismatic or Transformational leadership is a **charismatic communication style.** Those who are charismatic tend to have a number of common traits: a captivating tone of voice, direct eye contact with the listener, animated facial expressions, and a powerful, confident, and dynamic communication style. This type of communication style obviously helps a leader to communicate his or her vision and to generate enthusiasm for it. It also helps more generally by increasing the leader's appeal to his or her followers. Charismatic leaders have great "presence" and make a tremendous impression on those around them.

Research over the years has shown that characteristics of Charismatic and Transformational leaders are associated with positive outcomes such as employees' performance, satisfaction, and perceptions of leaders (Bass & Avolio, 1993; Shamir, House, & Arthur, 1993). A major limitation of research in this area, however, is that most studies are cross-sectional, and some are descriptions based on historical documents (e.g., House, Spangler & Woycke, 1991).

Studies that have used stronger methodologies, such as laboratory experimentation (e.g., Kirkpatrick & Locke, 1996), have also been supportive, although this support is not as strong as in field investigations and descriptive studies. It is unclear, however, whether all aspects of Charismatic and Transformational leadership lend themselves to laboratory experimentation. Although laboratory studies such as those of Kirkpatrick and Locke (1996) have used very careful procedures in manipulating characteristics of charismatic and transformational leadership (e.g., use of a professional actor), it is unclear whether these characteristics have the same impact in an actual organization that they do in a laboratory setting.

The major practical implications of Charismatic and Transformational leadership appear to be in the selection and assessment of leaders; that is, organizations may wish to identify individuals who have the potential to be Charismatic or Transformational leaders. However, leaders who are not charismatic could possibly be trained to act that way. An organization might work with leaders to make them communicate in a more dynamic and captivating manner. At present, it is unclear whether charismatic behaviors can be taught. It is also unclear whether Charismatic and Transformational leadership behaviors are needed in all situations. Most research in this area has focused on leaders in high-level positions in business and government, so it is unclear whether charismatic and transformational leadership would be as effective at lower organizational levels.

POWER AND INFLUENCE IN ORGANIZATIONS

Regardless of whether one is a chief executive officer of a Fortune 500 company or the supervisor of a janitorial crew, a big part of one's job is influencing others to behave in ways that are consistent with the goals of the organization. Furthermore, the extent to which a leader can influence others depends, to a large extent, on his or her social power over others. In this section, power will be discussed first, followed by influence tactics.

Defining Power

The term "power" is often used in a negative fashion, even though power is not inherently bad or evil. Power simply represents a person's *potential or capacity to influence others* (French & Raven, 1959). When one attempts to influence another person's behavior, the outcome of that influence attempt generally takes one of three forms (Kelman, 1958): compliance, identification, and private acceptance. **Compliance** represents a situation in which an influence attempt is successful to the extent that the target of influence does what is requested, but does not necessarily do it willingly. When a child is told by a parent that he or she cannot have a cookie, the child typically complies with this directive but, if given the choice, would certainly eat the cookie (at least that's the way it works in my house!). An example of compliance in the workplace might be an employee's wearing a piece of safety equipment, even though he or she doesn't want to.

The second potential outcome of influence is referred to as **identification**. In this case, the employee does what the leader wants, primarily because he or she likes the leader. As with compliance, when behavior is changed on the basis of identification, there is a change in behavior but not in attitudes; that is, the employee still does not really want to do what the leader wants done. A work-related example of identification might be: to help their well-liked leader meet an impending deadline, a group of employees works late even though they are not required to do so.

The third result of influence is referred to as **private acceptance** or **internalization**. In this case, the employee does what the leader wants because he or she believes that it is the right thing to do. Compared to compliance and internalization, private acceptance is, in the long run, much more efficient for leaders. Therefore, if subordinates believe that what the leader wants them to do is correct, the leader will need to spend much less time either monitoring to insure compliance, or making sure that subordinates still like him or her. Keep in mind, however, that it is not always necessary for a leader to obtain private acceptance from subordinates. For example, employees often must comply with safety guidelines, even if they don't agree with them.

The fourth and final outcome of influence that might occur is **resistance.** In this case, the employee simply does not do what the leader asks. Resistance may take the form of an overt refusal but, more typically, an employee will simply be evasive when the leader inquires about whether the subordinate has carried out the request. This can be a very frustrating situation for a leader, and it is obviously the least desirable outcome from a leader's perspective.

Bases of Power

Leaders are not automatically endowed with an unlimited amount of power over subordinates. Leaders also differ in terms of the *sources* or *bases* upon which power over subordinates can be exerted. The most widely cited model was proposed by French and Raven (1959) over 40 years ago. According to this model, power rests upon six bases. Some readers may recognize the fact that most treatments of French and Raven's model describe only the first five bases, but the original model did contain six. The first base of power is labeled **coercive power.** The basis of the influence is the fact that one person can punish another. Thus, a subordinate may do what a leader requests because the leader has the power to fire the subordinate. Although the threat of punishment may give a leader considerable power over subordinates, coercive power generally is not a very efficient base of power. If subordinates do what the leader wants only because they are threatened with punishment, the leader's power is diminished considerably if he or she is not around to monitor the ongoing behavior and administer punishment if necessary.

The second power base described by French and Raven is labeled **reward power.** This is essentially the opposite of coercive power. That is, subordinates do what the leader wants because the leader has the ability to reward them in some way. For example, a subordinate may comply with a leader's request that he or she work overtime because the leader has the power to grant this employee a larger pay increase when raises are given out. Unfortunately, as with coercive power, reward power is not a highly efficient power base. It requires the leader to monitor subordinates' behavior and reward it at the appropriate time.

The third power base is labeled **legitimate power.** This power emanates from the position that one holds in an organization. In most organizational settings, the fact that one employee is another employee's supervisor means that the supervisor has a legitimate right to make requests of the other person. Note that this legitimate right is independent of the person holding the position. Compared to coercive and reward power, legitimate power is more efficient. It does not require surveillance on the leader's part because, in most organizations, the level of legitimate authority that goes with any given position is typically known. In fact, in many cases, it is even documented in job descriptions and other formal documents. A limitation of legitimate power, however, is that if it is used exclusively, it may elicit only compliance from subordinates and, in the long run, may engender a great deal of resentment among them. People generally do not like to be told to do something simply because "I'm your supervisor."

The fourth power base is **expert power.** This is power based on the fact that an individual is perceived as an expert on something that is important to the target of influence. If the leader of a group of design engineers is also an expert design engineer, this will make subordinates more likely to do what he or she says. One thing that is important to note about expert power is: it is the *perception* that is important. For this to be a viable power base, subordinates must perceive that the leader is an expert. Regardless of the level of one's true expertise, if this is not perceived, then no expert power exists.

The fifth base of power in French and Raven's model is **referent power.** This is power based on subordinates' liking of a leader; that is, subordinates do what the leader wants because they like him or her. Although this form of power does not require surveillance, it is also somewhat more tenuous than expert power because interpersonal attraction is considerably more volatile than expertise. If subordinates no longer have positive feelings toward the leader, then a great deal of his or her power over subordinates is lost.

The sixth and final base of power is referred to as **informational power.** As stated earlier, this is typically not presented as one of the bases of power in the French and Raven model but was included in the initial model (Raven, 1993). A leader has informational power to the extent that he or she has high-quality information that will be convincing to subordinates. For example, a person trying to convince someone else to wear a seatbelt would have a great deal of informational power if valid data could be cited showing that the odds of being fatally injured are much lower if a seatbelt is being worn.

After the development of the initial model of power bases, French and Raven made a number of further refinements to the model (Raven, 1993). For example, they differentiated between *personal* and *impersonal* forms of reward and coercive power—that is,

rewards and punishments can come in the form of personal approval or disapproval. Conversely, they can also come in more impersonal forms such as a raise or a formal reprimand. French and Raven also refined the concept of legitimate power considerably. They proposed, for example, that legitimate power was based not just on one's formal organizational position, but also on the principle of *reciprocity* ("I did this for you, so you should feel obligated to do this for me"), *equity* ("I have worked hard and suffered, so I have the right to ask you to do something to make up for it"), and *responsibility* or *dependence* ("I cannot help myself, so you are responsible for helping me").

Expert and referent power were further distinguished in terms of being positive and negative. As originally conceived, both expert and referent power were positive. French and Raven, however, later pointed out that both could be negative as well. Negative expert power represents situations where a person is seen as having superior knowledge but, at the same time, is seen as using the superior knowledge only to further his or her own interests. Negative referent power occurs when a person is seen as someone who is disliked rather than liked. If this person were a leader, subordinates may be inclined to do the opposite of what this individual wants them to do.

Informational power was distinguished in terms of being direct or indirect. When informational power is direct, this means that the leader presents logical arguments to subordinates directly. When it is indirect, the information does not come from the leader directly, but may instead come from another subordinate or another leader. This distinction is important because social psychological research on influence (e.g., Petty & Cacioppo, 1981) has shown that, in some circumstances, information that is conveyed *indirectly* is given greater weight by the target of influence than information communicated directly.

No competing models of power bases have been proposed, but there has been at least one effort to add to the power bases originally proposed by French and Raven. Finkelstein (1992) examined bases of power within top management teams and, although some of the power bases he proposed corresponded to those in French and Raven's model, there were two that were unique. **Ownership power** represents the extent to which the member of a top management team has an ownership stake in the organization, through either stock ownership or family relations. Within a top management team, an executive who is a significant shareholder or is related to the organizational founder often wields tremendous power.

The other unique power base proposed by Finkelstein (1992) was **prestige power.** This represents the extent to which the member of a top management group has acquired prestige and status outside of the organization. Finkelstein measured this by the number of corporate boards a manager serves on, the level of prestige of those organizations, the number of nonprofit boards one serves on, and, finally, the prestige of the university where the executive received his or her education. Generally speaking, an executive has greater prestige power if he or she serves on the corporate boards of a number of successful organizations, also serves on the boards of nonprofit organizations, and graduated from a prestigious university (e.g., Ivy League).

Influence Tactics

To this point, we have discussed the *potential* of leaders to influence their subordinates. However, to truly understand the dynamics of power and influence, we must go beyond the *potential* to influence and examine the *specific tactics* that leaders use to influence subordinates. According to Yukl and Tracey (1992), nine distinct tactics can be used to influence. These are presented in Table 10.3. As can be seen, **rational persuasion** simply involves providing, to the target of influences, a logical explanation of why a given request is being made. For example, a foreman in a factory may advise a subordinate to wear protective earphones because chronic exposure to loud noises can lead to gradual hearing loss.

When **inspirational appeals** are used, the leader or person doing the influencing attempts to appeal to the target's values or ideals, and to persuade that person that he or she *will* be able to get something done. As an example of inspirational appeals, a military commander might attempt to encourage his or her troops to continue fighting after they are fatigued. The commander could explain the strategic need to carry on, or could appeal to the troops' sense of patriotism or of military duty.

In using **consultation,** the leader influences subordinates by seeking their assistance in an activity for which their participation is crucial. Essentially, the leader is trying to establish a situation in which it will be inconsistent for the subordinate to refuse whatever request is being made. This tactic is often used when changes are introduced in organizations. For example, if an organization wants to redesign jobs and must persuade employees to accept these changes, a good way to start is to seek the employees' assistance in the job redesign effort.

By using **ingratiation,** a leader attempts to influence subordinates by putting them in a good mood before making a request. This can be done in a variety of ways such as complimenting the subordinate, agreeing with his or her views or opinions, or doing favors for this person. A supervisor who is getting ready

TABLE 10.3
A Summary of Nine Common Influence Tactics Used by Leaders

Tactic	Definition
1. Rational persuasion	The person uses logical arguments and factual evidence to persuade you that a proposal or request is viable and likely to result in the attainment of task objectives.
2. Inspirational appeal	The person makes a request or proposal that arouses your enthusiasm by appealing to your values, ideals, or aspirations or by increasing your confidence that you can do it.
3. Consultation	The person seeks your participation in planning a strategy, activity, or change for which your support and assistance are desired, or the person is willing to modify the proposal to deal with your concerns and suggestions.
4. Ingratiation	The person seeks to get you in a good mood or to think favorably of him or her before asking you to do something.
5. Exchange	The person offers you an exchange of favors, indicates a willingness to reciprocate at a later time, or promises you a share of the benefits if you help to accomplish a task.
6. Personal appeal	The person appeals to your feelings of loyalty and friendship toward him or her before asking you to do something.
7. Coalition	The person seeks the aid of others to persuade you to do something or uses the support of others as a reason for you to agree also.
8. Legitimating	The person seeks to establish the legitimacy of a request by claiming the authority or right to make it or by verifying that it is consistent with organizational policies, rules, practices, or traditions.
9. Pressure	The person uses demands, threats, or persistent reminders to influence you to do what he or she wants.

Source: G. Yukl and J. B. Tracey. (1992). Consequences of influence tactics used with subordinates, peers, and the boss. *Journal of Applied Psychology, 77,* 525–535. Copyright © 1992 by the American Psychological Association. Reprinted with permission.

to ask a group of subordinates to work on a weekend may bring the group doughnuts before making the request. Ingratiation must be used carefully, however; it may make people less likely to comply with a request if it is seen as insincere. Some readers may recall the movie *Office Space,* in which the corporate vice president complimented his subordinates but did so in such an obnoxious and phony way that it had little influence on their behavior.

When **exchange** is used as an influence tactic, the leader offers subordinates something in return for complying with a request, or perhaps offers them a share of the benefits that will accrue when a task is accomplished. In some companies, forms of exchange are actually mandated by organizational policies. For example, when hourly employees work

more than 40 hours per week, they may receive overtime pay for doing so. However, this exchange may be strictly between the leader and his or her subordinates. For example, if the manager of a fast-food restaurant wants employees to come for an early-morning crew meeting, one way of getting employees to be there is to provide another incentive, such as an extra 30-minute break.

When a **personal appeal** is used as an influence attempt, the leader appeals to a subordinate's sense of personal loyalty and friendship before making a request. This influence tactic can only be used if two people do in fact share some degree of loyalty and friendship. Prior to making a request of a subordinate, the leader may first state: "We've been friends for a long time, and been through some tough times together, so I know you're someone I can really count on." After hearing that, most people would find it difficult to turn down the subsequent request.

Forming a **coalition** to influence involves seeking the aid of others to directly persuade a subordinate to comply with a request, or using others as examples of why a request should be honored. A good example: Get a subordinate to comply with a requirement to wear safety equipment by having other subordinates, who are wearing the equipment, persuade this individual that safety equipment is needed.

When **legitimating** is used, the leader seeks to establish the legitimacy of his or her request by falling back on his or her authority to make the request, or, in some cases, citing organizational policies or rules. In the military, the leader frequently points out that he or she outranks the subordinate; in military organizations, this form of influence tends to work very well because of the emphasis on rank. In other types of organizations, use of legitimating may be less successful and, if used frequently, may ultimately engender animosity among one's subordinates.

The final influence tactic listed in Table 10.3 is **pressure.** This involves the use of demands, threats, or persistent monitoring to make subordinates comply with a request. Suppose a supervisor wants to make sure a subordinate is on time every morning. One way to do this would be to check the person's desk to see if he or she is present by the required time. Although pressure may, at times, get leaders the behavior they desire, this almost always comes in the form of compliance on the part of the employee. Thus, using pressure typically requires a good deal of energy on the part of the leader because subordinates' behavior must be frequently monitored.

Although research on influence tactics is still relatively new, there are some reasonably consistent research findings. If a leader wishes to obtain behavior change in the form of "private acceptance," the most effective way to do so is through inspirational appeals and consultation (Falbe & Yukl, 1992; Yukl, Kim, & Falbe, 1996; Yukl & Tracey, 1992). Tactics such as coalition formation, legitimating, and pressure are unlikely to lead to private acceptance, and, in fact, may even lead to resistance. The reason simply may be that people are generally more enthusiastic about doing things when they feel that they have some freedom of choice in the matter.

Another rather consistent finding from this literature is that influence tactics may impact others' behavior in an additive fashion. For example, Falbe and Yukl (1992) found that the use of combinations of some tactics was more effective at facilitating behavior change than were tactics used alone. For example, an inspirational appeal combined with consultation was more effective than using either of these tactics alone or using single "hard" tactics such as pressure or legitimating. This suggests that, in some cases, the influence process takes time, and the leader must be prepared to use multiple tactics to influence subordinates' behavior.

The research on influence tactics is still relatively new, but it has produced some very important practical insights for leaders. Perhaps the most important of these is that if leaders want their subordinates to do things willingly, in the long run they are much better off *asking* them do it rather than simply relying on their position or using more coercive techniques. Although asking may take longer, it will produce more long-lasting behavioral change than will the use of more coercive tactics.

Politics in Organizations

The term "organizational politics" often conjures up images of very negative forms of behavior; therefore, most people want to avoid the politics of an organization. Nevertheless, political behavior is a fact of life and, in many cases, represents an important form of influence within organizations. Organizational politics has been defined as influence behavior, within organizations, that falls outside of the recognized legitimate power system (Yoffie & Bergenstein, 1985). Political behavior is often aimed at benefiting an individual or group at the expense of the organization as a whole, and acquiring more power.

According to Miles (1980), one of the major factors motivating political behavior is *uncertainty*. For example, when employees are uncertain about the goals of the organization, political behavior often results. Another factor that strongly contributes to political behavior is *scarcity of resources*. Although technically everyone in the same organization is "on the same team," obtaining scarce resources is a highly competitive process in many organizations. Thus, the manager of a department may have to engage in considerable political behavior in order to obtain even minimally acceptable resources.

Other conditions that motivate political behavior are: technological change, ambiguity in decision making, and organizational change. Often, the introduction of new technologies in organizations creates considerable uncertainty with respect to work roles and lines of authority; both conditions are ripe for political maneuvering. In many organizations, decisions are made with incomplete information; thus, it is not clear which alternative is "correct." When this is the case, political behavior often results because advocates of different positions may attempt to influence the decision-making process. Finally, political behavior is very common during times of organizational change because things are often "up for grabs" and readily amenable to such forms of influence.

Having defined what it means by organizational politics, we now turn to specific tactics that people use when they engage in political behavior. Although many tactics could be used to promote one's political agenda, some tactics are more commonly used, and many of these are similar to the general influence tactics discussed in the previous section. According to Allen, Madison, Porter, Renwick, and Mayes (1979), six commonly used political tactics include two that were discussed previously (ingratiation and forming coalitions and networks), and four that are somewhat different from more general influence tactics.

1. **Impression management** represents behaviors that are designed to enhance one's visibility or stature within the organization. An employee may manage his or her impression through physical appearance, or possibly through publicizing his or her accomplishments.

2. Another commonly used political tactic is **information management.** In many organizations, "information is power"; thus, one way to advance one's political agenda is to control others' access to information. This may include simply controlling whether others ever receive information, and the timing of the information's release. In political campaigns, for example, candidates often withhold negative information about their opponent until just before the election. By doing so, they leave the opposition little time to engage in any form of "damage control" that might save the election.

3. A political tactic that is somewhat counterintuitive, but often highly effective, is **promotion of the opposition.** This may involve eliminating a political rival by helping the person become so successful that he or she is promoted to a higher position in the organization and no longer poses a threat.

Using this tactic has a double advantage: the employee appears to be gracious, and an individual who may be a roadblock en route to the desired political objectives is eliminated.

4. A final political tactic used in organizations is an employee's promotion of his or her own agenda by **pursuing line responsibility**—actively seeking a position within the organization that makes it easier to exert one's influence. In most organizations, some positions are crucial to the main business of the organization, and others are considered peripheral. As a general rule, positions that are close to the core technology of an organization (e.g., production, resources acquisition) carry higher levels of influence than positions in departments designed to *support* that technology (e.g., research and development, human resources).

The political tactics described to this point are relatively benign, but certain tactics reflect the "dark side" of political behavior in organizations. According to DuBrin (1993), more destructive political tactics include the elimination of one's political rivals, use of a "divide and conquer" strategy, and exclusion of one's political adversaries. Political battles in organizations can be brutal. In some cases when members of organizations are competing with each other, the "winner" is able to facilitate the exit of rivals by getting them fired or making their life so difficult that they leave voluntarily.

The "divide and conquer" strategy may surface in situations where one individual is at odds with a group of other employees. It is often difficult for an individual to impose his or her will on such a group because of the numerical difference. Thus, one way to overcome this situation is to induce conflict within the group, to make it less likely that these individuals will put up a united front. Managers in many types of organizations often bemoan the lack of interpersonal harmony within work groups. However, the irony is that the existence of interpersonal conflict often makes it much easier for managers to control their groups and to advance their personal agenda.

Excluding one's political rivals simply involves making sure that they are "out of the loop" and thus less likely to influence their agenda. As stated earlier, in many organizations, information is power. Thus, one way to undercut one's rivals is to make sure that they do not receive crucial information that would make it easier for them to exert influence. In practice, this form of influence may involve making sure that one's rivals are not invited to important meetings, or perhaps seeing to it that they receive job assignments in remote areas of the organization.

Unfortunately, not a great deal of empirical research has been devoted to the study of organizational politics. The little research that has been done, however, suggests that political behavior has a negative impact on organizations, particularly when employees lack an understanding of the political landscape (e.g., Ferris, Gilmore, & Kacmar, 1990). When one considers the tactics described above, this is not surprising. The atmosphere in an organization with a great deal of political behavior is likely to be characterized by tension, mistrust, and, in extreme cases, downright paranoia.

It is not realistic to think that political behavior can be eliminated from organizations. However, there may be things that organizations can do to cut down on it. Political behavior is often the byproduct of uncertainty and ambiguity, so being clear about organizational goals and individual employees' job assignments is an important step toward reducing destructive political behavior. Organizations can also reduce political behavior by breaking up obvious cliques or coalitions through transfers or through job rotation. If individuals consistently engage in destructive political behaviors, organizations may be able to reduce these behaviors by confronting the offenders. Often, employees in organizations will "get away with" destructive political behaviors simply because they are never confronted about it.

Perhaps the most important way that managers can decrease political behavior is by setting a good example for subordinates. If a manager is honest and above board in his or her dealings with others in the organization, handles conflicts with others in a constructive manner, and conveys to subordinates that highly destructive political behavior will not be tolerated, this sends a powerful message. Although political behavior in organizations may not be eliminated, it may be possible to decrease it to a nondestructive level.

CHAPTER SUMMARY

This chapter focused on leadership and the closely related topic of influence processes. The study of leadership has been approached from trait, behavioral, and contingency perspectives. Although most modern theories of leadership can be considered contingency theories, the trait and behavioral approaches are by no means dead; they still offer some insight into leadership processes.

Fiedler's Contingency Theory proposes that the effectiveness of a leader hinges on the match between situational favorability and whether the leader is task- or relationship-oriented. This theory has received only mixed support, but it has generated a considerable body of leadership research. It also served as the impetus for other contingency-based leadership theories in subsequent years.

Path–Goal Theory also proposes that leader effectiveness depends on the leader–situation match. It differs from Fiedler's theory, however, in the manner in which effectiveness is defined, and in proposing that leaders are able to adapt different forms of leadership behavior to different situations. Although Path–Goal Theory still awaits more empirical scrutiny, it serves as a useful guide to the understanding of leadership and may have considerable practical benefits as well.

The Vroom–Yetton–Jago model of leadership is focused on one aspect of leadership behavior: decision making. This theory is somewhat different from the others in that it is largely *prescriptive* in nature; that is, it provides managers with guidelines for decision making. Support for this model has been strong when managers have been asked to recall decisions, but results have been more equivocal when other sources of data are used.

The Leader–Member Exchange (LMX) Theory proposes that leaders develop, with each of their subordinates, a unique relationship that is largely based on social exchange. This theory represents a vast departure from previous theories that were based on the rather naïve assumption that leaders treat all subordinates the same. Research on LMX Theory has yielded very interesting findings on both the determinants and the consequences of differences in exchange relationship quality. Further work, however, appears to be needed to define the dimensions of the exchange relationship and to broaden the scope of LMX research.

The final leadership theory described was Transformational/Charismatic Leadership. To some extent, this approach represents a return to the trait approach that dominated leadership research in the early twentieth century. Transformational/Charismatic leaders not only lead others but inspire them. These individuals also are capable of facilitating meaningful change in organizations. Research in this area has been largely descriptive. Future research needs to determine whether this form of leadership emerges largely from traits, behaviors, or some combination of the two.

Power and influence are at the core of leadership; therefore, both topics were covered in conjunction with leadership theories. Research has shown that leaders typically have multiple bases from which to exert power, and, in some cases, these bases may be situationally specific. Influence tactics represent the various ways in which leaders exert their power in organizations. Research has shown that the most effective tactics are those that give subordinates some freedom of choice, and the least effective tactics are those that involve pressure and appeals to one's formal authority.

Organizational politics represents a distinct form of influence that, in many cases, can be destructive. Political behavior may occur in any organization, but it is typically more prevalent in organizations that have a great deal of uncertainty and scarce resources. Specific political tactics may take a variety of forms—some more negative than others. Although relatively little research on organizational politics exists, there is some evidence that the impact of political behavior is negative. Although political behavior can never be eliminated completely, organizations can reduce it by improving communication and, in some cases, increasing resources. Ultimately, the most effective way for managers to reduce political behavior is to set a positive example in their dealings with subordinates and others in the organization.

SUGGESTED ADDITIONAL READINGS

Graen, G. B., & Uhl-Bien, M. (1995). Development of leader-member exchange (LMX) theory over 25 years: Applying a multi-level multi-domain perspective. *Leadership Quarterly, 6,* 219–246.

Hochwarter, W. A., Witt, L. A., & Kacmar, K. M. (2000). Perceptions of organizational politics as a moderator of the relationship between conscientiousness and job performance. *Journal of Applied Psychology, 85,* 472–478.

Karakowski, L., & Siegel, J. P. (1999). The effects of proportional representation and gender orientation of the task on emergent leadership behavior in mixed-gender work groups. *Journal of Applied Psychology, 84,* 620–631.

Klein, H. J., & Kim, J. S. (1998). A field study of the influence of situational constraints, leader-member exchange, and goal commitment on performance. *Academy of Management Journal, 41,* 88–95.

Waldman, D. A., & Yammarino, F. J. (1999). CEO charismatic leadership: Levels-of-management and levels-of-analysis effects. *Academy of Management Review, 24,* 266–285.

Chapter Eleven

Introduction to Group Behavior

Most employees belong to some formal work group, and organizations often establish temporary or ad hoc groups to accomplish many important tasks. Thus, a great deal of behavior in organizations takes place within group situations. It is therefore essential to examine behavior in groups in order to obtain a complete understanding of behavior in organizational settings. The prevalence of groups in organizations simply mirrors the fact they are also prevalent in everyday life. For example, most people are part of a family and belong to groups in their community or church, or within their profession. It is a good bet that most readers belong to a variety of groups, and that membership in these groups has an important impact on their behavior and attitudes.

Organizations make frequent use of groups for an obvious reason: a group can accomplish more than an individual. For example, a group of five firefighters can obviously bring a fire under control faster than one firefighter.

Groups are also used because the output of several people working on a task may be better—or, in some cases, more creative—than if each person approached the task individually. A third reason that groups are frequently utilized is simply *convention*. Organizational scholars (e.g., Hackman, 1992) have noted that behavior in organizations is often driven by "social inertia," or relying on familiar ways of doing things. Because groups have been used in the past, they are sometimes used without much thought as to whether they are appropriate for a given task.

Given the importance of groups in organizations, three chapters are devoted to this topic. The present chapter serves as an introduction to group behavior and draws largely from the social psychological literature. Chapter 12 focuses specifically on the effectiveness of groups in organizations, and draws largely (though not exclusively) from the organizational psychology literature. In Chapter 13, we shift to intergroup relations. This is an important, though often neglected, aspect of group behavior because different groups often must coordinate their efforts if their organization is to be successful. After reading these three chapters, students should have a firm understanding of the impact of groups in organizational settings.

WHY DO PEOPLE JOIN GROUPS?

People join groups for a multitude of reasons. A major reason is that group membership often results in some form of *need satisfaction* on the part of the individual. If one takes an evolutionary perspective (e.g., Buss, 1996), group membership may appeal to individuals' basic need for survival. Activities that enhance survival, such as hunting and defense against predators, are often better accomplished collectively than individually. Because of this, some have argued, the tendency to affiliate and form groups has become an adaptive behavior and thus has endured over many centuries.

At the present time, basic survival is not at issue for most people; thus, group membership often allows the fulfillment of other types of needs. One that is typically satisfied by group membership is the **need for affiliation.** Although there is not a clear consensus in the psychological literature as to whether humans have an innate biological need for social contact (e.g., Bowlby, 1973), most people do desire some form of it. Thus, people often join groups simply to be in the company of other people. In fact, when people do not affiliate

with others for prolonged periods of time, this may lead to psychological adjustment problems or even more severe forms of psychopathology (see Comment 11.1).

Another need that is often satisfied through group membership is the **need for power.** As was stated in Chapter 10, social power involves the capacity or potential to influence the behavior of others. If one has a strong need to exert power over others, that person needs to be in the company of other people. (It's pretty hard to boss yourself around! Actually, it can be done, but you might get some funny looks!) Thus, people often do join groups so they can hold leadership positions that allow them to exert power and influence over other group members.

Besides providing the opportunity for need satisfaction, group membership often gives people a greater opportunity to achieve goals than they would have if they were acting alone. For example, people often join labor unions because they believe they can achieve higher wages and more favorable working conditions by acting collectively rather than negotiating with their employer as individuals. Other examples of organizations joined for this reason include political parties, criminal organizations, churches, lobbying organizations, and consumer advocacy groups. These organizations seek vastly different goals, but they are similar in their use of the power of collective action to achieve some goal or higher purpose.

A final reason that people often join groups is that being around other people often provides comfort and support (Cohen & Wills, 1985). Particularly when people are anxious, or when they are experiencing stressful periods in their lives, being around other people can offer a great deal of support. This is especially true when the other people comprising a group are experiencing the same difficulties (Schacter, 1959). Examples of group membership can be seen in the numerous support

COMMENT 11.1

PEOPLE NEEDING PEOPLE: THE IMPACT OF SOCIAL ISOLATION

DO PEOPLE HAVE a strong *need* to be around other people? That is, do people suffer when they are deprived of contact with others? The answer to this question is rather complex, but there are many reasons to believe that social isolation may be detrimental to mental and physical health. Research in developmental psychology, for example, has shown that children often have severe developmental delays and other long-term difficulties when they are deprived of social contact as infants. Also, studies of individuals such as explorers, scientists working in seclusion, and prisoners document the psychological suffering that often accompanies seclusion from others. This suffering is often greater then the physical hardships these individuals face.

Another indication of the need for social contact (and hence the pain associated with isolation) is the comfort people often find when they are with other people, particularly in times of distress or turmoil. Often, when something traumatic happens in someone's life (e.g., loss of a spouse), the first words of concerned friends or relatives are: "He/She shouldn't be alone." The soothing effect of social contact also explains, at least partially, why many people regularly go to churches, synagogues, and mosques to practice their religious faith. It is certainly *possible* to practice one's religious faith in isolation; however, doing so with others often provides a great deal of comfort.

Despite the well-documented negative effects, isolation from others can provide people an opportunity for reflection and personal growth. Writers, artists, and others engaged in creative endeavors often find inspiration through solitude and isolation. It is important to note, however, that, for these individuals, the isolation is *self-imposed* and they are typically able to break their isolation if they want to. This element of choice appears to be a key element in whether social isolation is detrimental.

Source: D. R. Forsyth. (1999). *Group dynamics* (3rd ed.). Belmont, CA: Brooks/Cole-Wadsworth.

groups for people with certain diseases (e.g., cancer), survivors of tragedies (e.g., loss of a spouse), or people who are going through other major life transitions (e.g., divorce).

The major point to be gleaned from this section is that, typically, people do not randomly join groups; usually, they do so for more instrumental reasons. Another important point is that membership in a particular group may serve several purposes at the same time. Although organizations typically form groups in order to accomplish work-related tasks, work groups may serve a variety of other purposes for their members, such as affiliation and social support. This point is often overlooked in organizational psychology, but it is important in understanding the behavior of work groups.

DEFINING CHARACTERISTICS OF GROUPS

Psychologists who study group behavior are much more precise in their definition of what constitutes a group, as compared to the way most people use this term in everyday conversation. Although there is no "universal" accepted definition of what constitutes a group (Forsyth, 1999), there is actually a good deal of consensus on the most important defining characteristics. A term that is found in most definitions of a group is **interdependence.** Specifically, to be considered a group, a collection of people must, in some way, be interdependent. This simply means that the outcomes each member of a collective receives depend, to some degree, on the other members of the collective. In work situations, interdependence may be seen when one person may need information from other employees in order to do his or her job. Interdependence may also exist in social situations; that is, people may depend on each other for having fun.

Another key defining characteristic of a group is **social interaction.** To be considered a group, people must interact with each other in some way. This typically takes the form of verbal and nonverbal communication. If people are not in the same physical location, this interaction may take other forms (e.g., phone, e-mail, and so on). On the other hand, people who do not interact are typically not considered to be a group. Consider, for example, five people standing in an elevator. The people in this situation are essentially ignoring each other and would not be considered a group.

A third defining characteristic of a group is the **perception of being a group,** on the part of the actual group members and those external to the group. There may be instances where people interact with each other, and may even be somewhat interdependent, but do not perceive themselves as a group. Consider, for example, the members of a wedding party. These individuals certainly embody the first two characteristics of a group: they interact, and their behavior is somewhat interdependent (e.g., there is usually some predetermined order in which they must walk down the aisle). In most cases, though, these individuals probably perceive themselves as a collection of individuals rather than a group.

Furthermore, even if some level of group identity does develop among these individuals, it is very short-lived (see Comment 11.2).

A key defining characteristic of groups is **commonality of purpose.** For a collection of people to be a group, they must have some common goal or other reason for existence. Common goals may be quite formal—for example, for a work group—or quite informal, as would be the case for a group of friends who get together simply because they enjoy each other's company. The major point is: For a collection of people to be a group, they must have, at some level, something they are trying to accomplish collectively.

Based on these defining characteristics of groups, two important points are worth mentioning. First, clearly dividing collections of people into "groups" and "nongroups" is often difficult to do. Some collections of people are more "grouplike" than others. Thus, whether a collection of people constitutes a group is more a matter of degree than it is an absolute judgment. Second, within organizational settings, we often use the term *group* incorrectly. A formal work "group" may simply be a collection of people who are linked for administrative purposes but exhibit few of the defining characteristics of a group. In universities, for example, academic departments are typically considered "groups," even though the work of the "members" (professors) is not usually interdependent. They may interact very infrequently, may not perceive themselves as a group, and may disagree vehemently about departmental goals.

The other side of this, however, is that, within organizations, *informal* groups may develop, and the impact of these groups may be powerful. For example, people may develop friendship groups based on their level of seniority within the organization or their common interests (e.g., running, playing golf).

COMMENT 11.2

CAMARADERIE IN TEMPORARY GROUPS: INTENSE BUT SHORT-LIVED

IN WRITING THIS section, I was taken back to the days when my wife Robin and I began dating in the early 1980s. We were both in our early 20s at the time and, like many people our age, had a circle of "couples" with whom we regularly socialized. Many of these couples were dating seriously and ultimately married. Thus, for about a two-year period, it seemed that our social agenda was dominated by attending weddings. Given the free food and drink that go with weddings, this would have been quite enjoyable, except for one thing—at most of these weddings and receptions, I had to sit alone! Robin, being the very friendly person that she was (and still is), was asked by *every one* of her friends (and a few who seemed like strangers) to be a bridesmaid in their weddings. If there is a section in the *Guinness Book of World Records* entitled "Wedding Participation," Robin is at least in the top ten.

At most receptions, I had to sit with cousins of the bride, or with the groom's college fraternity brothers, but this experience was actually quite valuable because it provided an opportunity to watch group development in action. One of the things that I found interesting about the wedding parties, of which Robin was a part, was that they appeared to develop a great deal of camaraderie and cohesion, despite being formed very quickly. This may have had to do with strong commonality of purpose (they wanted to see the bride and groom tie the knot), similarity of dress, or the fact that they were required to engage in many activities together (e.g., the wedding ceremony, pictures, and sitting at the head table). I always detected a subtle sense of superiority as they received their food while the rest of the guests (including yours truly) were still munching on rolls in order to tame our hunger.

The camaraderie and cohesion of the wedding party were quite intense but also very short-lived. I noticed that, toward the end of dinner, the social fabric of this group would begin to fray. Members of the wedding party would visit friends and relatives at their tables, and some of us lowly "commoners" would actually visit people we knew at the head table. This loosening of social ties continued throughout the evening. By the time the band played the last song, members of the wedding party were strangers once more.

These informal groups are important because they may impact employees' attitudes and can ultimately impact whether employees stay with an organization. They are certainly as real as formal groups created by organizational structures.

GROUP STRUCTURE

To understand anything, it is helpful to have a set of dimensions or characteristics with which to describe it. For example, we can describe and compare physical objects according to physical dimensions such as height, weight, and function. To understand groups, it is useful to consider **group structure**, which represents a set of dimensions along which any group can be described. These dimensions also help when we are describing differences between groups. The most important elements of group structure are roles, norms, values, communication patterns, and status differentials. Each of these is discussed next.

Roles

Roles represent prescribed patterns of behavior that are specific to a particular individual, or to the position the individual occupies (King & King, 1990). In organizations, role-related behaviors are often communicated to employees through formal documents such as job descriptions, but may also be communicated by more informal means. As an element of group structure, roles are quite relevant. When groups first form, there is a great deal of uncertainty and ambiguity surrounding what individual groups' members are supposed to do (Tuckman, 1965). Over time, individual group members' roles are defined through the process of **role differentiation** (Hackman, 1992). Role differentiation simply represents the process by which (1) role-related expectations are communicated to group members, and (2) the various roles within the group take shape. Groups tend to form role structures primarily because this method is much more efficient than having "everyone do everything."

Although the specific roles played by group members may be highly specific and task-dependent, more general roles are enacted in all groups. For example, in most groups, a member or members plays what might be described as the **task role**. Behaviors associated with the task role might include clarifying task requirements, providing performance-related coaching and assistance to group members, and, at times, keeping the group focused on the task at hand. In many (but not all) cases, behaviors associated with the task role are performed by a formally designated group leader. It is not unusual, for example, for senior members of a work group to share their expertise with newer members,

even when the groups have formally designated leaders.

A second role that is commonly seen in most groups is the **socio-emotional role.** Behaviors associated with the socio-emotional role are aimed at maintaining the "social fabric" of the group. At various points in the life of any group, there is a need for someone to encourage others, to lighten the atmosphere with a joke, or to diffuse conflicts among group members. Socio-emotional behaviors could obviously be performed by any member of a group, but often are *not* performed by a formally designated leader when one is present. Exhibiting socio-emotional behaviors often puts leaders in an awkward position, given that they are also typically responsible for judging the performance of the members of their group. In professional sports, teams often acquire veteran players because they are able to perform aspects of the socio-emotional role, such as keeping morale high and diffusing personality conflicts among other players.

The third role that is common to most groups is labeled the **individual role.** In all groups, individual members have individual needs and desires that may or may not be compatible with those of the group as a whole. Individual group members pursue these needs to varying degrees, but (hopefully) not to the detriment of the larger group goals. However, these needs could be problematic when they conflict with the goals of the group. In many organizations, for example, employees have incentives that are based purely on individual performance.

Norms

The normative standards ("norms") that are adopted by the group represent a second important dimension of group structure. Norms are simply explicit or implicit standards that govern behavior. According to Hackman (1992), groups adopt norms primarily to increase the predictability of group members' behavior and, more generally, to keep things running smoothly within the group. Groups may adopt norms governing a number of aspects of group behavior, such as the format of meetings, the openness of communication, and even the way people dress. Typically, though, groups adopt norms only for behaviors that are deemed *important* for the functioning of the group.

Once norms are adopted, group members typically "fall in line" and behave in accordance with those normative standards. In some cases, however, a group member may behave in direct violation of those norms. If such a violation is unintentional, politely bringing it to the person's attention may be all that's needed to correct the behavior. For example, if a new group member arrives at a meeting 15 minutes late because he or she didn't realize the starting time, this type of norm violation can be dealt with simply by bringing it to the person's attention or making light of the infraction.

What happens when norm violation is more intentional and occurs repeatedly? Research suggests that, in these types of situations, group members should try to modify the norm violator's behavior—but only to a point. If repeated attempts fail to bring the norm violator's behavior in line with the prevailing group norms, one of three things can happen. First, the group may eliminate the norm violator. Evidence suggests, however, that this is a fairly drastic step; groups typically expel norm violators only as a last resort. There may even be instances in which a group simply does not have this option.

A second option is to allow the norm violator to remain a member of the group—but a very marginal member. Stated differently, the norm-violating group member may become an **institutionalized deviant** who is essentially ignored by the other members of the group (Dentler & Erikson, 1959). When this happens, the group essentially "gives up" on the norm violator and ignores his or her behavior. In some cases (but not all), being relegated to the role of institutionalized deviant may be enough to prompt a person to leave a group. The negative part of having a person in the role of institutionalized deviate is that the group has essentially lost the contributions of one of its members.

A final possibility is that the norm violator may ultimately change the relevant group norm. One of the positive things about norm violation is that it may force a group to take a critical look at its prevailing norms. Although, in many cases, norms help groups to function more effectively, they may also have negative effects. For example, a group that adopts a norm of never acknowledging internal conflict may function well on the surface but have problems in the long run. Thus, taking a critical look at prevailing group norms may reveal some that are either outdated or dysfunctional for the current group. As Hackman (1992) aptly points out, "Just as it has been said that the unexamined life is not worth living, so it may also be said that an unexamined norm is not worth enforcing" (p. 248).

For a norm violator to actually change prevailing group norms, however, a number of conditions must be present (Moscovici, 1994). Specifically, normative change is much more likely if there is at least one other group member violating the prevailing norm; one group member going against the grain will typically not be enough to change a group norm. It has also been found that the norm violator must be consistent in his or her behavior over time, and that the other members of the group must see this consistency as evidence of the strength of his or her convictions. Normative change is also more likely when the difference between the prevailing norm and the behavior of the norm violator is reasonably consistent with prevailing cultural values. Finally, members of the minority must avoid being cast into the role of institutionalized deviants. All in all, one may conclude that prevailing group norms can be changed by a norm violator, but this is not an easy process.

Values

Values represent things or ideas that the group deems as important (Rokeach, 1973). When new members are socialized into any collective body, the values of that collective body are communicated either explicitly or implicitly. For example, a group producing a product may strongly value quality, a group that deals with customers may strongly value customer satisfaction, and a group that forms for social reasons may strongly value group members' enjoyment.

Regardless of whether a group communicates its values explicitly through written documents or on a more ad-hoc basis, new members must accept them in order to remain part of the group. For membership in most groups, new members are not required to become completely committed to all the values of the group. At some level, however, a new group member must accept some of the group's values in order to remain part of the group.

Like norms, values may be functional because they often serve as "rallying points" for a good deal of group members' behavior. For example, the fact that a group strongly values customer service may motivate group members to "go the extra mile" for customers. Values, however, can also be dysfunctional. A group that values conformity and agreement over all else may, at times, make very poor

decisions and ultimately be ineffective (Janis, 1982). Thus, like norms, the values of a group must be periodically made explicit and critically examined.

Communication Patterns

Another way that groups can be described is by the characteristic patterns group members use to communicate with each other. In the group dynamics literature, the most typical distinction regarding communication is between **centralized** and **decentralized** communication networks (Leavitt, 1951; Shaw, 1964, 1978). When a centralized communication network is adopted in a group, communication tends to flow from one source to all group members. A typical form of centralized communication, termed the "hub and spokes" model, is depicted in Figure 11.1. Notice that in this type of communication network, one individual (often the group leader) is the focal point. This individual takes in information and disseminates it to the other members of the group. The advantage of this type of centralization is that it allows information to be standardized; that is, all

FIGURE 11.1
The Hub-and-Spokes Communication Network

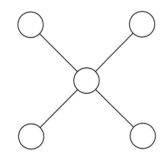

The lines with no arrows indicate that communication flows in a bidirectional manner.
Adapted from: M. E. Shaw. (1964). Communication networks. *Advances in Experimental Social Psychology, 1,* 111–147.

group members can obtain the same information. This is particularly important when groups are working on tasks that are fairly standardized and routine.

As one looks at Figure 11.1, an obvious disadvantage is that centralized communication tends to restrict and discourage the flow of communication among group members. Depending on the nature of the task, this may ultimately have a negative impact on the performance of individual group members and the group as a whole. For example, it has been shown that performance on highly complex tasks is hindered by highly centralized communication flow (Hackman, 1990; Leavitt, 1951). For example, if a group of researchers is working on developing a new product, communicating only through a supervisor would be highly inefficient.

Highly centralized communication also has a less obvious problem: It puts a great deal of reliance on one person; that is, the "hub" of any centralized communication network must take in and disseminate a great deal of information and may simply overload the person with too much information. This form of communication network is also based on the premise that the information that is disseminated by the person occupying the focal point will be accurate and consistent. In a highly centralized communication network, there is a great deal of potential for the person occupying the focal point to disseminate information in a way that enhances his or her political agenda without enhancing the productivity of the group.

In direct contrast to centralized communication networks, in a decentralized network, communication flows freely within the group. The network depicted in Figure 11.2, which is referred to as a "Comcon," depicts decentralized communication quite clearly. Note that everyone in this five-person group communicates with everyone else. Compared to a

FIGURE 11.2
The "Comcon" Communication Network

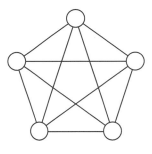

The lines with no arrows indicate that communication flows in a bidirectional manner.
Adapted from: M. E. Shaw. (1964). Communication networks. *Advances in Experimental Social Psychology, 1,* 111–147.

centralized network, a clear advantage of decentralization is that it allows communication to flow wider and faster. If two members of a group need to communicate with each other about an important issue, they can do so without having to go though an immediate supervisor. Research has shown that this type of free-flowing communication is an asset, especially when a group is working on a highly complex interdependent task (Leavitt, 1951). The primary disadvantage of decentralization is the sheer amount of information that is communicated. This is particularly true with the widespread use of electronic communication. Groups using highly decentralized communication must develop ways of managing the flow of information that do not restrict it, but, at the same time, introduce some level of consistency.

Other than their degree of centralization, groups can often be distinguished according to whether group members communicate with each other. In some groups, members communicate a great deal of information. However, in other groups, communication is very restricted and group members often find themselves "out of the loop" on important issues. A low level of communication among group members is often (but not always) symptomatic of an inability or unwillingness of a leader to grapple with the issue of communication. It may also be symptomatic of more serious problems within a group (Hackman, 1990).

Another aspect of communication can be seen in groups: the differences between formal and informal communication patterns. Formal communication methods include things such as written memos and directives, formal statements of policy, and information provided at group meetings. Virtually all groups engage in some formal communication, although the degree to which they stay in touch varies considerably. Formal communication is often necessary for dissemination of important information and policies to group members.

Communication within groups may also be quite informal. Group members may engage in small talk before beginning their workday, or may discuss work-related matters while socializing after work. Organizations obviously have less control over informal communication than they do over more formal modes of communication. Indeed, the "grapevine" can be a very important source of communication for group members. A key issue, however, is the accuracy of information that is communicated within informal communication networks. When the information is accurate, informal communication networks can be a highly efficient way to communicate information. On the other hand, when it is *inaccurate,* this can create big problems within groups or even within entire organizations (see Comment 11.3).

COMMENT 11.3

INFORMAL COMMUNICATION NETWORKS: THE "GRAPEVINE"

MOST OF THE research on communication in groups and organizations deals with *formal* systems of communication, but we know that much of the communication that takes place in groups and organizations is informal. The term "grapevine" is often used to describe such informal communication networks. Anyone who has worked in an organization has probably acquired or distributed information through the grapevine.

Managers in organizations are often leery of grapevine communication; they fear that such information is often inaccurate. Are managers justified in their distrust of the grapevine? Not a great deal of research has been done on this form of communication, so the evidence is somewhat mixed. Some research has shown that managers' distrust of the grapevine is justified; information communicated through the grapevine *is* often inaccurate. Other research,

however, has shown that the accuracy of grapevine communication is quite high, especially when the information being communicated is not controversial.

We know one thing for sure about the grapevine: It is much quicker than more formal communication channels. News often travels fast in organizations. Thus, rather than completely avoid it, managers can sometimes use the grapevine as a way to quickly communicate information. This obviously must be done carefully, but may be a very useful way to work around more cumbersome formal communication channels when information must be communicated rapidly.

Sources: R. Hershey. (1966). The grapevine—Here to stay but not beyond control. *Personnel, 20,* 64; and B. Smith. (1996). Care and feeding of the office grapevine. *Management Review, 85,* 6.

Status Differentials

As groups develop, there are typically differences in status among the various group members. The reasons for such status differences are generally classified into two general categories: **diffuse status characteristics** and **task-specific status characteristics.** Diffuse status characteristics are those that are not directly related to the task the group is performing but are still seen as legitimate bases on which to attribute status. In many societies, status is based on one's occupation. In American society, those employed in professional occupations, such as medicine, law, and engineering, are typically accorded higher status than individuals in occupations such as sales or manual labor. Many societies also attribute status based on demographic variables such as age, gender, and ethnic origin. Evidence of the impact of diffuse status characteristics can clearly be seen in studies of jury deliberations (e.g., Schneider & Cook, 1995).

Groups may also attribute status based on differences in group members' relative contributions to the task the group is performing. As one would expect, an individual who has contributed a great deal to the group's task performance, or is capable of doing so in the future, is typically accorded higher status than a group member whose contributions are more limited (Strodtbeck & Lipinski, 1985). For example, in a military combat team, prior combat experience might be seen as a relevant basis on which to attribute status.

In work situations, one obvious and very tangible consequence of status differentials is that higher status group members are typically paid more than those with lower status. Whether such differentials are based on diffuse or task-specific status characteristics, they are typically reflected in employees' paychecks and, in some cases, these differences are quite dramatic. For example, in

professional sports, star players are often paid several million dollars more than players of lower status.

A somewhat less tangible consequence of status differentials is that they typically impact a group's level of tolerance for norm violation. Put simply, compared to lower-status group members, high-status group members are given greater latitude in violating group norms. Hollander (1971) introduced the concept of **idiosyncrasy credits** to explain this process. Idiosyncrasy credits are akin to financial currency that group members "bank" and may use in the event that they must violate a group norm. The more idiosyncrasy credits one has accrued, the more latitude one is given in violating a group norm. In most group situations, high-status members have considerably more idiosyncrasy credits than lower-status members do and thus are able to violate group norms with fewer repercussions.

One important thing to note about idiosyncrasy credits is that even high-status group members do not have an infinite supply. Each time a high-status group member violates a norm, his or her idiosyncrasy credits are reduced by an amount proportionate to the importance of the norm. Thus, even high-status group members may eventually run out of idiosyncrasy credits and risk being sanctioned by the group for norm violations. This often occurs in professional sports, when teams initially accept unconventional behavior on the part of talented players, but ultimately reach a point where such behavior is not tolerated and the player is released or traded.

In addition to running the risk of depleting their supply of idiosyncrasy credits, high-status group members must be careful that their norm violations do not negatively impact the group. Research has shown that when a norm violation on the part of a high-status group member negatively impacts a group, this behavior is viewed more negatively than similar behavior on the part of a low-status group member (Forsyth, 1999). This is most likely due to the fact that high-status group members have much greater potential than lower-status members to positively impact a group. Thus, a norm violation on the part of a high-status group member that negatively impacts the group is much more visible and salient than similar behavior coming from low-status members.

STAGES OF GROUP DEVELOPMENT

Now that the basic dimensions of group structure have been described, we turn to the issue of how groups develop and change over time. All groups are somewhat unique in the way they are formed and the manner in which they may change over time. Despite this uniqueness, group dynamics researchers and theorists have identified a great deal of commonality in the way group behavior unfolds over time. Three of the most popular theoretical models describing the process of group development are described below.

Tuckman's (1965) Stage Model

Tuckman (1965) reviewed 50 articles dealing with development processes in a variety of groups (e.g., therapy groups, sensitivity training groups, naturally occurring groups, and laboratory groups) and concluded that there was a good deal of commonality in the processes by which these groups developed over time. Based on these findings, he proposed a stage model of group development that ultimately became quite popular and has endured very well over time. The stages in this model, presented in Figure 11.3, are essentially based on the major issues that a group must grapple with at various points in its development.

FIGURE 11.3
Tuckman's (1965) Model of Group Development

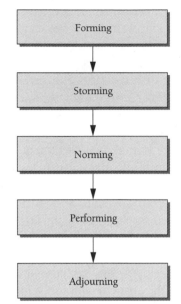

As can be seen, the first stage in the model is **forming.** This is the beginning point in the life of a group and is typically characterized by a great deal of uncertainty, or even anxiety, on the part of group members. This occurs because members of a group may be unfamiliar with each other and may have vastly different expectations about what to expect from membership in the group. At this point in the life of a group, members may deal with such uncertainties by depending heavily on the group leader for information and direction. Ultimately, though, the uncertainties that accompany membership in a new group gradually dissipate over time as group members acquire information and feel more comfortable being part of the group.

After issues associated with being in a new group are resolved, the next stage in group development is labeled **storming.** As one might guess from its name, this stage is characterized by conflict over a number of issues. For example, group members may disagree over important group norms, or perhaps over who should assume leadership responsibilities. This stage may be rather unpleasant, but it is also necessary if the groups hope to ultimately function effectively. If group members never acknowledge their disagreements, these may ultimately come out in subtler ways and prevent the group from ever performing effectively. It should be noted, however, that it is also possible for group members to be too vigorous in airing their differences. If conflicts are too intense and personal, group members may simply be unable to work together and never move past this stage.

Assuming that the conflicts identified during the storming stage can be resolved, the group next moves into the **norming** stage. In a very real sense, this is the point where a "collection of people" becomes a "group." Some level of role differentiation in group members' behavior occurs, and the behavior of the group develops some consistent patterns. For example, different group members may serve different functions, and the group may develop norms with regard to meetings, modes of communication, and, perhaps, the way group members are expected to dress. Once the norming stage is reached, the group is capable of functioning as a collective body, rather than simply as a collection of individuals.

After a group has reached the norming stage and is capable of working as an integrated unit, the next stage in group development is **performing**. This is the point at which a group accomplishes the major task or tasks for which it was formed. For example, if a group was formed to develop a strategic plan for an organization, this would be the point at which the group would actually come up with that plan. As Tuckman (1965) and others (e.g., Hackman, 1990, 1992) point out, not all groups reach this stage in group development. Problems during the earlier stages of group development (e.g., unresolved conflicts)

may prevent a group from accomplishing its major tasks. All groups, however, have the potential to reach this stage.

What happens when a group ultimately performs the task for which it was formed? A group may simply keep on performing this same task or move on to another one. In many other cases, a group is disbanded and the individuals move on to other activities. In recognition of this fact, Tuckman and Jensen (1977) added a fifth stage, **adjourning,** to the original model. In some cases, particularly when groups are formed for a very short duration, the adjourning phase is relatively mundane. That is, group members simply move on. However, when group members are together for a long period or the group experience is very intense, this can be a difficult time. Group members may genuinely miss each other and have feelings of loss or abandonment. Over time, group members will usually overcome these feelings, but initially it may be very difficult.

During the adjourning stage, the group members may reflect on their experiences in the group. Did they feel that the group was successful? Was working in the group a rewarding experience? Did they enjoy working with the other members of the group? These types of reflections are important, for two reasons. First, they may impact members' general views about working in groups. People who have negative experiences may be hesitant to work in groups in the future. Second, such reflections may strongly impact whether the members of a particular group can work together in the future. In organizations, ad-hoc groups often have to form and adjourn several times. If the members of a group have very negative reflections of being in a group, they may be unable to reconvene the group and function effectively in the future.

Tuckman's (1965) model is certainly useful in describing developmental processes in a great many groups. However, there are instances where groups do not strictly adhere to the sequence described in the model. For example, a group of individuals may have to come together and perform immediately, and address other issues later. There may also be cases in which a group of individuals immediately adheres to a strong set of norms, and deals with other issues later. The important point for readers to understand is that this model explains group development *in general.*

A second and related point is that Tuckman's (1965) model is best thought of as cyclical. For example, a group may progress all the way to the performing stage, but may have to digress to storming if important conflicts among group members arise. Also, in many instances, the composition of a group may change over time. Each time a new member joins a group, certain elements of the forming stage are replayed. For the new member, this period may be fraught with uncertainty and anxiety. However, longer-tenured group members may also have apprehensions about the new group member(s), and thus may experience a good deal of uncertainty of their own. The important point here is that real groups in organizations do not develop in a lock-step fashion. Over time, they cycle back and forth between different stages.

Moreland and Levine's (1982) Model

Group development can also be viewed in terms of the manner in which new group members are socialized into—and ultimately out of—a group. Moreland and Levine (1982) proposed a model to explain this socialization process. Although not a model of group development per se, this model is useful in helping to understand many of the important transitions that occur in groups over time.

The major premise underlying Moreland and Levine's (1982) model is that the socialization

of group members occurs in five unique stages. These stages are demarcated by the transitions an individual makes progressing from first being an outsider, then a group member, and, ultimately, an ex-member. The other important portion of Moreland and Levine's model, especially with respect to group development, is that each stage in the model is characterized by unique processes on the part of the individual seeking group membership and the group itself.

The full model is depicted in Figure 11.4. As can be seen, the first stage in the model is **investigation.** At this point in time, an individual is only a *prospective* member of a group. From the individual's point of view, this period is focused on gathering information about the group because information of this sort will help the individual decide whether he or she will ultimately seek membership in the group. The group, at this point, is trying to recruit or attract prospective members. To

FIGURE 11.4
Moreland and Levine's (1982) Model of Group Socialization

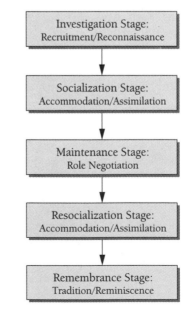

do this, the group may provide prospective members with information and, in most cases, emphasize the positive aspects of group membership and downplay the negative ones.

If a prospective member decides that membership in a group is attractive, he or she may decide to seek membership. Assuming that the individual is allowed by the group to do so, the individual moves on to the next stage in the model, which is **socialization.** At this point, the individual enters the group and makes the important transition from being an *outsider* to being a *new member.* The major task for the new member at this point is trying to "fit in" with the group and assimilate its norms and values. The major task for the group at this point is to facilitate this assimilation process by educating the new group member. This may also be a time of adjustment for the group, however, because they may have to accommodate or adjust to some of the unique characteristics of new group members. New members will not give up all of their individuality. Thus, the major issue at this point is balancing conformity to group norms with new members' individuality.

Assuming that such a balance can be achieved, the individual is accepted into the group as a full member. This is represented by the **maintenance** stage in the model. The major issue at this stage is for the group member to carve out his or her niche through the process of role negotiation. Through the "give and take" process, the individual ultimately settles into a comfortable pattern of behavior as a group member. Depending on the nature of the group, this stage may last for a long period of time. An individual may remain a member of a group for several years, although the specific roles he or she plays may vary over time, depending on this role negotiation process.

Eventually, an individual's views may diverge from those of the group, and the individual may become a *marginal* member of the group. This is represented by the **resocialization** stage. This is a critical period because it represents a point at which the individual diverges from the group in important ways. If such divergence cannot be resolved through the same assimilation and accommodation processes that were operating during the initial socialization, the individual may ultimately leave the group. On the other hand, if the individual can be successfully resocialized, he or she will again become a full member of the group.

If resocialization is not successful and the individual ultimately decides to leave the group, this leads to the final stage in the model: **remembrance.** At this point, the individual assumes the role of an ex-member and reflects on his or her experience in the group. Such reflections may be positive or negative, but they will undoubtedly have an impact on the individual's subsequent behavior in group settings. From a group's perspective, the major task at this point is to maintain some level of stability or tradition, even though the exit of a member represents an important change (see Comment 11.4).

Although Moreland and Levine's (1982) model is designed primarily to explain the process of group member socialization, it is also useful in helping to understand how groups develop over time. Most groups go through this cyclical process of bringing in new members, socializing them, and ultimately seeing them leave. Thus, this model provides useful insight into the processes that groups engage in, at least relative to the entry and exit of specific group members.

Gersick's Punctuated Equilibrium Model

In the group dynamics literature, the idea that groups strive to maintain an equilibrium

COMMENT 11.4

GROUPS THAT LIVE ON: DAVE, SAMMY, GARY, . . . AND DAVE?

STUDENTS WALKING BY my office often notice that I am wearing headphones and listening to music while I am writing. I am a college professor, so they undoubtedly assume that I am listening to Mozart, Bach, or some other titan of refined classical music. Actually, what I'm typically listening to (turned up to maximum volume, of course) is music from the rock group Van Halen. I've been a big fan of this group since I was in high school, and I continue to enjoy their music a great deal.

In terms of group dynamics, one of the things that is interesting about Van Halen is how they have been able to remain highly successful, despite having to replace a key member of the group three times. When the group started in the 1970s, David Lee Roth was the lead vocalist. He remained with the group until the mid-1980s, when he left to pursue a solo career. After Roth's exit, the group hired Sammy Hagar, who remained with the group until the mid-1990s. Like Roth, Hagar left the group to pursue a solo career. Following Hagar's departure, the group turned to Gary Cherone. Cherone had the shortest tenure with the group; he recorded only one album. Since Cherone has left, the group remains without a lead singer. However, in a somewhat odd twist of fate, it has been rumored that David Lee Roth will be returning to the group

after an absence of nearly 15 years. As of this writing, the group has yet to record with Roth.

Throughout these key personnel changes, the group has still managed to be highly successful. Why? One of the reasons is that, despite having three lead vocalists, the other members of the group have remained constant. Eddie Van Halen, Alex Valen, and Mike Anthony have been members of the group from the start. They have provided the group with stability and a distinctive sound that is independent of the lead vocalist. Another key to the group's success is that, along with stability, they have had the ability to adapt. The style and lyrics of the group's music have changed somewhat with each of the changes in the lead vocalist.

Perhaps the lesson here is that, in order for a group to be successful over time, its members need to have some level of stability in their membership. This serves to maintain continuity and perhaps reinforces important norms and values. However, when groups have changes in personnel, they must be flexible and willing to utilize the unique talents of these new group members.

Source: http://www.van-halen.com.

---

point between task accomplishment and the interpersonal needs of group members has been proposed for some time (e.g., Bales, 1965). Building on this general principle, Gersick (1988) proposed that groups might go through periods of relative inertia—or, conversely, periods of rapid change—based on group members' awareness of time and

deadlines. For example, if a task force has two months to develop a strategic plan for an organization, Gersick's (1988) model proposes that this group may spend a good portion of the first month "spinning their wheels" in an attempt to define the task, decide on how best to approach the task, and possibly deal with internal conflicts. However, once the halfway point is reached, the model predicts that group members will recognize that their time is limited, and a great deal of progress will be made in a relatively short period of time.

Gersick's (1988) model is well suited to organizational settings, because groups in organizations are typically formed to accomplish meaningful tasks, and often have to do so within a specific time frame. In contrast, groups in laboratory settings often do not have meaningful tasks to perform, and deadlines have little relevance because the duration of their activity is very limited. Furthermore, this model has received support using a variety of methodological approaches (e.g., Gersick, 1989; Hackman, 1990; Page, Davis, Berkow, & O'Leary, 1989).

The major practical implication of Gersick's (1988) Punctuated Equilibrium Model is that managers should be patient with groups when they are beginning to work on a task. This model also suggests that it is desirable for the members of task-performing groups to be aware of deadlines. Based on Gersick's (1988) model, one would assume that if group members are not made aware of deadlines, this will increase the probability that the group will flounder indefinitely and, ultimately, will never become productive.

THE IMPACT OF GROUPS ON INDIVIDUALS

People obviously behave and think differently in group situations than they do when acting alone. Not so obvious, however, are the *specific* effects that groups have on the behavior and attitudes of individual group members. Fortunately, a great deal of research, most of it conducted by social psychologists, has examined the specific effects of groups on individuals. In this section, we briefly review some of the major findings from this literature.

Social Loafing

One of the most important effects group membership has on individuals is that it impacts the effort people put forth when performing tasks. This is a particularly relevant issue for groups performing tasks in organizations. **Social loafing** is defined as the tendency for individuals to exert less effort on a task when they are performing in groups, compared to when they are performing the same task alone (Latane, Williams, & Harkins, 1979). This tendency toward social loafing has been found for a variety of tasks, in a variety of settings, and even across cultures.

Although explanations for social loafing have been proposed (see Williams & Karau, 1991), the one most widely accepted is that social loafing occurs in many group situations because the contributions (good or bad) of individual group members cannot be easily identified. Such anonymity often results in group members' exerting less effort than they would if they were acting alone. This explanation has received considerable support because making individuals' performance identifiable has been shown to reduce or eliminate social loafing for a variety of tasks (e.g., Latane et al., 1979).

Another possible explanation for social loafing has to do with the nature of the task that a group is performing. In much of the initial laboratory research on social loafing, groups performed relatively mundane tasks. More recently, however, it has been shown that social loafing tends to be reduced when groups are performing intrinsically interesting and meaningful tasks (Williams & Karau, 1991).

Although identifiability and task meaningfulness have been two of the most heavily examined causes of social loafing, there may be a number of other contributing factors as well. Karau and Williams (1993) conducted what has been the most comprehensive meta-analysis of the social loafing literature and found a number of factors that impact the likelihood of social loafing's occurring in groups. In addition to the two factors described earlier, they found that the tendency toward social loafing is decreased when group membership is important to group members, when the performance of the entire group will be evaluated, when group members do not expect their fellow group members to perform well, when individuals feel that they make unique contributions to the group, when the task performed by the group is complex, and when group members are from more collectivist Eastern cultures.

From an organizational point of view, Karau and Williams' (1993) findings are important because they suggest a variety of ways in which social loafing can be reduced. Organizations can go a long way toward reducing social loafing by redesigning the work of groups so that it is more intrinsically interesting and ultimately "counts for something" to group members. These findings also suggest that it is important for organizations to make group experiences meaningful to employees so that being part of the group is important. Organizations must also work hard to persuade employees working in groups that each of their contributions is important to the performance of the group, even if it is not the basis for formal evaluation. This "line of sight" issue can be challenging, particularly when a group's task is highly complex and there is a great deal of interdependence among group members.

Although it is widely assumed that social loafing should be reduced or eliminated in organizations, there is not a great deal of empirical evidence that social loafing has a negative impact on group and organizational effectiveness. What has been shown, however, is that social loafing may have negative effects on

those who are *not* loafing (Mulvey & Klein, 1998), and this may ultimately undermine a group's effectiveness. In many cases, it may be very difficult for group members to tell who is loafing and who is not.

Group Polarization

In many different settings, groups are required to evaluate information and, based on that information, make a decision or render some sort of judgment. This is certainly true of juries, governmental task forces, tenure and promotion committees, and many other policy-making groups in organizations. Individuals comprising these groups typically have their own views or opinions on the topic or issue on which the group will render a decision. Group dynamics researchers have found that as a group discusses an issue, the views of individuals tend to shift in a more extreme direction, compared to their view prior to the discussion. According to Lamm (1988), this tendency is termed **group polarization** and is defined as "the discussion-induced extremization of the group members' average position in the initially preferred direction" (p. 807). An example of group polarization might be a jury whose members are all moderately convinced of the guilt of a defendant but, after having a discussion, all become strongly convinced.

There are basically two explanations for group polarization that researchers have put forth over the years. According to the *social-comparison theory* explanation, a group discussion provides an opportunity for individual group members to compare their views with those of other group members. This comparative process will pull some group members toward more extreme positions than they had held prior to the discussion. Implicit in this explanation is the assumption that there is something socially desirable about being seen by others in the group as holding an extreme position on a relevant issue. Group situations may also lower group members' inhibitions regarding the expression of more extreme views and positions (Lamm, 1988).

The other most frequently cited explanation of group polarization is the *persuasive arguments theory*. According to this explanation, group members' shift in views is due to the preponderance of arguments during group discussions that favor the dominant tendency. Furthermore, the more valid and novel these arguments are, the greater the shift will be. A simple illustration shows how this works. Let's say that three people are in a group and they all hold moderately favorable attitudes toward gun control, though for slightly different reasons. During the course of group discussions on gun control, each member will provide the other group members with novel reasons for favoring gun control and, as a result, their attitudes may become more positive than they were when they started out.

The next issue to consider is the potential impact of group polarization in organizations. This represents a shift of individual group members' views in a more extreme direction, so the result often includes more extreme and riskier decisions. For example, if the members of an organizational task force all have moderately favorable attitudes toward acquiring a struggling competitor, discussing this issue may result in a shift toward more favorable attitudes and may ultimately result in the acquisition's going forward. This may occur despite the fact that there may be valid reasons why this is not a good idea. Obviously, shifts toward more extreme views will not always lead to poor decisions. On the other hand, if most members of a group enter with only moderately favorable attitudes toward a given course of action, there may in fact be valid reasons to be cautious.

Perhaps the most foolproof way of avoiding group polarization is simply to avoid having group discussions. For example, if the members of a task force must make an important decision, a group leader may poll individual group members separately and present this feedback to group members as the decision is made. This obviously may be more time-consuming, but by eliminating group discussions, group members may not be persuaded by others' views or social comparison processes. An obvious downside to this is that it prevents group members from expressing their views and perhaps building on each other's ideas.

Another potential way to avoid making a poor decision due to group polarization is to build in a time lag between when a decision is made and when it is implemented. If group members have this type of "cooling off" period, they may reflect on the decision and realize that it may have been too extreme. It is also possible that, during this period, new information will surface that will necessitate a change in the group's extreme decision. A good example can be seen in states where the law allows for the death penalty. Typically, when a jury invokes the death penalty, a period of several months passes before that sentence is carried out. During this period, many mechanisms can be used to stop or delay an execution. Given the extremity and irrevocability of such a decision, states want to be absolutely sure of the guilt of the defendant, and to have the opportunity to consider any information that may have a bearing on whether the sentence should ultimately be carried out.

Conformity

It is well known that people often do things as members of groups that they would not do as individuals. Perhaps one of the most famous examples of this notion is the response provided by a Nazi war criminal at the Nuremberg trials following World War II. When asked why he participated in war-related atrocities, his response was that he was simply "following orders," suggesting that the responsibility for his behavior rested with his superior officers. Indeed, conformity to group pressure can often bring out the dark side of human behavior, although conformity can also lead to positive and even heroic behavior.

A great deal of social psychological research has been devoted to explaining why people often are impacted by conformity pressures. In fact, three of the most famous studies ever conducted in social psychology have provided insight into conformity processes. Solomon Asch (1955, 1957) conducted a study in which a subject, along with several other individuals, was asked to perform a relative simple judgment task that involved deciding which of three lines matched a fourth reference line. Unknown to the subject, all the other individuals in the study were actually confederates and were instructed to make the *wrong* judgment. Unfortunately for the subject, he or she was the last person to publicly state this judgment.

As Asch predicted, many (though not all) subjects went along with the rest of the group and made the same incorrect judgment. The most widely cited reason for this is simply that these individuals knew their answer was wrong, but did not want to look foolish by disagreeing with the others. This is really "classic" conformity but, as it turns out, it is not the only form. When interviewed after the study, many subjects indicated that they went along with the group's judgment because they questioned the validity of their own judgments. Some subjects honestly believed that the incorrect judgments of the majority were correct.

Asch's study thus provides two explanations for conformity. People conform because they do not want to appear foolish or risk being socially ostracized by other group members. Furthermore, in subsequent research using essentially the same paradigm, Asch found this tendency was strongest when one individual faced a substantial majority. If even one member of the majority broke with the prevailing view (i.e., gave the correct judgment), this reduced conformity considerably. This explains why, for example, a member of a gang may engage in behavior that is against the law. This individual may know the behavior is wrong, but still go along in order to win the approval of fellow gang members.

The second explanation is rooted in the fact that the fellow members of a group play an important role in defining each individual's social reality. Asch was able to show that individuals will even look to others to validate their judgments of the physical properties of an object (e.g., the length of a line). In most group situations, deciding whether to conform involves much more subjective judgments. A work group member who is deciding whether to go along with others and falsify production records is making a judgment of right and wrong, not one of whether a line is a given length. These judgments are inherently more subjective, and thus more amenable to conformity. Thus, people often conform and go along with a group because they feel the group knows better than they do.

Additional insight into conforming processes was provided by a second classic study performed by Stanley Milgram at Yale University (Milgram, 1974). Milgram was interested in the conditions under which people would obey authority and engage in behavior that was harmful to others. This interest stemmed largely from the atrocities that were committed by the Nazis during World War II. To investigate obedience, Milgram led subjects to believe they were participating in a study of the effects of punishment on learning.

When subjects came into the laboratory, they were paired with another individual who was supposedly a subject but was actually a confederate of the experimenter. The experimenter conducted a drawing to determine which of the two "subjects" would be the teacher. The drawing was rigged so that the naïve subject was always the teacher and the confederate was always the learner.

Both subjects were then told that the teacher would present pairs of words to the learner, and the learner's task was to remember the associated words when only one of the word pairs was subsequently presented. The teacher was instructed to administer an electric shock as punishment for wrong answers, and to increase it by an increment of 15 volts for each successive wrong answer. The maximum voltage that could be administered was 450. To increase the realism of the situation and provide subjects with a sample of the punishment they were about to administer, they were required to experience a 45-volt shock.

Subjects did not actually inflict these electric shocks on the learners, but they were led to believe they were doing so (Milgram, 1974). During this situation, an experimenter was always close to the subject, repeating phrases such as "Please continue" and "The experiment requires that you continue" if subjects expressed any concern about the learner or showed any hesitation about the magnitude of the shocks they were inflicting. Under these conditions, 65% of the subjects ultimately administered the maximum voltage to the learner, despite expressions of discomfort and even screams of pain from the learner.

These findings came as a complete surprise to Milgram, who had estimated that no subjects would administer the maximum voltage. Further, in a survey of psychiatrists and psychological researchers that Milgram conducted prior to the experiment, the vast majority agreed with this hypothesis (Elms, 1995). How, then, can we account for Milgram's findings? In the most general sense, Milgram's findings illustrate the power of situational pressures in leading people to do things they would never do on their own. Anyone who has ever been "egged on" by other members of a group surely understands the intensity of this pressure. Milgram's findings also showed that pressure to conform can be especially intense when the persons applying the pressure are in positions of authority, are in very close proximity, and are representatives of prestigious organizations. Because the experimenter (an authority figure) ostensibly worked for Yale University (a prestigious institution), was always present, and told them to go on, they obeyed and went on, despite their misgivings. Subsequent variations of the study showed that obedience went down when the experimenter was made to seem less authoritative and was not as close to each subject, and when the study was conducted in a less prestigious organization (Milgram, 1974).

A third classic social psychological study that provides insight into conformity was performed by Phillip Zimbardo at Stanford University (Zimbardo, 1969). Zimbardo was interested in studying the impact of occupying a given role on conformity to the behavioral expectations of that role. To study this, he created a simulated prison and randomly assigned research participants to the roles of "prisoner" and "guard" for the duration of the study. Needless to say, Zimbardo found that research participants' behavior conformed to the role expectations. For example, prisoners became withdrawn and depressed, and some guards became physically abusive with prisoners. Zimbardo ultimately had to terminate the study prematurely, fearing for the physical and psychological well-being of the participants.

Perhaps the most important finding from this study is that people conform not only in response to authority, but to the demands associated with the roles they occupy in groups. In organizational settings, for example, an employee may engage in a number of behaviors because he or she occupies the role of supervisor. In fact, Zimbardo's results suggest that, in some cases, people may get so caught up in the roles they are playing that they do not consider the moral or ethical consequences of this role-related behavior.

Groupthink

According to Janis (1982), **groupthink** is defined as ". . . a mode of thinking that people engage in when they are deeply involved in a cohesive in-group, when the members' striving for unanimity overrides their motivation to realistically appraise alternative courses of action. . . . Groupthink refers to a deterioration of mental efficiency, reality testing, and moral judgment that results from in-group pressures" (p. 9). Notice in this definition that groupthink often results in flawed group decisions, but ultimately it is something that happens to the *individuals* that comprise a group.

The three primary causes of groupthink, according to Janis (1982), are: a high level of group cohesiveness, structural organizational flaws, and a provocative situational context. Cohesiveness represents the level of attraction that members have toward the group. Members of very highly cohesive groups value group membership to such an extent that they become extremely reluctant to disagree. The most common organizational flaw that leads to groupthink is a leader's stating his or her preferred decision alternative prior to a group's discussion of issues. Finally, the term "provocative situational context" is really a euphemism for a high-stress or high-pressure situation. In these types of situations, the stakes are typically high, and a group may have to make a decision very quickly.

If these antecedent conditions are present, they will lead to a concurrence-seeking tendency within a group; that is, members of a group will gloss over their differences and strive to agree with each other at all cost. This concurrence-seeking tendency may lead to more direct symptoms of groupthink, such as the active suppression of information that goes against the majority, ridicule of those who dissent, a belief that whatever the group does is moral or just, and devaluing the views or capabilities of anyone outside of the group. If these symptoms of groupthink are present, they may lead to defective decision making on the part of the group. The group may make incorrect or unrealistic assumptions, or use a decision-making scheme that is not very effective. For example, a group may ask members for a public vote on the decision when it would be more appropriate to have them express their views in private. The end result of groupthink is that it increases the potential for poor decisions, or, as Janis (1982) stated, "decision fiascoes."

Janis's (1982) primary support for the groupthink hypothesis came from an analysis of historical records associated with decision fiascoes. For example, based on such analyses, Janis proposed that groupthink played a role in the decisions to ignore repeated advance warnings associated with Japan's attack on Pearl Harbor, and to launch the ill-fated Bay of Pigs invasion during the Kennedy administration, among others. More recently, groupthink has been proposed as a possible factor contributing to the decision to launch the Challenger space shuttle (Moorhead, Ference, & Neck, 1991). Such historical analyses are provocative, but they are somewhat limited methodologically because they are based purely on the retrospective accounts of the events of interest. According to Aldag and Fuller (1993), more rigorous tests of the groupthink hypothesis have been less supportive than those based on retrospective historical analysis.

Whyte (1998) concluded that groupthink is a valid phenomenon, but proposed that the key to groupthink may be "collective efficacy," rather than group cohesiveness, as originally proposed by Janis (1982). Collective efficacy represents the beliefs that group members hold about the capability of the group to execute different courses of action. It is analogous to self-efficacy, which represents *individuals'* beliefs about executing different courses of action. According to Whyte, increased risk for groupthink occurs when the members of a group believe that the capabilities are higher than they actually are. An unrealistically high level of collective efficacy may lead a group to take undue risks and to fall into many of the decision-making traps proposed by Janis (1982). As yet, little empirical research has examined Whyte's (1998) revised conceptualization of groupthink, but this appears to be a fruitful direction for further research into the groupthink phenomenon.

How can organizations prevent or reduce the risk of groups' falling victim to groupthink? Based on historical analyses (e.g., Janis, 1982), we know that groupthink is less likely to occur when a leader does not strongly state his or her preferences prior to the group's discussing an important issue. Groupthink is also less likely to occur when leaders encourage free and open debate among group members and, in some cases, allow group members to discuss decision-making alternatives without the leaders' being present.

Another key to reducing groupthink is: a group should avoid isolating itself. Bringing in outsiders can help to provide a group with a realistic assessment of its own capabilities, as well as many of the parameters associated with the decision being made. According to Janis (1982), one thing that distinguished the decision-making process associated with the Bay of Pigs invasion (a decision-making fiasco) from that associated with the Cuban Missile Crisis (a decision-making success) was the inclusion of outside information. When deciding on how best to respond to the deployment of ballistic missiles in Cuba by the Soviets, Kennedy's group brought in a number of outsiders to provide information and, perhaps more importantly, to provide critical reactions to many of the group's assumptions about the situation. Despite such attempts to reduce groupthink, the pressure on group members to go along with a decision, despite their misgivings, can be intense. Decision-making groups will probably always have to grapple with this issue and make conscious attempts to avoid groupthink.

CHAPTER SUMMARY

The purpose of this chapter has been to introduce group behavior and provide a foundation for the next two chapters. We began by examining the defining characteristics of a group. Despite the numerous definitions proposed over the years, most maintain that the key features are interdependence, interaction, perception of being a group, and some commonality of purpose among group members.

Group structure represents a number of dimensions that can be described. The most common dimensions of group structure include roles, norms, values, status differentials, and communication patterns. Group members' behavior comes to be differentiated; normative behavior patterns develop; behaviors that are consistent with certain values are emphasized; status hierarchies emerge; and, finally, consistent modes of communication are adopted.

A number of models have been developed to describe the manner in which groups develop over time. The best known of these is Tuckman's (1965) model, which is based on the issues that must be dealt with at various points in the life of a group. Moreland and Levine's (1982) model approaches group development from the perspective of the socialization of new group members. Gersick's (1988) Punctuated Equilibrium Model focuses specifically on task groups. Each of these provides somewhat different and unique insights into group development.

Much of the social psychological research on groups has focused on the impact of groups on the behavior and attitudes of individual group members. Research on social loafing has shown that individuals may withhold effort when performing as part of a group; research on group polarization has shown that being in a group may lead individuals to more extreme views; research on conformity has shown that

people often engage in behavior simply to go along with the rest of the group; and, finally, group members may become part of faulty decision-making processes when they are part of a group.

SUGGESTED ADDITIONAL READINGS

Johnson, D. W., & Johnson, F. P. (2000). *Joining together: Group theory and group skills* (7th ed.). Boston: Allyn and Bacon.

Levine, J. M., & Moreland, R. L. (1998). Small groups. In D. T. Gilbert, S. T. Fiske, & G. Lindzey (Eds.), *The handbook of social psychology* (Vol. 2, pp. 415–469). New York: McGraw-Hill.

McGrath, J. E. (1984). *Groups: Interaction and performance.* Englewood Cliffs, NJ: Prentice-Hall.

Naper, R. W., & Gerschenfeld, M. K. (1999). *Groups: Theory and experience* (6th ed.). Boston: Houghton Mifflin.

Chapter Twelve

Group Effectiveness

In Chapter 11, we examined the impact of group membership on members' effort, their level of conformity and extremity of opinions, and, ultimately, their decision-making capabilities. These are certainly important processes in organizations. Thus, the field of organizational psychology has benefited greatly from the work of social psychologists who were the early pioneers of group dynamics research. However, two characteristics of early social psychological group dynamics research place limitations on its usefulness to organizational psychologists. First, very little social psychological group dynamics research *directly* examined the determinants of group effectiveness. Rather, the dependent variables examined in this research have typically been attributes of individuals rather than of performance groups. The fact that individuals are impacted by group membership may have implications for performance. However, research that *directly* examines group effectiveness is inherently more useful to organizational psychologists.

Second, the overwhelming majority of social psychological group studies have been conducted in laboratory settings. As was pointed out in Chapter 2, organizational phenomena are often replicated quite well in laboratory settings; thus, generalizability is often robust (Locke, 1986). Group effectiveness, however, may be one organizational variable for which generalizing from laboratory to field settings may be problematic because *the environmental context in which a group performs is an important key to understanding group effectiveness.* In laboratory settings, groups are formed randomly, and they perform tasks in relatively standardized settings. In fact, proper experimental methodology dictates that the environmental conditions under which different groups perform must be as similar as possible (Cook & Campbell, 1979).

In real organizations, however, there are important differences in the environmental context in which various groups perform. For example, even within the same organization, there are important differences among work groups in staffing levels, the manner in which rewards are distributed, the way leaders set goals with group members, and the way groups interface with other groups. Also, in real organizations, members often have known each other prior to their present group assignment, and those prior relationships may promote collegiality or lead to conflict. These *contextual* factors are difficult to simulate in laboratory research, yet there is little denying that they impact the effectiveness of groups.

Due to the importance of organizational context, what has been described as an "organizational psychology" group literature has developed during the past 25 years. In fact, many have come to the conclusion that when it comes to the study of group effectiveness, "the torch has been passed" from social to organizational psychology. Levine and Moreland (1990)—who, incidentally, are both social psychologists—make the point by stating: "Despite all the excellent research on small groups within social psychology, that discipline has already lost its dominance in this field. The torch has effectively been passed to (or, more accurately, picked up by) colleagues in other disciplines, particularly organizational psychology. They have no doubts about the importance of small groups and are often in the forefront of group research. So, rather than lamenting the decline of interest in groups, we should all be celebrating the resurgence, albeit in a different locale" (p. 620).

The purpose of this chapter is essentially to pick up where we left off in Chapter 11 and explore more recent group research that has focused more and more on the factors contributing to group effectiveness. We begin by examining a basic question: What constitutes group effectiveness? The focus then shifts to examining several influential models of group effectiveness. These models have helped to guide much of the organizational research on group effectiveness, and have served as a foundation for many organizational efforts to improve the performance of groups.

Across these models, several variables seem to "pop up" repeatedly as determinants of group effectiveness. These include group composition, task design, organizational resources, organizational rewards, group goals, and group processes. Each of these will be examined individually, and some of the most common methods organizations use to improve the performance of groups will be described. The chapter concludes with a brief discussion of the role that groups are likely to play in organizations in the future.

DEFINING GROUP EFFECTIVENESS

To say that groups now represent an important part of organizational life is certainly an understatement. Nearly all organizations use small groups to accomplish at least some tasks (Guzzo & Shea, 1992), and it has become increasingly popular for small groups to be the "basic foundation" upon which organizations are built (Peters & Waterman, 1982).

Despite the importance of group effectiveness, it is not necessarily easy to define what is meant by an "effective" group. Steiner (1972) proposed one of the earliest theoretical propositions bearing on group effectiveness:

$$\text{Actual productivity} = \text{Potential productivity} - \text{Process losses}$$

The *potential productivity* of a group represents the highest level of performance that is attainable by a group. Consider the following example. If each of the five starting players on a basketball team is capable of scoring 20 points per game, those players collectively should be able to score at least 100 points per game. The term **process losses** represents less-than-optimal ways of combining the inputs of group members into a group product. Process losses generally occur because of a lack of coordination among group members, or because the motivation of individuals may change when they are performing in a group setting. The team described above may not reach its scoring "potential" because the styles of the individual players do not mesh well, or because individual players may not feel a great deal of personal responsibility for the team's performance and, as a result, may reduce their effort.

Steiner's (1972) basic model is certainly useful in helping us to understand, in a very general sense, what determines group performance, but it also has some serious limitations. The most serious flaw is that this model doesn't specify which aspect(s) of the group, or the organizational context, can be used to enhance the coordination of group members or to prevent process losses. The other problem with this model is that it is based on the rather naïve assumption that organizational goals and group goals are perfectly aligned (Hackman, 1992). For example, if a group's goal is to produce a high-*quality* product, and the organization's goal is for the group to produce a large *quantity,* the group may appear to suffer from process loss, but in fact may be quite successful; the group is simply succeeding on its own terms.

The definition of group effectiveness that has been used most often by researchers was put forth by Hackman (1987) in a comprehensive review of the work group design literature. According to Hackman, group effectiveness is a multidimensional construct consisting of three interrelated dimensions. The first of these dimensions is related to the *output* of the team, the second has to do with the long-term viability of the group as a performing unit, and the third has to do with the impact of the group experience on individual group members. Each of these will be discussed below.

The vast majority of groups in organizations are formed to fulfill some specific charge or purpose; that is, they are formed to *do something.* For example, a top management team may be formed to create a long-range strategic plan, a surgical team may be assembled to perform a delicate cardiac bypass operation, or a rescue team may be formed to evacuate hurricane victims from their homes. Thus, one way to measure the effectiveness of a group is to judge whether its "output" is satisfactory. As Hackman (1987) states, for a group to be judged successful, "The productive output of the work group should meet or exceed the performance standards of the people who receive and/or review the output" (p. 323). In the previous examples, the top management team would hardly be considered a success if it failed to produce a viable strategic plan, the surgical team would be unsuccessful if the patient's arteries remain blocked, and the rescue team would be unsuccessful if the hurricane victims are not evacuated. Task accomplishment is thus an important component of group effectiveness.

Vince Lombardi, the legendary football coach of the Green Bay Packers, told his team: "Winning isn't everything, it's the *only* thing." In many organizations, a variant of this attitude prevails in that the quality of a group's output is seen as the *only* indicator of its effectiveness. According to Hackman (1987), a second indication of the effectiveness of a group is whether the social processes used in performing the task maintain or enhance the capability of the group members to work together in the future. In some cases, groups accomplish their assigned tasks, but they do so in such a contentious manner that they are incapable of working together in the future. According to Hackman, a group would hardly be considered effective if it essentially "burns itself up" while performing its assigned task, even if that task is performed successfully. In some cases, a group comes together only once to perform a task (e.g., a search committee is selecting a new college president). In most organizations, however, this is more the exception than the rule.

Working as part of a group can be an extremely rewarding experience. Often, a great deal of satisfaction goes with collective accomplishment, and the social relationships that often develop in groups can be extremely rewarding. Unfortunately, there is also a downside to working in groups. Depending on others to get things done can be extremely frustrating, high-performing individuals may not receive their full share of the credit for a group's performance, and relationships with other group members may go sour. According to Hackman (1987), if the experiences of group members are largely negative and frustrating, this is an indication that the group is unsuccessful. Thus, the third dimension of group effectiveness is group member satisfaction. This is really related to the second point about viability, but goes somewhat further. Specifically, those who are largely negative about group work may be loath to work in *any* group within the organization in the future. When a group performs its task well, while completely ignoring the needs of group members, it can hardly be considered effective (see Comment 12.1).

MODELS OF GROUP EFFECTIVENESS

As with many of the topics covered in this book, there have been a number of attempts to model the factors that contribute to group effectiveness. Like any theoretical models, the models of group effectiveness are incomplete; that is, they do not include *every* possible factor that contributes to group effectiveness. They are useful, however, in highlighting the general factors that differentiate between successful and unsuccessful groups. They also help us to understand the *processes* by which these general factors combine to impact group effectiveness. This aids in organizing research findings and may also guide organizational efforts toward improving the performance of groups. In this section, we examine five of the most influential models in the group effectiveness literature.

McGrath's (1964) Model

McGrath (1964) proposed that group effectiveness is determined by a basic **input–process–output** sequence; that is, certain inputs lead to differences in group process, which eventually lead to differences in group output. This basic idea is expanded in Figure 12.1 as a model of group effectiveness. Notice that McGrath included Individual-Level Factors, Group-Level Factors, and Environment-Level Factors in the input column. Individual-Level Factors include characteristics of group members that may have an impact on group effectiveness, such as their level and mix of skills, attitudes, and personality characteristics.

Group-Level Factors are essentially structural properties of groups themselves. These

COMMENT 12.1

WINNING ISN'T EVERYTHING: A BROADER VIEW OF GROUP EFFECTIVENESS

IN CLASSES I have taught over the years, describing Hackman's (1987) multidimensional view of group effectiveness has generated a great deal of discussion and, at times, vigorous debate. Typically, these discussions center around a question: "If a group performs its task well, does it *really* matter if people can work together in the future, or whether they have enjoyed working as part of the group?" After all, most organizations exist primarily to make a profit, not to provide psychological gratification to their employees.

This point of view is certainly compelling, but it is also rather shortsighted and it ignores some of the realities of organizational life. There may be crisis situations in which individuals must come together, perform very quickly, and disband immediately after their task is finished. For example, an international crisis may require that a number of national security officials come together to decide whether military intervention is warranted. In such a case, one could argue that making the correct decision is far more important than the satisfaction of the group members or the viability of the group.

In most organizations, however, group membership is more stable; thus, long-term viability and member satisfaction are important issues. Groups that repeatedly accomplish their primary task, but create a great deal of dissatisfaction among their members, often cannot survive over the long haul. Furthermore, when employees have bad experiences in a work group, these incidents will often carry over to other situations. The employees may even be reluctant to work in groups in the future. Thus, a group leader who is concerned about the psychological needs of the group members may appear to be compromising task performance, at least in the short term. Ultimately, though, groups under this type of direction are often much more successful than those governed by a "win-at-all-cost" philosophy.

Source: J. R. Hackman. (1987). The design of work teams. In J. W. Lorsch (Ed.), *Handbook of organizational behavior* (pp. 315–342). Englewood Cliffs, NJ: Prentice-Hall.

may include elements of group structure (e.g., roles, authority structure, norms, and so on), the level of cohesiveness within the group, and the number of individuals within the group. What McGrath (1964) was trying to convey here is that all groups are not created equal; that is, some are designed in a more optimal fashion than others. Thus, some groups are more "primed" for success than others.

Environment-Level Factors represent aspects of the organizational context under which the group works. Perhaps the most

important of these is the *task* that the group is performing. The nature of the task will dictate, to a large degree, the most appropriate strategies to be used by the group. The task may also be important for motivational reasons. Recall from Chapter 11 that social loafing, one of the problems inherent in group work, is less likely to occur when a group is performing a complex and stimulating task. More will be said about task characteristics later in the chapter.

Two other important aspects of the environment are the Reward Structure and the

FIGURE 12.1
McGrath's Model of Group Effectiveness

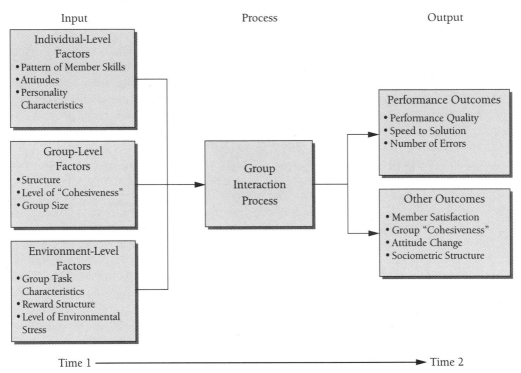

Adapted from: J. E. McGrath. (1964). *Social psychology: A brief introduction.* New York: Holt. Reprinted by permission of the author.

level of Environmental Stress under which the group performs. Rewards are important in shaping individual performance, so it should come as no surprise that this was proposed as a determinant of group performance as well. The most important consideration is whether the performance of the *group* is rewarded, rather than simply the performance of individual group members. The level of environmental stress may be determined by a number of factors, such as the criticality of work the group is performing and the time pressure under which it must be performed. A high level of environmental stress may lead to problems in a group's decision-making processes (e.g., Janis, 1982) or to conflicts surrounding

the distribution of authority within the group (e.g., Driskell & Salas, 1991).

Given all of these Input factors, the model proposes that they combine to determine Group Interaction Process, which represents the *manner* in which a group performs its task. Obviously, this may cover a good deal of territory, but the most crucial aspects of group process are likely to be things such as the performance strategies adopted by the group, the level of interpersonal harmony within the group, and the manner in which the group handles conflicts when they occur. Given the location of Group Interaction Process in the model, one can surmise that it is a key variable that distinguishes effective from ineffective groups. In models described subsequently, it will be evident that group process is believed to play a critical role in group effectiveness.

The model then proposes that Group Interaction Process will have a direct effect on the output of groups. The Output of a group can be viewed in two ways. First and foremost, a group's output can be viewed in terms of the level of performance. This would include factors such as the judged quality of the group's output, the time it takes for the group to make a decision or develop a solution to a problem, or, possibly, the number of errors that are made in performing the task. The category titled Other Outcomes represents social aspects of the group experience, such as the satisfaction of group members, the level of cohesiveness within the group after the task is performed, the attitudes of group members, and, finally, the pattern of relationships following the group's performance. Although these do not represent group performance per se [Hackman (1987) would later argue that they are part of it], they are still important outcomes.

Gladstein's (1984) Model

Gladstein (1984) proposed a model of group effectiveness which, in many ways, is quite similar to McGrath's (1964). As can be seen in Figure 12.2, this model follows the same general Input–Process–Output sequence. The Inputs in this model are also very similar to those proposed by McGrath. Notice that, at the Group level, these include characteristics of individual group members as well as elements of group structure. At the Organizational level, however, the model differs somewhat from McGrath's. The critical factors proposed by Gladstein include the resources available to groups (training and technical

consultation are available to groups and to the markets of customers they serve), as well as aspects of organizational structure (rewards and supervisory control).

Gladstein (1984) proposed that all of these inputs contribute directly to group process. The critical elements of group process include communication, level of support, handling of conflict, discussion of performance strategies, weighing of individuals' outputs, and "boundary management," or the manner in which the group interfaces with other units both inside and outside of the organization. Group process is then proposed to lead to group effectiveness (indicated by performance and satisfaction), as it does in McGrath's model.

This model differs from McGrath's in two important ways. First, Gladstein proposes that Inputs have a *direct* impact on group effectiveness, in addition to the effect that is mediated by group process. For example, a group with extraordinary levels of skill may be effective, regardless of the quality of group process. A second important difference is that Gladstein proposed that a group's task *moderates* the relationship between group process and group effectiveness. For example, a very unstructured, freewheeling style of interaction may be useful for a group creating a new product, but inappropriate for a group that is merely required to follow directions. This suggests that some forms of group process will be more or less effective, depending on the complexity, uncertainty, and interdependence present in the group's task. Recall that McGrath (1964) proposed that the nature of the task represented an input that contributed directly to group process and, subsequently, to effectiveness.

When Gladstein (1984) tested her model of group effectiveness, she used a sample of sales teams from the marketing division of

FIGURE 12.2
Gladstein's Model of Group Effectiveness

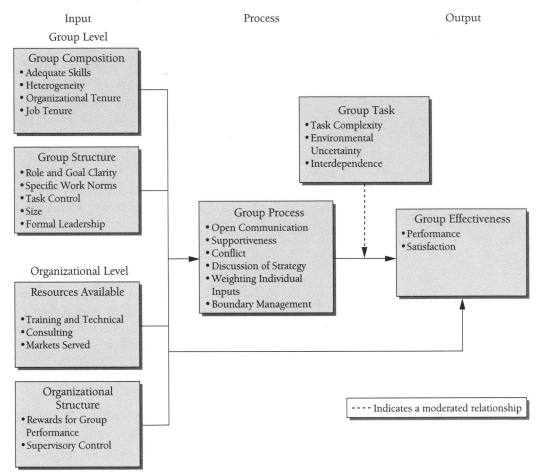

Adapted from: D. Gladstein. (1984). Groups in context: A model of task group effectiveness. *Administrative Science Quarterly, 29,* 499–517. Copyright © 1984, Cornell University Press. Reprinted by permission.

an organization in the communications industry and found mixed support. The model received the strongest support for the prediction of group members' perception of effectiveness, but support was much weaker when predicting actual sales revenue. This suggests that perhaps the model is more reflective of individuals' "implicit theories" of the determinants of group effectiveness than of actual group effectiveness. Another important finding from this study was that task characteristics did not moderate the relations between group process and effectiveness (perceived or sales revenue). This finding is difficult to interpret, given the fact that the study was cross-sectional and there was not a great deal of variation in the nature of the tasks that these groups performed.

Hackman's (1987) Model

Building again on the general Input–Process–Output framework, Hackman (1987) developed what he termed a "normative" model of group effectiveness. The term "normative" was used because Hackman's intent was clearly to develop a model that explicitly revealed the most important "performance levers" that organizations could use to enhance group effectiveness. Stated differently,

Hackman's purpose in developing this model was more to serve as a guide to improving group performance rather than merely facilitating an understanding of why a group fails.

As can be seen in Figure 12.3, the two "input" factors in the model are organizational context and group design. Under organizational context, the most important factor proposed by Hackman is the reward system under which groups work. One important aspect of an organizational reward system, with

FIGURE 12.3
Hackman's Normative Model of Group Effectiveness

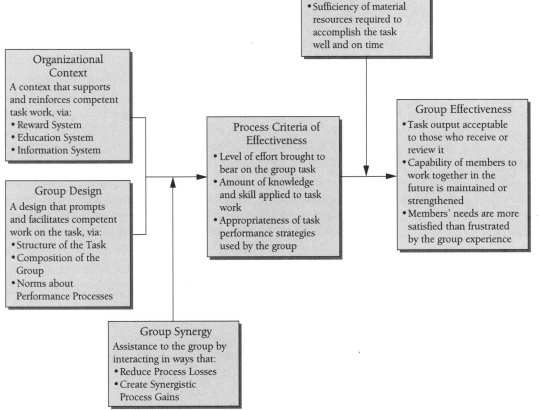

Adapted from: J. R. Hackman. (1987). The design of work teams. In J. W. Lorsch (Ed.), *Handbook of organizational behavior* (pp. 315–342). Englewood Cliffs, NJ: Prentice-Hall.

respect to groups, is whether challenging and specific performance objectives exist. The failure to provide performance objectives often plagues individual-level reward systems but is particularly problematic with groups simply because most organizational performance management systems are designed with individuals, not groups, in mind.

A second important aspect of organizational reward systems is that they must be designed so that groups receive positive consequences for excellent performance. The reinforcement value of positive consequences on individual behavior is well known (e.g., Luthans & Kreitner, 1985; Weiss, 1990). According to Hackman (1987), this same principle applies to groups, even though individual group members must ultimately see the connection between the performance of the group and the potential rewards it may obtain. If there are few positive consequences for excellent group performance, this will have an adverse motivational effect on groups.

The third aspect of organizational reward systems that is important, according to Hackman, is that rewards and objectives must focus on group, not individual, behavior. This is admittedly a tricky route for organizations to navigate because most organizational reward systems are designed for individuals, and many employees may be averse to completely giving up the possibility of having their performance rewarded. However, it is also true that, in some cases, individual and group-level reward systems work at cross-purposes. For example, in professional sports, it is becoming increasingly popular for teams to put incentive clauses, based purely on individual performance, into players' contracts. Unfortunately, in some cases, the behaviors reinforced by these incentive clauses do not support *team* performance.

In the organizational context, two other factors that contribute to group effectiveness

are the educational and informational systems present in the organization. People do not automatically know how to work as part of a group; thus, groups often need educational and training assistance. In addition, groups often need valid information so that they can competently make decisions and carry out tasks. To the extent that either of these is lacking or is of poor quality, it will undermine group effectiveness.

The group design component has to do largely with the structural features of the work group. Chief among these factors is the structure of the task that the group is performing. According to Hackman (1987), the design of a group's task has important implications for motivation (e.g., Hackman & Oldham, 1980), but may also be important for other reasons. Some tasks simply do not lend themselves well to group work (e.g., solving a highly technical problem); thus, an organization may have to face the fact that a given task may not be appropriate for groups.

The other features of the group design component are: the composition of the group and the group's performance-related norms. Groups obviously need individuals who possess the skills and abilities necessary to do the work. They also need individuals who possess at least a minimal level of compatibility in terms of personality and temperament. As was shown in Chapter 11, norms can have a powerful impact on behavior within groups. Most critical is whether groups develop norms that favor a high level of performance and effort.

As can be seen in Figure 12.3, the model proposes that both organizational context and group design contribute to what is termed the process criteria of effectiveness. These criteria are represented by the level of effort the group members exert, the amount of knowledge and skill they apply to the task, and the appropriateness of task performance strategies. Hackman (1987), in effect, turned what is group process in other models into an intermediate or **proximal criterion of effectiveness.** For example, the fact that group members are working hard on a task is an intermediate indicator that they will be successful.

Notice, however, that the impact of both organizational context and group design on the process criteria of effectiveness depends on group synergy. According to Hackman (1987), group synergy relates to the extent to which a group avoids "process losses" (e.g., wasting or misdirecting time), or whether the group takes the initiative to create innovative strategic plans. Specifically, the group may create synergistic "process gains" by building on each other's ideas. By putting this in, Hackman (1987) reminds us that groups may squander a favorable performance situation, or, conversely, they may do great things with only an average one.

The next step in the model is from process criteria of effectiveness to actual group effectiveness, which was defined previously. This represents the familiar link between group process and group effectiveness, which is part of the previous two models. Hackman (1987) adds a somewhat different wrinkle, however, by proposing that material resources moderate the relation between the process criteria of effectiveness and group effectiveness. A group can operate in a very favorable organizational context, have favorable design features, translate these favorable conditions into positive group processes, and, ultimately, *not* be successful. For example, a production team will not be successful if it does not have the tools necessary to produce the required product(s).

Shea and Guzzo's (1987) Model

Shea and Guzzo (1987) proposed a model of group effectiveness that is much less extensive than those previously described but nonetheless highlights some important determinants of group effectiveness. According to their model, group effectiveness is a consequence of three key factors: (1) *outcome interdependence,* (2) *task interdependence,* and (3) *potency.* Outcome interdependence reflects the extent to which members of a group share a common fate. An example of high outcome interdependence would occur if all of the members of a group were to receive a cash bonus because the group performed well. As one might expect, outcome interdependence is impacted, to a large extent, by organizational compensation practices. According to Shea and Guzzo (1987), a high degree of outcome interdependence will foster many of the behaviors necessary for groups to be effective—for example, cooperation, workload sharing, and so on. On the other hand, if group members' outcomes are largely independent, they will reduce the chances that group members will act cooperatively, and, hence, will undermine group effectiveness.

Task interdependence involves the degree to which members of a group have to depend on each other to get their work done. Interdependence is typically cited as one of the crucial characteristics that define groups. Thus, task interdependence can be seen more as a test of the appropriateness of groups than as a direct determinant of effectiveness per se. As one might expect, groups will generally be more effective when the tasks they are performing require a certain amount of interdependence. If there is very little interdependence, this is a sign that a group may not be appropriate or that the task may need to be redesigned (see Comment 12.2).

Potency reflects the *collective* belief, among group members, that the group can be effective (Guzzo, Yost, Campbell, & Shea, 1993). It is analogous to the individual-level construct of self-efficacy, which represents individuals' beliefs that they can carry out various

COMMENT 12.2

TO GROUP OR NOT TO GROUP?: A CRUCIAL QUESTION

ALTHOUGH ORGANIZATIONS ARE often quite rational, they are also subject to fads and fashion. After all, decisions in organizations are made by *people,* and people are certainly persuaded by fad and fashion to make a variety of personal choices. (What else could *possibly* explain the popularity of leisure suits in the '70s!).

The use of groups in organizations has literally skyrocketed in the past 20 years, and there is no sign that this trend will be reversed. The trend's positive aspect is that, for many organizational tasks, groups are highly appropriate. That is, much of the work performed in today's organizations requires a high degree of coordination and interdependence. Furthermore, the speed at which the competitive environment changes often makes it unlikely that one person can keep up with everything; thus, knowledge sharing among group members is often critical.

Despite all of the positive aspects of groups, they are certainly not appropriate for every task, nor do they fit well with the culture of every organization. Generally speaking, groups tend *not* to work well when tasks require highly independent work, or in organizations that do not encourage and value participation among their employees. The author has seen many cases, both as an employee and an external consultant, where groups are formed with very little consideration as to whether they are appropriate. It is as if managers often form groups as a "reflex action," which suggests that, in some instances, the use of groups is due to fad or fashion ("Everybody uses groups") rather than serious task-related considerations. This is unfortunate because, in such instances, groups may actually create more problems than they solve.

Does this mean that organizations should not use groups? Not at all. It does mean, however, that organizations need to think very carefully about task-related demands, and realistically appraise their culture before they create groups to perform tasks.

---

courses of action (Bandura, 1997). According to Shea and Guzzo (1987), potency is the most proximal determinant of group effectiveness—a proposition that has received some empirical support (e.g., Riggs & Knight, 1994). Presumably, potency positively impacts group effectiveness because it fosters persistence and may also lead to greater cooperation and cohesion among group members (cf. Jex & Bliese, 1999). In reality, however, relatively little is known about the specific mechanisms that link potency (and similar constructs) to group effectiveness.

Shea and Guzzo (1987) proposed that three key variables contribute to group potency: (1) *resources,* (2) *rewards,* and (3) *goals.*

As one would expect, when a group has access to numerous resources, their availability will reinforce group members' perceptions that they are capable of performing any task and responding to any challenge. Rewards are an important determinant of potency because they signal that performance means something, and this signal provides a group with an incentive to develop the internal capabilities necessary to perform well. To the extent that groups have challenging, specific goals, this enhances effort and persistence, as well as performance strategy development. All of these, in turn, should enhance potency. The contribution of rewards, resources, and goals to potency, and ultimately to effectiveness, has been supported empirically (Guzzo & Campbell, 1990), although clearly more work needs to be done.

Campion's Synthesis of Group Effectiveness Models

Campion, Medsker, and Higgs (1993) provided an extensive review of the group effectiveness literature and, based on that review, provided a model of group effectiveness that represents a synthesis of all of the models covered up to this point (as well as some others). Thus, what is presented in this section is not a new model; rather, it might be described as a "meta" model of group effectiveness because it represents a hybrid of many others.

This synthesis of group effectiveness models is presented in Figure 12.4. Notice that this model is clearly simpler than the first three that were described. Only factors that directly impact group effectiveness are proposed; thus, many of the intermediate linkages and moderator variables described in previous models are not included. The column labeled "Themes/Characteristics" indicates that there are essentially five general direct determinants of group effectiveness. The first of these, *job design,* centers around the nature of the task that the group is performing. According to Campion et al. (1993), the key aspects of a group's task environment include the degree of self-management and participation among group members, as well as the level of variety, significance, identity, and opportunity for feedback that is built into a group's task. High levels of effectiveness are associated with high degrees of all of these factors, although for different reasons. Self-management and participation enhance the group's sense of ownership of their work, and the task characteristics are likely to have their effects through enhanced intrinsic motivation.

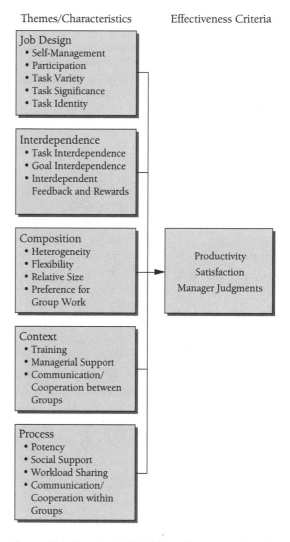

FIGURE 12.4
Campion's Synthesis Model of Group Effectiveness

Source: M. A. Campion, G. J. Medsker, and A. C. Higgs. (1993). Relations between work group characteristics and effectiveness: Implications for designing effective work groups. *Personnel Psychology, 46,* 823–850. Reprinted by permission.

The second determinant of effectiveness is labeled *interdependence.* This represents the degree to which group members are interdependent in terms of the tasks that they perform, the goals that the group adopts, the feedback they receive, and the rewards they strive for. As with Shea and Guzzo's (1987) model, Campion et al. (1993) proposed that higher levels of interdependence in all of these areas should enhance effectiveness. This is proposed primarily because a high level of interdependence will tend to foster cooperation and will also lead group members to coordinate their efforts.

The third determinant, labeled composition, largely involves the characteristics of the group members themselves. One key aspect of this is the degree to which groups are composed of members who possess heterogeneous skills and are flexible enough to cover for each other when required. Another important factor here is the relative size of the group. Although there is no magic number that is recognized as the "correct" group size, the general rule of thumb is that groups should be large enough to do the work, but not too large (i.e., more is not better). Finally, the variable preference for group work is somewhat unique because it is not contained in the previous models. Some people simply like or dislike working in some groups more than others.

The third category, labeled *context,* is comprised of factors in the organizational environment in which the group performs. These include the training available to groups, the degree to which managers support groups, and the extent to which there is cooperation and communication among different groups. Groups will be most effective when the organizational context provides plentiful training opportunities, when managers support groups, and when there is a high degree of cooperation and communication among groups.

The last determinant of group effectiveness in this model is *process.* This represents potency, or group members' collective perceptions of the group's capabilities, as well as the levels of social support, workload sharing, and communication/cooperation within the group. As with previous models of group effectiveness, Campion et al. (1993) proposed that a positive group process directly facilitates group effectiveness. That is, groups are more successful when there are high levels of potency (i.e., members believe in the group's capabilities), social support, workload sharing, and communication/cooperation among members.

The final notable feature of the Campion et al. (1993) model is the category of "effectiveness criteria." These criteria are largely based on Hackman's (1987) definition of group effectiveness; however, notice that the one component of Hackman's definition that is missing is *viability,* or the likelihood that members of a group will work together in the future.

The Campion et al. (1993) model provides a comprehensive account of the major factors that impact group effectiveness, and has received empirical support. Specifically, Campion et al. (1993) and Campion, Papper, and Medsker (1995) showed that many of the characteristics proposed to be related to group effectiveness were related to effectiveness criteria among employees in a large insurance company. Thus, like Gladstein (1984), Campion et al. (1993) not only proposed a model but tested it as well. The most obvious weakness in the Campion et al. (1993) model is that it proposed direct relations only between themes/characteristics and effectiveness criteria.

A Summary of the Group Effectiveness Models

In this section, we examined four of the most widely cited models of group effectiveness, and one recent attempt to synthesize these models. The common characteristic in all of these is that they follow the familiar

Input–Process–Output sequence—that is, they propose that aspects of the organizational context (e.g., rewards, interdependence, and task design) directly impact the *way* a group works, and this, in turn, impacts effectiveness. The critical role attributed to group process is somewhat ironic, for two reasons. First, there does not appear to be a high level of agreement among theorists as to the most important characteristics of group process. For example, in Hackman's (1987) model, group process is described primarily in terms of a group's approach to its task. In contrast, Campion et al. (1993) highlight variables such as social support and cooperation. This implies that the crucial elements of group process center around interpersonal relations among group members. Second, although empirical research is somewhat limited, there does not appear to be a great deal of support for the idea that group process (however one defines it) is a critical proximal cause of group effectiveness (Campion et al., 1993, 1995; Gladstein, 1984; see Comment 12.3).

COMMENT 12.3

GROUP PROCESS: CAUSE, CONSEQUENCE, OR CORRELATE?

AT THIS POINT, it is undoubtedly evident to readers that *group process* is considered an important variable in the group effectiveness literature. For example, this variable occupies a prominent position in most models of group effectiveness and has been examined extensively in empirical research (Guzzo & Shea, 1992).

Despite the proposed importance of group process, it is also problematic in some respects. In the most general sense, group process reflects *how* a group does its work or performs its task. Unfortunately, this general definition can be represented by a variety of specific dimensions (e.g., communication, level of effort, resolution of conflicts, etc.), and researchers have yet to agree on a common definition. This makes it very difficult to compare findings across studies, because each researcher's measure of group process may be quite different.

Another difficulty with group process is that there is considerable disagreement regarding the *role* it plays in determining group effectiveness. Some view it as having a direct impact on effectiveness, others as a key mediating variable, and still others as a moderator variable (Hackman, 1992). It is also possible that group process has no causal impact on group effectiveness; it may be a byproduct of the structural characteristics of groups that has no relation to group effectiveness, or it may simply be a way for group members to retrospectively explain their success (Staw, 1975).

Despite the difficulties surrounding group process, it is unlikely that this variable will fade away. Thus, a major task in future group effectiveness research is to more clearly define this variable and determine the role it plays in group life.

Sources: R. A. Guzzo and G. P. Shea. (1992). Group performance and intergroup relations in organizations. In M. D. Dunnette and L. M. Hough (Eds.), *Handbook of industrial and organizational psychology* (2nd ed., Vol. 3, pp. 269–313). Palo Alto, CA: Consulting Psychologists Press; J. R. Hackman. (1992). Group influences on individuals in organizations. In M. D. Dunnette and L. M. Hough (Eds.), *Handbook of industrial and organizational psychology* (2nd ed., Vol. 3, pp. 199–267). Palo Alto, CA: Consulting Psychologists Press; and B. M. Staw. (1975). Attribution of the "causes" of performance: A general alternative interpretation of cross-sectional research on organizations. *Organizational Behavior and Human Performance, 13,* 414–432.

Despite their possible overreliance on group process, these models are valuable because they highlight a number of organizational and group factors that impact group performance. Furthermore, there appears to be a good deal of consensus on what these contextual factors are. For example, most models highlight the composition of the group, the reward systems under which groups work, the design of the task that the group is working on, the resources available to the group, the goals that are set for a group (or those that it sets for itself), and internal processes such as cohesiveness, communication, and conflict management. Organizations have some degree of control over all of these variables and thus may be able to change them in order to improve group effectiveness. Given their importance, each of these factors is examined in greater detail in the following section.

IMPORTANT DETERMINANTS OF GROUP EFFECTIVENESS

Although models of group effectiveness are useful in highlighting important variables that contribute to group effectiveness and in mapping out the processes by which they have such an impact, they are often short on detail. In this section, we take a closer look at several of the most common general determinants of group effectiveness. This treatment is not meant to be exhaustive; it will provide a reasonably comprehensive coverage of specific variables within these categories that impact group effectiveness.

Group Composition

Perhaps one of the most robust findings in the group effectiveness literature is that groups staffed with more highly skilled members are more effective than groups possessing lower absolute skill levels (Guzzo & Shea, 1992;

Hackman, 1987). For example, a football team with more skilled players will generally win more games than a team with less skilled players. This finding is consistent with the literature on individual-level performance that has shown a very robust relation between cognitive ability and performance (Schmidt & Hunter, 1998).

Given that group members' skill/ability is positively related to group effectiveness, does this mean that organizations need only hire talented people in order to make groups effective? Probably not. Another relatively consistent finding in the literature is that, although the *absolute* level of skill/ability in a group is important, organizations must also consider the *mix* of skills/abilities within groups (Campion et al., 1995). For example, if a basketball team is to be effective, it is certainly necessary to have players who are capable of scoring a lot of points. On the other hand, it is also important to have players who rebound well, and others who are defensive specialists. A team composed only of scorers would probably not do very well. In fact, it has been shown that diversity of group skills is positively related to group performance (Guzzo & Shea, 1992).

Despite the importance of group members' skill/ability, there are instances where even groups composed of highly talented members are ineffective. Thus, composition factors other than skill/ability must be considered. One of these is the personality of group members, which may be important for a number of reasons. As with individual-level performance (e.g., Barrick & Mount, 1991), the *absolute* levels of certain personality traits may relate directly to performance. That is, groups composed of some members with high levels of conscientiousness may be more effective than groups with members who have lower levels (Barrick, Stewart, Neubert, & Mount, 1998).

Another reason that group members' personality may be important is that it may impact the climate within the group. George (1990), for example, found that groups could be distinguished in terms of their "affective tone," which was determined by the personalities of individual group members. Groups with more positive affective tones were found to provide higher levels of service to customers—an important aspect of performance for these groups, who were employed in a retail environment. The fact that personality impacts the climate of groups should not be surprising, given that the climates of entire organizations are impacted by the personalities of individual employees (Schneider, 1987).

In addition to the direct impact of group members' personalities, as well as the impact on group climate, the particular *mix* of personalities within a group may also have an important impact on group effectiveness. Within group settings, individual group members may have personalities that "clash," thus leading to negative conflict. It is also possible that having *one* group member who possesses a very negative personality trait can have a negative impact on the processes within a group and may ultimately have a negative impact on performance. For example, in the previously mentioned study by Barrick et al. (1998), groups that had at least *one* member with a very low level of emotional stability reported lower levels of social cohesion, flexibility, communication, and workload sharing, and higher levels of conflict compared to groups that did not have such a member. Interestingly, though, having at least one group member with low emotional stability did not have a negative impact on group performance.

A final aspect of group composition that may contribute to group effectiveness is the attitudes of group members. The impact of group members' attitudes can be seen in one of two ways. The most direct way is what Campion et al. (1993) termed "preference for group work," which reflects whether people like working in group settings. Despite the proliferation of groups in organizations, it is still likely that *not everyone* enjoys working in group settings. Despite the camaraderie that is often found in collective work, group work can be frustrating because of social loafing, conflict, and other difficulties. Campion et al. (1993) found that where the average level of preference for group work was low, groups performed lower on several performance criteria.

Another way that attitudes may come into play involves the similarity of group members' attitudes. Social psychological research has shown conclusively that people tend to like people who are perceived as being similar to themselves (Byrne, 1971). Thus, groups are likely to function more effectively when there is at least a moderate level of similarity in their attitudes toward important things such as the effectiveness of the group leader, or the supportiveness of the organization (Bliese & Britt, 2001). Despite the potential value of agreement, it is also possible that agreement may be too high. When the members of a group agree on everything, this may suppress needed debate and may cause the group to become extremely resistant to change. Recall that this is one of the explanations of the groupthink phenomenon (Janis, 1982; Whyte, 1998).

Task Design

Another consistent theme among the models reviewed is that the design of a group's task is a key variable that impacts group effectiveness. The exact manner in which task design is proposed to impact group effectiveness varies considerably between models, however. At the most basic level, task design is important because it speaks to the issue of whether the task a group is performing is appropriate for groups. Generally speaking, tasks involving a high level of interdependence are best accomplished by groups. Conversely, tasks that require primarily independent work are best performed by individuals. The zeal to use groups may blind organizations to the fact that some tasks are best accomplished by individuals.

Assuming for the moment that the task a group is performing is appropriate for groups, in what other ways does task design impact group effectiveness? One way is through its motivational impact. Individuals' motivation can be increased by redesigning jobs to enhance features such as autonomy, feedback, skill variety, task significance, and task identity (Hackman & Oldham, 1980). This same basic logic applies to groups; thus, members of groups that are performing tasks that are challenging, interesting, and engaging are likely to be more motivated than members of groups performing more mundane tasks.

The design of a group's task is also important; it should dictate which task-related strategies are most appropriate. Even tasks that are well suited for groups can be approached in a variety of ways; thus, some task-related strategies will be more effective than others. Therefore, an important determinant of group effectiveness is the extent to which strategies and approaches are appropriate for the task(s) they are performing. It has been shown that groups (a) tend *not* to allocate much of their time to discussions of task-related strategies (Hackman & Morris, 1975), and (b) tend to be more effective when they do, especially when they are performing complex tasks (Hackman, Brousseau, & Weiss, 1976).

Beyond the important impact it has on effectiveness, the nature of a group's task is often a key to understanding group interactions and processes. Many of the behavioral

dynamics that occur within groups can be understood only within the context of the work that a group performs. For example, Denison and Sutton (1990) describe many of the dynamics (e.g., loud music, joking) that occur in an operating room. To a large extent, these behaviors represent group members' mechanism for reducing tension because the work they do often has life-and-death consequences.

Organizational Resources

Just as *individuals* need organizational resources to perform well, so do groups. Given this need for organizational resources, an important question is: "What specific organizational resources do groups need in order to be effective?" To a certain degree, groups need many of the same resources that individuals need. Consider, for example, Peters and O'Connor's (1988) classification of organizational conditions that constrain individual performance. Many of these conditions also apply to groups. For example, groups often need equipment, information, budgetary resources, and time, in order to accomplish their assigned tasks.

Groups may also have some important and unique resource needs. Chief among these are training and consultation on how to work as a group. Members of groups may need training and assistance in learning how to work cooperatively with others, understanding how to coordinate their efforts with other group members, and, perhaps, training in how to resolve task-related disputes. In the author's experience, many organizations form work groups and instruct group members to "work out the details" with respect to task completion, but the organizations ignore issues associated with the internal dynamics of the group. Such an approach is based on the rather naïve assumption that group work comes naturally to people and they will be able to adapt to it naturally. Even a collection of highly intelligent, reasonable individuals may perform very poorly as a group.

Another resource need that is unique to groups is *meeting space/time*. For a group to be successful, the members need to be more than a collection of individuals working on their own. To be a collective entity, groups need to come together face-to-face, communicate with each other about task-related matters, and develop some level of cohesion. If an organization provides no meeting space, or very limited time, a group may never fully develop into a mature performing unit.

A final resource to consider is leadership. Just as individuals often rely on leaders in order to be successful, groups need leadership in order to be effective. Leaders of groups, however, must strike a delicate balance between being too detached and unavailable and being too directive, particularly in "self-managed" or autonomous work groups. Hackman (1990) likens the leadership of groups to being on a "balance beam" to show how leaders must often strike this delicate balance. What, then, is the appropriate balance? That is a difficult question; the answer depends, to a large extent, on the nature of the group one is leading and the organization in which the group resides. For groups that are largely self-directed, Hackman suggests that leaders essentially need to provide the group with a "clear, engaging direction," provide task-related assistance and consultation as needed, and work within the organization to obtain resources for the group. For anyone who has filled this role, these are demanding activities that are quite different from more traditional forms of supervision.

Rewards

One of the most consistent findings with respect to individual-level performance is that rewards tend to enhance effort and, as a result, often lead to high levels of performance (Luthans & Kreitner, 1985). Rewards are also an important determinant of group performance, although the issues organizations face in designing group-level reward systems are vastly different from those faced when designing rewards for individuals. Many organizations make the mistake of espousing the value of "teamwork" while rewarding employees solely on the basis of their individual accomplishments. Under such conditions, it is unlikely that groups will perform very effectively. Recognizing this, more and more organizations have been developing group-based compensation plans (Lawler, Mohrman, & Ledford, 1995).

One of the most fundamental issues organizations face in designing reward systems for groups is the extent to which the work they do is truly interdependent. If the work that groups do *is* truly interdependent, then rewarding groups rather than individuals is appropriate (Wageman & Baker, 1997). But what if a group performs a task that is not highly interdependent? Group-level reward systems are then less appropriate and, in fact, may be downright unfair. Consider, for example, a group of five individuals who perform independently. If rewards are based on group performance and the group performs well, less competent group members are rewarded because they are lucky enough to be in a group with others who are highly competent. On the other hand, if the group performs poorly, highly competent individuals are penalized because they happen to be in a group with fellow employees who are much less competent than they are.

Another important issue that organizations must consider in the design of group-level reward systems is the interplay between individual and group-level rewards. It is rare to find organizations in which employees are rewarded *solely* on the basis of group-level performance. In most organizations that have group-level reward systems, these must co-exist with individual-level reward systems (DeMatteo, Eby, & Sundstrom, 1998). Furthermore, in most cases, individual-level reward systems are better established than those based on group performance. In the author's opinion, it is unrealistic to think that individual-level reward systems can be eliminated, even in organizations that depend heavily on the performance of groups.

It is important to *not* have individual and group-level reward systems work against each other. If a group-level reward system is going to be effective, it is important to *not* have behaviors encouraged by the individual-level reward system undermine group performance, and vice versa. This may seem to be a rather obvious proposition, but it is actually quite common in organizations. For example, in sales organizations, individuals are typically rewarded largely on the basis of the dollar value of their own sales. Thus, individuals are highly motivated to make as many sales as possible, and will likely allocate their time accordingly.

On the other hand, when one considers the performance of a sales *group,* each individual's effort to maximize his or her sales volume may not necessarily maximize the group effort. In the long run, the group may be better served if individual salespeople devote at least some of their time to servicing existing accounts, providing training and guidance to less experienced salespeople, and making sure they keep current on emerging product lines. Unfortunately, the prospect of earning high sales commissions may induce a form of "tunnel vision" in employees that ultimately undermines group performance. Furthermore, organizations are often quite naïve about this conflict between employees' maximizing their own rewards and contributing to

the performance of the group or of the organization as a whole (see Comment 12.4).

A third consideration in the design of group-level reward systems is the degree to which groups have control over their own performance. This is an issue in the design of individual-level reward systems, but it is especially salient with group-level reward systems because the performance of groups may be highly dependent on the efficiency and reliability of the technology they employ (Goodman, 1986), or may be limited by organizational resource constraints (Shea & Guzzo, 1987). Holding groups to high performance standards while, at the same time, providing them with faulty technology or very limited resources is unfair and counterproductive. Groups may be able to overcome such performance barriers (Tesluk & Mathieu, 1999), but it is questionable whether this can be done in the long run without having adverse motivational effects on group members and ultimately undermining the group's viability (Hackman, 1987).

Group Goals

In many ways, the impact of goals on group performance mirrors the impact on individual-level performance. For example, O'Leary-Kelly, Martocchio, and Frink (1994) conducted a meta-analysis of the group goal-setting literature and found strong support for the impact of goals on group performance. This finding has been reinforced by individual studies that have been conducted subsequent to this review (e.g., Whitney, 1994). Given such findings, it is tempting to simply conclude that there is a one-to-one correspondence between group and individual goal setting.

There are, however, some important differences in the dynamics associated with individual and group-level goal setting. For example, an important consideration in

COMMENT 12.4

ORGANIZATIONS GET WHAT THEY REWARD

ONE OF THE first courses that I took as a graduate student in the Master's program in I/O Psychology at the University of New Haven nearly 20 years ago was Organizational Behavior. The course was taught by Michael Morris, a Community Psychologist who had a great deal of knowledge about organizations, as well as a great sense of humor. Mike was, by far, one of the finest professors I had as a graduate student. I mention this class because in one of the first class meetings, Morris made the statement: "Organizations don't get what they *want,* they get what they *reward.*" After nearly 20 years, I don't remember if he was quoting someone else, but I do know that this statement made a big impression on me at the time. Furthermore, it is a statement I have found to be true in my own experience.

Unfortunately, the wisdom of this statement is often ignored when organizations utilize groups; that is, the reward systems in many organizations are designed to motivate and reward individual performance, despite the fact that a high level of group performance is needed and desired. To be sure, a high level of individual performance is not always incompatible with a high level of group performance. For example, a quarterback who has a banner year often leads his team to more victories. In other cases, however, individuals are often forced to make difficult tradeoffs between maximizing their individual accomplishments (and, in many cases, rewards) and contributing to the overall performance of the group. For a salesperson working on commission, taking time to help a new group member means lower financial rewards.

It is highly unlikely that even organizations making extensive use of groups will ever eliminate individual-level rewards. It is possible, though, to design systems in which individual-level rewards are compatible with group rewards. By doing this, organizations can avoid the hypocrisy of telling employees they should work as a group, but only rewarding them as individuals.

---

setting goals for groups is the interplay between these and individual-level goals. This is analogous to the dilemma organizations face in developing group-level reward systems. It has been found, for example, that group-level goals are much more effective when individuals either do not have goals, or have goals that are compatible with group goals (Mitchell & Silver, 1990). Thus, organizations must be cognizant of the overall goal system when they are developing performance-related goals for groups.

Another important divergence between the individual and group goal-setting literature has to do with the intervening mechanisms between goals and performance. Because the impact of goals is so well established, goal-setting researchers have recently focused the majority of their attention on explaining *why* goal setting works. Most explanations for the effects of goal setting have centered on the fact that goals serve as an important focal point for self-regulation (Klein, 1989), and goal commitment is a crucial intervening step between goals and performance (Ambrose & Kulik, 1999).

While comparatively less research has examined the processes responsible for group goal-setting effects, there is some evidence that the mechanisms responsible for these effects are quite different from those responsible at the individual level. For example, there is some evidence that "collective efficacy" may be an important intervening mechanism between group goals and performance. Whitney (1994) found that groups that were assigned difficult goals reported higher levels of collective efficacy, compared to groups with easier or "do your best" goals. Thus, groups given difficult goals may take this as a sign that the organization considers them more capable than other groups (e.g., "We have a difficult goal, therefore we must be good."). These enhanced feelings of competence may then subsequently lead to a high level of performance through many of the same mechanisms by which goals enhance individual-level performance (e.g., increased effort, commitment, strategy development).

Another important difference between individual and group-level goal processes is that difficult goals may enhance members' attraction to the group or to group cohesion (Whitney, 1994); that is, a difficult goal may serve to "draw group members together" in a way that enhances attraction to the group and ultimately enhances performance. It is important to point out, however, that for enhanced cohesiveness and attraction to facilitate group performance, a group must have norms that support high levels of performance (Seashore, 1954).

Group Process

Recall that nearly all models of group performance reviewed included *group process* as a key variable mediating the relation between structural characteristics of groups and group performance. Given the centrality of group process in such models, it is surprising that group process is not defined more precisely. Currently, different models of group effectiveness tend to highlight different features of group process as being more important than others. The purpose of this section is not to resolve this issue, but merely to focus on certain elements of group process that seem to be more important than others.

In the most general sense, group process represents *the way in which groups accomplish their tasks*. Group process is not concerned with *what* a group does or produces; rather, it is concerned with *how* a group does its work. Given this general definition, a number of different elements of group process may be important to group effectiveness. However, three that seem to stand out, at least with respect to group effectiveness, are communication, cohesiveness, and conflict management.

Communication within a group reflects both the amount of information flow and the manner in which information is disseminated. Groups in which members share little information with each other and communicate very infrequently tend to perform more poorly than groups with more free-flowing communication (Hackman, 1987). The size of this difference, however, depends to a large extent on the nature of the task that a group is performing. Highly interdependent and complex tasks have much greater information requirements than tasks that are simple or require very low levels of interdependence.

Another aspect of communication, which was discussed in the previous chapter, is the extent to which a group's style of communication is either highly centralized or highly decentralized. Recall that centralized forms of communication have been found to be effective when groups are performing tasks that are relatively simple and have few coordination requirements. Decentralization, however, tends to facilitate performance when a group is working on highly complex tasks or tasks that have high coordination requirements.

A manifestation of this issue (centralization versus decentralization) that the author has observed over the years when conducting team development activities is the extent to which all members of a group participate. Although no data can be presented to back this up, one of the most common attributes of teams that appeared to be performing well has been that *all* members tended to participate and voice their opinions. On the other hand, in more dysfunctional groups, it was common to find participation very uneven among group members. Typically, one or two highly vocal group members dominated a great deal of the group's deliberations. This may lead a group to become dysfunctional because those who are the most vociferous may not always have the best ideas (in fact, in the author's experience, the opposite is often the case). Thus, many potentially good ideas never see the light of day.

With respect to communication, a final issue that has only recently become important is groups' use of electronic communication (e.g., e-mail). Employees in many organizations rely heavily on electronic communication, and there has been some research on this form of communication. For example, although electronic communication is highly efficient for transmitting factual information (Carey & Kacmar, 1997), it is much less effective when a group's task is highly interdependent, or the information to be communicated is emotive in nature (Straus & McGrath, 1994). Also, because users of electronic communication may feel a certain degree of anonymity that is not possible in face-to-face encounters, electronic communications may be more blunt and less tactful (Dubrovsky, Keisler, & Sethna, 1991).

Research on electronic communication within groups is still relatively new, but some consistent findings are beginning to emerge. For example, it has been found that members of groups generally prefer *not* to use electronic communication media when important, task-related information must be communicated (Straus & McGrath, 1994). The reason: Electronic communication is a rather limited communication medium. It is not possible to use physical gestures and other forms of nonverbal communication, so it may take longer for a person to get a point across (McGrath, 1990).

Despite this somewhat negative assessment of electronic communication, there are some instances when it may be superior to have face-to-face communication. For example, if the purpose of the communication is simply to disseminate information, electronic communication is much more efficient than a face-to-face meeting. Some readers have probably had the experience of attending a meeting that was merely an "information dump" and could have been accomplished by other means (e.g., electronic transmission of information).

Another instance in which electronic communication may be effective is when groups are working on "brainstorming" tasks. Brainstorming is often used when groups need to come up with creative or novel ideas. The major ground rules of brainstorming are that participants should be encouraged to generate as many ideas as possible (e.g., quantity is more important than quality), ideas should not be evaluated as they are generated, and participants should try to build on the ideas of others. Certainly, under the right conditions, brainstorming can be done very well face-to-face. However, in many cases, participants may experience **evaluation apprehension,** or become hesitant at the prospect of sharing novel ideas in front of others. There is some evidence that when brainstorming is done through electronic communication, participants may overcome such apprehension (Gallupe et al., 1992). This is due largely to the anonymity that electronic communication allows.

The research on electronic communication, although still fairly new, is important. As more and more organizations make use of groups in which members are geographically dispersed (e.g., "virtual" groups), it will become crucial to understand the limitations of such arrangements. The little research done so far suggests that groups may lose something if they are allowed to communicate only electronically. Clearly, more research is needed to strengthen these findings and communicate other limitations of various communication media.

Group cohesiveness is another variable that is measured in most group effectiveness models, although not all models consider it to be an aspect of group process. Although cohesiveness has been defined in a variety of ways, most group researchers see it as the degree to which the members of a group are attracted to the group, and place a high value on group membership (Mudrack, 1989). In everyday language, cohesiveness is often described as the level of "team spirit" or "espirit de corps" that we see within groups.

It has been demonstrated that highly cohesive groups tend to be more effective when prevailing norms support high performance (Seashore, 1954). However, we also know that it may be possible for groups to be *too* cohesive. As was stated in Chapter 11, Janis (1982) believed that "groupthink" is likely to occur when groups are so cohesive that they lose the capacity to realistically appraise their capabilities. In terms of group process, this is manifested in the suppression of dissent and inaccurate appraisals of the environment.

More recent research suggests that group cohesiveness may be multidimensional, and that this may have an impact on group effectiveness. According to Hackman (1992), it is possible to distinguish between **interpersonal-based cohesiveness** and **task-based cohesiveness**. When cohesiveness is interpersonal, this suggests that members' attraction to the group is based largely on the fact that they like the other group members and enjoy their company. Members of a college fraternity are likely to be cohesive for largely interpersonal reasons. The same would apply to more informal groups and friendship cliques. When cohesiveness is task-based, this suggests that members' attraction to the group is largely based on their attraction to the task that the group is performing. The members of a presidential campaign staff may develop a high level of cohesiveness because of their mutual support for the candidate they are supporting. Members of professional sports teams may also develop this form of cohesiveness as they strive to win a championship.

Distinguishing between interpersonal and task-based cohesiveness may have important consequences for group effectiveness. According to a study conducted by Zaccaro and Lowe (1988), task-based cohesiveness was positively associated with group effectiveness. In contrast, interpersonal cohesiveness was unrelated to group effectiveness, although it did lead to more communication and attraction among group members. This suggests that just because people like each other and enjoy being together, they will not necessarily be an effective group. In fact, it would not be hard to imagine a scenario in which a very high level of interpersonal cohesiveness could even be counterproductive. Members of a group may enjoy each other so much that they allocate very little time to their task.

According to Hackman (1992), this distinction in forms of cohesiveness highlights very clearly the importance of a group's task design. If tasks are designed so that they are interesting, challenging, and psychologically engaging, this will likely increase the chances that group members will develop high task-based cohesiveness that will ultimately enhance a group's performance. On the other hand, if a group's task is very mundane and uninteresting, there is less chance that high levels of task-based cohesiveness will develop. Ultimately, group members may be very "lukewarm" about what they are doing, and this may be reflected in the group's performance. In the future, more research on the dimensionality of cohesiveness, and the implications of this, is needed.

A third very important component of group process that may impact group effectiveness is the manner in which groups handle conflicts. Any time people come together to accomplish a task collectively, some level of conflict is inevitable. Members of a group may disagree over a variety of issues, such as who should play a leadership role in the group or how the task should be approached. Some individuals may simply not like each other because of fundamental personality and value differences. In addition to the sources of conflict, the *level* of conflict may vary from very minor friendly disagreement all the way to physical aggression.

Although conflict is consistently negatively associated with group member attitudes, it is not always negatively associated with lower levels of group performance. According to Jehn (1994), conflict within groups can be characterized as being **task-related** and **emotion-related.** When conflict is task-related, group members have differences over task-related issues. For example, they may disagree on the way a group should prioritize its work; which work methods are most appropriate; or, perhaps, which group members should be performing which tasks. According to Jehn, task-based conflict does not detract from group effectiveness and, in many cases, can actually enhance it. When group members' disagreements center around task-related issues, this may facilitate communication about these issues and ultimately generate innovative ideas that enhance effectiveness.

In contrast, when conflict is emotion-related, group members have differences over more personal issues. Even reasonable people may "see the world differently" because of fundamental value differences, and thus not get along well. According to Jehn (1994), emotion-related conflict can and often does detract from group performance. In fact, if such conflicts are allowed to escalate to extremely high levels, they may ultimately lead to the abolishment of a group. Why is this form of conflict so destructive? One reason is that it is simply unpleasant for all group members. Being in a heated conflict with another person is unpleasant, and it is also unpleasant to *watch* such conflicts unfold. Thus, in many cases, group members may simply withdraw from such unpleasant situations.

Perhaps a more important reason that emotion-related conflicts reduce effectiveness is that they distract group members' attention away from important task-related matters. When two people in a group become bitter enemies, they may become so focused on "one upping" each other that they pay little attention to the task that they are supposed to be performing. A good example of this is in the movie *Tin Men.* Actors Richard Dreyfuss and Danny DeVito portray two aluminum siding salesmen who are embroiled in a conflict that continually escalates. The conflict takes on a life of its own and, by the end of the movie, the conflict essentially becomes the major focus of each character's life.

ENHANCING THE EFFECTIVENESS OF GROUPS

Assuming for the moment that an organization has identified tasks that are appropriate for groups, what specific steps can organizations take to increase the odds that groups will be effective? In this section, we examine three general approaches that organizations can take to enhance group effectiveness. As readers will note, these steps correspond to activities that are typically conducted by Human Resources departments in organizations. This was done intentionally, to emphasize that they are not just general concepts; they are concrete, "actionable" steps.

Selection

Based on research by Barrick et al. (1998), it appears that one way of improving group effectiveness is to simply use some of the same factors that have been found to be robust predictors of individual performance (Barrick & Mount, 1991; Schmidt & Hunter, 1998). Specifically, they found that average levels of general mental ability within groups were positively related to performance. In addition, it was found that average levels of conscientiousness were also positively related. Thus, to some degree, organizations can use selection to improve group performance in much the same way that they enhance individual performance.

Although much less research has accumulated on group performance as compared to individual performance, individual characteristics such as general mental ability and personality appear to explain much less variance in group than in individual performance. For example, Schmidt and Hunter (1998) found that general mental ability explained approximately 31% of the variance in individual performance. In comparison, Barrick et al. (1998) found that average general mental ability explained approximately 5% of the variance in group performance. Therefore, there are probably other group composition factors that need to be considered when selecting people for group work.

Recall that Campion et al. (1993) proposed and found evidence for a positive relation between "preference for group work" and several group-level performance criteria. Thus, organizations selecting people for

groups might be wise to consider whether these individuals prefer working in group settings. In Campion et al.'s study, there was a reasonable amount of variance in preference for group work, suggesting that people do indeed vary in the degree to which they enjoy working as part of a group. However, a potential problem with using such a measure, particularly with job applicants, is that they may not be truthful in reporting their preferences. That is, if they know that a job requires group work, they may report that they enjoy working in groups (even if they do not), to enhance their chances of being hired. Although little research to date has addressed this issue, Nagel (1999) found evidence, in a laboratory simulation, for this type of distortion. One way to deal with this issue might be to use other selection methods, such as personal history, to measure applicants' affinity for working in group situations.

Instead of considering individuals' preferences, selection efforts might be aimed at assessing the knowledge, skills, and abilities (KSAs) needed in order to work in groups. Stevens and Campion (1999) used this approach to develop a selection instrument that they labeled the *Teamwork Test*. The specific KSAs measured by this instrument are presented in Table 12.1. As can be seen, these are grouped into two general categories: Interpersonal KSAs and Self-Management KSAs. In the Interpersonal category, the KSAs deemed most important have to do with conflict resolution, collaborative problem solving, and communication. The Self-Management KSAs have to do with goal setting/time management and planning/task coordination.

Stevens and Campion (1999) also attempted to provide predictive validity evidence for this instrument in two organizations. Overall, their findings provided support for the predictive validity of this instrument. More specifically, their instrument explained variance

TABLE 12.1
Dimensions Comprising the Stevens and Campion (1999) Teamwork Test

I. Interpersonal KSAs
  A. Conflict Resolution KSAs
    1. The KSA to recognize and encourage desirable, but discourage undesirable team conflict.
    2. The KSA to recognize the type and source of conflict confronting the team and implement and appropriate resolution strategy.
    3. The KSA to implement an integrative (win-win) negotiation strategy, rather than the traditional distributive (win-lose) strategy.
  B. Collaborative Problem Solving KSAs
    4. The KSA to identify situations requiring participative problem solving and to utilize the proper degree and type of participation.
    5. The KSA to recognize the obstacles to collaborative group problem solving and implement proper corrective actions.
  C. Communication KSAs
    6. The KSA to understand communication networks, and to utilize decentralized networks to enhance communication where possible.
    7. The KSA to communicate openly and supportively; that is, to send messages that are (a) behavior- or event-oriented, (b) congruent, (c) validating, (d) conjunctive, and (e) owned.
    8. The KSA to listen nonevaluatively and to appropriately use active listening techniques.
    9. The KSA to maximize the consonance between nonverbal and verbal messages and to recognize and interpret the nonverbal messages of others.
    10. The KSA to engage in small talk and ritual greetings as a recognition of their importance.
II. Self-Management KSAs
  D. Goal Setting and Performance Management KSAs
    11. The KSA to establish specific, challenging, and accepted team goals.
    12. The KSA to monitor, evaluate, and provide feedback on both overall team performance and individual team-member performance.
  E. Planning and Task Coordination KSAs
    13. The KSA to coordinate and synchronize activities, information, and tasks among team members.
    14. The KSA to help establish task and role assignments for individual team members and ensure proper balancing of workload.

Source: M. J. Stevens and M. A. Campion. (1999). Staffing work teams: Development and validation of a selection test for teamwork settings. *Journal of Management, 25,* 207–228. Copyright © 1999. Reprinted with permission from Elsevier Science.

in group performance beyond that explained by the general mental ability of group members. This suggests that this instrument may ultimately be a useful tool for organizations, although some further development may be needed. These findings are also interesting because they suggest that working in groups may require certain unique skills and abilities that may not be assessed by traditional selection instruments.

Organizational Reward Systems

Nearly all of the models of group effectiveness covered earlier in this chapter mentioned rewards as being an important factor contributing to group effectiveness. Quite simply, groups tend to be more effective when organizations reward their efforts. Unfortunately, in many organizations where groups are utilized, the rewards are focused almost exclusively at the individual level. In fact, even in organizations that do have group-level rewards, these must coexist with individual-level reward systems. How then do organizations make sure that individual and group-level reward systems complement each other?

According to Wageman and Baker (1997), two important considerations in the design of group-level reward systems are **task interdependence** and **outcome interdependence.** As defined earlier, task interdependence reflects the extent to which group members must work collaboratively in order to get their work done. Outcome interdependence reflects the extent to which the members of a group share a "common fate"; that is, do they all receive the same positive or negative outcome if the group performs well or poorly? For a group-level reward system to work well, there must be alignment between task and outcome interdependence. Group-level reward systems work best when both task and outcome interdependence are high. If a great deal of interdependence is required to perform a task, it stands to reason that the outcomes group members receive should be similar.

As Wageman (1996) points out, however, group reward systems are often ineffective because these two forms of interdependence are misaligned. Consider, for example, a situation in which the work performed by group members is highly interdependent, but the outcomes they receive are not. This will likely create disincentives for the members of a group to work cooperatively because those who receive the highest rewards will be seen as being overrewarded. On the other hand, what if there is very little task interdependence, but a great deal of outcome interdependence? In a case like this, those who perform well may resent sharing a common fate with those whose performance is far below theirs. The major point is that organizations often fail to consider these two forms

of interdependence when rewarding groups, and thus may inadvertently create a disincentive for people to work as a group.

In Chapter 9, we discussed specific ways in which organizations may reward the performance of groups, so they will be mentioned only briefly here. The most common of these include profit sharing and gain sharing, although Employee Stock Ownership Plans may also be used for this purpose. The specifics of all of these compensation plans differ, but they all share one common characteristic: *They are appropriate primarily in situations where employees in groups work on highly interdependent tasks.* Thus, when they are designing group reward systems, organizations must pay particular attention to the nature of the work that groups are performing.

Organizations can also attempt to enhance the performance of groups through nonmonetary rewards such as awards and recognition. Again, as with monetary compensation, it is important that the awards and recognition that are provided to individuals do not negate the effects of those at the group level. In professional team sports, individual-level honors and recognition are often viewed as more important than collective achievement. After all, *individuals* are inducted to sports halls of fame, not *teams*. Thus, organizations not only need to reward group performance, but must also create a climate in which collective achievement is viewed as being at least as important as individual accomplishments.

Team Development Interventions

A final way that organizations may enhance the effectiveness of groups is through training or team development activities. Team development will be discussed in much more detail in Chapter 16, so only a brief overview will be provided here. According to Dyer (1987), team development represents a variety of team-based training interventions that are aimed at one or more crucial aspects of group functioning. For example, team development activities may be aimed at clarifying roles with a group, establishing goals and priorities, and tackling more sensitive interpersonal issues (Beer, 1976; French & Bell, 1995).

Specific forms of team development may be carried out quite differently, but most involve some common generic steps. For example, in most cases, groups participate in team development activities with the assistance of an external consultant or facilitator; "outside," in this case, means someone from outside the group (this can be either someone who is external to the organization, or someone who is an organizational member). Compared to a group member, an individual from outside the group can be much more objective about the group and its process.

Another characteristic common to most team development activities is that they are data-based; that is, some data about the function of the group are collected prior to the actual intervention. Typically, preintervention data are collected through surveys and interviews of group members, although other methods may also be used (e.g., archival data, observations). After data are collected and summarized, they are usually used as the basis for choosing the specific team development intervention. For example, if data indicate a lack of role clarity among group members, the focus of team development would typically be on role clarification (for an example, see Schaubroeck, Ganster, Sime, & Ditman, 1993).

While not a great deal of research has examined the impact of team development on group performance, there is some indication that it may improve group effectiveness. For example, in a review of the work group literature, Sundstrom, DeMeuse, and Futrell

(1990) found that team development activities, particularly those focused on task-related issues, have a positive effect on group performance. In contrast, when team development activities are focused on *interpersonal* issues, the results are much less positive. This may be due to the fact that the underlying causes of interpersonal problems within groups (e.g., personality and value differences) are much less amenable to changes, as compared to the causes of task-related problems.

THE FUTURE OF GROUPS IN ORGANIZATIONS

One of the reactions that I frequently encounter when I teach about group effectiveness in my courses is that students become somewhat let down or disillusioned when they realize all of the things that must "fall into place" for groups to be effective. They seem to approach the study of group effectiveness with the notion that groups are the answer to every organizational problem, but quickly realize that they are not. In fact, in some cases, groups may create many problems of their own.

Given the challenges associated with designing and managing groups, it might be tempting to conclude that groups are just another fad that will pass with time. In the author's opinion, this is not the case; groups are now a permanent part of organizational life and will continue to be in the foreseeable future. One reason for this is the fact that more and more of the work being performed in organizations is becoming complex and mentally demanding (i.e., "knowledge work"). Often, groups can be much more effective in tackling such complex tasks because they offer variety in the skills and knowledge of group members.

Another reason that groups will continue to flourish in organizations of the future is that they are highly compatible with the changing nature of employee–employer relationships. Organizations are becoming leaner; they are relying less and less on formal job descriptions and more and more on temporary employees. In this type of environment, it is very convenient for organizations to retain a small "core staff" of permanent employees and bring in temporary employees on an "as needed" basis. Furthermore, when temporary employees are brought into an organization, it is often advantageous to create project groups to accomplish tasks.

Given this trend, a future challenge for organizations is their ability to assemble groups and have them working effectively within a very short time frame. This may involve many of the factors discussed in this chapter, but those likely to be most important in the future are the characteristics of the individuals comprising groups. More specifically, in the future, it may be especially crucial for individuals to have a set of generic knowledge, skills, and abilities (Stevens & Campion, 1999) that facilitates group effectiveness. This obviously raises the issue of where individuals will acquire these generic KSAs. They might be trained by organizations, but it is unlikely that this would be effective if temporary employees are being used. Perhaps, in schools of the future, "teamwork" will be as common as reading, writing, and arithmetic.

CHAPTER SUMMARY

In this chapter, we focused specifically on the issue of group effectiveness. In doing so, the relative emphasis shifted from predominantly laboratory-based social psychological research to the organizational psychology group literature. Although many definitions of group effectiveness have been proposed, Hackman's (1987) is the most well accepted. This defines effectiveness in terms of task performance, group viability, and the satisfaction of group members.

There have also been a number of group effectiveness models; several were reviewed in the chapter. We began by examining McGrath's model (1964) and ended up with Campion's attempt to synthesize many group effectiveness models. Although the specifics of the models described are different, a common characteristic of most is the idea that group process is a key mediating variable. Nevertheless, the importance of group process has not been supported well empirically, and it is possible that causal sequences other than the familiar Input–Process–Output may explain group effectiveness.

From the group effectiveness models described, several specific determinants of group effectiveness were chosen for further review. These included group composition, task design, reward systems, and group process. As with individual performance, groups need members with relevant skills/abilities in order to be successful. However, research has also shown that it is important to have the right mixture of abilities/skills, and that personality and attitudes are important as well.

Task design is an important determinant of group effectiveness, for several reasons. Groups are often ineffective because they are performing tasks that are not well suited for groups; organizations often overlook this fact in their zeal to utilize groups. Task design is important in determining the most important strategies for groups to use, and it may also have motivational effects on group members.

As with individual performance, rewards are a very important determinant of group performance. Simply put, if organizations want groups to perform well, reward systems must be designed so that the group's accomplishments are rewarded. In designing group reward systems, however, organizations must consider the level of both task and outcome interdependence. It is also crucial that the individual and group reward systems do not work against each other.

Group process is ubiquitous in the group effectiveness literature. Ironically, despite its importance, there is a lack of consensus on what actually constitutes the most important dimensions of group process. No attempt is made to resolve this issue here; rather, three aspects of group process are highlighted: (a) the level of communication within the group, (b) the degree to which a group is cohesive, and (c) the manner in which a group manages and resolves conflict.

Based on the determinants of group effectiveness, three general approaches to enhancing group effectiveness were offered: (a) selection, (b) reward system administration, and (c) team development activities. As with individual performance, organizations can enhance the performance of groups by selecting highly skilled individuals. Selection for group work, however, may require a consideration of individuals' preferences as well as specific group-related skills. The most fundamental issue with regard to reward administration is simply to make sure that *groups* are rewarded for their performance. Organizations must also make sure that group-level reward systems fit the tasks that groups perform, and that they are aligned with individual-level reward systems.

In the chapter, the final method of enhancing group effectiveness was team development. Team development activities represent training interventions that are designed to improve various aspects of group functioning (e.g., definition or roles, setting goals). Most team development interventions utilize the services of an outside consultant/facilitator, and most are data-based. Research has shown that team development activities may enhance group effectiveness. It appears, however, that interventions focused on task-related issues are more successful than those focused on interpersonal issues.

SUGGESTED ADDITIONAL READINGS

Alper, S., Tjosvold, D., & Law, K. S. (2000). Conflict management, efficacy, and performance in organizational teams. *Personnel Psychology, 53,* 625–642.

Forbes, D. P., & Milliken, F. J. (1999). Cognition and corporate governance: Understanding boards of directors as strategic decision making groups. *Academy of Management Review, 24,* 489–505.

Forrester, R., & Drexler, A. B. (1999). A model for team-based organizational performance. *Academy of Management Executive, 13,* 36–49.

Simons, T. L., & Peterson, R. S. (2000). Task conflict and relationship conflict in top management teams: The pivotal role of intragroup trust. *Journal of Applied Psychology, 85,* 102–111.

Wheelan, S. A. (1999). *Creating effective teams: A guide for members and leaders.* Thousand Oaks, CA: Sage.

Chapter Thirteen

Intergroup Behavior in Organizations

At this point, readers should have a good understanding of general principles governing group behavior, as well as specific factors impacting group effectiveness in organizations. There is, however, another important aspect of group behavior: interrelationships *between* groups. In the social and organizational psychology literature, the vast majority of research and theory is focused on behavior *within* groups; that is, groups are portrayed as self-contained entities. *Intra*group behavior is important and contributes greatly to organizational effectiveness. However, we also know that different groups often must work *together* if organizations are to prosper.

To highlight the importance of intergroup behavior, consider an example of a fairly typical organizational activity: hiring a new employee. In most organizations, a decision to hire a new employee typically begins in the department or unit that is doing the hiring. For example, in a university setting, if a psychology department wants to hire a new

organizational psychologist, that department would typically send a hiring request to a university or college committee that is set up to handle faculty staffing issues. Assuming that the request to hire is approved, the psychology department would then work with the human resources department, and perhaps the college dean's office, throughout the hiring process. Notice that throughout this process, a great deal of intergroup cooperation is needed to successfully complete the task of hiring a new faculty member.

In this chapter, intergroup behavior is covered by first describing the various forms of intergroup transactions that typically occur in organizations. Discussion then shifts to a variety of factors that impact both the frequency and the quality of intergroup interactions. From there, we address the issue of intergroup conflict by describing both the causes and the consequences of conflict between groups, as well as a number of strategies that can be used to keep intergroup conflict to manageable levels. The chapter concludes with a description of ways in which organizations can decrease the level of interdependence between groups and, by doing so, decrease the potential for conflict.

TYPES OF INTERGROUP INTERACTIONS

Given the vast array of organizational tasks that may require interactions among two or more groups, intergroup behavior might take a variety of forms. According to Thomas (1976), the nature of intergroup interactions depends largely on the degree to which groups *must* interact in order to achieve their goals (i.e., their interdependence), and the degree of *compatibility* between the goals of different groups. Crossing these two factors yields the matrix in Figure 13.1.

As can be seen at the bottom of the matrix, there are some instances in which groups simply do not have to interact in order to achieve their goals. Groups can accomplish some goals by acting more or less autonomously. If this is the case, and if the goals of two groups are reasonably compatible, interaction between these two groups can best be described as **accommodation**. This means that there is some cordial "give and take" between the two groups. An example of accommodation might be two baseball teams' deciding the order in which

FIGURE 13.1

Conceptual Map of the Various Forms of Intergroup Behavior

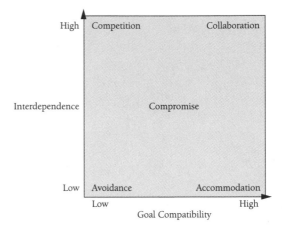

they are going to use the field for pregame practice. This is obviously not a crucial issue, so the coaches of the two teams might have a cordial discussion and make a decision.

Where interaction is not crucial and the goals of two groups are *incompatible,* the typical interaction is best described as **avoidance**; the groups can simply avoid interacting with each other. In many organizations, there are groups or departments that are pursuing vastly different and, to a large extent, conflicting goals. A group of researchers working on new product development is pursuing a goal that is far different from that of a group of engineers attempting to streamline current production processes. Such groups obviously have different goals, and these goals are largely independent. Thus, in many organizations, these types of groups can avoid interacting with each other.

Given the level of complexity in today's organizations, and the interdependence of many tasks, the reality is that groups often must interact with other groups in order to accomplish their goals. This state of affairs is reflected in the top portion of the matrix in

Figure 13.1. As can be seen, when interaction is crucial to goal accomplishment and the goals of two groups are largely compatible, the interactions between groups can best be described as **collaboration.** An example of this might be two research groups that are researching the same phenomenon. One group may possess expertise that the other does not have. Thus, by working together collaboratively, these two research groups accomplish more than they would if each was to work independently.

Where interaction is crucial to goal attainment, yet the goals of groups are incompatible, the interactions are typically characterized by **competition.** Two top collegiate football teams that are striving for a national championship are interdependent in the sense that they must play each other in order to achieve their goal. However, their goals are obviously diametrically opposed—there can only be *one* national champion. Thus, when these two teams play, there is a very high level of competition. There may also be instances in organizations when groups compete with each other. Sales groups may compete for awards, different academic departments may compete for scarce resources, and different political parties may compete for the right to govern. One negative aspect of competition is that it may lead to destructive conflict among groups. On the other hand, if approached in a positive manner, competition has the potential to bring out the best in a group (see Comment 13.1).

The final form of intergroup interaction depicted in Figure 13.1 is **compromise.** This form occurs when interaction is *moderately* important to goal attainment and there is also a *moderate* degree of goal compatibility between groups. Probably the best example of this form of interaction is that which occurs between unions and management within unionized organizations. It is not crucial for these groups to interact frequently in order for each to achieve its goals. However, there obviously must be a certain degree of interaction in order to produce a collective bargaining agreement and to periodically resolve disputes. With regard to goal compatibility, there is probably what could be described as a modest level. A union's goal of obtaining higher wages and benefits for its membership would appear to be incompatible with an organization's goal of controlling personnel costs. However, a union has a vested interest in an organization's staying in business and, for that reason, may at times compromise on issues. Conversely, an organization may make concessions to a union at times because its employees are needed to produce a product or perform a service for customers.

PREDICTORS OF INTERGROUP INTERACTION PATTERNS

Although interactions between groups in organizations are obviously influenced by the goals being pursued, many other factors impact the quality and frequency of intergroup interactions. In the intergroup literature, those that have been shown to have the most consistent effect are interdependence, organizational culture, past history, and the social networks that evolve within organizations. Each of these is reviewed below.

Interdependence

A relatively consistent theme, in reviews of the intergroup literature (see Alderfer & Smith, 1982, and Brett & Rognes, 1986), is that a major factor impacting the interactions between groups is *interdependence*. The degree to which groups depend on each other increases the frequency of interaction and, in some cases, heightens the potential for conflict.

COMMENT 13.1

THE PROS AND CONS OF INTERGROUP COMPETITION

As with individuals, groups in an organization often find themselves in competition. This is often due to a scarcity of organizational resources, but may also be due to the fact that the goals of different groups may be incompatible. For example, if one work group gains approval from upper management, this often means that others do not. Thus, groups in organizations are often in a position of competing against each other and, typically, are keenly aware of this competition.

Is competition between groups a bad thing? Not necessarily. When groups are competing, this may serve as an important source of motivation to group members. They may work harder, come up with more innovative ideas, and behave more cooperatively toward each other when they are competing with other groups. These types of behaviors, if widely prevalent, have the potential for enhancing *organizational* effectiveness. There are, however, some negative aspects of intergroup competition. For example, members of competing groups may communicate very little and develop distorted perceptions of each other. It is also not unusual for groups in competition to actively try to thwart each others' efforts in order to "win."

Can organizations foster some level of intergroup competition, but not let it escalate to destructive levels? This is a difficult question to answer, but, in this author's opinion, it is possible. The most likely way to accomplish this is by focusing competition primarily on the *tasks* that groups are performing, rather than on the personalities of individual group members. People should be able to compete without having to dislike each other. Competition can also be more positive when organizations move away from a "winner takes all" mentality. When groups perform better by competing with each other, there may in fact be many "winners." Ultimately, the question really revolves around how organizations manage intergroup competition.

There are, however, different *forms* of interdependence and these may have very different consequences for group interactions. According to Thomas (1976), **pooled interdependence** exists when groups are relatively independent of each other but their combined outputs contribute to the organization as a whole. A good example of pooled interdependence is the organizational structure of automotive manufacturers such as General Motors. Divisions such as Chevrolet, Buick, and Pontiac operate relatively independent of each other, yet they combine to determine the profitability of the corporation as a whole. To some extent, it is a misnomer to call this arrangement *interdependence* because these divisions run fairly autonomously. Keep in mind, however, that even when there is pooled interdependence, groups are not *completely* independent of each other. For example, if the Pontiac Division of General Motors is performing poorly, the other divisions may be negatively impacted.

A second common form of interdependence in organizations is referred to as **sequential interdependence.** In this form, the *outputs* of one group serve as the *inputs* to another. In many organizations, a good example of sequential interdependence can be seen when new products are developed. For instance, the market research department may conduct a study and determine that consumers desire a product that the organization currently does not offer. This information may then be passed on to the research and development department, which is responsible for the actual development of this new product. Once the new product has been developed and tested, the information from research and development may be passed on to the production engineers who will determine how this new product will be manufactured.

Reciprocal interdependence is commonly found among groups in organizations. This form of interdependence involves a series of continuous mutual exchanges among groups. As one might guess, reciprocal interdependence is highly complex and requires the most interaction among groups. In many organizations, reciprocal interdependence commonly exists between groups involved in manufacturing and maintenance. A manufacturing department depends on maintenance to repair equipment in order to minimize production delays and machine downtime. Conversely, a maintenance department relies heavily on the cooperation of those on the manufacturing side when repairs must be made and when preventative maintenance measures are taken. Note that one of the hallmarks of reciprocal interdependence is that there is a relatively equal status among the groups. Thus, with this form of interdependence, it is less likely that one group can gain the "upper hand" on another. The dependence is mutual.

What determines the type of interdependence that exists between any two groups? One obvious determinant is the nature of the *task*(s) that different groups are performing. Different tasks, by their very nature, require different levels and forms of interaction between groups. Generally speaking, groups that perform relatively complex tasks will often require higher levels of interaction compared to groups performing simpler tasks. Complex tasks may have greater information requirements that can only be satisfied through interaction with other groups.

Another important determinant of the form of interdependence between groups is *organizational structure*. As will be shown in Chapter 14, an organization can be structured in a variety of ways, ranging from very hierarchical, bureaucratic forms to structures that revolve primarily around important organizational projects. Often, when organizations are very formal and there are rigid boundaries around groups, the need and desire for intergroup interaction may be decreased. Hence, groups can operate fairly autonomously. Conversely, when such boundaries are more permeable, a great deal more intergroup interaction may be required, and, consequently, higher levels of interdependence will result.

A final potential determinant of interdependence is the authority system that predominates within an organization. Meyer and Allen (1997) draw a distinction between **control** and **commitment** organizations. In control organizations, the primary authority mechanisms center on formal rules and monitoring mechanisms. In such an environment, interdependence may be discouraged because it makes control more difficult. In commitment organizations, much more authority rests with individual employees, and there is less emphasis on formal rules and monitoring. In this type of environment, communication may flow very freely among groups, and there is a great deal more potential for interdependence.

Organizational Culture

Organizational culture essentially represents the set of implicitly shared norms and values that predominate within a given organization (Schein, 1990). With respect to intergroup relations, some organizations may develop cultures that encourage and value positive intergroup interactions. For example, some universities have cultures that encourage and facilitate interdepartmental cooperation. Individuals in such a culture may engage in a great deal of interdisciplinary work without even thinking about it, because it is so ingrained in the culture of the institution. Conversely, in other organizations, the culture may discourage most forms of intergroup interaction. For example, in some universities, the culture makes academic departments very "compartmentalized." Communication with other academic departments is infrequent and they are viewed with suspicion. In this type of culture, it is doubtful that productive cross-departmental collaboration will occur.

It is interesting to note that the effects of culture become particularly salient during the socialization of new employees. The newcomers are informed very quickly about group customs regarding expected behaviors toward other groups. If a new employee mistakenly behaves the wrong way in this regard, he or she is quickly "brought into line" and reminded of the prevailing norms regarding interaction with other groups. Given the power of norms to shape behavior (e.g., Hackman, 1992), such messages will typically have a very important effect on the general quality of intergroup relations.

Past History with Intergroup Relations

Another important factor that influences the quality of relations between pairs of groups is *past history*. If the members of two groups have generally had positive experiences working together, they are likely to approach future interactions in a positive manner. Conversely, if interactions have been contentious, groups will tend to approach future interactions with a great deal of apprehension and suspicion. Unfortunately, apprehension and suspicion on the part of one group tend to evoke similar feelings in members of other groups (see Comment 13.2).

Readers may wonder whether the influence of history tends to decay over time as new members, who do not have the "baggage" associated with past interactions, are brought into groups. As noted in Chapter 3, one of the major dimensions of socialization into organizations is being "educated" about the past history of the organization and, in many cases, of the specific work group that a new employee joins (Van Maanen & Schein, 1979). This education often includes a detailed history of events that have involved other organizational groups. Thus, in many cases, new employees are expected to "carry the baggage" associated with past conflicts and adjust their behavior accordingly. Employees who resist such pressures may encounter very negative sanctions from their more experienced coworkers, or, perhaps, may never become fully integrated into the group.

Social Networks in Organizations

When all is said and done, much of the quality of intergroup interaction depends on the nature of the relationships (i.e., the social network) that develop between individual members of groups. To the extent that individual members of a group develop cordial relationships with individual members of another group, this should enhance the quality of intergroup relationships. Evidence of this principle can often be seen in the area of international relations. For example, when leaders of nations get along well and have rewarding interpersonal relationships, this

COMMENT 13.2

THE IMPACT OF PAST HISTORY: A NEGLECTED TOPIC

BECAUSE A GREAT deal of research on intergroup behavior has been carried out in laboratory settings, there is very little empirical evidence on the impact of past history on intergroup relations. However, anyone who has joined an established group in an organization would likely attest to the powerful impact that past history has on intergroup relations. As with individuals, groups in organizations often have histories of dealing with each other that may even transcend the tenure of individual group members.

If groups have had a positive history of working together to get things done, interactions will be approached positively by the members of both groups. Furthermore, these positive interactions will likely be mutually reinforcing and the positive relations between groups will continue. In contrast, when two groups have a negative history, it may be difficult for them to work productively in the future. Members of each group may be taught to view each other with a great deal of suspicion and mistrust. Unfortunately, when people are treated with suspicion and mistrust, this evokes similar feelings and a negative spiral may begin.

Future research is needed on the mechanisms that are involved in communicating the "past history" of intergroup relations to new group members. The greatest need, however, is future research that examines how groups that have negative histories can reverse this negative spiral and develop positive working relations.

compatibility often positively influences diplomatic relations (see Comment 13.3).

Although not a great deal of research has linked personal relationships within organizations with quality of intergroup relations, there is some evidence that they do have an impact. For example, LaBianca, Brass, and Gray (1998) examined the social networks within a large health care facility, and found that *negative* relations among individual members of different groups had an impact on the quality of intergroup relations. When one member of a group had a negative encounter with a member of another group, this negatively impacted the quality of the relations between the two groups. Interestingly, positive social ties between individuals from different groups had no impact on intergroup relations. These findings suggest that when group members form impressions of other groups, they utilize information that is derived from the direct experience of their own group members. This may be much easier than approaching encounters with other group members objectively and, on that basis, forming an impression of the other group. These findings also suggest that individuals weigh *negative* information more heavily than *positive* information in forming their impressions of other groups. One reason for this may simply be that negative information is more distinctive and thus is more "attention getting" than positive information (Taylor, 1991). Another related reason may be that most people generally approach interpersonal interactions in a positive manner. Thus, negative interactions run counter to our expectations and thus receive more weight in the impression formation process.

THE IMPACT OF PERSONAL RELATIONSHIPS ON INTERGROUP RELATIONS

PEOPLE OFTEN THINK of international relations as being governed by highly formal mechanisms such as treaties and collective alliances such as NATO. Such formal mechanisms do exist and do influence the transactions between nations. We also know, however, that international relations are influenced by highly personal relationships that develop between national leaders.

A good example of this is the relationship that ultimately developed between U.S. President George Bush and Soviet leader Mikhail Gorbachev during the first term of Bush's presidency. Interestingly, the first meeting between these two men, which occurred in 1988 when Bush was president-elect, did not go very well. Despite getting off on the wrong foot initially, Bush and Gorbachev ultimately developed a genuine friendship. Furthermore, the friendship that developed between these two world

leaders may have been one of the reasons that the U.S. supported Gorbachev, even when it became obvious that he was losing his grip on power. Complementing this strong relationship between Bush and Gorbachev was an equal, if not stronger, relationship between U.S. Secretary of State James Baker and Soviet Foreign Minister Eduard Shevardnadze.

Although events in most organizations are not as dramatic as those that occurred between the United States and the former Soviet Union, it is true that relations between groups in any setting are strongly impacted by the interpersonal relations that develop between group leaders or members. When all is said and done, intergroup relations, like most forms of social behavior, are a "relationship business."

Source: G. H. W. Bush and B. Skowcroft. (1999). *A world transformed.* New York: Knopf.

INTERGROUP CONFLICT

Even a cursory perusal of the intergroup literature reveals that much of it is focused on *conflict* between groups. That is not to say that all intergroup encounters are negative. However, as we will see in this section, many conditions surrounding intergroup transactions in organizations greatly increase the potential for relations between groups to be highly contentious. In this section, we focus on the conditions that lead to intergroup conflict, describe the potential effects of intergroup conflict, and finally explore ways to diffuse or reduce it.

Causes of Intergroup Conflict

As one might imagine, conflict between groups in organizations may be caused by a number of different factors. Thus, pinning down the causes of conflict to a manageable number is no easy task. However, within organizations, a small number of factors seem to contribute disproportionately to intergroup conflict. These include competition for resources, goal incompatibility, time incompatibility, and contentious influence tactics. Each is discussed briefly below.

One of the realities of life in most organizations is that *resources are scarce.* Most organizations cannot provide groups with lavish support in the form of budgets, personnel, or even physical space. As a result, groups are often in the position of competing very hard with each other for these scarce resources. Like any competitive situation, there are often "winners" and "losers" in the resource game. Furthermore, the fact that there are winners and losers in the competition for resources has the potential to create very intense and long-standing conflicts between groups.

To a certain extent, the fact that groups must compete for resources is unavoidable. If members of groups understand and accept this, conflicts may be kept from escalating to destructive levels. However, another way that organizations can help to prevent such competition from escalating to destructive levels is to make sure that the resource allocation process is fair. When resource allocation procedures are fair, groups will not always be pleased with the resources allocated to them; however, the *procedures* used to allocate resources are seen as fair. Ways of doing this may include making sure that all groups have equal access to the resources allocation process, and that political considerations are minimized as much as possible. However, the reality is that, in most organizations, resources will never be in abundance, and competition for them will always be an issue that organizations must face.

A second common cause of intergroup conflict is *goal incompatibility*. The notion of goal incompatibility was touched on briefly at the beginning of the chapter, where we discussed the factors that determine the general intergroup interaction patterns. At the most general level, goal incompatibility exists when the goals of two or more groups are in direct opposition—that is, one group accomplishes its goals at the direct expense of another group's achieving its goals. For example, in a democratic system of government, the goal of each political party is to assume control over various branches of government, but this can only be done by thwarting the same goal of other political parties. In an organizational setting, a common example of goal incompatibility often exists between marketing and production. The primary goal of the marketing function is to satisfy customers by giving them what they want, when they want it. The production function, however, attempts to achieve efficiency and economies of scale—both of which are tough to do if products are tailored to individual customers and delivered very quickly.

One important thing to consider about goal incompatibility is the distinction between *real* goal incompatibility versus *perceived* goal incompatibility. In many instances such as the one described above, there are real incompatibilities in the goals of different groups. In many other cases, however, the extent of incompatibility is much more a matter of perception. For example, in colleges and universities, many people believe that educating students and encouraging faculty research are completely incompatible goals. In contrast, a good number of people in higher education believe that educating students and encouraging faculty research may actually be highly compatible goals. It is obviously beyond the scope of this chapter to decide which of these two positions is correct. The more important point is that this, along with many other forms of goal incompatibility, is largely a matter of perceptions and opinions.

A third cause of intergroup conflict, which is actually closely related to goal incompatibility, is **time incompatibility.** Due to the pursuit of different goals and the performance of different tasks, work groups may work under very different time frames. In a research and development department, for example, current product development projects ultimately may not come to fruition for a decade or longer. As a result, those who work in research and development may take their time and accumulate considerable data before making important decisions.

In contrast to research and development, those whose jobs revolve around the production of products typically work under a much different time frame. Production schedules are typically made in a very short time span, and the major concern is what is happening at the moment rather than what may occur 10 years hence. Because of this short time frame, those in production may need information very quickly and may not have the luxury of taking the time needed to consider every possible alternative before they make a decision.

Often, in organizational settings, the issue of time incompatibility is dealt with by making sure that there is little interdependence between groups that operate under very different time frames. This can be done in a number of ways, but, most typically, it is accomplished through physical separation. For example, the Xerox research and development center in Palo Alto, California, is credited with groundbreaking advances in computer technology and is located far from the company's East Coast corporate headquarters.

In some cases, it is not possible for organizations to create such "buffer zones" between groups with differing time frames. For example, a sales group must deal frequently with a market research group to gauge customers' needs, or a production group may need crucial information from a research and development group to plan future production processes. Where such groups depend on each other, the potential for conflict is quite evident. Groups that operate on a very short time frame may see the other group as being indecisive and overanalyzing problems. In contrast, groups operating under a long-term

perspective may see the other group as reckless and not caring about the quality of the information it is issuing.

Disputes like these are often difficult to resolve because they may have been going on for many years and, in some cases, may even be part of an individual's professional socialization before entering the organization. For example, people trained in production management may be taught to be leery of "R & D types." Conversely, those likely to enter research and development fields may be socialized to assume that those in areas such as marketing do not appreciate the scientific value of their work.

A final factor that may lead to conflict between groups is the use of **contentious influence tactics** by members of one group toward members of another. Recall from Chapter 5 that the use of contentious influence tactics is a general determinant of conflict in organizations, and the fact that they may lead to intergroup conflict may come as no surprise. The term "contentious influence tactics" simply means trying to influence another individual or individuals through the use of threats, demands, or other negative methods.

One obvious reason that contentious influence tactics heighten the potential for intergroup conflict is that they tend to invite retaliation. When someone requests something in a rude or abrasive manner, the natural response of the person on the receiving end is to respond to the request in a rude or abrasive manner, or simply refuse to comply (Falbe & Yukl, 1992). This can lead to a negative cycle of escalation and, ultimately, bitter conflict. In some cases, status differences may prevent *direct* retaliation (e.g., a subordinate cannot directly retaliate when a supervisor is rude), but retaliation may occur nonetheless. The author can recall an instance in which a former faculty colleague was very demanding (and, at times, rude) about his clerical work requests.

The clerical person assigned to him accepted such requests without being rude, but his clerical requests typically went to "the bottom of the pile" when she was prioritizing her work.

Another reason that such influence tactics lead to intergroup conflict has to do with the social networks that exist in groups (LaBianca et al., 1998). Employees in organizations obviously do not work in a social vacuum. Thus, when a person from one group attempts to influence a member of another group in a contentious manner, this individual will often relay news of a bad experience to members of his or her own group. As a result, some individuals may develop "bad reputations" before ever having any direct contact with members of another group. Unfortunately, when this is the case, the potential for conflict is greatly heightened.

Consequences of Intergroup Conflict

Most organizations would prefer to have different groups work well together, because the alternative is unpleasant. However, to merely say that intergroup conflict is "unpleasant" begs the question: What really happens within a group when it is in conflict with another group? Fortunately, a fair amount of social psychological research has examined this very issue, although some of the research has not been conducted in formal organizational settings (e.g., Sherif, 1966).

One thing we know very clearly is that conflict changes group members' perceptions of each other (Roccas & Schwartz, 1993). As one might expect, members of groups in conflict view each other in a negative manner. It is also clear from the intergroup literature that members of groups in conflict tend to adopt a "we" versus "they" mentality. Members of the other group are viewed as being very different but very similar to each other (e.g., "They're

all alike in accounting"). Conversely, members of one's own group are viewed as positive and as having a much greater degree of individuality than the "out-group." Making this "in-group" versus "out-group" distinction may not actually reflect the complexity of situations, but it is cognitively much easier for the members of groups embroiled in conflict.

Another thing that typically happens when groups are in conflict is that, within groups, members often become more cohesive—that is, when groups see a threat from an outside group, they may pull together and become highly cohesive. A good example of this is the intense social bonds that often develop between soldiers who are involved in combat. It is not unusual for such individuals to develop friendships that far outlast their military service. This "common enemy" effect also occurs in organizations; the members of a group band together when faced with an outside threat.

Beyond the perceptual changes that have been discussed to this point, intergroup conflict may also have tangible negative effects in organizations. If groups are completely independent and have little need to interact, conflict will have little tangible impact other than perhaps a bit of discomfort here and there. However, in most organizations, it is unlikely that any one group could be completely independent of other groups. Thus, in most cases where there is intergroup conflict, the groups involved in such conflict must interact. What, then, does intergroup conflict do to the quality of intergroup interactions?

One thing most of us certainly know from experience is that when two groups are embroiled in a conflict, the interaction between members of these groups is certainly strained and often unpleasant. Because of this, members of groups in conflict may actively try to avoid each other, even if they are highly interdependent. By their doing this, the quality of work may be compromised. For example, it is not unusual for students in universities to ask faculty from more than one academic department to serve on thesis or dissertation committees. If different academic departments represented in a committee are in conflict, this may greatly decrease the communication between faculty and ultimately make it more difficult for students. Put differently, the student may be caught in the middle of such a conflict.

The other thing that may occur when groups are in conflict is that members of each group may go out of their way to make things as difficult as possible for the other group. Phone calls from members of the other group may be returned late, or requests for information may be ignored. The most troubling thing about this is that contentious behavior tends to breed contentious behavior. As a result, groups (like individuals) may get caught up in a vicious cycle of conflict that is difficult to break. Thus, the conflict may take on a life of its own, often to the detriment of customers or the quality of the work in general.

Another troubling aspect of intergroup conflict is that groups often pass on these conflicts to newcomers. That is, when a new member enters a group, he or she is "educated" about the history of the conflict and is expected to adjust his or her behavior accordingly. If the newcomer is seen fraternizing with members of the "other" group, or expresses positive views toward them, his or her own group members may react very sternly in order to bring the newcomer "back into line." In very extreme cases, a newcomer who refuses to embrace the group's conflicts and act accordingly may be forced to leave the group or may do so voluntarily.

A final problem caused by intergroup conflict is that when groups are in conflict with each other, their goals focus primarily inward and less toward the organization as a whole.

Put differently, what happens in the group may become more important than what happens in the organization as a whole. This may not be a problem if the goals of a group are perfectly aligned with the goals of the organization. However, it could be a major problem if the goals of a group are unrelated to or are in conflict with the major goals of the organization. For example, a group that has a primary goal of maintaining intergroup harmony and stability may be a liability to an organization that places a strong emphasis on quickly adapting to change in the environment.

IMPROVING THE QUALITY OF INTERGROUP RELATIONS

Given the potentially dysfunctional effects of intergroup conflict, organizations have a vested interest in keeping it to a manageable level. In fact, organizations would ideally like to create conditions that foster positive intergroup relations so that destructive conflicts do not occur in the first place. In this section, we examine some of the most commonly used methods for improving intergroup relations. These include superordinate goals, negotiation, group member exchanges, intergroup team development, and, finally, decreasing the interdependence among groups.

Superordinate Goals

One of the dangers of intergroup conflict is that groups will focus inward and become more focused on their own goals than on those of the organization as a whole. Thus, one way of improving relations between groups is to introduce **superordinate goals**—goals that both groups endorse and that often require cooperative intergroup behavior to be achieved. The notion of superordinate goals comes from the Robbers Cave study, which was conducted over 40 years ago by Muzafer and Carol Sherif and their colleagues at the University of Oklahoma (Sherif, Harvey, White, Hood, & Sherif, 1961). In this study, groups of boys believed they were participating in a summer camp at Robbers Cave in Oklahoma, but they were actually participating in a study of intergroup conflict. The researchers assigned these boys to two groups and created all the conditions that would likely foster intergroup conflict. For example, the two groups had different names ("Eagles" and "Rattlers"), were physically separated, and competed against each other in a variety of athletic contests. These manipulations were largely successful at creating a good deal of intergroup conflict.

After creating this state of intergroup conflict, the researchers then set about testing various methods of reducing it. One approach, which was largely unsuccessful, was simply to get the two groups together for a meal. The groups' reaction to this intervention was rather messy: They engaged in a food fight! This finding has also been supported in subsequent research (e.g., Brown, Condor, Matthews, Wade, & Williams, 1986) and thus suggests that simply getting groups together will not diffuse conflict.

The other approach employed by the researchers, however, met with much greater success. They staged a series of "incidents" that required the cooperation of both groups in order to solve a problem. For example, when both groups were being transported to a certain area of the camp, the bus they were riding in broke down and required the combined efforts of both groups to fix it. The groups were also forced to cooperate to fix a staged plumbing problem in the cabin in which they both ate. In both incidents, the groups were forced to work together to solve a problem that negatively impacted both groups.

What lessons can organizations learn about managing intergroup conflict from groups of boys at a summer camp? One is that simply getting conflicting groups to interact with each other will probably not reduce the conflict. In fact, the findings from the Robbers Cave study, and subsequent research, suggest that such efforts may actually intensify conflicts (although it's unlikely, in organizations, that food fights would break out!). The more practical implication, for example, is that simply locating conflicting groups in close physical proximity will probably not successfully diffuse conflicts.

The other important lesson from this study is that conflict *can* be reduced if members of groups must cooperate in order to achieve superordinate goals. Thus, for example, if two groups must cooperate to produce a product or prepare an important report, this may go a long way toward diffusing conflict. Furthermore, what makes this very feasible in organizational settings is that opportunities to introduce superordinate goals typically abound. For example, an organization can always point out the fact that the "superordinate goal" is the success of the organization.

It is also possible, in many organizations, to evoke the concept of superordinate goals through the introduction of a "common enemy" that the groups must band together to fight. In professional sports, coaches often build team unity by focusing on opponents or, in some cases, on criticism of the team by the news media. In organizations, this "common enemy" approach could obviously target a competitor, but could also focus on the poor economic environment, or perhaps on government regulators. Organizations, however, need to be careful in using this approach. If an organization becomes too internally focused and adopts an extreme "them versus us" mentality, important external cues may be missed, which may ultimately reduce the effectiveness of the organization as a whole.

Negotiation

In any type of conflict, one of the problems is that the parties involved avoid each other and, as a result, do not communicate. The irony, of course, is that conflicts can often be resolved if the parties sit down and communicate rationally about their differences. One way of doing this is through some form of **negotiation,** typically between the leaders of the groups in conflict (Brett & Rognes, 1986).

Negotiation involves a discussion of the issues causing conflict between the groups, and, ultimately, a resolution of those issues in a manner that is acceptable to both groups. Why is negotiation a potential mechanism for reducing intergroup conflict? First, negotiation facilitates communication. Negotiation is a **bilateral influence technique**; it involves a *mutual* exchange between parties (Kipnis, 1984). During this mutual exchange, it is possible for misunderstandings and misperceptions to be corrected.

Another reason that negotiation can be successful is that it is generally seen as a fair method of dispute resolution. Often, when groups are in conflict in organizations, the managers of the conflicting groups will make their case to someone at a higher level and a decision will be made that favors one group or the other. In another common way of handling disputes between groups, a higher-level manager serves as a mediator, much in the way mediators help to resolve labor disputes. In the first method, the dispute is resolved but there is often a "winner" and a "loser." Thus, members of one of the two groups involved in the dispute may feel that they have been treated unfairly. In the second scenario, where a higher-level manager mediates disputes, the problem that caused the dispute may never be resolved. There is also a chance, in this scenario, that a higher-level manager may favor one group over the other

and effectively "force" a resolution that is unfavorable to one of the groups.

Although negotiation can be used effectively to resolve intergroup disputes, not all forms of negotiation are equally effective. Fischer and Ury (1981) coined the term **principled negotiation** to refer to a style of negotiating whereby parties strive to achieve *resolution* to problems, rather than to stake out positions. This "problem-solving" approach to negotiating is likely to result in creative resolutions to problems that may in fact be quite palatable to both groups. In contrast, when groups in conflict approach a negotiation with a mentality that states "This is my position, and I'm not going to compromise," they are doing little to resolve the dispute and may even be heightening the conflict. Unfortunately, according to Brett and Rognes (1986), many managers of groups are not trained in principled negotiation techniques and may lack more general negotiation skills. Thus, organizations that want to encourage managers to resolve intergroup conflict through negotiation should provide managers with training in negotiation.

Member Exchanges

As we've seen, one of the things that happens when groups are in conflict is that group members distort their perceptions. Members of their own group are seen positively, and members of the other group are seen negatively. One way to combat such biased perceptions is for groups to periodically engage in **member exchanges:** for a stated period of time, members of the conflicting groups will switch and reverse roles. This type of intervention may initially be uncomfortable for those working in the "enemy camp," but it can also be very instrumental in reducing intergroup conflict. As an example, at a university where the author once worked, there was a program whereby faculty could become "administrative interns" for one year. These individuals essentially worked as administrators for one year, although they were still responsible for a small portion of their other faculty duties. The program was designed primarily for faculty considering administrative careers, but it also helped to educate the faculty "interns" about some of the challenges faced by administrators. Although not a member-exchange program, per se, it did help the participants to increase their understanding and therefore may have had the effect of reducing conflict between faculty and the university's administration.

There are obviously some situations in which member exchanges cannot occur. If the tasks performed by groups require vastly different skills, or if large geographic differences exist, exchanges may be impractical. There may also be some cases where conflict is so bad that the individual being exchanged may have a very difficult time or may even be harassed. However, when they are possible, member exchanges can be an excellent way of correcting misperceptions and, ultimately, diffusing conflict.

Intergroup Team Development

In Chapter 12, team development was discussed as an intervention that could potentially be used to improve performance *within* groups. There are also team development activities designed to facilitate or improve relations *between* different groups (Dyer, 1987; French & Bell, 1999). Team development will be described in greater detail in Chapter 16, but two specific intergroup team development interventions are relevant here.

One intervention, which was developed by Blake, Shephard, and Mouton (1964), is a structured way of highlighting possible areas of misperception and encouraging groups to

work through their misperceptions. Figure 13.2 provides a summary of the basic steps involved in this intervention. The first step is to have the members of both groups meet separately and, collectively, generate two lists. The first list is designed to reflect how each group views the other group. This includes perceptions of the other group, what the other group does that "gets in our way," and so on. The second list reflects each group's prediction of what the *other* group will say about them; that is, each group is trying to anticipate what the other group dislikes about them, or how they are perceived.

After each group generates these two lists separately, they reconvene to "compare notes" on their perceptions. This can be a quite revealing exercise because it highlights important issues and problems that are preventing the groups from working together, and it can serve as the basis for concrete actions designed to improve relations between the groups. As an example, let's say that the members of one group see the other group as unresponsive

FIGURE 13.2
Summary of the Steps Involved in a Typical Intergroup Team Development Intervention

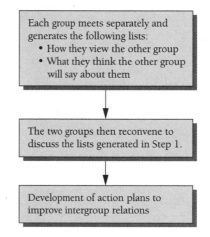

Each group meets separately and generates the following lists:
• How they view the other group
• What they think the other group will say about them

The two groups then reconvene to discuss the lists generated in Step 1.

Development of action plans to improve intergroup relations

and unwilling to provide service to them, and the other group has similar perceptions. Discussing these perceptions may allow both groups to develop a greater understanding of the pressures faced by the other group. It may also lead to concrete action plans designed to improve the situation.

A variation of this intervention, the **organizational mirror technique,** can also be used very effectively for correcting the misperceptions of conflicting groups. With this technique, one group forms a circle around the perimeter of the other group. The group "inside the fishbowl" is instructed to discuss its self-perceptions and its perceptions of the other group. During this time, the group observing is instructed not to interrupt, even if they feel that the perceptions of the group are not correct. The groups then may reverse roles; the group seeking feedback may discuss what they have heard and may possibly seek clarification. Following this step, the groups reconvene and ultimately generate a master list of action plans for improving the relations between the two groups.

As with the previous intervention, the organizational mirror may provide unique opportunities for members of groups in conflict to correct misperceptions and resolve misunderstandings. The advantages of the organizational mirror technique, however, are that it may be less time consuming and more adaptable. A consultant may be able to employ this technique at several points during a day-long intergroup team development intervention. A potential disadvantage of the fishbowl technique is that it is potentially very confrontational. Therefore, this method should only be used in conjunction with a consultant who is well trained in group facilitation and conflict management. The technique probably should not be used when groups are embroiled in highly intense, personalized conflicts.

Reducing the Need for Intergroup Interaction

Despite well-intentioned efforts to improve intergroup relations, there may be times when groups simply cannot work well together. This may be due to irreconcilable personality conflicts, or, at times, the nature of the work that groups perform is so different that cooperation may be difficult. One way of dealing with intergroup conflict is creating conditions in which two groups have little or no need to interact. This can generally be done in one of two ways. The first approach is to change the structure of an organization, or the flow of work, so that the level of interdependence between two groups is greatly reduced. A way of doing this is to create a "coordinating group" to manage the interactions between groups. In this type of structure, each group needs to communicate only with the coordinating group. This eliminates the need to interact with the other group. To decrease interdependence, organizations frequently "outsource" products or services that are currently being performed internally. The auto industry has relied heavily on outsourcing for many of the parts that they used to produce internally. This has proved to be cost effective and undoubtedly has reduced the level of interdependence among internal groups.

A second general way to reduce interdependence among groups, particularly in sequential production systems, is to build some level of "slack" into the system. If one group supplies parts to a second group, for example, maintaining a reserve inventory of these parts will decrease the interdependence of the groups. Creating slack resources of this type results in somewhat less sequential interdependence. This decrease in interdependence may ultimately decrease tensions between the two groups, because one is not so dependent on the other.

The Resource Allocation Process

A final way that organizations can potentially reduce conflict between groups is through the resource allocation process. As was noted earlier in the chapter, a very common cause of intergroup conflict is that groups are often in competition for scarce organizational resources. Thus, one way to reduce conflict is to reexamine the resource allocation process to make sure that groups have the resources they need to be effective.

At first glance, the suggestion that organizations "give groups more resources" may be a rather simplistic and naïve way of decreasing intergroup conflict. After all, the vast majority of organizations operate under conditions whereby resources are scarce. This may be true, but organizations do have control over *where* those scarce resources are allocated, and the *process* by which resource allocation decisions are made. Thus, organizations can choose to allocate resources in a manner that is commensurate with group needs, or they can do so on the basis of political gamesmanship and "back-room dealing." Similarly, organizations can make the choice to allocate resources in a fair, rational manner, or they can do so in a highly secretive, clandestine fashion.

When organizations allocate resources in a fair, rational, and open manner, this will not necessarily eliminate the problem of resources' scarcity. However, based on what is known about procedural justice (e.g., Folger & Cropanzano, 1998), it is certainly possible that even when groups come up short on resources, they will still see the resource allocation process as fair. Another more general benefit of fair resource allocation procedures is that these may simply foster a more positive organizational climate. When people feel they are being treated fairly by the organization, this will tend to foster a climate of openness and trust as opposed to mistrust and paranoia.

Such a climate certainly does not guarantee positive intergroup relations, but it certainly makes them more likely.

CHAPTER SUMMARY

In this chapter, we examined a relatively neglected topic in the group literature: intergroup relations. This neglect is unfortunate because, in most organizations, groups must work together collaboratively to accomplish many important tasks. The chapter began with a discussion of the various types of interactions that may occur between groups. These range from avoidance to collaboration, and depend largely on the compatibility of goals and the level of interdependence that exists between two groups. Other factors that determine the nature of intergroup interactions include the type of interdependence, task-related demands, the culture of the organization, past events that have transpired between groups, and the nature of the individuals that comprise each of the groups.

Given that different groups in organizations may have different goals, operate on different time frames, and employ different types of people, the potential for intergroup conflict is often high. Thus, it is not surprising that a great deal of the intergroup literature has focused on conflict. Conflict between groups—due to biases in perceptions and a tendency to adopt an "us" versus "them" mentality—clearly has a negative impact on relations between groups. While negative in and of themselves, biases may ultimately have a negative impact on organizational effectiveness. Thus, organizations have a vested interest in keeping intergroup conflict at manageable levels.

From the social psychological literature, a method that has been shown to reduce intergroup conflict is the adoption of "superordinate goals." These are goals that transcend the interests of individual groups and often require collaborative efforts in order to achieve them. Among other methods of reducing intergroup conflict, the chapter discussed member exchanges, intergroup team development interventions, decreasing interdependence among groups, and improvement of the resource allocation process. Given the realities of organizational life, it is doubtful that intergroup conflict can ever be completely eliminated. However, it is certainly possible for organizations to keep it to manageable levels.

SUGGESTED ADDITIONAL READINGS

Brett, J. M., Goldberg, S. B., & Ury, W. L. (1990). Designing systems for resolving disputes in organizations. *American Psychologist, 45,* 162–170.

Nelson, R. E. (1989). The strength of strong ties: Social networks and intergroup conflict in organizations. *Academy of Management Journal, 32,* 377–401.

Pruitt, D. G., & Carnevale, P. J. (1993). *Negotiation in social conflict.* Pacific Grove, CA: Brooks/Cole.

Worchel, S. (1986). The role of cooperation in reducing intergroup conflict. In S. Worchel & W. G. Austin (Eds.), *Psychology of intergroup relations* (2nd ed., pp. 288–304). Chicago: Nelson-Hall.

Chapter Fourteen

Organizational Theory and Design

A major theme throughout this book is that the primary focus of organizational psychology is *individual behavior*. Consistent with this theme, we have explored a number of factors that impact that behavior. Some of these (e.g., compensation programs) are aimed directly at individuals; others (e.g., groupthink) reside primarily at the group level. In this chapter, we raise the level of analysis one step higher, and explore the impact of the design of organizations on employee behavior and overall organizational effectiveness.

Organizational psychologists have tended to shy away from "macro-level" issues such as organizational theory and design. This is due, at least partially, to the difficulty of seeing the "fuzzy" connection between organizational design and individual behavior. As a result, over the years, these topics have gradually become the province of those trained in macro-level organizational behavior, organizational theory, and strategic management. This tendency of organizational psychologists to leave the "macro stuff" to these other fields is troubling, for two reasons. First, anyone who has worked in an organization knows that organizational structure *does* impact individual employees, although such influences are admittedly often indirect. For example, in a university setting, the manner in which academic departments are grouped often has implications for resource allocations.

A second reason is that those trained in macro-organizational behavior, organizational theory, and strategic management often provide an incomplete picture of the impact of

371

organizational design. Just as organizational psychologists tend to focus (or, some would say, overfocus) on individual behavior, the analyses provided by those trained in other fields often *exclude* individual behavior. To say that the design of an organization contributes to its effectiveness begs the question: How, specifically, does the design of an organization impact the behavior of those in the organization, and does it make the organization more, or less, effective? Therefore, an interdisciplinary approach to organizational design that includes the contributions of macro-level organizational behavior, organizational theory, strategic management, and organizational psychology will be taken in the present chapter.

The chapter will begin by discussing the broad field of organizational theory. Organizational theories are simply different approaches to organizing human endeavors such as work. Organizational theories are important because they form the basis for concrete organizational designs. The focus of the chapter then shifts to a discussion of the major factors that impact the decisions organizations make with respect to organizational design. The chapter will then examine recent innovations in the design of organizations; these designs depart widely from traditional organizational theories. The chapter concludes with a brief summary of empirical research on the impact of organizational design on organizational effectiveness, and a description of factors that will likely impact the design of organizations of the future.

WHAT IS AN "ORGANIZATIONAL THEORY"?

In the organizational sciences (e.g., organizational behavior, organizational psychology), one of the more misunderstood terms is "organizational theory." To some, organizational theory is a field of study; to others, it is the process of using metaphors to describe organizational processes (e.g., McKenna & Wright, 1992; Morgan, 1986), or it represents an attempt to determine the *best* way to organize work organizations. The term is used to indicate all of these things, but an "organizational theory" is really just a way of organizing purposeful human action. Given the diversity of purposeful human endeavors, there are numerous ways to organize them, and, hence, a great many organizational theories.

In terms of academic roots, the field that really has taken the lead in theorizing about the organization of purposeful human behavior is sociology. Sociology is essentially the study of macro-level forces (e.g., social stratification, social institutions) on human behavior (e.g., Merton, 1968; Parsons, 1951). A classic illustration of the manner in which this interest was manifested was sociologist Emil Durkheim's classic studies of the determinants of suicide (Durkheim, 1951). Durkheim proposed and found support for the idea that some forms of social structure result in alienation and a sense of hopelessness (called "anomie"), which ultimately leads to higher rates of suicide. Given this historical backdrop, it is natural that sociologists would be more interested in the impact of the structure and design of organizations than psychologists would be. In fact, the Hawthorne studies, which are considered one of the most important historical events contributing to the development of organizational psychology, were conducted under the direction of sociologist Elton Mayo.

Given that organizational theory deals with different ways of organizing human activity, how does one "theorize" about organizations? In most scientific disciplines, if one wants to theorize about something and ultimately study it, the most common approach is to bring it into a laboratory for closer inspection. Unfortunately, organizational theorists cannot do this because organizations are largely abstractions, and thus cannot be subjected to laboratory investigations. Although we can draw elegant organization charts to represent reporting relationships, and so on, what keeps an organization together is the fact that an organization's employees understand it and adapt their behavior accordingly (Katz & Kahn, 1978).

Given these constraints, organizational theorists have been forced to adopt more indirect methods of investigation. Perhaps the most common of these methods has been the use of *metaphors* to describe and understand organizational structures (McKenna & Wright, 1992). A metaphor is simply a type of figurative language; that is, using words or phrases to communicate anything other than their literal meaning. For example, if I say that my eight-year-old son is always "hungry as a horse" (which he is!), I am using a metaphor.

The most common metaphor used in the organizational theory literature has been to liken organizations to *biological organisms* and apply **general systems theory** to describe them (Katz & Kahn, 1978; von Bertalanffy, 1956). If we liken organizations to biological organisms, this leads to several important conclusions that may have powerful implications for organizational functioning. Perhaps the most important of these is that organizations are in constant interaction with the environment, just as any biological system must interact with the larger ecosystem in which it is embedded. If organizations ignore the larger environment, they may cease to exist; like biological organisms that ignore the ecosystem, they may risk extinction. Because of this, organizations often spend considerable time and financial resources attempting to understand (and sometimes control) the external environment.

A second major implication of the biological organism metaphor is that organizations consist of a series of subsystems that must work in concert in order for the organization to function optimally. As an analogy, the human body, which is a highly complex biological system, consists of a number of systems that control physiological activities such as circulation, digestion, and respiration. Most of the coordination among these systems is controlled by a complex array of chemical messengers that are released by the brain. In organizations, coordination among subsystems is often achieved through the structural arrangements themselves, but, in some cases, special mechanisms (e.g., coordinating committees) are established for it.

Another metaphor that is quite common in organizational theory is that of the organization as a *machine.* Like machines, organizations take environmental input, transform the input in some fashion, and return that input, in an altered form, back into the environment. Many of the implications of the "organization as machine" metaphor are quite similar to the "organization as biological organism" metaphor. That is, organizations must pay attention to the external environment and to the coordination of its internal components. An additional implication of the machine metaphor, however, is the importance of making sure that the "components" of the machine (i.e., people) are performing properly. This is typically accomplished in a number of ways, including selection, performance appraisal, performance coaching, and, in some cases, redesign of jobs in order to maximize the unique capabilities of individuals.

Although the biological organism and machine metaphors have the longest histories in organizational theory, McKenna and Wright (1992) point out that other metaphors may also be useful to organizational theorists. For example, they point out that organizations can be likened to the brain, with all its complex interconnections, and to families, with their complex relationships, and to political areas, with all of their influence and power dynamics. These metaphors have yet to be used extensively by organizational theorists. The major point, however, is that organizational theorists may limit themselves by focusing only on the biological organism and machine metaphors. By widening the scope of metaphorical thinking about organizations, new and important insights into organizing human activities may be developed.

MAJOR ORGANIZATIONAL THEORIES

Having provided a brief overview of the general field of organizational theory, we now move on to a consideration of the major organizational *theories* themselves. Organizational theories simply represent ideas about the form in which human activity can be organized. Obviously, there could be an almost infinite number of ideas about organizing human activity; however, over the years, three general types of organizational theories have been developed. These three types are described next.

Classical Organizational Theories

Historically, the term "classical" organizational theory has been used to denote models of organizing that were developed from approximately the early twentieth century until the mid-1940s. The best known of these classical theories were **scientific management** (Taylor, 1911), **ideal bureaucracy** (Weber, 1947), and **administrative management** (Fayol, 1984). Each is discussed briefly below.

The term "scientific management" was first introduced in describing the history of organizational psychology (Chapter 1) and was examined further in our discussion of job design (Chapter 9). We resurrect this term one more time because it also has implications for the way organizations are designed.

As might be remembered from our earlier discussion, one of the fundamental principles of scientific management was that *those who design the work should be separate from those who actually perform the work.* The implications of this, as an organizing principle, are quite important. For example, it implies that there should be distinct status or hierarchical differences among employees. In Taylor's writings, it is fairly obvious that those who *design* the work occupy a higher status than those who *perform* it. An organization that is designed from a scientific management perspective has many levels and many ways to distinguish among those levels.

Recall that one of the other fundamental principles of scientific management is that work should be broken down into the smallest and simplest components possible. For example, the various steps involved in the production of an automobile would be broken down into the simplest possible instructions. The implication of this emphasis on simplification is that an organization should consist of similar groups of employees, all performing highly specialized tasks. Furthermore, in most cases, the best way to manage these groups of employees is to create departmental structures that are based on these highly specialized activities. Thus, an organization that is designed according to scientific management will consist of a large number of highly specialized departments.

Beyond these more concrete organizational design implications of scientific management, there are also a number of less tangible implications. Perhaps one of the most important of these is that a scientifically managed organization will have a great number of rules and procedures for employees to follow. Frederick Taylor became famous for using empirical research to determine the most efficient way to carry out work tasks. The underlying assumption behind this quest for efficiency was that there is "one best way" to do any job or accomplish any task. The trick is to find it. This tendency is likely to be generalized to other organizational tasks; thus, such organizations are likely to have thick "policies and procedures" manuals that have scripted procedures for employees to follow in the event of any contingency.

The term "ideal bureaucracy" may strike some as an oxymoron, because the term "bureaucracy" is often used sarcastically to denote organizational inefficiency and inflexibility. In reality, however, ideal bureaucracy simply represents one idea or theory of how human activity should be organized. The development of ideal bureaucracy is typically attributed to Max Weber, who is generally credited with being one of the pioneers of the macro side of organizational psychology. Weber, as you may recall, wore many intellectual hats and made contributions to history, economics, political science, and sociology during his lifetime. In Weber's time, there were few organizations in the form that we see them today. Instead, a great many "organizations" of his era were loosely run family businesses, or individual craftsmen who worked relatively independently. Given these organizational forms, there was not a great need for organizing, per se.

With the advent of the Industrial Revolution, however, there began to be a great need for organizing the large numbers of people who had left rural areas and come to cities to work in factories. Furthermore, the organizational models that were predominant in the late nineteenth and early twentieth centuries were not adequate for handling these large organizations. For example, at that time, a great deal of one's success was based on social connections or the nature of one's family relations; not surprising, given that a good number of organizations of that era were family run. The problem with this model's being implemented in industrial settings was that those who possessed the best social or family connections were not always capable of performing the tasks required by the work.

Weber proposed ideal bureaucracy as an alternative that would result in more efficient operations and more effective use of talent in organizations. One of the primary assumptions behind ideal bureaucracy (and one that many people forget) is a noble one: Rewards should be based on one's contributions to the organizations, as opposed to social or familial connections. Unfortunately, many of the more negative assumptions underlying bureaucracy have tended to overshadow this one.

As in scientific management, there is, in ideal bureaucracy, a strong reliance on previously developed rules and procedures to guide behavior. In a truly efficient ideal bureaucracy, there should be a rule or procedure to govern almost any situation that employees may encounter. This may often explain why bureaucracies have so much difficulty when there is a highly novel situation. This is also likely to be the reason many people have a negative view of this organizational form.

Another hallmark of ideal bureaucracy is that there is very close supervision of employees. Bureaucratic organizations typically are characterized by very narrow **spans of control**; that is, each supervisor does not supervise a large number of employees. One thing is accomplished by a narrow span of control: It is easier for a supervisor to meet the needs of his or her subordinates. Answering questions and helping to train four employees is obviously much easier than doing the same tasks with 40. A narrow span of control also makes it far easier for supervisors to monitor the behavior of their subordinates. This has led many to draw the conclusion that bureaucracy is based on the assumption that employees will not work unless their behavior is tightly monitored. This is not a particularly positive view of human nature.

Another important principle of ideal bureaucracy is **unity of command.** In a bureaucratic structure, each employee should ideally have one (and only one) direct supervisor. For anyone prone to cynicism, a logical conclusion would be that this principle, like the narrow span of control, would make it easier for an organization to control its employees. Unity of command, however, may have some tangible positive benefits for employees. If an employee reports to only one supervisor, this reduces the odds that he or she would have to meet the combined and potentially conflicting expectations of more than one individual. As will be discussed later in this chapter, one of the problems with some modern organizational designs that violate this principle is that they increase role conflict among employees (e.g., Joyce, 1986).

A third important principle of ideal bureaucracy is **unity of direction,** with respect to information flow. This means that information within a bureaucratic organization flows in one direction—typically, from the top of the organization down to lower levels. The primary benefit of the unity of direction principle is that it increases the predictability and stability of information flow. This makes everyone's life easier when vast amounts of information must be processed. This principle also makes it much easier for the top management of an organization to control the nature of the information that employees have access to. Top managers can make sure that employees "know only what they need to know," and nothing more. This principle, like the others previously discussed, make it far easier for employees to be controlled than would be the case if information within an organization flowed freely.

Ultimately, like any other organizational theory, ideal bureaucracy is neither good nor bad. The extent to which it enhances or detracts from organizational effectiveness depends to a large extent on how it is implemented, and whether it is appropriate for the organization's environment. As will be shown later, in the section on contingency theories, there are some situations in which bureaucracy is very appropriate. In other situations, however, organizations that use it are highly prone to failure.

The term *administrative management* was first coined by Henri Fayol, who was an engineer by training and eventually became the chief executive of a French mining company. Fayol (1984) sought to develop a relatively universal set of organizing principles for managers to apply in organizations. To give these principles meaning, however, Fayol presented them in the context of the activities of managers, or behaviors he called **management functions.** According to Fayol, the major functions of managers included planning, organizing, commanding, coordination, and controlling. The principles that Fayol proposed were designed to assist managers in carrying out these essential functions.

Table 14.1 presents Fayol's 14 organizing principles. As can be seen, many items on this list are similar to the principles of ideal bureaucracy that were described earlier. For example, Fayol advocated, among other bureaucratic principles, the division of work, having a well-defined authority structure, unity of command, unity of direction, order, and equity in the way individuals are rewarded. Among the unique principles that Fayol added were: stability of personnel, encouraging people to take initiative, and having a high level of cohesion and camaraderie among employees. These three additions are interesting, simply because they seem very *un*bureaucratic. In fact, they seem more compatible with organizational theories that were

TABLE 14.1
Fayol's Classic Principles of Organizing

Principle	Fayol's Comments
1. Division of work	Individuals and managers work on the same part or task.
2. Authority and responsibility	Authority: right to give orders; power to exact obedience; goes with responsibility for reward and punishment.
3. Discipline	Obedience, application, energy, behavior. Agreement between firm and individual.
4. Unity of command	Orders received from one supervisor.
5. Unity of direction	One head and one plan for activities with the same objective.
6. Subordination of individual interest to general interest	Organizational objectives come before the objectives of the individual.
7. Remuneration of personnel	Fairness of pay to the organization and the individual; discussed various forms.
8. Centralization	Amount of discretion held by the manager compared to that allowed to subordinates.
9. Scalar chain	Line of authority from lowest to top.
10. Order	A place for everyone, and everyone in his or her place.
11. Equity	Emphasis on kindness and justice.
12. Stability of tenure of personnel	Ability in managerial ranges; time to adapt to work.
13. Initiative	Power of thinking out and executing a plan.
14. Esprit de corps	Harmony and union among personnel is strength.

Adapted from: From H. Fayol. (1984). *General and industrial management.* Belmont, CA: Lake Publishing.

developed due to perceived limitations of bureaucracy.

Although many of Fayol's principles are useful, and in fact put into practice in many organizations to this day, they have also been widely criticized on a number of counts. Perhaps the most vigorous criticism of these principles, and classical theories in general, is that they ignore the "human element" in organizations (e.g., McGregor, 1960). That is, these principles paint a picture of employees in organizations being interchangeable cogs in a grand machine, rather than humans with emotions, desires, and creative talents. The other major criticism of Fayol's principles has been that they are simply too general. To take

one example, Fayol advocates fairness in the remuneration of employees, which most managers would likely agree is a desirable principle. However, even though he does offer some suggestions on how to accomplish this (Fayol, 1984), these suggestions are rather vague. The same problem plagues many of the other principles as well.

Humanistic Organizational Theories

Recall from Chapter 1 that the Human Relations movement began in the 1940s, largely as a response to the classical theories that were described in the previous section. According to those at the forefront of the

Human Relations movement, most notably Douglas McGregor and Rensis Likert, the application of the principles of classical design to organizations had created a dehumanized workplace that vastly underutilized the creativity and initiative of employees. The primary reason for this negative impact of classical theory can be traced largely to its underlying assumptions about human nature. With their strong emphasis on order and control, classical organizational theories are based on the assumption that employees will not work unless they are prodded to do so, and they lack the creativity and initiative to define their roles on their own. The best known of these humanistic organizational theories were McGregor's **Theory X/Y Leadership Distinction** and Likert's concept of **The Human Organization.**

In his 1960 book, *The Human Side of Enterprise,* McGregor made a distinction between two types of managers: Theory X and Theory Y. Managers characterized as Theory X operate under the assumption that most people have an inherent dislike for work and, as a result, need to be coerced and supervised very closely if they are to work toward the goals of the organization. Another fundamental assumption of the Theory X manager is that people have little ambition, are not self-directed, and value security over all else. This again suggests the need for high levels of managerial control and close supervision of employees.

In direct contrast to the Theory X manager, the Theory Y manager operates under the assumption that work is a natural part of peoples' lives and, rather than avoid it, most people seek greater meaning in it. As a result, individuals are capable of some degree of self-control and will work toward the goals of the organization to the extent that they find doing so personally rewarding. Another fundamental Theory Y assumption is that, under the right conditions, many people will seek out

responsibility and will creatively solve organizational problems if they are allowed to do so. A final key assumption of Theory Y is that the conditions in most organizations result in the underutilization of employees' skills and talents. Given that classical organizational designs were still dominant at the time McGregor wrote this book, this was a not-so-subtle criticism of classical organizational theory.

Although the Theory X/Y distinction is made at the individual manager level and thus is not technically a theory of organizing, these ideas can be extended to the organizational level. An organization that is populated with Theory X managers is likely to have very narrow spans of control, strict lines of authority, and a vast number of rules and procedures—in short, its design would be based largely on classical organizational design principles. In contrast, in the Theory Y organization, spans of control would be wider, lines of authority would not be as strictly defined, and there would only be rules when necessary. These are logical design features if one assumes that employees are capable of doing their work without close supervision, and that they are bright enough to engage in creative problem solving when novel problems occur.

The primary benefit of the Theory Y organization is that such organizations are inherently more humane and potentially more psychologically fulfilling for employees. Within such an organization, work can be a source of personal growth rather than a "necessary evil" that one must endure in order to have life's necessities. There are, however, potential downsides to the Theory Y organization that must be taken into account. Specifically, many have argued that it is rather naïve to assume that *all* employees want to achieve personal growth through their work experience (e.g., Hackman & Oldham, 1980), and that everyone can work productively with only minimal supervision. Another potential drawback associated with the Theory Y organization is that, because lines of authority are not as clear as in classical organizations, there is a great deal of potential for confusion and conflict regarding employees' roles and responsibilities.

The other organizational theory that has come to be seen as highly representative of the humanistic perspective is Likert's idea of the human organization. In his 1961 book, *New Patterns of Management,* Likert proposed that organizations could be classified into four different types, which corresponded to System 1 through System 4. A System 1 organization was described by Likert as an **exploitive authoritarian** type. This type of organization was very similar to Theory X because it is characterized as having very little trust in employees, scant communication between employees and management, very centralized decision making, and control achieved in a very "top-down" manner. This type of organization, according to Likert, would result in largely dissatisfied employees and, ultimately, a low level of organizational performance.

The System 2 organization, which was labeled **benevolent authoritative,** was proposed to be much like the System 1 organization, although some notable differences were present. For example, in this organizational form, there is *some* level of trust in employees, and, at times, management uses their ideas. There is also a little more communication in this type of organization, and, on occasion, employees have an opportunity to communicate their ideas to upper management. To sum up this type, employees are still treated in a largely authoritative manner, but the organization is a bit nicer to them. According to Likert, employees in this type of organization may derive some moderate level of satisfaction toward their work, and organizational performance may be "fair to good."

The System 3 organization was labeled **consultative** by Likert. This type of organization is very different from System 1 in that there is substantially greater trust in employees, and their ideas are used a great deal more. In addition, there is more overall communication in such an organization, and, compared to the other organizational forms, much more of it flows from the bottom up. Decision making is still primarily in the hands of those at higher organizational levels, but the manner in which this authority is exerted is different than in the System 1 and System 2 organizations. Those at the top of the organization set broad policies, and more specific operational decisions are made by those at lower organizational levels. Employees in the consultative organization work on goals that they adopt after some discussion, and, at times, they may resist organizational goals. Some level of control resides at lower organizational levels, and the information that flows within the organization is accurate. According to Likert, the consultative organization is capable of "good" performance, although it may never reach a level of extremely high excellence.

System 4, the final type of organization in Likert's typology, is labeled **participative group.** This type of organization is essentially the mirror opposite of the System 1 or exploitive authoritarian organization. For example, in this type of organization, managers have complete trust in subordinates and, as a result, always seek their input before making decisions. Communication in this type of organization is free-flowing in all directions, and there is often a great reliance on teamwork. As might be expected, decision making occurs at all organizational levels and with a high level of involvement. Employees in the participative group organization work on goals that they have a say in developing and, as a result, there is a great deal of acceptance of them. Control mechanisms are applied at all levels of the organization, and the information available to employees is complete and accurate.

According to Likert, the participative group organization is the only one of the four that is truly capable of "excellent" performance. Therefore, it is probably not a coincidence that descriptions of organizations considered excellent (e.g., T. Peters & Waterman, 1982) have much in common with Likert's System 4 organization.

R. Likert (1961) originally proposed four organizational types. More recently, J. G. Likert and Araki (1986) proposed that there is also a System 5. The System 5 organization is essentially identical to System 4, but differs in one important respect. Specifically, in a System 5 organization, leadership is truly a shared enterprise. Essentially, the organization has no "bosses." Such organizations are extremely rare, although they may eventually become more prevalent.

Although many would agree that the System 4 or 5 organizations are most likely to be successful, it is questionable whether this would always be the case. For example, having completely free-flowing information may be an advantage in some ways, but it also may lead to problems such as information overflow or distortion. Similarly, having complete trust in employees may be a good policy, provided people are in fact trustworthy. Furthermore, in the more recently developed System 5 organization, although the absence of bosses may contribute to an egalitarian atmosphere, it may also be problematic at times when someone needs to take charge.

The overall point is that there is much about McGregor's Theory Y or Likert's System 4 or 5 organizations that can lead to organizational effectiveness. However, the major weakness in these organizational theories is the notion that there is *one* most effective way to run an organization. That was essentially the problem with classical organizational theories. This dissatisfaction with the "one best way"

approach to organizations led to the development of *contingency* theories of organization.

Contingency Organizational Theories

Recall from Chapter 10 that contingency theories of leadership developed largely because leadership theorists recognized that there is no singular set of personal traits, nor is there one set of behaviors that will *always* distinguish good leaders from poor ones. Similarly, organizational theorists gradually came to the realization that neither a classical nor a humanistic organizational form was appropriate *all* of the time. Thus, the basic premise of contingency organizational theories is that design of an organization must be consistent with the situation (Lawrence & Lorsch, 1967). Given this premise, the obvious question then becomes: *What* aspects of the situation do organizations need to pay most attention to when making organizational design decisions? In the following section, we discuss five factors that have most often been cited as driving organizational design decisions.

DETERMINANTS OF ORGANIZATIONAL DESIGN

Organizational design decisions should be made on some rational basis; that is, the design of an organization should serve some purpose. Keeping this in mind, there are many purposes that organizational design decisions can serve. Most commonly, design decisions are made to support an organization's strategy, to help it cope with environmental uncertainty, to reflect the beliefs and assumptions of those in power, and to support its core technology. In some cases, however, design is essentially preordained because of the size of an organization. Each of these factors is discussed next.

Strategy

An organization's strategy is represented by its long-range goals and the tactics it uses to reach those goals. Strategic differences in organizations have a number of implications for organizational issues such as staffing, compensation and reward systems, and performance appraisal. According to Galbraith (1995), the aspects of organizational structure that tend to have the greatest impact on strategy implementation include the level of specialization, the shape of the organization, the distribution of power within the organization, and the form of departmentalization present. Specialization refers simply to the types and numbers of specialties that an organization uses in performing its work. When organizations have a high degree of specialization, this tends to improve the performance of various subtasks—excellence in engineering is more likely when there is a high concentration of engineers. The downside to high specialization, however, is that it becomes difficult to integrate all the various specialties. If an organization's strategy is to produce a highly specialized product—and produce it very consistently over time—then high specialization is preferred. On the other hand, if an organization pursues a strategy that involves changing products quickly in response to consumer demand, then specialization is a liability because it is slow. The trend in recent years has been away from specialization, largely because more and more organizations are pursuing strategies that require quick responses to changes in market conditions, and because many highly specialized tasks can be automated.

A second organizational design factor that impacts strategy implementation is the *shape* of the organization. According to Galbraith (1995), the shape of an organization is reflected by the number of people who form departments at each hierarchical level. A *narrow* organization is one that has a relatively large number of levels but relatively few individuals at each level. In contrast, a very flat organization is one that has a relatively few number of levels, but each level is comprised of a large number of employees. Figure 14.1 highlights this distinction.

From a strategic point of view, the shape of an organization may have some extremely important consequences. When organizations are narrow, a great deal of time and energy is typically invested in communication, supervision, and, especially, decision making. Stated differently, a narrow organization expends a great deal of resources "running itself." This time spent on internal issues obviously takes time away from externally focused activities such as interfacing with customers or determining trends in the competitive market. As a result, a narrow organization is most appropriate for an organization pursuing a strategy that involves producing highly specialized products or services in markets that do not change rapidly.

A very flat organization, in contrast, spends far less time on internal processes such as supervision and decision making. With such large spans of control, these types of organizations often rely on teams or co-ordinating committees to provide typical supervisory functions. Also, with a flatter organizational structure, decisions can be made without having to go through many organizational layers. Flatter organizations are thus much more adept at supporting strategies that involve quick responses to consumer demand, or penetration of highly volatile market segments.

A third organizational design principle that impacts strategy implementation is *distribution of power* within an organization. As Galbraith

FIGURE 14.1

Contrast between a Flat and Narrow Organizational Structure

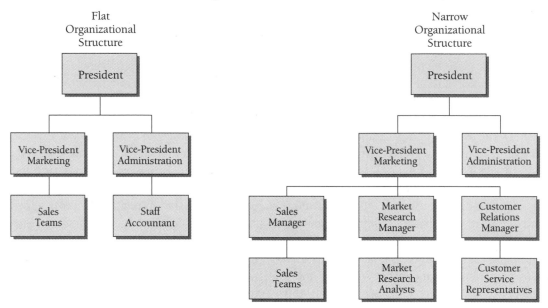

(1995) notes, the most typical manifestation of power distribution in organizations is the manner in which decisions are made. Furthermore, this can be reflected both vertically and horizontally. Vertical distribution of decision-making power is the extent to which the decision making in an organization is centralized versus decentralized. Centralization, for example, would be present if the headquarters of an organization made all important decisions; decentralization would be present if decision making was pushed down to the level of those who either produce the product or directly interact with the customers.

Horizontal distribution of power is a different concept and is reflected in whether managers shift decision-making power to the department that has the best information or is in the best position to make a decision. An example of horizontal decision-making power that is becoming increasingly common is organizations' shift of decision making to units that have the *most customer contact,* particular in highly volatile customer-driven industries.

In terms of strategy implementation, an organization that concentrates power in the hands of a few top managers is not well situated to implement a strategy involving quick responses to market conditions. This type of strategy requires decisions to be made very quickly—often, by those who are close to consumers (e.g., salespeople, customer service employees). Similarly, an organization that is very hesitant to share power horizontally is often unable to take advantage of cost-saving opportunities associated with contracting out aspects of their business. They simply lack the knowledge to take advantage of such opportunities.

The final aspect of structure that will impact strategy implementation is an organization's *departmental structure.* According to Galbraith (1995), departments may be formed according to a number of criteria, including function, product line, customer segments, geographical areas, or work flow processes. Departmentalization by function (e.g., marketing, production, and human resources) has traditionally been the most common form in organizations (see Figure 14.2). The primary advantage of this form of departmentalization is that it promotes a high level of specialization and, as a result, a high level of excellence in each particular function. Under this type of structure, it is easier for groups of product engineers to exchange ideas that will potentially lead to new and creative products.

Despite this benefit, a functional departmental structure has two primary weaknesses. First, this type of organization is very good if an organization produces a single product or a very limited product line. However, as the number of products increases, managers who lead functional teams can easily become overwhelmed because of the complexity that is introduced. A second disadvantage of this type of structure is that it does not promote a great deal of cross-fertilization of ideas among functional groups. There is a tendency, in this type of structure, for employees to become very compartmentalized and thus not take advantage of the ideas of other specialties in the development of new products or services.

In terms of strategy, a functional structure is likely to work best in a relatively stable environment—one in which technological change is not rapid. Organizations with functional structures have a difficult time in industries where competitive advantage is determined largely by the speed with which organizations are able to respond to market demands.

A second manner in which many organizations today create departmental structures is based on products. Figure 14.3 provides an illustration of how such an organization might look. Notice that immediately below the CEO are the finance and human resources departments. The departments at the next level, however, correspond to the various products or services in which this organization specializes (e.g., electronic instruments, medical instruments, and computers). In this type of

FIGURE 14.2
Example of a Functional Department Structure

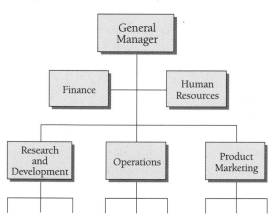

Source: J. R. Galbraith. (1995). *Designing organizations: An executive briefing on strategy, structure, and process.* San Francisco: Jossey-Bass. Copyright © 1995 Jossey-Bass. Reprinted by permission of John Wiley & Sons, Inc.

FIGURE 14.3
Example of a Product-Based Structure

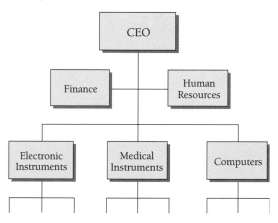

Source: J. R. Galbraith. (1995). *Designing organizations: An executive briefing on strategy, structure, and process.* San Francisco: Jossey-Bass. Copyright © 1995 Jossey-Bass. Reprinted by permission of John Wiley & Sons, Inc.

structure, the functional specialties that were described earlier are included under each of the product groupings. That is, there would be a marketing group for electronic instruments, another for medical instruments, and so on.

Departmental structures based on product lines are an advantage if an organization's strategy is to penetrate many markets or to have a highly diverse set of products. As stated earlier, a functional departmental structure would quickly be overwhelmed if an organization pursued this type of strategy. According to Galbraith (1995), however, two principal disadvantages are associated with this type of structure. First, general product managers often tend to think of themselves as entrepreneurs, and thus want considerable autonomy and independence. Although this may be desirable in some ways, it also can result in an organization's consistently "reinventing the wheel" because these individuals act independently of each other.

A second and related problem is that, under product structures, it is difficult to achieve functional "economies of scale" that benefit the organization as a whole. Note in Figure 14.3 that there is a marketing department for *each* of this organization's three product lines. While beneficial in some ways, this can also be wasteful because it precludes the organization's taking advantage of complimentary approaches to marketing or advertising. In effect, each marketing department focuses on its own product and may not have the larger interests of the organization as its first priority.

A third type of structure that is often employed is based on the various *markets* that an organization serves. This may lead to a departmental structure based on the customers the organization serves or the various industries in which the organization operates. Market-driven departmental structures are

becoming increasingly popular, given the decline in large-scale heavy manufacturing and the increasing number of firms in the service sector. This type of structure is particularly advantageous in the service sector because it enables the organization to react very quickly when, for some reason, customers' preferences change. The primary concern, as with the product-based structure, is that organizations may waste a considerable amount of time duplicating functional activities within each market.

A fourth type of departmental structure that may be used by organizations is based on geographic location. For example, an organization may create a "Northeast" division that is responsible for all operations in the New England states, and a "Midwest" division that is concerned with all business in the Great Lakes region. Most typically, geographical structures are found in industries where service is provided on-site and regional differences may be important to the business. Fast-food companies such as McDonald's or Burger King are organized in this fashion. The primary service is provided on-site (you can't e-mail someone a Big Mac!) and there may be important regional differences in food preferences.

The primary advantage of a geographic structure is that organizations can more easily provide personal services to customers and adjust those services to meet regional preferences. A potential disadvantage of this structure, however, is duplication of functional activities. Also, geographical dispersion makes it more difficult to maintain consistency and company-wide quality standards. Recent advances in communication technology have made consistent quality somewhat less of a concern, but it still remains a problem.

A final way that organizations may structure their departments is according to major *work-flow processes*. According to Galbraith (1995), this is the newest type of departmental structure. Figure 14.4 shows an example of a departmental structure that is process based. Notice that the three departments in this organizational structure correspond to the processes of new product development, order fulfillment, and customer acquisition/maintenance. Functional groups would reside within each of these process-related departments.

When compared to the functional organizational structure, the process-based structure has one advantage: potentially, it results in a lower amount of duplication of effort because there is less need to duplicate functions across departments responsible for different processes. For example, customer service personnel would reside exclusively in the customer acquisition and maintenance department, so these efforts would not be duplicated *across* departments. Another advantage of this structure is that it forces an organization to take a hard look at its major work-flow process; in fact, this type of structure cannot be created unless an organization does so. By looking at major processes, an organization may gain valuable insights into

how to make such processes more effective and efficient. For example, by gaining a greater understanding of its work-flow processes, a consumer product company may be able to adopt a strategy of reducing costs by maintaining small inventories.

Level of Environmental Uncertainty

There are vast differences among organizations in terms of the extent to which they must deal with uncertainty in the environment. One obvious factor that impacts uncertainty is the level of competition an organization faces. An organization in an industry with few competitors will face a far more certain environment compared to one in an industry that has heavy competition. A related factor that impacts uncertainty is the degree of stability in an organization's competitive environment. Some organizations produce goods and services that have rather stable demand; for others, the demand may fluctuate very widely. A third factor impacting an organization is the extent to which its markets are affected by external factors such as government regulations. Examples of very stable environments would include government and regulated utilities. Examples of very uncertain environments would include computer software, consumer products, and transportation.

Uncertainty is related to organizational design because the degree of uncertainty often impacts the speed at which organizations must adapt to external conditions. A computer software company, for example, must be constantly prepared to bring new products to market, to satisfy the rapid changes in technology. A regulated utility, on the other hand, typically does not have to adapt nearly as quickly because it has much less volatility in its environment. Given this consideration, as a general rule, organizations

FIGURE 14.4
Example of a Work-Flow Process Structure

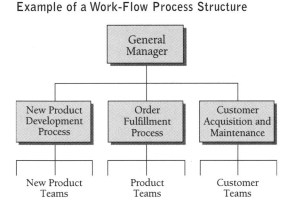

Source: J. R. Galbraith. (1995). *Designing organizations: An executive briefing on strategy, structure, and process.* San Francisco: Jossey-Bass. Copyright © 1995 Jossey-Bass. Reprinted by permission of John Wiley & Sons, Inc.

that operate in highly uncertain environments need organizational structures that allow them to act quickly when change occurs (Burns & Stalker, 1961).

Based on the organizational theories that have been discussed up to this point, it seems fairly clear that highly bureaucratic organizational structures are not very adaptable in highly uncertain environments. Having a large number of rules and procedures, clear lines of authority, and small spans of control may keep things humming along very smoothly in stable environments. When things change, however, it is very difficult for highly bureaucratic organizations to change course quickly. More humanistic organizations fare much better in uncertain environments. In these types of organizations, power is shifted to lower levels, and employees at these levels are empowered to make decisions without first having lengthy deliberations with superiors.

Beliefs and Assumptions of Those in Power

Although organizations are institutions, they are ultimately creations of people; therefore, they reflect the beliefs and assumptions of people. One of the fundamental judgments that managers in organizations must make is whether their employees can be trusted (Dansereau, Graen, & Haga, 1975). Organizations run by managers who place little trust in their employees will likely favor organizational designs that allow for high levels of managerial control. These designs offer very small spans of control, limited and highly centralized communication, and other mechanisms that discourage independent action on the part of employees.

A somewhat related issue is the extent to which managers respect their employees' job-related skills or believe in their competence (Liden & Maslyn, 1998). This is obviously related to trust but is not the same thing. For example, it is possible for managers to believe that employees are trustworthy, and yet have little confidence in their skills. Managers may also see some employees as highly competent, yet have little trust in them. Organizations run by managers who have little confidence in their employees will probably be designed to resemble organizations where there is low trust. The similar designs achieve the same goal: a high level of control over employees. Conversely, when managers in organizations have a great deal of confidence in employees, the organizational designs selected will more easily allow employees to use their unique skills and abilities. Organizational arrangements may allow employees to exercise independent judgment and decision making, and to communicate freely with each other. Furthermore, in some cases, organizations create designs that specifically facilitate creativity. A good example of an organization with a long history of doing this is 3M (see Comment 14.1).

A final fundamental belief or assumption of those in power may impact organizational design: the level of organizational performance that is expected or desired. As we saw earlier, R. Likert (1961) proposed that there is a strong connection between the desire to maintain managerial control and organizational performance. In the System 1 organization, managers maintain very high levels of control, yet the price they pay for this control is high—such organizations will likely only be mediocre. In contrast, in the System 4 and System 5 organizations, managers give up a good deal of control, which is risky. However, the rewards that go along with doing so are potentially very high because organizations are capable of truly excellent performance.

Although it seems illogical, there could be a number of reasons why managers in an organization would be comfortable with minimal

---

COMMENT 14.1

THE 3M PATH TO INNOVATION

THE MINNESOTA MINING and Manufacturing Company, more commonly known as 3M, was founded in 1902 by five businessmen whose original intent was to mine the mineral corundum and sell it to grinding-wheel manufacturers. The manufacturers needed this mineral to make abrasive materials such as sandpaper. Unfortunately, the mineral found in the mine they purchased in Crystal Bay, Minnesota, contained another material that was not suitable for abrasives; thus, they were not able to carry out their original plan. The company ultimately decided to manufacture abrasives themselves, and, after several years of struggle, expanded into the production of adhesives. Ultimately, as most readers are well aware, 3M became the leader in both industries. Today, 3M is one of the most successful corporations in existence. Annual sales are approximately $15 billion, half of which comes from outside the United States.

By any measure, 3M's credentials as an innovative company are impressive. For example, 30% of the company's sales come from products that have been introduced within the past four years. In 1998 alone, 3M gained 611 patents, and consistently ranks in the top 10 U.S. companies in patents granted. How do they do it? One obvious factor is their recruitment and hiring of top scientific talent. Another factor that has been widely cited is 3M's long-standing "15% rule" among its research personnel. More specifically, researchers are encouraged to spend up to 15% of their time on projects that are based purely on their own interest. The most visible outcome of the 15% rule is the ubiquitous "post-it"® note. Many other product innovations have resulted from this policy as well.

Another major factor in 3M's success as an innovator is its organizational structure. Research personnel are organized into Corporate Laboratories, Divisional Laboratories, and Technology Centers. Researchers in each of these areas are focused on somewhat different activities (e.g., "basic" research, modification of existing products and technologies), but they are encouraged to communicate freely with each other and with customers. This type of structure facilitates the sense of scientific community that is needed for innovation, and the probability that innovations have market potential.

Source: E. Gundling. (2000). *The 3M way to innovation: Balancing people and profit.* Tokyo: Kodansha International.

---

performance. For example, managerial compensation packages often provide disincentives for taking steps to create long-term organizational excellence. Specifically, stock option plans often reward managers for taking steps to boost short-term stock prices (e.g., layoffs, cuts in research and development expenditures) at the expense of long-term excellence. Thus, managers may sacrifice long-term success for short-term gains.

Another potential reason has to do with the culture of the organization. According to L. H. Peters and O'Connor (1988), over time, many organizations develop a "culture of justification": employees' primary concern becomes justifying minimal levels of performance. In such an organizational culture, high levels of performance are not rewarded; in fact, they may actually be punished. As a result, over time, those who strive for excellence either leave the organization or simply retreat to a minimal level of performance themselves. A logical corollary to this sequence is that managers who demand excellence typically do not fare well in such an environment.

Organizational Size

As a general rule, organizational design and structure become more important issues as organizations increase in size. An organization that consists of five family members probably has little need for departmental or divisional structures. However, as organizations grow in size, coordinating the efforts of individuals with a "free form" organizational structure becomes increasingly difficult. Thus, as organizations grow in size, the level of formalization in organizational structure tends to increase.

Empirical research has consistently supported the link between organizational size and structure. Perhaps the best known research was conducted by the Aston research group, in Great Britain (Hickson, Pugh, & Pheysey, 1969). These researchers found that organizational size, along with major organizational technology (which will be described next), determined the structure of these organizations. As organizations increased in size (as measured by number of employees), they were more likely to exhibit the characteristics of bureaucracy, or what has also been labeled "mechanistic" organizational structure (Burns & Stalker, 1961). In contrast, smaller organizations tended to resemble characteristics of humanistic organizations, or what has been labeled "organic" organizational structure.

Larger organizations gravitate toward more bureaucratic organizational designs because they make it much easier to cope with the complexities that are inevitable when large numbers of people are involved. For example, having free-flowing communication in a large organization could potentially lead to information overload and, ultimately, chaos. Unfortunately, many organizations face a competitive environment that is not well served by having a highly bureaucratic organizational structure. Thus, many organizations deal with this issue by creating what may be described as a "hybrid" type of organizational structure, in which the organization as a whole might be described as a bureaucracy. However, within smaller organizational units, the structure and culture are more like those of a humanistic organization.

Small organizations obviously have less need for coordination, and thus are able to adopt a purer version of humanistic organizational structure. For example, in these organizations, communication is more free-flowing, roles are less well defined, and employees are consulted on a regular basis. Highly organic structures often work very well, but there may be a point at which more formalization is necessary. As an example, many highly successful Internet start-up companies were populated primarily by employees in their early twenties, who had little, if any, formal managerial experience. Most of these companies adopted highly informal organizational structures and cultures. As their sales revenues increased, many of these organizations hired seasoned managers who imposed more formalized structures. The challenge for these organizations is to reap the benefits of these more formal structures without losing the creativity and entrepreneurial spirit that initially made them successful (see Comment 14.2).

Major Technologies

The word "technology" typically conjures up images of complex machinery and manufacturing processes. Although this applies to some forms of technology, it is not always the case. Many formal definitions exist (e.g., Scott, 1990), but technology is generally seen

COMMENT 14.2

THE SECOND COMING OF BOTH APPLE AND STEVE JOBS

IN THE LATE 1970s and early 1980s, Apple Computer became one of the clear leaders in the newly emerging personal computer industry. Much of the success of Apple was attributed to its founder, Steve Jobs, whose goal was to make computing accessible to everyone—and fun. Ironically, as Apple grew, the innovative, free-wheeling style that initially contributed to Apple's success nearly led to its undoing. In 1985, after a well-publicized power struggle with John Scully, Steve Jobs was asked by Apple's board of directors to leave the company.

In the years after his exit from Apple, Jobs was determined to prove that he was not just a technological "visionary" but was also an effective leader. The start of Jobs' first post-Apple venture, NeXT Computer, was highly publicized but ultimately turned out to be a failure. Ironically, what ultimately changed Jobs' fortunes was his acquisition of Pixar, a small film animation studio owned by film producer George Lucas. With the release of the movie *Toy Story*, Pixar became a great success, and Jobs' wealth increased considerably.

In the years following Jobs' exit, Apple continued on a downward spiral. By 1996, its stock price had fallen to $17 a share (com-pared to $60 a share in 1992), and its share of the personal computer market fell from 12%, which had once made it the leader, to only 4%. Finally, in 1996, Apple acquired Jobs' company NeXT and allowed him to once again take it over, although he was only an "informal adviser" (he would be named CEO in 2000). In Jobs' second stint with Apple, some things remained the same—he relied on product innovation, in the form of the iMac, to boost profits. What was different, however, was that Jobs imposed a level of structure and discipline that was not seen during the early years. Employees were outraged, for example, when he banned smoking on the Apple campus and would not allow them to bring their dogs to work. Despite the grumbling, Jobs' leadership worked. Profits soared, and Apple's stock price more than tripled.

What can we learn from this story? For starters, people *can* change and can learn from failure. In terms of organizational structure, the lesson is clear: different *times call for different levels of structure.*

Source: A. Deutschman. (2000). *The second coming of Steve Jobs.* New York: Broadway Books.

---

as the primary means by which inputs from the environment are converted into something tangible that can be returned to the environment. For an organization that makes paper products, for example, technology represents the processes used to convert wood to products such as paper napkins and tissue paper. The technology of a drug treatment center represents the therapeutic methods and interventions that are used to "convert" people from being addicted to alcohol and drugs to being free from these addictions.

An organization's technology is related to organizational design in several ways. At the most general level, the two must be compatible. Since an organization's technology is typically established prior to its structure, the structure is typically created to support technology rather than the reverse. One of the most widely cited studies relating structure and technology was conducted by Woodward (1965). In this study, a number of organizations were classified as having one of three primary technologies. **Large-batch technology** organizations were those that used traditional assembly-line production processes; that is, products were mass-produced, and this was done in a sequential fashion. The second type of organization was described as having **small-batch technology.** This type of organization produced products that were essentially custom made, and thus it was not possible to obtain the economies of scale that are possible with mass production. The third type of technology in this study was described as **continuous process technology.** Organizations using this type of technology are not mass-producing a product; they are converting material from one state to another.

Based on this classification of technology types, Woodward (1965) found a distinct relationship between technology and organizational design. The largest difference in organizational design was found between organizations that used large-batch and small-batch technology. Organizations that used large-batch technology tended to have bureaucratic or mechanistic organizational structures. Presumably, the need to maintain control and certainty during the production process would be responsible for this finding. Organizations using small-batch technology tended to have humanistic or organic structures. One would assume that this would be due to the fact that custom-made products require a high level of adaptability and flexibility in an organization—both of which are hard to achieve in a typical bureaucratic organization. The third type of organization, the one using continuous-process technology, was found to be a hybrid between bureaucratic and humanistic structures.

Although Woodward's (1965) findings have been widely cited over the years, they have also received their fair share of criticism. Perhaps the most serious criticism is that her findings confounded organizational technology with organizational size. Because technology tends to covary quite strongly with organizational size, it has been asserted that her findings are due primarily to organizational size. Researchers in the Aston project empirically tested this idea and found that, although size was a predictor of organizational design, it was not completely confounded with technology (Hickson et al., 1969)—that is, technology and organizational design had independent effects on the design of organizations.

Another potential limitation of Woodward's (1965) research is that many organizations do not use single technologies; they utilize multiple technologies. Universities, for example, typically use different instructional methodologies for undergraduate education than they do for doctoral programs. This leads to a question: What type of organizational structure would be present in an organization that utilizes very different technologies at the same time? At present, there are no definite answers to this question. However, it is probably logical to assume that organizations often deal with this issue by having several structures.

A final limitation is that the classification developed by Woodward nearly 40 years ago may not be applicable today. For example, because of changes in manufacturing technology, organizations are often capable of producing customized versions of products that at one time were mass-produced (e.g., Zammuto & O'Connor, 1992). In addition, many tasks that were once performed by assembly-line workers have now been automated. Thus, employees involved in mass production today are much more likely to be involved in monitoring tasks as opposed to repetitive tasks. As a result, the organizational structure needed for mass production may be quite different today than it was 40 years ago; for example, it may be more similar to structures that support continuous process technology.

RECENT INNOVATIONS IN ORGANIZATIONAL DESIGN

It is becoming increasingly common for organizations to adopt organizational designs that resemble neither the classical nor the humanistic types. These different organizational designs have evolved for a number of reasons. One reason is that many organizations have found that purely bureaucratic or humanistic organizational designs have not allowed them to meet the challenges of their competitive environment. Also, different organizational designs have developed as a way to better leverage both employee skills and organizational resources, and still remain competitive. Finally, evolution of these different organizational forms has corresponded to recent changes in managerial philosophy. In this section, we examine three of the most common recent innovations in organizational design: (1) the team-based organization, (2) the matrix organization, and (3) the virtual organization.

The Team-Based Organization

In the past 20 years, research on group or team effectiveness within organizational psychology has grown rapidly (Guzzo & Shea, 1992). Along with this increasing interest, organizations have dramatically increased their use of teams. Most organizations utilize teams under the assumption that teams represent a much more effective way to utilize and combine employees' skills than simply having employees work as individuals. Teams can be very effective tools in organizations, yet they are certainly not the answer to all problems. In fact, teams may create problems of their own.

A **team-based organization** is one that goes beyond the occasional ad-hoc use of teams and uses them as the basis for their organizational structure. Figure 14.5 illustrates an organizational design that is based entirely on teams. As can be seen, this small organization consists of four cross-functional teams that correspond to the organization's four primary product lines. According to Mohrman and Quam (2000), in a team-based organization, teams are used to "carry out their core work, to develop and deliver the products and services that provide value to customers" (p. 20). In this type of organization, teams have responsibility for activities such as planning work, staffing, and compensating team members.

According to Galbraith (1995), a number of important issues must be addressed for even a simple team-based organizational structure to work effectively. One of the most important of these is *coordination* of the activities of the different teams comprising the structure. This is important because the activities of one team often impact the activities of others. As an example, let's say that the marketing efforts of each of the teams in Figure 14.5

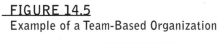

FIGURE 14.5
Example of a Team-Based Organization

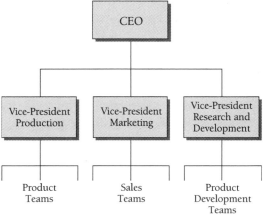

lack coordination. This could actually result in sales representatives from each team calling on customers at the same time, thus decreasing the chances of *any* sale being made. This is obviously bad for the teams and embarrassing for the organization as a whole.

One of the most common ways to achieve coordination is to create what is essentially an "executive committee" that consists of the leaders of each of the teams. That is, the leader of each team belongs to a higher-level team that meets periodically to consider issues of coordination between teams. Given the size and complexity of an organization, there may be several such executive or coordinating committees at various levels of the organization. A variant of this method would be to create various coordinating committees from different organizational levels.

Many academic departments utilize this mechanism by having an executive committee comprised of the chairperson, the directors of the undergraduate program, and the directors of the graduate programs. These individuals are often responsible for setting overall departmental policy in a way that balances the needs of the various programs offered by the department. Another potential activity of such a committee might be to create long-term strategic plans. Such a committee is often very useful because those who comprise it must look beyond their own interests and make policy decisions that are based on the department as a whole. This can also be an excellent mechanism for training members of an academic department to assume leadership positions in the future.

Along with coordination, perhaps the other most crucial issue in implementing a team-based organizational structure is creating a compatible reward system. As was stated in Chapter 12, a common problem with the use of teams in general is that organizational reward systems are often aimed primarily at individual-level performance. As a result, individuals often have little incentive to behave in ways that maximize the performance of the team. This issue becomes even more important with a team-based structure because overall organizational performance is intimately tied to the performance of individual teams.

One obvious way to align reward systems with a team-based structure is to base rewards primarily on the *team* performance or even the *organizational* performance. Compensation methods such as profit sharing and gain sharing are common ways of accomplishing this objective. This is not to say that organizations should completely ignore individual performance. However, if organizational performance depends primarily on team performance, this should be the focal point of the reward system.

Another reward system practice that is consistent with team-based organizational structure is skill-based compensation (Lawler, 1990). Recall from Chapter 6 that, in this type of compensation plan, employees have the opportunity to achieve pay increases by demonstrating the acquisition of additional job-relevant skills. Skill-based compensation is compatible with a team-based organizational structure because it provides a team with much greater staffing flexibility than it would have if each team member performed a highly specialized task. Skill-based pay systems provide team members with an incentive to develop the multiple skills that are needed in such an environment.

Another important consideration in the implementation of the team-based organization is the nature of the work that is performed by the teams. One obvious question must be asked before implementing a team-based organizational structure: Does the work lend itself to a team-based structure? This may seem like a rather obvious point, yet many organizations overlook it. In their zeal to reap the benefits of teamwork, many organizations overlook the fact that the work being performed does not lend itself to a team-based structure. If the work does not lend itself to a team-based structure, an organization can either abandon this structure or redesign the work.

Finally, organizations committed to implementing a team-based organizational structure must take a hard look at their selection procedures. As with any organization, employees must be selected based on whether they are able to perform important job-related tasks. However, team-based organizations must also confront the fact that not all individuals want to work within a team-based structure. Some individuals are more comfortable than others working in a team-based environment (Campion, Medsker, & Higgs, 1993). There is also evidence that some individuals possess better team-based skills than others do (e.g., Stevens & Campion, 1999).

The Matrix Organization

A matrix organization is one in which there are essentially two separate organizational structures at the same time (Davis & Lawrence, 1977). One of these structures may be represented by traditional functional departments such as Marketing, Engineering, Accounting, and so on. At the same time, a second structure is superimposed on this traditional departmental structure. Most typically, this second structure is based on organizational *projects,* although there are many other bases for creating this second structure. Consumer product companies often have secondary structures based on brands or, in some cases, different markets that they serve.

Typically, in a matrix structure, managers in charge of different projects draw employees from each of the functional departments until a project is completed. Figure 14.6 provides a simple illustration of how this might work in practice. Notice that project A draws employees from all three functional departments, project B draws employees from both Marketing and Engineering, and project C draws employees from both Marketing and Accounting. Often, but not always, projects in matrix organizations are of limited duration. For example, in consumer product companies that have matrix structures based on brands, these structural arrangements are more or less permanent. It is highly likely, however, that the specific needs of each of the brands may change over time, and thus the specific functional resources devoted to each brand may also fluctuate over time.

The primary advantage of a matrix structure is that it allows an organization the flexibility needed to quickly shift the focus of its design on the most important part of its business. As an example, the lifeblood of an organization that is a major defense contractor is obviously defense contracts. Therefore, if such an organization receives a large contract to develop an advanced weapons system, a matrix structure allows it to quickly shift a great deal of its internal resources to that project. When the project is completed, resources

FIGURE 14.6
Example of a Matrix Organizational Structure

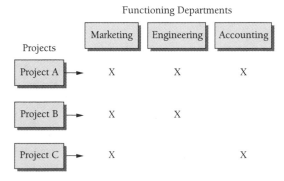

can then be quickly reallocated to other projects as needed.

Matrix structures based on products or product lines allow an organization to use a unique approach in the way it handles each product. For example, a well-established product line may require a vastly different advertising approach than a product that has just emerged on the scene. In the consumer product environment, matrix structures also help to guard against complacency. Having people assigned to products (e.g., brand managers) makes it more likely that the organization will continue trying to improve them through research and development efforts, and through the use of consumer data.

Beyond these more obvious benefits, there are also intangible benefits. For example, regardless of whether a matrix structure is based on projects or brands, being a project or brand manager can be a highly developmental experience for managers. In fact, Procter and Gamble, one of the largest consumer product companies in the world, is known to use brand management positions explicitly for developmental purposes. Brand managers not only learn a great deal about a particular product or product line, they also learn a great deal about the organization as a whole as they draw resources for their brand. Project or brand managers in any organization also learn a great deal about negotiation and compromise because, in many cases, they are not simply handed resources; instead, they must negotiate with functional managers in order to get them.

Matrix structures also pose a number of challenges. One of the biggest challenges is that, in many cases, matrix structures end up pitting project or brand managers *against* functional managers. This can result in a great deal of dysfunctional conflict and political gamesmanship (e.g., de Laat, 1994). Some organizations address this issue by establishing that the needs of projects take priority over the needs of functional departments. This may help to clarify things a bit, but it introduces some dysfunctional effects of its own. Functional managers may come to see themselves as "second-class citizens" in comparison to project or brand managers. As a result, functional management is often seen as an undesirable position, particularly if one wants to be promoted to upper management.

Matrix structures can also have deleterious effects on employees working in functional departments. In a large organization with a matrix structure, it is very likely that an employee working in a functional department will be working on several projects simultaneously. This may result in work overload and can often impose conflicting demands on employees (Joyce, 1986). Beyond these workload issues, a by-product of matrix structure is that employees may have to work for several "bosses" at the same time. Furthermore, these different bosses may have very different performance standards and interpersonal styles. Thus, from an employee's point of view, working under a matrix structure could be highly stressful. Functional managers must communicate frequently with project managers to ensure that they are not overworking employees.

The Virtual Organization

The term "virtual organization" is sometimes used to refer to organizations in which employees are in different physical locations. For example, a research organization that is based in Boston may employ an individual who lives in Los Angeles and works out of her home. When this is done on a limited basis, the term to describe it is typically *telecommuting*. In the organizational design literature, the term *virtual organization* is used differently. According to Galbraith (1995), a virtual organization is one, for example, in which an organization decides to produce a product or service but contracts with other firms to provide a key part of that product or service. The auto companies have, to a large extent, become virtual organizations. Although they continue to assemble automobiles, parts that were once produced internally are now produced by external suppliers.

The primary motivation for forming virtual organizations is cost reduction. For auto companies, the capital and other internal resources needed to produce automotive parts have simply increased to a level that is prohibitive. A second motivation is that contracting out more peripheral functions allows an organization to concentrate all of its energy on its core business. In Peters and Waterman's (1982) classic book, *In Search of Excellence,* one of the key characteristics of companies they identified as being excellent was labeled "Stick to the knitting." That is, excellent organizations do not try to do *everything;* rather, they stick to what they know.

Despite the potential advantages of virtual organizations, this type of organizational design also has its drawbacks. When an organization enters into a partnership with a supplier, it is assuming some degree of risk. For example, when auto companies do not produce most of their own parts, it is more difficult to ensure that those parts meet quality standards. Organizations obviously do have some degree of leverage because it is certainly in suppliers' interests to maintain the relationship. Nevertheless, entering into such a relationship is, to some extent, entering into the unknown. According to Galbraith (1995), organizations typically deal with this uncertainty by thoroughly investigating potential business partners before entering into relationships. Another way is to build "escape clauses" into business partnerships, as consultants often do.

Another potential drawback of virtual organizations is that they make it difficult for an organization to maintain a coherent culture. In the extreme, an organization that contracts out nearly everything ceases to become a distinct organizational entity; instead, it becomes a rather large conglomeration of different organizational cultures. This status may make it very difficult to instill a sense of commitment and loyalty in employees. This may also explain why some organizations known to have very strong and distinct cultures (e.g., 3M) have not made extensive use of the virtual organization concept. As the virtual organization concept becomes more prevalent, it is possible that organizations will find effective ways to deal with this issue.

RESEARCH ON ORGANIZATIONAL DESIGN

Perhaps one of the clearest themes in the organizational design literature over the years is that *organizational designs come about largely as adaptive responses to the environment.* For example, it has been shown that organizations differ as a function of environmental uncertainty (Burns & Stalker, 1961), technology (Scott, 1990; Woodward, 1965), strategy (Galbraith, 1995), and sheer organizational size (Hickson et al., 1969). Thus, one thing that empirical research has shown is that organizational designs do not just *appear;* rather, they typically come about as a response to an organization's environment. Interestingly, though, it has also been proposed that organizational design may at times reflect the personality quirks of individual managers (Kets de Vries & Miller, 1986). Therefore, the driving forces behind organizational design decisions may not always be rational or functional.

One thing that has clearly *not* been shown in empirical organizational design research is that there is *one best way to design an organization.* Granted, research has shown that organizational designs come about as a result of environmental factors; unfortunately, there is scant evidence that organizations with designs matching their environment are always successful. If anything, organizational design research has shown, with respect to design, that there are many paths to organizational success. It appears, though, that a key factor in whether a given organizational design leads to success is whether internal policies and procedures are congruent with the design. Perhaps the best example of this is the literature on team-based organizations, which has shown that organizations using this type of design are much more successful if their compensation practices are congruent with it (Mohrman & Quam, 2000).

A third major theme is clearly evident in organizational design research: *The design of organizations has tangible effects on employee behavior.* Perhaps the best example of this is the previously cited study in which Joyce (1986) found that employees working under a matrix organizational design experienced greater levels of role conflict, compared to employees working under a more traditional design. It has also been found that organizational structure has an impact on individual employees' perceptions of fairness (Schminke, Ambrose, & Cropanzano, 2000). Centralized decision making was negatively associated with procedural fairness, and organizational size was negatively associated with interactional fairness. This may be due to the fact that larger organizations tend to treat employees in a very impersonal manner.

Findings of this sort are important because they suggest possible mediating mechanisms by which organizational designs—or any other organizational intervention, for that matter—impact organizational effectiveness. More importantly, they shift our thinking from viewing organizational designs as "boxes and arrows" to seeing them for what they really are—purposeful interventions that are designed to shape and influence human behavior in a particular direction. For those in the field of psychology, this is important because it drives home the point that macro-level factors such as organizational design are important. Conversely, for those trained in organizational theory or strategy, it suggests that something very important is in the "black box" between macro-level variables such as design and organizational effectiveness.

A final theme in organizational design research is that *organizational designs are not static and therefore can be changed.* This is really a logical corollary to the first theme discussed earlier; namely, that organizational designs are the result of conscious decisions on the part of organizational policy makers. Thus, if organizational decision makers are capable of making conscious decisions about the initial structure of an organization, it follows that they are capable of changing the design of an organization in response to other changes in the organization. Studies have shown, however, that changing the design of an organization is not easy (e.g., Porras & Robertson, 1992). As with any organizational change, there may be problems of employee resistance. An additional challenge with changing organizational design is that, compared to many other aspects of organizations, employees tend to think of design as a fixed entity.

THE FUTURE OF ORGANIZATIONAL DESIGN

How will organizations be designed in the future? This question obviously cannot be answered with complete certainty. We do know, however, that a number of trends will clearly shape organizations in the future. One trend that has impacted many aspects of organizational functioning is the ever-increasing sophistication of information technology. Business transactions that used to take weeks to accomplish can now be completed in a matter of seconds. This increased sophistication of information technology has been a double-edged sword for organizations. On the positive side, it has resulted in a level of efficiency and speed that is unprecedented. At the same time, however, it has contributed to a highly volatile environment in many business sectors that were previously much more stable.

With respect to organizational design, the most general impact of information technology is that it places a premium on speed and flexibility. Thus, based on the organizational designs that were discussed in this chapter, there will likely continue to be an increasing trend toward designs that resemble Likert's System 4 and System 5, as well as the team-based structure. The reason for this is that speed often demands that lower-level employees must be empowered to make many decisions that were once reserved for management. Organizations simply will not have time to go up through a large chain of command to make every decision.

The other implication of information technology is that it will likely increase the use of more flexible organizational designs. It will become increasingly common for organizations to consist of individuals who spend some or all of their time "off site" through telecommuting. This will also make virtual organizations much more appealing, and therefore more likely to be used. For example, through videoconferencing, regular meetings can take place between those at organizational headquarters

and suppliers in different parts of the country, or even the world. Thus, in the future, we may need to seriously rethink what an *organization* actually is.

A second trend, which is actually somewhat related to the first, is the globalization of the economy. With the fall of communism in the early 1990s, coupled with free trade agreements and a trend toward standardization of currency, the world has increasingly embraced free-market capitalism. Furthermore, countries that were at one time essentially closed to Western society (e.g., China) are now becoming active trading partners with the West. Obviously, the extent to which this globalization of the economy will lead to global prosperity depends on a number of factors (e.g., maintaining world peace, stabilizing new free-market economies). However, it will have a major impact on organizations.

With respect to organizational design, globalization will clearly increase the incentive of organizations to expand their markets beyond national borders. Thus, an increasing number of organizations will add foreign subsidiaries to their existing structures. A major issue in the future is how these foreign subsidiaries are managed and integrated with the existing structure. More specifically, organizational design issues will focus primarily on determining the appropriate combination of direction and autonomy to give these foreign subsidiaries. Globalization will also likely force more and more organizations to adopt geographically based or regional organizational structures.

A third trend that will likely impact organizational design is the growing contingent workforce (Beard & Edwards, 1995). Recall from Chapter 1 that this was described as an important trend that was predicted to have an impact on many areas of organizational psychology. In the realm of organizational design, the increasing availability of a contingent workforce, combined with the previously discussed trends, will make the virtual organization much more prevalent in the future. Having contingent employees readily available makes it much easier for organizations to quickly reconfigure themselves in order to take advantage of market opportunities. In the past, more permanent bureaucratic structures made this type of flexibility nearly impossible. Of course, with these new opportunities comes a number of challenges, such as maintaining consistent performance standards, and instilling a coherent sense of organizational culture in these transient employees.

CHAPTER SUMMARY

In this chapter, we shifted the focus from individual and group-level phenomena to a broader level. This shift is important because a complete understanding of behavior in organizations requires that we look at it from all three vantage points. The chapter began with a discussion of the field of organizational theory, primarily focusing on its intellectual roots and its linkage to the closely related field of organizational design. The focus then shifted to a description of the three most general types of organizational designs. Classical organizational designs are represented by Scientific Management, Ideal Bureaucracy, and Administrative Management. Humanistic organizational designs are best represented by McGregor's Theory X/Y, and Likert's System 4 organization. Classical and humanistic organizational designs have both advantages and disadvantages. Furthermore, the appropriateness of each of these organizational types depends largely on situational factors, and this leads to the third type of organizational design: contingency organizational design.

Based on the premise that contingency theory is the dominant paradigm in organizational

design today, the chapter then shifted to the major factors that are taken into consideration when organizations make design decisions. These included strategy, level of environmental uncertainty, beliefs and assumptions of those in power, organizational size, and the dominant technology. Given this number of factors, there will obviously be a variety of organizational designs. Furthermore, it very likely that different organizational designs may coexist within the same organization.

The chapter then shifted to focus on three relatively recent trends in the design of organizations: (1) team-based organizational structure, (2) matrix organizational structure, and (3) the virtual organization. Although each of these organizational designs is different, they all allow organizations to respond more quickly to market opportunities and to make better uses of their internal resources. Furthermore, all three of these organizational designs require that other organizational subsystems must be properly aligned in order for them to work well.

There has been considerable research on the impact of organizational design, and this was summarized according to the dominant themes. One of these themes is that designs appear to be at least partially traceable to adaptive responses to the environments in which organizations operate. Research has also shown that there is no "right way" to design an organization; however, organizations that tend to align their various subsystems with their structure tend to be the most effective. A third theme is that organizational designs do influence the behavior of employees. This serves as an important linkage between micro- and macro-level organizational behavior.

The chapter concluded with a brief discussion of factors that are likely to influence organizational designs of the future. These include information technology, globalization of the economy, and the increasing number of contingent employees. These trends may have many influences on organizations, but their most likely impact on design will be to increase the use of virtual organizational designs. Organizations will then be better able to expand and contract quickly, and to move much more quickly into previously untapped global markets.

SUGGESTED ADDITIONAL READINGS

Galbraith, J. (1994). *Competing with flexible lateral organizations* (2nd ed.). Reading, MA: Addison-Wesley.

Humphrey, R. H., & Ashforth, B. E. (2000). Buyer-supplier alliances in the automobile industry: How exit-voice strategies influence interpersonal relationships. *Journal of Organizational Behavior, 21,* 713–730.

McKinley, W., Mone, M. A., & Moon, G. (1999). Determinants and development of schools of thought in organizational theory. *Academy of Management Review, 24,* 634–648.

Steensma, H. K., & Corley, K. G. (2000). On the performance of technology-sourcing partnerships: The interaction between partner interdependence and technology attributes. *Academy of Management Journal, 43,* 1045–1067.

Chapter Fifteen

Organizational Culture

Perhaps the best way to appreciate organizational culture is to imagine entering an unfamiliar organization for the very first time—maybe as a new employee. In some ways, this experience is similar to entering a foreign country. For example, members of the organization may use words and phrases we don't understand; they may engage in behaviors that they take quite seriously but have little meaning to outsiders, and tell jokes and stories that only they can fully understand. If we were to stay in the organization long enough to make the transition to full-fledged organizational member, many of the things that we initially observed would become much more meaningful.

As a topic of study in organizational psychology, organizational culture is very new. In fact, most researchers have traced its beginning to the late 1970s (Pettigrew, 1979). However, the fact that organizational psychologists have studied organizational culture for only a short period of time does not decrease its

importance. To the contrary, culture is an extremely important key to understanding many behavior patterns in organizations. In fact, all behavior in organizations occurs in a cultural context. This may explain why things (e.g., incentive pay) that work well in some organizations fail miserably in others. Culture may also help us to understand why some organizations are successful and why others are not.

This chapter provides an overview of organizational culture and many of its implications. We begin by defining what is meant by organizational culture—no small feat, considering that this concept comes not only from psychology, but also from cultural anthropology and sociology. The chapter then shifts to an explanation of the various ways in which culture is reflected in organizations. As we'll see, some of these are rather obvious, but culture is often reflected in very subtle ways. We then explore the factors that shape the culture of an organization. The chapter will then focus on the various methods that can be used to study organizational culture. As we'll see, there are many ways to examine the culture of an organization, and strong opinions on their appropriateness. The chapter then shifts to a discussion of organizational culture change, and concludes with an examination of the impact of organizational culture, both on the success of the organization as a whole and on individual organizational members.

DEFINING ORGANIZATIONAL CULTURE

Organizational culture is a far easier concept to *experience* than it is to define. At the most general level, culture can be thought of as the "view of the world" under which the members of an organization operate. By "view of the world," we mean that culture essentially represents the "lens" through which employees of an organization learn to interpret the environment. According to Schein (1985, 1992), there are essentially three levels of an organization's culture, and each succeeding level is more difficult for outsiders to decipher. The most visible level of organizational culture is reflected in **artifacts, technology, and behavior patterns.** Artifacts, which will be discussed in more depth later, are simply aspects of the physical environment that are meant to communicate cultural meaning. Technology simply represents the means by which organizations transform input from the outside environment. Behavior patterns, of course, simply represent what employees in the organization do.

The next level of culture, according to Schein (1992), is represented by the **shared values** within the organization. According to Hofstede (1980), values simply represent individuals' broad tendencies to prefer certain things, or states of affairs, over others. The values that might be salient within an organization could be a number of things: loyalty, customer service, collegiality, and self-preservation, to name a few. According to Schein (1992), values are less accessible to an outsider than are things such as behavior patterns, and, typically, they must be *inferred* by the outsider through symbolic means. For example, if an organization depends very heavily on seniority to reward and promote employees, it might be inferred that the organization tends to place a high value on employee loyalty and retention.

One of the things that is interesting about values in organizations is that, to truly understand this concept, we must distinguish between the values that are *espoused* by the organization, and those that are actually in operation (e.g., the "true" values). Obviously, in some organizations, there is a very strong relationship between the espoused and the true values. For example, innovation has always been an espoused value at 3M, and studies of this organization (e.g., Gundling, 2000; Peters & Waterman, 1982) have revealed that many company practices are consistent with it.

In many organizations, however, there is a disconnect between what an organization *claims* to value, and the values that appear to be guiding overt behavior. For example, many organizations claim to place a high value on diversity, yet have few minority employees in management positions; many organizations claim to place a high value on performance, yet tolerate consistently poor performance from employees; and many organizations claim that customer service is one of their core values, yet customers are treated rudely. What organizations *say* they value isn't always the same as the values in operation.

The third layer of culture, according to Schein (1992), is represented by the **basic assumptions** held by the members of an organization. These are ideas, or ways of looking at situations, that are so deeply ingrained that people take them for granted. To better understand basic assumptions, let's consider a basic assumption that we operate under in our daily lives, at least in western society. For example, when people greet each other, it is fairly common for one or both persons involved in such an encounter to ask the other, "How are you doing?" or "How's it going?" Most people understand that these questions, particularly when people do not know each other very well, are merely forms of greeting, and the appropriate response is "Fine, thanks" or "Not bad; how are you?" Most people are very uncomfortable when a person gives a lengthy, detailed response to such a question.

What are the basic assumptions that people hold in organizational settings? This is a difficult question to answer because organizations, and the people in them, differ so widely. However, if one thinks about it, there are probably some "basic truths" that may be salient, regardless of the situation. For example, employees in organizations have basic assumptions about whether the organization can be trusted, whether the organization supports them, whether the psychological environment is threatening or supportive, or whether hard work and dedication pay off. There are obviously other basic assumptions that are quite specific to a given organizational setting. For example, members of an accounting firm may have basic assumptions about the ethics surrounding the tax deductions they seek for their clients, or the teachers in an elementary school may hold common basic assumptions regarding the benefits of parental involvement in children's education.

Compared to the other two levels of culture discussed, basic assumptions are clearly the most difficult to study because they are so ingrained; in fact, Schein (1992) argued that they are not at a conscious level. Because of this, it is extremely difficult for a naïve organizational outsider to determine what these assumptions are. Furthermore, it is nearly equally difficult to *ask* people to tell you what these basic assumptions are. People generally perceive the world based on what is observable and accessible to them—by definition, basic assumptions are not. Typically, basic assumptions are determined only through painstaking research processes such as field observation, use of informants, and careful study of organizational archives. More will be said about studying organizational culture later in the chapter.

Having covered what is generally the most widely accepted definition of organizational culture, two important points must be addressed. The first is that, although Schein's (1992) definition of organizational culture is the most widely accepted, it is certainly not the only one. For example, organizational culture has been defined in terms of the common "cognitive maps" that are used by employees to navigate the organizational world (Weick, 1979), the systems of knowledge that bind organizational members together (Argyris & Schon, 1978), and even the nature of communication processes in organizations (Pacanowsky & O'Donnell-Trujillo, 1983). This variety of definitions should not be surprising, considering that cultural anthropologists and sociologists have also come up with many definitions of culture (Geertz, 1973; Ouchi & Wilkins, 1985). Schein's (1992) definition was highlighted because it is the most widely utilized in organizational psychology.

A second important point is that even though most organizations have what could be described as an "organization-wide" culture, they also contain a number of identifiable *subcultures*. Janson (1994) proposed that, in most organizations, there are six subcultures; these are presented in Table 15.1. As can be seen, the first subculture is labeled "Elite culture/corporate culture" and is essentially represented by those at the highest levels of the organization. The subculture in which the chief executive and the top executive group of an organization live is much different than most other employees. These individuals typically have more pleasant surroundings than other employees, and have a great deal of control over information dissemination in the wider organization.

The next form of subculture described by Janson is labeled "Departmental." Individuals within the same department work very closely together, face many of the same challenges, and collectively experience success and failure. Because of this, individuals within departments may develop many of the same views, and thus have many of the same basic assumptions about the organization. In universities, this is very evident when one looks at the different cultures that develop in academic departments (see Comment 15.1).

The next level of subculture development is at the Division level. In a business organization, for example, the Marketing Division may consist of the Sales, Market Research, and Advertising departments. In a university, the equivalent of a Division is a College that is composed of several academic departments. Divisional subcultures develop for essentially the same reasons as departmental subcultures. Employees in the same division may work under many of the same policies, and may experience many of the same challenges. As a result, individuals within the same division may begin to develop many of the same basic assumptions, and hence a subculture develops.

The next level of subculture that may develop is labeled "Local Culture" and is based on geographic regions. Local subcultures may be identical to Divisional subcultures where an organization's structure is based on geographic region. However, this is not always the case. Local subcultures develop largely based on local customs and norms of the region in which a unit works. For example, as a graduate student, the author worked as a contractor in the Florida division of a large telecommunications company. Based on conversations with others in that organization, it

TABLE 15.1
Possible Subcultures within an Organization Proposed by Janson (1994)

Elite culture/corporate culture—"For your eyes only" or "For public consumption"
Departmental culture—Horizontal slice; for example, sales department
Divisional culture—Vertical slice; for example, a division
Local culture—Within a geographical location/unit
Issue-related culture—Metaphorical, related to an important issue throughout the organization; for example, safety culture or quality culture
Professional culture—On the basis of professional background and training

Source: J. V. Mbijen. (1998). Organizational culture. In P. J. Drenth and H. Thierry (Eds.), *Handbook of work and organizational psychology* (2nd ed., Vol. 4, pp. 113–131). Hove, England: Psychology Press. Reprinted with permission of publisher.

ACADEMIC DEPARTMENT CULTURES AND SUBCULTURES

LIKE MOST UNDERGRADUATE students, the first two years of my college career were spent taking a broad range of courses in order to fulfill general education requirements. Although the primary goal of having these requirements is to facilitate liberal arts education, they also provide the opportunity for students to interact with faculty from a variety of academic disciplines and observe various departmental cultures. For a budding organizational psychologist like me, being able to compare these cultures was actually quite interesting.

As I recall (even though it's been quite a few years), there did appear to be a great deal of variation in the cultures of various academic departments. For example, I can remember visiting a faculty member in the English department and getting myself tangled in the beads that hung over his door. In fact, I can recall many of the faculty offices in that department looking more like coffeehouses or head shops than offices (remember, this *was* the mid-70s). This is no doubt consistent with the fact that a large part of writing is self-discovery and free expression—both of which were at the core of many of the social movements of the 1960s.

The cultures that I found to be the most different from English were Management and Marketing. Since both of these departments were in the School of Business, there was an emphasis on maintaining a businesslike culture. For example, most of the faculty dressed formally (many business schools *require* that faculty wear business attire when teaching), and many of their offices resembled those in corporations. Considering that most of the faculty members were trained in business schools, and that their primary mission was to train students for business careers, it is understandable that a businesslike culture would develop.

Psychology departments tend have very interesting cultures because of the dominance of subcultures. Particularly in large psychology departments with several doctoral programs, the subcultures that develop in each of the areas may be quite different. For example, the culture of a clinical psychology faculty might be very different from the culture of an industrial/organizational psychology faculty. The cultures of both groups, in turn, may be very different than the culture of a social psychology faculty.

The next time you're in an academic department, look around and see if you can find any clues about the culture of that department. Better yet, do this with two or more departments and see what the differences are. You might be surprised, fascinated, and even a bit amused by what you find!

became evident that there were distinct regional differences between this division and other regional divisions of the company. Due to the warm weather in Florida, the dress code was a bit more relaxed, and the manner in which people dealt with each other was a bit more informal than in other parts of the organization.

Subcultures may also develop due to some important issues faced throughout the organization. Recently, much work has been done on the construct of "safety culture" in organizations (Hofmann & Stetzer, 1998). In reality, in most organizations, there are probably many safety "subcultures"; that is, safety is likely to be viewed and practiced quite differently in many different parts of an organization. Other important issues that may be the basis for subculture development may include affirmative action, whether pay should be based on performance, and views of the trust-worthiness of management, to name a few.

The final basis for subculture development proposed by Janson is the professional training of employees. In some organizations, this could be the basis for the wider organizational culture (e.g., accounting firms, law firms, consulting firms), but, in many other cases, organizations employ groups of individuals who have obtained very different forms of professional training. For example, an organization that hires groups of chemical engineers may find that these individuals constitute a distinct subculture within the organization. In fact, in some cases, employees may have a much greater identification with their professional subculture than with the organization or division in which they work. Physicians, for example, often identify more strongly with the medical profession than they do with the hospitals or clinics in which they are employed.

MANIFESTATIONS OF ORGANIZATIONAL CULTURE

Now that we have some idea of what organizational culture is, the next issue is determining how organizational culture is manifested in organizations. Anyone who has visited several organizations, even within the same industry, can tell that each has a different "feel" to it. However, this begs the question of how a culture actually reveals itself in organizations. Fortunately, organizational culture researchers have come up with a number of ways, and they are described in this section.

Symbols and Artifacts

Symbols and artifacts are objects or aspects of the organizational environment that convey some greater meaning. In most organizations, symbols provide us with information on the nature of the culture. Perhaps one of the most

revealing symbols in an organization is the physical layout in which employees work. In some organizations, employees' "offices" are located in large open areas; in others, however, employees are given a great deal more privacy by having their offices placed in more remote locations. In the former setting, the office layout may be symbolic of a culture that places a high value on sociability and openness of communication. In the latter, the layout may be symbolic of a culture characterized by a high degree of secrecy or perhaps just a great deal of respect for privacy.

Another aspect of the physical environment that may provide symbolic information is the pervasiveness of status symbols. In recent years, it has become popular for organizations to de-emphasize status differentials; however, there are undoubtedly differences between organizations in this regard. An organization that has separate dining facilities for its executives, and carefully makes sure that the size of offices reflects employees' location in the status hierarchy, reflects a very status-conscious culture. On the other hand, organizations that have none of these status symbols are conveying a more egalitarian culture.

An **artifact,** as described earlier, is a material object that is created by people *specifically* to facilitate culturally expressive activities (Schein, 1983). An artifact is very similar to a symbol; the only difference is that artifacts represent a more direct attempt to convey cultural meaning, whereas symbols are more indirect. As with symbols, artifacts are most easily found in the physical environment of organizations. One of the most typical cultural artifacts in organizations is the physical manifestation of the major technology that is used. In educational settings, for example, classrooms are symbolic artifacts in that they convey the fact that students are to be reasonably obedient recipients of the knowledge that is passed down to them. In the Army, the fact that everyone wears uniforms, regardless of the settings in which they work, is a powerful artifact to remind everyone that they are all soldiers.

Rites and Rituals

Rites represent "relatively elaborate, dramatic, planned sets of activities that consolidate various forms of cultural expressions into one event, which is carried out through social interactions, usually for the benefit of an audience" (Trice & Beyer, 1984, p. 655). The most common rites carried out in organizations are summarized in Table 15.2. As can be seen, *rites of passage* are typically conducted in order to socialize individuals—from organizational outsiders to full-fledged organizational members—although these may be used for other types of transitions as well. The military's use of basic training is probably the most dramatic organizational rite of passage, but other organizations have these as well. For example, in academia, a familiar rite of passage is the oral defense of one's doctoral dissertation.

In some cases, rites are designed to sanction or, in a more general sense, to convey negative information to employees. *Rites of degradation* often occur when there is a problem in the organization or when there must

be a change in personnel. In the military, for example, when someone is relieved of his or her command, there is a great deal of symbolism in the change-of-command ceremony. When someone is denied tenure in a university, the year following the denial of tenure is a type of degradation ceremony. During this year, a faculty member must face his or her peers each day, knowing that he or she has failed to meet tenure standards and thus will not be employed there the following year.

In direct contrast, *rites of enhancement* are designed to convey positive information. This can be positive information about the organization, or public recognition of individuals for exceptional levels of performance. To illustrate this type of rite, Trice and Beyer (1984) provide the example of the employee seminars conducted by the Mary Kay cosmetics company. During these seminars, the company legacy is celebrated, and individual employees are recognized for outstanding sales performance—all of which is done with a great deal of fanfare and glamour. Many of the activities at the annual meetings of professional organizations often serve this purpose as well (see Comment 15.2).

In most organizations, there are times when problems need to be addressed and employees need to renew their sense of purpose

TABLE 15.2
A Summary of Organizational Rites

Type of Rites	Example
Rites of passage	Induction and basic training in the U.S. Army
Rites of degradation	Firing and replacing top executives
Rites of enhancement	Mary Kay seminars
Rites of renewal	Organizational development activities
Rites of conflict reduction	Collective bargaining
Rites of integration	Office Christmas party

Source: H. M. Trice and J. M. Beyer. (1984). Studying organizational culture through rites and ceremonials. *Academy of Management Review, 9,* 653–669. Reprinted with permission of the Copyright Clearance Center.

COMMENT 15.2

WHY IS IT IMPORTANT TO GO TO SIOP?

FOR OVER A decade, a familiar activity for me has been attendance at the annual conference of the Society for Industrial and Organizational Psychology (SIOP) in late April. Attending this conference has taken me to Boston, Miami, St. Louis, Montreal, San Francisco, San Diego, Nashville, Dallas, Atlanta, and New Orleans. In fact, each year, it seems that more and more people attend this three-day event.

Why do I, and so many other people in the profession, make the SIOP conference a regular event? One reason is that going to the conference allows one to keep up on the latest developments in both the science and practice of industrial/organizational psychology. Each year, the conference program includes symposia and poster sessions that allow researchers and practitioners to discuss their findings and exchange ideas. This is particularly important for researchers, because much of what appears in academic journals is often one or two years old!

Another important (and perhaps less understood) function of the SIOP conference is that it serves a socialization function. Each year, many graduate students attend this conference for the first time, and receive their first taste of what it is like to be in this profession. They learn who the important people in the profession are and how to conduct themselves as professionals, and they are educated about the major issues facing the profession. These things are obviously important in transmitting a professional culture that will live on far longer than any individual. Furthermore, in my experience, graduate students attending this conference for the first time leave feeling very enthused about the profession they have chosen, and eager to attend the next year.

So, if you are a graduate student, try your best to attend the SIOP conference. You won't be disappointed!

within the organization. *Rites of renewal* serve this purpose. Trice and Beyer (1984) cite the use of organizational development interventions as a prime example of rites of renewal in organizations. For example, interventions such as team building, survey feedback, and Management by Objectives (MBO), which are often part of organizational development programs, can be seen as ritualistic activities that ultimately serve to renew employees' sense of purpose. Such activities provide employees with reassurance that something is being done about the problems in the organization. Ultimately, though, such activities may distract employees from the *real* causes of problems. By doing this, they may reinforce the existing power structure and social arrangements within the organization.

This view of organizational development proposed by Trice and Beyer (1984) is certainly provocative, although many organizational development professionals would probably disagree with it. In fact, there is some empirical evidence that organizational development interventions can facilitate positive change in organizations (e.g., French & Bell, 1995) and thus are not merely expensive "feel good" rituals. On the other hand, organizational development is often applied in a somewhat ritualistic fashion—an employee opinion survey is conducted, a report is written and filed away, and everyone feels good about the process. Meanwhile, none of the substantive problems within the organization are even addressed, much less solved.

Rites of conflict reduction are often conducted in organizations when there is potentially debilitating conflict that needs to be addressed. Perhaps the best example of this type of rite in unionized organizations is the collective bargaining process. According to Trice and Beyer (1984), this activity is a rite because, in most cases, each side knows that an agreement is ultimately going to be reached. However, on the way to getting there, each side must "play a game" that is consistent with its role. For example, representatives of the company must initially present an unacceptable contractual offer in order to show that they are good stewards of organizational resources. The union representatives, in turn, must reject that offer and make contractual demands that they know the organization cannot agree to, just to show that they are protecting the interests of the union membership. Ultimately, this give-and-take process will produce a contract that is acceptable, though often not ideal, to both sides.

The final type of rites described by Trice and Beyer (1984) are *rites of integration*. The major purpose behind rites of integration is to encourage and revive common feelings that serve to bind members of the organization together. In most organizations, the common example of this form of rite is the annual office Christmas party. In most annual Christmas parties, employees typically suspend normal rules of protocol and simply have fun together. This experience of having fun together presumably serves to make the social ties that bind these people together that much stronger, even if it is only for an afternoon or evening.

Rituals are closely related to rites because they are also enacted through behavior patterns. Trice and Beyer (1984) define a ritual as "a standard, detailed set of techniques and behaviors that manage anxieties, but seldom produce intended, technical consequences of practical importance" (p. 655). Perhaps the most visible examples of ritualistic behavior come from the world of sports—in particular, from baseball. Many baseball players, for example, believe that it is bad luck to step on the chalk lines when running onto the field, and often make a visible effort to avoid doing so (just watch closely sometime!). More elaborate rituals could be seen in the behavior of former major league baseball player Wade Boggs. Boggs would eat only chicken on the day of a game, and he had to field a certain number of ground balls during pregame practice. In Boggs's case, however, these might not be considered rituals because they evidently did him some good—he was a lifetime .300 hitter and ended his career with over 3,000 hits!

Employees in most organizations obviously do not engage in ritualistic behaviors similar to those of professional athletes. Organizational rituals, however, do exist and they do convey information about the organizational culture. For example, employees in many organizations develop nearly ritualistic behavior that centers around daily breaks and lunch time. Each day, employees may congregate in the same location, or eat at the same restaurant at precisely the same time. In contrast, in some organizations, individuals may spend these times eating at their desk or perhaps reading a book. In the former case, such rituals convey strong social bonds within the organization; in the latter case, they may suggest a culture that values privacy and solitude.

Another form of ritualistic behavior common in most organizations is that which occurs at the beginning and end of the workday. Employees, for example, may congregate around the coffee machine and exchange pleasantries, or perhaps talk about sports. In other organizations, each employee may begin the day by quickly going to his or her desk and immediately beginning to work.

In the former case, one might presume again that the social ties are a bit stronger; in fact, they reach to the point where employees may feel that such daily activities are highly vital to their work, even though the information exchanged may actually be quite trivial. In the latter case, this behavior, at least on the surface, may convey a high level of diligence and a desire to accomplish tasks. It may also be indicative of a high level of conflict and suspicion among the employees of an organization.

At the end of the day, some organizations are very lively places, with employees talking cheerfully to each other and bidding farewell. In other organizations, the best description that can be given is that employees literally attempt to "escape" without having to talk to anyone. In the first organization, the culture would likely be characterized by a high degree of camaraderie and social integration. The exit behavior in the latter case conveys a much different message about the organization's culture. In this case, the culture of an organization is unlikely to be positive. If it were, people wouldn't be dying to get out. The culture of the organization may not be experienced by employees as positive and, in fact, may feel very threatening.

Another ritual that can be very revealing about the culture of organizations—or, in many cases, subcultures within larger organizations—is that associated with socializing after work hours. In the author's first academic position after completing graduate school, a common ritual on Friday afternoons was socializing over beer and peanuts at a local bar. Although the conversation in these "faculty development sessions," as they were called, would occasionally turn to work-related issues, most of the time was just spent socializing. In contrast, in some academic departments, faculty rarely, if ever, socialize outside of work hours. In the former case, the weekly ritual likely conveyed the fact that the members of this department saw themselves as more than just coworkers, and sought to extend the social bonds beyond the confines of the work environment. A lack of socializing outside of work may signify that coworkers do not find each other's company appealing, and thus do not want to extend it beyond normal work hours. It may also signify an organizational culture in which employees get along quite well, but place a very high value on spending time with their families.

Stories and Legends

It is certainly well documented, from fields such as cultural anthropology (e.g., Geertz, 1973) and communication theory (Pacanowsky & O'Donnell-Trujillo, 1983), that a very important mechanism for transmitting culture from one generation to another is through story telling and passing on legends. As a personal example of this, when my oldest son was preschool age, one of his favorite books was *The Little Engine That Could*. Reading this book to him could be viewed as purely entertainment, but it could be viewed as cultural transmission as well. As most readers know, the story contained in this book teaches values that are central to American culture, such as persistence and altruism.

In organizational settings, stories are defined as "narratives based on true events—often a combination of truth and fiction" (Trice & Beyer, 1984, p. 655). Employees in organizations tell many stories, some of which may be completely irrelevant to cultural transmission. What makes a story a vehicle for cultural transmission is that it is intentionally meant to convey something important about the culture of the organization—in many cases, to organizational newcomers. For example, employees of a retail store may tell newcomers stories about former employees who went to extraordinary lengths to satisfy customers' requests or needs. These stories communicate to new employees that an important value in the organization is customer service.

A **legend** is a "handed-down narrative of some wonderful event that is based in history, but is embellished with fictional details" (Trice & Beyer, 1984, p. 655). In schools throughout the United States, children are required to learn about how the founding fathers, such as Thomas Jefferson, Benjamin Franklin, and Alexander Hamilton, cooperated to produce the Constitution, and what this signifies about our national culture. As historical analysis has shown, however, the processes surrounding the development of the U.S. Constitution were anything but cooperative (Founding Rivalries, 2001). Many of the framers of the Constitution were very political and self-interested. In fact, today's partisan politics is relatively tame in comparison. Notice, however, that teaching this slightly inaccurate version of history does serve to transmit cultural values that are important in a democracy such as the United States.

Legends are also used in organizations to convey important cultural details. The specific legends passed on typically focus on important milestones such as the founding of the organization, a critical organizational crisis, or an important innovation that has had a great impact on the organization. Within 3M, the details surrounding many product innovations, such as a Post-it® note, take on a legendary status, and the individuals responsible for these innovations are seen as almost larger than life (Gundling, 2000). Passing on these legends to new employees within 3M serves the purpose of communicating the fact that innovation and creativity are important parts of the culture.

Language and Communication

Spoken language is one of the key things that distinguish humans from lower-order primates and from other species. It would seem logical, then, that the culture of an organization would be reflected in the language of organizational employees; in fact, each organization typically has its own unique vocabulary. A related mechanism is the manner in which employees communicate with each other. Organizations typically differ widely on this, and these differences may be revealing about underlying cultural properties.

With respect to spoken language, organizational terminology can be quite revealing. The author once conducted a brief training seminar in an organization in which virtually all employees referred to their various departments as "worlds" rather than by more standard terms such as "departments" or "units." Although use of this terminology may have been completely coincidental, it also could have been indicative of a great deal of "turf battles" and compartmentalization within the organization. A more familiar example of how terminology reflects organizational culture is Disney's practice of referring to park visitors as "guests" rather than customers (Van Maanen, 1991). This signifies that people who pay to visit the Disney theme parks should be treated by employees as though they were visitors in their homes. Disney also uses theatrical terminology (e.g., employees are "cast members") to reinforce the point that they are in the business of providing entertainment.

The *mode of communication* used by employees in organizations can also provide insights into organizational culture. In some organizations, employees often favor highly impersonal one-way modes of communication such as written messages, voice mail, and electronic communication. This is particularly

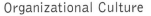
true with the advent of e-mail in most organizations. What do these forms of communication suggest about organizational culture? Heavy reliance on these impersonal modes of communication is very efficient, but may also get employees into the habit of "issuing directives" and making "declarations" to their fellow employees rather than engaging in real communication and dialogue. As a result, this may lead to a relatively high level of suspicion and a great deal of conflict.

In some organizations, the preferred mode of communication is much different. Employees may tend to favor highly personal, face-to-face communication rather than more impersonal modes such as e-mail or written memos. In terms of organizational culture, this may indicate that there is a great deal of emphasis on interpersonal harmony and on making sure that others' feelings are considered when making decisions. This may also indicate a highly participative culture in which a great deal of consultation must take place prior to decisions' being made.

THE DEVELOPMENT OF ORGANIZATIONAL CULTURE

According to Schein (1992), the two major functions of organizational culture are **external adaptation** and **internal integration.** The notion of external adaptation reflects an anthropological, or even an evolutionary approach to organizational culture. To cultural anthropologists, the totality of a culture reflects behaviors and beliefs that have survived over time because they have helped a group of people adapt more successfully to their environment. This obviously has evolutionary overtones because adaptation is a central part of the evolutionary process.

When we apply the concept of external adaptation, we come up with the rather obvious proposition that cultures develop and

persist in organizations because they facilitate an organization's adaptation to the external environment. Organizational cultures develop and persist because they help an organization to survive. This concept is quite easy to illustrate if one looks at organizations that possess cultural attributes that most observers would consider very positive. For example, developing a culture that emphasizes innovation kept 3M from going out of business and continues to help it remain one of the most successful corporations in the world. Similarly, developing a culture that puts customer service and comfort above all else helped Disney make the transition from a small film-animation company to a large entertainment conglomerate.

External adaptation can also explain why some organizations ultimately develop cultures that possess what some would consider negative attributes. For example, over the years, many have criticized the Central Intelligence Agency (CIA) for having a highly secretive, internally focused culture (e.g., Kessler, 1992). If in fact this is true, consider the adaptive value that such a culture might have. Those in the intelligence field must constantly be skeptical about the quality of the information they obtain, and must be on the lookout for threats from foreign intelligence services. The CIA has in fact been victimized by serious breaches of security from within its own ranks (Wise, 1996), and most recently from an employee of the Federal Bureau of Investigation (FBI) (Spy vs. Spy, 2001). In this type of environment, being highly secretive and internally focused may be a highly adaptive response for an organization. In fact, if the CIA were not like this, it is possible that the number of security breaches over the years might have been much higher.

Another example in which negative cultural attributes may have adaptive value is the level of secrecy in many consumer product companies. One of the key levers of competitive advantage in consumer product industries is whether an organization can develop innovative products, and subsequently bring them to market ahead of its competitors. In this type of competitive environment, it is perfectly logical that secrecy would be adaptive. Why would an organization want to give its competitors a good idea?

In addition to facilitating external adaptation, Schein (1992) proposed that organizational culture facilitates internal integration. To understand what this means, consider for a moment how an organization could function if it had no identifiable culture. In such a scenario, how would new members be integrated into the organization and taught how to assume their new roles? Thus, culture can be thought of as a sort of "glue" that bonds the social structure of a larger organization together. This is critical because, when all is said and done, organizations are ultimately social constructions and, without social integration, they would cease to exist (Katz & Kahn, 1978).

This integrative function can be seen at various levels of an organization and thus serves as an explanation for the development of organizational subcultures. Furthermore, some of these subcultures may result from the fact that individuals in a particular department or function have had common experiences or similar academic training. Within large psychology departments, for example, the various areas that are represented by graduate programs (e.g., Clinical, I/O, Social, Experimental) often develop very distinct subcultures that are based on commonality of academic training and experiences. The development of these subcultures, provided they don't clash with each other, tends to increase social cohesion within these areas and more generally enhances the professional socialization of graduate students. This does not mean, however, that there is no *overall* departmental

culture. This is based on the fact that all faculty typically have had at least some overlap in their training as doctoral-level psychologists, regardless of their specialty.

A final factor that often shapes culture is the personality of the organization's founder. This may not be relevant to all organizations, but, in some instances, culture may reflect characteristics of the founder or even of the top executives. Readers can probably think of several examples of organizations that have either been founded, or are run, by very strong, high-profile individuals. At Microsoft, this individual would obviously be Bill Gates; at Intel, this would be Andrew Grove; at Apple Computer, this would be Steve Jobs; at Dell computer, this would be Michael Dell.

How do influential founders and high-level executives put their own "personal stamp" on the culture of an organization? This question has not achieved a great deal of empirical attention, but several mechanisms are possible. One is obviously the fact these individuals have a great deal of control over who is hired, particularly at the highest levels. In fact, when Steve Jobs started his ill-fated NeXT computer company, he essentially hand-picked and interviewed *every* employee of the company. Because people generally like to be in the company of others whom they perceive to be similar to them (Byrne, 1971), it is highly likely that employees hand-picked by a founder such as Jobs were at least able to communicate values that were similar to his. Furthermore, because those who really *didn't* share his values either declined to join the company or ultimately left (Schneider, 1987), those remaining probably shaped a culture that was very similar to his personality.

Founders and influential executives also have a great deal of influence over the strategy an organization decides to pursue (Finkelstein, 1992). Choice of strategy, in turn, may ultimately impact the culture that develops in the organization. For example, an organization that chooses to pursue a strategy of offering a very limited number of highly specialized products will likely develop a very different culture, compared to an organization where the primary source of competitive advantage is high-quality customer service. In the former case, the culture that develops may place a premium on technical expertise. In contrast, in the latter case, a culture may develop that places a much higher value on social skills and the reduction of conflict.

A final issue to consider, particularly with respect to founders, is whether they continue to impact the culture of an organization when they are no longer involved with it on a day-to-day basis (e.g., after retirement or death). Again, there is not a great deal of empirical research examining this issue. However, based on what we do know about culture, the *legacy* of an organizational founder may be reflected in the culture for quite some time. That is, through processes of cultural transmission (e.g., rites, stories, and so on), cultures will typically perpetuate themselves, and thus outlive the founding member of the organization. This is particularly true if the original culture of the organization has led to *success* and thus is seen as having some adaptive value. Disney is a good example of an organization that has worked hard to preserve the legacy of the founder, Walt Disney, and has been very successful in doing so.

MEASURING ORGANIZATIONAL CULTURE

To scientifically determine the effect of organizational culture, we need to be able to measure it and to do so with a great deal of precision. Like many variables in organizational psychology, organizational culture is very complex and thus very difficult to measure. In this section,

we examine common approaches to measuring organizational culture.

Self-Report Assessments of Culture

The most direct way to measure the culture of an organization is to create some type of self-report measure, administer this measure to a sample of organizational employees, and then create a numerical index to describe the culture. One of the more popular self-report measures of organizational culture is the Organizational Culture Profile (OCP), which was developed by O'Reilly, Chatman, and Caldwell (1991). The OCP measures culture primarily in terms of the values that tend to predominate within the organization. The specific values assessed by the OCP include innovation, detail orientation, aggressiveness, outcome-orientation, supportiveness, nature of rewards, decisiveness, and team-orientation. Because the OCP provides measures of *organizations* and not *individuals,* the scores for each of these values are formed by aggregating individual employees' ratings.

Another relatively common self-report measure of organizational culture is Hofstede's (1980) measure of organizational values. This self-report instrument, which is based on Hofstede's work on differences in national cultures, assesses the following potential organizational values: Process-oriented vs. Results-oriented; Employee-oriented vs. Job-oriented; Parochial vs. Professional; Open System vs. Closed System; Loose Control vs. Tight Control; Normative Control vs. Tight Control. As with the OCP, individual employees' scores are aggregated to come up with the scores for the organization. The organization's unique culture is then determined by examining the pattern of the scores.

Self-report measures of organizational culture are relatively easy to administer, and they provide quantitative indexes that researchers can use to describe and compare organizational cultures. However, some serious limitations are associated with self-report assessments of organizational culture. Recall, from Schein's (1992) definition, that the deepest and more fundamental component of organizational culture is represented by the *basic assumptions* shared by the employees in an organization. Because these basic assumptions are rarely questioned by employees, they are, to a large extent, unconscious. Thus, employees who are immersed in the culture of an organization are probably going to be able to report only the surface aspects of that culture, such as values, which are exactly assessed by self-report measures.

Another problem with self-report measures of culture is that they impose a somewhat arbitrary structure on the respondent. Although researchers have found that certain values are important components of culture *in general,* there may be other values that are more specific to a given organization and contribute greatly to its culture. For example, the organizational culture of an educational institution may be heavily influenced by highly unique external factors such as the level of educational funding that is provided by the state government. These highly specific factors are typically not measured in standard self-report culture measures.

A final and perhaps a most serious problem with self-report is that we have no way of assessing whether the culture the respondents are describing is the *actual* culture or the *idealized* culture of the organization. In many organizations, there may be a great deal of difference between what employees would like the culture to be and what it actually is. Furthermore, employees completing self-report measures may very well report what is essentially an idealized version, and not the

reality, of the culture. This occurs simply because of the many weaknesses inherent in self-report measurement (e.g., Spector, 1994) and the fact that employees, particularly those at higher organizational levels, may have "blind spots" regarding the culture.

Ethnographic Methods of Culture Assessment

Ethnography is the use of qualitative, observational methods of assessing behavior. Researchers conducting ethnographic assessment of organizational culture (herein referred to as "ethnographers") typically do so through observing and recording behavior in an organization for an extended period of time. In some cases, ethnographers present themselves as outside researchers. In other cases, however, ethnographers may actually become members of the organizations they are trying to analyze. The most notable example of this type of research in the organizational literature was Van Maanen's analysis of police culture (Van Maanen, 1975). To conduct this study, Van Maanen actually went through a police academy as a recruit and recorded his observations.

Other than direct observation, a common tool used in ethnographic research is the use of *informants* (Johnson, 1990). An informant is a member of the organization to whom ethnographers can go for information. In many cases, informants help by making sense out of what they have observed in the organization. According to Johnson (1990), there is no *ideal* informant in any ethnographic study; however, it is obviously important that any informant should possess a detailed knowledge of the organization being studied.

When they must choose an organizational informant, researchers often seek out long-tenured employees. Indeed, these individuals may be very helpful because they are able to provide a historical context for understanding much of what goes on in an organization. A potential drawback of long-tenured employees, though, is that they may be so immersed in the culture that they are unable to describe it accurately. The "first impressions" of a relatively new employee may ultimately provide as much (or more) insight into an organization's true culture. The best course of action for ethnographers, if possible, is to seek organizational informants who represent a variety of tenure levels.

The obvious benefit of ethnographic assessment of organizational culture is that it does not require the researcher to *ask* employees about the culture of the organization. If we accept Schein's (1985) notion that the core of organizational culture is represented by shared "basic assumptions" of employees, then qualitative methods are more likely than self-report questionnaires to capture these assumptions, simply because basic assumptions are at a level of consciousness that is very difficult for employees to access. Thus, more information about culture can probably be gleaned from observing their behavior, rather than directly asking them questions. Unfortunately, ethnography is a labor-intensive and, at times, painstaking process. Many researchers do not have the time to observe an organization for long periods, or the capability of coding all of those observations. There is also a potential for observer bias in ethnographic research. There are ways that ethnographers can address this issue (e.g., via informants or multiple observers), but observation ultimately involves a good deal of subjectivity.

Other Methods of Cultural Assessment

By far, the most common methods of culture assessment are self-report surveys and ethnography. Given the vast methodological toolkit available to organizational psychologists, however, there are certainly other ways culture could be assessed. One method, which is not used very often in organizational culture research, is the use of *archival information* from the organization. Most organizations produce a good deal of archival information, and some of this may provide clues about culture. For example, an organization's annual report could be analyzed through **content analysis** to provide information about culture. If a good portion of the text of the annual report deals with customer service, this is a sign that customer service is a major part of an organization's culture. Similarly, if all of an organization's top executives are long-tenured employees, this may be a sign that, in the organization, a strong value is placed on experience.

Another method, which has not been used frequently, is to assess culture through measuring employees' **cognitive maps** of the organizations (see Silvester, Anderson, & Patterson, 1999). Cognitive mapping is simply a way of determining the underlying heuristics that employees use to process information about the organization. To construct cognitive maps, employees are interviewed, and the information from these interviews is subjected to a standardized coding process. Although this is a relatively new process, it certainly holds great promise for future researchers as a method of culture assessment.

CHANGING ORGANIZATIONAL CULTURE

So far, in defining organizational culture, we have emphasized the values and basic assumptions that are shared among employees and may have been passed down through many generations. Another key point in the previous discussion is that organizational cultures do not develop in a random fashion;

rather, they develop and are sustained over time because they help an organization adapt to its competitive environment. However, what happens when that competitive environment changes? The attributes of an organization's culture that helped it compete in the previous competitive environment may be irrelevant, or perhaps even counterproductive, in the new environment. Thus, an organization will have to change its culture in order to survive in the new competitive environment.

Even in a relatively stable competitive environment, organizations may attempt to change their cultures for other reasons. Often, the desire for culture change accompanies significant changes in the top management team of an organization. Change is then driven more by the desires of those in top management than by necessity. Cultures also change because the composition of an organization changes over time. Although some have argued that this process favors cultural stability (e.g., Schneider, 1987), it may not always be the case. When different people come into an organization, they may gradually change its interpersonal dynamics and, ultimately, its culture.

Many of the organizational development interventions that will be described in Chapter 16 are ultimately aimed at changing the culture of an organization, so the topic will not be covered in great depth here. In this section, however, two important questions about culture change are addressed:

1. Why is changing the culture of an organization so difficult?
2. What are some of the common mechanisms by which organizational cultures change?

Why Is Culture Change Difficult?

In almost any comprehensive treatment of organizational culture it is concluded that or-

ganizational culture is hard to change once it has been established (Hatch, 1993; Ouchi & Wilkins, 1985; Schein, 1985, 1992). That's not to say that organizational culture is completely intractable; in fact, all organizational cultures change naturally over time, due to a number of factors that will be covered in the next section. What is difficult, however, is for organizations to change their cultures very quickly. A manager cannot simply write a memo to employees on a Friday informing them that, as of Monday, the culture will be different (though some organizations may naïvely think this is possible).

One reason that culture change is difficult has to do with the definition of culture that was presented at the beginning of the chapter. As Schein (1992) pointed out, the essence of organizational culture resides in the *basic assumptions* shared by employees. Recall that basic assumptions can be about anything, but those relevant to organizational culture typically have something to do with the organization and its major activities. What makes these assumptions "basic" is the fact that they are shared among employees and, as such, are rarely if ever questioned or put under objective scrutiny.

Because of this, "basic assumptions" are highly resistant to change. Furthermore, in the rare cases when basic assumptions are challenged in organizations, the challenge may actually serve to strengthen employees' beliefs in those basic assumptions. If a new employee comes into an organization and refuses to accept the basic assumptions that are inherent in its culture, this will typically force other employees to "bring that person into line." In the process of doing so, the core values and assumptions may be strengthened, regardless of whether that person eventually accepts them, actively resists them, or ultimately leaves the organization. Although basic assumptions are viewed by most organizational culture experts as being highly resistant to change, it should be noted that this view is not shared by all (see Comment 15.3).

Organizational culture is difficult to change because there are always those who benefit from the culture's remaining static. A logical corollary to this is: There are often some who stand to *lose* if the culture is changed. Perhaps the best way to illustrate this is through one of the most fundamental assumptions shaping organizational culture: whether rewards should be based on performance, as opposed to other factors. Let's say that one of the most basic assumptions of an organization's culture is that rewards should be based primarily on seniority. Further assume that a new organizational president is

hired and is determined to change the culture to one in which rewards are based primarily on performance.

Given this scenario, consider first the issue of who benefits from the present culture of this organization. Very clearly, those who have been employed in the organization for a long period of time benefit from the organization's present culture, assuming of course that this part of the culture is reflected in the organization's reward policies. Now consider who stands to lose if the culture of the organization changes and performance is then valued above all else. Not all long-tenured employees will be hurt by this change, because some of these individuals may be among the organization's best performers.

COMMENT 15.3

IS ORGANIZATIONAL CULTURE REALLY SO DIFFICULT TO CHANGE?

IN NEARLY ALL reviews of organizational culture, one of the common assertions is that once the culture of an organization is established it is extremely difficult to change. This is because, by definition, culture represents beliefs and assumptions that are so rarely questioned that they are not even conscious. Thus, it takes a lot of effort to get people to question basic assumptions and, in the process, change culture.

Although this is by far the dominant viewpoint, there are some organizational culture researchers that disagree. Wilkins and Ouchi (1983), for example, point out that the idea of organizational culture being difficult to change comes from cultural anthropology. Cultural anthropologists, as many readers know, are primarily interested in *societal* cultures. Societal cultures are obviously very difficult to change because most people become totally immersed in their societal culture.

In the case of organizational culture, however, there is a great deal of variation in the degree of "enculturation." Some employees do become "true believers" and faithfully espouse the values and assumptions of their organization. On the other hand, employees may be very much opposed to the values and assumptions of their organization. Most employees are probably somewhere between these two extremes. Given this variation in employee enculturation, it is probably *easier* to change the culture of an organization than an entire society.

Source: A. L. Wilkins and W. G. Ouchi. (1983). Efficient cultures: Exploring the relationship between culture and organizational performance. *Administrative Science Quarterly, 28,* 468–481.

Rather, employees who perform their jobs poorly, regardless of tenure, stand to lose the most from such a culture change.

Among those actively resisting such a change, however, long-tenured poor-performing employees would probably be the most vigorous. These individuals may resist such a culture change by actively arguing against it, or even failing to follow policies that are based on it. These individuals not only must give something up (rewards based on seniority), but may also be hurt again (based on their performance, they will not be highly rewarded) by the culture change. Regardless of how bad or dysfunctional an organizational culture may appear, there are typically those who benefit from having it remain that way, and those who stand to lose by changing it. Many attempts to change organizational culture end up in failure because those initiating the change haven't recognized this.

A final reason that organizational culture cannot be easily changed goes back to the factors that shape culture in the first place. Recall that one of the most important of these is *adaptation*. Cultures ultimately develop and are sustained over time because they serve some purpose, or help some group adapt more effectively to its environment. That's not to say that maladaptive cultures never develop. For the most part, though, cultures remain stable because they serve some adaptive function. It follows, then, that superficial or misguided attempts to change organizational culture would probably encounter resistance.

The Nature of Organizational Culture Change

According to Schein (1992), organizations are like individuals in that they pass through distinct "life" stages. The stages that organizations go through are important because they help us to understand how organizations change and evolve over time. During the *Birth and Early Growth* phase, the organization is founded and is essentially beginning to develop a distinct culture. As one might imagine, during this phase, organizational culture is strongly impacted by the organizational founder or the family of the founder. This individual can often literally hire or fire at will and is in a position to demand a great deal of loyalty. Furthermore, just to survive, organizations at this stage may demand a great deal of commitment on the part of employees. Also, at this stage, when the organization is most vulnerable, external events can potentially have great effects on the organization and, in fact, become part of organizational folklore.

In the second stage, *Organizational Midlife*, an organization typically becomes "bigger" structurally. This may also be a time of growth and expansion, as organizations decide to explore new markets or product lines. With respect to organizational culture, the great structural complexity that often accompanies this stage may result in a number of organizational "subcultures." These subcultures may be based on a number of things, such as geographic location, product lines or divisions, or even functional specialties. The obvious danger at this stage is that the subcultures may become so distinct that the organization begins to lose its more general, overarching culture.

The third and final stage in this model is *Organizational Maturity*. This is essentially the "crossroads" in the life of an organization. At this point, an organization is essentially faced with the choice of renewal (e.g., continuing on indefinitely), or stagnation and, ultimately, death. In this sense, organizations have an advantage over people—they can live on indefinitely whereas people cannot. Organizational culture is a key factor in determining this choice between renewal and stagnation. Organizations that fail to change any aspect of their culture stand a good chance of failure. On the other hand, organizations that live on indefinitely must decide which aspects of their culture need to be changed and which ones need to be preserved over time.

Schein (1985, 1992) proposed a number of mechanisms by which organizational cultures change over time in the context of these organizational life stages. These are summarized in Table 15.3. During the Birth and Early Growth phase, organizational culture may change through any of four primary mechanisms. The mechanism of *natural evolution* can be seen as the processes that shape an organizational culture when it attempts to adapt to its environment. When viewed in a general sense, this simply represents those aspects of organizational culture that contribute to its survival. For example, during the early life of an organization, changing from a highly autocratic to a highly collaborative culture is adaptive, and this becomes part of the organization's permanent culture.

A second mechanism that frequently leads to culture change in the early stages of an or-ganization is referred to as *self-guided evolution through organizational therapy*. Changes in organizational culture are not driven by natural forces; they are more deliberate. In this case, organizational decision makers decide what they want the culture to be and take steps to change it accordingly. The term "organizational therapy" is used to refer to a variety of interventions (some of which will be described in Chapter 16) that are designed to facilitate culture change. As an example, the top management of a relatively new organization may decide that the culture of the organization should be very team-oriented. In this case, the "therapy" used to achieve this culture change might be in the form of training on topics such as team decision making, or resolving interpersonal conflict in teams.

Another mechanism by which culture change can be initiated is referred to as *managed evolution through hybrids*. In this case, culture change is initiated intentionally, although the mechanism is much different from the one in the previous example. In this case, the mechanism is through the appointment of

TABLE 15.3
Culture Change Mechanisms at Different Stages of the Organizational Lifecycle

Stage	Change Mechanisms
1. Birth and Early growth	1. Natural evolution 2. Self-guided evolution through organizational therapy 3. Managed evolution through hybrids 4. Managed "revolution" through outsiders
2. Organizational midlife	1. Planned change and organizational development 2. Technological seduction 3. Change through scandal and explosion of myths 4. Incrementalism
3. Organizational maturity	1. Coercive persuasion 2. Turnaround 3. Reorganization, destruction, and rebirth

Source: E. H. Schein. (1985). *Organizational culture and leadership: A dynamic view.* San Francisco: Jossey-Bass. Copyright 1985, Jossey-Bass. Reprinted by permission of John Wiley & Sons.

"hybrids" in key positions within the organization. A "hybrid" is an individual who has grown up in the present culture, but, at the same time, may not accept all of the underlying assumptions on which it is based. By putting these types of individuals in key positions, the culture may not change radically, but it may shift in a way that is ultimately more adaptive for the organization.

The final mechanism by which culture is typically changed during the early life of an organization is referred to as *managed "revolution" through outsiders*. This mechanism is like the one just described, except for one important detail. Here, the "agents of change" are individuals from outside of the organization who are essentially unfamiliar with the organizational culture. Bringing these types of individuals into an organization can potentially initiate a great deal of culture change because they will probably question many of the basic assumptions on which the current culture is based. This may be a difficult process, however, for both current employees and the outsiders that are brought in. Such individuals may encounter considerable resistance to any changes they initiate.

By the time an organization reaches the midlife stage, the culture is relatively well established, and different mechanisms may be needed to initiate change. The first of these, in Table 15.3, is referred to as *planned change and organizational development*. This represents a deliberate attempt to guide and facilitate the change process. On the part of the organization, this is a sign of maturity because it shows a recognition that adaptation is necessary for success. While all organizational development programs have somewhat different goals, the fundamental purpose of many is to change the culture of the organization, or at least provide the capability to be able to do so. Organizations using this type of strategy typically bring in outside consultants, although, in some large organizations, an organizational development function may be established.

The second change mechanism in organizational midlife is referred to as *technological seduction*. This refers to the use of technology as a lever for organizational culture change, and may occur in two different ways. For example, technology may drive organizational change because of the technologies that emerge within the organization. That is, a "high tech" culture may develop in a computer company, due to the types of people needed to fill many of the positions in such an organization. In addition, organizations can sometimes induce culture change by introducing new and unfamiliar technology. The idea that technology can shape the social environment is well known and can be traced back to the sociotechnical systems perspective and the Tavistock studies of coal mining (Trist & Bamforth, 1951).

A third mechanism of culture change during organizational midlife is through *scandal, and explosion of myths*. For example, a scandal involving an organization may force organizational members to rethink some of their basic assumptions. Ultimately, scandal leads to culture change. This may occur, for example, when a charismatic leader in an organization is caught engaging in illegal behavior. On a societal level, one could certainly argue that the Watergate scandal in the early 1970s led many to rethink their assumptions about government officials. Ultimately, this has led to a great deal of mistrust and skepticism toward these people.

The explosion of myths occurs when one of the generally accepted organizational myths is publicly proven to be false. As an example, a common organizational myth is that employees' jobs are secure, and that the organization would do anything to avoid layoffs. If layoffs do occur, this results in an explosion of this myth, and the culture of an organization may be changed forever. At the social level, a myth that persisted among Americans was that there was little possibility of terrorism being carried out on our own soil. Terrorism was something that went on only in the Middle East. The bombing in Oklahoma City and the destruction of the World Trade Center obviously shattered this myth and is probably one of the reasons that people were so shocked by these acts.

The final mechanism for change during organizational midlife is referred to as *incrementalism*. Essentially, this means that change does occur, but it occurs very slowly. For example, most organizations in the midlife stage have employees who represent a variety of tenure levels. Some have been with the organization for a long time, others have been around for a few years, and others are new. Over time, as new employees come into an organization and others either retire or leave, the organization will undoubtedly change, although in subtle ways. As an example, academic departments in many universities are changing because a large number of faculty hired during the late 1960s and early 1970s are retiring. These changes are incremental, however, because all of these individuals will not retire at once. New faculty are brought in gradually, and the change is often very subtle and hard to detect.

During the final stage, *organizational maturity,* an organization is really faced with the choice of stagnation/decline or changing in ways that will facilitate its renewal. Thus, change in organizational culture may be a very critical issue. One way that change may be achieved at this point is through what Schein (1985) described as *coercive persuasion*. In this case, organizations use a variety of coercive

tactics to facilitate changes in individuals, which will ultimately lead to changes in the culture. A common way that organizations use this mechanism is by providing long-tenured employees with the option of early retirement. Another way that organizations may facilitate change in this manner is through the threat of undesirable work assignments, or by altering working conditions in ways that are undesirable to any employees who will not change.

The second change mechanism during Organizational Maturing is described by Schein (1985) as *turnaround*. To a large extent, turnaround embodies many of the change mechanisms that were previously described. During turnaround, the organization recognizes the need for a cultural change and takes the steps necessary for the change to occur. In many cases, this may be through the application of organizational development methods, but could also be through a change in personnel. As Schein (1985, 1992) points out, for turnaround to be successful, it must be a comprehensive effort and involve all members of the organization.

The final change mechanism in organizational maturing is referred to as *reorganization, destruction, and rebirth*. This is probably the most extreme form of culture change because it essentially involves destroying the present culture and instituting a new one. Given the extremity of this method, it is typically reserved for times of crisis or times when the only alternative to culture change is failure. An example of this change mechanism can often be seen when a president is reelected to a second term in office. Specifically, many of the cabinet members and key members of the administration from the first term resign or are replaced with new appointees. The impact of such changes, one would assume, is to change the culture surrounding the administration, and hence enhance its effectiveness.

MODELS OF ORGANIZATIONAL CULTURE

Anyone who has worked in several different organizations knows that, to a large extent, no two organizational cultures are completely alike. Therefore, it is probably futile to develop a finite typology of all organizational culture types or dimensions. Over the years, however, researchers have discovered what they have considered to be meaningful clusters of cultural attributes. For example, there seem to be a number of characteristics that are common among successful organizations and among organizations that operate in different national cultures. In this section, we examine two of these common models of organizational culture.

The Peters and Waterman Model

Peters and Waterman's 1982 bestseller, *In Search of Excellence,* was based on a study of the management practices of a sample of highly successful organizations. In the course of studying these highly successful organizations, Peters and Waterman noticed a number of common characteristics. They were not policies or work practices; rather, they were aspects of the cultures of these organizations that appeared to contribute to their success. The eight characteristics found by Peters and Waterman are presented in Table 15.4.

The first attribute of excellent organizations presented in Table 15.4 is **bias for action.** Employees in excellent organizations are not afraid to make decisions with incomplete information. This does *not* mean that decision making is haphazard. Rather, excellent organizations

TABLE 15.4
Peters and Waterman (1982) Characteristics of Excellent Organizations

1. Bias for action
2. Stay close to the customer
3. Autonomy and entrepreneurship
4. Productivity through people
5. Hands-on management
6. Stick to the knitting
7. Simple form, lean staff
8. Simultaneously loosely and tightly organized

Source: T. J. Peters and R. H. Waterman, Jr. (1982). *In search of excellence.* New York: Harper & Row.

encourage employees not to delay making decisions until every possible piece of information is available. It may never be available. Bias for action can be an advantage because, in many industries, a key factor that distinguishes success from failure is the speed at which an organization can offer services or bring products to market. Organizations that encourage employees to procrastinate are likely to fail.

Peters and Waterman also found that excellent organizations tend to **stay close to the customer.** That is, they engage in practices that allow a great deal of communication with customers. By staying close to the customer, organizations have a much better idea of customers' preferences and become quickly aware when they change. This is important because all organizations have customers, and their survival depends on satisfying those customers. In terms of organizational culture, this principle is embodied in the view that customers are important and their views should be taken seriously.

The third common characteristic of excellent organizations is a combination of **autonomy and entrepreneurship.** Specifically, in excellent organizations, employees have a great deal of freedom to do their jobs, and this often involves acting as entrepreneurs by promoting their ideas. In some organizations, many employees are actually *discouraged* from being entrepreneurial because of the belief that good ideas can only come from certain employees (e.g., senior management). In excellent organizations, however, all employees are given the freedom to come up with good ideas and run with them.

Excellent organizations also tend to have cultures that stress **productivity through people.** Many organizations have slogans such as "Our people are our greatest asset," but in excellent organizations, this is a real part of the organizational culture. How is this principle reflected in practice? Although it may come through in a variety of ways, the basic idea is that employees are treated with respect and dignity. One very concrete way that this value often comes to life in organizations is through the amount spent on training and development activities. Because excellent organizations believe that productivity is achieved through people, they tend to offer a great collection of training opportunities to employees.

Excellent organizations also adopt what can be described as a **hands-on management** style. Stated differently, in excellent organizations, managers are not simply detached observers. They understand the organization's business activities, and are visible in the organization. Hands-on management should not be mistaken for micromanagement, however. Because managers understand what is going on in the organization, that does not mean that it is desirable for them to be involved in *all* aspects of the organization.

The principle of **stick to the knitting** means that excellent organizations tend to only be involved in business activities that they understand and have expertise in. Therefore, excellent organizations tend to shy away from acquiring and operating businesses outside of their area of expertise, even when doing so might appear to be highly profitable. By doing so, organizations cut down on the risk of failing because they simply do not understand the business they are operating in.

In terms of structure, excellent organizations tend to operate according to the principle of **simple form, lean staff.** Obviously, as organizations become more and more successful, there is a temptation to increase the layers of management and to increase the complexity of the entire organizational structure. Excellent organizations resist this temptation and are rewarded for it because organizations with very complex structures often can be very difficult to manage. Having a lean staff is advantageous in terms of cost, but also makes communication and decision making much easier.

The final characteristic of excellent organizations proposed by Peters and Waterman is that they are **simultaneously loosely and tightly organized.** This means that excellent organizations have a set of core values that are widely understood and accepted by employees; in this sense, they are tightly organized. In day-to-day operations, though, these organizations are leaner and typically have fewer rules and regulations to govern employee behavior; in this sense, they are loosely organized. This is important because employees are more likely to be committed to their organization and its mission if their commitment is achieved voluntarily and not through coercion.

Overall, Peters and Waterman's work has been highly influential with managers and is cited frequently in academic circles. This is undoubtedly due to the fact that their work makes a good deal of sense, and there are many anecdotal examples of successful organizations that embody these characteristics of excellent companies. It must be remembered, however, that Peters and Waterman's model has yet to be subjected to a rigorous empirical testing. Such a test would require many organizations, and many aspects of culture would have to be measured.

The Ouchi Framework

Like Peters and Waterman, William Ouchi was the author of a bestseller in which he described a number of organizational characteristics of Japanese organizations. In his book, *Theory Z,* Ouchi (1981) also described a number of U.S. organizations that had adopted Japanese management practices. This was a very hot topic in the late 1970s and early 1980s because U.S. firms were consistently losing out to their Japanese competitors.

The Ouchi Framework is an effort to compare the cultural values of typical Japanese companies, U.S. companies that have adopted some of the cultural values of Japanese companies (Theory Z), and typical U.S. companies. Table 15.5 compares three types of organizations on the basis of seven cultural values. As can be seen in Table 15.5, the first value on

which these three organizations differ is **commitment to employees.** Most (though not all) Japanese companies have lifetime employment, indicating a great deal of commitment to the employees. Theory Z companies also show a high level of commitment to employees by typically having long-term employment. Typical U.S. companies have the lowest level of commitment toward employees, and are often resigned to the fact that employment will be short-term.

The second cultural value on which these organizations differ is in the area of **employee evaluation.** Japanese and Theory Z organizations tend to take their time in evaluating employees, and they do so qualitatively. For example, in these types of organizations, employees typically would not be evaluated until they had been on the job for quite some time. In addition, the nature of the evaluation would be extensive comments and feedback from their supervisor (and perhaps from others familiar with their performance, e.g., peers, subordinates). In typical U.S. companies, Ouchi observed that evaluation is usually done very quickly and is typically stated in

TABLE 15.5
The Ouchi Framework

	Expression in		
Cultural Value	*Japanese Companies*	*Type Z U.S. Companies*	*Typical U.S. Companies*
Commitment to employees	Lifetime employment	Long-term employment	Short-term employment
Evaluation	Slow and qualitative	Slow and qualitative	Fast and quantitative
Careers	Very broad	Moderately broad	Narrow
Control	Implicit and informal	Implicit and informal	Explicit and formal
Decision making	Group and consensus	Groups and consensus	Individual
Responsibility	Group	Individual	Individual
Concern for People	Holistic	Holistic	Narrow

Source: W. G. Ouchi. (1981). *Theory Z.* Reading, MA: Addison-Wesley.

quantitative terms. This is probably related to the fact that employees in typical U.S. companies may only be with the company for a short period of time.

Another aspect of culture that differs among these three types of organizations has to do with the **breadth of career paths** of employees. In Japanese companies, the careers of employees tend to be very broad. For example, it is not unusual for management personnel in Japanese companies to have had experience in nearly all major organizational functions before assuming high-level executive positions. In typical Theory Z organizations, career paths may not be quite as broad as in Japanese companies, but employees are still provided with a fair amount of breadth in their careers. In U.S. companies, career paths are typically narrow. An employee is typically hired for a specific job, such as accountant, and gains very little organizational experience outside of that specialty.

In terms of **control mechanisms,** both Japanese and Theory Z organizations rely primarily on both implicit and informal control. These are what Walton and Hackman (1986) have termed "high commitment" organizations because they rely primarily on the commitment and loyalty of employees to maintain control of behavior, and thus have little need for more external control mechanisms. In contrast, typical U.S. organizations often rely on very explicit and formal mechanisms to maintain control. These often come in the form of rules, directives from management, explicit control policies (e.g., keeping track of hours worked), as well as thick policies-and-procedures manuals. The underlying assumption in using such mechanisms is that employees cannot be trusted to monitor their own behavior and to act in a way that is in the interests of the organization.

Ouchi also found that there are distinct differences in **decision making** among these three types of organizations. In Japanese and Theory Z organizations, primary responsibility for decision making is at the group level, and the decision rule most often used is consensus. This has the advantage of high commitment to decisions once they are made, but unfortunately can greatly increase the time needed for decision making (Guzzo, 1986). In contrast, primary responsibility for decision making in typical U.S. companies is at the individual level, often after consulting the views of others. This form of decision making has the advantage of expediency, but it also may result in a lack of commitment to decisions after they are made.

One area in which Ouchi proposed that Japanese companies differ from both Theory Z and typical U.S. companies was in the **location of responsibility.** In Japanese companies, responsibilities typically lie with the *group* and not with the individual. In contrast, in these other two types of organizations, responsibilities typically lie with *individuals* and not with groups. The difference on this dimension is probably due largely to a fundamental difference between the Japanese and American cultures. As a result, this is probably one aspect of Japanese organizational culture that cannot be duplicated even in Theory Z organizations.

The final cultural dimension on which these three types of organizations differ is **concern for people.** Japanese and Theory Z organizations tend to exhibit what Ouchi described as a "holistic" concern for their employees. Stated differently, these types of organizations understand that employment in the organization is only one part of their employees' lives. Thus, they tend to exhibit concern for the overall health and well-being of employees, beyond the work-related area. In typical U.S. organizations, the health and well-being of employees is a concern only as it is related to work.

Like the Peters and Waterman model, the Ouchi framework is supported by a good deal of anecdotal evidence and is certainly provocative—and is yet to be rigorously tested. One interesting fact about Ouchi's framework, however, is that, going back to the time he developed it, there is some evidence that his description of Japanese organizations may not be as accurate as was once thought. For example, because of economic problems in Japan, Japanese employees have had to deal with some of the same insecurity as U.S. workers. It is also unclear whether Japanese companies have quite the high level of holistic concern for their employees that Ouchi claimed. Japanese organizations are known to demand extremely long hours from their employees, and this scheduling has led to serious health problems among Japanese workers.

THE IMPACT OF ORGANIZATIONAL CULTURE

So far, we have examined a variety of issues pertaining to organizational culture—how it is defined, how it is measured, how it changes—and two models that provide a comparison of different organizational cultures. However, some important questions have yet to be examined: *Does organizational culture make a difference in important organizational outcomes?* Do organizations with certain cultural attributes tend to be more successful than organizations without such attributes? Do organizations with cultural attributes tend to attract, hire, and retain better employees than organizations without such attributes? Do employees in organizations with certain cultural attributes tend to be more satisfied and to have a better quality of work life than employees in organizations without such attributes? In this section, a brief summary of research evidence bearing on each of these questions will be provided.

Culture and Organizational Performance

The issue of linking organizational culture with organizational performance has certainly received some attention (e.g., Denison, 1984; Wilkins & Ouchi, 1983). Kotter and Heskett (1992) conducted what is perhaps the most comprehensive empirical study. They investigated 207 U.S. organizations spread among 25 different industries. They measured the *strength* of organizational culture and examined how this related to a number of performance indexes, such as revenues, stock price, expansion of the work force, and net income. The fact that culture and performance were measured using different sources is important because it decreases the possibility that culture and performance were related simply because of a common method bias.

The results of this study suggest that organizational culture does make a difference in bottom-line organizational performance. For example, organizations with cultures that these authors labeled "adaptive" performed much better than organizations with cultures labeled "unadaptive." The major differences between adaptive and unadaptive cultures are highlighted in Table 15.6. When one looks at these differences, it becomes fairly clear that an organization with an adaptive culture would be a much more enjoyable place to work, compared to an organization that is unadaptive. Furthermore, from the results of this study, it appears an adaptive culture translates into organizational success.

Probably the most important issue in future research in this area will be an attempt to explain the mediating linkages between culture and organizational performance. It has been proposed, for example, that organizational culture may impact the level of employee creativity (Tesluk, Farr, & Klein, 1997), the strength of employee motivation (Weiner

TABLE 15.6
Key Differences between Adaptive and Unadaptive Corporate Cultures

	Adaptive Corporate Cultures	*Unadaptive Corporate Cultures*
Core values	Managers care deeply about customers, stockholders, and employees. They place a high value on people and processes that create useful change.	Managers care about themselves, their immediate work group, or some product or technology. They value the orderly and risk-reducing management processes.
Common behavior	Managers pay close attention to all their constituencies, especially customers; initiate change when needed; take risks.	Managers behave politically and bureaucratically. They do not change their strategies quickly to adjust to or take advantage of changes in their business environments.

Source: J. P. Kotter and J. L. Heskett. (1992). *Corporate culture and performance.* New York: Free Press. Reprinted with the permission of The Free Press, a division of Simon & Schuster, Inc. Copyright © 1992 by Kotter Associates Inc. and James L. Heskett.

& Vardi, 1990), and the reporting of unethical behavior (Ellis & Arieli, 1999). Much more work is needed, however, to explain *why* culture makes a difference in organizational performance.

The Impact of Culture on Recruitment and Retention

Compared to the literature on organizational culture and performance, there has actually been much more empirical research investigating the impact that organizational culture has on attracting, recruiting, and retaining employees. (This issue was examined in some detail in Chapter 3 and will not be covered extensively here.) The basic finding in both of these areas is that individuals tend to be attracted to organizations that possess cultures that they perceive to be compatible. Furthermore, once people are in organizations, they will tend to *remain* in organizations that they perceive to be compatible.

There is no denying that the "fit" between individuals and culture is important, but there appears to be less consensus on which dimensions of fit are most important when individuals make decisions about organizations.

For example, it has been proposed that attraction is impacted by the degree to which culture is compatible with an applicant's personality (e.g., Judge & Cable, 1997), and other studies have examined the compatibility between organizational culture and core values (e.g., O'Reilly et al., 1991). Further work is needed to clarify the specific elements that are important in determining fit, although there is little denying that it is important in the recruitment process.

In terms of retention, fit is probably also important but far less theoretical and empirical work has been done, compared to the work on attraction. One of the reasons for this lack of information is that theoretical models of turnover (e.g., Mobley, 1977) have typically focused on characteristics of the *job* rather than *organizational-level* variables such as culture. Furthermore, we know that turnover is a complex process and is affected by variables (e.g., economic conditions, family considerations) that have little to do with the job or the organization (e.g., Cartsen & Spector, 1987; Lee & Mitchell, 1994). It seems plausible, though, that if an employee perceives that the culture is incompatible with his or her values or personality, this would certainly prompt a search for a new job. High turnover may be one mediating factor in the relationship between culture and organizational performance (Kotter & Heskett, 1992). Further research needs to be done to address these issues.

Culture and Employee Satisfaction/Well-Being

Given the pervasiveness of organizational culture, to say that it impacts employee satisfaction and well-being seems to be a statement of the obvious. Surprisingly, there is not a great deal of empirical evidence bearing on this issue—perhaps because of the difficulty of conducting the multiorganizational studies necessary to test such hypotheses. What little evidence exists, however, suggests that culture makes a difference in the quality of employees' work lives. For example, Hatton et al. (1999) found that a *mismatch* between the actual culture of the organization and what employees felt that culture should be was associated with a number of negative outcomes. For example, perceived mismatch was associated with lower job satisfaction, higher job strain, general stress, and turnover intent. These findings suggest that there is no universally appropriate culture. Rather, the key again appears to be whether the culture meets employees' expectations.

FIGURE 15.1
Model of the Relation between Culture, Work, and Health

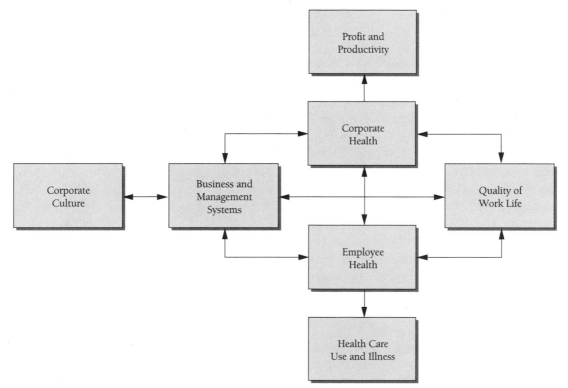

Source: M. Peterson and J. Wilson. (1998). A culture-work-health model: A theoretical conceptualization. *American Journal of Public Health, 22,* 378–390. Reprinted by permission of PNG Publications.

To provide more explanation of the impact of organizational culture on employees' quality of life, Peterson and Wilson (1998) proposed the model presented in Figure 15.1. Note that the key mediating factor in the relation between culture and employee health is *business and management systems*. Culture directly impacts the business and management systems that are deployed by the organization. These, in turn, may then impact employee health. As an example, an organization with a very controlling culture may have a human resources system that requires employees to account very carefully for their time. There is, in fact, evidence that culture does impact organizational choices of human resources systems (Aycan, Kanungo, & Sinha, 1999). This high level of control, in turn, may detract from quality of life and ultimately detract from employees' health.

Although it clearly needs empirical assessment, the connection between organizational culture and employee well-being has certainly been recognized (e.g., Monroy, Jonas, Mathey, & Murphy, 1998; Murphy, 1996). More specifically, there has been increasing emphasis on examining the characteristics of "healthy organizations"—those that are economically successful and possess healthy employees. Extensive models of organizational health await development, and a key factor in that development is likely to be organizational culture. In the future, linking macro-level variables such as organizational culture to employee health and well-being will likely become a major focus of the employee health literature (e.g., Bliese & Jex, 1999).

CHAPTER SUMMARY

This chapter examined the important topic of organizational culture. Although culture has been defined in a variety of ways, the essence of culture lies in the basic assumptions and values held by the members of an organization. This definition is widely accepted in organizational psychology, and it reflects the impact that cultural anthropology and sociology have had on the study of organizational culture.

The culture of an organization is reflected in a variety of ways; some are understandable to outsiders and others are more difficult to comprehend. Symbols and artifacts represent the major physical manifestations of culture; rites and rituals represent behavioral manifestations. Language and stories can also be an important window into culture, both directly and for more symbolic reasons. Ultimately, culture is difficult to comprehend and an outsider needs a long time to decipher it.

The culture of an organization may be shaped by a number of factors. For most organizations, the organizational founder(s) is the most important factor in initially shaping the organization. Over time, however, culture will also be impacted and shaped by the extent to which it facilitates organizational adaptation and survival. Cultures tend to develop and ultimately persist over time because they have adaptive value for the organization.

Studying organizational culture can be challenging, but it is necessary in order to fully understand it. There are certainly instances of the use of self-report measures of culture, although many organizational culture researchers are wary of this method. As a result, the most typical method of studying organizational culture has been ethnography. Using a qualitative assessment of a culture is consistent with the notion that members of a culture are not good at reporting their basic assumptions. This methodology is also consistent with the anthropological roots of this field. In the future, other methods will probably be available for studying culture as well.

Changing the culture of an organization is difficult, given that culture is reflected in basic assumptions. Nevertheless, organizational cultures do change over time, and, in most cases, the mechanisms responsible for change depend on the life stage of the organization. Clearly, though, organizational culture change is not something that occurs quickly or easily in organizations. True organizational culture change usually occurs only in response to extreme environmental conditions.

All organizational cultures are unique to some degree, but there have been efforts to develop "models" of organizational culture. Peters and Waterman's model is based on the cultural factors that distinguish successful from unsuccessful organizations. Ouchi's model is aimed at distinguishing typical Japanese organizations from typical U.S. firms and from U.S. firms that have incorporated Japanese management principles. Both models are useful, but they are rather narrow in scope. Also, the methodology underlying both is not highly rigorous.

A final factor to consider in examining organizational culture is its impact on important outcomes. Not a great deal of empirical research has been done on the effects of organizational culture, most likely because multiple organizations are needed to do such research. Nevertheless, empirical research has shown that organizational culture may impact a number of important outcomes such as performance, attraction and recruitment of employees, employee retention, and employee satisfaction and well-being. Although a great deal of research is yet to be done in this area, it appears that there is no one type of culture that is ideal. Rather, the most important factor appears to be a *match* between organizational culture and characteristics of employees rather than what is considered to be the idealized culture.

SUGGESTED ADDITIONAL READINGS

Maierhofer, N. I., Griffin, M. A., & Sheehan, M. (2000). Linking management values and behavior with employee values and behavior: A study of values and safety in the hairdressing industry. *Journal of Occupational Health Psychology, 5,* 411–416.

Shalley, C. E., Gilson, L. L., & Blum, T. C. (2000). Matching creativity requirements and the work environment: Effects on satisfaction and intentions to leave. *Academy of Management Journal, 43,* 215–223.

Trice, H. M., & Beyer, J. M. (1993). *The cultures of work organizations.* Englewood Cliffs, NJ: Prentice Hall.

Van Vianen, A. E. M. (2000). Person-organization fit: The match between newcomers' and recruiters' preferences for organizational cultures. *Personnel Psychology, 53,* 113–150.

Chapter Sixteen

Organizational Change and Development

I t is often said that *change* is one of the few constants in today's organizations. In this final chapter, we cover the various ways in which organizations seek to become more effective through the use of organizational development. Organizational development is the process by which organizations use the theories and technology of the behavioral sciences to facilitate changes that enhance their effectiveness. Another way to view organizational development is: It applies much that has been covered in this book, in order to facilitate change and enhance effectiveness in organizations. Thus, it is fitting that organizational development is the focus of this final chapter.

The chapter will begin by defining organizational development, and will then focus on why organizations seek to change. Many organizations seek to change simply to be able to survive. If they don't change, they'll go out of business. Change, however, may also be necessary for more proactive reasons. We will then discuss the theoretical models that have

been most influential in guiding the work of organizational development practitioners. The discussion will be followed by descriptions of the most popular organizational development interventions.

After describing organizational development interventions, the focus of the chapter will shift to a more general discussion of process issues in organizational development. Perhaps the most important of these issues is the conditions necessary to sustain meaningful organizational change, as well as the conditions that prevent it. This will be followed by a discussion of the evaluation of organizational development interventions—an important topic, considering the cost of organizational change. The chapter will conclude with an exploration of some of the most common ethical issues faced by organizational development professionals.

WHAT IS ORGANIZATIONAL DEVELOPMENT AND WHY IS IT USED?

Organizational development has been defined in a variety of ways, by a number of authors (French & Bell, 1995; Porras & Robertson, 1992). Porras and Robertson (1992), however, attempted to integrate the numerous definitions of organizational development and stated that: "Organizational development is a set of behavioral science-based theories, values, strategies, and technologies aimed at planned change of the organizational work setting for the purpose of enhancing individual development and improving organizational performance, through the alteration of organizational members' on-the-job behaviors" (p. 722).

Several aspects of this definition are noteworthy. First, the focus of organizational development is facilitating organizational changes that enhance *both* organizational performance and individual development. This distinguishes organizational development from organizational interventions that focus exclusively on either organizational performance or individual development. Second, organizational development is rooted in the theories and methodology of the behavioral sciences. This distinguishes organizational development from approaches to organizational change that may be based on changes in manufacturing technology or, perhaps, information systems. Finally, this definition makes it very clear that the key to organizational change is changing the behavior of employees.

Now that organizational development has been defined, the next issue to explore is why organizational development is used. One of the most common motivating factors behind organizational development programs can be described as *survival*. Organizational decision makers may realize (hopefully, not too late) that change is necessary in order for the organization to remain competitive. Consider the following example. The author once worked for a large telecommunications company that was engaged in a fairly comprehensive organizational development program. The motivating force behind this program was actually quite simple. Prior to the program, the organization (like others in that industry) operated in a very stable, regulated environment. When this industry was deregulated, top management recognized that the organization had to become more marketing-oriented and customer-focused, in order to remain competitive.

Another factor that can often serve as a powerful motivator of change through the use of organizational development is poor organizational performance. When an organization fails to show a profit over an extended period of time, or sees its market share being steadily eroded, this event will often facilitate organizational change. This factor was undoubtedly at work at the Chrysler Corporation in the late 1970s. During that period, Chrysler had lost market share and was literally in danger of going out of business. The fact that Chrysler was performing so poorly made it easier for Lee Iaccoca to institute a number of organizational changes that ultimately turned the company around (Iaccoca, 1984).

The desire for survival is often the motivating factor behind many organizational development programs, but there are certainly other factors as well. In some cases, relatively effective organizations will engage in programs of planned change, and could do so for a variety of reasons. For example, an effective organization may engage in change for strategic reasons (e.g., Buller, 1988). A manufacturing organization that decides to enter the consumer products business, perhaps through an acquisition, may have to institute a number of organizational changes in order to make this strategy work effectively. An organization that competes primarily on the basis of product quality may decide that it wants to put greater emphasis on customer service. Again, organizational changes may very well be necessary if this strategy is successful.

Some organizations may simply anticipate changes in the external environment and proactively respond to those changes. For example, in many fast-food restaurants, anticipated changes in the demographic population have led to greater utilization of retirees as employees. As another example, several years ago, many universities put considerable resources into distant education programs because they anticipated changes in technology and an increase in the number of working professionals who would be attending college. In both instances, organizational development was the tool of choice for facilitating these changes.

A final reason for organizations' engaging in programs of planned change can simply be described as *self-improvement;* that is, no external pressure for change exists, and there are no concrete strategic reasons for changing. Instead, a well-functioning organization may just want to improve itself in some way. An example of this motivation for change occurs when a major-league baseball team wins the World Series and then is very active, during the off-season, acquiring new players and making some changes in the coaching staff. This response may be due to the fact that, despite its success, the team had a high number of fielding errors and needs improvement in its defense. Organizations that are always striving to get better will remain competitive longer than organizations in which success leads to complacency (Ferrier, Smith, & Grimm, 1999).

A BRIEF HISTORY OF ORGANIZATIONAL DEVELOPMENT

There is no recognized "father of organizational development," but the person who would probably be most deserving of that title would be Kurt Lewin, whose contributions to the broader field of organizational psychology were described in Chapter 1. With respect to organizational development, Lewin made a number of contributions, but two stand out as being most important. First, Lewin was the first psychologist to provide the field of organizational development with a theoretical base. His Three-Step Model of Change and Action Research Model continue to serve as important theoretical guides to organizational development practitioners. Second, Lewin played a key role in the establishment of both the Center for the Study of Group Dynamics, at Massachusetts Institute of Technology (MIT), and the National Training Laboratories (NTL), in Bethel, Maine.

The Center for the Study of Group Dynamics was a fertile site for the study of many group processes that are important to organizations. It also served as the training ground for many individuals who played important roles in shaping the emerging field of organizational development (French & Bell, 1995).

Although Lewin died before the establishment of the National Training Laboratories (NTL), he was instrumental in their development. The major purpose of the NTL was to provide laboratory or **T-group training** to managers and educators. T-groups are essentially unstructured groups in which participants learn both through their interactions and through the evolving group dynamics.

Although there has been considerable criticism of T-groups over the years (e.g., Campbell & Dunnette, 1968), the purported goals of T-group training—enhancement of interpersonal skills, and awareness of group dynamics—are certainly worthwhile. In the early 1950s, T-groups were synonymous with organizational development, and nearly all of the early practitioners of organizational development were either laboratory trainers, or had gone through such training.

Along with Lewin and the development of T-groups, a major factor in the history of organizational development was the application of survey research methods in organizations. This was begun in 1946 when the Survey Research Center (SRC) was established at the University of Michigan under the direction of Rensis Likert. Likert, along with individuals such as Floyd Mann, devoted considerable attention to the development and refinement of survey research methodology. This technique became part of the field of organizational development in 1947, when Likert was able to interest Detroit Edison in conducting a survey on employee attitudes, perceptions, reactions, and behaviors.

What made this project at Detroit Edison unique, however, was that the SRC staff not only conducted the survey and compiled the results, but also helped the company to present the results back to the employees. The approach taken by the SRC researchers, which is now commonplace, was to use what was termed an "interlocking chain of conferences" to feed the data back. The top management team would first receive the survey results. Each individual in this group would then present the results back to his or her own group, with the assistance of a consultant. This process would then be repeated until the results of the survey had been presented to everyone in the organization. From these beginnings, survey feedback has become one of the most

common and most effective (Bowers, 1973) organizational development interventions.

A third major historical foundation of organizational development was the development and use of action research methods. Action research, as mentioned earlier, is attributed to Kurt Lewin and is often used to describe the more general process by which organizations change. Action research also has an applied side and, during the mid-1940s and early 1950s, many action research projects were conducted not only in business organizations but also in educational institutions and community settings. In addition to the general process of action research, one of the important principles that came out of the action research movement was the idea that research is a *collaborative effort* between the researcher and the members of an organization. Indeed, organizational development practitioners today stress the importance of participation of members of the client system in the organizational development process.

The final historical foundation of organizational development was the sociotechnical systems and socioclinical work that emerged in Great Britian. The center of this activity was the Tavistock Clinic, which was established in 1920 to provide psychotherapy and to treat the battle neuroses resulting from World War I. The work at Tavistock that contributed the most to the field of organizational development was a series of experiments, by Trist and Bamforth (1951), in the redesign of work in coal mines. These researchers found a strong link between the design of the work and the social structure and group dynamics within the mines. This work was important on its own merits, and it served as one of the first applications, in an actual industrial setting, of the ongoing U.S. work on group dynamics. Trist conducted many subsequent investigations of the interaction between the design of work and the social environment. The Tavistock work has served as a foundation for many work redesign interventions, and has helped to provide more general insight into the relationship between the technological and social environments.

As will be evident throughout this chapter, many of the interventions and approaches in organizational development can be traced to the historical foundations discussed above. Like any field, however, organizational development is not static; thus, a number of more recent trends in the field will shape the future. One clear recent trend in organizational development is the increased interest in interventions aimed at improving team functioning. Small teams represent the building blocks of many organizations today, and the success of entire organizations depends heavily on the success of individual teams. It is no surprise, then, that team building has become by far one of the most popular organizational development interventions.

A second recent trend is the increased use of large-scale, broad-based organizational change interventions. This trend toward more large-scale change efforts is probably due to a number of factors. For example, because of the volatile competitive environments many organizations face, change often needs to be comprehensive and must occur quickly. Thus, organizations often cannot wait for individual or team-focused interventions to lead to more general organizational change. This trend also reflects, to some degree, a maturing of the field of organizational development. Over time, the accumulated wisdom of organizational development researchers and practitioners has shown that, for real change to occur in an organization, *the entire system must be involved* (e.g., Beckhard, 1967). What better way to get total system involvement than to make the whole organization the focus of an intervention?

A current trend in organizational development is that the extent of application has grown widely. Organizational development is used in a wide variety of organizations (see, e.g., Athey & Hautaluoma, 1988) and has become truly international in scope (e.g., Perlaki, 1994; Rao & Vijayalakshmi, 2000). Perhaps the only negative fact associated with the growth of organizational development is that it makes the establishment of common ethical and professional standards quite difficult. Although many organizational development practitioners are trained specifically in organizational development and in closely related fields such as industrial/organizational psychology, organizational behavior, and human resources management, there is no specific "credential" that one must have as a practitioner of organizational development. As a result, few safeguards exist to protect organizations against incompetent or unethical organizational development practitioners. However, in recent years, organizational development professionals have taken some steps to establish firm standards of professional practice (see Comment 16.1).

THE THEORY BASE OF ORGANIZATIONAL DEVELOPMENT

In most comprehensive treatments of organizational development, the author(s) inevitably point out that organizational development is a field without a strong theoretical base (e.g., Beer, 1976; Porras & Robertson, 1992; Porras & Silvers, 1991). Often, consultants apply organizational development interventions based much more on empiricism, or even a trial-and-error approach, than on solid theoretical grounding. This has led some observers to view organizational development more as a *technology* than as a legitimate subtopic within organizational psychology. Such views are certainly provocative and may have some merit, but organizational development practitioners do in fact have a theory base that practitioners can look to for guidance. In this section, we review that theory base.

Lewin's Three-Step Model

The oldest theory of the general organizational change process is referred to as Lewin's Three-Step Model (Lewin, 1947). Lewin used a physical metaphor to explain the process by which social systems change. The use of metaphor in theory development was introduced in Chapter 14 on organizational design (e.g., McKenna & Wright, 1992) and is also quite useful in

describing organizational change. Like organizational design, organizational change is a highly abstract process that cannot be readily simulated or modeled in a laboratory setting.

The three steps in Lewin's model are presented in Figure 16.1. In the first step in the change process, the stage labeled **unfreezing,** an organization *begins to recognize the need for change.* This is a crucial step in the change process, according to Lewin (1947), because an organization cannot, and will not, change unless there is some recognition of the need for change. Many factors described earlier as motivators of organizational change (e.g., loss

FIGURE 16.1
Lewin's Three-Step Model of the Organizational Change Process

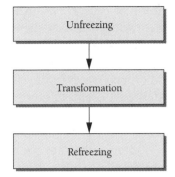

in profits, major environmental changes) would qualify as "unfreezing events." That is, if an organization is unprofitable or faces dramatic changes in its operating environment, this *could* make its employees recognize the need for change. The word "could" is italicized because it is certainly possible for an organization to recognize these unfreezing events, yet not connect them to the need for organizational change.

Assuming that a sufficient level of organizational unfreezing has occurred, the second step in Lewin's model is **change** or **transformation.** This is also a crucial step in the process because it represents tangible changes in the way an organization operates. For example, an organization may convert to a team-based structure, or redesign jobs to enhance customer satisfaction, or engage in any number of other changes. In addition to being a crucial step, this is also a very difficult step. Changes introduced at this point may require that employees do things very differently than in the past. For some, this may be invigorating; for most people, however, changing the way they have done things in the past is a very difficult process.

When an organization changes or transforms itself in some way, the next step is **refreezing.** The changes that are enacted during

the second step in the model become a relatively permanent part of an organization's behavioral repertoire. Refreezing may also be a difficult step because employees may be resistant to the organizational changes. For example, it is quite common for employees to initially be very enthused about enacting organizational changes. However, after their initial enthusiasm wears off, employees may revert to old ways of doing things. For true refreezing to occur, employees must see that it is in their best interest to maintain the organizational changes that are carried out in the transformation phase.

Perhaps the greatest strength of Lewin's Three-Step model is its simplicity. This model is easy to understand and, in fact, provides an organization with some useful guidance in carrying out organizational changes. For example, an organization must consider the need to prepare its employees prior to introducing changes (e.g., unfreezing), and must anticipate some degree of resistance before these changes become a permanent part of the culture (e.g., refreezing). Organizations that do not pay attention to these factors are unlikely to have successful change efforts.

Ironically, simplicity is also one of the primary *weaknesses* of Lewin's model. The model does not provide a great deal of insight into how, for example, the process of unfreezing actually works; for that matter, it provides little insight into how organizations can actually facilitate the processes of change or refreezing. Thus, although Lewin's model is good as a *description* of organizational change, it falls somewhat short as a comprehensive model of the organizational change process because it lacks explanatory power.

The Action Research Model

A second general theoretical model of the organizational change process, also attributed to

Kurt Lewin, is the **Action Research Model.** The general idea behind action research is that the process of organizational change is likened to a cyclical research process. Action research also emphasizes that throughout all phases of the research process, there is active collaboration between the researcher and the members of the client system. The major steps in the action research process, as delineated by Lewin (1951), are presented in Figure 16.2.

As can be seen, the first step in the action research process is **problem identification.** For any research to be undertaken, or any change to occur, there has to be some recognition of a problem that people care about. In organizations, what qualifies as a "problem" may vary greatly from setting to setting. In the most general sense, a problem exists any time there is a *difference between the current state of affairs and the desired state of affairs.* For example, an organization's profits may be lower than they should be; the level of employee turnover may be higher than the organization feels is desirable; or the number of employee grievances filed may be higher than the organization feels it should be.

FIGURE 16.2
Lewin's Action Research Model

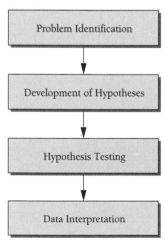

The second step in the Action Research Model is **development of hypotheses.** Obviously, for any particular problem, there could be a multitude of causes. Fortunately, based on prior theory and, perhaps, the experience of organizational members, it is often possible to focus heavily on some causes and pay less attention to others. For example, if the problem area identified is employee turnover, we know from many years of research that turnover is impacted by factors such as employees' job attitudes and the economic environment (Hulin, 1991). Based on this knowledge, it may be useful to examine employee attitudes and, possibly, explore the external job market to develop some hypotheses about turnover.

After hypotheses have been specified, the next step in the action research process is to collect the data needed to engage in **hypothesis testing.** This is an important step because it distinguishes action research from less scientific forms of inquiry. For example, the previously described hypotheses could be tested by asking experts, or perhaps even through introspective methods. When action research is used, however, the scientific method is used, and it requires that hypotheses be tested by gathering empirical data.

After empirical data are collected, the next step in the action research process is **data interpretation.** The critical question the action researcher is trying to answer at this point is: Do the empirical data support, or fail to support, the proposed hypotheses? The biggest dilemma for the researcher at this point is essentially "deciding how to decide" whether the data support the hypotheses. Fortunately, inferential statistical methods are available (e.g., Hays, 1988) to assist the action researcher in making such decisions.

After the data are interpreted and a decision is made about whether the hypotheses are supported, is the action research sequence complete? The researcher may possibly lose interest in a particular problem, but, more typically, the action research process will repeat itself once more. For example, if the researcher collects data and finds that job satisfaction is inversely related to turnover (as suspected), this raises other important questions. What measures could the organization take toward raising employees' levels of job satisfaction and, by inference, reducing turnover? Are certain facets of job satisfaction more important than others in determining turnover? These are empirical questions that could certainly be tested through further research projects. Put differently, the action research cycle can be repeated once again in order to answer these questions.

Thus, according to the Action Research Model, the process of organizational change can be characterized as a continuing cyclical process of hypothesis generation, data collection, data evaluation, and, ultimately, intervention. Another important aspect of the Action Research Model was alluded to earlier: The research process is a *collaborative effort* between the researchers and members of the client system. In a more traditional research project, there is a distinct power or status differential between researchers and the "subjects" of studies. Although researcher–participant collaboration can pose some difficult dilemmas at times (e.g., Mirvis & Seashore, 1979), its positive benefit is that the client system assumes ownership of the organizational change process—an important ingredient in maintaining organizational change over time.

To a certain extent, the advantages and disadvantages associated with the Action Research Model are similar to those associated with Lewin's Three-Step Model. That is, the action research provides a very useful *guide* to understanding organizational change. However, like the Three-Step Model, it also does

not directly explain the most important factors that are involved in the change process. For example: Does change begin with the leadership of an organization or with lower-level employees? What are the factors that lead to resistance to change? How does an organization sustain organizational change over the long term? In fairness to Lewin, the Action Research Model was never really intended to be a theory of organizational change. Rather, it is probably most appropriate to think of the Action Research Model more as a general "theory of intervention" than as a theory of organizational change.

General Systems Theory

A third general theoretical base upon which much of organizational development rests is **General Systems Theory.** General Systems Theory, which was briefly covered in Chapter 14, was developed by von Bartalanffy in 1950 but only made its way into organizational psychology in 1966, through the work of Katz and Kahn. The basic idea of general systems, as applied to organizations, is that organizations import material from the environment, transform that input, and ultimately return it to the environment in some altered form. As a result, organizations are constantly in a dynamic interaction with the external environment. More often than not, organizations change in reaction to, or in anticipation of, changes in the external environment. If organizations were "closed systems" and therefore could ignore the external environment, there would be little need to engage in organizational change and development activities.

Another aspect of General Systems Theory that has greatly influenced the field of organizational development is the idea that any system is comprised of a series of smaller "subsystems." As an analogy, the human body is composed of a number of "subsystems" that guide functions such as circulation, digestion, and so on. Katz and Kahn (1966) pointed out that organizations also consist of a number of interrelated subsystems that guide such functions as importing materials from the environment (e.g., purchasing), transforming those materials (e.g., production), and making sure that the transformed materials are returned to the external environment (e.g., marketing).

The idea of interrelated subsystems is relevant to organizational development because whenever a change is introduced in one part of an organization, those guiding the change must be on the lookout for the "system-wide" ramifications of that change. If an organization decided to change to a team-based structure (a change that is, in fact, becoming increasingly popular), there would be many system-wide implications of this change. Within a team-based structure, supervisors become more like "advisers" or "consultants" rather than bosses. It is also quite likely that working in teams may require fundamentally different skills and abilities than are found in more traditional structures. Finally, for a team-based structure to be effective, a vastly different compensation system is needed. Thus, one change may require changes in the way that leaders and other employees are selected and trained, as well as changes in the organization's compensation system.

Theories of Organizational Change

The theories that have been covered to this point are useful and provide some insight into the general processes involved in organizational change and development, but they do not describe the specific organizational factors that are involved in the change process. Perhaps one of the reasons there are so few specific theories of organizational change is that organizations are so diverse. As a result, it is quite difficult to create a model that serves as a generalized guide to change in all organizations. Fortunately, some theories of this type have been developed, and two are reviewed in this section.

Burke (1994) developed a theory of the organizational transformation process that is general enough to apply to a great variety of organizational types. As can be seen in Figure 16.3, the model proposes that organizational transformation is the result of interrelated factors. Starting at the top of the model, the *external environment* is often a key factor in initiating organizational transformation because change is often motivated by survival or by the desire to capitalize on a new opportunity. The model proposes that the external environment has a direct impact on *leadership,* the *mission and strategy* of an organization, and *organizational culture.* Note, however, that in each of the three cases, these effects are *reciprocal.* For example, the external environment impacts leadership, but leadership could also shape the external environment. The same could be said for mission and strategy and for organizational culture. Note that all three of these organizational factors are interrelated.

The model further proposes that mission and strategy, leadership, and organizational culture have a direct impact on *individual and organizational performance.* Note, however, that, as in the first portion of the model, all relations are reciprocal. That is, mission and strategy, leadership, and organizational culture impact performance but are also impacted by the performance of individuals and the organization as a whole. The other notable feature of the model is the dynamic feedback loop between performance and the external environment. It is possible for the external environment to have a *direct* impact on individual and organizational performance. Also, the performance of individuals and the organization as a whole impacts the external environment.

FIGURE 16.3
Burke's Theory of Organizational Change

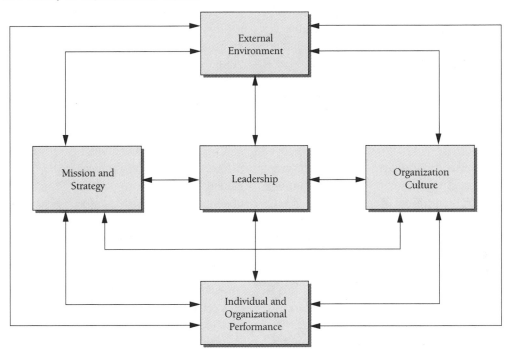

Burke's (1994) model tells us several important things about the process of organizational change. First, it clearly shows that the external environment plays a key role in the organizational change process. This is certainly consistent with General Systems Theory, and it reinforces the point that organizations cannot afford to be out of touch with the external environment. The model also suggests that there are three key "levers of change" that organizations can look to if they want to sustain meaningful change over time. These levers are the interrelated factors of mission and strategy, leadership, and organizational culture. Let's consider each of these respective factors.

Mission and strategy dictate what an organization's purpose is, and how it plans to achieve this purpose. It follows, then, that a *change* in mission and strategy will serve as a powerful catalyst for broader organizational change. Furthermore, at the individual-employee level, mission and strategy are important because they help to provide individuals with a sense of purpose and coherence. Therefore, if mission and strategy are changed, this will serve as a powerful message to employees that change is necessary.

The leadership within an organization is important for a number of reasons. Organizational leaders play a key role in developing organizational mission and strategy, as well as culture, but they also make key contributions to the development of internal policies and procedures and the representation of the organization to the external environment. Thus, it should come as no surprise that organizations are only as effective as their leaders and that top management's involvement is a key factor in successful organizational change.

Organizational culture, as discussed in the previous chapter, represents the underlying values and basic assumptions that are present in an organization. Culture can have powerful effects, both positive and negative, on the performance of individuals and entire organizations. It follows, then, that culture would play a key role in organizational change. This might occur very directly; that is, organizational change might be viewed as culture change.

Culture may also play a more indirect role in organizational change. It is much more likely that changes in an organization will be sustained or will "take hold" if they are compatible with the prevailing culture. For example, an organization that decides to redesign jobs to enhance employee autonomy, yet retains a highly authoritarian culture, will probably not be successful in sustaining this form of organizational change. In this case, the organization may have the option of implementing less dramatic organizational change, or attempting to change to a more participative culture prior to implementing the job design intervention.

Porras and Robertson (1992) have proposed a theoretical framework from which to view the organizational change and development process. This model, presented in Figure 16.4, is a bit more detailed than Burke's (1994), although there are some similarities. For example, Porras and Robertson (1992) propose that the external environment is an important factor in driving organizational change. They also propose that the overall purpose of the organization (represented by *vision*) drives many of the tangible interventions that are designed to facilitate organizational change. Based on the vision that is being carried out, several interrelated variables proposed in the model may be used as levers of change for an organization. These include organizational arrangements, social factors, the physical setting, and the organization's technology.

Changes in these aspects of the work setting should ultimately lead to improved organizational performance and enhanced individual development. Notice, in the model, that these changes are fully mediated by individual cognitions and the behavior of employees. This is perhaps the most important and fundamental proposition in Porras and Robertson's model: *Behavior change is the key mediating variable in organizational change.* At first glance, this would appear to be a rather obvious statement, but it is also a very important one. Many times, when we speak of the "organizational change process," we tend to forget that organizations are *collections of people*. An organization becomes more innovative only if *individuals* come up with new product designs and creative solutions to problems; an organization becomes more customer-service oriented if *individuals* place high priority on serving customers.

The major practical implication of Porras and Robertson's (1992) model is that organizations must pay attention only to issues associated with behavior change when instituting organizational change. Often, failure to consider individual behavior change amounts to organizational decision makers' failure to see the perspective of employees, which is: "What's in it for me?" Some employees may stand to gain very little by changing their behavior, even if organizational decision makers believe that the associated changes are needed.

The organizational change theories presented in this section are still quite general. However, compared to the more general models of the change process presented earlier, they tell us a great deal more about specific things that an organization can do to facilitate and sustain change. With that in mind, we now change the focus to specific organizational development interventions.

FIGURE 16.4
Porras and Robertson's Model of the Organizational Change Process

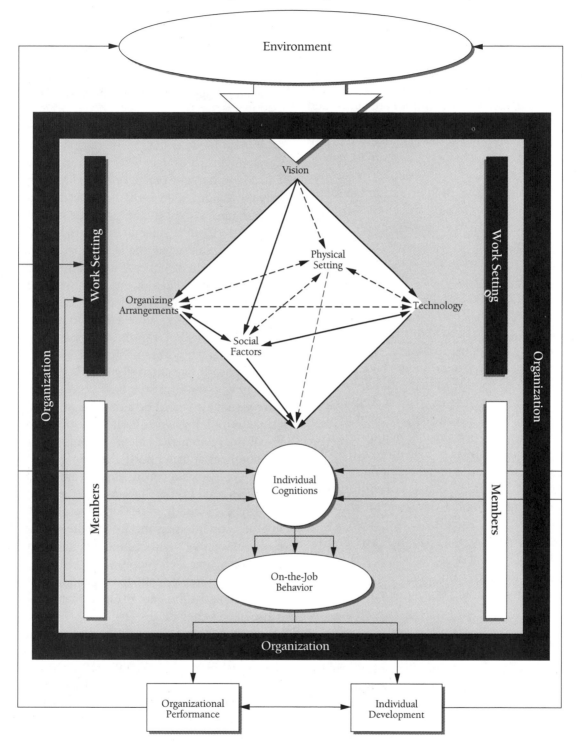

Source: J. I. Porras and P. J. Robertson. (1992). Organizational development: Theory, practice, and research. In M. D. Dunnette and L. M. Hough (Eds.), *Handbook of industrial and organizational psychology* (2nd ed., Vol. 3, pp. 719–822). Palo Alto, CA: Consulting Psychologists Press, Inc. Reprinted by permission.

ORGANIZATIONAL CHANGE INTERVENTIONS

Generally speaking, organizational change interventions differ in terms of (1) the level in the organization at which they are aimed and (2) the process(es) they are designed to impact. Organizational development interventions are typically aimed at *individuals, groups,* or *the organization as a whole.* Of these, the most popular level of intervention is groups, largely because most organizations have realized how important groups are to the success of organizations. Despite the popularity of group-level interventions, another trend is occurring in organizational development: the use of broad, system-wide interventions (French & Bell, 1995). Individual-level interventions are also used frequently, although, in many organizations, these are presented simply as training programs rather than as organizational development interventions.

In terms of *processes* that interventions are designed to impact, essentially anything that can impact the performance of individuals, or the organization as a whole, could be the focus of an organizational development intervention. Common examples of processes on which organizational development interventions are focused are: the roles that employees are asked to play; the goals that drive individual employees and organizations as a whole; group and intergroup processes; organizational structure; and organizational strategy.

Individual-Level Interventions

In reviewing the history of organizational development, one of the first organizational development interventions was **sensitivity training**, also known as **T-group training**. Although T-group training is carried out as a group activity, it is aimed at the individual rather than the group. This is because the goals of T-group training are: enhancement of interpersonal skills and competence, enhanced awareness of the impact of one's behavior on others, and a greater general understanding of group dynamics (Forsyth, 1999).

Although T-groups was at one time the most popular intervention in organizational development, it is rarely used by organizational development practitioners today. Probably the major reason is that the effectiveness of T-groups is doubtful (Campbell & Dunnette, 1968). It is difficult to transfer back to the workplace what one has learned in the T-group. The total honesty and authenticity that are the hallmarks of the T-group movement may not play well in most real-world work settings. Also, some ethical questions surround the use of T-groups—in particular, *requiring* that employees participate.

Despite the fact that T-groups are rarely used now as an organizational development intervention, it would be a mistake to underestimate its impact on the field of organizational development. Many organizational development interventions that are popular today (e.g., process consultation, team building) are rooted in the T-group movement. Although team-building sessions typically do not focus on interpersonal issues, the ground rules that govern team-building meetings quite often parallel those of T-group sessions—for example, participant candor is encouraged, and efforts are made to maintain a sense of "psychological safety."

Another common individual-level organizational development intervention is **job redesign** (Hackman & Oldham, 1980; Parker & Wall, 1998). Job redesign was discussed in some detail in Chapter 6, so it will not be covered in depth here. Job redesign can be a powerful individual-level organizational development intervention because employees typically spend more time on performing their jobs than on any other activity in the work-place. Thus, job redesign can be a very efficient way to change the behavior of employees. The primary limitation of job redesign is that it does not typically address more "macro" issues in the work environment; that is, re-designing jobs will not address the fact that the culture in an organization is one of mistrust and hostility. Another drawback of job re-design is that it is costly. The expense neces-sary to diagnose and change jobs may be prohibitive for some organizations, and the system-wide effects of job redesign may be far-reaching.

Another commonly used organizational development intervention that is focused on individual employees is **Management By Ob-jectives (MBO)** (Carroll & Tosi, 1973). Al-though the specifics of MBO programs vary widely among different organizations, certain features are common to most. Specifically, most involve some level of joint goal setting between employees and their supervisors. In addition, in most MBO programs, the perfor-mance of individual employees is assessed in relation to their progress in accomplishing these objectives. Overall, empirical research has shown that MBO programs have a posi-tive effect on employee performance (Rodgers & Hunter, 1991). It appears, though, that top management support is necessary for MBO programs to be successful.

Group-Level Interventions

As stated earlier, the group or team is the most common level at which organizational devel-opment interventions are focused. This is due to the fact that more and more organizations are adopting team-based structures (Gordon, 1992). It may also reflect the key role that T-groups played in the history of organizational development. By far the most common group-level organizational development intervention

is **team building** (Covin & Kilman, 1991). According to Liebowitz and DeMeuse (1982), team building is defined as "a long-term, data-based intervention in which intact work teams experientially learn, by examining their structures, purposes, norms, values, and in-terpersonal dynamics, to increase their skills for effective teamwork. It is a direct attempt to assist the group in becoming more adept at *identifying, diagnosing, and solving its own problems,* usually with the aid of a behavioral science consultant" (p. 2, italics added). This is obviously a very general definition, and there is a great deal of variation in the way team building is carried out in organizations (Offermann & Spiros, 2001).

The italicized portion of this definition—*"identifying, diagnosing, and solving its own problems,"* captures the essence of the team-building process. A work group that success-fully engages in a team-building intervention is not necessarily going to be problem-free. Rather, this group will be capable of recogniz-ing when things are not going well, diagnos-ing the root causes of the problem(s), and taking steps to solve them.

Although team-building programs do vary considerably from organization to organiza-tion, Liebowitz and DeMeuse (1982) describe a series of eight steps that are typical in most team-building interventions. These steps are presented in Figure 16.5. The first step in the team-building process is labeled **scouting**. This is a preliminary step that involves an ex-change of information between a consultant and a potential client organization. The con-sultant would typically describe his or her ex-pertise, values, and style of operation. The organization, in this step, would normally de-scribe the nature of its problem(s) as well as its views regarding the potential causes of these problem(s). If it is determined that team building is an appropriate intervention, the process moves ahead. If team building is

FIGURE 16.5
Major Steps in the Team-Building Process

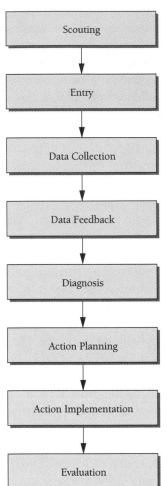

Scouting

Entry

Data Collection

Data Feedback

Diagnosis

Action Planning

Action Implementation

Evaluation

will perform; others are more open-ended (e.g., Schein, 1987). Regardless of how the actual contract is worded, what is important at this point is that the consultant and the client organization must forge a common understanding on the major dimensions of the consulting relationship (e.g., activities of the consultant, fees, time frame of the work, method of billing, and so on). It is also important at this point that the consultant establishes credibility with the client organization, and that there is enough managerial support to sustain the project.

When the preliminary steps of scouting and entry have been completed, the consultant begins the process of **data collection.** This simply involves collecting information, from a variety of sources, on the current functioning of the work groups in an organization. This may also involve personal interviews of group members, although consultants often obtain data from a variety of other sources, such as surveys, observations, and archival records (e.g., minutes of meetings, performance records). The major objective here is to get as complete a picture of the functioning of groups as possible. Thus, the more methods and sources of information that can be used, the better.

After data on the functioning of groups are collected, the next steps are to summarize these data, and then to engage in some form of **data feedback.** This involves holding meetings with each of the work groups in the client organization, and presenting the data that have been collected. Although at first glance this may appear to be just "telling people what they already know," this is often not the case. For example, some group members may have a much more positive picture of their group's functioning than is indicated by the data. Ideally, such discrepancies serve as "unfreezing experiences" for the group members, and prompt a desire for a closer

inappropriate, the consulting relationship may be terminated, unless the consultant can offer other services.

Assuming that team building is appropriate, the process then moves on to the next step: **entry.** This is the point at which the client–consultant relationship begins to be formalized. Although this is typically done through written contracts, there is considerable variation in the way consulting contracts are drawn up. Some contracts are very specific about the nature of the work the consultant examination of the team's functioning. Group members may deny these discrepancies by questioning the accuracy of the data, or may even turn hostile toward the process or the consultant. (The author has experienced both of these responses.)

During data feedback, certain themes or areas of concern will typically surface. For example, group members may be dissatisfied with the level of communication or with the way decisions are made. Unfortunately, data are simply numbers; typically, they do not tell a group *why* a particular issue continues to surface. Thus, at this point, the group needs to engage in **diagnosis,** which represents the group's attempt to explain why the data came out the way they did. This is a very crucial step in the team-building process because, for many groups, it may be the first time they have ever taken a serious look at their work methods and internal processes (Hackman & Morris, 1975).

Ultimately, the diagnosis stage is a series of problems that are preventing the group from performing up to their full capabilities. One could also think of these as "barriers to performance." Developing a list of performance barriers is an important step because once these problems are identified, the group can begin to develop solutions. This is the purpose of the next step: **action planning**. During this phase, one or more action plans are developed for each of the important problems identified. For example, if one of the problems identified in the diagnosis stage is "Poor communication among group members," a corresponding action plan might be "Increase the number of group meetings from once a month to once every two weeks."

Action plans are very important because they represent the most tangible products of a team-building meeting—particularly, what a group has committed to do (often in writing) to make it function more effectively. One

thing is important to consider, however: Not all action plans are of equal value. Generally speaking, action plans are much more useful if they are specific and measurable, have an identifiable time frame associated with them, and hold an individual or individuals responsible for implementing them. Typically, when one or more of these attributes is missing, the action plan will be forgotten soon after the team-building meeting adjourns.

After the team-building meeting is over, the group goes back to its normal routine and thus enters the next phase: **action implementation.** This involves implementing the action plans that were agreed on during the team-building meeting. This is perhaps the most challenging part of the team-building process because even if the action plans the group generates are very good (e.g., specific, measurable), they often require group members to give up old habits and engage in new behaviors. It may be easy for a leader to *talk* about letting group members have more input into decisions, but it's quite another thing to actually relinquish a portion of his or her control over decision making.

The final stage in the team-building process is **evaluation,** which normally takes place after some period of time has passed since the team-building meeting. Evaluation involves assessing the group's progress on the implementation of the action plans. This step is important because it serves to hold the group to its action plans. If there is no follow-up, groups will either fail to implement action plans or will begin to implement them and lose interest. Often, the evaluation portion of the process comes in the form of a follow-up meeting in which the groups, with the assistance of a consultant, review progress on each of the action plans generated during the initial team-building meeting. Ideally, this meeting will reveal that the group is implementing the action plans as written. In some cases, though, it may reveal that the action plans need to be revised, or that external factors may have prevented the group from implementing them as written.

As with many organizational development interventions described in this chapter, not a great deal of empirical research exists on the effectiveness of team-building interventions. The little empirical research that has been done provides mixed support for the effectiveness of team building. Some empirical data have failed to support the effectiveness of team building (e.g., Eden 1985), but there is also evidence that team building can be a very effective method of improving a number of group processes (e.g., Cohen & Bailey, 1997). A key factor in determining the success of team building is whether there is a need for it in the first place. If a team is functioning very well, or works under conditions of very low interdependence, team building may have little effect on group processes or outcomes.

A second organizational development intervention that is often aimed at the group level is **process consultation** (Schein, 1969, 1987), which is both a philosophy of consulting and an organizational development intervention. As a consulting philosophy, process consultation emphasizes that the role of the consultant is primarily to guide an organization through the process of discovering what its problems are, and finding solutions to those problems. In doing so, the emphasis is on "how things are done" (e.g., process issues) rather than "what" is actually done. Readers eager to learn more about process consultation as a consulting philosophy are strongly urged to read Edgar Schein's various works on the topic.

Process consultation also represents a set of interventions that a consultant can implement. Although these interventions do not necessarily have to be applied in group settings, this is the context in which they are often used. Schein (1987) classified interventions on a continuum, based on how confrontational they are vis-à-vis the client. The least confrontational type of intervention that a process consultant can use is an **exploratory inquiry.** For example, a process consultant may ask a group: "How have things been going the past few months?" or "Tell me a little bit about things that are important to the group's success."

The second general type of intervention described by Schein (1987) is a **diagnostic intervention.** The process consultant in this case does not tell the client what to do, although the questions being asked about the problem are more focused than in the exploratory inquiry stage. If a group decides that its primary problem is poor communication among group members, a diagnostic inquiry might be: "What do you think contributes to this poor communication within your group?" or "What can I do to help you improve communication?" It is doubtful that members of such a group would perceive either of these questions as being confrontational. On the other hand, they do focus on a specific aspect of group functioning, both in terms of isolating the problem and determining whether the consultant will be able to help them solve it.

The third level proposed by Schein (1987) is called **action alternative interventions.** This type of intervention does not involve telling the client what to do. It is potentially more confrontational than the first two types of interventions because the process consultant is asking the group: *"What have you done about the problem?"* So, for example, if a group feels that internal communication is a problem and that the nature of their work roles contributes to this problem, the process consultant might ask, as an action alternative intervention: "What have you done to improve the situation?" or "If roles are the problem, have you done anything to change the roles of group members in a way that would facilitate communication?"

Why does Schein (1987) consider these questions to be potentially confrontational? The key to answering this question really lies in the difference between the roles of client and consultant. According to Schein, consulting is really all about *helping,* and therefore we can think of consultants as professional *helpers.* If one accepts this notion, a logical corollary is that the client organization is in the position of *seeking help,* primarily because it cannot solve a particular problem on its own. The idea that an organization needs help potentially puts it in a dependent or lower status position vis-à-vis the consultant. Therefore, when the process consultant asks, "What have you done about this problem?", the client organization risks embarrassment by saying that it has done the wrong thing or, worse yet, has done nothing to solve the problem.

The final type of intervention described by Schein (1987) is labeled **confrontive interventions.** In interventions of this type, the process consultant makes recommendations as to how to solve the problem. For example, a process consultant may say: "Why don't you try _____ as a way to solve the problem?" or "I would recommend trying _____ ." Notice that these statements are much more directive than the previous three. They are also potentially more confrontational, because the client may assume that the way he or she had been doing things is incorrect. Intervening in this way also tends to reinforce the status differences between the client and the process consultant that were described above.

According to Schein (1987), a key issue in process consultation is how far and how quickly one moves along this intervention from exploratory inquiries to confrontive interventions. Many consultants begin with confrontive interventions or move to that point very quickly, often because the client expects or even demands it. Many organizations see consultants as bright experts to whom they can essentially "hand off" their problems. Unfortunately, handing off problems is often counterproductive because even extremely bright consultants rarely have enough information to immediately make concrete recommendations to an organization. Most problems in organizations are too complex and are embedded in a cultural context that an outside consultant cannot completely understand.

Another reason problems are handed off is simply because it is reinforcing to a consultant. The author has personally experienced the positive feelings associated with being seen as an expert by employees of an organization, and having one's advice taken seriously. When members of an organization ask for advice, consultants are often compelled to offer something more concrete than "What do *you* think the problem is?" The irony, of course, is that, in the long run, a consultant is often much more helpful to the client organization by keeping his or her interventions at the exploratory or diagnostic levels. By doing so, the consultant ultimately obtains much more information about the organization and its problems than he or she would obtain by immediately being confrontational. Therefore, if the consultant needs to make recommendations in the future, these will be based on much more solid information.

Staying at the exploratory or diagnostic levels is also beneficial because these interventions force members of a client organization to *think.* As a result, these types of interventions help to sharpen employees' analytical and diagnostic skills so that they ultimately develop the capacity to solve some of the problems on their own. It also increases the chances that, although the members of the client organization are being helped by the process consultant, they will ultimately come up with the solution to whatever problem(s) are identified. This is important because members of the client organization are typically in a much better position than the consultant to judge what will and what will not work in that organization.

In addition to this general typology of interventions, Schein (1987) proposed a number of more specific interventions that fit into this typology. These are presented in Table 16.1. To reiterate a point made earlier, these interventions are not specific to groups, but they are often used when helping groups. Notice that many of these interventions are so simple, and are used so frequently, that we don't really think of them as being organizational development interventions. Terms such as *active, interested listening, forcing historical reconstruction, forcing concretization, forcing process emphasis,* and *diagnostic questions and*

TABLE 16.1

A Listing and Categorization of Process Consulting Interventions

Intervention	Category
1. Active, interested listening	Exploratory
2. Forcing historical reconstruction	Diagnostic
3. Forcing concretization	Diagnostic
4. Forcing process emphasis	Diagnostic
5. Diagnostic questions and probes	Diagnostic, action oriented
6. Process management and agenda setting	Confrontive
7. Feedback	Confrontive
8. Content suggestions and recommendations	Confrontive
9. Structure management	Confrontive
10. Conceptual inputs	Potentially confrontive

Adapted from: E. H. Schein. (1987). *Process consultation: Lessons for managers and consultants* (Vol. II). Reading, MA: Addison-Wesley.

probes are used all the time as a way to help people figure out what their problems are.

Items 6 through 10 in Table 16.1 are more specific to group settings and require a bit more explanation. With *process management and agenda setting,* the process consultant would perhaps provide suggestions as to how group meetings might be conducted or how the agenda might be structured. While potentially confrontational, it may also be very helpful to a group that is doing some things that are very clearly causing it problems. For example, one of the problems that the author has observed in group meetings over the years is poor management of the group's time—that is, the group may consistently get through only one or two agenda items during its meetings. One way to deal with this problem is to be very structured in setting the meeting agenda and allocating a certain number of minutes to each agenda item.

Providing *feedback* is also a potentially confrontational intervention, yet it may also be quite useful to a group. A process consultant sitting in a group meeting can observe many things about the group's functioning. Probably the most visible thing is the manner in which the group communicates. Is communication very formal, or do group members feel free to jump in at any time? Do all members of the group communicate, or does a small number of very vocal group members tend to dominate the discussions? If a group's discussions are dominated by a small number of vocal employees, having a consultant point this out could be highly confrontational. This is particularly true if this behavior pattern is indicative of other problems in the group. Despite being potentially confrontational, this type of feedback may be highly useful because a group may not even be aware that this is happening.

When a consultant makes *content suggestions and recommendations,* he or she is being even more directive and potentially "confrontive." A process consultant, for example, may recommend that a work group should have all group members discuss concerns at the end of its meetings. He or she may also make recommendations about the frequency of team meetings—a process consultant may suggest that a group that meets only once a month should start meeting twice a month. This type of intervention is potentially confrontational because, although the process consultant is not explicitly saying that things have been done wrong, the recommendations given to the work group may convey that opinion.

With *structure management,* the process consultant may make recommendations regarding the design of a group's task, or perhaps the manner in which a group carries out its tasks. For example, in a group where each group member performs a highly specialized task, a consultant may recommend combining tasks in order to increase the meaningfulness of the work. This is again potentially confrontational because the process consultant is directing the client to accept a solution to a problem that he or she, rather than the client, has proposed.

The final intervention listed in Table 16.1 is labeled *conceptual inputs.* It is common for process consultants to present relevant conceptual material during group-related interventions. For example, if a consultant is helping a group improve its effectiveness, he or she may, at some point, provide the group with a "lecturette" covering conceptual material on group effectiveness. Although conceptual inputs can be quite useful, they can also be counterproductive, particularly if they are overused. As Schein (1987) points out, conceptual inputs may be confrontational because they may highlight weaknesses in a group's processes. A group that does not encourage a great deal of debate and open communication may become uneasy when it hears

that research has shown that both of these are positively related to group effectiveness.

Given the generality of process consultation, there is little empirical evidence as to whether this approach is effective. It would seem, however, that there would be a number of advantages in using this method, as opposed to more traditional forms of consultation. As Schein (1987) points out, organizations often know that something is "not right," but they are not sure where the problems lie. Thus, they often need help and guidance in discovering what those problems are, and how best to solve them. Process consultation is ideal in this type of situation because the primary assumption behind this model is that the client owns the problem and is ultimately the one who knows the organization well enough to figure out the problems—and the solutions to the problems.

Organization-Wide Interventions

Interventions that target the organization as a whole are becoming increasingly popular, for a number of reasons. For example, we know that organizational change is most likely to occur and be sustained when the entire organization is involved in the change effort. Also, given the rapid rate of change in the business environment today, many organizations do not have the luxury of intervening with groups or individuals and then expecting their interventions to be translated into organization-wide change. Thus, interventions that focus on the organization as a whole are becoming increasingly popular.

The organization-wide intervention that is probably most widely used is **survey feedback.** In a typical survey feedback program, a survey is administered to all employees. It may address issues such as attitudes, perceptions of organizational climate, perceptions of management, and perceived level of organizational effectiveness, among other things. After the survey is administered and returned, the results are tabulated and then presented back to employees, typically within their own work group.

As with most organizational development interventions, the precise manner in which survey feedback is carried out varies widely. A common practice, though, is for consultants to first conduct personal interviews with at least a random sample of employees. Based on the themes that emerge from these interviews, survey items are then developed (e.g., Gavin, 1984). Other consultants may have a standardized instrument that they administer to employees. An advantage of using a standardized approach is that an organization's results can be compared with those of other organizations in the same industry or the same geographical location. A disadvantage of this type of survey instrument is that because the items are not specific to the particular organization, many issues that are important to employees may be missed.

Although survey development is important, the feedback process is the key part of survey feedback, and thus it will be discussed in a bit more detail. In a model survey feedback program, the data are fed back to *every* employee in the organization, in a "water falls down" procedure. That is, the top management team of an organization first reviews the survey results. Each member of the top management team then shares the data with his or her direct reports. This process is repeated until everyone in the organization has had an opportunity to review the data. This feedback process makes survey feedback an organization-wide intervention and distinguishes *true* survey feedback from many employee opinion surveys conducted in organizational settings. For example, if a consultant conducts a survey of organizational employees and prepares a written summary report for top

management, but the process essentially ends at this point, this is *not* true survey feedback.

In terms of research, there is some evidence that survey feedback is an effective organizational change intervention. In fact, Bowers (1973) compared several organizational development interventions and found that survey feedback was the most effective. More recent evidence has also shown that survey feedback is effective (Neuman, Edwards, & Raju, 1989). Research has also investigated more specific factors that impact the feedback process. For example, Klein, Kraut, and Wolfson (1971) found that employees are most responsive to feedback when it comes from their managers and is perceived as relevant to their actual work group. Because of this, in many survey feedback interventions, two types of data are presented back to employees: (1) data that represent the opinions of the entire organization, and (2) data that represent the opinions of the department in which the work group may reside.

A second organization-wide intervention that has become increasingly popular in the past twenty years is **Total Quality Management (TQM).** Based on the statistical process control principles pioneered by the late W. Edwards Deming, TQM is a comprehensive effort that has a number of components (Flynn, Sakakibara, & Schroeder, 1995). One of the major principles of TQM is that an organization must measure quality if it wants to improve it. Thus, organizations that have adopted TQM typically spend a great deal of time both collecting and analyzing data on the quality of their products and services.

Another important principle of TQM is that even the lowest level employees should feel empowered to take steps toward quality improvement when necessary. This is one of the factors that truly makes TQM an organization-wide intervention and a powerful management philosophy. In a manufacturing environment, all employees have access to quality control data, and they are encouraged to act on problems in order to improve the product quality. In a service organization, all employees should have the authority to do whatever it takes to make customers satisfied.

Although many organizations have had success with TQM and similar programs—Continuous Quality Improvement (CQI)—these interventions are not without critics. A frequent criticism of TQM and related interventions is that they do not translate well to nonmanufacturing settings. In recent years, TQM has been applied in organizations such as public schools, universities, and hospitals. Unlike manufacturing organizations, "quality" is a much more nebulous concept in these organizations. Therefore, by focusing on numerical data, TQM could be directing employees' efforts in the wrong direction.

Another typical problem that arises in TQM programs is that they often generate considerable union resistance. Unions may see TQM as undercutting them in a number of ways. For example, employees may have to engage in a considerable amount of work to collect and analyze quality information, and to suggest solutions to problems. Both of these activities are typically not covered under collective bargaining agreements, and unions often see them as being management's responsibilities. Despite these potential disadvantages, many organizations have adopted TQM. Furthermore, most of these organizations maintain a very high level of commitment to these programs and feel convinced that they are effective. Over time, more empirical data will be accumulated on the effectiveness of TQM and similar programs.

A third form of comprehensive organizational change is through a **change in structure**. As discussed in Chapter 14, orga-

nizations have numerous options when it comes to organizational structures. As a method of organizational change, changing structure is certainly enticing. If all of the departments in an organization are restructured, employees have no choice but to engage in at least some form of change. Unfortunately, though, the changes that are brought about by structural changes may ultimately be only "pseudo" changes. Unless a change in structure is accompanied by changes in employees' behavior, this is a relatively ineffective method of organizational change. For example, if an organization changes to a team-based structure, this will not result in meaningful organizational change if individual employees continue to act primarily in their own self-interest.

Other common ways of facilitating broad-based organizational change are through **strategic planning**, and **visioning** interventions. Strategic planning is simply an organization's plan for what it is going to accomplish, and the mechanisms that will be used to accomplish it. Strategic planning is an important function in an organization because it drives important activities such as human resources planning and compensation, and it influences key decisions such as acquisitions. Given this importance, one obvious way for an organization to effect change would be to change its strategic objectives. For example, the top management of an organization that had once relied primarily on getting its products to market quickly may decide that it wants to be seen as a technological innovator. This type of strategic decision is highly significant and would likely lead to a number of organizational changes capable of carrying out this new strategy. For example, this organization might decide to hire the best technical talent available, or perhaps acquire a small but highly innovative competitor. It may also require a fundamental change in organizational culture, or perhaps even in structure.

The process of visioning simply requires the members of an organization (usually top management) to decide: (1) what the organization would look like if it were ideal, (2) what the organization currently looks like, and (3) what strategic steps need to be taken in order to get the organization from where it is to where it could begin an ideal state. An example of this visioning process is depicted in Figure 16.6. This type of activity can be very useful, particularly prior to strategic planning, because it forces organizational decision makers to think about where they are headed and, perhaps more importantly, how to get there.

Most typically, strategic planning and visioning processes will represent the beginning of a long-term, large-scale organizational change process. These two macro-level interventions will necessitate many other interventions at many other organizational levels. At Harley-Davidson, for example, a long-term process of organizational change essentially began with a simple visioning exercise (Teerlink & Ozley, 2000) and then "branched out" to a variety of other interventions needed to help that organization get from where it was to where it ultimately wanted to be (see Comment 16.2). When looked at in this way, it is probably more accurate to think of very global interventions (such as visioning) as *precursors* to organizational change rather than interventions themselves.

FIGURE 16.6
Example of the Visioning Process

CONDITIONS NECESSARY FOR SUCCESSFUL ORGANIZATIONAL CHANGE

Up to this point, we have defined organizational development, covered the theoretical base of this field, and described some of the more commonly used organizational development interventions. In this section, we shift the focus to the more general process of organizational development. More specifically, we examine organizational factors that have been found to impact the success of organizational change and development interventions. These include top management support, the consultant who guides the organization through the change process, general resistance to change, and organizational ownership of the change and development process.

Top Management Support

For most initiatives in organizational settings to succeed, support from top management personnel is crucial. Conversely, a *lack* of top management support is almost a guarantee of failure. Thus, it should come as no surprise that top management support is a key factor in determining whether programs of planned organizational change are successful. In this section, we examine why top management support is so important to the success of organizational change.

One of the most fundamental reasons that top management support is so crucial is that *top management personnel have a great deal of control over organizational resources*. This is important because organizational change and development programs are *very expensive*. Not only does an organization typically have to pay the fees of outside consultants; in most cases, organizational change and development programs require a great deal of employees' time. Employees' time is a finite resource;

COMMENT 16.2

ORGANIZATIONAL CHANGE AT HARLEY-DAVIDSON

IN TERMS OF brand loyalty and identification, few organizations have been as successful as motorcycle manufacturer Harley-Davidson. Its products not only provide transportation, but have really come to symbolize a lifestyle as well. Harley-Davidson endured some very tough times in the early 1980s due to Japanese competition and labor problems. Remarkably, the company pulled together, weathered this crisis, and by the late 1980s was again very profitable. Unfortunately, to get through this crisis, the organization adopted a very rigid "command and control" culture in which employees obeyed orders but took little personal initiative. This culture helped save the company, but, unfortunately, changes were needed if the company was to continue to grow in the *absence* of an external crisis.

In the book *More than a Motorcycle: The Leadership Journey at Harley-Davidson,* Rich Teerlink and Lee Ozley describe the difficult, long-term process of moving from a "command and control" culture to one in which employees are empowered and feel a sense of ownership. What's striking about this process is that it began with a very simple visioning exercise. Specifically, the top executives at Harley-Davidson, with the assistance of a consultant, discussed how the company was currently functioning and how the company *ideally* should be functioning. An examination

of the differences between these two (current vs. ideal) began a process that has gone on for over 10 years and has led to significant changes in organizational structure, performance appraisal, compensation practices, and labor relations.

A number of important lessons about organizational change can be learned from this book. Perhaps most important is: For organizational change to be meaningful, it must be *comprehensive*. Another important lesson is that organizational change must be supported by top management in order to succeed. Rich Teerlink, one of the authors, was the Chief Executive Officer of Harley-Davidson through most of this change process, and strongly supported it. Without his support, it is doubtful that this process would have survived. Finally, in reading this book, it becomes very obvious that this change process did not always go smoothly. There were times when union support of the change process was low, and other times in which more immediate crises took higher priority. Ultimately, though, the organization kept at it and produced meaningful, positive organizational changes.

Source: R. Teerlink and L. Ozley. (2000). *More than a motorcycle: The leadership journey at Harley-Davidson.* Boston, MA: Harvard Business School Press.

therefore, during the time that employees are engaged in organizational development activities, they are not producing products, serving customers, or doing other things that directly support the mission of the organization. Top managers in an organization are typically the only ones who can authorize resource expenditures of this magnitude.

Top management support is also crucial because, in most organizations, top management is the level that provides broad strategic direction. Organizations do not change in a random fashion—rather, they typically change for some logical reason. Top management's involvement and support are essential in order to give an organizational change effort proper direction. If an organizational change effort were to be conducted without this involvement, it is quite possible that change might occur, but it might be counterproductive.

A final reason that top management's support is so crucial is that it has symbolic value. Although employees in most organizations may not feel personally connected to members of the top management team, they do look to these individuals for guidance. If an organizational development program is initiated and members of the top management team are indifferent toward it, this signals to employees that the program is unimportant. On the other hand, if top managers enthusiastically support it, this communicates to employees that the organizational effort is important and they should be committed to it.

The Consultant Guiding the Process

Many students see organizational development consulting as a glamorous profession characterized by high earnings, interesting work, and exciting travel opportunities. There is certainly some truth to this, but organizational development consulting is also very *hard work*. Facilitating day-long meetings can be both physically and mentally draining, and consultants must constantly be aware of the ethical implications of their behavior.

Organizational development consultants have a very strong impact on whether an organizational change program is successful. A highly skilled organizational development consultant will greatly enhance the odds that an organizational change program will be successful, even if the organization may initially be vague about what it is trying to accomplish. On the other hand, a poorly trained organizational development consultant who is lacking in skill will most certainly increase the odds that an organizational change program will be a failure.

Given the importance of the organizational development consultant, the question that naturally arises is: "What are the attributes of an effective organizational development consultant?" This is a difficult question to answer because the success of a consultant often depends on the fit between his or her skills and personality, and the attributes of the client organization. A consultant may be a smashing success in one organization but a miserable failure in another. Despite this situational specificity, it is possible to come up with a set of general attributes that tend to characterize successful consultants.

One characteristic that may seem obvious to readers is that consultants need to have a well-developed *knowledge of organizational development and, more generally, behavior in organizations*. This is important because consultants observe behavioral processes in organizations and, based on these observations, often make recommendations about organizational development interventions. Such knowledge often (but not always) comes from graduate study in the behavioral sciences or related fields (e.g., organizational behavior, industrial relations, human resources management). An individual, for example, may acquire such knowledge through several years of working in a corporate training and development department, or through continuing education.

In addition to knowledge, several *skills* are needed in order to develop a successful consulting relationship with an organization. Probably the most basic skill consultants need to have is *listening*. Particularly when a consultant first makes contact with an organization, it is important that he or she gathers as much information about that organization as is possible. The only way to do that is for the consultant to actively listen to members of the organization as they describe their culture and explain why they want to embark on a program of organizational change.

It is also important for consultants to possess very well-developed *communication skills*. Consulting involves a great deal of verbal communication with the members of a client organization, but it also requires that the consultant can communicate in writing and nonverbally. Consultants must be highly skilled communicators because much of their communication to the client organization comes in the form of feedback about problems and process issues. If an organization is going to change successfully, the consultant's feedback must be frequent and easy for members of an organization to understand.

Organizational development consultants also need to have skill in *research methodology and data analysis*. Organizational development consulting almost always involves the collection of empirical data about the client organization, analysis of those data, and a summary of the data in a form that members of the client organization can readily understand. Consultants who do not possess at least minimal skills in methods of data collection and analysis, and who are unable to summarize data for nontechnical audiences, are at a distinct disadvantage compared to those who can. Consultants who lack these skills may rely on less rigorous methods of data gathering and ultimately may compromise the quality of an organizational change effort.

In addition to knowledge and skill, some intangible qualities are important for organizational development consultants to possess. For example, any type of consulting demands *a very strong sense of ethics*. Inevitably, consultants are told things "in confidence," and may even detect that organizational members are attempting to use their services for political purposes. These are difficult situations, but they will be less difficult for consultants who have strong sets of ethical standards, and who clearly communicate these standards to clients before accepting a consulting assignment.

Another highly important, yet intangible quality of successful organizational development consulting is *flexibility*. Effective consultants are flexible enough to see an organization and its problems as they really are, not as they are seen through the lens of a particular theory or favorite intervention. This type of flexibility at times demands that a consultant must assess the situation in an organization and conclude that he or she is not appropriate for the consulting assignment. In the short term, this may result in lost consulting revenue; in the long run, it helps to build a consultant's credibility. Flexibility also requires a willingness to see multiple sides of an issue, and occasionally to admit that one is wrong. If a consultant offers advice, or an assessment of a problem, that ultimately turns out to be wrong, he or she needs to be flexible enough to admit the error and learn from it.

A final intangible characteristic that is crucial in effective consulting is *credibility*. How does a consultant establish and maintain credibility with an organization? When consultants initially come into contact with organizations, they are often sought out because of their academic credentials, prior work they have done, or an influential book that they have written. In such cases, the organization certainly has a positive view of the consultant, and positive expectations about his or her capabilities, but the consultant does yet have credibility. This is because credibility is an earned commodity, not a professional entitlement. Credibility is earned over time as the consultant interacts with the organization.

Perhaps the most important factor in determining credibility is whether the consultant keeps his or her word. When the consultant tells an employee that what he or she says will be held in confidence, is this information *really* held in confidence? When the consultant tells an organization that a report summarizing an employee attitude survey will be completed

by a certain date, is the report delivered on *that date?* When a client organization is told that a project will cost a certain amount, does the consultant bill for *that* amount? These are obviously hypothetical examples, but they serve to underscore the point that credibility is something that consultants accrue each time they meet (or, ideally, exceed) the expectations of the client organization.

General Resistance to Change

Humans are basically creatures of habit, and as such, they take a great deal of comfort in routine and familiarity. Consequently, even the idea of change often evokes a great deal of apprehension and anxiety. This general principle certainly applies in the workplace as well. People develop routines and rituals surrounding many behaviors and have a great deal of difficulty changing them, even if such changes are positive. As stated in Chapter 15, this fear of change often comes from a belief that changes will have a negative impact, or from just general fear of the unknown.

It is unlikely that organizations can ever completely eliminate resistance to change. What can be done, though, is to introduce organizational changes in a way that decreases the potential for resistance. One way of doing this is to provide the opportunity for employee participation in the implementation of the organizational changes. As was shown over 50 years ago by Coch and French (1948), employees are much more receptive to changes when they have the opportunity to participate in their implementation. Autocratic methods of organizational change may appear to be much quicker and easier than participative methods, but, in the long run, organizations stand a much greater chance of encountering employee resistance if changes are imposed on employees.

Change can also be made less threatening to employees if organizations maintain a high level of communication with employees throughout the change process. Employees typically want to know *why* the organization is initiating the changes, what specifically the organization is attempting to change, what implications the proposed changes will have for them personally, and whether other changes will occur in the future. Willingly sharing this type of information with employees will go a long way toward calming their fears about the change process. On the other hand, if employees feel that they have to "pull teeth" to get information, they will be much more likely to assume the worst and resist the organizational changes.

Although resistance to change is typically perceived as something that must be "overcome" in order to implement organizational change, in some cases it may be a sign that the organization should rethink the changes it is implementing. The reaction of employees to proposed changes may be a good "reality check" for an organization. This may especially be true in organizations where top management has sought out little input from rank-and-file employees prior to going ahead with organizational change programs.

Organizational Ownership of the Change and Development Process

Why do organizations at times abdicate responsibility for organizational development programs to outside consultants? One reason is that, if done correctly, organizational development is *hard work*. Developing a new vision for an organization, participating in team building activities, or conducting survey feedback meetings are all mentally and physically draining activities. It is much easier to simply have a consultant take care of these chores and submit a report to the organization. Ultimately, though, the solutions that come strictly from consultants may not mesh well with the realities of an organization's culture (Schein, 1987). Employees may also have little enthusiasm for implementing changes recommended by a consultant.

Organizations may also resist ownership because organizational development can be very *threatening*. During the course of an organizational development program, employees may be faced with the reality that their organization is not functioning as well as it could. It is even more threatening for employees to be confronted with the possibility that they may bear some of the responsibility for this suboptimal performance. Viewing an organizational development program as "something the consultant does" may be a way of sparing employees the difficult task of confronting the organization's (and, by implication, their own) shortcomings.

One thing consultants can do to increase ownership is to stress its importance at the beginning of the organizational development process. Often, in an effort to win a consulting contract with an organization, a consultant is tempted to portray the role of the organization as being very minimal (e.g., the consultant will take care of everything). However, in the long run, this model is often counterproductive because the change process rarely works without the participation of members of the client organization.

The other thing that consultants can do to increase organizational ownership is to truly make the client a partner in the change process. It is often tempting for consultants to give organizations advice in a very "top down" or authoritative manner, particularly when they see things being done in the organization that are obviously counterproductive. If consultants can resist this temptation, however, and explore such counterproductive practices in a collaborative manner, this will ultimately be of greater help to the organization. It is also much more empowering to the client organization, because when problems occur in the future, the organization will be able to solve them.

EVALUATION OF ORGANIZATIONAL DEVELOPMENT PROGRAMS

At this point in the chapter, some readers may find the organizational development process, and the various interventions that often go with it, to be quite interesting. In fact, in the author's experience, many students get "hooked" on organizational development very quickly, and often want to focus their career in that direction. More skeptical readers, however, may be asking themselves: "Does any of this stuff actually work?" This is certainly an important question, given the large amount of resources that are required to implement an organizational development program.

In this section, we tackle the difficult question of whether organizational development actually "works." We do this by first examining the issue of evaluative criteria. One of the problems in evaluating anything is that we are often vague in specifying the criteria by which we judge effectiveness. We then discuss the most common research designs that are used in the evaluation of organizational development programs, and the difficulty of measuring change. Finally, a brief review of the published literature on the effectiveness of various organizational development interventions is provided.

The Problem of "Evaluative Criteria"

Within the field of industrial/organizational psychology, what has been termed "the criterion problem" is typically associated with personnel selection (e.g., Campbell, 1990). To be sure, when organizations attempt to systematically validate employee selection procedures, deciding on appropriate criteria is a major challenge. What does it mean to say that an employee is *effective?* How do we gauge the contribution of an employee to an organization's success? To the extent that we *can't* answer either of these questions very well, it is much more difficult to assess the value of employee selection procedures.

Fortunately, due to a great deal of theoretical and empirical work, we know considerably more about predicting employee performance than we did 50 years ago. One of the unfortunate consequences of this work, however, is that it has led to the misperception that "the criterion problem" is unique to personnel selection. In fact, nothing could be farther from the truth. The criterion problem is alive and well in many areas of organizational psychology and, more specifically, in the evaluation of organizational development programs.

If an organizational development program is viewed in a holistic manner (e.g., the diagnosis, interventions, follow-up), the criterion problem becomes particularly acute. This is because the goal of most, if not all, organizational development programs is essentially the same: *enhanced organizational effectiveness.* How, then, can we show that an organization is more effective after the implementation of an organizational development program? One way this could be done is through standard financial measures such as stock price, sales revenues, return on assets, market share, or any number of other measures that have been developed through cost accounting procedures.

Financial performance data are appealing because they have the feel of objectivity. When an organization improves its financial performance following the implementation of an organizational development program, it is hard to argue that such results were due

to methodological artifacts. A disadvantage of the financial indexes mentioned above is that they represent a fairly narrow view of organizational effectiveness. Is an organization truly effective if its stock price goes up, but it lays off 30% of its workforce? Is an organization truly effective if its market share increases by 5%, but its rate of turnover is one of the highest in its industry?

Another way to assess organizational effectiveness, which can be equally as narrow, is to do so primarily in terms of employee behaviors and attitudes. For example, organizations might use the results of employee opinion surveys, rates of turnover, or number of grievances filed to indicate how well the organization is performing. These effectiveness criteria may be much more relevant to the aims of an organizational development program than financial performance data are. Unfortunately, though, these criterion measures may be as narrow as the financial indexes described above. Is an organization effective if its employees are highly satisfied with their jobs, yet its stock price declines steadily over a three-year period? Is an organization effective if its turnover rate is extremely low, yet it continues to lose market share to its competitors?

The best approach to measuring overall organizational effectiveness is to utilize *multiple* criteria measures. This provides the most complete picture of organizational effectiveness, and, in fact, yields the most comprehensive view of the impact of organizational development programs. Also, if such data are collected over a relatively long period of time, they may be particularly revealing. For example, in some cases, the initial impact of organizational development programs on traditional financial measures is actually negative (e.g., Griffin, 1991) but, over time, may ultimately end up being positive. Conversely, with attitudinal measures, employees' initial reactions to organizational development may be very positive.

Over time, however, the novelty of an organizational development program may wear off, and attitudes may return to baseline levels.

Deciding on the proper criterion measure is a bit easier if evaluation efforts are focused on specific organizational development interventions, as opposed to programs in general. For example, evaluating an organizational development program that features team building would logically call for some assessment of group or team effectiveness as the criterion. Furthermore, within the group effectiveness literature, there exists some excellent guidance as to the criteria that define group effectiveness (e.g., Guzzo & Shea, 1992; Hackman, 1987). Even with such guidance, however, coming up with the actual criterion measures may be more easily said than done.

Evaluation Research Designs

A research design is simply a plan for data collection (Cook, Campbell, & Perrachio, 1990). When any organizational intervention is evaluated, some form of research design is needed because the evaluator typically needs to collect some data to assess the impact of that intervention. In organizational settings, researchers typically have much less control than laboratory researchers. As a result, when conducting evaluation research, a number of methodological "compromises" have to be made in order to obtain any data showing the effectiveness of interventions. For example, in organizational settings, it is rare to be able to randomly assign research participants to conditions, and researchers have little control over either the implementation of intervention or the variables that are extraneous to the intervention.

The most typical way that organizational development practitioners deal with these challenges is simply not to conduct any form of systematic evaluation at all (Porras &

Robertson, 1992). Often, if an organizational development intervention *seems* like it might be helping, that is good enough for upper management. For those trained in the behavioral sciences, this apparent disregard for rigorous evaluation of organizational development programs is troubling. However, when one considers that evaluation can be a very human, and often a political process, this disregard for evaluation makes much more sense (see Comment 16.3).

One of the most typical designs used in evaluation research—and, unfortunately, one of the *least* powerful, research designs—is the **One Group, Posttest Only** design. In this type of design, participants in an organizational development intervention may simply indicate whether they felt the intervention was useful or effective. The obvious disadvantage of this type of design is that there is no baseline from which to evaluate the impact of the intervention. There is also no way of knowing whether there would have been a positive change in the criterion measure if the organizational development intervention had not been implemented. Due to these weaknesses, Cook and Campbell (1979) refer to this design as generally "uninterpretable."

Another common design used in the evaluation of organizational development interventions is the **One Group, Pretest–Posttest** design. In this case, a baseline measure is obtained both prior to and after an organizational development intervention or program is implemented. For example, measures of group process may be obtained prior to, and three months after, the implementation of a team-building intervention. Although this represents some improvement over the previous design, it still has important limitations. Because there is no control group, it is impossible to tell whether the observed effects would be

THE POLITICS OF EVALUATION

In most discussions of evaluation, including the one in this chapter, the bulk of the material deals with technical issues such as evaluative criteria and research designs. Furthermore, these technical issues are important to consider if organizational interventions are to be evaluated properly. Unfortunately, however, in focusing on the technical aspects of evaluation, we often overlook the politics of the evaluation process.

Why is evaluation often a political process? The key to answering this question is to understand what is actually occurring when an evaluation takes place. When we evaluate something, we are literally determining its *value*. For example, if we are evaluating a team-building program, what we are really doing is determining whether this program has any *value* to the organization. One of the reasons that organizations often do not want to know the true value of organizational development interventions is that they're afraid of what they might find out. Obviously, if an intervention is evaluated and found to be very effective, everyone's happy.

However, what happens when an intervention is evaluated and found to be very ineffective? In this case, everyone is unhappy, particularly if the organization has invested considerable resources in the intervention. There may also be cases where a particular individual (e.g., a Human Resources Director) initiates an intervention. If this is the case, such an individual has a great deal riding on the success or failure of that intervention. Thus, for political reasons, it may not be in this person's best interests to conduct a thorough, methodologically rigorous evaluation.

The major point is that even though evaluation is a technical process, it is also a very human process. Useful evaluation can only take place in organizations where people are willing to accept negative outcomes, to learn from them, and ultimately to improve the implementation of future interventions. Unfortunately, based on my own experience and the low prevalence of rigorous evaluation, such organizations are probably more the exception than the rule.

obtained in the absence of the intervention. With the team-building example, it is possible that as team members get to know each other better over time, their interactions and subsequent group processes would improve even in the absence of a team-building intervention.

To address this issue, the researcher actually has several options. One is to add a control group and thus create a **Pretest–Posttest with Control Group** design. By doing this, the effects of the intervention can be compared against those of a group that does not

take part in the intervention, thus providing the researcher with a firmer base for judging the effectiveness of the intervention. Unfortunately, in most organizational settings, control groups are hard to come by because of a limited number of employees, and the unwillingness of management to withhold a potentially valuable intervention.

When faced with the prospect of no control group, a researcher still has some viable options. For example, he or she can use the **Pretest–Posttest with Multiple Dependent Measures** design. This design is similar to the previously described One Group, Pretest–Posttest design except that the researcher measures two sets of dependent measures: one set that should be impacted by the intervention, and another set that should not be. If, for example, a team-building intervention has a positive impact on group process measures, yet has no impact on participants' satisfaction with fringe benefits, this suggests that the intervention was effective.

A second option is a **One Group, Interrupted Time Series** design. This is similar to the One Group, Pretest–Posttest design except that several measures of dependent variable are obtained prior to and after the intervention. By obtaining these multiple measures, the researcher is able to statistically model the behavior of the dependent measure over time, and, more importantly, determine whether the intervention has any impact on that measure. This design is also useful because it allows the researcher some assessment of whether the effects that are observed persist over time.

The research designs briefly described in this section represent only a small sample of those available for the evaluation of organizational development interventions or entire programs. Readers seeking more information about research designs are urged to consult Cook and Campbell (1979) or Cook et al. (1990). Given the large number of research designs available, in most cases it is possible to conduct some form of evaluation of organizational development programs even in the most challenging of field situations.

The Challenge of Measuring Change

The aim of evaluation research is essentially to measure *change*. Although much has been written about the statistical issues surrounding the measurement of change (e.g., Cronbach & Furby, 1970), conceptual issues surrounding the *meaning* of change impact the evaluation of organizational development programs. In this section, we focus on the conceptual meaning of change in organizational development research.

Golembiewski, Billingsley, and Yeager (1976) proposed that "change" in response to organizational development interventions and programs can come in three varieties, which they labeled as Alpha, Beta, and Gamma change, respectively. **Alpha change** represents what we typically think of as "true" change. The meaning of the dependent measures used, as well as the manner in which participants perceive the measures, remain the same both prior to and after an organizational development intervention. As an example, an organization may implement a survey feedback program, and the levels of job satisfaction of employees may improve as a result.

Beta change represents a situation in which the participants' frame of reference changes with respect to the dependent measure being assessed. Thus, beta change can be thought of as a methodological artifact rather than a true form of change. As an example, suppose an organization implemented a team-building intervention designed to improve communication within work groups. To evaluate this intervention, group members' perceptions of communication may be measured prior to and following the intervention. One reason that the researcher might find that the level of communication is rated higher following the intervention is that, by going through this intervention, participants develop a greater awareness of the various ways in which people in groups communicate. Thus, what seemed to participants like a "small" amount of communication prior to the intervention, may seem like an "above-average" amount following the intervention.

Note that in this example the *actual* level of communication has not changed. What has changed, however, is participants' definition of the various points on the scale measuring communication.

Gamma change represents a situation in which participants essentially redefine or reconceptualize key dependent or outcome variables. This can also be thought of as a methodological artifact, although Golembiewski et al. (1976) argued that because one of the goals of organizational development is really to change employee perspectives, this may actually be a legitimate form of change. As an example, an organization may implement a *participative decision making* (PDM) intervention designed to increase employee input into organizational decision making. To evaluate this intervention, the level of participation may be assessed prior to and after the program has been implemented. Prior to the intervention, employees may conceptualize participation as being somewhat narrow, and something that is not their role. As a result, they may rate this very low. After the intervention, however, they may view participation in a much broader sense, see it as something that is part of their job, and, consequently, rate it higher than they did in the pretest. Note that in this example the *actual* level of participation has not changed. Rather, employees have changed the way they define participation.

How does the researcher distinguish among Alpha, Beta, and Gamma change when evaluating an organization program? One way is obviously to decrease reliance on self-report criterion measures, or at least utilize *both* self-report and nonself-report criterion measures (e.g., Spector & Jex, 1991). Both Beta and Gamma change effects have to do with the cognitive *perceptions*. Thus, these artifacts can be avoided by utilizing at least some nonperceptual measures in the evaluation process.

For example, archival measures of performance could be used in addition to perceptual measures when evaluating the impact of an organizational development intervention.

To assess whether Gamma change has occurred, one recommendation that has been advanced requires comparing the factor structures of scales used to measure key dependent measures at pretest and posttest (Armenakis, Bedeian, & Pond, 1983; Armenakis & Zmud, 1979). Recall that Gamma change represents a change in respondents' conceptualization of key dependent measures. Given this change in conceptualization, it is possible that the dimensionality of scales may change from pretest to posttest measurement. While this is certainly logical, at least from a statistical point of view, in practice it is often difficult to apply. Individual scale items contain a good deal of measurement error (Nunnally & Bernstein, 1994), and evaluation studies often have sample sizes that severely limit the usefulness of such analyses.

Evidence on the Effectiveness of Organizational Development

As was stated earlier, many organizational development programs are conducted without the benefit of any formal evaluation. Fortunately, enough empirical evaluations of organizational development programs have been conducted over the years and they have yielded several summaries, using both qualitative and quantitative methods. The most widely cited qualitative summary of the effectiveness of a number of organizational development interventions was conducted by Bowers (1973). The most important finding from this review was that when a number of organizational development interventions were compared, survey feedback appeared to be the most effective.

Another widely cited qualitative review of organizational development studies was conducted by Terpstra (1981), who summarized 52 published organizational development studies. Compared to Bowers' (1973) review, Terpstra's was more systematic because he coded each study reviewed, in terms of whether the effects of the organizational development program were positive, neutral, or negative. Based on this classification, his conclusion was that the effects of organizational development are generally positive. This effect, however, was found to be moderated by methodological rigor; positive findings were most likely to be found in studies that were lacking in methodological rigor. Subsequent studies, however, have not supported Terpstra's claim of a pervasive "positive findings" bias in organizational development evaluation (e.g., Bullock & Svyantek, 1983; Woodman & Wayne, 1985).

In more recent years, researchers have applied meta-analytic methods to the evaluation of organizational development interventions. For example, meta-analytic reviews have supported the effectiveness of Management By Objectives (Rodgers & Hunter, 1991), as well as a number of other organizational development interventions (e.g., Guzzo, Jette, & Katzell, 1985; Neuman et al., 1989). For the most part, these quantitative reviews suggest that many organizational development interventions positively impact a number of employee attitudes and behaviors. It is also true, however, that in all of these meta-analyses, a portion of variance in the effects is left unexplained after accounting for statistical artifacts such as sampling error, unreliability, range restriction, and so on. This suggests that while organizational development interventions can have positive effects, these effects may vary considerably across organizations.

SPECIAL ISSUES IN CLIENT–CONSULTANT RELATIONSHIPS

At this point, a relatively comprehensive coverage of organizational development has been provided. However, one aspect of the organizational development process that has *not* been covered is the relationship between the organizational development consultant and the organization. This is an important omission because some readers may ultimately assume the role of organizational development consultant at some point in their careers. Therefore, in this final section, we briefly examine some of the important issues that a consultant faces in facilitating organizational development programs.

Balancing the Needs of Multiple Clients

When providing consulting services to an organization, the first client an organizational development consultant encounters is a member of the top management team or, in some cases, a human resources executive. One of the reasons is that these individuals tend to focus on "big picture" issues such as overall organizational effectiveness and change. In addition, individuals at this level are typically able to authorize the budgetary resources needed for consulting services.

Once a consultant is in an organization, however, the list of "clients" begins to grow very quickly. For example, depending on the size of the organization, a consultant may very well come into contact with employees ranging from division heads to hourly workers. One of the challenges that consultants often face, particularly as they deal with employees at lower levels of the organization, is the perception that they are serving primarily the interests of those in upper management. This is a difficult challenge, especially because consultants are typically brought into organizations by upper-management employees.

Probably the most effective way to balance the needs of multiple clients is to address the issue in the earliest stages of the consulting relationship. That is, when a consultant first enters an organization, he or she needs to make his or her initial contact aware that there will likely be multiple, and often competing, interests among various employees in the organization. After making the client aware of this, the next issue that needs to be confronted is how the consultant will handle such competing interests.

In the author's opinion, consultants are best served by maintaining a neutral stance when faced with such situations. If a consultant appears to be too "pro-management," he or she risks losing credibility with lower-level employees, and may then find it very difficult to obtain their cooperation in carrying out the organizational development program. Conversely, becoming too aligned with lower-level employees may put a consultant in the awkward position of going against the individual(s) who facilitated his or her entry into the organization. Ultimately, consultants are best served by assuming that conflicts of interests *will* occur, and making it clear to all parties involved that the consultants will not take sides.

Maintaining Confidentiality

A very simple rule of thumb for consultants regarding confidentiality: If you assure someone that the information he or she is giving you is confidential, *be prepared to honor that commitment.* In actuality, though, maintaining confidentiality in consulting relationships can be a very complex issue that poses some serious ethical dilemmas. One of the reasons that

maintaining confidentiality is a challenge is that consultants are often tempted to violate it. For example, a member of upper management may want to know what a particular vice president said about her leadership style. A group of hourly employees may want to know what upper management is planning to do with regard to a rumored merger. In both of these hypothetical cases, it is tempting for the consultant to reveal confidential information, primarily because it would please the party receiving the information and is reinforcing to the consultant.

Another reason that confidentiality is often compromised is carelessness on the part of the consultant or those working for the consultant (e.g., Gavin, 1984). For example, a consultant may provide the top management group with written comments from a survey and forget to first delete the names or other identifying information of the respondents. A consultant may unknowingly leave the notes from an interview of an employee in a place where anyone can see them. Obviously, in both cases, the violation of confidentiality is completely unintentional. However, regardless of the intent, such lapses are embarrassing to the consultant and could severely damage a consulting relationship.

Perhaps the most typical reason for consultants' being pressured to reveal confidential information is through some misunderstanding regarding the confidentiality of the information that the consultant collects. For example, the organization's top echelon may feel that they should be given copies of the completed questionnaires that employees have filled out, but the consultant plans to provide them with only summary data. Or, perhaps the manager of a group wants to know "who said what" during the personal interviews of group members prior to a team-building session, but the consultant plans to report only the general themes that emerged during these interviews.

The best way to avoid such misunderstandings is for the consultant to *clarify all issues surrounding confidentiality prior to formally entering into the consulting relationship.* Often, when consultants begin working with an organization, there is a temptation to "dive right in" and simply deal with issues such as confidentiality as they arise. In the long run, though, consultants and organizations are much better served by taking the time to thoroughly address issues such as confidentiality prior to beginning a project.

Terminating a Consulting Relationship

Some consulting assignments are short-term in nature, so there are clear starting and ending points. However, consultants also develop relationships with organizations that are more long-term in nature, and the services provided are less well defined in scope. A consultant may essentially be "on retainer" and be utilized by an organization in a variety of ways. This is helpful to an organization because, over time, the consultant may develop considerable knowledge of the organization and its problems. Long-term relationships with organizations can also be very advantageous for a consultant. They may be quite lucrative, and may also result in the development of some very satisfying relationships with members of the organization. However, what happens if relationships like these go sour?

Deciding when to terminate a consulting relationship is obviously one of the most difficult issues a consultant faces, and there are no easy solutions. A common criterion that consultants use for making this decision is whether the consulting relationship is professionally satisfying. Particularly for part-time consultants, providing consulting services is done more out of interest in the activity than for financial gain. Therefore, some consultants will decide to terminate a consulting relationship when the consulting activity is no longer of interest.

Another common basis on which a consultant may decide to terminate a consulting relationship is whether he or she is helping an organization. Recall from the discussion of process consultation (Schein, 1987) that consulting is essentially a form of professional helping. Given this definition, a consultant may conclude that although he or she is *trying* to be helpful, the services being provided are not really doing the organization any good. This may be due to the fact that different services may be needed, or perhaps the organization has improved to a certain level and further improvement is unlikely.

Finally, a consultant may decide to terminate a consulting relationship due to philosophical or value differences with the client organization. A consultant may terminate a relationship upon discovering that the organization condones sexual harassment of its female employees, or that it "looks the other way" in response to other unethical behaviors. Making the decision to terminate an otherwise satisfying consulting relationship for these types of reasons is obviously difficult. However, in the long run, a consultant is probably better off terminating such a relationship and working with organizations in which such conflicts do not exist.

CHAPTER SUMMARY

In this chapter, we examined the important area of organizational change and development. We began by defining organizational development and describing the typical reasons that organizations engage in programs of planned change. The focus of the chapter then shifted to a discussion of the historical roots of organizational development. As was shown, this field has a rich history and bene-fited from the contributions of many organiza-tional psychologists.

The chapter then shifted to a discussion of the theoretical foundations of organiza-tional development. Some theories focus on the general phenomenon of organizational change, and others serve as a foundation for more specific interventions. Although theo-ries can be useful guides in the implementa-tion of organizational development programs, organizational development practioners must be careful not to depend too heavily on theory.

The next section of the chapter focused on organizational development interventions. Given the number of interventions, this was not intended to be a comprehensive coverage; rather, the goal was to highlight for readers the most widely used organizational develop-ment interventions. Typically, interventions focus on the individual, the group, or broad organizational levels. Of these three, interven-tions at the group level are presently the most popular; therefore, interventions at this level were covered in the greatest depth. Regardless of the level at which interventions take place, however, some level of behavior change has to occur if these interventions are to enhance or-ganizational effectiveness.

A number of the factors that were dis-cussed impact on the success of organiza-tional development programs. These included top management support, consultant compe-tence, and organizational ownership of the change process. Top management personnel typically have the power to authorize the re-sources needed for an organizational change effort to occur, and employees often look to top management in deciding what is and what is not important. The competence level of the consultant is a crucial factor because even a useful intervention will not be effective if it is applied incompetently. Finally, if an organization does not take ownership of the organizational development process, then such efforts are reduced to being passing fads rather than catalysts for change.

Evaluation of organizational development programs is challenging, for a number of rea-sons. Specifically, it is often difficult to come up with appropriate criteria; a good deal of creativity may be needed to produce appro-priate research designs; and it may be difficult to assess whether the changes observed are caused by the organizational development program rather than artifacts. Despite these challenges, considerable evaluation research has been conducted in the field of organiza-tional development. Generally speaking, the re-sults of organizational development have been shown to be positive, although there is consid-erable organization-to-organization variation.

The final section of the chapter discussed some of the common challenges in client–consultant relationships. These include bal-ancing the needs of various clients within an organization, maintaining confidentiality of information, and deciding when to termi-nate a consulting relationship. As with most other difficult issues, there are no formulas or easy solutions. In most cases, though, taking the time to address these issues prior to for-mally beginning the consulting process is the best way to ensure that they do not become major problems down the road.

SUGGESTED ADDITIONAL READINGS

Church, A. H., Burke, W. W., & Van Eynde, D. F. (1994). Values, motives, and interven-tions of organization development practition-ers. *Group and Organization Management, 19,* 5–10.

Detert, J. R., Schroeder, R. G., & Mauriel, J. J. (2000). A framework for linking culture and improvement initiatives in organizations. *Academy of Management Review, 25,* 850–963.

Dyer, W. (1994). *Team building: Current issues and new alternatives* (3rd ed.). Reading, MA: Addison-Wesley.

Lawler, E. E., III, Mohrman, S. A., & Ledford, G. E., Jr. (1995). *Creating high performance organizations: Practices and results of employee involvement and total quality management in* *Fortune 1000 companies.* San Francisco: Jossey-Bass.

Ryan, A. M., Chan, D., Ployhart, R. E., & Slade, L. A. (1999). Employee attitude surveys in a multinational organization: Considering language and culture in assessing measurement equivalence. *Personnel Psychology, 52,* 37–58.

References

Abelson, M. A., & Baysinger, B. D. (1984). Optimal and dysfunctional turnover: Toward an organizational level model. *Academy of Management Review, 9,* 331–341.

Abramis, D. J. (1994). Work role ambiguity, job satisfaction, and job performance: Meta-analysis and review. *Psychological Reports, 75,* 1411–1433.

Ackerman, P. L. (1989). Within-task correlations of skilled performance: Implications for predicting individual differences? (Comment on Henry & Hulin, 1987). *Journal of Applied Psychology, 74,* 360–364.

Adams, G. A., & Beehr, T. A. (1998). Turnover and retirement: A comparison of their similarities and differences. *Personnel Psychology, 51,* 641–665.

Adams, G. A., King, L. A., & King, D. W. (1996). Relationship of job and family involvement, family social support, and work-family conflict with job and life satisfaction. *Journal of Applied Psychology, 81,* 411–420.

Adams, J. S. (1965). Inequity in social exchange. In L. Berkowitz (Ed.), *Advances in experimental social psychology* (Vol. 2, pp. 267–299). San Diego, CA: Academic Press.

Adler, S., Skov, R. B., & Salvemini, N. J. (1985). Job characteristics and job satisfaction: When cause becomes consequence. *Organizational Behavior and Human Decision Processes, 35,* 266–278.

Aguinis, H., & Stone-Romero, E. F. (1997). Methodological artifacts in moderated multiple regression and their effects on statistical power. *Journal of Applied Psychology, 82,* 192–206.

Ajzen, I., & Fishbein, M. (1977). Attitude-behavior relations: A theoretical analysis and review of empirical research. *Psychological Bulletin, 84,* 888–918.

Albanese, R., & Van Fleet, D. D. (1985). Rational behavior in groups: The free riding tendency. *Academy of Management Review, 10,* 244–255.

Aldag, R. J., & Fuller, S. R. (1993). Beyond fiasco: A reappraisal of the groupthink phenomenon and a new model of group decision processes. *Psychological Bulletin, 113,* 522–533.

Alderfer, C. P. (1969). An empirical test of a new theory of human needs. *Organizational Behavior and Human Performance, 4,* 142–175.

Alderfer, C. P., & Smith, K. K. (1982). Studying intergroup relations embedded in organizations. *Administrative Science Quarterly, 27,* 35–65.

Aldred, C. (1994, December 5). U.K. ruling focuses attention to job stress. *Business Insurance,* pp. 55–56.

Allen, N. J., & Meyer, J. P. (1990). The measurement and antecedents of affective, continuance, and normative commitment to the organization. *Journal of Occupational Psychology, 63,* 1–18.

Allen, N. J., & Meyer, J. P. (1996). Affective, continuance, and normative commitment to the organization: An examination of construct validity. *Journal of Vocational Behavior, 49,* 252–276.

Allen, R. W., Madison, L. W., Porter, L. W., Renwick, P. A., & Mayes, B. T. (1979). Organizational politics: Tactics and characteristics of its actors. *California Management Review, 12,* 77–83.

Amabile, T. M. (1983). The social psychology of creativity: A componential conceptualization. *Journal of Personality and Social Psychology, 45,* 357–376.

Ambrose, M. L., & Kulik, C. T. (1999). Old friends, new faces: Motivation research in the 1990s. *Journal of Management, 25,* 142–175, 231–292.

Americans with Disabilities Act of 1990, Publ. L. No. 101–336, 104 Stat. 328 (1990). Codified at U.S.C.A. § 12101 *et seq.*

Ames, G. M., Grube, J. W., & Moore, R. S. (1997). The relationship of drinking and hangovers to workplace problems: An empirical study. *Journal of Studies on Alcohol, 57,* 37–47.

Argyris, C., & Schon, D. A. (1978). *Organizational learning.* Reading, MA: Addison-Wesley.

Armenakis, A., Bedeian, A. G., & Pond, S. (1983). Research issues in OD evaluation: Past, present, and future. *Academy of Management Review, 8,* 320–328.

Armenakis, A., & Zmud, R. W. (1979). Interpreting the measurement of change in organizational research. *Personnel Psychology, 32,* 709–723.

Arvey, R. D., Bhagat, R. S., & Salas, E. (1991). Cross-cultural and cross-national issues in personnel and human resources management: Where do we go from here? In G. R. Ferris & K. M. Rowland (Eds.), *Research in personnel and human resources management* (Vol. 9, pp. 367–407). Greenwich, CT: JAI Press.

Arvey, R. D., Bouchard, T. J., Segal, N. L., & Abraham, L. M. (1989). Job satisfaction: Environmental and genetic components. *Journal of Applied Psychology, 74,* 187–192.

Arvey, R. D., & Jones, A. P. (1985). The use of discipline in organizational settings. In B. M. Staw & L. L. Cummings (Eds.), *Research in organizational behavior* (pp. 367–408). Greenwich, CT: JAI Press.

Asch, S. E. (1955). Opinions and social pressures. *Scientific American, 193,* 31–35.

Asch, S. E. (1957, April). An experimental investigation of group influence. In *Symposium on preventive and social psychiatry.* Symposium conducted at the Walter Reed Army Institute of Research, Washington, DC: U.S. Government Printing Office.

Ashforth, B. E., & Humphrey, R. H. (1993). Emotional labor in service roles: The influence of identity. *Academy of Management Review, 18,* 88–115.

Athey, T. R., & Hautaluoma, J. E. (1988, Winter). Team building in religious organizations. *Organization Development Journal,* 62–65.

Atkinson, J. W. (1964). *An introduction to motivation.* Princeton, NJ: Van Nostrand.

Austin, J. T., Humphreys, L. G., & Hulin, C. L. (1989). Another view of dynamic criteria: A critical reanalysis of Barrett, Caldwell, and Alexander. *Personnel Psychology, 42,* 583–596.

Austin, J. T., & Vancouver, J. B. (1996). Goal constructs in psychology: Structure, process, and content. *Psychological Bulletin, 120,* 338–375.

Averill, J. E. (1973). Personal control over aversive stimuli and its relationship to stress. *Psychological Bulletin, 80,* 286–303.

Aycan, Z., Kanungo, R. N., & Sinha, J. B. (1999). Organizational culture and human resource management practices: The model of culture fit. *Journal of Cross-Cultural Psychology, 30,* 501–526.

Bachrach, D. G., Bendoly, E., & Podsakoff, P. M. (2001). Attributions of the "Causes" or group performance as an explanation of the organizational citizenship behavior/organizational performance relationship. *Journal of Applied Psychology, 86,* 1285–1293.

Bachrach, D. G., & Jex, S. M. (2000). Organizational citizenship and mood: An experimental test of perceived job breadth. *Journal of Applied Social Psychology, 30,* 641–663.

Bagozzi, R. P., & Yi, Y. (1990). Assessing method variance in multitrait-multimethod matrices: The case of self-reported affect and perceptions at work. *Journal of Applied Psychology, 75,* 547–560.

Bales, R. F. (1965). The equilibrium problem in small groups. In A. P. Hare, E. F. Borgatta, & R. F. Bales (Eds.), *Small groups: Studies in social interaction.* New York: Knopf.

Bandura, A. (1986). *Social foundations of thought and action: A social-cognitive theory.* Englewood Cliffs, NJ: Prentice-Hall.

Bandura, A. (1997). *Self-efficacy: The exercise of control.* New York: Freeman.

Barkema, H. G., & Gomez-Mejia, L. R. (1998). Managerial compensation and firm performance: A general research framework. *Academy of Management Journal, 41,* 135–145.

Barling, J. (1996). The prediction, experience, and consequences of workplace violence. In G. R. VandenBos & E. Q. Bulatad (Eds.), *Violence on the job: Identifying risks and developing solutions* (pp. 29–49). Washington, DC: American Psychological Association.

Barling, J., Dupre, K. E., & Hepburn, C. G. (1998). Effects of parents' job insecurity on children's work beliefs and attitudes. *Journal of Applied Psychology, 83,* 112–118.

Baron, R. A., & Bell, P. A. (1976). Aggression and heat: The influence of ambient temperature, negative affect, and a cooling drink on physical aggression. *Journal of Personality and Social Psychology, 33,* 245–255.

Baron, R. M., & Kenny, D. A. (1986). The moderator-mediator variable distinction in social psychological research: Conceptual, strategic and statistical considerations. *Journal of Personal and Social Psychology, 51,* 1173–1182.

Barrett, G. V., Caldwell, M., & Alexander, R. (1985). The concept of dynamic criteria: A critical reanalysis. *Personnel Psychology, 38,* 41–56.

Barrick, M. R., & Mount, M. K. (1991). The big five personality dimensions and job performance: A meta-analysis. *Personnel Psychology, 44,* 1–26.

Barrick, M. R., Mount, M. K., & Strauss, J. P. (1993). Conscientiousness and performance of sales representatives: Test of the mediating effects of goal setting. *Journal of Applied Psychology, 78,* 715–722.

Barrick, M. R., Stewart, S. L., Neubert, M. J., & Mount, M. K. (1998). Relating member ability and personality to work-team processes and team effectiveness. *Journal of Applied Psychology, 83,* 377–391.

Bass, B. M., & Avolio, B. J. (1993). Transformational leadership: A response to critiques. In M. M. Chemers & R. Ayman (Eds.), *Leadership theory and research: Perspectives and directions* (pp. 49–80). San Diego, CA: Academic Press.

Bauer, T. N., & Green, S. G. (1998). Testing the combined effects of newcomer information seeking and manager behavior on socialization. *Journal of Applied Psychology, 83,* 72–83.

Baugh, S. G., & Roberts, R. M. (1994). Professional and organizational commitment among professional engineers: Conflicting or complementing? *IEEE Transactions on Engineering Management, 41,* 108–114.

Beach, L. R. (1993). *Making the right decision.* Englewood Cliffs, NJ: Prentice-Hall.

Beard, K. M., & Edwards, J. R. (1995). Employees at risk: Contingent work and the psychological experience of contingent workers. In C. L. Cooper & D. M. Rousseau (Eds.), *Trends in organizational behavior* (Vol. 2., pp. 109–126). Chichester, England: Wiley.

Becker, H. S. (1960). A note on the concept of commitment. *American Journal of Sociology, 66,* 32–42.

Becker, T. E. (1992). Foci and bases of commitment: Are they distinctions worth making? *Academy of Management Journal, 35,* 232–244.

Beckhard, R. (1967). The confrontation meeting. *Harvard Business Review, 45,* 149–153.

Beehr, T. A. (1986). The process of retirement: A review and recommendations for future investigation. *Personnel Psychology, 39,* 31–55.

Beehr, T. A. (1995). *Psychological stress in the workplace.* London: Routledge.

Beehr, T. A. (1998). Research on occupational stress: An unfinished enterprise. *Personnel Psychology, 51,* 835–844.

Beehr, T. A., & Bhagat, R. S. (1985). Introduction to human stress and cognition in organizations. In T. A. Beehr & R. S. Bhagat (Eds.), *Human stress and cognition in organizations* (pp. 3–19). New York: Wiley.

Beehr, T. A., & Franz, T. M. (1987). The current debate about the meaning of job stress. In J. M. Ivancevich & D. C. Ganster (Eds.), *Job stress: From theory to suggestion* (pp. 5–18): New York: Haworth Press.

Beehr, T. A., Jex, S. M., & Ghosh, P. (2001). The management of occupational stress. In C. M. Johnson, W. K. Redmon, & T. C. Mawhinney (Eds.), *Handbook of organizational performance: Behavior analysis and management* (pp. 225–254). New York: Haworth Press.

Beehr, T. A., Jex, S. M., Stacy, B. A., & Murray, M. A. (2000). Work stress and co-worker support as predictors of individual strains and performance. *Journal of Organizational Behavior, 21,* 391–405.

Beehr, T. A., & Newman, J. E. (1978). Job stress, employee health, and organizational effectiveness: A facet analysis, model, and literature review. *Personnel Psychology, 31,* 665–699.

Beehr, T. A., Walsh, J. T., & Taber, T. D. (1980). Relationship of stress to individually and organizationally valued states: Higher order needs as a moderator. *Journal of Applied Psychology, 61,* 35–40.

Beer, M. (1976). The technology of organization development. In M. D. Dunnette (Ed.), *Handbook of industrial and organizational psychology* (pp. 937–993). Chicago: Rand McNally.

Bellarosa, C., & Chen, P. Y. (1997). The effectiveness and practicality of stress management interventions. *Journal of Occupational Health Psychology, 2,* 247–262.

Bem, D. J. (1972). Self-perception theory. In L. Berkowitz (Ed.), *Advances in Experimental Social Psychology* (Vol. 6, pp. 1–62). New York: Academic Press.

Bemmels, B., & Foley, J. R. (1996). Grievance procedure research: A review and theoretical recommendations. *Journal of Management, 22,* 359–384.

Bennett, J. B., & Lehman, W. E. K. (1998). Workplace drinking climate, stress, and problem indicators: Assessing the influence of teamwork (group cohesion). *Journal of Studies on Alcohol, 59,* 608–618.

Berkowitz, L., & Donnerstein, E. (1982). External validity is more than skin deep. *American Psychologist, 37,* 245–257.

Bialek, H., Zapf, D., & McGuire, W. (1977, July). *Personnel turbulence and time utilization in an infantry division* (Hum RRO FR-WD-CA 77-11). Alexandria, VA: Human Resources Research Organization.

Blake, R., & Mouton, J. (1964). *The managerial grid.* Houston, TX: Gulf.

Blake, R. R., Shephard, H. A., & Mouton, J. S. (1964). *Managing intergroup conflict in industry.* Houston, TX: Gulf.

Bliese, P. D., & Britt, T. W. (2001). Social support, group consensus, and stressor-strain relationships: Social context matters. *Journal of Organizational Behavior, 22,* 425–436.

Bliese, P. D., & Jex, S. M. (1999). Incorporating multiple levels of analysis into occupational stress research. *Work and Stress, 13,* 1–6.

Blum, T. C., Roman, P. M., & Martin, J. K. (1993). Alcohol consumption and work performance. *Journal of Studies on Alcohol, 54,* 61–70.

Bolino, M. C. (1999). Citizenship and impression management: Good soldiers or good actors? *Academy of Management Review, 24,* 82–98.

Borman, W. C. (1991). Job behavior, performance, and effectiveness. In M. D. Dunnette & L. M. Hough (Eds.), *Handbook of industrial and organizational psychology* (2nd ed., Vol. 2, pp. 271–398). Palo Alto, CA: Consulting Psychologists Press.

Borman, W. C., & Motowidlo, S. J. (1993). Expanding the criterion domain to include elements of contextual performance. In N. Schmitt & W. C. Borman (Eds.), *Personnel Selection in Organizations* (pp. 71–98). San Francisco: Jossey-Bass.

Bouchard, T. D., Jr. (1976). Field research methods: Interviewing, questionnaires, participant observation, systematic observation, unobtrusive measures. In M. D. Dunnette (Ed.), *Handbook of industrial and organizational psychology* (pp. 363–413). Chicago: Rand McNally.

Bowen, D. E., Ledford, G. E., & Nathan, B. R. (1991). Hiring for the organization, not the job. *Executive, 4,* 35–51.

Bowers, D. G. (1973). OD techniques and their results in 23 organizations: The Michigan ICL study. *Journal of Applied Behavioral Science, 9,* 21–43.

Bowlby, J. (1973). *Separation: Anxiety and anger.* New York: Basic Books.

Boye, M. W., & Wasserman, A. R. (1996). Predicting counterproductivity among drugstore applicants. *Journal of Business and Psychology, 10,* 337–348.

Bramel, D., & Friend, R. (1981). Hawthorne, the myth of the docile worker, and class bias in psychology. *American Psychologist, 36,* 867–878.

Brannick, M. T., & Spector, P. E. (1990). Estimation problems in the block diagonal model of the multitrait-multimethod matrix. *Applied Psychological Measurement, 14,* 325–339.

Breaugh, J. A., & Colihan, J. P. (1994). Measuring facets of job ambiguity: Construct validity evidence. *Journal of Applied Psychology, 79,* 191–202.

Brett, J. M., & Rognes, J. K. (1986). Intergroup relations in organizations. In P. S. Goodman (Ed.), *Designing effective work groups* (pp. 202–236). San Francisco: Jossey-Bass.

Bridges, W. (1994). *JobShift: How to prosper in a workplace without jobs.* Reading, MA: Addison-Wesley.

Broadbent, D. E. (1985). The clinical impact of job design. *British Journal of Clinical Psychology, 24,* 33–44.

Brockner, J., Grover, S., Reed, T. F., & DeWitt, R. L. (1992). Layoffs, job insecurity, and survivors' work effort: Evidence of an inverted-U relationship. *Academy of Management Journal, 35,* 413–425.

Brockner, J., Grover, S., Reed, T. F., DeWitt, R. L., & O'Malley, M. (1987). Survivors' reactions to layoffs: We get by with a little help from our friends. *Administrative Science Quarterly, 32,* 526–542.

Brown, R., Condor, S., Matthews, A., Wade, G., & Williams, J. A. (1986). Explaining intergroup differentiation in industrial organization. *Journal of Occupational Psychology, 59,* 273–286.

Buch, K., & Aldrich, J. (1991). O.D. under conditions of organizational decline. *Organizational Development Journal, 9,* 1–5.

Buckley, M. R., Fedor, D. B., Veres, J. G., Weise, D. S., & Carraher, S. M. (1998). Investigating newcomer expectations and job-related outcomes. *Journal of Applied Psychology, 83,* 452–461.

Buell, P., & Breslow, L. (1960). Mortality from coronary heart disease in California men who work long hours. *Journal of Chronic Diseases, 11,* 615–626.

Buller, P. F. (1988). For successful strategic organizational change: Blend OD practices with strategic management. *Organizational Dynamics, 16,* 42–55.

Bullock, R. J., & Svyantek, D. J. (1983). Positive-findings bias in positive-findings bias research: An unsuccessful replication. *Academy of Management Proceedings,* 221–224.

Buono, A. F., & Bowditch, J. L. (1989). *The human side of mergers and acquisitions: Managing collision between people, cultures, and organizations.* San Francisco: Jossey-Bass.

Burke, W. W. (1994). *Organization development* (2nd ed.). Reading, MA: Addison-Wesley.

Burns, T., & Stalker, G. M. (1961). *The management of innovation.* London: Tavistock.

Buss, D. M. (1996). The evolutionary psychology of human social strategies. In E. T. Higgins & A. W. Kruglanski (Eds.), *Social psychology: Handbook of basic principles* (pp. 3–38). New York: Guilford Press.

Byrk, A., & Raudenbush, S. (1992). *Hierarchical Linear Models: Applications and data analysis methods.* Newbury Park, CA: Sage.

Byrne, D. (1971). *The attraction paradigm.* New York: Academic Press.

Byrne, J. E. (1988, September 12). Caught in the middle. *Business Week,* 80–88.

Campbell, D. (1999). Innovative strategies to thrive in today's health care environment. *ADVANCE for Speech-Language Pathologists and Audiologists, 9,* 9–10.

Campbell, D. T., & Fiske, D. W. (1959). Convergent and discriminant validation by the multi-trait-multimethod matrix. *Psychological Bulletin, 56,* 81–105.

Campbell, J. P. (1990). Modeling the performance prediction problem in industrial and organizational psychology. In M. D. Dunnette & L. M. Hough (Eds.), *Handbook of industrial and organizational psychology* (2nd ed., Vol. 1, pp. 687–732). Palo Alto, CA: Consulting Psychologists Press.

Campbell, J. P. (1994). Alternative models of job performance and their implications for selection and classification. In M. G. Rumsey, C. B. Walker, & J. H. Harris (Eds.), *Personnel selection and classification* (pp. 33–51). Hillsdale, NJ: Erlbaum.

Campbell, J. P., & Dunnette, M. D. (1968). Effectiveness of t-group experiences in managerial training. *Psychological Bulletin, 70,* 73–104.

Campion, M. A. (1993). Editorial. Article review checklist: A criterion checklist for reviewing research articles in applied psychology, *Personnel Psychology, 46,* 705–718.

Campion, M. A. (1996). A message from your president: How to publish the results of applied projects (or how two needles can find each other in a haystack). *Industrial-Organizational Psychologist, 33,* 9–10.

Campion, M. A., & Berger, C. J. (1990). Conceptual integration and empirical test of job design and compensation relationships. *Personnel Psychology, 43,* 525–554.

Campion, M. A., Cheraskin, L., & Stevens, M. J. (1994). Career-related antecedents and outcomes of job rotation. *Academy of Management Journal, 37,* 1518–1542.

Campion, M. A., & McClelland, C. L. (1991). Interdisciplinary examination of the costs and benefits of enlarged jobs: A job design quasi-experiment. *Journal of Applied Psychology, 76,* 186–198.

Campion, M. A., Medsker, G. J., & Higgs, A. C. (1993). Relations between work group characteristics and effectiveness: Implications for designing effective work groups. *Personnel Psychology, 46,* 823–850.

Campion, M. A., Papper, E. M., & Medsker, G. J. (1995). Relations between work team characteristics and effectiveness: Replication and extension. *Personnel Psychology, 49,* 429–452.

Campion, M. A., & Thayer, P. W. (1985). Development and field evaluation of an interdisciplinary measure of job design. *Journal of Applied Psychology, 70,* 29–43.

Campion, M. A., & Thayer, P. W. (1987). Job design: Approaches, outcomes, and trade-offs. *Organizational Dynamics, 15,* 66–79.

Cannon, W. B. (1914). The interrelations of emotions as suggested by recent physiological researches. *American Journal of Psychology, 25,* 256–282.

Caplan, R. D. (1987). Person-environment fit in organizations: Theories, facts, and values. In A. W. Riley & S. J. Zaccaro (Eds.), *Occupational stress and organizational effectiveness* (pp. 103–140). New York: Praeger Press.

Caplan, R. D., Cobb, S., French, J. R. P., Jr., Harrison, R. V., & Pinneau, S. R. (1975). *Job demands and worker health: Main effects and occupational differences.* Washington, DC: U.S. Government Printing Office.

Caplan, R. D., & Jones, K. W. (1975). Effects of workload, role ambiguity, and Type A personality on anxiety, depression, and heart rate. *Journal of Applied Psychology, 60,* 713–719.

Carey, A. (1967, June). The Hawthorne Studies: A radical criticism. *American Sociological Review,* 403–417.

Carey, J. M., & Kacmar, C. J. (1997). The impact of communication mode and task complexity on small group performance and member satisfaction. *Computers in Human Behavior, 13,* 23–49.

Carroll, S. J., & Tosi, H. L. (1973). *Management by objectives.* New York: Macmillan.

Carsten, J. M., & Spector, P. E. (1987). Unemployment, job satisfaction, and employee turnover: A meta-analytic test of the Muchinsky model. *Journal of Applied Psychology, 72,* 374–381.

Cartwright, S., & Cooper, C. L. (1997). *Managing workplace stress.* Thousand Oaks, CA: Sage.

Carver, C. S., & Scheier, M. F. (1981). *Attention and self-regulation: A control theory approach to human behavior.* New York: Springer.

Cascio, W. F. (1998). *Applied psychology in human resource management* (5th ed.), Upper Saddle River, NJ: Prentice-Hall.

Chadwick-Jones, J., Nicholson, N., & Brown, C. (1982). *Social psychology of absenteeism.* New York: Praeger.

Champoux, J. E. (1991). A multivariate test of the job characteristics theory of work behavior. *Journal of Occupational Behavior, 12,* 431–446.

Chan, D. (1998). Functional relations among constructs in the same content domain at different levels of analysis: A typology of composition models. *Journal of Applied Psychology, 83,* 234–246.

Chao, G. T., O'Leary-Kelly, A. M., Wolf, S., Klein, H. J., & Gardner, P. D. (1994). Organizational socialization: Its content and consequences. *Journal of Applied Psychology, 79,* 730–749.

Chatman, J. (1991). Matching people and organizations: Selection and socialization in public accounting firms. *Administrative Science Quarterly, 36,* 459–484.

Chattopadhyay, P. (1998). Beyond direct and symmetric effects: The influence of demographic dissimilarity on organizational citizenship behavior. *Academy of Management Journal, 42,* 273–287.

Chemers, M. M. (1983). Leadership theory and research: A systems/process integration. In R. R. Paulus (Ed.), *Group process* (pp. 9–39). New York: Springer-Verlag.

Chemers, M. M., Hays, R. B., Rhodewalt, F., & Wysocki, J. (1985). A person-environment analysis of job stress: A contingency model explanation. *Journal of Personality and Social Psychology, 49,* 628–635.

Chen, P. Y., & Spector, P. E. (1992). Relationships of work stressors with aggression, withdrawal, theft, and substance use: An exploratory study. *Journal of Occupational and Organizational Psychology, 65,* 177–184.

Cleyman, K. L., Jex, S. M., & Love, K. G. (1995). Employee grievances: An application of the leader-member exchange model. *International Journal of Organizational Analysis, 3,* 156–174.

Coch, L., & French, J. R. P., Jr. (1948). Overcoming resistance to change. *Human Relations, 1,* 512–532.

Cohen, J. (1992). A power primer. *Psychological Bulletin, 112,* 155–159.

Cohen, J., & Cohen, P. (1983). *Applied multiple regression/correlation for the behavioral sciences.* Hillsdale, NJ: Erlbaum.

Cohen, S., & Wills, T. A. (1985). Stress, social support, and the buffering hypothesis. *Psychological Bulletin, 98,* 310–357.

Cohen, S. G., & Bailey, D. E. (1997). What makes teams work: Groups effectiveness research from the shop floor to the executive suite. *Journal of Management, 20,* 239–290.

Colarelli, S. M. Dean, R. A., & Konstans, C. (1987). Comparative effects of personal and situational influences on job outcomes of new professionals. *Journal of Applied Psychology, 72,* 558–566.

Conti, R., Amabile, T. M., & Pollak, S. (1995). The positive impact of creative activity: Effects of creative task engagement and motivational focus on college students' learning. *Personality and Social Psychology Bulletin, 21,* 1107–1116.

Conway, J. M. (1999). Distinguishing contextual performance from task performance for managerial jobs. *Journal of Applied Psychology, 84,* 3–13.

Cook, T. D., & Campbell, D. T. (1979). *Quasi-experimentation: Design and analysis issues for field settings.* Chicago: Rand McNally.

Cook, T. D., Campbell, D. T., & Perrachio, L. (1990). Quasi experimentation. In M. D. Dunnette & L. M. Hough (Eds.), *Handbook of industrial and organizational psychology* (2nd ed., Vol. 1, pp. 491–576). Palo Alto, CA: Consulting Psychologists Press.

Cooper, M. L., Russell, M., & Frone, M. R. (1990). Work stress and alcohol effects: A test of stress-induced drinking. *Journal of Health and Social Behavior, 31,* 260–276.

Cotton, J. L. (1995). Participation's effect of performance and satisfaction: A reconsideration of Wagner. *Academy of Management Review, 20,* 276–278.

Covey, S. R. (1997). *The 7 habits of highly effective families.* New York: Golden Books.

Covin, T., & Kilman, R. (1991). Profiling large scale change efforts. *Organizational Development Journal, 9,* 1–8.

Cox, M. H., Shephard, R. J., & Corey, P. (1981). Influence of employee fitness, productivity and absenteeism. *Ergonomics, 24,* 795–806.

Crampton, S. M., & Wagner, J. A., III. (1994). Percept-percept inflation in micro organizational research: An investigation of prevalence and effect. *Journal of Applied Psychology, 79,* 67–76.

Cronbach, L. J., & Furby, L. (1970). How should we measure "change"—or should we? *Psychological Bulletin, 74,* 68–80.

Cropanzano, R., & James, K. (1990). Some methodological considerations for the behavioral genetic analysis of work attitudes. *Journal of Applied Psychology, 75,* 433–439.

Crowne, D. P., & Marlowe, D. (1964). *The approval motive: Studies in evaluative dependency.* New York: Wiley.

Crystal, G. S. (1991). *In search of excess.* New York: Norton.

Crystal, G. S. (1995, December, 3). Turner's compensation stirs executive pay criticism. *CompFlash.*

Cvetanovski, J., & Jex, S. M. (1994). Locus of control of unemployed people and its relationship to psychological and physical well-being. *Work and Stress, 8,* 60–67.

Daily, C. M., Johnson, J. L., Ellstrand, A. E., & Dalton, D. R. (1998). Compensation committee composition as a determinant of CEO compensation. *Academy of Management Journal, 41,* 209–220.

Damanpour, F. (1991). Organizational innovation: A meta-analysis of effects of determinants and moderators. *Academy of Management Journal, 34,* 555–590.

Dansereau, F., Alutto, J. A., & Yammarino, F. J. (1984). *Theory testing in organizational behavior: The variant approach.* Englewood Cliffs, NJ: Prentice-Hall.

Dansereau, F., Graen, G., & Haga, W. (1975). A vertical dyad approach to leadership within formal organizations. *Organizational Behavior and Human Performance, 13,* 46–78.

Davis, S. M., & Lawrence, P. R. (1977). *Matrix.* Reading, MA: Addison-Wesley.

Davis-Blake, A., & Pfeffer, J. (1989). Just a mirage: The search for dispositional effects in organizational research. *Academy of Management Review, 14,* 385–400.

Dawis, R. V. (1990). Vocational interests, values, and preferences. In M. D. Dunnette & L. M. Hough (Eds.), *Handbook of industrial and organizational psychology* (2nd ed., Vol. 1, pp. 833–871). Palo Alto, CA: Consulting Psychologists Press.

Day, D. V., & Bedeian, A. G. (1991). Predicting job performance across organizations: The interaction of work orientation and psychological climate. *Journal of Management, 17,* 589–600.

Deadrick, D. L., & Madigan, R. (1990). Dynamic criteria revisited: A longitudinal study of performance stability and predictive validity. *Personnel Psychology, 43,* 717–744.

de Laat, P. B. (1994). Matrix management of projects and power struggles: A case study of an R&D laboratory. *Human Relations, 47,* 1089–1119.

DeMatteo, J. S., Eby, L. T., & Sundstrom, E. (1998). Team-based rewards: Current empirical evidence and directions for future research. *Research in Organizational Behavior, 20,* 141–183.

Denison, D. (1984). Bringing corporate culture to the bottom line. *Organizational Dynamics, 13,* 5–22.

Dennison, D. R., & Sutton, R. I. (1990). Operating room nurses. In J. R. Hackman (Ed.), *Groups that work (and those that don't)* (pp. 293–308). San Francisco: Jossey-Bass.

Dentler, R. A., & Erikson, K. T. (1959). The functions of deviance in groups. *Social Problems, 7,* 98–107.

Dickter, D. N., Roznowski, M., & Harrison, D. A. (1996). Temporal tempering: An event history analysis of the process of voluntary turnover. *Journal of Applied Psychology, 81,* 705–716.

Dillman, D. A. (2000). *Mail and Internet surveys: The tailored design method* (2nd ed.). New York: Wiley.

Dipboye, R. L., & Flanagan, M. F. (1979). Research settings in industrial and organizational psychology: Are findings in the field more generalizable than in the laboratory? *American Psychologist, 34,* 141–151.

Driskell, J. E., & Salas, E. (1991). Group decision making under stress. *Journal of Applied Psychology, 76,* 473–478.

DuBrin, A. J. (1993, Fall). Deadly political sins. *National Business Employment Weekly,* 11–13.

Dubrovsky, V. J., Keisler, S., & Sethna, B. N. (1991). The equalization phenomenon: Status effects in computer-mediated and face-to-face decision making groups. *Human-Computer Interaction, 6,* 119–146.

Durkheim, E. (1951). *Suicide* (J. A. Spaulding & G. Simpson, Trans.). Glencoe, IL: Free Press.

Dyer, W. G. (1987). *Team building: Issues and alternatives* (2nd ed.). Reading, MA: Addison-Wesley.

Eastman, K. K. (1994). In the eyes of the beholder: An attributional approach to ingratiation and organizational citizenship behavior. *Academy of Management Journal, 37,* 1379–1391.

Eden, D. (1985). Team development: A true field experiment at three levels of rigor. *Journal of Applied Psychology, 70,* 94–100.

Eden, D., & Aviram, A. (1993). Self-efficacy training to speed reemployment: Helping people help themselves. *Journal of Applied Psychology, 78,* 352–360.

Edwards, J. R. (1992). A cybernetic theory of stress, coping, and well-being in organizations. *Academy of Management Review, 17,* 238–274.

Edwards, J. R. (1994). The study of congruence in organizational behavior research: Critique and a proposed alternative. *Organizational Behavior and Human Decision Processes, 58,* 51–100.

Edwards, J. R., & Parry, M. E. (1993). On the use of polynomial regression equations as an alternative to difference scores in organizational research. *Academy of Management Journal, 36,* 1577–1613.

Edwards, J. R., Scully, J. A., & Brtek, M. D. (1999). The measurement of work: Hierarchical representation of the Multimethod Job Design Questionnaire. *Personnel Psychology, 52,* 305–334.

Eisenberger, R., Huntington, R., Hutchison, S, & Sowa, D. (1986). Perceived organizational support. *Journal of Applied Psychology, 71,* 500–517.

Ekman, P. (1973). Cross-cultural studies of facial expression. In P. Ekman (Ed.), *Darwin and facial expression: A century of research in review* (pp. 169–222). New York: Academic Press.

Ellis, S., & Arieli, S. (1999). Predicting intentions to report administrative and disciplinary infractions: Applying the reasoned action model. *Human Relations, 52,* 947–967.

Elms, A. C. (1995). Obedience to authority in retrospect. *Journal of Social Issues, 51,* 21–31.

Equal Employment Opportunity Commission. (1980). *Guidelines on sexual harassment in the workplace* [No. 45 FR 74676–74677]. Washington, DC: Author.

Eskew, D., & Hennemen, R. L. (1996). Survey of merit pay plan effectiveness: End of the line for merit pay or hope for improvement. *Human Resource Planning, 19,* 12–19.

Evans, M. G., & Ondrack, D. A. (1991). The motivational potential of jobs: Is a multiplicative model necessary? *Psychological Reports, 69,* 659–672.

Fahr, J. L., Dobbins, G. H., & Cheng, B. S. (1991). Cultural relativity in action: A comparison of self-ratings made by Chinese and U.S. workers. *Personnel Psychology, 44,* 129–147.

Falbe, C. M., & Yukl, G. (1992). Consequences for managers of using single influence tactics and combinations of tactics. *Academy of Management Journal, 35,* 638–652.

Falkenberg, L. W. (1987). Employee fitness programs: Their impact on the employee and organization. *Academy of Management Review, 12,* 511–522.

Farrell, D., & Stamm, C. L. (1988). Meta-analysis of the correlates of employee absence. *Human Relations, 41,* 211–227.

Fayol, H. (1984). *General and industrial management.* Belmont, CA: Lake Publishing.

Feldman, D. C. (1976). A contingency theory of socialization. *Administrative Science Quarterly, 21,* 433–452.

Feldman, D. C. (1981). The multiple socialization of organizational members. *Academy of Management Review, 6,* 309–318.

Ferrier, W., Smith, K., & Grimm, C. (1999). The role of competitive action in market share erosion and industry dethronement: A study of industry leaders and challengers. *Academy of Management Journal, 42,* 372–388.

Ferris, G. R., Gilmore, D. C., & Kacmar, K. M. (1990, April). *Potential moderators of the organizational politics-job anxiety relationship.* Paper presented at the annual Society for Industrial and Organizational Psychology Convention, Miami, FL.

Festinger, L. (1954). A theory of social comparison processes. *Human Relations, 7,* 114–140.

Fiedler, F. E. (1967). *A theory of leader effectiveness*. New York: McGraw-Hill.

Fiedler, F. E. (1978). Recent developments in research on the contingency model. In L. Berkowitz (Ed.), *Group processes* (pp. 59–112). New York: Academic Press.

Fiedler, F. E., & Garcia, J. E. (1987). *New approaches to leadership: Cognitive resources and organizational performance*. New York: Wiley.

Field, R. H. G., & House, R. J. (1990). A test of the Vroom-Yetton model using manager and subordinate reports. *Journal of Applied Psychology, 75*, 362–366.

Finkelstein, S. (1992). Power in top management teams: Dimensions, measurement, and validation. *Academy of Management Journal, 35*, 505–538.

Finkelstein, S., & Boyd, B. K. (1998). How much does the CEO matter? The role of managerial discretion in setting of CEO compensation. *Academy of Management Journal, 41*, 179–199.

Finkelstein, S., & Hambrick, D. C. (1988). Chief executive compensation: A synthesis and reconciliation. *Strategic Management Journal, 9*, 543–558.

Fischer, R., & Ury, W. (with B. Patton, Ed.). (1981). *Getting to YES: Negotiating agreement without giving in*. Boston: Houghton-Mifflin.

Fishbein, M. (1979). A theory of reasoned action: Some applications and implications. In H. Howe & M. Page (Eds.), *Nebraska symposium on motivation* (pp. 65–116). Lincoln: University of Nebraska.

Fisher, C. D., & Gitelson, R. R. (1983). A meta-analysis of the correlates of role conflict and role ambiguity. *Journal of Applied Psychology, 68*, 320–333.

Fitzgerald, L. F. (1993). Sexual harassment: Violence against women in the workplace. *American Psychologist, 48*, 1070–1076.

Fitzgerald, L. F., Drasgow, F., Hulin, C. L., Gelfand, M. J., & Magley, V. J. (1997). Antecedents and consequences of sexual harassment in organizations: A test of an integrated model. *Journal of Applied Psychology, 82*, 359–378.

Flannery, T. P., Hofrichter, D. A., & Platten, P. E. (1996). *People, performance, and pay: Dynamic compensation for changing organizations*. New York: Free Press.

Fleishman, E., Harris, E. F., & Burtt, H. E. (1955). *Leadership and supervision in industry*. Columbus: Bureau of Educational Research, Ohio State University.

Florkowski, G. W. (1987). The organizational impact of profit sharing. *Academy of Management Review, 12*, 622–636.

Florkowski, G. W., & Schuster, M. H. (1992). Support for profit sharing and commitment: A path analysis. *Human Relations, 45*, 507–523.

Flynn, B. B., Sakakibara, S., & Schroeder, R. G. (1995). Relationship between JIT and TQM: Practices and performance. *Academy of Management Journal, 38*, 1325–1360.

Folger, R., & Cropanzano, R. (1998). *Organizational justice and human resource management*. Thousand Oaks, CA: Sage.

Ford, R. N. (1973, September/October). Job enrichment lessons from AT&T. *Harvard Business Review*, 96–106.

Forsyth, D. R. (1999). *Group dynamics* (3rd ed.). Belmont, CA: Brooks/Cole-Wadsworth.

Foti, R. J., & Rueb, J. (1990, April). *Self-monitoring, traits, and leadership emergence*. Paper presented at the annual meeting of the Society for Industrial and Organizational Psychology, Miami, FL.

Fowler, F. J., Jr. (1984). *Survey research methods*. Beverly Hills, CA: Sage.

Fox, M. L., Dwyer, D. J., & Ganster, D. C. (1993). Effects of stressful demands and control on physiological and attitudinal outcomes in a hospital setting. *Academy of Management Journal, 36,* 289–318.

Frank, L. L., & Hackman, J. R. (1975). A failure of job enrichment: The case of the change that wasn't. *Journal of Applied Behavioral Science, 11,* 413–436.

Frankenhaeuser, M. (1979). Psychoneuroendocrine approaches to the study of emotion as related to stress and coping. In H. E. Howe & R. A. Diensbier (Eds.), *Nebraska symposium on motivation* (pp. 123–161). Lincoln: University of Nebraska Press.

French, J. R. P., Caplan, R. D., & Harrison, R. V. (1982). *The mechanisms of job stress and strain.* Chichester, England: Wiley.

French, J. R. P., Jr., & Kahn, R. L. (1962). A programmatic approach to studying the industrial environment and mental health. *Journal of Social Issues, 18,* 1–47.

French, J. R. P., Jr., & Raven, B. H. (1959). The bases of social power. In D. Cartwright (Ed.), *Studies in social power* (pp. 150–167). Ann Arbor, MI: Institute for Social Research.

French, W. L., & Bell, C. H. (1995). *Organization development: Behavioral science interventions for organization improvement* (5th ed.). Englewood Cliffs, NJ: Prentice-Hall.

Frese, M. (1985). Stress at work and psychosomatic complaints: A causal interpretation. *Journal of Applied Psychology, 70,* 314–328.

Frese, M., Kring, W., Soose, A., & Zempel, J. (1996). Personal initiative at work: Differences between East and West Germany. *Academy of Management Journal, 39,* 37–63.

Fried, Y., & Ferris, G. R. (1987). The validity of the job characteristics model: A review and meta-analysis. *Personnel Psychology, 40,* 287–322.

Fried, Y., Rowland, K. M., & Ferris, G. R. (1984). The physiological measurement of

work stress: A critique. *Personnel Psychology, 37,* 583–615.

Friedland, N., Keinan, G., & Regev, Y. (1992). Controlling the uncontrollable: Effects of stress on illusory perceptions of controllability. *Journal of Personality and Social Psychology, 63,* 923–931.

Galbraith, J. R. (1995). *Designing organizations: An executive briefing on strategy, structure, and process.* San Francisco: Jossey-Bass.

Gallupe, R. B., Dennis, A. R., Cooper, W. H., Valacich, J. S., Bastianutti, L. M., & Nunamaker, J. F., Jr. (1992). Electronic brainstorming and group size. *Academy of Management Journal, 35,* 350–369.

Gannon, M. J. (1971). Sources of referral and employee turnover. *Journal of Applied Psychology, 55,* 226–228.

Ganster, D. C., & Schaubroeck, J. (1991). Work stress and employee health. *Journal of Management, 17,* 235–271.

Gavin, J. F. (1984). Survey feedback: The perspectives of science and practice. *Group and Organization Studies, 9,* 29–70.

Geertz, C. (1973). *The interpretation of cultures.* New York: Basic Books.

George, J. M. (1990). Personality, affect, and behavior in groups. *Journal of Applied Psychology, 75,* 107–116.

George, J. M., & Bettenhausen, K. (1990). Understanding prosocial behavior, sales performance, and turnover: A group-level analysis. *Journal of Applied Psychology, 75,* 689–709.

George, J. M., & Brief, A. P. (1992). Feeling good-doing good: A conceptual analysis of the mood at work-organizational spontaneity relationship. *Psychological Bulletin, 112,* 310–329.

Gerhart, B. (1987). How important are dispositional factors as determinants of job satisfaction? Implications for job design and other personnel programs. *Journal of Applied Psychology, 72,* 366–373.

Gerhart, B. (1990). Voluntary turnover and alternative job opportunities. *Journal of Applied Psychology, 75,* 467–476.

Gerhart, B., & Milkovich, G. T. (1990). Organizational differences in compensation and financial performance. *Academy of Management Journal, 33,* 663–691.

Gerhart, B., & Milkovich, G. T. (1992). Employee compensation: Research and practice. In M. D. Dunnette & L. M. Hough (Eds.), *Handbook of industrial and organizational psychology* (2nd ed., Vol. 3, pp. 481–569). Palo Alto, CA: Consulting Psychologists Press.

Gersick, C. G. (1988). Time and transition in work teams: Toward a new model of group development. *Academy of Management Journal, 31,* 9–41.

Gersick, C. J. G. (1989). Marking time: Predictable transitions in task groups. *Academy of Management Journal, 32,* 274–309.

Gerstner, C. R., & Day, D. V. (1997). Meta-analytic review of leader-member exchange theory: Correlates and construct issues. *Journal of Applied Psychology, 82,* 827–844.

Gilliland, S. W., & Landis, R. S. (1992). Quality and quantity goals in a complex decision task: Strategies and outcomes. *Journal of Applied Psychology, 77,* 672–681.

Gladstein, D. (1984). Groups in context: A model of task group effectiveness. *Administrative Science Quarterly, 29,* 499–517.

Glick, W. H., Jenkins, G. D., Jr., & Gupta, N. (1986). Method versus substance: How strong are underlying relationships between job characteristics and attitudinal outcomes? *Academy of Management Journal, 29,* 441–464.

Goff, S. J., Mount, M. K., & Jamison, R. L. (1990). Employer supported childcare, work/ family conflict, and absenteeism: A field study. *Personnel Psychology, 43,* 793–810.

Goldstein, I. L. (1993). *Training in organizations* (3rd ed.). Pacific Grove, CA: Brooks/ Cole.

Golembiewski, R. T., Billingsley, K., & Yeager, S. (1976). Measuring change and persistence in human affairs: Types of change generated by OD designs. *Journal of Applied Behavioral Science, 23,* 295–313.

Gomez-Mejia, L. R. (1994). Executive compensation: A reassessment and future research agenda. In G. R. Ferris (Ed.), *Research in personnel and human resource management* (Vol. 12, pp. 161–222). Greenwich, CT: JAI Press.

Gomez-Mejia, L. R., Welbourne, T. M. (1989). The strategic design of executive compensation programs. In L. R. Gomez-Mejia (Ed.), *Compensation and benefits* (pp. 216–260). Washington, DC: Bureau of National Affairs.

Goodale, J. G., & Aagaard, A. K. (1975). Factors relating to varying reactions to the four-day work week. *Journal of Applied Psychology, 60,* 33–35.

Goodman, P. S. (1986). The impact of task and technology on group performance. In P. S. Goodman (Ed.), *Designing effective work groups* (pp. 120–167). San Francisco: Jossey-Bass.

Gordon, J. (1992). Work teams: How far have they come? *Training, 29,* 59–65.

Graen, G. (1976). Role making process within complex organizations. In M. D. Dunnette (Ed.), *Handbook of industrial and organizational psychology* (pp. 1201–1245). Chicago: Rand McNally.

Greenberg, J. (1990). Employee theft as a reaction to underpayment inequity: The hidden cost of pay cuts. *Journal of Applied Psychology, 5,* 561–568.

Greenhaus, J., & Buetell, N. (1985). Source of conflict between work and family roles. *Academy of Management Review, 10,* 76–88.

Griffeth, R. W., & Hom, P. W. (1987). Some multivariate comparisons of multinational managers. *Multivariate Behavioral Research, 22,* 173–191.

Griffin, R. W. (1991). Effects of work redesign on employee perceptions, attitudes, and behavior: A long-term investigation. *Academy of Management Journal, 34,* 425–435.

Griffin, R. W., & McMahan, G. C. (1994). Motivation through job design. In J. Greenberg (Ed.), *Organizational behavior: State of the science* (pp. 23–44). New York: Erlbaum and Associates.

Gruber, J. E. (1998). The impact of male work environments and organizational policies on women's experiences of sexual harassment. *Gender and Society, 12,* 301–320.

Gundling, E. (2000). *The 3M way to innovation: Balancing people and profit.* Tokyo: Kodansha International.

Gupta, N., & Jenkins, D. G. (1985). Dual career couples: Stress, stressors, strains, and strategies. In T. A. Beehr & R. S. Bhagat (Eds.), *Human stress and cognition in organizations* (pp. 141–176). New York: Wiley.

Gutek, B., Cohen, A., & Konrad, A. (1990). Predicting social-sexual behavior at work: A contact hypothesis. *Academy of Management Journal, 33,* 560–577.

Guzzo, R. A. (1986). Group decision making and group effectiveness in organizations. In P. S. Goodman (Ed.), *Designing effective work groups* (pp. 34–71). San Francisco: Jossey-Bass.

Guzzo, R. A., & Campbell, R. J. (1990, August). *Conditions for team effectiveness in management.* Paper presented at the annual meeting of the Academy of Management, San Francisco.

Guzzo, R. A., Jette, R. D., & Katzell, R. A. (1985). The effects of psychologically based intervention programs on worker productivity: A meta-analysis. *Personnel Psychology, 38,* 275–291.

Guzzo, R. A., & Shea, G. P. (1992). Group performance and intergroup relations in organizations. In M. D. Dunnette & L. M. Hough (Eds.), *Handbook of industrial and organizational psychology* (2nd ed., Vol. 3, pp. 269–313). Palo Alto, CA: Consulting Psychologists Press.

Guzzo, R. A., Yost, P. R., Campbell, R. J., & Shea, G. P. (1993). Potency in groups: Articulating a construct. *British Journal of Social Psychology, 32,* 87–106.

Hackett, R. D. (1989). Work attitudes and employee absenteeism: A synthesis of the literature. *Journal of Occupational Psychology, 62,* 235–248.

Hackett, R. D., & Guion, R. M. (1985). A reevaluation of the absenteeism-job satisfaction relationship. *Organizational Behavior and Human Decision Processes, 35,* 340–381.

Hackman, J. R. (1987). The design of work teams. In J. W. Lorsch (Ed.), *Handbook of organizational behavior* (pp. 315–342). Englewood Cliffs, NJ: Prentice-Hall.

Hackman, J. R. (Ed.). (1990). *Groups that work (and those that don't): Creating the conditions for effective teamwork.* San Francisco: Jossey-Bass.

Hackman, J. R. (1992). Group influences on individuals in organizations. In M. D. Dunnette & L. M. Hough (Eds.), *Handbook of industrial and organizational psychology* (2nd ed., Vol. 3, pp. 199–267). Palo Alto, CA: Consulting Psychologists Press.

Hackman, J. R., Brousseau, K. R., & Weiss, J. A. (1976). The interaction of task design and group performance strategies in determining group effectiveness. *Organizational Behavior and Human Performance, 16,* 350–365.

Hackman, J. R., & Lawler, E. E. (1971). Employee reactions to job characteristics. *Journal of Applied Psychology, 55,* 259–286.

Hackman, J. R., & Morris, C. G. (1975). Group tasks, group interaction process, and group performance effectiveness: A review and proposed integration. In L. Berkowitz (Ed.), *Advances in experimental social psychology* (Vol. 9). New York: Academic Press.

Hackman, J. R., & Oldham, G. R. (1975). Development of the Job Diagnostic Survey. *Journal of Applied Psychology, 60,* 159–170.

Hackman, J. R., & Oldham, G. R. (1976). Motivation through the design of work: Test of a theory. *Organizational Behavior and Human Performance, 16,* 250–279.

Hackman, J. R., & Oldham, G. R. (1980). *Work redesign.* Reading, MA: Addison-Wesley.

Hale, A. R., & Hale, M. (1972). *A review of the industrial accident literature.* London: Her Majesty's Stationery Office.

Hall, D. T., & Nougaim, K. E. (1968). An examination of Maslow's need hierarchy in an organizational setting. *Organizational Behavior and Human Performance, 3,* 12–35.

Hammer, M., & Champy, J. (1993). *Reengineering the corporation: A manifesto for business revolution.* New York: HarperCollins.

Hammer, T. H., & Landau, J. (1981). Methodological issues in the use of absence data. *Journal of Applied Psychology, 66,* 574–581.

Hansen, C. P. (1988). Personality characteristics of the accident involved employee. *Journal of Business and Psychology, 2,* 346–365.

Hansen, C. P. (1989). A causal model of the relationships among accidents, biodata, personality, and cognitive factors. *Journal of Applied Psychology, 74,* 81–90.

Hatch, M. J. (1993). The dynamics of organizational culture. *Academy of Management Review, 18,* 657–693.

Hatcher, L., & Ross, T. L. (1991). From individual incentives to an organization-wide gain sharing plan: Effects on teamwork and product quality. *Journal of Organizational Behavior, 12,* 169–183.

Hatton, C., Rivers, M., Mason, H., Mason, L., Emerson, E., Kiernan, C., et al. (1999). Organizational culture and staff outcomes in services for people with intellectual disabilities. *Journal of Intellectual Disability Research, 43,* 206–218.

Hays, W. L. (1988). *Statistics.* New York: Holt, Rinehart and Winston.

Heinisch, D. A., & Jex, S. M. (1997). Negative affectivity and gender as moderators of the relationship between work-related stressors and depressed mood at work. *Work and Stress, 11,* 46–57.

Hellervik, L. W., Hazucha, J. F., & Schneider, R. J. (1992). Behavior change: Models, methods, and a review of evidence. In M. D. Dunnette & L. M. Hough (Eds.), *Handbook of industrial and organizational psychology* (2nd ed., Vol. 3, pp. 823–895). Palo Alto, CA: Consulting Psychologists Press.

Henkoff, R. (1990, April 9). Cost cutting: How to do it right. *Fortune,* 40–46.

Henry, R., & Hulin, C. L. (1987). Stability of skilled performance across time: Some generalizations and limitations on utilities. *Journal of Applied Psychology, 72,* 457–462.

Henry, R., & Hulin, C. L. (1989). Changing validities: Ability-performance relations and utilities. *Journal of Applied Psychology, 74,* 365–367.

Hershey, R. (1966). The grapevine—Here to stay but not beyond control. *Personnel, 20,* 64.

Herzberg, F. (1968, January/February). One more time: How do you motivate employees? *Harvard Business Review, 52*–62.

Herzberg, F., Mausner, B., & Snyderman, B. (1959). *The motivation to work.* New York: Wiley.

Hickson, D. J., Pugh, D. S., & Pheysey, D. (1969). Operations technology and organization structure: An empirical reappraisal. *Administrative Science Quarterly, 14,* 378–397.

Hochschild, A. R. (1979). Emotion work, feeling rules, and social structure. *American Journal of Sociology, 85,* 551–575.

Hochschild, A. R. (1983). *The managed heart: Commercialization of human feeling.* Berkeley: University of California Press.

Hochschild, A. R. (1989). *The second shift: Working parents and the revolution at home.* New York: Viking.

Hofmann, D. A., & Morgeson, F. P. (1999). Safety-related behavior as a social exchange: The role of perceived organizational support and leader-member exchange. *Journal of Applied Psychology, 84,* 286–296.

Hofmann, D. A., & Stetzer, A. (1998). The role of safety climate and communication in accident interpretation: Implication from negative events. *Academy of Management Journal, 41,* 644–657.

Hofstede, G. (1980). *Culture's consequences: International differences in work-related values.* Beverly Hills, CA: Sage.

Hofstede, G. (1984). *Culture's consequences: International differences in work-related values* (Abridged ed.) Newbury Park, CA: Sage.

Hogan, E. A., & Overmeyer-Day, L. (1994). The psychology of mergers and acquisitions. In C. L. Cooper & I. T. Robertson (Eds.), *International review of industrial and organizational psychology 1994* (Vol. 9, pp. 247–280). Chichester, England: Wiley.

Hogan, J., & Hogan, R. (1989). How to measure employee reliability. *Journal of Applied Psychology, 74,* 273–279.

Hollander, E. P. (1971). *Principles and methods of social psychology* (2nd ed.). New York: Oxford University Press.

Hollenbeck, J. R., Ilgen, D. R., & Crampton, S. M. (1992). Lower back disability in occupational settings: A review of the literature from a human resource management view. *Personnel Psychology, 45,* 247–278.

Hom, P. W., Caranikas-Walker, F., Prussia, G. E., & Griffeth, R. W. (1992). A meta-analytic structural equations analysis of a model of employee turnover. *Journal of Applied Psychology, 77,* 890–909.

Hom, P. W., & Griffeth, R. W. (1991). Structural equation modeling test of a turnover theory: Cross-sectional and longitudinal analysis. *Journal of Applied Psychology, 76,* 350–366.

Homans, G. C. (1958). Social behavior as exchange. *American Journal of Sociology, 63,* 597–606.

House, R. J. (1971). A path-goal theory of leader effectiveness. *Administrative Science Quarterly, 16,* 321–339.

House, R. J. (1977). A 1976 theory of charismatic leadership. In J. G. Hunt & L. L. Larson (Eds.), *Leadership: The cutting edge.* Carbondale: Southern Illinois University Press.

House, R. J., & Mitchell, T. R. (1974). Path-goal theory of leadership. *Contemporary Business, 3,* 81–98.

House, R. J., Spangler, W. D., & Woycke, J. (1991). Personality and charisma in the, U.S. presidency: A psychological theory of leader effectiveness. *Administrative Science Quarterly, 36,* 364–396.

Hugick, L., & Leonard, J. (1991). Job dissatisfaction grows; "moonlighting" on the rise. *Gallop Poll News Service, 56,* 1–11.

Hulin, C. L. (1991). Adaptation, commitment, and persistence in organizations. In M. D. Dunnette & L. M. Hough (Eds.), *Handbook of industrial and organizational psychology* (2nd ed., Vol. 2, pp. 445–505). Palo Alto, CA: Consulting Psychologists Press.

Hunter, J. E., Schmidt, F. L., & Judiesch, M. K. (1990). Individual differences in output variability as a function of job complexity. *Journal of Applied Psychology, 75,* 28–42.

Hurrell, J. J., Jr. (1995). Commentary: Police work, occupational stress, and individual coping. *Journal of Organizational Behavior, 16,* 27–28.

Iacocca, L. (1984). *Iacocca: An autobiography.* New York: Bantam Books.

Iaffaldano, M. T., & Muchinsky, P. M. (1985). Job satisfaction and job performance: A meta-analysis. *Psychological Bulletin, 97,* 251–273.

Ilgen, D. R., Mitchell, T. R., & Frederickson, J. W. (1981). Poor performers: Supervisors' and subordinates' responses. *Organizational Behavior and Human Performance, 27,* 386–410.

Ironson, G. H., Smith, P. C., Brannick, M. T., Gibson, W. M., & Paul, K. B. (1989). Constitution of a job in general scale: A comparison of global, composite, and specific measures. *Journal of Applied Psychology, 74,* 193–200.

Ivancevich, J. M., & Matteson, M. T. (1980). *Stress and work: A managerial perspective.* Glenview, IL: Scott, Foresman.

Ivancevich, J. M., Schweiger, D. M., & Power, F. R. (1987). Strategies for managing human resources during mergers and acquisitions. *Human Resource Planning, 10,* 19–35.

Jackofsky, E. F. (1984). Turnover and performance: An integrated process model. *Academy of Management Review, 9,* 74–83.

Jackson, S. E., & Schuler, R. S. (1985). A meta-analysis and conceptual critique of research on role ambiguity and role conflict in work settings. *Organizational Behavior and Human Decision Processes, 36,* 16–78.

Jackson, S. E., Schwab, R. L., & Schuler, R. S. (1986). Toward an understanding of the burnout phenomenon. *Journal of Applied Psychology, 71,* 630–640.

Jackson, S. E., Stone, V. A., & Alvarez, E. B. (1992). Socialization amidst diversity: The impact of demographics on work team old-timers and newcomers. In L. L. Cummings & B. M. Staw (Eds.), *Research in organizational behavior* (Vol. 15, pp. 45–109). Greenwich, CT: JAI Press.

James, L. R., & Brett, J. (1984). Mediators, moderators, and tests for mediation. *Journal of Applied Psychology, 69,* 307–321.

James, L. R., Demaree, R. G., & Wolf, G. (1984). Estimating within-group interrater reliability with and without response bias. *Journal of Applied Psychology, 69,* 85–98.

James, L. R., & Jones, A. P. (1974). Organizational climate: A review of theory and research. *Psychological Bulletin, 81,* 1096–1112.

James, L. R., Mulaik, S., & Brett, J. (1982). *Causal analysis: Assumptions, models, and data.* Beverly Hills, CA: Sage.

Janis, I. L. (1982). *Groupthink: Psychological studies of policy decisions and fiascoes* (2nd ed.). Boston: Houghton Mifflin.

Janson, N. (1994). *Safety culture: A study of permanent way staff at British Rail.* Amsterdam: Vrije University.

Jeanneret, P. R. (1991). Growth trends in I/O psychology. *Industrial-Organizational Psychologist, 29,* 47–52.

Jehn, K. A. (1994). Enhancing effectiveness: An investigation of advantages and disadvantages of value-based intragroup conflict. *International Journal of Conflict Management, 5,* 223–238.

Jenkins, G. D., Jr., Mitra, A., Gupta, N., & Shaw, J. D. (1998). Are financial incentives related to performance? A meta-analytic review of empirical research. *Journal of Applied Psychology, 83,* 777–787.

Jex, S. M. (1988). *The relationship between exercise and employee responses to work stressors: A test of two competing models.* Unpublished doctoral dissertation, University of South Florida, Tampa.

Jex, S. M. (1991). The psychological benefit of exercise in work settings: A review, critique, and alternative model. *Work and Stress, 5,* 133–147.

Jex, S. M. (1998). *Stress and job performance: Theory, research, and implications for managerial practice.* Thousand Oaks, CA: Sage.

Jex, S. M., Adams, G. A., Bachrach, D. G., & Rosol, S. (2001, April). *Relations between stressors and altruism: Commitment as a moderator.* Paper presented at the annual Society for Industrial and Organizational Psychology Convention, San Diego, CA.

Jex, S. M., Adams, G. A., Elacqua, T. C., & Bachrach, D. J. (1998, May). *Type A as a moderator: An examination using component measures.* Paper presented at the 1998 annual conference of the American Psychological Society, Washington, DC.

Jex, S. M., & Beehr, T. A. (1991). Emerging theoretical and methodological issues in the study of work-related stress. In G. R. Ferris & K. M. Rowland (Eds.), *Research in personnel and human resources management* (Vol. 9, pp. 311–364). Greenwich, CT: JAI Press.

Jex, S. M., Beehr, T. A., & Roberts, C. K. (1992). The meaning of occupational "stress" items to survey respondents. *Journal of Applied Psychology, 77,* 623–628.

Jex, S. M., & Bliese, P. D. (1999). Efficacy beliefs as a moderator of the impact of work-related stressors: A multilevel study. *Journal of Applied Psychology, 84,* 349–361.

Jex, S. M., Cvetanovski, J., & Allen, S. J. (1994). Self-esteem as a moderator of the impact of unemployment. *Journal of Social Behavior and Personality, 9,* 69–80.

Jex, S. M., & Elacqua, T. C. (1999). Self-esteem as a moderator: A comparison of global and organization-based measures. *Journal of Occupational and Organizational Psychology, 72,* 71–81.

Jex, S. M., & Heinisch, D. A. (1996). Assessing the relationship between exercise and employee mental health: Some methodological concerns. In J. Kerr, A. Griffiths, & T. Cox (Eds.), *Workplace health: Employee fitness and exercise* (pp. 55–67). London: Taylor & Francis.

Jex, S. M., & Spector, P. E. (1988, April). *Is social information processing a laboratory phenomenon?* Paper presented in M. Deselles (Chair), Job attitude measurement: Variations on a theme. Symposium presented at the 1988 Society for Industrial and Organizational Psychology Convention, Dallas, TX.

Jex, S. M., & Spector, P. E. (1989). The generalizability of social information processing to organizational settings: A summary of two field experiments. *Perceptual and Motor Skills, 69,* 883–893.

Jex, S. M., & Spector, P. E. (1996). The impact of negative affectivity on stressor-strain relations: A replication and extension. *Work and Stress, 10,* 36–45.

Johns, G. (1991). Substantive and methodological constraints on behavior and attitudes in organizational research. *Organizational Behavior and Human Decision Processes, 49,* 80–104.

Johns, G., & Xie, J. L. (1998). Perceptions of absence from work: People's Republic of

China versus Canada. *Journal of Applied Psychology, 83,* 515–530.

Johns, G., Xie, J. L., & Fang, Y. (1992). Mediating and moderating effects in job design. *Journal of Management, 18,* 657–676.

Johnson, J. G. (1990). *Selecting ethnographic informants.* Newbury Park, CA: Sage.

Johnson, P. R., & Indvik, J. (1994). Workplace violence: An issue of the Nineties. *Public Personnel Management, 23,* 515–523.

Johnson, W. B., & Packer, A. H. (1987). *Workforce 2000: Work and workers for the 21st century.* Indianapolis, IN: Hudson Institute.

Jones, B., Flynn, D. M., & Kelloway, E. K. (1995). Perception of support from the organization in relation to work stress, satisfaction, and commitment. In S. L. Sauter & L. R. Murphy (Eds.), *Organizational risk factors for job stress* (pp. 41–52). Washington, DC: American Psychological Association.

Jones, J. W., & Boye, M. W. (1992). Job stress and employee counterproductivity. In J. C. Quick, J. J. Hurrell, & L. R. Murphy (Eds.), *Stress and well-being at work* (pp. 239–251). Washington, DC: American Psychological Association.

Jordan, M., Herriot, P., & Chalmers, C. (1991). Testing Schneider's ASA theory. *Applied Psychology: An International Review, 40,* 47–54.

Joyce, W. F. (1986). Matrix organization: A social experiment. *Academy of Management Journal, 29,* 536–561.

Judge, T. A., & Cable, D. M. (1997). Applicant personality, organizational culture, and organizational attraction. *Personnel Psychology, 50,* 359–394.

Kahn, R. L., & Byosiere, P. (1992). Stress in organizations. In M. D. Dunnette & L. M. Hough (Eds.), *Handbook of industrial and organizational psychology* (2nd ed., Vol. 2, pp. 571–650). Palo Alto, CA: Consulting Psychologists Press.

Kahn, R. L., Wolfe, D. M., Quinn, R. P., Snoek, J. D., & Rosenthal, R. A. (1964). *Organizational stress: Studies in role conflict and ambiguity.* New York: Wiley.

Kanfer, R. (1990). Motivation theory and industrial/organizational psychology. In M. D. Dunnette & L. M. Hough (Eds.), *Handbook of industrial and organizational psychology* (2nd ed., Vol. 1, pp. 75–170). Palo Alto, CA: Consulting Psychologists Press.

Kanfer, R. (1992). Work motivation: New directions in theory and research. In C. L. Cooper & I. T. Robertson (Eds.), *International review of industrial and organizational psychology 1992* (pp. 1–53). Chichester, England: Wiley.

Kanfer, R., Ackerman, P. L., Murtha, T. C., Dugdale, B., & Nelson, L. (1994). Goal setting, conditions of practice, and task performance: A resource allocation perspective. *Journal of Applied Psychology, 79,* 826–835.

Karambayya, R. (1989). *Contexts for organizational citizenship behavior: Do high performing and satisfying units have better "citizens"?* York University Working Paper, North York, Ontario, Canada.

Karasek, R. A. (1979). Job demands, job decision latitude, and mental strain: Implications for job redesign. *Administrative Science Quarterly, 24,* 285–308.

Karasek, R. A., Baker, D., Marxer, F., Ahlbom, A., & Theorell, T. (1981). Job decision latitude, job demands, and cardiovascular disease: A prospective study of Swedish men. *American Journal of Public Health, 71,* 694–705.

Karau, S. J., & Williams, K. D. (1993). Social loafing: A meta-analytic review and theoretical integration. *Journal of Personality and Social Psychology, 65,* 681–706.

Kasl, S. V., & Cobb, S. (1970). Blood pressure changes in men undergoing job loss: A preliminary report. *Psychosomatic Medicine, 32,* 19–38.

Kasl, S. V., & Cobb, S. (1980). The experience of losing a job: Some effects on cardiovascular functioning. *Psychotherapy and Psychosomatics, 34,* 88–109.

Katz, D., & Kahn, R. L. (1966). *The social psychology of organizations.* New York: Wiley.

Katz, D., & Kahn, R. L. (1978). *The social psychology of organizations* (2nd ed.). New York: Wiley.

Katzell, R. A., & Austin, J. T. (1992). From then to now: The development of industrial-organizational psychology in the United States. *Journal of Applied Psychology, 77,* 803–835.

Keenan, A., & Newton, T. J. (1985). Stressful events, stressors and psychological strains in young professional engineers. *Journal of Occupational Behavior, 6,* 151–156.

Kelley, H. H. (1973). The process of causal attribution. *American Psychologist, 28,* 107–128.

Kelley, H. H., & Thibaut, J. W. (1978). *Interpersonal relations: A theory of interdependence.* New York: Wiley.

Kelman, H. C. (1958). Compliance, identification, and internalization: Three processes of attitude change. *Journal of Conflict Resolution, 2,* 51–60.

Keppel, G. (1982). *Design and analysis: A researcher's handbook* (2nd ed.). Englewood Cliffs, NJ: Prentice-Hall.

Kerr, J. (1975). On the folly of rewarding A, while hoping for B. *Academy of Management Journal, 18,* 769–783.

Kerr, J. H., & Vos, M. C. (1993). Employee fitness programs, absenteeism, and general well-being. *Work and Stress, 7,* 179–190.

Kessler, R. (1992). *Inside the CIA: Revealing the secrets of the world's most powerful spy agency.* New York: Simon & Schuster.

Kets de Vries, M. F. R., & Miller, D. (1986). Personality, culture, and organization. *Academy of Management Review, 11,* 266–279.

King, L. A., & King, D. W. (1990). Role conflict and role ambiguity: A critical assessment of construct validity. *Psychological Bulletin, 107,* 48–64.

Kipnis, D. (1984). The use of power in organizations and interpersonal settings. *Applied Social Psychology Annual, 5,* 179–210.

Kirkpatrick, S. A., & Locke, E. A. (1996). Direct and indirect effects of three core charismatic leadership components on performance and attitudes. *Journal of Applied Psychology, 81,* 36–51.

Klaas, B. S. (1989). Determinants of grievance activity and the grievance system's impact on employee behavior: An integrated perspective. *Academy of Management Review, 14,* 445–458.

Klaas, B. S., & Wheeler, H. N. (1990). Managerial decision making about employee discipline: A policy capturing approach. *Personnel Psychology, 43,* 117–134.

Klein, H. J. (1989). An integrated control theory model of work motivation. *Academy of Management Review, 14,* 150–172.

Klein, K. J. (1987). Employee stock ownership and employee attitudes: A test of three models [Monograph]. *Journal of Applied Psychology, 72,* 319–332.

Klein, K. J., Dansereau, F. J., & Hall, R. J. (1994). Levels issues in theory development, data collection, and analysis. *Academy of Management Review, 19,* 195–229.

Klein, S. M., Kraut, A. I., & Wolfson, A. (1971). Employee reactions to attitude survey feedback: A study of the impact of structure and process. *Administrative Science Quarterly, 16,* 497–514.

Koestner, R., Zuckerman, M., & Olsson, J. (1990). Attributional style, comparison focus of praise, and intrinsic motivation. *Journal of Research in Personality, 24,* 87–100.

Kohler, S. S., & Mathieu, J. E. (1993). Individual characteristics, work perceptions, and affective reactions influences on differentiated absence criteria. *Journal of Organizational Behavior, 14,* 515–530.

Kokotovich, M., Jex, S. M., & Adams, G. A. (2000, April). *Leader-member exchange: A moderator of the stressor-satisfaction relationship.* Paper presented at the annual meeting of the Society for Industrial and Organizational Psychology, New Orleans, LA.

Komaki, J., Barwick, K. D., & Scott, L. R. (1978). A behavioral approach to occupational safety: Pinpointing and reinforcing safe performance in a food manufacturing plant. *Journal of Applied Psychology, 63,* 434–445.

Komaki, J., Heinzmann, A. T., & Lawson, L. (1980). Effective training and feedback: Component analysis of a behavioral safety program. *Journal of Applied Psychology, 65,* 261–270.

Konovsky, M. A., & Cropanzano, R. (1991). Perceived fairness of employee drug testing as a predictor of employee attitudes and health. *Journal of Applied Psychology, 76,* 698–707.

Konovsky, M. A., & Pugh, S. D. (1990). Citizenship behavior and social exchange. *Academy of Management Journal, 37,* 656–669.

Kossek, E. E., & Ozeki, C. (1998). Work-family conflict, policies, and the job-life satisfaction relationship: A review and directions for organizational behavior-human resources research. *Journal of Applied Psychology, 83,* 139–149.

Kotter, J. P., & Heskett, J. L. (1992). *Corporate culture and performance.* New York: Free Press.

Kozlowski, S. W. J., Chao, G. T., Smith, E. M., & Hedlund, J. (1993). Organizational downsizing: Strategies, interventions, and research implications. In C. L. Cooper & I. T. Robertson (Eds.), *International review of industrial and organizational psychology* (Vol. 8, pp. 263–332). London: Wiley.

Kristof, A. L. (1996). Person-organization fit: An integrative review of its conceptualization, measurement, and implications. *Personnel Psychology, 49,* 1–50.

Kuhn, R. (1988). Psychological tests reduce counterproductive acts by employees. *Assets Protection, 9,* 9–12.

Kunin, T. (1955). The construction of a new type of attitude measure. *Personnel Psychology, 8,* 65–67.

LaBianca, G., Brass, D. J., & Gray, B. (1998). Social networks and perceptions of intergroup conflict: The role of negative relationships and third parties. *Academy of Management Journal, 41,* 55–67.

Lamm, H. (1988). A review of our research on group polarization: Eleven experiments on the effects of group discussion on risk acceptance, probability estimation, and negotiation positions. *Psychological Reports, 62,* 807–813.

Landy, F. J., & Farr, J. L. (1980). Performance rating. *Psychological Bulletin, 87,* 72–107.

Latack, J. C., & Foster, L. W. (1985). Implementation of compressed work schedules: Participation and job redesign as critical factors. *Personnel Psychology, 38,* 75–92.

Latane, B., Williams, K., & Harkins, S. (1979). Many hands make light the work: The causes and consequences of social loafing. *Journal of Personality and Social Psychology, 37,* 822–832.

Latham, G. P., & Huber, V. L. (1992). Schedules of reinforcement: Lessons from the past and issues for the future. *Journal of Organizational Behavior Management, 12,* 125–149.

Latham, G. P., & Locke, E. A. (1991). Self-regulation through goal setting. *Organizational Behavior and Human Decision Processes, 50,* 212–247.

Lawler, E. E. (1990). *Strategic pay: Aligning organizational strategies and pay systems.* San Francisco: Jossey-Bass.

Lawler, E. E., & Jenkins, D. G. (1992). Strategic reward systems. In M. D. Dunnette & L. M. Hough (Eds.), *Handbook of industrial and organizational psychology* (2nd ed., Vol. 3, pp. 1009–1035). Palo Alto, CA: Consulting Psychologists Press.

Lawler, E. E., Koplin, C. A., Young, T. F., & Fadem, J. A. (1968). Inequity reduction over time in an overpayment situation. *Organizational Behavior and Human Performance, 3,* 253–268.

Lawler, E. E., Mohrman, S., & Ledford, G. (1995). *Creating high performance organizations: Practices and results of employee involvement and TQM in Fortune 1000 companies.* San Francisco: Jossey-Bass.

Lawrence, P. R., & Lorsch, J. W. (1967). *Organization and environment: Managing differentiation and integration.* Boston: Harvard Business School, Division of Research.

Lazarus, R. S. (1966). *Psychological stress and the coping process.* New York: McGraw-Hill.

Leana, C. R., & Feldman, D. D. (1992). *Coping with job loss.* New York: Lexington Books.

Leavitt, H. J. (1951). Some effects of certain communication patterns on group performance. *Journal of Abnormal and Social Psychology, 46,* 38–50.

Lee, T. W., & Mitchell, T. R. (1994). An alternative approach: The unfolding model of voluntary employee turnover. *Academy of Management Review, 19,* 51–89.

Lee, T. W., Mitchell, T. R., Holtom, B. C., McDaniel, L. S., & Hill, J. W. (1999). The unfolding model of voluntary turnover: A replication and extension. *Academy of Management Journal, 42,* 450–462.

Lee, T. W., Mitchell, T. R., Wise, L., & Fireman, S. (1996). An unfolding model of employee turnover. *Academy of Management Journal, 39,* 5–36.

Lehman, W. E., Farabee, D. J., Holcom, M. L., & Simpson, D. D. (1995). Prediction of substance use in the workplace: Unique contributions of personal background and work environment variables. *Journal of Drug Issues, 25,* 253–274.

Lehman, W. E., & Simpson, D. D. (1992). Employee substance use and on-the-job behaviors. *Journal of Applied Psychology, 77,* 309–321.

Levin, I., & Stokes, J. P. (1989). Dispositional approach to job satisfaction: Role of negative affectivity. *Journal of Applied Psychology, 74,* 752–758.

Levine, E. L. (1983). *Everything you always wanted to know about job analysis.* Tampa, FL: Mariner.

Levine, J. M., & Moreland, R. L. (1990). Progress in small group research. In M. R. Rosenzweig & L. W. Porter (Eds.), *Annual Review of Psychology, 41,* 585–634.

Lewin, K. (1947). Frontiers in group dynamics. *Human Relations, 1,* 26–41.

Lewin, K. (1951). *Field theory in social science.* New York: Harper.

Liden, R. C., & Maslyn, J. M. (1998). Multidimensionality of leader-member exchange: An empirical assessment through scale development. *Journal of Management, 24,* 43–72.

Liden, R. C., Wayne, S. J., Judge, T. A., Sparrowe, R. T., Kraimer, M. L., & Franz, T. M. (1999). Management of poor performance: A comparison of manager, group member, and group disciplinary decisions. *Journal of Applied Psychology, 84,* 835–850.

Liden, R. C., Wayne, S. J., & Stilwell, D. (1993). A longitudinal study on the early development of leader-member exchanges. *Journal of Applied Psychology, 78,* 662–674.

Liebowitz, S. J., & DeMeuse, K. P. (1982). The application of team building. *Human Relations, 35,* 1–18.

Likert, J. G., & Araki, C. T. (1986). Managing without a boss: System 5. *LODJ, 7,* 17–20.

Likert, R. (1961). *New patterns of management.* New York: McGraw-Hill.

Likert, R. (1967). *The human organization.* New York: McGraw-Hill.

Locke, E. A. (1968). Toward a theory of task motivation and incentive. *Organizational Behavior and Human Performance, 3,* 157–189.

Locke, E. A. (1976). The nature and causes of job satisfaction. In M. D. Dunnette (Ed.), *Handbook of industrial and organizational psychology* (pp. 1297–1349). Chicago: Rand McNally.

Locke, E. A. (1982). The ideas of Frederick, W. Taylor: An evaluation. *Academy of Management Review, 7,* 14–24.

Locke, E. A. (1986). Generalizing from laboratory to field: Ecological validity or abstraction of essential elements. In E. A. Locke (Ed.), *Generalizing from laboratory to field studies* (pp. 3–9). Lexington, MA: Heath.

Locke, E. A., & Henne, D. (1986). Work motivation theories. In C. L. Cooper & I. T. Robertson (Eds.), *International review of industrial and organizational psychology 1986* (pp. 1–35). Chichester, England: Wiley.

Locke, E. A., & Latham, G. P. (1990a). *A theory of goal setting and task performance.* Englewood Cliffs, NJ: Prentice-Hall.

Locke, E. A., & Latham, G. P. (1990b). Work motivation and satisfaction: Light at the end of the tunnel. *Psychological Science, 4,* 240–246.

Long, R. G., Bowers, W. P., Barnett, T., & White, M. C. (1998). Research productivity in graduates in management: Effects of academic origin and academy affiliation. *Academy of Management Journal, 41,* 704–714.

Lord, R. G., & Hanges, P. J. (1987). A control system model of organizational motivation: Theoretical development and applied implications. *Behavioral Science, 32,* 161–178.

Lord, R. G., & Hohenfeld, J. A. (1979). Longitudinal field assessment of equity aspects on the performance of major league baseball players. *Journal of Applied Psychology, 64,* 19–26.

Louis, M. R. (1990). Acculturation in the workplace: Newcomers as lay ethnographers. In B. Schneider (Ed.), *Organizational climate and culture* (pp. 85–129). San Francisco: Jossey-Bass.

Lowin, A. (1968). Participative decision making: A model, literature critique, and prescriptions for research. *Organizational Behavior and Human Performance, 3,* 68–106.

Luthans, F., & Kreitner, R. (1985). *Organizational behavior modification and beyond: An operant and social learning approach* (2nd ed.). Glenview, IL: Scott, Foresman.

Maidani, E. A. (1991). Comparative study of Herzberg's Two-Factor Theory of job satisfaction among public and private sectors. *Public Personnel Management, 20,* 441–448.

Majchrzak, A. (1987). Effects of management policies on unauthorized absence behavior. *Journal of Applied Behavioral Science, 23,* 501–523.

Mann, R. D. (1959). A review of the relationships between personality and performance in small groups. *Psychological Bulletin, 56,* 241–270.

Margerison, C., & Glube, R. (1979). Leadership decision-making: An empirical test of the Vroom-Yetton model. *Journal of Management Studies, 16,* 45–55.

Marion-Landis, C. A. (1993). *A cross-cultural study of leader-member exchange quality and job satisfaction as correlates of inter-dyadic work-value congruence.* Unpublished master's thesis, University of South Florida, Tampa.

Martocchio, J. J. (1994). The effects of absence culture on individual absence. *Human Relations, 47,* 243–262.

Martocchio, J. J., & Harrison, D. A. (1993). To be there or not to be there: Questions, theories, and methods in absenteeism research. *Research in Personnel and Human Resources Research, 11,* 259–329.

Maslow, A. H. (1943). A theory of human motivation. *Psychological Review, 50,* 370–396.

Mathieu, J. E., & Kohler, S. S. (1990). A cross-level examination of group absence influences on individual absence. *Journal of Applied Psychology, 75,* 217–220.

Mathieu, J. E., & Zajac, D. M. (1990). A review and meta-analysis of the antecedents, correlates, and consequences of organizational commitment. *Psychological Bulletin, 108,* 171–194.

Matteson, M. T., & Ivancevich, J. M. (1987). *Controlling work stress.* San Francisco: Jossey-Bass.

May, D. R., & Schwoerer, C. E. (1994). Employee health by design: Using employee involvement teams in ergonomic job design. *Personnel Psychology, 47,* 861–876.

Mayo, E. (1933). *The human problems of an industrial civilization.* New York: Macmillan.

McCabe, D. M. (1988). *Corporate nonunion complaint procedures and systems: A strategic human resources management analysis.* Westport, CT: Praeger.

McClelland, D. (1961). *The achieving society.* Princeton, NJ: Van Nostrand.

McClelland, D. (1965). Toward a theory of motive acquisition. *American Psychologist, 20,* 321–333.

McCloy, R. A., Campbell, J. P., & Cudeck, R. (1994). A confirmatory test of a model of performance determinants. *Journal of Applied Psychology, 79,* 493–505.

McDaniel, M. A., Schmidt, F. L., & Hunter, J. E. (1988). Job experience correlates of job performance. *Journal of Applied Psychology, 73,* 327–330.

McEvoy, G. M., & Cascio, W. F. (1985). Strategies for reducing employee turnover: A meta-analysis. *Journal of Applied Psychology, 70,* 342–353.

McEvoy, G. M., & Cascio, W. F. (1987). Do good or poor performers leave? A meta-analysis of the relationship between performance and turnover. *Academy of Management Journal, 30,* 744–762.

McGrath, J. E. (1964). *Social psychology: A brief introduction.* New York: Holt.

McGrath, J. E. (1976). Stress and behavior in organizations. In M. D. Dunnette (Ed.), *Handbook of industrial and organizational psychology* (pp. 1351–1396). Chicago: Rand McNally.

McGrath, J. E. (1990). Time matters in groups. In J. Galegher, R. E. Kraut, & C. Egido (Eds.), *Intellectual teamwork: Social and technological foundations of cooperative work* (pp. 23–61). Hillsdale, NJ: Erlbaum.

McGrath, J. E., & Beehr, T. A. (1990). Time and the stress process: Some temporal issues in the conceptualization and measurement of stress. *Stress Medicine, 6,* 93–104.

McGregor, D. (1960). *The human side of enterprise.* New York: McGraw-Hill.

McKenna, D. D., & Wright, P. M. (1992). Alternative metaphors for organizational design. In M. D. Dunnette & L. M. Hough (Eds.), *Handbook of industrial and organizational psychology* (2nd ed., Vol. 3, pp. 901–960). Palo Alto, CA: Consulting Psychologists Press.

McMahon, J. (1972). The contingency theory: Logic and method revisited. *Personnel Psychology, 25,* 697–710.

McMullen, T. J. (1991). *Personality correlates of on-the-job substance use: Exploring an alternative to urinalysis.* Unpublished master's thesis, Central Michigan University, Mount Pleasant.

McNamara, R. S., Blight, J., Brigham, S., Biersteker, T., & Schandler, H. (1999). *Argument without end: In search of answers to the Vietnam tragedy.* New York: Public Affairs.

Meichenbaum, D. (1977). *Cognitive-behavior modification: An integrated approach.* New York: Plenum Press.

Merton, R. K. (1968). *Social theory and social structure.* New York: Free Press.

Meyer, H. H., Kay, E., & French, J. R. P., Jr. (1965). Split roles in performance appraisal. *Harvard Business Review, 43,* 123–129.

Meyer, J. P., & Allen, N. J. (1991). A three-component conceptualization of organizational commitment. *Human Resource Management Review, 1,* 61–89.

Meyer, J. P., & Allen, N. J. (1997). *Commitment in the workplace: Theory, research, and application.* Thousand Oaks, CA: Sage.

Michaels, C. E., & Spector, P. E. (1982). Causes of employee turnover: A test of the Mobley, Griffeth, Hand, and Meglino model. *Journal of Applied Psychology, 67,* 53–59.

Miles, R. H. (1980). *Macro organizational behavior.* Glenview, IL: Scott, Foresman.

Milgram, S. (1974). *Obedience to authority.* New York: Harper & Row.

Milkovich, G. T., & Newman, J. (1990). *Compensation.* Homewood, IL: Irwin.

Miller, V. D., & Jablin, F. M. (1991). Information seeking during organizational entry: Influences, tactics, and a model of the process. *Academy of Management Review, 16,* 92–120.

Milliken, F. J., Martins, L. L., & Morgan, H. (1998). Explaining organizational responsiveness to work-family issues: The role of human resource executives as interpreters. *Academy of Management Journal, 41,* 580–596.

Mirvis, P., & Seashore, S. (1979). Being ethical in organizational research. *American Psychologist, 34,* 766–780.

Mitchell, T. R. (1974). Expectancy models of job satisfaction, occupational preferences and effort: A theoretical, methodological, and empirical appraisal. *Psychological Bulletin, 81,* 1053–1077.

Mitchell, T. R., & Kalb, L. S. (1982). Effects of job experience on supervisor attributions for a subordinate's poor performance. *Journal of Applied Psychology, 67,* 181–188.

Mitchell, T. R., & O'Reilly, C. A. (1983). Managing poor performance and productivity in organizations. *Research in Personnel and Human Resources Management, 1,* 201–234.

Mitchell, T. R., & Silver, W. R. (1990). Individual and group goals when workers are interdependent: Effects on task strategy and performance. *Journal of Applied Psychology, 75,* 185–193.

Mobley, W. H. (1977). Intermediate linkages in the relationship between job satisfaction and employee turnover. *Journal of Applied Psychology, 62,* 237–240.

Mobley, W. H., Griffeth, R. W., Hand, H. H., & Meglino, B. M. (1979). Review and conceptual analysis of the employee turnover process. *Psychological Bulletin, 86,* 493–522.

Mohrman, S. A., & Quam, K. (2000). Consulting to team-based organizations: An organizational design and learning approach. *Consulting Psychology Journal: Practice and Research, 52,* 20–35.

Mone, M. A., & Shalley, C. E. (1995). Effects of task complexity and goal specificity on change in strategy and performance over time. *Human Performance, 8,* 243–252.

Mone, M. A., Mueller, G. C., & Mauland, W. (1996). The perceptions and usage of statistical power in applied psychology and management research. *Personnel Psychology, 49,* 103–120.

Monroy, J., Jonas, H., Mathey, J., & Murphy, L. (1998). Holistic stress management at Corning, Incorporated. In M. K. Gowing, J. D. Kraft, & J. C. Quick (Eds.), *The new organizational reality: Downsizing, restructuring, and revitalization.* Washington, DC: American Psychological Association.

Moorhead, G., Ference, R., & Neck, C. P. (1991). Group decision fiascoes continue: Space Shuttle Challenger and a revised framework. *Human Relations, 47,* 929–952.

Moorhead, G., & Griffin, R. W. (1998). *Organizational behavior: Managing people and organizations* (5th ed.). Boston: Houghton Mifflin.

Moorman, R. H. (1991). Relationship between organizational justice and organizational citizenship behaviors: Do fairness perceptions influence employee citizenship? *Journal of Applied Psychology, 76,* 845–855.

Moreland, R. L., & Levine, J. M. (1982). Socialization in small groups: Temporal changes in individual-group relations. *Advances in Experimental Social Psychology, 15,* 137–192.

Morgan, G. (1986). *Images of organization.* Beverly Hills, CA: Sage.

Morris, L. A., & Feldman, D. C. (1996). The dimensions, antecedents, and consequences of emotional labor. *Academy of Management Review, 21,* 986–1010.

Morrison, E. W. (1993). Longitudinal study of the effects of information seeking on newcomer socialization. *Journal of Applied Psychology, 78,* 173–183.

Morrison, E. W. (1994). Role definitions and organizational citizenship behavior: The importance of the employee's perspective. *Academy of Management Journal, 37,* 1543–1567.

Morrison, E. W., & Robinson, S. L. (1997). When employees feel betrayed: A model of how psychological contract violation develops. *Academy of Management Review, 22,* 226–256.

Moscovici, S. (1994). Three concepts: Minority, conflict, and behavioral styles. In S. Moscovici, A. Mucchi-Faina, & A. Maas (Eds.), *Minority influence* (pp. 233–251). Chicago: Nelson-Hall.

Motowidlo, S. J., Packard, J. S., & Manning, M. R. (1986). Occupational stress: Its causes and consequences for job performance. *Journal of Applied Psychology, 71,* 618–629.

Mowday, R. T., Porter, L. W., & Steers, R. M. (1982). *Organizational linkages: The psychology of commitment, absenteeism, and turnover.* San Diego, CA: Academic Press.

Mowday, R. T., Steers, R. M., & Porter, L. W. (1979). The measurement of organizational commitment. *Journal of Vocational Behavior, 14,* 224–247.

Muchinsky, P. M. (1977). A comparison of within- and across-subjects analyses of the expectancy-value model for predicting effort. *Academy of Management Journal, 20,* 154–158.

Muchinsky, P. M., & Morrow, P. C. (1980). A multidisciplinary model of employee turnover. *Journal of Vocational Behavior, 17,* 263–290.

Mudrack, P. E. (1989). Defining group cohesiveness: A legacy of confusion. *Small Group Behavior, 20,* 37–49.

Muijen, J. V. (1998). Organizational culture. In P. J. Drenth & H. Thierry (Eds.), *Handbook of work and organizational psychology* (2nd ed.,

Vol. 4, pp. 113–131). Hove, England: Psychology Press.

Mulcahy, C. (1991, May 20). Workplace stress reaches "epidemic" proportion. *National Underwriter, 4,* 20.

Mulvey, P. W., & Klein, H. J. (1998). The impact of perceived loafing and collective efficacy on group goal processes and group performance. *Organizational Behavior and Human Decision Processes, 74,* 62–87.

Murphy, K. R. (1989a). Dimensions of job performance. In R. Dillion & J. W. Pelligrino (Eds.), *Testing: Theoretical and applied perspectives* (pp. 218–247). New York: Praeger.

Murphy, K. R. (1989b). Is the relationship between cognitive ability and performance stable over time? *Human Performance, 2,* 183–200.

Murphy, K. R. (1994). Toward a broad conceptualization of jobs and job performance: Impact of changes in the military environment on the structure, assessment, and prediction of job performance. In M. G. Rumsey, C. B. Walker, & J. H. Harris (Eds.), *Personnel selection and classification* (pp. 85–102). Hillsdale, NJ: Erlbaum.

Murphy, K. R., & Cleveland, J. N. (1990). *Performance appraisal: An organizational perspective.* Boston: Allyn & Bacon.

Murphy, K. R., Thornton, G. C., III., & Reynolds, D. H. (1990). College students' attitudes toward employee drug testing programs. *Personnel Psychology, 43,* 615–631.

Murphy, L. R. (1984). Occupational stress management: A review and appraisal. *Journal of Occupational Psychology, 57,* 1–15.

Murphy, L. R. (1996). *Future directions for job stress research and practice: Expanding the focus from worker health to organizational health.* Opening keynote speech at the 2nd National Occupational Stress Conference 1996, Brisbane, Queensland, Australia.

Murray, B., & Gerhart, B. (1998). An empirical analysis of a skill-based pay program and plant performance outcomes. *Academy of Management Journal, 41,* 68–78.

Murray, H. A. (1938). *Explorations in personality.* New York: Oxford University Press.

Nagel, C. M. (1999). *The perception of fit within the interview process.* Unpublished master's thesis, University of Wisconsin, Oshkosh.

National Council on Compensation Insurance. (1988). *Emotional stress in the workplace: New legal rights in the eighties.* New York: Author.

National Council on Compensation Insurance. (1991). *Issues report, 1991.* Boca Raton, FL: Author.

Neuman, G. A., Edwards, J. E., & Raju, N. S. (1989). Organizational development interventions: A meta-analysis of their effects on satisfaction and other attitudes. *Personnel Psychology, 42,* 461–483.

Nielsen, I. K., Jex, S. M., & Adams, G. A. (2000). Development and validation of scores on a two-dimensional workplace friendship scale. *Educational and Psychological Measurement, 60,* 628–643.

Normand, J., Lempert, R. O., & O'Brien, C. P. (Eds.). (1994). *Under the influence? Drugs and the American work force.* Washington, DC: National Academy Press.

Nunnally, J. C., & Bernstein, I. H. (1994). *Psychometric theory* (3rd ed.). New York: McGraw-Hall.

O'Donnell, M. P. (1986). Definition of health promotion. Part II: Levels of programs. *American Journal of Health Promotion, 1,* 6–9.

Offermann, L. R., & Spiros, R. K. (2001). The science and practice of team development: Improving the link. *Academy of Management Journal, 44,* 376–392.

O'Leary-Kelly, A. M., Griffin, R. W., & Glew, D. J. (1996). Organization-motivated aggression:

A research framework. *Academy of Management Review, 21,* 225–253.

O'Leary-Kelly, A. M., Martocchio, J. J., & Frink, D. D. (1994). A review of the influence of group goals on group performance. *Academy of Management Journal, 37,* 1285–1301.

Ones, D. S., & Viswesvaran, C. (2000). Most published authors in *Journal of Applied Psychology and Personnel Psychology* during the 1990s. *Industrial-Organizational Psychologist, 37,* 26–35.

Ones, D. S., Viswesvaran, C., & Schmidt, F. L. (1993). Comprehensive meta-analysis of integrity test validities: Findings and implications for personnel selection and theories of job performance. *Journal of Applied Psychology Monograph, 78,* 679–703.

O'Reilly, C. A., & Caldwell, D. (1979). Information influences as a determinant of task characteristics and job satisfaction. *Journal of Applied Psychology, 64,* 157–165.

Organ, D. W. (1977). A reappraisal and reinterpretation of the satisfaction-causes-performance hypothesis. *Academy of Management Review, 2,* 46–53.

Organ, D. W. (1994). Organizational citizenship behavior and the good soldier. In M. G. Rumsey, C. B. Walker, & J. H. Harris (Eds.), *Personnel selection and classification* (pp. 53–67). Hillsdale, NJ: Erlbaum.

Organ, D. W., & Ryan, K. (1995). A meta-analytic review of attitudinal and dispositional predictors of organizational citizenship behavior. *Personnel Psychology, 48,* 775–802.

Ostroff, C. (1992). The relationship between satisfaction, attitudes, and performance: An organizational level analysis. *Journal of Applied Psychology, 77,* 963–974.

Ostroff, C., & Kozlowski, S. W. J. (1992). Organizational socialization as a learning process: The role of information acquisition. *Personnel Psychology, 45,* 849–874.

Ostrovsky, V., & Hoy, C. (1990). *By way of deception: The making and unmaking of a Mossad officer.* New York: St. Martin's Press.

Ouchi, W. G. (1981). *Theory Z.* Reading, MA: Addison-Wesley.

Ouchi, W. G., & Wilkins, A. L. (1985). Organizational culture. *Annual Review of Sociology, 11,* 457–483.

Pacanowsky, M. E., & O'Donnell-Trujillo, N. (1983). Organizational communication as cultural performance. *Communication Monographs, 50,* 126–147.

Page, R. C., Davis, K. C., Berkow, D. N., & O'Leary, E. (1989). Analysis of group process in marathon group therapy with users of illicit drugs. *Small Group Behavior, 20,* 220–227.

Parker, C. P. (1999). The impact of leaders' implicit theories of employee participation on tests of the Vroom-Yetton model. *Journal of Social Behavior and Personality, 4,* 45–61.

Parker, S., & Wall, T. (1998). *Job and work redesign: Organizing work to promote well-being and effectiveness.* Thousand Oaks, CA: Sage.

Parsons, T. (1951). *The social system.* New York: Free Press.

Paul, R. J., & Ebadi, Y. M. (1989). Leadership decision-making in a service organization: A field test of the Vroom-Yetton model. *Journal of Occupational Psychology, 62,* 201–211.

Pedalino, E., & Gamboa, V. U. (1974). Behavior modification and absenteeism: Intervention in one industrial site. *Journal of Applied Psychology, 59,* 694–698.

Pelletier, K. R. (1991). A review and analysis of the health and cost effective outcome studies of comprehensive health promotion and disease preventive programs. *American Journal of Health Promotion, 5,* 311–315.

Perlaki, I. (1994). Organizational development in Eastern Europe: Learning to build culture-specific OD theories. *Journal of Applied Behavioral Science, 30,* 297–312.

Perrewe, P. L., & Ganster, D. C. (1989). The impact of job demands and behavioral control on experienced job stress. *Journal of Organizational Behavior, 10,* 213–229.

Peters, L. H., & O'Connor, E. J. (1980). Situational constraints and work outcomes: The influences of a frequently overlooked construct. *Academy of Management Review, 5,* 391–397.

Peters, L. H., & O'Connor, E. J. (1988). Measuring work obstacles: Procedures, issues, and implications. In F. D. Schoorman & B. Schneider (Eds.), *Facilitating work group effectiveness* (pp. 105–123). Lexington, MA: Lexington Books.

Peters, T. J., & Waterman, R. H. (1982). *In search of excellence: Lessons from America's best-run companies.* New York: Harper & Row.

Peterson, M., & Wilson, J. (1998). A culture-work-health model. *American Journal of Health Behavior, 22,* 378–390.

Peterson, M. F., Smith, P. B., Akande, A., Ayestaran, S., Bocher, S., Callan, V., et al. (1995). Role conflict, ambiguity, and overload: A 21-nation study. *Academy Management Journal, 38,* 429–452.

Pettigrew, A. M. (1979). On studying organizational cultures. *Administrative Science Quarterly, 24,* 570–581.

Petty, M. M., Singleton, B., & Connell, D. W. (1992). An experimental evaluation of an organizational incentive plan in the electrical utility industry. *Journal of Applied Psychology, 77,* 427–436.

Petty, R. E., & Cacioppo, J. T. (1981). *Attitudes and persuasion: Classic and contemporary approaches.* Dubuque, IA: Brown.

Pierce, J. L., & Dunham, R. B. (1992). The 12-hour work day: A 48-hour, eight day week.

Academy of Management Journal, 35, 1086–1098.

Pierce, J. L., & Newstrom, J. W. (1982). Employee responses to flexible work schedules: An inter-organization, inter-system comparison. *Journal of Management, 8,* 9–25.

Pierce, J. L., Newstrom, J. W., Dunham, R. B., & Barber, A. E. (1989). *Alternative work schedules.* Needham Heights, MA: Allyn & Bacon.

Pinder, C. C. (1998). *Work motivation in organizational behavior.* Upper Saddle River, NJ: Prentice-Hall.

Ployhart, R. E., & Hakel, M. D. (1998). The substantive nature of performance variability: Predicting interindividual differences in intraindividual performance. *Personnel Psychology, 51,* 859–901.

Podsakoff, P. M. (1982). Determinants of a supervisor's use of rewards and punishments: A literature review and suggestions for further research. *Organizational Behavior and Human Performance, 29,* 58–83.

Podsakoff, P. M., Ahearne, M., & MacKenzie, S. B. (1997). Organizational citizenship behavior and the quantity and quality of work group performance. *Journal of Applied Psychology, 82,* 262–270.

Podsakoff, P. M., & Williams, L. J. (1986). The relationship between job performance and job satisfaction. In E. A. Locke (Ed.), *Generalizing from laboratory to field settings* (pp. 207–253). Lexington, MA: Heath.

Porras, J. I., & Robertson, P. J. (1992). Organizational development: Theory, practice, and research. In M. D. Dunnette & L. M. Hough (Eds.), *Handbook of industrial and organizational psychology* (2nd ed., Vol. 3, pp. 719–822). Palo Alto, CA: Consulting Psychologists Press.

Porras, J. I., & Silvers, R. C. (1991). Organization development and transformation. *Annual Review of Psychology, 42,* 51–78.

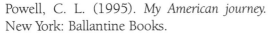

Powell, C. L. (1995). *My American journey.* New York: Ballantine Books.

Powers, W. T. (1973a). Feedback: Beyond behaviorism. *Science, 179,* 351–356.

Powers, W. T. (1973b). *Behavior: The control of perception.* Chicago: Aldine.

Powers, W. T. (1978). Quantitative analysis of purposive systems: Some spadework at the foundations of scientific psychology. *Psychological Review, 85,* 417–435.

Primeau, J. (2000). *Type A behavior pattern as a moderator of the relationship between job complexity and job outcomes.* Unpublished master's thesis, University of Wisconsin, Oshkosh.

Pritchard, R. D. (1969). Equity theory as a predictor of productivity and work quality. *Psychological Bulletin, 70,* 596–610.

Pritchard, R. D. (1992). Organizational productivity. In M. D. Dunnette & L. M. Hough (Eds.), *Handbook of industrial and organizational psychology* (2nd ed., Vol. 3, pp. 443–471). Palo Alto, CA: Consulting Psychologists Press.

Puffer, S. M. (1999). Global statesman: Mikhail Gorbachev on globalization. *Academy of Management Executive, 13,* 8–14.

Pulakos, E. D. (1984). A comparison of rater training programs: Error training and accuracy training. *Journal of Applied Psychology, 69,* 581–588.

Quinones, M. A., Ford, J. K., & Teachout, M. S. (1995). The relationship between work experience and job performance: A conceptual and meta-analytic review. *Personnel Psychology, 48,* 887–910.

Rao, T. V., & Vijayalakshmi, M. (2000). Organization development in India. *Organization Development Journal, 18,* 51–63.

Raven, B. H. (1993). The bases of power: Origins and recent developments. *Human Relations, 49,* 227–251.

Rawlinson, H. (1989). Pre-employment testing. *Small Business Reports, 14,* 20–27.

Reid, G. L. (1972). Job search and the effectiveness of job-finding methods. *Industrial and Labor Relations Review, 25,* 479–495.

Reilly, R. R., Brown, B., Blood, M. R., & Malatesta, C. (1981). The effect of realistic previews: A study and discussion of the literature. *Personnel Psychology, 34,* 823–834.

Renn, R. W., & Vandenberg, R. J. (1995). The critical psychological states: An underrepresented component in job characteristics model research. *Journal of Management, 21,* 279–303.

Rentsch, J. R., & Schneider, B. (1991). Expectations for postcombination organizational life: A study of responses to merger and acquisition scenarios. *Journal of Applied Social Psychology, 21,* 233–252.

Riggs, M. L., & Knight, P. A. (1994). The impact of perceived group success-failure on motivational beliefs and attitudes: A causal model. *Journal of Applied Psychology, 79,* 755–766.

Riordan, C. M., & Griffeth, R. W. (1995). The opportunity for friendship in the workplace: An underexplored construct. *Journal of Business and Psychology, 10,* 141–154.

Roberts, C. K. (1995). *The role of personality in perceived free riding.* Unpublished doctoral dissertation, Central Michigan University, Mount Pleasant.

Roccas, S., & Schwartz, S. H. (1993). Effects of intergroup similarity on intergroup relations. *European Journal of Social Psychology, 23,* 581–595.

Rodgers, R., & Hunter, J. E. (1991). Impact of management by objectives on organizational productivity. *Journal of Applied Psychology, 76,* 322–336.

Rokeach, M. (1973). *The nature of human values.* New York: Free Press.

Rosen, C., Klein, K. J., & Young, K. M. (1986). *Employee ownership in America: The equity solution.* Lexington, MA: Lexington.

Rosen, T. H. (1987). Identification of substance abusers in the workplace. *Public Personnel Management, 16,* 197–205.

Rosenthal, R. (1991). *Meta-analytic techniques for social research* (Rev. ed.). Newbury Park, CA: Sage.

Ross, L. (1977). The intuitive psychologist and his shortcomings: Distortions in the attribution process. In L. Berkowitz (Ed.), *Advances in experimental social psychology.* New York: Academic Press.

Rotter, J. B. (1966). Generalized expectancies for internal versus external control of reinforcement. *Psychological Monographs* (Entire issue, No. 609).

Rousseau, D. (1985). Issues of level in organizational research: Multi-level and cross-level perspectives. In L. L. Cummings & B. M. Staw (Eds.), *Research in organizational behavior* (Vol. 7, pp. 1–38). Greenwich, CT: JAI Press.

Runkel, P. J., & McGrath, J. E. (1972). *Research on human behavior.* New York: Holt, Reinhart and Winston.

Rynes, S. L. (1991). Recruitment, job choice, and post hire consequences: A call for new research directions. In M. D. Dunnette & L. M. Hough (Eds.), *Handbook of industrial and organizational psychology* (2nd ed., Vol. 2, pp. 399–444). Palo Alto, CA: Consulting Psychologists Press.

Rynes, S. L., & Boudreau, J. W. (1986). College recruiting in large organizations: Practice, evaluation, and research implications. *Personnel Psychology, 39,* 729–757.

Rynes, S. L., Bretz, R. D., Jr., & Gerhart, B. (1991). The importance of recruitment in job choice: A different way of looking. *Personnel Psychology, 44,* 487–522.

Rynes, S. L., & Miller, H. E. (1983). Recruiter and job influences on candidates for employment. *Journal of Applied Psychology, 68,* 147–154.

Sackett, P. R., & Larsen, J. R., Jr. (1990). Research strategies and tactics in industrial and organizational psychology. In M. D. Dunnette & L. M. Hough (Eds.), *Handbook of industrial and organizational psychology* (2nd ed., Vol. 1, pp. 419–490). Palo Alto, CA: Consulting Psychologists Press.

Sagie, A. (1995). Employee participation and work outcomes. *Academy of Management Review, 20,* 278–280.

Salancik, G. R., & Pfeffer, J. (1977). An examination of need satisfaction models of job attitudes. *Administrative Science Quarterly, 22,* 427–456.

Salancik, G. R., & Pfeffer, J. (1978). A social information processing approach to job attitudes and task design. *Administrative Science Quarterly, 23,* 224–253.

Sales, S. M., & House, J. (1971). Job dissatisfaction as a possible risk factor in coronary heart disease. *Journal of Chronic Diseases, 23,* 189–194.

Salvendy, G. (1978). An industrial engineering dilemma: Simplified versus enlarged jobs. In R. Muramatsu & N. A. Dudley (Eds.), *Production and industrial systems* (pp. 965–975). London: Taylor & Francis.

Scandura, T. A., & Williams, E. A. (2000). Research methodology in management: Current practices, trends, and implications for future research. *Academy of Management Journal, 43,* 1248–1264.

Scarpello, V., & Jones, F. F. (1996). Why justice matters in compensation decision making. *Journal of Organizational Behavior, 17,* 285–299.

Schacter, S. (1959). *The psychology of affiliation.* Stanford, CA: Stanford University Press.

Schaubroeck, J., Ganster, D. C., & Jones, J. R. (1998). Organization and occupation influences in the attraction-selection-attrition process. *Journal of Applied Psychology, 83,* 869–891.

Schaubroeck, J., Ganster, D. C., & Kemmerer, B. E. (1994). Job complexity, Type A behavior, and cardiovascular disorder: A prospective study. *Academy of Management Journal, 34,* 966–975.

Schaubroeck, J., Ganster, D. C., Sime, W. E., & Ditman, D. (1993). A field experiment testing supervisory role clarification. *Personnel Psychology, 46,* 1–25.

Schaubroeck, J., & Merritt, D. E. (1997). Divergent effects of job control on coping with work stressors: The key role of self-efficacy. *Academy of Management Journal, 40,* 738–754.

Schein, E. H. (1969). *Process consultation: Its role in organization development.* Reading, MA: Addison-Wesley.

Schein, E. H. (1980). *Organizational psychology.* Upper Saddle River, NJ: Prentice-Hall.

Schein, E. H. (1983, Summer). The role of the founder in creating organizational culture. *Organizational Dynamics,* 13–28.

Schein, E. H. (1985). *Organizational culture and leadership: A dynamic view.* San Francisco: Jossey-Bass.

Schein, E. H. (1987). *Process consultation: Lessons for managers and consultants* (Vol. 2). Reading, MA: Addison-Wesley.

Schein, E. H. (1990). Organizational culture. *American Psychologist, 45,* 109–119.

Schein, E. H. (1992). *Organizational culture and leadership: A dynamic view* (2nd ed.). San Francisco: Jossey-Bass.

Schmidt, F. L., & Hunter, J. E. (1998). The validity and utility of selection methods in personnel psychology: Practical and theoretical implications of 85 years of research findings. *Psychological Bulletin, 124,* 262–274.

Schmidt, F. L., Hunter, J. E., & Outerbridge, A. N. (1986). The impact of job experience and ability on job knowledge, work sample performance, and supervisory ratings of performance. *Journal of Applied Psychology, 71,* 432–439.

Schminke, M., Ambrose, M. L., & Cropanzano, R. S. (2000). The effect of organizational structure on perceptions of procedural fairness. *Journal of Applied Psychology, 85,* 294–304.

Schmitt, N., & Coyle, B. W. (1976). Applicant decisions in the employment interview. *Journal of Applied Psychology, 61,* 184–192.

Schneider, B. (1987). The people make the place. *Personnel Psychology, 40,* 437–454.

Schneider, B., Smith, D. B., Taylor, S., & Fleenor, J. (1998). Personality and organizations: A test of the homogeneity of personality hypothesis. *Journal of Applied Psychology, 83,* 462–470.

Schneider, J., & Cook, K. (1995). Status inconsistency and gender: Combining revisited. Special issue: Extending interaction theory. *Small Group Research, 26,* 372–399.

Schriesheim, C. A., & Kerr, S. (1977). Theories and measures of leadership: A critical appraisal of current and future directions. In J. G. Hunt & L. L. Larson (Eds.), *Leadership: The cutting edge* (pp. 9–45). Carbondale: Southern Illinois University Press.

Schriescheim, C. A., Tepper, B. J., & Tetrault, L. A. (1994). Least preferred co-worker score, situational control, and leadership effectiveness: A meta-analysis of contingency model performance predictions. *Journal of Applied Psychology, 79,* 561–573.

Schwab, D. P. (1991). Contextual variables in employer performance-turnover relationships. *Academy of Management Journal, 34,* 966–975.

Schweiger, D. M., & DeNisi, A. S. (1991). Communication with employees following a merger: A longitudinal field experiment. *Academy of Management Journal, 34,* 110–135.

Scott, W. R. (1990). Technology and structure: An organizational-level perspective. In P. S. Goodman & L. S. Sproull (Eds.), *Technology and organizations* (pp. 109–143). San Francisco: Jossey-Bass.

Seashore, S. E. (1954). *Group cohesiveness in the industrial work group.* Ann Arbor: University of Michigan Press.

Sederberg, C. H., & Clark, S. M. (1990). Motivation and organizational incentives for high vitality teachers: A qualitative perspective. *Journal of Research and Development in Education, 24,* 6–13.

Selye, H. (1956). *The stress of life.* New York: McGraw-Hill.

Shamir, B., House, R. J., & Arthur, M. B. (1993). The motivational effect of charismatic leadership: A self-concept based theory. *Organization Science, 4,* 577–594.

Shaw, M. E. (1964). Communication networks. *Advances in Experimental Social Psychology, 1,* 111–147.

Shaw, M. E. (1978). Communication networks fourteen years later. In L. Berkowitz (Ed.), *Group processes.* New York: Academic Press.

Shea, G. P., & Guzzo, R. A. (1987). Groups as human resources. In K. M. Rowland & G. R. Ferris (Eds.), *Research in personnel and human resources management* (Vol. 5, pp. 323–356). Greenwich, CT: JAI Press.

Sherif, M. (1966). *In common predicament: Social psychology of intergroup conflict and cooperation.* Boston: Houghton Mifflin.

Sherif, M., Harvey, O. J., White, B. J., Hood, W. R., & Sherif, C. W. (1961). *Intergroup conflict and cooperation: The Robbers Cave experiment.* Norman, OK: Institute of Group Relations.

Shim, W., & Steers, R. M. (1994). *Mediating influences on the employee commitment-job performance relationship.* Unpublished manuscript.

Silvester, J., Anderson, N. R., & Patterson, F. (1999). Organizational culture change: An inter-group attributional analysis. *Journal of Occupational and Organizational Psychology, 72,* 1–23.

Skinner, B. F. (1971). *Beyond freedom and dignity.* New York: Knopf.

Small, M. (1999). *The presidency of Richard Nixon.* Lawrence: University of Kansas Press.

Smith, B. (1996). Care and feeding of the office grapevine. *Management Review, 85,* 6.

Smith, J. C. (1993). *Understanding stress and coping.* New York: Macmillan.

Smith, P. B., & Misumi, J. (1989). Japanese management: A sun rising in the West. In C. L. Cooper & I. T. Robertson (Eds.), *International review of industrial and organizational psychology, 1989* (pp. 330–369). Chichester, England: Wiley.

Smith, P. C., Kendall, L. M., & Hulin, C. L. (1969). *Measurement of satisfaction in work and retirement.* Chicago: Rand McNally.

Sparks, K., Cooper, C., Fried, Y., & Shirom, A. (1997). The effect of hours of work on health: A meta-analytic review. *Journal of Occupational and Organizational Psychology, 70,* 391–408.

Spector, P. E. (1982). Behavior in organizations as a function of employees' locus of control. *Psychological Bulletin, 91,* 482–497.

Spector, P. E. (1985). Measurement of human service staff satisfaction: Development of Job Satisfaction Survey. *American Journal of Community Psychology, 13,* 693–713.

Spector, P. E. (1986). Perceived control by employees: A meta-analysis of studies concerning autonomy and participation at work. *Human Relations, 11,* 1005–1016.

Spector, P. E. (1987a). Interactive effects of perceived control and job stressors on affective reactions and health outcomes for clerical workers. *Work and Stress, 1,* 155–162.

Spector, P. E. (1987b). Method variance as an artifact in self-reported affect and perceptions at work: Myth or significant problem? *Journal of Applied Psychology, 72,* 438–443.

Spector, P. E. (1994). Using self-report questionnaires in OB research: A comment on the use of a controversial method. *Journal of Organizational Behavior, 15,* 385–392.

Spector, P. E. (1996). *Industrial and organizational psychology: Research and practice.* New York: Wiley.

Spector, P. E. (1997a). *Job satisfaction: Application, assessment, causes, and consequences.* Thousand Oaks, CA: Sage.

Spector, P. E. (1997b). The role of frustration in anti-social behavior at work. In R. A. Giacalone & J. Greenberg (Eds.), *Anti-social behavior in the workplace* (pp. 1–17). Thousand Oaks, CA: Sage.

Spector, P. E. (2000). *Industrial and organizational psychology: Research and practice* (2nd ed.). New York: Wiley.

Spector, P. E., Dwyer, D. J., & Jex, S. M. (1988). Relations of job stressors to affective, health, and performance outcomes: A comparison of multiple data sources. *Journal of Applied Psychology, 73,* 11–19.

Spector, P. E., & Jex, S. M. (1991). Relations of job characteristics from multiple data sources with employee affect, absence, turnover intentions, and health. *Journal of Applied Psychology, 76,* 46–53.

Spector, P. E., & Jex, S. M. (1998). Development of four self-report measures of job stressors and strain: Interpersonal Conflict at Work Scale, Organizational Constraints Scale, Quantitative Workload Inventory, and Physical Symptoms Inventory. *Journal of Occupational Health Psychology, 3,* 356–367.

Spector, P. E., & O'Connell, B. J. (1994). The contribution of individual dispositions to the subsequent perceptions of job stressors and job strains. *Journal of Occupational and Organizational Psychology, 67,* 1–11.

Spielberger, C. D. (1979). *Preliminary manual for the State-Trait Personality Inventory (STPI).* Unpublished paper, University of South Florida, Tampa.

Spy vs. Spy: How accused double agent Robert Hanssen beat the FBI at it's own game—and what finally led to his arrest. (2001, March 5). *U.S. News & World Report,* 17–24.

Staw, B. M. (1975). Attribution of the "causes" of performance: A general alternative interpretation of cross-sectional research on organizations. *Organizational Behavior and Human Performance, 13,* 414–432.

Staw, B. M., Bell, N. E., & Clausen, J. A. (1986). The dispositional approach to job attitudes: A lifetime longitudinal test. *Administrative Science Quarterly, 31,* 56–77.

Staw, B. M., & Boettger, R. D. (1990). Task revision: A neglected form of work performance. *Academy of Management Journal, 33,* 534–559.

Staw, B. M., & Ross, J. (1985). Stability in the midst of change: A dispositional approach to job attitudes. *Journal of Applied Psychology, 70,* 469–480.

Steel, R. P. (1996). Labor market dimensions as predictors of the reenlistment decisions of military personnel. *Journal of Applied Psychology, 81,* 421–428.

Steel, R. P., & Griffeth, R. W. (1989). The elusive relationship between perceived employment opportunity and turnover behavior: A methodological or conceptual artifact? *Journal of Applied Psychology, 74,* 846–854.

Steel, R. P., & Rentsch, J. R. (1995). Influence of cumulation strategies on the long-range prediction of absenteeism. *Academy of Management Journal, 6,* 1616–1634.

Steers, R. M., & Rhodes, S. R. (1978). Major influences on employee attendance: A process model. *Journal of Applied Psychology, 63,* 391–407.

Steiner, I. D. (1972). *Group process and productivity.* New York: Academic Press.

Stevens, M. J., & Campion, M. A. (1999). Staffing work teams: Development and validation of a selection test for teamwork settings. *Journal of Management, 25,* 207–228.

Stogdill, R. M. (1948). Personal factors associated with leadership: A survey of the literature. *Journal of Psychology, 25,* 35–71.

Stone, D. L., & Kotch, D. A. (1989). Individuals' attitudes toward organizational drug testing policies and practices. *Journal of Applied Psychology, 74,* 518–521.

Storms, P. L., & Spector, P. E. (1987). Relationships of organizational frustration with reported behavioral reactions: The moderating effect of locus of control. *Journal of Occupational Psychology, 60,* 227–234.

Straus, S. G., & McGrath, J. E. (1994). Does the medium matter? The interaction of task type and technology on group performance and member reactions. *Journal of Applied Psychology, 79,* 87–97.

Strodtbeck, F. L., & Lipinski, R. M. (1985). Becoming first among equals: Moral considerations in jury foreman selection. *Journal of Personality and Social Psychology, 49,* 927–936.

Stroh, L. K., & Dennis, L. E. (1994). An interview with Madame Nguyen Minh Hoa: Vietnam's move to a market economy and the impact on women in the workplace. *Industrial-Organizational Psychologist, 31,* 37–42.

Sullivan, S. E., & Bhagat, R. S. (1992). Organizational stress, job satisfaction, and job performance: Where do we go from here? *Journal of Management, 18,* 353–374.

Sundstrom, E., DeMeuse, K. P., & Futrell, D. (1990). Work teams: Applications and effectiveness. *American Psychologist, 45,* 120–133.

Swanson, N. G., & Murphy, L. R. (1991). Mental health counseling in industry. In C. L. Cooper & I. T. Robertson (Eds.), *International review of industrial and organizational psychology* (pp. 265–282). New York & London: Wiley.

Swap, W. C., & Rubin, J. Z. (1983). Measurement of interpersonal orientation. *Journal of Personality and Social Psychology, 44,* 208–219.

Sweeney, P. D., & McFarlin, D. B. (1997). Process and outcome: Gender differences in the assessment of justice. *Journal of Organizational Behavior, 18,* 83–98.

Tabachnick, B. G., & Fidell, L. S. (1983). *Using multivariate statistics.* New York: Harper & Row.

Taylor, F. W. (1911). *Principles of scientific management.* New York: Harper.

Taylor, S. E. (1991). Asymmetrical effects of positive and negative events: The mobilization-minimization hypothesis. *Psychological Bulletin, 110,* 67–85.

Teerlink, R., & Ozley, L. (2000). *More than a motorcycle: The leadership journey at Harley-Davidson.* Boston: Harvard Business School Press.

Terpstra, D. E. (1981). Relationship between methodological rigor and reported outcomes in organization development evaluation research. *Journal of Applied Psychology, 66,* 541–543.

Tesluk, P. E., Farr, J. L., & Klein, S. R. (1997). Influences of organizational culture and climate on individual creativity. *Journal of Creative Behavior, 31,* 27–41.

Tesluk, P. E., & Jacobs, R. R. (1998). Toward an integrated model of work experience. *Personnel Psychology, 51,* 321–355.

Tesluk, P. E., & Mathieu, J. E. (1999). Overcoming roadblocks to effectiveness: Incorporating management of performance barriers into models of work group effectiveness. *Journal of Applied Psychology, 84,* 200–217.

Tett, R. P., Jackson, D. N., & Rothstein, M. (1991). Personality measures as predictors of job performance: A meta-analytic review. *Personnel Psychology, 44,* 703–742.

Theodory, G. C. (1982). The validity of Fiedler's contingency logic. *Journal of Psychology, 110,* 115–120.

Thomas, K. (1976). Conflict and conflict management. In M. D. Dunnette (Ed.), *Handbook of industrial and organizational psychology* (pp. 889–935). Chicago: Rand McNally.

Thomas, L. T., & Ganster, D. C. (1985). Impact of family-supportive work variables on work-family conflict and strain: A control theory perspective. *Journal of Applied Psychology, 80,* 6–15.

Tiegs, R. B., Tetrick, L. E., & Fried, Y. (1992). Growth need strength and context satisfaction as moderators of the relations of the Job Characteristics Model. *Journal of Management, 18,* 575–593.

Tierney, P., Farmer, S. M., & Graen, G. B. (1999). An examination of leadership and employee creativity: The relevance of traits and relationships. *Personnel Psychology, 52,* 591–620.

Tombaugh, J. R., & White, L. P. (1990). Downsizing: An empirical assessment of survivors' perceptions of a postlayoff environment. *Organization Development Journal, 8,* 32–43.

Trevino, L. K. (1992). The social effects of punishment in organizations: A justice perspective. *Academy of Management Review, 17,* 647–676.

Trevor, C. O., Gerhart, B., & Boudreau, J. W. (1997). Voluntary turnover and job performance: Curvilinearity and the moderating influences of salary growth and promotions. *Journal of Applied Psychology, 82,* 44–61.

Trice, H. M., & Beyer, J. M. (1984). Studying organizational culture through rites and ceremonials. *Academy of Management Review, 9,* 653–669.

Trist, E. L., & Bamforth, K. W. (1951). Some social and psychological consequences of the long-wall method of coal-getting. *Human Relations, 4,* 3–38.

Tubre, T. C., Sifferman, J. J., & Collins, J. M. (1996, April). *Jackson and Schuler (1985) revisited: A meta-analytic review of the relationship between role stress and job performance.* Paper presented at the annual meeting of the Society for Industrial and Organizational Psychology, San Diego, CA.

Tucker, L. A., Aldana, S., & Friedman, F. M. (1990). Cardiovascular fitness and absenteeism in 8,301 employed adults. *American Journal of Health Promotion, 5,* 140–145.

Tuckman, B. W. (1965). Developmental sequences in small groups. *Psychological Bulletin, 63,* 384–399.

Tuckman, B. W., & Jensen, M. A. C. (1977). Stages of small group development revisited. *Group and Organization Studies, 2,* 419–427.

Turner, A. N., & Lawrence, P. R. (1965). *Industrial jobs and the worker.* Cambridge, MA: Harvard University, Graduate School of Business.

U.S. Bureau of Labor Statistics. (1999). *National census of fatal occupational injuries, 1998.* Washington, DC: Author.

U.S. Chamber of Commerce. (1991). *Employee benefits 1990.* Washington, DC: Author.

U.S. Department of Health and Human Services. (2002). *National occupational research agenda: Update 2001.* Washington, DC: Author.

Vance, R. J., & Biddle, T. F. (1985). Task experience and social cues: Interactive effects on attitudinal reactions. *Organizational Behavior and Human Decision Processes, 35,* 252–265.

VandenHeuvel, A., & Wooden, M. (1995). Do explanations of absenteeism differ for men and women? *Human Relations, 48,* 1309–1329.

Van De Vliert, E., & Van Yperen, N. W. (1996). Why cross-national differences in role overload? Don't overlook ambient temperature! *Academy of Management Journal, 39,* 986–1004.

Van Eerde, W., & Thierry, H. (1996). Vroom's expectancy models and work-related criteria: A meta-analysis. *Journal of Applied Psychology, 81,* 575–586.

Van Maanen, J. (1975). Police socialization: A longitudinal examination of job attitudes in an urban police department. *Administrative Science Quarterly, 20,* 207–228.

Van Maanen, J. (1991). The smile factory: Work at Disneyland. In P. J. Frost, L. F. Moore, M. R. Louis, C. C. Lundberg, & J. Martin (Eds.), *Reframing organizational culture* (pp. 58–76). Newbury Park, CA: Sage.

Van Maanen, J., & Schein, E. H. (1979). Toward a theory of organizational socialization. In B. M. Staw (Ed.), *Research in Organizational Behavior* (Vol. 1, pp 209–264). Greenwich, CT: JAI Press.

Vecchio, R. P. (1977). An empirical examination of the validity of Fiedler's model of leadership effectiveness. *Organizational Behavior and Human Performance, 19,* 180–206.

Villanova, P., & Roman, M. A. (1993). A meta-analytic review of situational constraints and work-related outcomes: Alternative approaches to conceptualization. *Human Resource Management Review, 3,* 147–175.

Vinokur, A. D., van Ryn, M., Gramlich, E. M., & Price, R. H. (1991). Long-term follow-up and benefit-cost analysis of the Jobs program: A preventive intervention for the unemployed. *Journal of Applied Psychology, 76,* 213–219.

Viteles, M. S. (1932). *Industrial psychology.* New York: Norton.

Viteles, M. S. (1953). *Motivation and morale in industry.* New York: Norton.

von Bertalanffy, L. (1956). General systems theory. *General systems Yearbook of the Society for General Systems Theory, 1,* 1–10.

Vroom, V. H. (1964). *Work and motivation.* New York: Wiley.

Vroom, V. H. (1995). *Work and motivation* (2nd ed.). New York: Wiley.

Vroom, V. H., & Jago, A. C. (1988). *The new leadership: Managing participation in organizations.* Englewood Cliffs, NJ: Prentice-Hall.

Vroom, V. H., & Yetton, P. W. (1973). *Leadership and decision making.* Pittsburgh, PA: University of Pittsburgh Press.

Wageman, R. (1996). Interdependence and group effectiveness. *Administrative Science Quarterly, 40,* 145–180.

Wageman, R., & Baker, G. (1997). Incentives and cooperation: The joint effects of task and reward interdependence on group performance. *Journal of Organizational Behavior, 18,* 139–158.

Wagner, J. A. (1994). Participation's effect on performance and satisfaction: A reconsideration of research evidence. *Academy of Management Review, 19,* 312–330.

Wagner, J. A., & Gooding, R. Z. (1987). Shared influence and organizational behavior: A meta-analysis of situational variables expected to moderate participation-outcome relationships. *Academy of Management Journal, 30*, 524–541.

Waldman, D. A., & Spangler, W. D. (1989). Putting together the pieces: A closer look at the determinants of job performance. *Human Performance, 2*, 29–59.

Walton, R. E., & Hackman, J. R. (1986). Groups under contrasting management strategies. In P. S. Goodman (Ed.), *Designing effective work groups* (pp. 168–201). San Francisco: Jossey-Bass.

Wanberg, C. R. (1997). Antecedents and outcomes of coping behaviors among unemployed and reemployed individuals. *Journal of Applied Psychology, 82*, 731–744.

Wanous, J. P. (1973). Effects of a realistic job preview on job acceptance, job attitudes, and job survival. *Journal of Applied Psychology, 58*, 327–332.

Wanous, J. P. (1989). Installing realistic job previews: Ten tough choices. *Personnel Psychology, 42*, 117–134.

Wanous, J. P., Poland, T. D., Premack, S. L., & Davis, K. S. (1992). The effects of met expectations on newcomer attitudes and behaviors: A review and meta-analysis. *Journal of Applied Psychology, 77*, 288–297.

Wanous, J. P., & Zwany, A. (1977). A cross-sectional test of the need hierarchy. *Organizational Behavior and Human Performance, 18*, 78–97.

Watson, D., & Clark, L. (1984). Negative affectivity: The disposition to experience aversive emotional states. *Psychological Bulletin, 96*, 465–490.

Webb, E. J., Campbell, D. T., Schwartz, R. D., Sechrest, L., & Grove, J. B. (1981). *Nonreactive measures in the social sciences* (2nd ed.). Boston: Houghton Mifflin.

Weber, M. (1947). *The theory of social and economic organization* (A. M. Henderson & T. Parsons, Trans.) New York: Free Press.

Webster's new world dictionary. (1984). (2nd College ed.). New York: Simon & Schuster.

Weed, E. D. (1971). Job enrichment "Cleans up" at Texas Instruments. In J. R. Maher (Ed.), *Perspectives in job enrichment.* New York: Van Nostrand.

Weick, K. E. (1979). Cognitive processes in organizations. In B. M. Staw & L. L. Cummings (Eds.), *Research in organizational behavior* (Vol. 2, pp. 41–73). Greenwich, CT: JAI Press.

Weiner, Y., & Vardi, Y. (1990). Relationships between organizational culture and individual motivation—A conceptual integration. *Psychological Reports, 67*, 295–306.

Weiss, D. J., Dawis, R. V., England, G. W., & Lofquist, L. H. (1967). *Manual for the Minnesota Satisfaction Questionnaire* (Minnesota Studies in Vocational Rehabilitation, No. 22). Minneapolis: University of Minnesota.

Weiss, H. M. (1990). Learning theory and industrial and organizational psychology. In M. D. Dunnette & L. M. Hough (Eds.), *Handbook of industrial and organizational psychology* (2nd ed., Vol. 1, pp. 171–222). Palo Alto, CA: Consulting Psychologists Press.

Weiss, H. M., & Shaw, J. (1979). Social influences on judgments about tasks. *Organizational Behavior and Human Performance, 24*, 126–140.

Weitz, J. (1952). A neglected concept in the study of job satisfaction. *Personnel Psychology, 5*, 201–205.

White, S., & Mitchell, T. (1979). Job enrichment versus social cues: A comparison and competitive test. *Journal of Applied Psychology, 64*, 1–9.

Whitehead, T. N. (1935). Social relationships in the factory: A study of an industrial group. *Human Factor, 9*, 381–394.

Whitehead, T. N. (1938). *The industrial worker.* Cambridge, MA: Harvard University Press.

Whitney, K. (1994). Improving group task performance: The role of group goals and group efficacy. *Human Performance, 7,* 55–78.

Whyte, G. (1998). Recasting Janis's Groupthink Model: The key role of collective efficacy in decision making fiascoes. *Organizational Behavior and Human Decision Processes, 73,* 185–209.

Wickens, C. D., & Hollands, J. G. (2000). *Engineering psychology and human performance* (3rd ed.). Upper Saddle River, NJ: Prentice-Hall.

Wilkins, A. L., & Ouchi, W. G. (1983). Efficient cultures: Exploring the relationship between culture and organizational performance. *Administrative Science Quarterly, 28,* 468–481.

Williams, C. R., & Livingstone, L. P. (1994). Another look at the relationship between performance and voluntary turnover. *Academy of Management Journal, 37,* 269–298.

Williams, K. D., & Karau, S. J. (1991). Social loafing and social compensation: The effects of expectations of co-worker performance. *Journal of Personality and Social Psychology, 61,* 570–581.

Williams, L. J., & Anderson, S. E. (1991). Job satisfaction and organizational commitment as predictors of organizational citizenship and in-role behavior. *Journal of Management, 17,* 601–617.

Williams, L. J., & Anderson, S. E. (1994). An alternate approach to method effects using latent variable models: Applications in organizational behavior research. *Journal of Applied Psychology, 79,* 323–331.

Williams, L. J., Cote, J. A., & Buckley, M. R. (1989). Lack of method variance in self-reported affect and perceptions at work: Reality of artifact? *Journal of Applied Psychology, 74,* 462–468.

Wilson, M., Northcraft, G. B., & Neale, M. A. (1985). The perceived value of fringe benefits. *Personnel Psychology, 38,* 309–320.

Wilson, T. B. (1995). *Innovative reward systems for the changing workplace.* New York: McGraw-Hill.

Wise, D. (1996). *NIGHTMOVER: How Aldrich Ames sold the CIA to the KGB for $4.6 million.* New York: HarperCollins.

Wofford, J. C., & Liska, L. Z. (1993). Path-goal theories of leadership: A meta-analysis. *Journal of Management, 19,* 857–876.

Wood, R. E. (1986). Task complexity: Definition of the construct. *Organizational Behavior and Human Decision Processes, 37,* 60–82.

Woodman, R. W., & Wayne, S. J. (1985). An investigation of positive findings bias in evaluation of organization development interventions. *Academy of Management Journal, 28,* 889–913.

Woodward, J. (1965). *Industrial organization: Theory and practice.* London: Oxford University Press.

Worchel, S., Cooper, J., Goethals, G. R., & Olson, J. M. (2000). *Social psychology.* Belmont, CA: Wadsworth.

Wright, P. M. (1992). An examination of the relationships among monetary incentives, goal level, goal commitment, and performance. *Journal of Management, 18,* 677–693.

Wright, P. M., George, J. M., Farnsworth, S. R., & McMahan, G. (1993). Productivity and extra-role behavior: The effects of goals on spontaneous helping. *Journal of Applied Psychology, 78,* 374–381.

Xie, J. L. (1996). Karasek's model in the People's Republic of China: Effects of job demands, control, and individual differences.

Academy of Management Journal, 39, 1594–1618.

Yoffie, D., & Bergenstein, S. (1985, Fall). Creating political advantage: The rise of corporate enterpreneurs. *California Management Review,* 124–139.

Yukl, G. (1989). *Leadership in organizations.* Englewood Cliffs, NJ: Prentice-Hall.

Yukl, G., Kim, H., & Falbe, C. M. (1996). Antecedents of influence outcomes. *Journal of Applied Psychology, 81,* 309–317.

Yukl, G., & Tracey, J. B. (1992). Consequences of influence tactics used with subordinates, peers, and the boss. *Journal of Applied Psychology, 77,* 525–535.

Yukl, G., & Van Fleet, D. D. (1992). Theory and research on leadership in organizations. In M. D. Dunnette & L. M. Hough (Eds.), *Handbook of industrial and organizational psychology* (2nd ed., Vol. 2, pp. 147–197). Palo Alto, CA: Consulting Psychologists Press.

Zaccaro, S. J., Foti, R. J., & Kenney, D. A. (1991). Self-monitoring and trait-based variance in leadership: An investigation of leader flexibility across multiple group situations. *Journal of Applied Psychology, 76,* 308–315.

Zaccaro, S. J., & Lowe, C. A. (1988). Cohesiveness and performance on an additive task: Evidence for multidimensionality. *Journal of Social Psychology, 128,* 547–558.

Zammuto, R. F., & O'Connor, E. J. (1992). Gaining advanced manufacturing technologies benefits: The role of organization design and culture. *Academy of Management Review, 17,* 701–728.

Zanna, M. P., & Rempel, J. K. (1988). Attitudes: A new look at an old concept. In D. Bar-Tal & A. W. Kruglanski (Eds.), *The social psychology of knowledge* (pp. 315–334). Cambridge, England: Cambridge University Press.

Zickar, M. J. (2001). Using personality inventories to identify thugs and agitators: Applied psychology's contribution to the war against labor. *Journal of Vocational Behavior, 58,* 149–164.

Zimbardo, P. G. (1969). The human choice: Individuation, reason, and order versus deindividuation, impulse, and chaos. In A. W. Arnold & D. Levine (Eds.), *Nebraska Symposium on Motivation* (Vol. 17, pp. 237–307). Lincoln: University of Nebraska Press.

Author Index

Subject Index